ASPEN PUBLISHERS

AF710865

Emergency Department Compliance Manual

2008 Edition

Emergency Department Compliance Manual provides everything you need to stay in compliance with complex emergency department regulations, including such topics as legal compliance questions and answers—find the legal answers you need in seconds; Joint Commission survey questions and answers—get inside guidance from colleagues who have been there; hospital accreditation standard analysis—learn about Joint Commission standards as they apply to the emergency department; and reference materials for emergency department compliance. The *Manual* offers practical tools that will help you and your department comply with emergency department-related laws, regulations, and accreditation standards.

Highlights in the 2008 Edition

New and updated legal and regulatory information affecting your Emergency Department, including:

- Updated questions and answers, including compliance guidelines for PHS research awards, Board of Director responsibilities toward compliance, Joint Commission responsibilities for ED corporate leaders, on-call payments and the antikickback statute, and new Joint Commission emergency management standards focusing on a hazard vulnerability analysis, emergency operation plan, and the specifics of emergency communication, resource and asset management, safety and security, staff responsibility, and patient clinical and support activities.
- Updated sections on hospital accreditation standards.
- New forms, policies, and other reference materials to facilitate compliance, including:
    - — MRSA—Infection Control Policy and Checklist
    - — Delineation of ED Physician Privileges Policy
    - — Detoxification and Substance Abuse Treatment in the ED
    - — Steering Committee Leadership Communication Tool
    - — ED Open Medical Record Review Tool
    - — Employee Health Infection Control Policy and Procedures
    - — ED EMTALA Transfer Tracker

3/08

For questions concerning this shipment, billing, or other customer service matters, call our Customer Service Department at 1-800-234-1660.

For toll-free ordering, please call 1-800-638-8437.

Wolters Kluwer
Law & Business

ASPEN PUBLISHERS

Emergency Department Compliance Manual
2008 Edition

Consulting Editor
Rusty McNew, RN, MA, CPHQ

Contributors
Denise Atwood, RN, BSS
Ann H. Nevers, JD, LLM Health Law
Jane L. Conley, MS

Wolters Kluwer
Law & Business

AUSTIN BOSTON CHICAGO NEW YORK THE NETHERLANDS

Printed in the United States of America

ISBN 978-0-7355-7382-6
ISSN 1537-8438

1 2 3 4 5 6 7 8 9 0

About Wolters Kluwer Law & Business

Wolters Kluwer Law & Business is a leading provider of research information and workflow solutions in key specialty areas. The strengths of the individual brands of Aspen Publishers, CCH, Kluwer Law International and Loislaw are aligned within Wolters Kluwer Law & Business to provide comprehensive, in-depth solutions and expert-authored content for the legal, professional and education markets.

CCH was founded in 1913 and has served more than four generations of business professionals and their clients. The CCH products in the Wolters Kluwer Law & Business group are highly regarded electronic and print resources for legal, securities, antitrust and trade regulation, government contracting, banking, pension, payroll, employment and labor, and healthcare reimbursement and compliance professionals.

Aspen Publishers is a leading information provider for attorneys, business professionals and law students. Written by preeminent authorities, Aspen products offer analytical and practical information in a range of specialty practice areas from securities law and intellectual property to mergers and acquisitions and pension/benefits. Aspen's trusted legal education resources provide professors and students with high-quality, up-to-date and effective resources for successful instruction and study in all areas of the law.

Kluwer Law International supplies the global business community with comprehensive English-language international legal information. Legal practitioners, corporate counsel and business executives around the world rely on the Kluwer Law International journals, loose-leafs, books and electronic products for authoritative information in many areas of international legal practice.

Loislaw is a premier provider of digitized legal content to small law firm practitioners of various specializations. Loislaw provides attorneys with the ability to quickly and efficiently find the necessary legal information they need, when and where they need it, by facilitating access to primary law as well as state-specific law, records, forms and treatises.

Wolters Kluwer Law & Business, a unit of Wolters Kluwer, is headquartered in New York and Riverwoods, Illinois. Wolters Kluwer is a leading multinational publisher and information services company.

ASPEN PUBLISHERS SUBSCRIPTION NOTICE

This Aspen Publishers product is updated on a periodic basis with supplements to reflect important changes in the subject matter. If you purchased this product directly from Aspen Publishers, we have already recorded your subscription for the update service.

If, however, you purchased this product from a bookstore and wish to receive future updates and revised or related volumes billed separately with a 30-day examination review, please contact our Customer Service Department at 1-800-234-1660 or send your name, company name (if applicable), address, and the title of the product to:

ASPEN PUBLISHERS
7201 McKinney Circle
Frederick, MD 21704

Important Aspen Publishers Contact Information

- To order any Aspen Publishers title, go to *www.aspenpublishers.com* or call 1-800-638-8437.
- To reinstate your manual update service, call 1-800-638-8437.
- To contact Customer Care, e-mail *customer.care@aspenpublishers .com,* call 1-800-234-1660, fax 1-800-901-9075, or mail correspondence to Order Department, Aspen Publishers, PO Box 990, Frederick, MD 21705.
- To review your account history or pay an invoice online, visit *www.aspenpublishers.com/payinvoices*.

Wolters Kluwer
Law & Business

Editorial Board

Contributor

Jane L. Conley, MS
Risk Management Consultant
Carlisle, Pennsylvania

Contents

Acknowledgments

Developing and revising the *Emergency Department Compliance Manual* is a unique project, requiring the participation of many individuals. We are especially in debt to Consulting Editor Rusty McNew, who shares his expertise and creativity regarding strategies for preparing for Joint Commission surveys, as well as many sample materials from his organization. We also are immensely grateful to all Editorial Board members and contributors who aided in compiling examples of compliance documentation. Finally, we applaud the group of professionals who graciously consented to interviews about their recent Joint Commission survey experiences. Their candid comments bring a personal and practical section to the manual.

Introduction

Emergency department (ED) compliance issues can be overwhelming. Federal laws, state laws, local laws, liability concerns, and Joint Commission on Accreditation of Healthcare Organizations (Joint Commission) accreditation requirements affect nearly all aspects of patient care and departmental management. Leaders must balance their compliance obligations against patient care concerns, management time, and limited resources. The 2008 edition of this manual is designed to assist ED managers in finding that balance by providing urgently needed up-to-date information in a comprehensive, easy-to-use compliance tool that can be used to improve the care delivered to patients and meet various external requirements.

FEATURES OF THIS MANUAL

Legal Compliance Questions and Answers

This section of the manual provides an easy reference to legal issues commonly encountered in hospital EDs. A list of questions at the front of this section will enable you to quickly locate helpful and current information on a variety of difficult legal areas such as complying with fraud and abuse laws, patients' rights regulations, the Consolidated Omnibus Reconciliation Act (COBRA), negotiating consent requirements, obtaining reimbursement for ED services, avoiding employment law problems, and more. Citations to laws, regulations, and cases are provided for guiding additional research. Appendix 1-A provides a state-by-state summary of laws and regulations regarding exceptions to patient consent under emergency circumstances.

Joint Commission Survey Questions and Answers

This section contains valuable advice from staff members at hospitals that have recently and successfully navigated a Joint Commission survey. Interviewees provide frank and detailed information on what surveyors did and didn't look for, how they prepared staff for the survey, and how they demonstrated participation in performance improvement activities. This section is organized by topic, to allow you to readily compare the experiences of hospitals across the country.

Hospital Accreditation Standards Analysis

This section condenses applicable Joint Commission standards and elements of performance that are surveyed on the ED. Many standards are scored specifically in the ED while others are scored as a composite of the organization. This matrix allows ED managers to quickly find the standard or element of performance and understand how it is applicable to the ED.

Communication between the ED manager and the organization is a key component in the continuous Joint Commission readiness. ED managers are encouraged to be in the communication loop on all activities that impact all applicable standards.

- *Comment:* This column describes the relationship between ED and hospital responsibility for demonstrating compliance with the standard. It also indicates what the standard assesses.
- *Evidence:* This column lists the types of evidence that might be used to show compliance with the standard. Special emphasis is paid to documents that are developed or maintained in the ED.
- *Staff questions:* This column lists questions that the Joint Commission surveyor might ask the ED director, nurse manager, ED staff members, and others to assess compliance with the standard.

Reference Materials for Emergency Department Compliance

This section of the manual provides documentation that hospitals across the country have recently used to show compliance with Joint Commission standards, as well as documentation used to meet legal requirements discussed in Legal Compliance Questions and Answers.

CMS and Joint Commission Standards Checklist

This tool allows customers to cross reference the Medicare Conditions of Participation to the Joint Commission Standards and also provides a place for them to note any deviations in their own state law requirements. This checklist will simplify compliance efforts by highlighting duplications and inconsistencies in the many standards that emergency departments must follow.

Part 1

Legal Compliance Questions and Answers

INTRODUCTION TO COMPLIANCE

The emphasis on establishing corporate compliance programs for hospitals and other health care facilities is the direct result of the government's aggressive efforts to enforce legislative provisions governing health care fraud and abuse. Corporate compliance programs have been imposed on numerous providers by the government as part of settlements following fraud and abuse investigations, and many health care organizations have voluntarily implemented such programs to protect themselves from sanctions under fraud and abuse laws. As a result, compliance efforts have been closely linked with the subject of fraud and abuse legislation, even though an effective compliance program is much broader in scope and covers many other types of legislative requirements and prohibitions. In fact, compliance efforts should be directed at establishing a culture within a hospital that promotes prevention, detection, and resolution of all instances of conduct that do not conform to all federal and state laws, private payer health program requirements, as well as the hospital's ethical and business policies. [Department of Health and Human Services, Office of Inspector General, Compliance Program Guidance for Hospitals, Feb. 23, 1998]

Compliance recommendations should include a Code of Conduct that creates a culture of compliance and regular review of the effectiveness of the compliance program. Compliance effectiveness review can focus on the compliance officer role, adequacy of corporate policies, adequacy of open communication, regular training and education, internal monitoring and audits, response to detected deficiencies, and enforcement of disciplinary standards. [Department of Health and Human Services, Office of Inspector General, Supplemental Compliance Program Guidance for Hospitals, 70 Fed. Reg. 4858 (Jan. 27, 2005)]

What are the benefits of compliance?

Voluntary compliance can be a good way to demonstrate good faith efforts to comply with all relevant laws and regulations that impact hospital activities. Voluntary implementation of Compliance Program Guidance (CPG) recommendations can help the hospital demonstrate commitment to responsible corporate conduct, increases the chance to finding and correcting illegal or unethical behavior at an earlier point in time, and reduces subsequent financial loss to the hospital and government agencies. [Department of Health and Human Services, Office of Inspector General, Supplemental Compliance Program Guidance for Hospitals, 70 Fed. Reg. 4858 (Jan. 27, 2005)]

What types of activities are governed by health care fraud and abuse legislation?

Both at the state and federal levels, statutory fraud and abuse prohibitions apply to the following categories of health care provider activities:

- false claims or other fraudulent billing activities;
- bribes or kickbacks, including a complex array of discounts, rebates, profit-sharing agreements, or other business relationships; and

- illegal referrals, prohibiting physicians or other types of health care providers from referring patients for health care services to entities in which the physician has a financial interest.

What are the fraud and abuse issues that are of particular concern to a hospital emergency department (ED)?

As the above list indicates, the broad language of many of the fraud and abuse provisions in federal law and numerous state statutes makes these provisions applicable to a very wide range of potentially illegal activities. Several areas of activity are of particular concern to physicians practicing in a hospital ED, especially if the physicians are part of an emergency department staffing organization that contracts with a hospital to provide services in its ED. Some of the areas of risk for fraud and abuse liability include:

- Procedural coding. The importance of accurate coding in avoiding fraud and abuse liability is significant for all health care providers. Emergency physicians are ultimately responsible for the coding and billing that is done on their behalf in a hospital ED and should periodically review the way their services are coded and billed. Billing practices which raise concerns include improper coding, upcoding, unbundling (billing separately for services), billing for medically unnecessary services or non-covered services, duplicate billing, billing for services not documented, or filing fraudulent cost reports. Recent hospital compliance program guidance (CPG) also focuses on areas of risk that may be underappreciated in industry such as outpatient coding, admissions and discharges, supplemental payments, and use of information technology.
- Reassignment. When providing emergency services as an employee or a contracting physician, an emergency physician may assign the right to set and collect fees for his or her services but only within the limits of federal and state law. Payment may be made to a hospital where emergency physician services are provided if there is a contractual arrangement between the facility and the physician under which the hospital bills for the physician's services. In these cases, the emergency physician should retain the right to review what is billed and collected on his or her behalf.
- Teaching physician billing. A probe launched in 1996 by the Department of Health and Human Services and the Office of the Inspector General (HHS and OIG) focused on Part B reimbursement to hospitals or faculty physicians for the services of attending physicians in cases where patients were actually treated by residents acting under the supervision of an attending physician. Emergency physicians that practice at teaching hospitals must make sure that they comply with current teaching physician billing rules. [Refer to Services Provided by Teaching Physicians and Residents, under Reimbursement in this Part.]
- Gainsharing and other financial arrangements with hospitals. Potential violations of the antikickback statute can occur in financial arrangements between hospitals and hospital-based physicians that require physicians to pay more than the fair market value for services provided by the hospitals (for example, billing services, personnel, utilities) or compensate physicians for less than the fair market value of goods and services that they provide to hospitals. An OIG Management Advisory Report issued in 1991 lists a number of arrangements between hospital-based

physicians and hospitals that would be suspect under the antikickback statute, including

1. payment by a group of ED physicians to a hospital of half of its cash receipts exceeding $600,000 per year;
2. payment by a physician group of 50 percent of their gross receipts to a hospital's endowment fund;
3. an agreement by a physician group to purchase equipment and donate the equipment to the hospital at the termination of the contract, where the hospital has the unrestricted right to terminate the contract at any time; and
4. payment by a physician group to a hospital of 33 percent of all its profits above a set amount, to cover the facilities capital improvements, equipment, and other departmental expenditures [OIG Management Advisory Report: Financial Arrangements between Hospitals and Hospital-Based Physicians, OEI-09-89-00330, Jan. 31, 1991]

The OIG has also issued a special advisory bulletin stating that gainsharing arrangements between hospitals and physicians are prohibited by federal law and are subject to civil monetary penalties. [Office of Inspector General Special Advisory Bulletin, "Gainsharing Arrangements and CMPs for Hospital Payments to Physicians to Reduce or Limit Services to Beneficiaries," issued July 1999, available on the Internet at ***http://www.oig.hhs.gov/fraud/docs/alertsandbulletins/gainsh.htm***] Gainsharing typically describes an arrangement where a hospital gives a physician a percentage share of any reduction in the hospital's costs for patient care attributable in part to the physician's efforts. For example, in an advisory opinion, the OIG found that a joint arrangement in which an ambulance company would purchase a helicopter and the hospital would provide a helipad and crew at no cost raised concerns under the antikickback statute; however, there was minimal risk of abuse because the arrangement (1) involved emergency services only, (2) did not involve steering to the hospital, (3) was overseen by a regional counsel, and (4) had a positive impact on quality of care. The OIG indicated that it would not impose sanctions on such an arrangement. [OIG Advisory Opinion No. 03-14]

Emergency medicine groups are encouraged to develop compliance programs of their own to protect against fraud and abuse liability in their contractual arrangements with hospitals. [See American College of Emergency Physicians, Strategic Plan and Environmental Assessment, 1999-2000]

- Quality Emergency Care: The HHS/OIG and the Department of Justice have successfully enforced the federal fraud and abuse laws by investigating and prosecuting nursing homes under the Civil False Claims Act for billing for inadequate patient care. The charges in these cases typically allege that the care provided to nursing home residents failed to meet federal and state requirements relating to the quality of care. In the 2005 supplemental compliance guidance, the OIG has indicated that it has authority to exclude providers from federal programs for providing substandard care. [Department of Health and Human Services, Office of Inspector General, Supplemental Compliance Program Guidance for Hospitals, 70 Fed. Reg. 4858 (Jan. 27, 2005)]
- Referrals: The Stark self referral law and antikickback statutes prohibit certain referrals. The Stark law prohibits payment for designated health services (DHS) if the referral is from a physician with whom the hospital has a prohibited relationship. The antikickback statute prohibits direct or indirect payments to induce referrals.

However, safe harbors can be met which protect the provider under the statute. Areas of concern under the antikickback statute include: joint ventures, physician compensation, relationships with other health care entities, recruiting arrangements, discounts, medical staff credentialing (based on referrals), and malpractice insurance subsidies.

In August 2007 the Stark Phase III final rule was issued that clarifies physicians' compensation arrangements and increases flexibility in nonabusive compensation arrangements. The indirect compensation is more limited and requires physicians to meet a specific Stark exception because any hospital contract with a medical group will be viewed as a direct compensation arrangement with the physician. The "stand in the shoes" provision considers a physician to "stand in the shoes" of his or her physician organization. Thus, if the ED contracts with a medical group for services, each physician will be presumed to receive direct compensation under the contract. The rule also makes changes to rural requirement for physicians and relaxes standards. The final regulation provides the opportunity to cure inadvertent violation of the Stark law by allowing parties who exceed the limit on nonmonetary compensation to satisfy the requirements of the exception if the excess compensation did not exceed 50 percent of the permitted amount and is repaid in 180 days. It also expands the nonmonetary compensation exception to allow organizations with formal medical staff to provide one local medical staff appreciation event per year. Thus, the hospital could provide an appreciation activity for ED medical staff on an annual basis. [*Stark Phase III Final Rule,* 72 Fed. Reg. 51012 (Sept. 5, 2007)] For academic medical centers (AMCs) and nonprofit organizations organized under 501(c)(3), implementation of the Stark III final rule is delayed until December 4, 2008. [72 Fed. Reg. 4162 (Nov. 15, 2007)]

- Ambulance restocking arrangements: Agreements between hospitals and ambulance suppliers under which hospitals restock drugs and medical supplies used during emergency runs at no charge could technically violate the antikickback statute if this practice is intended to induce ambulance personnel to steer patients to a particular hospital. However, if all the hospitals within a geographic area served by the same EMS council participate in ambulance restocking programs, it is unlikely that free ambulance restocking could influence the referral process. A safe harbor to the antikickback statute was finalized by HHS/OIG in December 2001 [66 Fed. Reg. 62,979 (2001)] To be covered by the safe harbor, a restocking arrangement must meet four general conditions relating to the appropriate billing of federal health care programs, documentation requirements, safeguards relating to referrals, and compliance with other applicable laws. In addition, each of the three safe harbor categories involves a set of specific conditions providers must meet. An earlier, proposed version of the safe harbor would have protected certain restocking arrangements where the ambulance provider pays the facility fair market value for replenished drugs or supplies used in connection with the transport or where free or discounted restocking is provided by the hospital under the oversight of an EMS council or similar organization. The final rule is more lenient, however, eliminating requirements involving monitoring by an oversight entity and easing certain restrictions involving billing.

Since publishing the final rule, the OIG has also issued advisory opinions regarding ambulance restocking arrangements. The first (OIG Advisory Opinion No. 02-2, issued April 4, 2002) involved a non-profit ambulance company that serves several counties and uses each ambulance at least three times a week on runs to two non-profit hospitals. After emergency runs the hospitals restock certain drugs and supplies for free under county and state protocols. Neither the hospitals nor the ambulance company bill for the restocked drugs or supplies, and the arrangement is not based on the volume or value of referrals. The OIG found that the arrangement satisfies the criteria for the general replenishing safe harbor. In another opinion (OIG Advisory Opinion No. 02-3, issued April 4, 2002), the OIG likewise found an arrangement would meet the criteria for the general replenishing safe harbor where a quasi-governmental agency composed of representatives of EMS providers, hospitals, and medical directors proposed a formal regional ambulance restocking program in which participating hospitals would restock all ambulances uniformly with the drugs and supplies used in treating emergency patients. Ambulance providers would not be charged, and hospitals would bill Medicare or other parties only to the extent allowed under the payor's rules and regulations. Recent advisory opinions have reviewed whether state or city owned ambulance services can bill insurers for reimbursement of services without collecting copayments from taxpayers, and the OIG has found that it was acceptable to consider the resident taxes as a copayment and that failure to collect copayments with each service would not violate antikickback provisions. However, this did not apply when the government contracted with a private ambulance supplier to provide services. A proposed exclusive arrangement for emergency ambulance services was allowable as it presented a minimal risk. [See the following OIG Advisory Opinions: 02-8 (June 19, 2002), 02-15 (Oct. 7, 2002), 03-09 (Apr. 25, 2003), 04-02 (Mar. 8, 2004), 04-10 (Aug. 11, 2004), 04-12 (Sept. 28, 2004), 04-13 (Oct. 12, 2004), 04-14 (Nov. 4, 2004), 05-07 (Feb. 25, 2005), 05-09 (June 13, 2005), 05-10 (June 16, 2005), 06-06 (May 8, 2006), 06-07 (June 29, 2006)]

An evaluation of "pay to play" contracts, which require the ambulance service to pay the city or contracting authority a flat fee per year as part of the exclusive contract arrangement, found them to have minimal risk under the antikickback statute. [OIG Advisory Opinions 06-11 (Sept. 25, 2006), 06-12 (Sept. 25, 2006)] A county exclusive contract requiring the ambulance provider to absorb the cost of transporting uninsured arrestees was found to have minimal risk since it was part of a county-wide plan, dispatch varied referrals, it only partially compensated the county for costs, it did not negatively impact competition, it provided a public benefit, it didn't change EMS response, and it provided free service for indigent arrestees. [OIG Advisory Opinion 07-14 (Oct. 19, 2007)] However, an arrangement that provided for a hospital to subsidize the cost of ambulance transport not covered by public or private insurance from facilities outside the locality was found to violate the antikickback statute as a subsidy to the patient and as an arrangement that would influence the patient's choice of hospitals. [OIG Advisory Opinion 07-02 (Mar. 7, 2007)]

What other types of legal issues are implicated in a comprehensive hospital compliance program?

The OIG's Model Compliance Guidance for Hospitals sets forth the basic elements of an effective hospital compliance program and lists a number of risk areas that are of particular concern to hospitals. While many of these risk areas focus on practices that could implicate fraud and abuse laws, other legal issues that should be addressed in an effective compliance program include:

- medical records documentation practices
- patient confidentiality

- patient dumping and EMTALA compliance
- employment, licensure, and staffing issues
- environmental compliance issues
- informed consent issues
- quality of care issues
- antitrust issues
- tax exempt status issues [Department of Health and Human Services, Office of Inspector General, Compliance Program Guidance for Hospitals, Feb. 23, 1998]

In January 2005 supplemental compliance program guidance (CPG) set forth new compliance recommendations and risk areas for hospitals. These voluntary guidelines focus on the following risk areas:

- accuracy of claims information
- compliance with referral and antikickback statutes
- gainsharing arrangements that may reduce or limit services
- EMTALA compliance
- substandard care
- relationship with federal program beneficiaries, i.e., gifts, cost sharing waivers, or free transportation
- HIPAA privacy and security
- excess billing of Medicare or Medicaid recipients, and
- other issues such as discounts to uninsured, preventative care, and professional courtesy billing waivers. [Department of Health and Human Services, Office of Inspector General, Supplemental Compliance Program Guidance for Hospitals, 70 Fed. Reg. 4858 (Jan. 27, 2005)]

Can the emergency room physician rent office space from the hospital?

The OIG has issued a special fraud alert in regard to physician rental of office space from a person or entity to which the physician might refer because of the concerns that the rental may induce referrals. Emergency room physicians renting space from the hospital would be in a position to refer patients to the hospital as inpatients. Therefore, care needs to be taken in establishing rental agreements. If the OIG were to review the rental agreement it would look at the appropriateness of the agreement, the amount paid for rent, and time and space considerations. While not required, complying with the elements of the space rental safe harbor can provide protection because then the agreement will be considered appropriate. To comply with the safe harbor, the agreement must be (1) in writing and signed, (2) must cover all the premises rented and include all the terms of the rental agreement, (3) the rental must be for specific time intervals, (4) the term of the rental agreement must exceed one year, (5) the charge for rent must be set in advance based on fair market value, and (6) the space rented must not exceed the area needed for business purposes. If the emergency room physician was to rent space from any other entity that the physician was in a position to make referrals to, the same provisions would apply. [OIG Special Fraud Alert, *Rental of Space in Physicians Offices by Persons or Entities to Which Physicians Refer* (Feb. 3, 2000) & 64 Fed. Reg. 63,518 (Nov. 19, 1999)]

Can emergency room physicians participate in a joint venture with the hospital?

One of the original safe harbors set forth by the OIG was for joint ventures in which the physician provided personal services when opportunities to make referrals were limited and the contract was based on fair market value for the services. [56 Fed. Reg. 35,952 (July 29, 1991)] Since then the OIG has issued special fraud alerts in regards to certain types of joint ventures. The OIG has expressed concern that there may be opportunities for referrals in joint ventures where the investor is in a position to make a referral, when the joint venture business structure is a "shell" with an ongoing business entity, or when the physician investment is small or based on amounts borrowed from the entity the physician is in a position to refer to. [59 Fed. Reg. 65,372 (Dec. 19, 1994)]

More recently the OIG has expressed concern with joint ventures in which the owner expands into a related line of business that depends upon referrals from the owner's existing business by contracting with an existing business competitor to manage the services on behalf of the owner. For safe harbor protection, the arrangement would need to be an arm's length transaction based on fair market value. Factors which would make the joint venture suspect include a joint venture which involves: (1) a new line of business, (2) a captive referral base, (3) little or no bona fide business risk on the part of the owner, (4) status of manager or supplier as a competitor, and (5) the manager or supplier's remuneration impacted by referrals. [OIG Special Advisory Bulletin: Contractual Joint Ventures (Apr. 23, 2003) available at *http://www.oig.hhs.gov*]

Can a hospital provide complimentary non-emergency local transport?

In a letter in regard to complimentary transport, the OIG indicated that a hospital can provide non-emergency complimentary transportation for patients and family members to and from the hospital or ambulatory care center when the transportation is valued at less that $10 per trip and less than $50 per year. The hospital transportation must comply with certain criteria; therefore, the program must have been in place prior to August 30, 2002, it must be offered uniformly without charge, the transportation can only be to and from the hospital and in the hospital service area, the cost of the transport cannot be claimed on federal cost reports, and the transportation cannot be ambulance transportation. [OIG Letter clarifying the provision of complimentary local transportation for program beneficiaries (Dec. 9, 2002)]

How do compliance guidelines for ambulance suppliers impact the ED?

In March 2003 the OIG issued final compliance program guidance (CPG) for ambulance suppliers who interact frequently with the emergency ED. The guidance sets forth voluntary provisions to assist ambulance suppliers to comply with fraud and abuse standards. Areas of concern for ambulance suppliers include: improper transportation, medically unnecessary trips, trips claimed but not provided, misrepresentation of destinations, false documentation, billing individual services when group transport was provided, upcoding basic life support to advanced life support, and payment kickbacks. Other risk areas include: transportation calls when someone has already died, multiple-patient transports, situations where multiple ambulances respond, and billing amounts that exceed usual charges. The ED personnel may be the ones who assist in identifying whether ambulance transport is necessary, the level of care needed during transport, and whether life support is needed and at what level. A physician certification statement (PCS) should indicate whether the ambulance service is medically necessary. Safe harbors generally available for fraud and abuse are also available for ambulance suppliers. [Final Compliance Program Guidance for Ambulance Suppliers (Mar. 24, 2003) available on the Internet at *http://www.oig.hhs.gov/fraud/complianceguidance.html*]

How do compliance guidelines for pharmacy manufacturers impact the ED?

In April 2003 the OIG issued voluntary compliance guidance for pharmacy manufacturers and identified three areas of risk: (1) data integrity, (2) kickbacks and illegal remuneration, and (3) compliance with drug sample laws. The concerns with data integrity relate to manufacturers' ability to manipulate average wholesale price (AWP) for drugs. Kickback concerns with purchasers such as an ED include product discounts, providing product support such as billing at no charge, educational grants to attend seminars about the manufacturers' product, research funding for product research, and reimbursement such as rebates and payments to convert to the manufacturers' drug. Kickback concerns with physicians include switching arrangements to encourage switching patients to the manufacturers' brand, consulting and advisory payments which must be for fair market value, payment for research, business courtesies such as entertainment and gifts, and educational and research grants such as for continuing medical education (CME) especially when it relates to the manufacturers' drug product. Drug sample concerns include concerns with compliance with the Prescription Drug Marketing Act (PDMA), which prohibits the sale or billing for drug samples provided by drug manufacturers. [Final Compliance Program Guidance for Pharmaceutical Manufacturers (Apr. 28, 2003), available on the Internet at *http://www.oig.hhs.gov/fraud/complianceguidance.html*]

Can a hospital participate in a pharmaceutical patient assistance program (PAP)?

In November 2005 CMS clarified pharmaceutical patient assistant programs' viability under the Medicare Part D drug program. These PAP programs typically provide cash, or free or reduced prices for drugs. When the recipient is a Medicare beneficiary, the PAP is acceptable, and any drug subsidy counts toward the patient out-of-pocket costs. While there are concerns about the antikickback statute, CMS indicated that the PAP would be acceptable as long as it was administered by a bona fide charity that was truly independent of the pharmacy and that decisions were based on legitimate financial need. For those participating in the PAP who are outside the Medicare program, the drug subsidy does not count toward the out-of-pocket costs. Notice must be given to beneficiaries that the subsidies won't count toward out-of-pocket costs and will be based on financial need. [Special Advisory Bulletin: *Patient Assisted Programs for Medicare Part D enrollees,* 70 Fed. Reg. 70,623 (Nov. 22, 2005) & Advisory Opinion 06-08 (June 30, 2006)]

How do compliance guidelines for PHS research awards impact the ED?

The OIG issued draft voluntary compliance guidance for recipients of Public Health Service (PHS) research awards in 2005 and identified three areas of risk: (1) time and effort reporting, (2) properly allocating charges to award projects, and (3) reporting financial support from other sources. When an ED department professional is involved in a PHS research project, the time spent focused on the research project will be compensated by the award and needs to be properly reported. Costs that accrue because of a specific project need to be separated and specifically allocated to the project. Finally, other financial support should be reported in order to prevent fraud or double billing for services. Like other compliance programs, there should be a focus on standards of conduct with written policies, a compliance officer and committee, education and training, good communication and role identification, regular audits, appropriate discipline of misconduct, and investigation of identified areas of noncompliance. [Draft OIG Compliance Guidance for Recipients of PHS Research Awards (Nov. 28, 2005)]

What are the compliance standards for electronic health records and e-prescribing?

The Medicare Part D prescription drug program (PDP) requires participating plans to use electronic health records (EHR) and e-prescribing. Physicians and pharmacies can voluntarily comply with the standards. The intent is to improve quality, reduce medical error, and reduce cost through electronic prescribing. For those who prescribe electronically, CMS has adopted the National Council for Prescription Drug Programs (NCPDP) SCRIPT standard for EHR. CMS also requires all Medicare Drug Integrity Contractors (MEDIC) to oversee prescription drug fraud and abuse. [CMS Prescription Drug Benefit Manual & Final Rule, 70 Fed. Reg. 67,568 (Nov. 7, 2005)] Stark and antikickback statutes generally prohibit referrals to entities where the physician or family have a financial interest; however, final rules relating to EHR and e-prescribing set forth exceptions and safe harbors.

The final rules create new Stark Phase III exceptions for e-prescribing and electronic health records (EHRs). The first exception focuses on e-prescribing and covers hardware, software, Internet connection, training, and support with no limit on cost. Donations of these items used in e-prescribing can be made from a hospital to medical staff, a group practice to its members, or a prescription drug plan (PDP) sponsor or a Medicare Advantage plan to a prescribing physician as long as the donation is not linked to the volume or value of referrals. Other technology used for billing or scheduling, admissions, or general office processes would not fall within the exception. The donor cost must be documented through a written agreement. The second exception is broad and focuses on arrangements involving interoperable EHR software, information technology, or training. There is no limit on the value of technology, but the physician must pay 15 percent of the donor cost. The technology can include other software such as patient administration, scheduling, billing, or clinic support software as long as the primary focus is EHR. The technology can be donated by any provider of DHS to any physician. Criteria that can be used in selecting physicians would include providing uncompensated care, total number of prescriptions, size of the physician practice, total hours the physician practices medicine, overall use of technology by the physician, whether the doctor is a medical staff member, and other reasonable and verifiable methods that don't relate to the volume or value of referrals or business generated. This exception expires on December 31, 2013. [71 Fed. Reg. 45,140 (Aug. 8, 2006) codified at 42 C.F.R. 411.357(v)(w)]

In conjunction with the Stark Phase III exceptions, the OIG has created new safe harbors under the antikickback statute for e-prescribing and EHR arrangements. The first safe harbor for electronic prescribing allows for hardware, software, IT, and training services to be donated by a hospital to medical staff, a group practice for a physician, or a physician drug plan (PDP) sponsor or a Medicare Advantage plan to a prescribing physician as long as it is "necessary and used solely" for e-prescribing. Donated items must be able to be used regardless of payor status, and donation must not be based on the volume or value of referrals. The second safe harbor for EHRs requires the recipient to provide health services under a federal program or health plan and the software to be interoperable and not related to the volume or value of referrals. A donor may be selected based on number of prescriptions written, size of the practice, use of technology, medical staff membership, the provision of uncompensated care, or other reasonable means. There must be a written agreement and technology must be useable for any payor. The recipient must pay 15 percent of the donor cost. [71 Fed. Reg. 45,110 (Aug. 8, 2006) codified at 42 C.F.R. 1001.952(x)(y)]

Proposed standards for e-prescribing include a uniform standard and a standard identifier. These would include Accredited Standards Committee (ASC) health care eligibility standards and National Council for Prescription Drug Program (NCPDP) standards, including the NCPDP SCRIPT 8.1 for medication histories and NCPDP formulary and benefit standard 1.0 for formulary and benefit information. It is also proposed that the National Provider Identifier (NPI) be used for e-prescribing. [72 Fed. Reg. 64,900 (Nov. 16, 2007)]

What is the responsibility of the Board of Directors in overseeing compliance?

The hospital Board of Directors has a fiduciary duty toward the hospital to act with a duty of care and to make reasonable inquiries in making decisions and overseeing corporate activities. This requires good faith actions to ensure that a corporate compliance program is in place that adequately identifies organizational risks and takes actions to prevent and respond to any violations in compliance. Legal counsel and the Chief Compliance Officer may play key roles in reporting to the Board of Directors. The Board needs to ensure that the corporate mission and purpose align with the actual conduct of hospital staff, medical staff, and professional standards of care. In this role, Board members may ask questions to determine how well compliance programs are operating. The ED may be asked to respond to inquiries from the Board regarding departmental compliance activities. [Department of Health and Human Services, Office of Inspector General, Corporate Responsibility and Corporate Compliance: A Resource for Health Care Boards of Directors (Apr. 2, 2003); Department of Health and Human Services, Office of Inspector General, An Integrated Approach to Corporate Compliance: A Resource for Health Care Boards of Directors (July 1, 2004); Department of Health and Human Services, Office of Inspector General, Corporate Responsibility and Health Care Quality: A Resource for Health Care Boards of Directors (Sept. 13, 2007)]

In 2009 the Joint Commission will update its leadership standards to require a strong leadership structure to be in place with governing body accountability for the safety and quality of treatment and services. Each hospital should have a Chief Executive, and medical staff should be accountable to the Board. Each organizational leader should have the knowledge needed for his/her role. The ED Directors and leaders play a key role to ensure that safe treatment and services provided are of high quality within the department.

[JCAHO Comprehensive Accreditation Manual for Hospitals LD 1.10-1.70 (2009 Prepublication Standards) available on the Internet at *http://www.jcaho.org*]

What are Joint Commission requirements for ED and corporate leaders?

The 2009 Joint Commission standards will update the leadership requirements and focus on leadership structure, leadership relations, organizational culture and system performance, and operations. The leadership requirements apply to the governing body (Board of Directors), medical staff leaders, and managers in the hospital leadership structure. Those with leadership roles within the ED will need to have the skills and knowledge needed to meet the standards. The leadership relations standards require that leaders identify and address any conflicts of interest, that the leaders regularly communicate with one another, and that processes are established to handle conflicts between leaders to protect the quality and safety of patient care. [JCAHO Comprehensive Accreditation Manual for Hospitals LD 1.10-1.70, LD 2.10-2.40 (2009 Prepublication Standards) available on the Internet at *http://www.jcaho.org*]

Organizational culture and system performance standards focus on five key elements: use of data, planning, communication, changing performance, and staffing. The intent is to create and maintain a culture of safety and quality; to use data and information to guide decision making; to understand data variations; to have hospital-wide planning to ensure safe processes; to communicate accurate information to those who need it, such as staff, practitioners, patients, and patients' family members; and for all employees to participate in initiatives to improve both the safety and quality of care within the organization. [JCAHO Comprehensive Accreditation Manual for Hospitals LD 3.10-3.60 (2009 Prepublication Standards) available on the Internet at *http://www.jcaho.org*]

Operations standards require the organization to comply with all laws and regulations; to ensure that all departments and programs are effectively managed; to ensure that policies and procedures are in place and guide patient services; to identify and address any conflicts of interest; to incorporate ethical principles in hospital business practices; to identify patient needs as a guide to govern patient care and treatment decisions; to provide comparable treatment to patients with similar needs; and to have space and equipment available to provide adequate services. The standards also require oversight and monitoring of contracted providers to insure safe care and treatment with plans for performance improvement as needed, to ensure that any new or modified processes are well-designed, to integrate patient safety into hospital programs, and to ensure that policies and procedures for organ donors are developed with medical staff participation. [JCAHO Comprehensive Accreditation Manual for Hospitals LD 4.10–4.270 (2009 Prepublication Standards) available on the Internet at *http://www.jcaho.org*]

PATIENTS' RIGHTS

Beginning in 2000, patients' rights issues came to the forefront, as legislators on the federal and state levels enacted new laws to ensure the safety and self-determination of patients following headlines concerning medical errors and managed care mistreatment in the popular press. Federal agencies responded as well, most notably by incorporating patients' rights guarantees in the Medicare Conditions of Participation, and issuing final regulations setting out standards for the privacy of patient health care information as required by the Health Insurance Portability and Accountability Act (HIPAA). Congress has continued to debate the scope and content of a series of proposed patients' rights bills with various provisions. In the meantime, current patient right provisions require the hospital to inform patients of their rights, and to establish processes for the prompt resolution of patient grievances including specific times, procedures, and decisions. The ED can participate with other hospital departments to establish these processes. Patients have the right to participate in their plan of care and be informed of decisions; they also have the right to privacy and safety in an environment free of abuse or harassment. (42 C.F.R. § 482.13)

Patients' right to be free of restraint and seclusion include specific ordering, documentation, and time requirements for restraint and seclusion as part of the Medicare patients' rights provisions. JCAHO includes patient rights in its hospital accreditation standards focusing on patient rights to: respect, be involved in treatment decisions, wishes of the patient in regard to life decisions, be informed of the outcome of care including unanticipated outcomes, confidentiality, privacy, security, to access protective and advocacy services, to be protected in human research, to receive information about care and treatment, to access and receive health information, to make decisions based on patient needs, and to be free from mental, physical, sexual and verbal abuse, neglect or exploitation. [JCAHO Comprehensive Accreditation Manual for Hospitals RI 2.10–2.190 (2007)]

Patient confidentiality, while of great importance, is often difficult to ensure in the ED setting, where the numbers of patients and urgency of care may make it difficult to safeguard patient information closely. However, it is crucial to do so, more than ever, as discussed below.

Consent to treatment is a basic concept that is second nature to health care providers. It is a more complex concept than it first appears, however, and can give rise to a variety of questions, such as what constitutes valid consent, whether consent must be in writing, and who can consent if the patient is not able. Finally, EDs are governed by a number of antidiscrimination laws that require hospitals to provide care to the public in a nondiscriminatory manner. ED administrators should review policies and staff conduct to determine whether patients are being discriminated against on the basis of race, national origin, gender, or disability. Federal and state laws prohibiting discrimination may create affirmative duties for EDs, such as providing foreign language or sign language interpreters or modifying the physical premises to increase accessibility for individuals with disabilities. This section discusses all of these patients' rights issues.

Restraint and Seclusion

Do any federal regulations address the use of restraints and seclusion?

In 2000, the Medicare Conditions of Participation were amended to incorporate a patients' bill of rights, which set standards for the use of restraint and seclusion of hospital patients. These standards must be met by hospitals that receive Medicare or Medicaid reimbursement. The regulations establish patients' right to be free from both physical restraints and drugs that are used as a restraint that are not medically necessary or are used as a means of coercion, discipline, convenience, or retaliation by staff. The standards distinguish between the use of restraint for medical and surgical care from the use of restraint or seclusion for behavior management, setting out separate criteria for each. [42 C.F.R. § 482.13]

What constitutes a restraint?

Under the regulations, a restraint is any manual method, physical device, mechanical device, material, or equipment attached or adjacent to the patient's body that he or she cannot easily remove, if it restricts freedom of movement or access to one's body. A drug constitutes a restraint if it is a medication used to control behavior or to restrict the patient's freedom of movement and is not a standard treatment for the patient's medical or psychiatric condition. [42 C.F.R. § 482.13]

According to the Centers for Medicare and Medicaid Services (CMS) guidance, what constitutes a restraint depends on whether the object or technique is being used for the purpose of limiting patient movement and access to their body. According to the guidance, devices that serve multiple purposes, such as a gerichair or side rails, constitute a restraint when they have the effect of restricting a patient's movement and cannot be easily removed by the patient. A drug qualifies as a restraint if it is used to restrict a patient's freedom of movement in medical post-surgical situations and is not a standard treatment for the patient's medical or psychiatric condition. Tucking a patient's sheets in so tightly that he or she cannot move is another example of a physical restraint under the standards. [CMS State Operations Manual, Interpretive Guidance, Appendix A, 482.13(e) (May 21, 2004)] However, the use of restraints for the purposes of law enforcement (for example, if a prisoner is in handcuffs and needs treatment) is not governed by the restraint regulations because in such cases the restraint is not related to the provision of health care.

The 2006 final rule published December 8, 2006, finalized the Patients' Rights Condition of Participation (CoP) applicable to restraint and seclusion. The final interpretive guidelines to assist hospitals in implementing the requirements have not been published as of Wednesday, December 12, 2007. [71 Fed. Reg., 236 (Dec. 8, 2006) (Rules and Regulations)]

How do the patients' rights standards limit the use of restraints for medical and surgical care?

The standards, which have generated much controversy in the hospital community,

- limit restraint use to those situations in which less restrictive interventions have been determined to be ineffective to protect the patient or others from harm;
- require the order of a physician or qualified licensed independent practitioner;
- prohibit the use of standing or PRN (as needed) orders for restraints;
- require consultation with the patient's treating physician as soon as possible (if the physician did not personally write the order);
- necessitate a written amendment of the patient's plan of care mandate that restraints be implemented in the least restrictive manner possible and in accordance with safe and appropriate restraining techniques;
- require the withdrawal of restraints at the earliest possible time;
- establish that restraint use must be continually assessed, monitored, and reevaluated;
- impose ongoing staff training requirements. [42 C.F.R. § 482.13]

What documentation is necessary with regard to restraint orders and evaluations?

The guidance states that the rationale that a patient might fall is an inadequate basis for using a restraint. Each individual patient's history of falls, medical condition, and symptoms must be evaluated on a case by case basis. According to the guidelines, restraints are not a substitute for adequate staffing and monitoring. The guidelines emphasize the importance of documentation of: continual reevaluation of patients in restraints, the rationale for ordering a restraint, the rationale for the time frame for the order, and that other less-restricting alternatives were considered. Consistency with hospital policy and reliance on current standards of safety and technique are also factors in evaluating whether restraint use is appropriate. [CMS State Operations Manual, Interpretive Guidance, Appendix A, 482.13(e) (May 21, 2004)]

What are the procedures that must be followed for ordering, monitoring, evaluating, and documenting the use of restraints or seclusion for behavior management?

Seclusion and restraints for behavior management can only be used in emergency situations if needed to ensure the patient's or others' physical safety when less restrictive interventions have been determined to be ineffective. According to the guidelines, an emergency is a situation where the patient's behavior is violent and aggressive and poses an immediate and serious danger to the safety of the patient or others.

Like restraints for medical or surgical care, seclusion and restraints for behavior management can only be used in accordance with the order of a physician or other authorized licensed independent practitioner. Standing orders and PRN orders are prohibited. The patient's treating physician must be consulted as soon as possible, unless that individual ordered the restraint or seclusion. The restraint or seclusion triggers a written modification of the patient's plan of care, must be implemented in the least restrictive manner possible, must be applied in accordance with safe appropriate restraining techniques, and must be ended at the earliest possible time. The condition of the patient must be continually assessed, monitored, and reevaluated. Staff must have ongoing education in the safe use of seclusion and restraint, as well as alternatives for handling behavior that would traditionally have been treated through the use of restraint or seclusion.

Unlike restraints for medical or surgical care, there are specific timelines for the duration of orders and reevaluation of patients under restraint or in seclusion for behavior management. A physician or other licensed independent practitioner (where permitted by state law) must evaluate in person the need for restraint or seclusion within one hour of initiation. Written orders are limited to 4 hours for adults, 2 hours for patients ages 9 to 17, and 1 hour for patients under age 9. Orders may only be renewed up to a total of 24 hours, at which time a second face to face evaluation by a physician or other licensed independent practitioner is required. In the event that a patient who is restrained for aggressiveness or violence quickly recovers and is released before the physician or licensed independent practitioner arrives to perform the assessment, the physician or practitioner must still see the patient face to face to perform the assessment. [42 C.F.R. § 482.13]

Further, seclusion may not be used simultaneously with restraint for behavior modification unless the patient is continually monitored face to face by an assigned staff member or continually monitored by staff in close proximity to the patient using both video and audio equipment. [42 C.F.R. § 482.13]

Documentation is crucial to demonstrating compliance, particularly with respect to changes in the patient's behavior, attempts to use other interventions first, the rationale for using restraint or seclusion, the patient's response, compliance with hospital policy, and the removal of the restraint or seclusion.

Confidentiality of ED Records

What rules of confidentiality apply to ED records?

General rules establishing the confidentiality of patient information apply to the information gathered and compiled in an ED record. These rules are frequently elaborated in state statutes or regulations. A few states simply specify that the medical record is confidential and impose a general obligation on hospitals to develop an appropriate policy for record confidentiality without further statutory or regulatory guidance. Enactments in other states similarly embody the principle of confidentiality and the patient's right of access. In Connecticut, for example, a statutory Patient's Bill of Rights provides that patients are entitled to confidential treatment of personal and medical records. [Conn. Gen. Stat. § 19a-550(b)(9)] Patients may approve or refuse their release to any individual outside the facility, except in the case of the patient's transfer to another health care institution or as required by law or a third party payment contract. Numerous other statutes provide that medical records are confidential and may be disclosed only with the patient's consent or as provided in the statutes. Note that while the general rule establishes that the medical record is a confidential document, numerous exceptions allow disclosure or impose mandatory reporting of patient information under specific circumstances.

In addition to state laws, in December 2000 the Department of Health and Human Services issued final regulations that set out standards for the privacy of individually identifiable patient health information that required compliance by April 2003. [65 Fed. Reg. 82,462, available on the Internet at *http://www.hhs.gov/ocr/hipaa/finalreg.html*] The rules apply to all communications regarding medical records that have been maintained by health care providers or plans, whether electronic, written, or oral. The rules generally provide that a health care provider may not disclose health information that identifies the patient unless authorized by the patient or is specifically allowed under the regulations. State law is generally preempted to the extent it conflicts with the federal privacy standards, but state laws that are more stringent (i.e., provide greater privacy protections) will take precedence over the federal regulations.

What does patient consent for disclosure consist of under the federal privacy rule?

The privacy rule was finalized August 14, 2002. The final rule clarified the need for individual written consent to use health information for marketing purposes, and it requires notice of privacy protections to all patients even though consent to use health information for regular health care is optional. Providers must make a good faith effort to obtain written acknowledgment that the patient received a copy of the provider's notice of privacy practice at the time of the first service, except in emergency situations. The intent of the rule is not to limit common health care communications as long as reasonable means are used to protect confidentiality. For example, the ED can continue to use sign in sheets and call names of people in the waiting room without violating the rule. When person health information (PHI) is released as appropriately authorized, only the minimum necessary information should be disclosed. Hospitals can establish criteria upon which disclosure will be made. The final rule also clarifies that parents acting as the personal representative of minor children have the right to access medical records of the minor children, but determination of when a child is emancipated and what disclosure is permissible is governed by state law. [67 Fed. Reg. 53,181 (Aug. 14, 2002)] Routine disclosure of private information is allowed for treatment and billing purposes and has been upheld by the court. [*Citizens for Health v. Leavitt,* 428 F.3d 167 (3d Cir. 2005), *cert. denied,* 127 S. Ct. 43 (2006)]

Whom does the Health Insurance Portability and Accountability Act (HIPAA) privacy rule apply to?

Health Insurance Portability and Accountability Act (HIPAA) applies to health care providers, such as a hospital unit, that bill for health care services electronically.

Three questions can be asked to determine if HIPAA applies:

1. Does the organization bill for a covered service, i.e., health care services?
2. Is the transaction covered, i.e., is the organization submitting a bill or claim or storing health data?
3. Is the covered transaction billed electronically?

If the answers to the questions are yes, then the organization is considered a "covered entity" and HIPAA applies. Privacy protections became effective April 2003. Each organization must designate a Privacy Officer who is responsible for meeting regulatory requirements on behalf of the facility. The ED should coordinate compliance efforts with the hospital Privacy Officer.

Who can be a business associate under HIPAA?

A business associate is a person or entity that performs activities on behalf of a covered entity using personal health information. For example, a business associate with the ED could include a billing manager, claims or utilization review or administration, practice manager, an accountant, lawyer, or consultant, or someone involved in data analysis, accreditation, or financial review. These business associates need access to personal health information to perform their activities on behalf of the hospital. A covered entity must have a contract with a business associate requiring the business associate to protect the privacy of the health information, describe the use of the health information and requiring protections to limit disclosure of personal health information. As of April 2004 all contracts must include the required business associate language. Sample contract language is available on the Internet at *http://www.hhs.gov/ocr/hipaa/contractprov.html.*

Situations in which an entity is exempted from the business associate include: disclosures by a covered entity to a health care provider to treat the patient such as disclosure from the emergency room physician to a specialist on-call or to a laboratory; disclosures to a health plan sponsor or insurer such as information required for payment purposes; incidental access to information such as the evening janitor; other entities that participate in an organized health care arrangement (OHCA); and disclosures for research purposes. An ED may give patient payment information to an ambulance service provider that transported the patient to the hospital in order for the ambulance provider to bill for its treatment services. [*OCR Guidance Explaining Significant Aspects of the Privacy Rule* (Dec. 4, 2002)]

What are the HIPAA requirements for data privacy?

HIPAA protects individually identifiable health information used by covered entities through the following requirements:

Privacy Notice—The organization should provide patients with notice of their privacy rights and the organizations privacy practices. The organization must make a good faith effort to obtain the patient's written acknowledgement of the notice. Consent for use of health information for routine health care delivery such as treatment, payment, and health care operations is optional.

Privacy Officer—The Privacy Officer is to develop and implement privacy policies and procedures and train all staff on privacy requirements. The organization is to limit data use to the minimum necessary use or disclosure for which there is authorization.

Marketing Use—A covered entity must obtain a patient's prior written authorization to use health information for marketing purposes unless there is a face to face encounter or communication involving a promotional gift of nominal value. Marketing includes selling lists of patients to a third party, thus precluded use of a patient list by a third party without patient consent. Marketing does not include discussion of treatment options, products, or services with a patient.

FDA Use—The organization allows disclosure of information to the Food and Drug Administration (FDA) for reporting purposes.

Incidental Data Use—Health providers can use data as part of treatment and decision making without violating privacy rules. For example, hospitals can keep charts at the bedside, doctors can talk to patients in semi-private rooms, and doctors and nurses can confer at nursing stations without violating the rule.

Authorization—Patients are required to grant permission in advance for nonroutine use of data or disclosure.

Parents and Minors—The rule clarifies that state law governs parents' access to health information in regards to their minor children.

Limited Data Set—Limited data that does not include identifiable information can be disclosed for research, public health, and health care operations if there is an agreement to ensure data security and privacy. [*Standards of Privacy of Individually Identifiable Health Information*, 45 C.F.R. §§ 160 & 164, *Modifications to the Standards for Privacy of Individually Identifiable Health Information—Final Rule*, DHHS Fact Sheet (Aug. 9, 2002)]

Are there situations where patient health information may be disclosed for other purposes?

The final rule provides that special authorization is not required for specific purposes where there is an "overriding public interest," such as disclosures to public health authorities that are authorized or required by law to collect information for public health purposes (for example, reporting of disease or injury, reporting deaths, investigating the occurrence and cause of injury and disease, and monitoring adverse outcomes related to food, drugs, biological products, and dietary supplements), disclosures for purposes of research, legal proceedings, or law enforcement, or to report abuse or neglect.

Who keeps track of HIPAA complaints?

The Office of Civil Rights (OCR) enforces HIPAA privacy and has information on compliance and enforcement on the Internet at *http://www.hhs.gov/ocr/privacy/enforcement*. Compliance issues most frequently investigated include impermissible use and disclosure of PHI, lack of safeguards for PHI, patients' inability to access their own PHI, disclosures of more than the minimum necessary, and lack of authorization for use of PHI. [*Privacy Rule Enforcement Highlights* (Oct. 31, 2007)]

The HIPAA administrative simplification provisions are tracked by the Office of E-Health Standards and Services (OESS), which has a HIPAA information tracking system (HITS) to store HIPAA complaint and investigation information. Disclosure of complaint information will be limited to the following needs: CMS in order to reach CMS goals, other state or federal agencies for HIPAA enforcement, members of Congress based on inquiry, Department of Justice (DOJ) for litigation, CMS contractors who administer health benefits, and federal agencies investigating fraud and abuse. [70 Fed. Reg. 38,944 (July 7, 2005)]

How will HIPAA be enforced?

In 2006, a final enforcement rule was issued that applies to all HIPAA administrative simplification rules, not just privacy. If HIPAA provisions are not in place, the entity should document why it was not reasonable to implement and then apply an equivalent alternative measure. It mandates the following:

- a health care entity be considered a person subject to enforcement;
- in an investigation there is a responsibility to provide records, cooperate and permit access to information;
- an entity is prohibited from retaliating or harassing someone who files a privacy complaint;
- when multiple organizations are involved and found to have violated the rule, joint and several liability will occur, but a covered entity may avoid liability if it is clear that another entity was responsible for the violation;
- fines are limited to $100 per violation and $25,000 for identical violations;
- the number of violations will be determined by the nature of the violation;
- factors that will be considered in setting a penalty include the nature of the violations, the circumstances, culpability, history of prior offenses, and the financial condition of the entity;
- an entity may raise affirmative defenses to the alleged violation including no knowledge of the violation, reasonable cause for the violation which is then corrected quickly, and that the violation was punishable as a wrongful disclosure of individually identifiable health information; and

- hearing and appeal rights are set forth. [HIPAA Administrative Simplification Enforcement Final Rule, 71 Fed. Reg. 8390 (Feb. 16, 2006)]

How do HIPAA disclosure clarifications impact the ED?

HIPAA rule clarifications have clarified that ambulance providers may report to health care providers on the status of transported patients as part of the health care treatment. ED personnel may leave a message at the home or on an answering machine for a patient, but should disclose as little information as possible.

Personal health information (PHI) may be disclosed to someone who can assist in notifying the family of the patient's location or condition either with patient approval, or in an emergency when it is in the best interest of the patient. For example, the ED could notify the Red Cross, police, or other emergency response personnel of the patient's location and condition. Similarly, the ED may disclose relevant information to the family or friends of a patient, even when the patient cannot signify approval because of incapacity, when it would be in the best interest of the patient to do so.

The hospital may inform callers and visitors of a patient's location and condition in the ED, and the patient's phone number and room can be released as part of a patient directory, even if the ED directory is separate from the rest of the hospital. Disclosure may also be made to law enforcement to comply with a court order, to report a violent crime, etc. [OCR HIPAA FAQ available at *http://www.hhs.gov/ocr/hipaa/*]

What are some examples of reporting requirements that could apply to health care professionals working in an ED?

Legislative reporting provisions, both state and federal, that allow or mandate the disclosure of patient information without the patient's consent frequently apply to health care professionals who treat patients in an ED. These provisions cover a variety of situations, including cases of suspected child abuse or neglect, abuse of adults and injuries to disabled persons, drug abuse, communicable diseases, and disclosure of patient information to law enforcement officials. For further discussion of reporting requirements that apply to these issues, see "Responsibilities Relating to Crimes outside the ED."

Under what circumstances does the duty to report communicable diseases typically arise?

All states have enacted communicable disease reporting laws, which variously require hospitals and practitioners to inform public health authorities of cases of infectious, venereal, or sexually transmitted diseases. The statutes usually list the particular diseases that must be reported and direct practitioners to give local public health officials the patient's name, age, sex, address, and identifying information, as well as the details of the illness. [*See, e.g.*, Ala. Code §§ 22-11A-1 through 22-11A-73] The health department may have the authority to request patient records for purposes of conducting epidemiological investigations. [*See, e.g.*, Fla. Stat. § 395.3025(5)] Only the information required by the statute should be disclosed.

A few states have laws authorizing hospitals to disclose confidential information when emergency medical personnel come into contact with a patient suffering from a reportable condition. [*See, e.g.*, Fla. Stat. § 395.1025] The procedures for notifying emergency personnel vary among the states, with some statutes allowing the hospital to directly notify the person at risk and others requiring the hospital to notify authorities at the state board of health, who then contact the emergency personnel. In either case, the hospital is usually precluded from revealing the name of the afflicted patient.

What types of rules govern the disclosure of human immunodeficiency virus (HIV) or acquired immune deficiency syndrome (AIDS) related information?

Many confidentiality statutes allow the release of HIV- or AIDS-related information without the patient's consent to medical technicians who provide emergency care to an HIV-positive patient. The statutes vary, however, in the purpose for such disclosure. Some link disclosure to the health of the patient, others indicate a concern for the safety of the emergency workers, and many reflect an ambiguous balance between the two concerns. In some states, for example, confidential HIV-related information may be released to medical personnel in a "medical emergency" to the "extent necessary to protect the health or life of the named party." [*See, e.g.*, Colo. Rev. Stat. § 25-4-1404(1)(c)] The Hawaii law defines "medical emergency" as any disease-related situation that threatens life or limb. [Haw. Rev. Stat. § 325-101] Other states authorize disclosure to health care providers rendering medical care when knowledge of HIV test results is necessary to provide appropriate emergency care or treatment to the patient. [Del. Code Ann. tit. 16, § 1203(a)(4)] Both types of laws demonstrate concern for the patient's treatment.

Other laws reflect a concern for the safety of rescue workers. Illinois allows release of the identity of the subject of an HIV test to "[a]ny health care provider or employee of a health facility" involved in an accidental contact with the blood or bodily fluids of an individual that could transmit HIV according to a physician's medical judgment. [410 Ill. Comp. Stat. Ann. § 305/9]

A few states impose an affirmative duty on an attending physician or health care facility to respond to inquiries by emergency rescuers as to contact with a patient later diagnosed with a contagious disease or virus including HIV. The rescuers entitled to receive such information include paid or volunteer firefighters, emergency medical technicians, rescue squad personnel, and law enforcement officers. The notification must occur within two days after confirmation of the patient's diagnosis. The information must be communicated in a manner that protects the confidentiality of both the patient and rescuer. [*See, e.g.*, Mich. Comp. Laws § 333.20191]

Are there reporting requirements that apply to diagnoses of drug abuse?

Some states require health care professionals to report diagnoses of drug abuse. In New Jersey, for example, the law requires health care practitioners to report the names of drug-dependent persons within 24 hours after determining that the person uses a controlled dangerous substance for purposes other than treatment of sickness or injury as prescribed and administered under the law. [N.J. Stat. § 24:21-39] In Texas, health care providers treating a patient for an overdose of a controlled substance must report the case at once to the state Department of Health. [Tex. Health & Safety Code § 161.042]

Is there a duty to report certain types of patient information to law enforcement authorities?

The new federal privacy regulations do not impose a duty on hospitals to furnish law enforcement authorities with patient information, but provide that limited information may be disclosed without patient consent in order to locate or identify a suspect, fugitive, or missing person, or regarding a victim of a crime who cannot agree to disclosure because of incapacity. A hospital may also disclose patient information if it believes that the disclosure is necessary for authorities to apprehend a participant in a violent crime or an escapee from custody. [45 C.F.R. § 164.512]

State law varies widely as to a hospital's duty to report certain kinds of patient-related information, such as cases involving gunshot or knife wounds [*see, e.g.*, Cal. Penal Code § 11161 and Tex. Health & Safety Code § 161.041], or disorders affecting a motorist's ability to drive safely to law enforcement authorities. In states having these types of reporting statutes, a patient's consent is not required in order to release the record. In fact, under some statutes, hospitals may be guilty of criminal misdemeanor if they fail to report certain cases. For further discussion of these reporting requirements, see "Responsibilities Relating to Crimes outside the ED."

As a general rule, however, hospitals should not release medical records or other patient information to law enforcement personnel without the patient's authorization. In the absence of statutory authority or legal process, a police agency has no authority to examine an ED record or other medical record. If a law enforcement official does provide the facility with a valid court order or subpoena, the hospital, upon the advice of counsel, may provide the information requested.

What specific confidentiality concerns arise with respect to patient information collected in an ED?

Specific confidentiality concerns arise with respect to patient information that is collected in an ED because of the physical setting in which treatment is delivered, the urgent nature of the treatment, and the high patient volume. In particular, the use of status boards to record the progress of patients through ED procedures, the prescription drug abuser lists that many EDs keep on 3 × 5 file card systems, and the physical layout of examination rooms can generate unique difficulties in protecting patient privacy.

A specific privacy concern that arises in the ED is the filming of patients for television productions. The telecast of several documentaries including footage of actual emergency room patients raised concerns with the Joint Commission on Accreditation of Healthcare Organizations (Joint Commission) that patient privacy was being violated. As a result, it issued a standards' clarification for patient rights and informed consent when videotaping or filming patients in a hospital ED. The standard clarification states that

- it is appropriate to film or videotape patient care activities in the ED if patients or surrogate decision makers give informed consent;

- if the patient is unable to give informed consent and no surrogate decision maker is available, patient care activities in the ED may be filmed as long as it is in accordance with a policy that requires a patient's informed consent before the film is used for any purpose;
- the film or video must remain in the physical possession of the hospital and not released to anyone for any purpose until such informed consent is obtained;
- if the patient does not give informed consent for the use of the film, then the relevant footage must be removed or the video destroyed; and
- the hospital must post a notice to the community it serves (in the public areas of the hospital) informing the public that filming or videotaping may be occurring while emergency services are being delivered [JCAHO Comprehensive Accreditation Manual for Hospitals RI 2.5 (2007)]

The CMS guidance interpreting the federal regulations also states that video or other electronic monitoring or recording methods should not be used during the examination of a patient without his or her consent. [CMS, State Operations Manual, Appendix U § 403.730(c)(1-2)]

Why does the use of status boards present confidentiality concerns?

Many EDs use a status board to track the progress of patients seeking care in the ED. A status board typically consists of a write-on/wipe-off or other erasable board that shows information including patient names, complaints or diagnoses, and room numbers. These boards, when placed in view of patients and visitors, present a serious breach of confidentiality concern. For example, although ED staff might not consider tracking diagnostic tests on the status board a confidentiality problem, a status board that says, "John Smith, curtain 3, shortness of breath, HIV test ordered" is a clear violation of patient privacy if other patients and visitors can read the information. The Joint Commission has repeatedly cited status boards as a patient privacy problem. Alternatives that better safeguard patient confidentiality include:

- using patient numbers rather than names. Many EDs find this method cumbersome.
- omitting medically sensitive information such as complaints, diagnoses, and diagnostic tests from the board. Simply including the patient's name and room or curtain number is not likely to violate confidentiality.
- implementing a computerized "status board" that requires staff members to log on to obtain patient information. If this method is adopted, the computer terminal must either be placed where access is strictly limited to ED staff, or the system should automatically "log off" after staff use, so that patient information is not readily visible.

What confidentiality concerns arise with the use of drug abuser lists?

Another ED practice that can raise confidentiality concerns is the establishment of a prescription drug abuser list that is compiled to alert department personnel of the identity of patients who have been diagnosed as drug abusers and who fraudulently seek treatment at the ED to obtain more drugs. These lists are often compiled on a 3 × 5 card file system, and are not always stored in a secure location.

These abuser lists raise significant liability risks not only under general confidentiality rules but also under federal legislation governing alcohol and drug abuse patient records. In particular, provisions in the Public Health Service Act state that records of the "identity, diagnosis, prognosis, or treatment" of any patient maintained in connection with these programs are confidential and may not be disclosed except for certain purposes and under certain circumstances. [42 U.S.C. § 290dd-2] The regulations define "patient" as any individual who has requested or received a diagnosis or treatment for drug abuse at a federally assisted program. [42 C.F.R. § 2.11] An earlier court has ruled that a person who enters a hospital ED for immediate treatment of conditions arising from a drug overdose is a "patient" under the regulations because that individual clearly "applied for treatment or diagnosis of drug abuse."[*United States v. Eide*, 875 F.2d 1429 (9th Cir. 1989)] The court further ruled that the ED qualified as a "program" because it provides diagnoses, treatment, and referrals and because many drug users enter the hospital through the ED as the first step to further drug treatment. However, a more recent case found that an ED was not a "program" and indicated that there were two ways an ED could be considered a "program" (1) when the primary function of the ED is to provide treatment for drug and alcohol abuse, and (2) when the ED held itself out to the community as providing drug and alcohol abuse treatment services. The later court decision was based on federal regulations stating that the regulation was not intended to apply to emergency department personnel who refer a patient for drug treatment unless the primary purpose of the staff is to provide drug and alcohol treatment. [*Center for Legal Advocacy v. Denver Health and Hosp. Auth.*, 320 F.3d 1107 (10th Cir. 2003) and 42 C.F.R. § 2.12(e)(1)]

Are there any special confidentiality concerns with regard to minors and their parents?

Under the federal privacy rule, a person's right to control his or her health information is based on the person's right under state law to control the health care itself. Because a parent usually has authority to make health care decisions about his or her minor child, a parent or legal guardian is generally the child's personal representative under the privacy rule and has the right to obtain the minor child's health information. Even where a child receives emergency medical care in the ED without a parent's consent, normally the parent would still be the child's representative and can get all information about the child's treatment and condition.

There are exceptions, however, where a parent might not be the minor child's "personal representative" with regard to certain health information about the child being treated in an ED. Such situations include

- when state law does not require parental consent before a minor can obtain a particular health care service (e.g., treatment for an STD or for sexual assault) and the minor consents to the health care service, the parent is not considered the minor's representative under the privacy rule, and information regarding that treatment can only be disclosed with the minor's consent;
- when a parent agrees that the minor and the physician may have a confidential relationship, the parent does not have access to the health information related to that relationship. For example, if an ED physician asks the parent of a 16-year-old if the physician may speak with the child confidentially about a medical condition and the

parent agrees, the parent has no right to information regarding that conversation unless the minor child consents to disclosure;

- when a physician believes in his or her professional judgment that the minor child has been or may be subjected to abuse or neglect, or that treating the parent as the child's representative could endanger the child, the physician may choose not to treat the parent as the minor's representative.

However, the standards of the federal privacy rule do not preempt state laws that specifically address disclosure of a minor's health information to a parent, whether the state law authorizes or prohibits the disclosure. Thus, for example, if an ED physician believes that disclosing information about a minor would endanger the minor, but a state law requires disclosure to a parent, the physician may comply with the state law without violating the privacy rule. [Complete Privacy Rule Text (Oct. 10, 2002) available on the Internet at *http://www.hhs.gov/ocr/combinedregtext.pdf*]

What other measures should ED personnel follow to ensure patient privacy and confidentiality?

ED personnel should ensure that patients are treated in separate rooms or that the beds are separated by curtains or screens. During oral communications among themselves and with patients and their family members, ED personnel should reasonably safeguard patient health information. Although overheard communications are unavoidable in a busy emergency room, where it may be necessary for ED personnel to speak loudly in order to ensure appropriate treatment, ED personnel should take reasonable precautions to minimize the chance of inadvertent disclosures to others who may be nearby. Examples of this would include speaking apart, speaking quietly when discussing a patient's condition with family members in a waiting room or other public area, and by avoiding using patients' names in public hallways and elevators. ED personnel should also be aware of the hospital's confidentiality policy and be aware of the specific ways the policy is put into practice in the ED.

What is the difference between data privacy and security?

Data privacy focuses on who can access personal health information (PHI), and it focuses on all patient information. The data privacy requirements include data safeguards to protect patient privacy and prevent unintentional disclosure or use of information. As part of complying with data privacy standards, some of the security standards may have been met.

Security requirements cover electronic personal health information (EPHI) only and focus on administrative, physical, and technical safeguards to protect confidentiality, data integrity, and available access to data by those who need it.

What are the HIPAA requirements for data security?

HIPAA data security requirements focus on the security of electronic personal health information (EPHI) for covered entities by setting required and addressable standards. If a standard is required, policies and procedures should be put in place to meet the standards. It the standard is addressable, the organization should implement the standard if it is reasonable. If it is not reasonable, the organization should (1) document the reasons for its decision not to implement the standard, and (2) implement an equivalent measure that is reasonable and appropriate unless in light of the assessment the standard can be met without implementation of the specification or the alternative. To determine whether a standard is reasonable, the organization should look at factors such as how probable and critical the data security risk is, the costs of security, and the size and complexity of the covered entity. Organizations should balance risk and capabilities to determine when to implement programs. [45 C.F.R. § 164.306]

Implementation of data security standards is required by all covered entities except small health plans by April 20, 2005. A hospital ED would be considered a covered entity. Small health plan data security implementation is required by April 20, 2006. [*Security Standards Final Rule*, 68 Fed. Reg. 8334 (Feb. 20, 2003)]

What administrative, physical, and technical safeguards are involved in data security?

Required administrative safeguards for data security include having a security management process, assigning security responsibilities, isolating health care clearinghouse functions, setting up security incident response and reporting, and implementing plans for data back-up, disaster recovery, and emergency mode operation. The program should be regularly evaluated and contracts should include appropriate data security provisions. Administrative safeguards that are addressable include workforce security issues such as clearance and authorization for personnel, access authorization, security awareness and training, and testing and revising procedures.

Required physical safeguards include workstation use and security, and device and media control of disposal and reuse of equipment. Addressable standards include contingency operations and security plans, access control and validation procedures, maintenance records, accountability, and data backup and storage plans.

Required technical safeguards include access control through unique user identifiers with emergency access procedures and authentication of the person accessing the data. Addressable technical standards include automatic logoff, encryption, audit controls, and transmission security. [45 C.F.R. §§ 164.308, 164.310, 164.312]

Who must obtain a National Provider Identifier (NPI)?

In order to improve electronic transactions, CMS requires all health care providers who are covered entities to obtain and use a National Provider Identifier (NPI). Beginning January 1, 2008, all 837I electronic and UB04 paper claims must include the NPI. As of March 1, 2008, all Medicare fee-for-service 837 claims and CMS-1500 claims require the NPI on the claim. As of May 23, 2008, only the NPI will be accepted on HIPAA electronic transactions. An NPI application can be completed online at *https://nppes.cms.hhs.gov.*

Consent to Treatment

Is patient consent always necessary for medical treatment?

The general legal principle is that patient consent to medical treatment is necessary. There are some situations, however, when patient consent is not required, for example,

- in an emergency;
- when the patient is not able to give consent due to minority;
- when the patient is not able to give consent due to mental incapacity;
- when the law designates a substitute decision maker, such as in the case of abused children; and
- when a court permits treatment without consent, such as in the case of taking a blood sample pursuant to a search warrant. In many of these situations, "substituted consent" of a decision maker other than the patient, such as the next of kin, a guardian, or a court, is required.

What is informed consent?

While patients presenting at the ED often require urgent medical treatment, in many cases there is time to obtain patient consent before initiating treatment. The consent obtained must be "informed consent"; that is, the patient must understand the procedure and its inherent risks and benefits and voluntarily give consent. The physician is ultimately responsible to obtain the informed consent for the procedure.

What information must be disclosed to the patient to obtain informed consent?

The law of informed consent has been shaped by years of court cases, with each state forming its own response regarding what information must be disclosed to the patient. An attestation that the patient or authorized representative has been given all the information to make an informed discussion must be documented in the medical record. Below is an attestation that contains the required CMS and Joint Commission requirements:

> *I have discussed and answered the patient's and/or legal guardian's questions related to the proposed anesthesia along with the potential benefits, risks, or side effects, including potential problems that might occur during recuperation, the likelihood of achieving goals, reasonable alternatives, the relevant risks, benefits, and side effects related to alternatives, including the possible results of not receiving care, treatment, and services and when indicated, any limitations on the confidentiality of information learned from or about the patient.*

For hospitals, including EDs, the importance of obtaining informed consent to medical treatment has been reiterated by the federal government's adoption of a patient's rights Condition of Participation, the requirements of which hospitals must meet to be approved for, or to continue participation in, the Medicare and Medicaid programs. [*See, e.g.*, 42 C.F.R. § 482.13] Among other requirements, the rule contains a standard on patients' rights requiring hospitals to establish policies and procedures directed at protecting the patient's right to participate in the development and implementation of his or her plan of care. The standard expressly provides that patients or their representatives (as allowed under state law) have the right to make informed decisions regarding their care, be informed of their health status, be involved in care planning and treatment, and be able to request or refuse treatment.

Do all states use the same method to determine whether the consent was informed?

There are two different standards that states use to define informed consent: the professional community standard and the reasonable patient standard. The first is a physician-based standard, while the second is a patient-based standard. It is important for ED staff to learn which standard applies in the state in which they practice.

The professional community standard focuses on the physician and states that a physician's duty to disclose information is limited to the information that a reasonable medical practitioner would disclose under the same or similar circumstances.

The reasonable patient standard focuses on the patient and states that the physician must disclose all information material to the patient's decision to accept the proposed treatment. This is considered the more modern standard. Some states have adopted this standard through legislation. In Pennsylvania, for example, state law requires physicians to inform a patient of the nature of the proposed treatment, its risks, and the alternatives that a reasonable patient would consider material to the decision about whether to undergo treatment. [40 Pa. Cons. Stat. § 1303.504] Similarly, the Alaska Supreme court focused on the reasonable patient standard when a physician recommended that a patient go to the emergency room for treatment. The court ordered the lower court to determine whether the physician had disclosed enough information for a reasonable patient to determine whether to seek treatment. The physician had disclosed that the emergency room would probably take x-rays and insert a nasogastric tube for this person with abdominal pain; however, it was claimed that he failed to disclose the seriousness of the situation, the risk she faced, and the need to seek immediate attention. [*Marsingill v. O'Malley*, 58 P.3d 495 (Ala. 2002)]

Does the failure to disclose relevant information to a patient automatically result in liability?

Even when relevant information is not disclosed, there is no liability unless a court is convinced that the patient, if given the information that should have been disclosed, would have chosen a different course of treatment and avoided physical injury. This link between the nondisclosure and the patient's injury is called proximate cause or causation.

Under the reasonable patient standard, the patient must prove that the specific danger that was not disclosed was material (important) to the patient's decision. Some courts measure this by determining what a reasonable person would find material to his or her decision, while other courts require the information to be tailored to the needs of the particular circumstances of the patient in the case at hand.

Is a signed consent form sufficient evidence of informed consent?

Simply requiring the patient to sign a form does not satisfy informed consent requirements, as the form serves merely as evidence of the informed consent process. For example, a general consent form, worded to permit a physician to perform whatever procedures are in the patient's best interest, is invalid because it does not illustrate that the patient made an informed decision after receiving adequate information. On the other hand, it is important to document consent or the lack of consent. While not legally conclusive, a well-written, properly executed consent form is strong evidence that informed consent was given.

A legally effective consent form must

- be signed voluntarily;
- show that the procedure performed was the one to which consent was given; and
- show that the consenting person understood the nature of the procedure, the risks involved, and the probable consequences.

Some state statutes create a presumption that a written informed consent is valid. For example, in Ohio, a consent is considered valid if it (1) sets forth the nature of the procedures, (2) the person making the consent acknowledges disclosure and that all questions were answered, and (3) is signed by the patient or his legal representative. To overcome this presumption of validity, a claimant must show by a preponderance of the evidence that the consent was not in good faith, was fraudulent, or made by someone who did not understand English. [Ohio Rev. Code § 2317.54] Other states place the burden of proof on the plaintiff to show that the medical provider did not supply appropriate information in obtaining the consent or did not inform the patient of the common risks and alternatives. [See Tenn. Code Ann. § 29-26-118 requiring appropriate information and Alaska Stat. 09.55.556 requiring discussion of risks and alternatives, and Utah Code Ann. § 78-14-5 requiring substantial and significant risks.] Note that generally, however, a patient does not need to be informed of every remote risk.

Other state statutes provide defenses to medical malpractice based on failure to obtain informed consent. These defenses include the fact that the risks not disclosed were remote, a statement by the patient that he would continue treatment regardless of risk, the fact that consent was not possible, or health care provider judgment and discretion that full disclosure would adversely impact the patient. [Alaska Stat. § 09.55.556]

Is consent required in a medical emergency?

A true medical emergency may obviate the need for consent. The two factors necessary to trigger the emergency care doctrine are the patient's incapacity to consent and the need for immediate treatment. When immediate treatment is required to preserve life or prevent a serious impairment to health and it is impossible to obtain the patient's consent or that of someone authorized to consent on the patient's behalf, the physician may perform the required procedure without liability. Consent is implied by law as a matter of public policy because the physician's inaction in an emergency might result in greater harm to the patient.

Some states have enacted laws that formalize this emergency exception to the informed consent requirement. In Pennsylvania, for example, the physician's duty to obtain informed consent does not apply in emergencies. [40 Pa. Cons. Stat. § 1303.504]

What if the patient is able to consent but the need for quick action does not permit full disclosure?

This situation may occur in the ED when, for example, a patient presents with a heart attack in progress, a snake bite, or a severe allergic reaction. These situations do not meet the strict parameters of the emergency doctrine because the patient may be competent and able to consent to treatment. The situation is exigent, however, and the physician may not have time to provide full disclosure of all possible treatment alternatives.

Some states have enacted laws recognizing an exception to the consent requirement in such circumstances. In Alaska, for example, failure to obtain consent is permissible when "under the circumstances, consent by or on behalf of the patient was not possible." [Alaska Stat. § 09.55.556]

In states that have not recognized this exception in either case law or statute, the physician will have to make a reasonable medical decision, communicate with the patient as much as possible while not delaying necessary treatment, and document the circumstances and his or her reasons for proceeding. One view is that the patient's coming to the ED in need of immediate treatment implies the patient's consent. Another view is that treatment in such circumstances is simply a logical and necessary extension of the emergency doctrine.

How serious must the patient's condition be to render care without consent?

The patient's condition must be so serious that the initiation of treatment cannot be delayed until consent is obtained or the patient would suffer death or serious permanent impairment. This is a medical judgment. In cases in which delay would not materially increase the hazards, although it is clear that the medical treatment in question will be needed in the near term, failure to obtain consent cannot be excused on the grounds that an emergency existed. Courts have ruled that no consent was needed in the following cases:

- A 17-year-old boy's elbow was crushed beyond repair, and three physicians agreed that amputation was necessary to protect his life. The patient was unconscious from anesthetic administered to allow suturing of a profusely bleeding head wound and his family could not be contacted. [*Jackovach v. Yocum,* 237 N.W. 444 (Iowa 1931)]
- A 15-year-old boy's foot was run over by a train. A physician and four surgeons agreed that it was necessary to amputate the foot to save the patient's life. Although there was evidence at trial that it was possible to save the foot, the court ruled that it was inconceivable that the patient's parents would have refused to consent to the amputation under the circumstances. [*Luka v. Lowrie,* 136 N.W. 1106 (Mich. 1912)]
- A physician amputated a patient's gangrenous lower leg without obtaining informed consent. The court ruled that the physician was not liable because the patient's condition constituted a life-threatening emergency. [*Stafford v. Louisiana State Univ.,* 448 So. 2d 852 (La. Ct. App. 1984)]

What should ED staff do to comply with consent requirements in an emergency?

As with all questions of fact, it is important that the need for haste in rendering treatment be documented fully and carefully. Whenever possible, the health care provider should seek confirmation that an immediate threat to life or health exists. Hospitals should insist that staff engage in such consultation as time and circumstances permit. Findings supporting the existence of an emergency should be noted on the patient's record, with particular emphasis on the nature of the threat, its immediacy, and its magnitude. The initialing of such notations by consultant physicians is advisable from an evidentiary standpoint; at the least, the consulting physicians' names should be recorded.

The attending physician should be particularly wary of proceeding when a difference of opinion surfaces about the need for immediate treatment. Unfortunately, such disagreements do arise from time to time, forcing providers to choose between a conservative course safeguarding their legal position and the professional and ethical imperative to attempt to preserve life and health. See **Appendix 1-A** for a state-by-state description of consent to emergency medical treatment.

Can health care providers rely on the emergency doctrine if a patient representative is available?

The emergency doctrine contemplates not only that a medical situation require immediate treatment but also that the provider be unable to consult with next of kin or others recognized by the law as capable of giving consent on the patient's behalf. The search for such proxy authorization must extend as far as available time reasonably allows. State law often defines who may act on the patient's behalf. If these persons are not available, or if trying to contact them would be impractical given the urgency of the situation, then treatment can be rendered without consent under the emergency doctrine.

What is administrative consent?

The attempt to locate next of kin frequently falls to the hospital's administrative officials, which explains in part the significance of the so-called administrative consent to emergency care. The administration's approval serves three basic purposes:

1. documenting that the fullest possible attempt was made to secure a proxy consent;
2. showing that someone with experience in emergency health care situations concurred with the physician's judgment that immediate care was needed (in fact, it might be used to provide additional proof that the hospital took all reasonable steps to ensure adequate medical consultation); and
3. preventing the hospital from later instituting any internal disciplinary action against the physician for proceeding without consent.

Administrative consent may be spelled out in a hospital policy or procedure and should be followed so that it protects both the institution and the practitioner. What must be recognized, however, is that the administration of a hospital has no special power to grant a legally effective consent; that must come from the patient, from a duly empowered representative, or from the circumstances. Administrative consent serves essentially an evidentiary function. Its significance and the procedures for its issuance should be clearly communicated to all members of the administrative and medical staffs.

What if the patient representative refuses to consent to treatment a provider considers essential to save the patient's life?

Where the circumstances clearly dictate immediate medical treatment but the person empowered to speak for the patient forbids it, the provider may not be absolutely bound by that decision. Assuming the necessity of treatment can be proved, the provider probably will not be held liable for proceeding. Such an approach is risky, however. It is much safer to secure a court order authorizing the treatment if there is time to do so. Some hospital administrations have set up channels for seeking court orders authorizing the provision of treatment when consent cannot be obtained in the regular manner. The court's power in this regard may be set forth by statute. Such procedures are often used for providing treatment to minors when their parents cannot be located to give consent or, more rarely, when the parents are available but refuse consent.

A New York case illustrates the use of a court order to avoid liability. A patient was unconscious and unable to either refuse or consent to needed surgical treatment. His wife refused to authorize treatment. A court authorized treatment, finding that the patient would die without surgery. The court pointed out that physicians should not be exposed to liability for either an unauthorized procedure if they render needed treatment or malpractice if they do not. By authorizing the treatment, the court insulated the physician from liability. [*Collins v. Davis*, 254 N.Y.S.2d 666 (Sup. Ct. 1964)]

What kind of treatment is authorized in an emergency?

Authorized treatment during an emergency when there is no patient consent is limited to whatever is reasonable under the circumstances. Reasonable treatment is dictated by the patient's condition. While exploratory surgery may be indicated for a patient who has sustained extensive abdominal injuries in a car accident, the surgeon is not justified in performing elective surgery that is not necessary to treat the emergency situation. Whatever treatment is necessary to alleviate the threat of death or serious permanent injury would be considered reasonable.

Can minors consent to medical treatment?

Generally, minors cannot consent to treatment. In most cases, the health care provider must secure the consent of the minor's parent or other person standing *in loco parentis* (in the place of the parents). There are several exceptions to this rule, however, including emergency situations, emancipated minors, and state laws that allow minors to consent to treatment for various conditions, such as sexual assault, sexually transmitted diseases (STDs), drug or alcohol abuse, and pregnancy-related care. See **Appendix 1-A** for a state-by-state description of when a minor can consent to emergency medical treatment.

What if there is a medical emergency and the parents cannot be located?

Parental consent is implied when there is a need for immediate action necessary to preserve a life or prevent permanent bodily harm, which is the definition of a true emergency.

Most states have statutes specifically addressing consent to emergency medical and surgical treatment of minors. A North Carolina statute, for example, authorizes medical treatment without parental consent if the minor's life or health is in jeopardy or if delaying treatment to seek consent would create a threat of serious injury to the minor. Surgical treatment under such circumstances requires consultation with another surgeon or physician, except in rural areas where consultation may not be promptly available. [N.C. Gen. Stat. §§ 90-21.1 through 90-21.4] Arizona and New Mexico have laws providing that consent may be given on behalf of a minor by anyone standing *in loco parentis* to the minor when an emergency exists and the parents cannot be located. [Ariz. Rev. Stat. § 44-133; N.M. Stat. Ann. § 24-10-2]

What is an emancipated minor?

Most states recognize the concept of the emancipated minor, that is, one who, although below the chronological age of majority, has assumed the lifestyle and responsibilities of an adult. Emancipation is generally accomplished by marriage and/or cessation of dependency on parental support. Having a separate home and independent means of financial support are key factors in assessing emancipation. In many states, a minor is automatically emancipated upon becoming a parent. Whether a minor is emancipated is a factual question that depends on the circumstances of the particular case.

Most states have statutes that allow married and emancipated minors to give effective consent to medical and surgical treatment. Many of these statutes also provide that parents of minors have the power to consent to care of their children. A Delaware statute states that consent for treatment of any minor by any licensed medical, surgical, dental, or osteopathic practitioner or any hospital or public clinic, and to hospitalization and other reasonably necessary care, may be given by

- a parent or guardian;
- a married minor or, if the married minor is unable to give consent by reason of physical disability, then by his or her spouse;
- a minor of the age 18 years or more;
- a parent of a minor for his or her child; and
- a minor or any person professing to be temporary custodian of the minor at the request of a parent or guardian, "for the examination and treatment of (i) any laceration, fracture, or other traumatic injury or (ii) any symptom, disease, or pathology" that may reasonably be expected to "threaten the health or life of such minor; provided that the consent given shall be effective only after reasonable efforts shall have been made to obtain the consent of the parent or guardian." [Del. Code Ann. tit. 13, § 707]

What is mental competency?

For consent purposes, competency is an ability to understand the nature and consequences of the treatment to which one is asked to consent. Mental incompetency is not limited to patients who have been legally declared incompetent. It also includes patients who, in the opinion of the treating physician, are either permanently or temporarily unable to give consent. Permanent inability to give consent may apply to patients who suffer from mental retardation or senility. Temporary inability to give consent may result from head injury, alcohol, or drugs.

Who can consent to treatment if the person is mentally incompetent?

If a person has been declared legally incompetent, and a legal guardian or conservator has been appointed, that person's consent must be obtained. The guardian or conservator should be asked to provide proof of legal authority to make medical decisions for the patient.

In many cases, the person has not been declared legally incompetent, but in the physician's medical judgment the person is either permanently or temporarily incompetent to provide consent to treatment. Whenever possible, a hospital or other provider contemplating treatment of a person arguably incompetent should try to obtain substituted consent from the person's next of kin or a court order authorizing the proposed treatment. If the next of kin refuses to consent, it may still be possible to obtain a court order allowing the treatment.

In some cases the patient, while competent, may have executed an advance directive (such as a durable power of attorney) relating to the provision of medical care if the person is incapacitated. Such a document may grant agents full power and authority to make health care decisions on behalf of the person who executed the document to the same extent as that person would make if he or she were competent.

In emergency situations, when death or serious harm is imminent, general rules regarding emergency treatment will protect the provider who acts reasonably and in good faith. See **Appendix 1-A** for a state-by-state description of capacity and consent to emergency medical treatment.

Who can refuse treatment when a person is mentally incompetent?

In light of legal battles over treatment refusal and the right to withdraw life support, a number of states have passed statutes that give surrogate decision makers the right to determine if treatment may be refused or withheld. These surrogate decision makers are typically the next of kin and can refuse treatment even if it will result in death. Statutes frequently specify that the person must be terminally ill or in a persistent vegetative state (PVS) in order for support to be withheld. Some statutes provide guidelines on how the decision will be made. The primary approaches to surrogate decision making include: (1) substituted judgment in which the surrogate makes the decision the person would make if competent and able to do so, (2) clear and convincing evidence standard in which the surrogate must set forth proof that the person wished to have life support terminated, and (3) the best interests of the patient standard in which objective criteria are used to determine if refusal or termination of life sustaining treatment is in the best interest of the person.

Some states also provide for the physician to make the decision. This typically occurs when no surrogate is available, no guardian has been appointed, and there is no advanced directive. The physician may be authorized to make the decision independently or may be required to obtain the consensus of a second physician. When a state has this kind of statute, the physician would be authorized to withhold treatment without court order. For example, the Utah statute requires the physician to obtain the written consent of another physician as well as the legal guardian or spouse, parent, or adult child to terminate a life-sustaining procedure. [Utah Code Ann. § 75-2-1107]

Have any courts applied mental incompetency analysis to intoxicated patients?

A Rhode Island case illustrates how incompetency to consent may be applied in an emergency when an intoxicated patient refuses medically necessary treatment. A patient arrived at the ED complaining of head, eye, back, and rib pain after a car accident in which he was not wearing a seat belt. He had consumed the equivalent of 16 alcoholic drinks and his blood alcohol level was 0.233, well above the state's legal limit for driving (0.10). The patient learned that a physician planned to perform a peritoneal lavage to check for abdominal bleeding. The patient refused to consent to the procedure. The physician explained to the patient that he was not in a position to appreciate his injuries and that the physician was following standard hospital procedure. The patient attempted to get up and began yelling and struggling with the physician. A security guard arrived, and the patient was restrained and administered anesthesia. The procedure was performed and the patient sued, arguing that he did not consent. The hospital defended that it properly administered emergency treatment to a patient who was not competent to refuse consent in accordance with hospital protocol and medical professional practice guidelines.

The highest court in Rhode Island considered whether intoxication could be presented to a jury as evidence of incompetence to consent. To consent to treatment, a patient should be able to reasonably understand his or her condition, the nature and effect of the proposed treatment, and the risks of pursuing and not pursuing the treatment. Determining whether a patient is in a mental condition to understand the risks and consequences of treatment includes an assessment of the effect of intoxication, the court ruled. Cautioning that intoxication does not make every patient incapable of informed consent, the court held that a particular patient's capacity is for the jury to assess. In this case, the jury should consider testimony that the hospital complied with the standards of the American College of Surgeons, the effects of a 0.233 blood alcohol content, the practices of physicians in similar situations, and hospital protocol for treating intoxicated patients injured in serious accidents. [*Miller v. Rhode Island Hosp.*, 625 A.2d 778 (R.I. 1993)]

Can a mental health patient give valid consent to treatment?

It is a medical judgment whether a patient is able to understand the information necessary for informed consent and make a rational decision regarding that information. There is no presumption of inability to give valid consent merely because the patient is a mental health patient. The medical determination of whether a patient is competent to consent to treatment should be well documented in the medical record. For additional discussion, see "What is mental competency?" For sample documentation, see **Part 4**.

What is an advance directive?

An advance directive is a witnessed, written (and in some states oral) statement voluntarily executed by a person who is mentally competent. An advance directive may appoint an agent who will render health care decisions on behalf of the patient and may indicate the type of treatment or withholding of treatment the patient wishes in the event he or she is unable to make such decisions when treatment is necessary. Advance directives include living wills and durable powers of attorney for health care. For sample documentation, see **Part 4**.

How do advance directives apply in emergency situations?

Several state laws include provisions that address the effect of an advance directive in an emergency situation. This usually arises in the case of a seriously or terminally ill patient who has executed an advance directive. Generally, when emergency medical services personnel are called, they initiate cardiopulmonary resuscitation (CPR) when necessary; however, this may be altered by an advance directive.

In Arkansas, for example, the EMS Do Not Resuscitate Act refers to a standardized card, form, necklace, or bracelet of uniform size and design used to indicate that the patient has executed an advance directive specifically addressing cardiopulmonary resuscitation or that the patient's attending physician has issued an EMS DNR order for the patient and has documented the grounds in the patient's medical record. Such identification authorizes qualified EMS personnel to withhold cardiopulmonary resuscitation in the event of a cardiac or respiratory arrest. [Ark. Code Ann. § 20-13-901]

The following is an example of how the advance directive would work in this situation. The caregiver of a seriously ill patient calls 911 when the patient begins to go into crisis. The EMS team arrives prepared to administer CPR if the patient's condition warrants it. Because the patient has previously executed an advance directive specifically prohibiting CPR, and the caregiver has approved documentation to that effect and presents it to the EMS team, CPR is not administered. The EMS team is still authorized to provide other types of support to ensure the patient's safety and comfort, including intravenous fluids, oxygen, nutrition, or hydration, and can transport the patient to a health care facility. In the absence of proper documentation regarding the advance directive, the EMS personnel would have begun CPR if the patient's condition warranted it, regardless of the caregiver's statements.

Should advance directives be followed in the ED?

If the attending physician is aware of the advance directive, it should be followed. According to the patients' rights Condition of Participation required by CMS, hospitals must take measures to protect a patient's right to have hospital staff and practitioners comply with advance directives in providing care to patients. [42 C.F.R. § 483.10] This regulation also specifies that a patient has a right to formulate advance directives, and therefore if the patient is competent upon arriving in the ED and requests assistance in drafting an advance directive, the hospital should be prepared to offer such assistance. If, however, the patient's condition and the circumstances do not allow for providing such assistance (i.e., the patient arrives at the ED unconscious with life-threatening medical condition), necessary treatment should not be delayed to permit extensive investigation into whether the patient has executed a legitimate advance directive.

What if a patient refuses to consent to treatment in the ED?

A competent adult patient who has been informed of the consequences of such a decision has the right to refuse to consent to treatment. To provide treatment in the face of refusal to consent would constitute battery. Courts have specifically recognized that the emergency treatment exception cannot override the refusal of treatment by a patient who is capable of providing consent, even if the attending physician is persuaded that, without treatment, the patient's life is threatened. [*See, e.g., Shine v. Vega,* 709 N.E.2d 58 (Mass. 1999)] Nor can a physician, after a patient's refusal, wait until the patient's condition worsens or until the patient lapses into unconsciousness and then commence treatment, basing such action on the existence of an emergency or the patient's lack of competence.

If the patient refuses care in the face of pressing need, this may be evidence of incompetence. The attending physician must make a medical judgment of whether the patient is competent. This assessment must be fully documented and medically supportable.

If the patient is not competent, there may be a patient representative who is authorized to consent to treatment. However, if a patient is not capable of giving consent and a relative refuses to consent to treatment that the provider considers essential to the patient's life or health, the provider should seek a court order authorizing such treatment.

Can a suicidal patient give a valid refusal of treatment?

As discussed under Mental Competency, above, certain patients lack the competency to consent to or refuse treatment. When patients are brought to the ED after a suicide attempt and refuse to consent to life-saving care, many clinicians deem the individual incompetent to refuse care on the basis of the suicide attempt alone and provide necessary emergency treatment despite their refusal. A risk assessment supports this view, as a wrongful treatment or false imprisonment suit poses a lesser risk of hospital liability than a wrongful death suit. Some courts have upheld the right of suicidal patients to refuse care, however, especially if those patients are terminally ill. Thus, ED leaders should consider requiring a competency evaluation, where time allows, before overriding these patients' refusals. If the patient is found competent, the refusal to accept treatment should be honored.

How should refusal of consent be documented?

Refusal of consent should be documented in the medical record, along with documentation that the consequences of the person's refusal to consent were explained to the patient and the physician's assessment that the patient was competent at the time of the refusal.

It is also good policy to obtain a signed release form that exculpates the hospital and its employees and staff from liability for any consequences flowing from the refusal. It should contain the information stated above. If the patient refuses to sign a release form, a note reflecting that should be added to the medical record.

Antidiscrimination Laws

What laws prohibit race, national origin, and gender discrimination?

A number of laws provide overlapping prohibitions against discrimination in hospitals. Public hospitals are subject to the federal Constitution, including the Equal Protection clause of the 14th Amendment. This clause prohibits state action (applied by some courts to include hospital care) from being used to deny individuals equal protection of the laws—making race and gender unlawful criteria for restricting or denying public hospital care.

Receipt of federal funding triggers a number of nondiscrimination provisions. Under Title VI of the Civil Rights Act of 1965, institutions that receive federal assistance (including Medicare, Medicaid, and Hill-Burton funds) must not discriminate on the basis of race, color, or national origin. [42 U.S.C. §§ 2000d through 2000d-7] Title II of the Civil Rights Act of 1964, which prohibits race, color, religion, and national origin discrimination, has also been applied to hospitals, as both public and private hospitals come within the definition of "public accommodation."[42 U.S.C. §§ 2000a through 2000a-6] Hospitals that receive Hill-Burton funds are prohibited from discriminating on the basis of race, color, national origin, creed, or any other grounds unrelated to the patient's need for the service or the availability of the needed service, presumably including gender. [42 C.F.R. § 124.603]

Finally, many states have enacted laws that preclude institutions serving the public from discriminating on the basis of race, ethnic background, and gender. Provisions specifically barring hospitals from discriminating on these grounds are incorporated in many hospital licensure laws.

What should hospitals do to avoid race, national origin, and gender discrimination suits?

Hospital admitting policies should be reviewed for compliance with antidiscrimination laws. Although it is not likely that policies explicitly condone disparate treatment of minorities, policies may disparately affect patients in protected minority groups in violation of antidiscrimination laws. For example, a policy automatically excluding all pregnant women from a drug detoxification program constituted discrimination on the basis of sex if the facility had the capacity to safely treat some pregnant women, a New York court has ruled. [*Elaine W. v. Joint Diseases N. Gen. Hosp. Inc.*, 613 N.E.2d 523 (N.Y. 1993)] Policies that limit Medicaid patients to a certain number of beds may also discriminatorily affect minority groups.

What federal laws govern discrimination on the basis of handicap or disability?

There are two major federal statutes that prohibit discrimination on the basis of handicap or disability. Under the Rehabilitation Act of 1973, individuals cannot be excluded from participating in or receiving the benefits of a federally financed program or activity (including Medicare, Medicaid, and Hill-Burton) solely because they have handicaps. [29 U.S.C. § 794(a)]

Title III of the Americans with Disabilities Act (ADA) of 1990 prohibits places of public accommodation from discriminating against individuals with disabilities in the provision of goods and services. Hospitals are specifically included within the definition of "public accommodation." Unlike the Rehabilitation Act, the ADA does not require receipt of federal funds to apply. [42 U.S.C. §§ 12182 through 12189]

What are an ED's legal duties toward disabled patients?

Under the ADA and the Rehabilitation Act, hospitals may not offer unequal services to individuals with disabilities. This prohibition requires not only that hospitals make nondiscriminatory treatment and admitting decisions, but also that hospitals accommodate disabled patients so that the services offered to disabled patients are equal to those offered to nondisabled patients. For example, hospitals may make the exchange of information between staff and deaf patients "equal" by providing sign language interpreters for deaf patients and their families so that they may participate in their health care to the same extent as a nondisabled individual. Other accommodations that may be necessary for disabled individuals to make comparable use of ED services include posted signs, Braille materials, a policy addressing service animals in the ED, and improved physical accessibility of hospital facilities.

Patients with Limited English Proficiency (LEP)

Emergency departments are frequently involved with patients and families who speak no English at all, or if they have some ability, their comprehension level in English makes communications difficult. This communication barrier makes obtaining informed consent difficult and makes active decision making by the family nearly impossible. In response to federal constitutional provisions, antidiscrimination laws, and court decisions, HHS's Office of Civil Rights (OCR) has issued requirements over the past 30 years on these issues, but hospitals have been very slow to adopt them, which has resulted in substantial compliance issues. In 2000, the OIG issued guidelines that outline the requirements for hospitals and their departments, including emergency services. [Title VI of the Civil Rights Act of 1964: Policy Guidance on the Prohibition against National Origin Discrimination as It Affects Persons with Limited English Proficiency. 65 Fed. Reg. 52,762-52,774 (Aug. 30, 2000)] The guidelines were subsequently modified and republished in 2002. [67 Fed. Reg. 4968 (Feb. 1, 2002)] Revised guidelines were published in 2003. [68 Fed. Reg. 47,311 (Aug. 8, 2003)]

Under the new federal guidelines, do hospitals have a responsibility to provide foreign language interpreters?

The 2003 OCR policy guidance focuses on the need to take reasonable steps to ensure meaningful access to programs and activities by LEP persons. Hospitals are expected to establish meaningful communication with "Limited English Proficient" (LEP) patients when reasonable based on a balancing of the need to make services accessible without creating an undue burden on small or nonprofit organizations. The guidelines, which apply to hospitals that receive federal funds such as Medicare and Medicaid, do not have the force of law or regulation, but should be closely considered, because they set forth the criteria that investigators will rely on when investigating claims of national origin discrimination based on failure to provide no cost interpretive services, and also suggest "safe harbors" that can be used to ensure that OCR will not find a facility in violation. The guidelines are clear that failure to comply with a safe harbor does not indicate noncompliance with the guidelines.

The 2003 guidelines focused on four factors to consider in determining the organization's LEP responsibility. These are: (1) The number or proportion of LEP persons eligible or likely to be served by the program or organization. The greater the number or percentage of LEP persons served, the greater the need for services. (2) The frequency with which the LEP individual comes into contact with the program. For these purposes, an organization can differentiate a language such as Spanish, which may be encountered frequently, from another language that is used less frequently. (3) The nature and importance of the program to people's lives. For example, emergency surgery and consent would be important with a high need for services, while consent for elective surgery might be delayed without a negative impact. (4) The resources available and costs involved to implement a program. Each organization will then determine the appropriate mix of LEP services through oral interpreters and written translated materials that is necessary under the four-factor test.

The need for translation of both written documents and oral communications must be assessed. The OCR outlined safe harbor guidelines to help a hospital determine when documents need to be translated into other languages. The safe harbor requires that

- the HHS recipient provides written translation of vital documents to each LEP group with five percent or 1,000 individuals, whichever is less, or
- when less than 50 individuals in a language group meet the five-percent standard the organization does not need to translate the vital document, but should provide written notice in the LEP person's primary language of the right to oral interpretation of materials free of cost.

A vital document is one such as an intake form, consent form, or test; non-vital documents include general information. [68 Fed. Reg. 47,311 (Aug. 8, 2003)]

How should notice be provided to LEP persons?

An organization has flexibility to determine how to provide notice to LEP persons based on the four-factor test. Methods of providing notice include, but are not limited to:

- posting and maintaining signs in regularly encountered languages other than English in waiting rooms, reception areas and other initial points of entry. These signs should inform applicants and beneficiaries of their right to free language assistance services and invite them to identify themselves as needing such services [general information is available in other languages on the Internet at *http://www.lep.gov*];
- using telephone and voice menu services with multiple languages;
- translation of application forms and instructional, informational, and other written materials into appropriate non-English languages by competent translators;

- inclusion of statements about the services available and the right to free language assistance services, in appropriate non-English languages, in brochures, booklets, outreach and recruitment information, and other materials that are routinely disseminated to the public; and
- through community outreach with non-English spots on television or radio or presentations at schools and churches.

May a hospital depend on the use of family as interpreters?

The guidance encourages a hospital or the care provider to determine the competence of an interpreter. Options for hospitals in regard to interpreters include:

- hiring bilingual staff
- hiring staff interpreters
- contracting with an outside interpreter service
- using telephone interpreters
- using community volunteers
- using family or friends.

When using family members, the provider should be aware of conflicts of interest that may arise or limits of ability that impact translation. For example, in the ED language assistance should not result in delay of medical emergency treatment. A family member may serve as a good interpreter in the ED. Extra caution should be taken when using a minor to interpret and in using a family member to interpret when there is a concern about possible abuse.

A recent study of medical errors and interpreters found that family and staff interpreters had a higher interpretation error rate than professional interpreters. These errors included omission of words or phrases (52 percent), addition of terms (8 percent), substitution with different phrases (13 percent), editorialization by adding their own view (10 percent), and false fluency—using a word or phrase that did not exist (16 percent). Sixty-three percent of the translation errors had medical consequences. For example, one interpreter told a family to begin topical steroids in four days when the physician said to start it immediately and administer it for four days. [Flores G., Laws M.B., Mayon S.J., et al., *Errors in Medical Interpretation and Their Potential Clinical Consequences in Pediatric Encounters,* Pediatrics, 2003 (111:6-14)] Thus, care should be taken in using family or staff interpreters who have not been trained.

In a non-emergency situation if the caregiver determines that the family member is unable to continue translating because of the technical medical terminology, the exam should be delayed while arrangements are made for another interpreter. This may be as simple as a locating a bilingual staff member or calling a telephone interpreter. [68 Fed. Reg. 47,311 (Aug. 8, 2003)]

How should hospital employees be made aware of the hospital's language assistance policies and procedures?

Over the years, OCR has observed that hospitals often develop effective language assistance policies and procedures but that employees are unaware of the policies, or do not know how to, or otherwise fail to, provide available assistance. Effective training is one means of ensuring that there is not a gap between a hospital's written policies and procedures, and the actual practices of employees who are in the front lines interacting with LEP persons.

It is important that this training be part of the orientation for new ED and other hospital employees and that all employees in client contact positions be trained properly. Given the high turnover rate among some employees, hospitals may find it useful to maintain a training registry that records the names and dates of employees' training.

What are the elements of an effective LEP plan?

An effective LEP plan should include the following components: (1) identification of LEP individuals who are in need of services, (2) language assistance measures, which are made available to staff who know how to obtain such services, (3) staff training, (4) notice to LEP persons that services are available and free of charge in the language the LEP person will understand, and (5) monitoring and updating the LEP plan to regularly determine if changes have occurred that would warrant a program change.

What monitoring or quality improvement programs should be utilized?

It is crucial for a hospital to monitor its language assistance program on a regular basis to assess the current LEP makeup of its service area, the frequency of contact with the language group, the importance of the activity to the LEP person, the available hospital resources, the assistance needed to meet the needs of the LEP person, whether staff members know of the LEP plan, and sources for assistance and whether they are still current and viable. One element of such an assessment is for a hospital to seek feedback from clients and advocates. OCR has stated that compliance with Title VI is most likely when a hospital continuously monitors its program, makes modifications where necessary, and periodically trains employees in implementation of the policies and procedures.

How will OCR enforce compliance with the LEP requirements of Title VI?

OCR's goal is to encourage voluntary compliance with the guidance policy in a way that balances the need for services with the costs of compliance. The guidelines are intended to encourage organizations to take reasonable steps to ensure meaningful access for LEP persons through use of the four-factor analysis. [68 Fed. Reg. 47,311 (Aug. 8, 2003)]

Have state laws addressed the issue of non-English-speaking patients?

Some states have enacted laws requiring hospitals to provide foreign language interpreters. A law in Massachusetts, for example, requires hospitals to provide emergency services in all emergency rooms to non-English speaking patients [105 Mass. Regs. 130.1103]. Hospitals in that state must designate a coordinator of interpreter services and notify ED patients of their right to an interpreter and may not use underage family members as interpreters.

How have courts and government investigators viewed the ED's duty to accommodate deaf and hard of hearing ED patients?

There have been a number of lawsuits brought by patients against hospitals for failing to provide sign language interpreters in the ED. The federal Department of Justice has prosecuted a number of these claims as well. Hospitals have set forth a number of arguments in defending charges of discrimination, contending that

- the patient suffered no adverse medical consequences;
- a relative of the patient was available to provide translation services;
- effective communication was established through writing notes, or with the help of a hospital staff member with limited sign language (i.e., finger spelling) skills;
- the hospital had a contract with an interpreter service, but an interpreter was not available promptly.

These arguments have been largely unsuccessful. Courts and investigating agencies have typically reasoned that the hospital cannot escape liability for disability discrimination by showing that adequate communication was established so that the patient received the care he or she needed. Rather, courts and the government have found that the ADA protects not only a deaf patient's right to receive the same medical care as hearing patients, but that the deaf patient be able to participate in his or her care to the same extent as hearing patients. Where hospitals have relied on relatives for translation services, courts have criticized the hospital for relying on an interpreter who may not understand medical terminology and compromising the patient's right to confidential medical care. Further, entering into a contract for translation services does not satisfy the hospital's duty; the services must be available and present when needed in connection with emergency care. [*See, e.g.*, *Negron v. Snoqualmie Valley Hosp.*, 936 P.2d 55 (Wash. Ct. App. 1997); *Naiman v. New York Univ.*, 95 Civ. 6469 (LMM) (S.D.N.Y. May 13, 1997)]

In 2000, the Justice Department issued a publication entitled "Sign Language Pictograms for Hospital Communication" to 1000 hospitals and hospital associations. This publication was developed in connection with a settlement against 32 hospitals throughout Connecticut that faced allegations under the ADA that they failed to communicate with deaf and hard of hearing patients. The publication consists of illustrations of sign language phrases with captions written in English. For more information, call the Department's toll free ADA information line at 1-800-514-0301. In 2003, the Justice Department issued communication recommendations for hospitals focusing on patients who were deaf or hard of hearing and recommended use of sign language, oral interpreters, cued speech interpreters, or computer-assisted real-time transcription. Interpreters are especially recommended when discussing medication conditions, tests, or treatment; obtaining informed consent; during ongoing physician communication; and when providing follow-up instructions. TTY devices are required at public pay phones for the emergency room and recovery area as well as other waiting areas. Visual alarms should be used to notify people of fire or safety concerns. [*Communicating with People Who Are Deaf or Hard of Hearing in Hospital Settings*, DOJ (Oct. 2003)]

Must a health care provider obtain authorization to disclose personal health information to an interpreter?

When an interpreter helps a covered entity with language services and provides services that are part of the health care operations, then personal health information can be disclosed under the privacy rule as long as the interpreter is part of the workforce as an employee, contract interpreter, or volunteer. If the interpretive services are arranged by contract, then the organization should be sure the contract meets the requirements of a business associate contract. [45 C.F.R. § 160.103] If a family member is used to interpret, then the agreement of the individual patient should be obtained prior to using the service. [45 C.F.R § 164.510 and DHHS FAQ on Sharing PHI with Interpreters (Mar. 8, 2005)]

Patients with HIV or AIDS

Do disability discrimination laws apply to patients with HIV or AIDS?

The ADA protects all individuals who are human immunodeficiency virus (HIV)-positive, even those individuals who are outwardly asymptomatic, the United States Supreme Court has ruled. An individual who was HIV-positive, but not exhibiting the infection's most serious symptoms, went to a dentist for an examination. When the dentist discovered a cavity, he informed the patient that he would not fill her cavity in his office and offered to treat her in the hospital. Although he agreed to charge his regular fee, the patient would be responsible for paying the hospital for the cost of using its facilities. The patient sued the dentist under the ADA. The Supreme Court ruled that the patient's HIV infection was a disability under the ADA. Stating that it was a "misnomer" to refer to HIV as asymptomatic in its early stages, the Court determined that HIV is a physical impairment from the moment of infection because of the immediacy with which the virus begins to damage the infected person's white blood cells and the severity of the disease. Further, HIV infection substantially limits reproduction, which is no less important than activities such as working and learning, which are listed as major life activities in the Rehabilitation Act's regulations defining disability, the Court reasoned. Thus, the Court affirmed that HIV infection is a disability under the ADA. [*Bragdon v. Abbott*, 524 U.S. 624 (U.S. 1998)]

Can EDs be liable for discrimination for exercising special precautions when treating patients with HIV or AIDS?

Courts have ruled that hospitals implementing blood and body fluid precautions when treating patients with HIV and acquired immunodeficiency syndrome (AIDS) are not liable under disability discrimination statutes. [*Doe v. District of Columbia Comm'n on Human Rights*, 624 A.2d 440 (D.C. 1993); *Syracuse Community Health Ctr. v. Wendi A. M.*, 604 N.Y.S.2d 406 (App. Div. 1993), *aff'd*, 659 N.E.2d 760 (N.Y. 1995)] EDs should treat all patients with similar conditions in accordance with hospital practice and procedure, however, and protocols should be based on prevailing medical knowledge. [*North Shore Univ. Hosp. v. Rosa*, 657 N.E.2d 483 (N.Y. App. Div. 1995)]

Treatment must not be delayed, however, or the hospital is at risk for liability under the Consolidated Omnibus Budget Reconciliation Act (COBRA). A federal court in Kansas ruled that a patient who was asked to undergo an HIV test before being treated in a hospital ED can sue under COBRA. The patient sought treatment for abdominal pain, later diagnosed as acute appendicitis. Before he was evaluated and admitted for surgery, however, a physician inquired into the patient's sexual orientation, and upon learning that the patient was homosexual, required him to consent to an HIV test and await the results before being treated. The patient later sued the hospital and the physician, claiming that he did not receive the appropriate medical screening exam required under COBRA, because he was treated differently than similarly situated patients. Rejecting the hospital's argument that COBRA did not apply because there was no proof that treatment was delayed due to an economic motive, the court allowed the claim to proceed. [*Blake v. Richardson*, No. 98-2576-JWL (D. Kan. Apr. 2, 1999)]

Breach of confidentiality is also a concern when special precautions are used for treating patients with infectious diseases. For a discussion of this issue, see "Under what circumstances does the duty to report communicable diseases typically arise?" under ED Records and Confidentiality.

Can hospitals and health care providers be liable for refusing to treat patients with HIV or AIDS?

Hospitals may be held liable for discrimination for refusing to treat or admit patients known or suspected to have HIV or AIDS. For example, an on-call admitting physician and a hospital violated the ADA when the physician refused to admit an HIV-positive man, a federal trial court in Ohio has ruled. The HIV-positive man was traveling when he had a severe allergic reaction to a new prescription medication. He sought treatment in the ED at the nearest hospital, where the attending physician determined that the reaction should be further treated. When the physician requested approval for admission, however, the hospital's on-call admitting physician expressed concern over whether the patient had progressed from HIV-positive to full-blown AIDS status, and he denied admission. Because the patient required prompt medical care, the attending physician arranged for admission at another hospital. The patient sued the hospital and the admitting physician. [*Howe v. Hull*, 873 F. Supp. 72 (N.D. Ohio 1994)]

The court ruled that both the hospital and the admitting physician were liable for discrimination under the ADA. The court found that the admitting physician could be personally liable, because he had the authority and discretion to admit the patient to the hospital and because his decision was not the implementation of an institutional policy at the hospital. The court ruled that the decision not to admit the patient was discriminatory, finding that the patient had been denied the opportunity to receive medical treatment and that the patient's HIV status was the motivating factor in the admitting physician's refusal to admit the patient to the hospital.

Does transferring the care of an HIV-positive patient constitute disability discrimination?

Transferring an HIV-positive patient to another physician or hospital may not constitute disability discrimination under certain circumstances, if the treatment is beyond the provider's expertise or the provider does not have the resources to properly treat the patient.

In one case, for example, a Massachusetts federal trial court ruled that an obstetrician who transferred a pregnant HIV-positive patient to another hospital better able to treat her did not violate the Rehabilitation act or a state disability discrimination statute. [*Lesley v. Chie*, 81 F. Supp. 2d 217 (D. Mass. 2000), *aff'd*, 250 F.3d 47 (1st Cir. 2001)] There the physician transferred the patient to a hospital with more expertise because the hospital where he practiced did not have an AZT program in place, he had never prescribed AZT, and he did not know how to manage its side effects.

Are there confidentiality concerns related to the treatment of patients with HIV or AIDS?

Many states have enacted laws specifically addressing the confidentiality of medical information concerning AIDS, reflecting the importance of protecting the type of medical information from disclosure. These laws prohibit disclosure of HIV status without patient consent, although all of the laws contain statutory exceptions to this blanket prohibition. [*See, e.g.*, Fla. Stat. Ann. § 381.004 and Haw. Rev. Stat. § 325-101] Several states also have general medical confidentiality statutes protecting HIV- or AIDS-related information. Protection of HIV-related information may be available through statutes establishing patient-physician privilege. [*See, e.g.*, N.Y. C.P.L R. 4504(a)] For a more detailed discussion of this issue, see above section, Patients' Rights, Confidentiality of ED Records.

In addition to statutory privileges, if confidential information is improperly revealed, the person could sue for invasion of privacy, defamation, or intentional infliction of emotional distress. In one case, for example, a hospital and physician were found liable for defamation when a newspaper printed the picture of an HIV-positive patient who was being treated at the hospital. [*Anderson v. Strong Mem'l Hosp.*, 531 N.Y.S.2d 735 (Sup. Ct. 1988), *aff'd*, 542 N.Y.S.2d 96 (App. Div. 1989)]

What are the reporting requirements for patients who are HIV-positive or have AIDS?

Laws in all 50 states require the names of people with AIDS to be reported to state or local health departments. In addition, all states have been required to report AIDS cases to the federal CDC since 1983. The reporting requirement is usually imposed on the physician who initially diagnoses AIDS, although it may apply to other health care providers, such as laboratories.

The majority of states also require some sort of HIV case reporting. Name-based reporting for individuals infected with HIV is a contentious issue, however. In order to allay concerns about patient confidentiality, some states report using unique-identifier codes or initials. At least 40 states require some sort of HIV case reporting. Because the reporting requirements differ among states, each hospital should check the requirements of its state law.

What does DHHS recommend when there is a non-occupational exposure to HIV?

The Department of Health and Human Services (DHHS) recommends antiretroviral drugs to prevent HIV infection after unanticipated exposure through sex or injection drug exposure. For those who seek care within 72 hours of exposure and there is substantial risk of transmission, a 28-day course of highly active antiretroviral therapy (HAART) is recommended. The drug therapy should begin as soon as possible after exposure. When the person seeks care more than 72 hours after exposure and there is substantial risk of transmission, no recommendation is made. Each physician should evaluate the risk and care on a case-by-case basis. When the benefits of drug treatment outweigh the risks and exposure is high, then non-occupational post exposure prophylaxis (nPEP) may be considered. When there is little risk of exposure and care is sought more than 72 hours after exposure, nPEP is not recommended. Further, the DHHS recommends counseling to reduce risk. [*Antiretroviral post-exposure prophylaxis after sexual, injection-drug use, or other non-occupational exposure to HIV in the U.S.*, DHHS Recommendations 54 MMWR RR02 (Jan. 20, 2005)]

CONTENT OF THE ED RECORD

The importance of properly charting patient information and the difficulties that arise in accurately recording this information are highlighted when medical services are delivered in an ED. In the ED, the limitations on time and space, the numbers of patients that are seen, and the urgency of medical intervention often make it difficult to properly document all significant findings. The following section discusses legal requirements governing the content of the ED record.

What types of information should an ED record contain?

Many ED record forms are only one page in length, sometimes double sided, and do not provide much space to record information. Even with these space limitations, however, a complete ED record should contain the following types of information:

- patient identification, including demographic information;
- means and time of arrival (although in practice, it is the patient's time of registration with the department that is usually recorded);
- consent signature;
- patient's vital signs;
- history of illness or injury;
- diagnosis;
- reports of procedures, tests, and results;
- medical orders and follow-up instructions;
- patient's condition on discharge or transfer.

For sample documentation, see **Part 4**.

Are there specific legal requirements that govern the content of an ED record?

Legal requirements governing the content of the patient records compiled in hospital EDs are found in state and federal statutes and regulations. In jurisdictions in which there are no state regulations spelling out the content of ED records, the general provisions relating to the content of medical records apply. Frequently, these provisions simply state that the content of a medical record must be adequate, accurate, and complete. The medical record documentation will provide the basis for proper billing that complies with fraud and abuse standards and billing coding requirements.

How does federal law govern the content of an ED record?

At the federal level, the enactment of COBRA significantly increased the importance of establishing complete and accurate emergency care records. Under this statute, any hospital with an ED must provide for an appropriate medical screening examination (MSE) to any individual who comes to the department and requests treatment for a medical condition, or at the request of someone acting on that individual's behalf. A hospital cannot delay an MSE, further medical examination, or treatment to inquire about the individual's method of payment or insurance status. Although the law contains no specific requirements for documentation of medical screening, a hospital should carefully document this type of patient care to defend against charges that it violated the law. The ED should create and retain a record of each medical screening it conducts. If the medical screening indicates that the individual does not have an emergency condition, the hospital will have satisfied its obligations under the law. For evidence purposes, however, its records should demonstrate that the screening was conducted and that such a conclusion was reached.

Proper documentation is particularly important if the individual refuses to consent to the screening or refuses to undergo recommended further treatment. The ED record should include written informed consent when an individual has refused an examination, treatment, or transfer. The law also prohibits transferring an individual who has not been stabilized unless certain consent and medical certification requirements are met. Documentation on the stabilization of a patient's condition or a transfer, therefore, should be accurate and complete in order to prove that the hospital complied with its duties under the law. The documentation should indicate the status of the individual's condition and the treatment provided to achieve stabilization. In the event of a transfer, the record should include a statement by medical personnel that within reasonable medical probability, no material deterioration of the patient's emergency medical condition will result from the transfer or will occur during the transfer process. The transferring hospital must send a copy of all medical records relating to the emergency condition that are available at the time of the transfer, including observations of signs or symptoms, preliminary diagnosis, treatment provided, results of any tests, the informed consent to transfer, the physician's certification, and the name and address of any on-call physician who refused or failed to appear within a reasonable time to provide necessary stabilizing treatment. Failure to do so may not only generate liability under COBRA, but also generate common law liability for the hospital. In a ruling by a federal appeals court, for example, a patient's widow was allowed to sue a hospital for negligence under state law, claiming that its ED failed to forward an X-ray of the patient's chest to the hospital where the patient was transferred. [*Dickey v. Baptist Mem'l Hosp.*, 146 F.3d 262 (5th Cir. 1998)] For a more detailed discussion of ED obligations under COBRA, see "Duty to Treat Patients Regardless of Ability to Pay" in this section. [Note that Medicare regulations on the conditions of participation formerly distinguished between ED records and medical records, but no longer do so.]

How does state law govern the content of an ED record?

Some state laws and regulations specify the information to be recorded in ED records. In Wisconsin, for example, regulations specify that the ED patient record must contain

- patient identification,
- a history of disease or injury,
- physical findings,
- laboratory and X-ray reports, if any,
- diagnosis,
- record of treatment,
- disposition of the case,
- authentication,
- appropriate notations regarding time of the patient's arrival, time of physician notification, time of treatments (including administration of medications), and time of patient discharge or transfer from the service. [Wis. Admin. Code § 124.24]

Similarly, Maine details the content of the ED record, specifying that in addition to the types of information listed above, the record must contain documentation of notification of appropriate authorities in suspected medicolegal cases. [Code of Me. Rules § 10-144-112] In Oklahoma, regulations require that an emergency medical record contain documentation if a patient leaves AMA. [Okla. Admin. Code § 310:667-19-11] Connecticut requires documentation of the reasons for transfer or discharge in the medical record. [Conn. Gen. Stat. § 19a-535]

STAFFING ISSUES

EDs encounter unique staffing issues arising from the necessity of providing 24-hour emergency services every day. State hospital licensure laws govern ED staffing, and on-call staffing requirements vary from state to state. Staffing and compensation requirements under federal laws may also raise legal concerns. For example, EDs are subject to COBRA requirements related to the availability of on-call physicians, as well as fair labor standards pertaining to payment for on-call hours. In addition, federal antidiscrimination law may come into play if ED employees are dissatisfied with an ED's grooming or dress code policies. The nature of providing emergency services may also generate special liability and employment issues, such as refusal to treat an HIV-positive patient, employee substance abuse, failure to respond to a call, and drug ordering by nonphysicians. The following questions and answers discuss state and federal laws as well as judicial decisions relevant to these ED staffing issues.

On-Call Staffing

Are hospitals required to staff the ED with on-call physicians and other employees at all times?

Hospital licensure laws generally require an ED to provide 24-hour services with adequate professional and ancillary staff coverage, including on-call staff, to ensure that all persons are treated within a reasonable length of time, depending on the priority of need for treatment. In some states, the hospital licensure law simply requires that the ED provide 24-hour staff coverage and have at least one physician on call at all times. [*See, e.g.*, Va. Code Ann. § 32.1-127, 12 Va. Admin. Code § 5-410-280] In many states, however, the hospital licensure regulations contain more detailed ED staffing requirements. In Rhode Island, for example, the ED must be staffed on a 24-hour basis by a physician or physicians with more than two years of practice following full licensure or, in hospitals that have an approved residency program, by residents with more than two years of training in specialties of medicine or surgery. [R.I. Code R. § 23-17-10] In Illinois and New Jersey, the ED must have a physician specialist on call and able to arrive within minutes for each major clinical service provided by the hospital. [Ill. Admin. Code tit. 77, § 250.710 ("within minutes")] In Wisconsin, if an on-call physician is unable to reach a patient within 15 minutes, he or she must provide specific instructions to the emergency staff on duty if emergency measures are necessary. [Wis. Admin. Code § 124.24] Many states also require that one registered nurse be on duty in the ED at all times and that ancillary departments, including laboratory, X-ray, and pharmacy, be staffed or provide on-call services at all times. [*See, e.g.*, Ill. Admin. Code tit. 77, § 250.710]

Although not as specific as some state law requirements regarding the availability and response time of on-call physicians, federal requirements under EMTALA (see extensive discussion of this statute later in Part I of this manual) specify that hospitals must maintain a list of on-call physicians who can provide treatment necessary to stabilize a patient with an emergency medical condition. [42 C.F.R. § 489.20(r)(2)] CMS does not require that a hospital's medical staff provide on-call coverage 24 hours a day, 365 days a year. CMS guidance has stated that if there comes a particular time when a hospital does not have on-call coverage for a particular specialty that hospital lacks capacity to treat patients needing that specialty service, and it is therefore appropriate to transfer the patient because the medical benefits of transfer outweigh the risks. [HHS/CMS Program Memorandum to Associate Regional Administrators, *On-Call Requirements-EMTALA,* June 13, 2002] It is desirable, but not mandatory, that when certain specialties are not available full-time, then EMS staff should be advised of times when certain specialties are not available to minimize transfer due to lack of complete on-call coverage. [*EMTALA Final Rule,* 68 Fed. Reg. 53,222 (Sept. 9, 2003)]

Can two hospitals in the same geographic area share on-call coverage so that together they provide full coverage in a particular specialty?

Federal law allows physicians to provide simultaneous on-call coverage at more than one hospital in order to maximize patient access to care; however, when a physician is providing simultaneous on-call coverage at several hospitals, all hospitals involved must be aware of the on-call schedule as each hospital independently has an obligation under EMTALA, and must have policies and procedures to follow when an on-call physician is not available to respond. Policies may include procedures for back-up on-call physicians or the implementation of an appropriate transfer under EMTALA, or any other policies that will meet the needs of emergency patients. [CMS Memorandum to Associate Regional Administrators, *On-Call Requirements-EMTALA*, #S&C-02-34 June 13, 2002; *EMTALA Final Rule,* 68 Fed. Reg. 53,222 (Sept. 9, 2003)]

How frequently is a hospital's medical staff of on-call physicians expected to provide on-call coverage?

Federal law does not set requirements on how frequently a hospital's on-call physician staff is expected to provide on-call coverage. Hospitals are expected to provide services based upon the availability of physicians required to be on-call. CMS has recognized that physician practice demands, conferences, and vacations must be incorporated into the availability of staff, and that some hospitals have limited financial means to maintain on-call coverage all the time. CMS acknowledges that hospitals have flexibility to comply with EMTALA obligations by maintaining a level of on-call coverage that is within their capability. [CMS Memorandum to Associate Regional Administrators, *On-Call Requirements-EMTALA*, #S&C-02-34, June 13, 2002] CMS requires no specific ratio for how many days a hospital must provide on-call physicians based upon the number of physicians on staff for a particular specialty. Rather, on-call coverage should be provided within reason depending on the number of physicians in a specialty. In determining whether a hospital is in compliance CMS has indicated that it will consider the facts of each individual case, including such relevant factors as the number of physicians on staff, other demands on these physicians, the frequency with which the hospital's patients typically require services of on-call physicians, and the provisions the hospital has made for situations in which a physician in the specialty is not available or the on-call physician is unable to respond. The hospital has flexibility to comply within its capability. [*EMTALA Final Rule,* 68 Fed. Reg. 53,222 (Sept. 9, 2003)]

Can senior medical staff be exempted from on-call activities?

The EMTALA final rule makes it clear that exemption of senior medical staff from on-call activities does not necessarily violate EMTALA. The hospital is required to keep an on-call list in a way that "best meets the needs of the hospital's patients." Exemption of senior medical staff based on years of service or age does not violate EMATLA as long as it does not adversely impact patient care. The hospital has flexibility in utilizing its ED personnel. [*EMTALA Final Rule,* 68 Fed. Reg. 53,222 (Sept. 9, 2003)]

What federal law affects payment for on-call hours?

The Fair Labor Standards Act (FLSA), a federal statute governing wage and hour issues, may affect the rate at which employees covered under the Act (or nonexempt employees) are paid for on-call hours. [29 U.S.C. §§ 201 through 219] Most employees are nonexempt and protected under the FLSA. Employers must compensate any nonexempt employee required to work in excess of 40 hours per week at an overtime rate of at least one and one-half times the employee's regular rate. Hospitals, however, may enter agreements with employees to establish an alternative work period of 14 consecutive days and to pay the overtime for hours worked in excess of 80 hours during that period. Even under this option, the employee must be paid overtime rates for hours worked in excess of eight in any one day.

Federal regulations interpreting FLSA requirements address whether employers must pay nonexempt employees for time spent on call. If the health care employer requires an employee to remain on call either at the institution or so close to it that the employee cannot effectively use the time for his or her own purposes, then the time spent on call must be compensated as working time. For example, when a hospital employee returns home after a normal shift with the understanding that he or she is expected to return to the hospital in the event of an emergency, the time spent at home is normally not compensable. If, however, the conditions placed on the employee's activities are so restrictive that the employee cannot use the time effectively for personal pursuits, then such time on call is compensable. [29 C.F.R. § 553.221]

How have courts determined whether on-call time constitutes working time under the FLSA?

Courts have also focused on whether restrictions placed on the employee during on-call hours prevented the employee from using the time for his or her own purposes. A Colorado appeals court, for example, ruled that four physician assistants (PAs) employed by a multiple-site state correctional facility were entitled to overtime compensation for time spent on call. The PAs each worked 40 hours per week and also rotated through on-call time, during which they would provide emergency medical services after regular working hours. The state paid the PAs one and one-half times their regular rate for hours when they were physically present at a facility on a call, but it did not compensate them for time spent waiting for calls. The PAs argued they should be paid for all on-call hours because the employer required a 20-minute response time to any of seven sites located within an 8-mile radius, and so they could not use the on-call time for personal pursuits. The appeals court agreed, concluding that the short response time, high volume of calls, number of facilities, and geographical radius between facilities placed severe restrictions on the PAs' activities during on-call hours. The court found that the time was used predominantly for the employer's benefit and therefore was working time. [*Casserly v. State*, 844 P.2d 1275 (Colo. Ct. App. 1992)]

Similarly, a federal trial court in Georgia has held that, under the FLSA, hospital respiratory therapists who were required to respond to pages during their 30-minute lunch period were entitled to be paid for that break. The therapists wore pagers on their lunch break and were required to respond to a page by calling in immediately. The test for whether a break is compensable is whether the employees are subject to limitations on their personal freedom that inure to the benefit of the employer, the court stated. In this case, such criteria have been met, the court concluded, because the hospital benefited from its requirement that therapists respond to pagers, and the therapists' use of their time during lunch breaks was significantly limited by this requirement. [*Hoffman v. St. Joseph Hosp.*, Civ. No. 1:97-CV-0753-RLV (N.D. Ga. Apr. 14, 1998)]

On the other hand, some courts have held on-call time noncompensable. A federal trial court in Kansas, for example, ruled that hospital emergency medical technicians who work a 24-hour on-call shift during which they must remain within city limits were not entitled to compensation for on-call time. Under the hospital's procedures, the on-duty crew would respond to an emergency call, and the on-call crew would be notified to maintain a heightened sense of readiness. If another emergency call came in while the on-duty crew was responding to the prior emergency, the on-call crew was required to report to the hospital in five minutes. The court reasoned that this notification system provided the technicians with a warning that lessened the restrictive nature of the five-minute call-back requirement. [*Burnison v. Memorial Hosp.*, 820 F. Supp. 549 (D. Kan. 1993); *see also, Sletten v. First Care Med. Servs.*, Civil No. 98-2446 (D. Minn. 2000)]

Similarly, emergency medical technicians with a seven-minute response time did not qualify for compensated time because they were able to pursue personal pursuits at home and were thus not considered working while on call. The entire rural town was within the seven-minute response time, there was less than a 50 percent chance the technicians would be called in, and the hospital credited the employees for two hours' work each time they responded at a rate of one and a half their regular salary. Thus, the employees were paid for three hours' work each time they responded even if the actual response was much shorter. If the call took more than two hours, they were compensated for actual time worked. The court found that the FLSA did not require a different arrangement. [*Dinges v. Sacred Heart St. Mary's Hosps.*, 164 F.3d 1056 (7th Cir. 1999)]

Courts have focused on whether someone is "engaged to wait" which would require compensation because other activities are restricted, or whether they are "waiting to be engaged" which time allows them to pursue other personal activities. When an operating nurse was on call with a pager and required to return the call within 5 minutes and report to work within 30 minutes, the court found that she was "waiting to be engaged" because she could pursue other activities at home or in the community during this time so that the on-call time was not compensable. [*Huskey v. Trujillo*, 302 F.3d 1307 (Fed. Cir. 2002)] Some courts have looked at several factors to determine whether on-call time should be compensable which include: whether there is an on-premises living requirement, whether there are excessive geographic restrictions on the employees' movement, whether the frequency of the calls was unduly restrictive, whether the fixed time limit to respond was unduly restrictive, whether call time could be traded, whether a pager could ease restrictions, and whether the person could engage in personal activities. [*Owens v. Local No. 169*, 971 F.2d 351 (9th Cir. 1992)]

What may a hospital ED do to ensure that its policy of payment for on-call employees does not violate the FLSA?

To avoid a potential violation of FLSA's wage and hour provisions, hospitals may wish to make a written request to the Wage and Hour Administrator for an interpretation of the FLSA as applied to the particular facts of the employer's policy of payment for on-call time spent on and off premises.

What may a hospital ED do to ensure that its policy of payment for on-call physicians does not violate the antikickback statute?

In a 2007 advisory opinion, the OIG analyzed a payment arrangement between a medical center and on-call physicians to determine whether there were antikickback concerns. The OIG found that the arrangement had sufficient protections in place to not raise antikickback concerns. While the opinion is specific to the arrangement proposed, it offers guidance on factors the OIG would look at to determine whether an arrangement was acceptable. The situation involved a medical center that had a difficult time getting physicians to take on-call coverage when one-fourth of ED patients had no insurance and one-tenth of those uninsured were admitted to the hospital for follow-up care. This situation created a burden of uncompensated care coupled with malpractice costs for physicians and kept the medical center from meeting its charity care obligation. Physicians in some specialties refused to provide uncompensated care, resulting in ED patient transfer to other facilities.

The hospital formed a committee to evaluate the situation. The committee recommended a two-year contract for providers that required (1) participation in the on-call rotation; (2) inpatient care and consultation follow-up as needed regardless of the patient's ability to pay; (3) provide a timely response to calls from the ED; (4) cooperation with hospital care management, risk management, and quality of care initiatives; and (5) medical record completion by the physician. Noncompliance with the contract requirements would result in termination of the physician. Each physician was paid a per diem rate for each day on call, except for one and one-half days per month (18 days per year) that the physician contributed gratuitously. The per diem rate was based on physician specialty and whether the on-call time was on a weekday or weekend. Specialty per diem rate differences were based on (1) severity of illness the specialty usually evaluated in the ED; (2) likelihood of the specialty's responding to an ED call; (3) likelihood of an inpatient consultation; and (4) degree of inpatient care typically required for the specialty.

The OIG noted that the personal services and management contract provided a safe harbor for arrangements that were in writing and signed; when the agreement covered all provided services; when for periodic or part time services the specifics such as the schedule, length, and charge for performance were spelled out; the agreement was for more than one year; the aggregate compensation was set in advance at fair market value; there was no promotion of a business arrangement to enhance referrals; and the total services compensated did not exceed what was reasonably necessary. This arrangement did not fall under the safe harbor because compensation was not set in advance and could vary from month to month.

The OIG analyzed the arrangement under the antikickback statute and indicated that ED on-call coverage issues based on EMTALA, scarcity of physicians, and the need for accessible care had to be balanced against concerns that physicians might demand on-call reimbursement as a condition of doing business with the hospital, or otherwise misuse payments. The general rule is that any remuneration of the physician by the hospital should be based on the fair market value of actual services provided. OIG is concerned about covert kickbacks that include payments that did not accurately reflect lost income from taking call, payments to compensate physicians when no identifiable services were provided, aggregate payments that are unusually high compared to usual practice income, or payments to the physicians that would be billed to insurers by physicians and paid twice. The OIG raised the issue that any on-call payment could be a disguised payment for referrals.

In this situation the medical center had an outside auditor review the per diem payments and methodology and certify that payments were based on the fair market value of services. The per diem rates were based on the physician's burden and risk of uncompensated services and also provided responsibilities for the physician to provide uncompensated care. There was low risk of referral misuse because the payments were uniform for physicians in each specialty without looking at the volume or value of referrals and the only variables in the payment were based on physician specialty and whether the on-call service was provided on a weekend or weekday. The arrangement also met a legitimate need to provide on-call coverage and uncompensated care. Other features of the arrangement that reduced the risk of an antikickback violation were that all physicians in a specialty were included, the responsibilities for on-call work were divided each month, and physicians had a responsibility for follow-up care regardless of the patient's ability to pay. There was a public benefit from enhanced on-call coverage and increased care for those unable to pay. These costs were assumed by the medical center and not billed to federal programs. Based on these reasons, the OIG found that sufficient safeguards were in place to avoid antikickback concerns. [OIG Advisory Opinion 07-10 (Sept. 27, 2007)]

What happens if a physician doesn't respond to a call?

The ED staff must carefully document what time the physician was called, the information presented to the physician, and the physician's response, including any requests for additional information and the nursing response. When a physician refuses to come in, the nurse attending the patient must follow procedures for appealing to department or hospital leadership and/or calling in an alternate physician. If staff members with concerns about a patient fail to advocate for that patient, the hospital may ultimately be held liable for a bad outcome. For example, Maryland's highest court sustained a verdict against both a hospital and a physician in a case in which a patient was brought to the hospital after he was struck by a car and the physician failed to respond to a call for assistance in the ED. Upon the patient's arrival in the ED, he was not personally attended to by a physician although he was in shock, as indicated by dangerously low blood pressure. There was telephone contact between an ED nurse and the physician who was providing on-call coverage, but the physician failed to come to the hospital until the patient was near death. The court found that the physician's failure to respond was clearly not reasonable care because the physician knew that wounds sustained as a result of a car accident could have been serious internal injuries that should be evaluated and treated by a physician. The court also held that the negligence of the nurse, who failed to contact the on-call physician after the patient's condition had worsened, did not relieve the physician of liability. Relying on the doctrine of respondeat superior, the court ruled that the hospital was liable for the nurse's negligence. [*Thomas v. Corso*, 288 A.2d 379 (Md. 1972)] A federal court in Missouri has also recognized the duty of physicians to respond to call, holding a general surgeon, who attended an out-of-town medical conference while on call without notifying the hospital, liable to a patient whose treatment was delayed as a result. [*Millard v. Corrado*, 14 S.W.3d 42 (E.D. Mo. 1999); but *see Anderson v. Houser*, 523 S.E.2d 342 (Ga. Ct. App. 1999), *cert. denied,* No. S00C0414 (Ga. Mar. 3, 2000) (no liability for on-call physician who was out of town because no doctor-patient relationship existed)]

A physician's failure to respond to a call also has ramifications under EMTALA, the federal statute discussed extensively later in Part 1 of this manual. Under that statute, the physician may be cited and fined up to $50,000 per violation. If CMS (the Centers for Medicare and Medicaid Services) finds that the violation was gross and flagrant or repeated, the physician is subject to exclusion from Medicare and Medicaid. [42 U.S.C. § 1395dd(d)(1)] If the hospital's attempts to call in an alternate physician fail and the patient must be transferred, the physician's refusal to respond and the steps taken to find another provider must be carefully documented, and the EMTALA transfer requirements closely followed.

Failure to respond to call may also trigger investigation or disciplinary proceedings under hospital rules or medical staff bylaws, or by the state medical board. Failure to respond to call may also constitute a breach of the physician's contract with the hospital. Internal reporting requirements and procedures should be closely followed.

Can an on-call physician be held liable to a patient if the physician is not actually called?

Some courts have determined that there is no duty on an on-call attending physician without a showing that the doctor accepted the patient, consulted with a physician about the patient, or was actually summoned for consultation for treatment, unless the on-call agreement between the hospital and the physician provides otherwise. [*Rivera v. Prince George's Cty. Health Dept.*, 649 A.2d 1212 (Md. Ct. Spec. App. 1994), *cert. denied*, 656 A.2d 772 (Md. 1995)] The Virginia Supreme Court recently adopted this reasoning in a case in which a child was brought to a teaching hospital's ED with chicken pox lesions in her mouth and was lethargic and not eating or drinking. Residents did not contact the on-call physician, who was not physically present in the emergency room, but was available to answer any questions from the treating residents. The residents treated the child for dehydration and released her the next morning with instructions to see her pediatrician. The child saw the pediatrician, but developed a serious respiratory condition and later died. In the malpractice suit that followed, the state Supreme Court agreed with the trial court that there was no physician-patient relationship between the child and the on-call physician, and therefore the physician owed the child no duty of care. The high court noted that the physician-patient relationship is a consensual relationship that exists if a patient entrusts her treatment to the physician and the physician accepts the case. Here there was no indication that the physician agreed to accept responsibility for the child's care. She had no direct contact with or consultation concerning the child, and there was no evidence that she assumed responsibility by contract with the hospital or by hospital policy. [*Prosise v. Foster*, 544 S.E.2d 331 (Va. 2001)].

One court, however, has taken a contrary position. The North Carolina Supreme Court held that an on-call attending physician had a common law duty to supervise residents who provided medical care to patients, even though the relationship did not fit traditional notions of the doctor-patient relationship, because of the increasingly complex modern delivery of health care. [*Mozingo v. Pitt County Mem'l Hosp.*, 415 S.E.2d 341 (N.C. 1992)]

Does a telephone consultation with an on-call physician create a physician-patient relationship that could result in liability?

A physician on call with an OB/GYN practice group spoke with a person by phone. The court found that this was not sufficient evidence that a physician-patient relationship had been established, nor was there evidence that the physician had acted negligently. The claim against the on-call physician was dismissed. [*Webb v. Nash Hosps. Inc.*, 133 N.C. App. 636 (N.C. Ct. App. 1999)]

Similarly, a court found that when a transferring hospital physician speaks with a physician at the hospital accepting transfer, the physician at the receiving hospital does not have an established physician-patient relationship to form a duty of care until care is rendered at the receiving hospital. [*Sterling v. John Hopkins Hosp.*, 145 Md. App. 161 (Ct. App. Md. 2001), *cert. denied*, 808 A.2d 808 (2002)]

What does developing an on-call schedule entail?

EMTALA final regulations require each hospital to maintain an on-call list of physicians that "best meets the needs of the hospital's patients who are receiving services" under EMTALA based on the hospital resources "including the availability of on-call physicians." Hospitals must have policies and procedures in place that specify response to situations where a particular specialty is not available or cannot respond due to circumstances beyond the physician's control. Final regulations were effective November 10, 2003. [42 C.F.R. § 489.24(j)]

Although COBRA requires a hospital to establish an on-call schedule for the specialties offered at the facility, the federal law and its implementing regulations do not require 24-hour coverage in all specialties offered. For example, a hospital with only one or two neurosurgeons on staff is required to have an on-call schedule for neurosurgery, but would not be required to have continuous on-call coverage for that specialty. Generally, on-call specialty coverage should be proportionate to care generally available at the hospital. However, when the sub-specialist is called and there is a disagreement about the need to come in, the specialist should defer to the ED physician's judgment. The hospital should ensure that the specialist or sub-specialist has the privileges needed to provide care while on-call. [*EMTALA Final Rule,* 68 Fed. Reg. 53,222 (Sept. 9, 2003)]

To safeguard patients, backup procedures should be in place in the event that an on-call physician becomes unavailable. The on-call lists should be posted and accessible to attending physicians, residents, and nurses, who should be trained on how to use the lists and backup procedures. When planning the on-call schedule, careful consideration should be given to how many backup physicians are necessary in light of the patient load, physician specialties, proportion of patients who present needing care in a particular specialty, whether the physicians take call at more than one facility, whether physician contracts or medical staff bylaws set forth requirements for on-call hours, whether state law requires 24-hour coverage for certain specialties, the physical health of on-call staff, the availability of nearby hospitals for transfer, and other relevant factors.

Joint Commission standards regarding the assessment of community and patient needs should also be considered with respect to the development of an on-call schedule. The Joint Commission standards require leaders to continually evaluate the relationship between patient needs and departmental resources. [For guidance on evaluating patient needs, refer to **Part 3**, under the headings Management of Human Resources and Leadership.]

What can the ED do to ensure adequate specialty call coverage?

Traditionally, on-call panels of physicians have been based on ethical responsibilities of physicians who voluntarily agree to be on-call or legal responsibilities established through medical staff bylaws. However, as the number of uninsured, underinsured, and out-of-plan patients in the ED have increased; as reimbursement has not been available for all ED services; as liability remains high for the ED professional; and as EMTALA rules have eased requirements of mandatory specialty on-call backup, adequate on-call coverage has become a serious problem. The growth of specialty hospitals has also reduced on-call specialty coverage, while EMS providers are left to determine whether specialty hospital care is appropriate based on presenting symptoms. [*ACEP Policy Compendium: Specialty Hospitals* (2004)]

An ACEP study released in 2006 found that three-fourths of EDs reported inadequate specialty coverage, up from two-thirds in 2004. Forty-five percent reported patients leaving without being seen, up from 29 percent in 2004. The top five shortage specialties are orthopedic, plastic surgery, neurosurgery, ear-nose-throat surgery, and hand surgery. One half of the emergency departments reported one to five patients a day were "boarding" while waiting for a hospital bed to become available for admission. [*Three-Fourths of Emergency Department Directors Report Shortages of Medical Specialists* (May 2006), *On-call Specialist Coverage in U.S. Emergency Departments*, ACEP Survey of Emergency Department Directors (Sept. 2004)]

While some hospitals have bylaws that require call panel participation as a condition of affiliation, mandating call can result in physicians choosing to practice at hospitals without mandates. Recommendations are to include policy changes on a global scale to encourage funding for emergency room safety net care while finding ways to limit liability for those who render care in good faith. On a hospital level, ACEP sets forth an EA program (established by Emergency and Acute Care Medical Corporation (EACMC) in California) as a best practice model to ensure adequate ED call coverage. This program based in California uses compensation agreements to improve on-call panel coverage. EA programs compensate on-call physicians at a fixed rate per RVU (relative value unit) for treatment of unassigned patients. Each hospital negotiates the RVU rate with medical staff. Other options include compensation to the doctors for their availability combined with a fee-for-service reimbursement for care rendered. The guaranteed reimbursement encourages physician participation with call panels. The hospital assumes financial responsibility for any billing shortfall, but can offset this by reducing length of stay in the ED and hospital. [*Ensuring Adequate On-Call Backup in the ED*, ACEP News Release 2005] A 2007 report noted hospital strategies to improve on-call coverage. These strategies include enforcing bylaws and requiring on-call duty, contracting with physicians for coverage, paying daily or monthly physician stipends, and/or employing physicians. [*Hospital Emergency On-Call Coverage: Is There a Doctor in the House?* HSC Issue Brief 115 (2007)]

The Role of Nonphysicians in the ED

What happens when nonphysicians in the ED transmit medical orders for other health care staff to follow?

The term "transmit orders" refers to orders written by a nonphysician (such as a PA) that convey the original intentions of a physician, who usually is also the nonphysician's supervisor. Supervising physicians may communicate these orders to nonphysician providers through any of several means, including conveying the order in person, over the phone, or by written protocols or standing orders. Other health care personnel, including nurses, must comply with transmit orders when the order is clearly made under the direction, direct or indirect, of a supervising physician. In one case, for example, a state nurses' association challenged a law allowing PAs to transmit orders from a physician, but the state supreme court upheld the law, reasoning that medical orders transmitted by a PA (under supervision of a physician) are in fact physician's orders and thus should be honored by nurses. [*Washington State Nurses Ass'n v. Board of Med. Exam'rs*, 605 P.2d 1269 (Wash. 1980)]

What is a standing order?

A standing order is a medical order written for use by nurses and other nonphysicians when a physician is not present. Another term often interchanged with "standing orders" is "protocols," which can be defined as a detailed template for treatment of a very specific medical problem. In most states, standing orders and protocols are a legal and convenient way for drugs and treatment to be given on a physician's order but within the discretion of the nurse or other nonphysician health care provider. Standing orders are commonly used in EDs, particularly as a mechanism for authorizing a nonphysician to prescribe medication or administer drugs to a patient in the physician's absence. Registered nurses and other appropriate personnel are generally allowed to transcribe oral orders of a physician or authorized nonphysician prescriber for the purpose of administering drugs to ED patients.

When might a standing order regarding a patient's medication treatment trigger potential legal problems?

A PA or nurse practitioner who has prescribing authority under a state practice statute might prescribe drugs in accordance with a hospital protocol but neglect to follow the prescribing requirements enumerated in the state practice statute. In that case, the PA or nurse practitioner would be subject to charges of exceeding his or her scope of practice. Similarly, complications arising as a result of a drug administered to a patient by a nonphysician who followed a standing order may give rise to claims that the nonphysician exceeded the scope of his or her legal authority in administering the drug or that the nonphysician's actions constituted practicing medicine without a license.

What should an ED do to ensure that nonphysician patient care does not give rise to legal liability?

- Review relevant state practice acts, as well as hospital licensure laws, to make sure that standing orders are in compliance with these statutes, particularly regarding requirements for documentation of physician oversight (i.e., countersignatures).
- Monitor the use of standing orders to determine whether the quantity and the scope of patient care being rendered without individual physicians' orders are appropriate.
- Assess whether patients are being discharged after nonphysicians alone provide care under standing orders. Implement a mechanism for "catching" these cases and ensuring an appropriate level of physician involvement prior to discharge.
- Educate ED staff members regarding the special legal risks associated with nonphysician drug ordering and the importance of following state scope of practice acts.

What factors impact ED overcrowding?

ED overcrowding occurs as a result of a number of factors. The number of ED visits has increased 20 percent over 10 years ending in 2001, while the number of EDs nationwide decreased by 15 percent. This has led to higher patient volumes and waiting times in EDs that have remained open. Average patient time spent in the ED is three hours. [*New Data Show Upward Trend in Emergency Department Visits*, ACEP Press Release (June 4, 2003)] A study of the impact of final EMTALA regulations in regard to on-call specialty coverage found that two-thirds of ED directors had shortages of on-call specialists in neurosurgery, orthopedics, and obstetrics with the more flexible EMTALA final regulations. This resulted in delayed treatment, increased transfers, and reduced access to specialty care. [*Two-Thirds of Emergency Department Directors Report On-call specialty coverage problems*, ACEP Press Release (Sept. 28, 2004)]

Some reasons for overcrowding are hospital specific, such as high volume of patients, lack of space, or delays in test results. Other reasons relate to the ED's ability to transfer patients to an inpatient bed once it has been decided to admit them. This leads to an increasing number of patients being "boarded" in the ED. There is especially inpatient demand for critical care and telemetry units. [*Hospital Emergency Departments: Crowding Conditions Among Hospitals and Communities* (GAO-03-460)] Other factors that impact overcrowding include staffing shortages and saturation of primary care networks with more patients with chronic diseases and more elderly patients accessing the ED. [*ED Overcrowding:* JCAHO News Release (Feb. 2003)] In addition, the total number of hospitals and inpatient beds decreased, while ED visits rose. Medicaid accounted for 81 percent of ED visits in 2003, up from 65 percent in 2002. [*Hospital-Based Emergency Care: At the Breaking Point*, IOM ED Report (June 14, 2006)]

What recommendations are in place for ED overcrowding?

A publication released in November 2004 entitled *Managing Patient Flow: Strategies and Solutions for Addressing Hospital Overcrowding* (available at *http://www.jcrinc.com*) focuses on the use of JCAHO leadership, emergency management, care planning, and staffing standards to mitigate the impact of overcrowding and improve patient flow.

Hospitals are already trying to address overcrowding through actions that expand the capacity of the ED or increase the efficiency of inpatient transfer. Overall, community-wide resources are needed to resolve overcrowding. [*Hospital Emergency Departments: Crowding Conditions Among Hospitals and Communities* (GAO-03-460)]

The 2006 IOM report recommends the following strategies to help with ED overcrowding:

- Improving operational efficiency by addressing patient flow problems,
- Increasing clinical decision unit payments from CMS,
- Developing standards to prohibit boarding and diversion,
- Improving IT solutions to enhance patient information availability,
- Providing funds to hospitals for uncompensated care,
- Increasing medical disaster preparedness funding,
- Regionalizing crucial on-call specialties,
- Implementing medical malpractice reform to lesson liability,
- Linking rural EDs to academic centers for consultation and referral,
- Increasing funding to emergency medicine research,
- Regionalizing ED trauma centers, and
- Using expert panels to develop evidence-based indicators for the ED.

[*Hospital-Based Emergency Care: At the Breaking Point,* IOM ED Report (June 14, 2006). *See also Emergency Care for Children: Growing Pains,* IOM ED Report (June, 2006) for issues related to pediatric ED care and *Emergency Medical Services: At the Crossroads,* IOM ED Report (June, 2006)] Success factors in changing patient flow through the ED include management support, hospital-wide teams to facilitate process change, and having a person champion improvements. Patient flow strategies include streamlining triage and registration processes, having a bed manager monitor patient flow, facilitating early discharge for patients who are ready, and involving hospital staff in moving boarders to inpatient care. Solid metric measurements can be used to document process improvements. [Wilson, Marcia and Nguyen, Khoa. *Bursting at the Seams: Improving Patient Flow to Help America's Emergency Departments,* Urgent Matters White Paper (Sept. 2004)]

Are there mandatory staffing ratios in the ED?

Some states have enacted statutes that require state agencies to establish minimum staffing ratios. For example, the California code requires the state to establish staffing ratios based on the licensure of the nurse as well as the type of hospital unit. For the ED, the state agency should consider regularly scheduled staff as well as additional nurses needed to care for critically ill persons. Other factors to consider in establishing staffing ratios include: patient care needs, illness, severity, use of equipment or technology, and complexity of clinical judgment. The hospital should also have policies and procedure for training and orientation of employees including orientation for temporary workers. [Cal. Health & Safety Code § 1276.4] Be sure to check with requirements in your state in setting minimum staffing standards.

California also allows the EMT who was caring for the patient prior to ED admission to remain and assist when there is a "patient crisis." Specifically, small and rural hospitals can use EMTs to provide patient care if they have completed hospital ED training, demonstrate competency annually, work according to protocols, and follow procedures for supervision. Hospitals and ambulance set up a contractual agreement for EMT services prior to ED use of EMTs. The hospital must provide for a process for care if the EMT is called off-site for an emergency. [Cal. Health & Safety Code § 1797.195]

Can the ED require mandatory overtime to meet staffing needs?

Some states have set limits on the amount of overtime an employer may require. For example, Maine limits overtime an employee can work to 80 hours in a consecutive two-week period. By agreement, the maximum overtime hours can be lowered. The Maine statute specifically addresses staffing for nurses indicating that a nurse cannot be disciplined for refusing to work more than twelve consecutive hours. If the nurse is mandated to work over twelve consecutive hours, then the nurse must be given ten hours off duty immediately afterward. A nurse can be disciplined for refusing mandatory overtime in the case of an unforeseen emergency when overtime is the last resort to protect patient safety. [26 Me. Rev. Stat. Ann. § 603]

The Maryland statute prohibits mandatory overtime for nurses beyond regularly scheduled shifts, while allowing the nurse to voluntarily agree to work more hours. However, the statute has a number of exceptions that allow a nurse to work mandatory overtime when: (1) there is an emergency situation that was not reasonably anticipated, (2) the emergency is not recurrent or due to lack of employer planning, (3) the employer makes good faith efforts to obtain voluntary workers, (4) the nurse has the skills and expertise to do the work, (5) the standard of care requires continuity of care, (6) the employer informs the nurse of the need for mandatory overtime, and (7) other general overtime requirements are satisfied. The statute further allows overtime when the employment includes an on-call rotation or community based care. The statute further limits liability for care to the regularly scheduled work hours of the nurse as long as she notifies another nurse of the patient status and effectively transfers care of the patient at the completion of the work shift. [Md. Labor & Empl. Code Ann. § 3-421] Similarly, Washington prohibits mandatory overtime for health care employees, while allowing employees to accept voluntary shifts. However, overtime can be required when "unforeseeable emergent circumstances" occur. [Rev. Code Wash. § 49.28.140]

Other states have taken a different view by exempting health care workers or hospital employees providing medical services from state overtime requirements. [*See, e.g.*, Mass. Gen. Laws ch. 151, § 1A] Because state laws differ, it is important to check local laws before implementing mandatory overtime.

How do fair pay regulations impact overtime?

Fair pay regulations effective August 23, 2004, require that workers who earn less than $23,660 a year or less than $455 a week be guaranteed overtime pay for hours worked. The regulations also clarify that first responders such as EMTs, paramedics, and ambulance personnel are not exempt from the FLSA because their primary duty is not management and therefore must be paid overtime when hours exceed forty in a week. Nurses may qualify for the learned profession exemption to overtime provisions if the compensation, salary, or fee is over $455 a week; if the nurse's primary duty required advanced knowledge that is predominantly intellectual in character and consists if discretion in judgment; if the advanced knowledge is in a field of science or learning; and if the advanced knowledge is customarily acquired by a prolonged course of intellectual instruction. Registered nurses (RNs) will generally meet the learned profession exemption and earn over $455 a week. However, licensed practical nurses (LPNs) generally do not meet the learned profession exemption because an advanced degree is not necessary for entry into the profession. [*Final Rule*, 69 Fed. Reg. 22,260 (Apr. 23, 2004); 29 C.F.R. § 541.301(e)]

What does JCAHO recommend to improve staffing effectiveness?

JCAHO has recognized that there is an evolving nursing crisis with patient acuity rising and the number of nurses falling. JCAHO recommends creation of an organizational culture to encourage staff retention by empowering staff, transforming work, setting competent staffing levels, establishing zero tolerance policies for verbal abuse, and encouraging diversity. It also recommends that the nursing educational infrastructure be bolstered and that federal monies be used to create financial incentives for hospitals to invest in nursing care. [*Health Care at the Crossroads: Strategies for Addressing the Evolving Nursing Crisis* (Sept. 2005)]

2007 JCAHO hospital accreditation standards for leadership include requirements that leadership define qualified and competence of staff, that the number of staff needed for competent care be reviewed, and that staffing be integrated into a patient safety program. [JCAHO Comprehensive Accreditation Manual for Hospitals HR 1.30, LD 3.70 (2007)]

Dress Codes

What legal claim might be triggered by an ED's grooming or dress code policies?

Grooming standards and dress codes have triggered lawsuits by employees claiming that the employer's policy violates Title VII's prohibition of gender discrimination. For a discussion of gender discrimination prohibitions in the context of claims by patients, rather than staff, see "What laws prohibit race, national origin, and gender discrimination?" under Antidiscrimination Laws.

How have courts responded to suits based on alleged discriminatory grooming or dress code policies?

Numerous courts have upheld the employer's right to enforce a dress code. In one case, a federal appeals court upheld a county ambulance department's grooming policy for male emergency medical technicians (EMTs) prohibiting mustaches, beards, and hair of certain lengths. The policy was not arbitrary, the court ruled, finding its purposes were to promote esprit de corps among EMTs, establish a uniform and professional image for EMTs, and minimize the possibility that the EMTs' hair would interfere with the performance of their jobs. [*Hottinger v. Pope County*, 971 F.2d 127 (8th Cir. 1992)]

Dress codes will be subjected to a different standard of scrutiny, however, in instances in which male and female employees who perform the same functions are expected to conform to two entirely different dress codes. Several courts have held that Title VII requires that similarly situated employees be treated in an equal manner with respect to dress code requirements. A state appeals court in Michigan, for example, ruled that a hospital's dress code requirements illegally discriminated on the basis of sex. The court rejected the hospital's argument that its policy of requiring female technologists to wear white or pastel-colored uniforms, while male technologists wore white lab coats over their street clothes, was justified because patients are used to seeing males dressed like physicians and females dressed like nurses. [*Michigan Dep't. of Civil Rights v. Sparrow Hosp.*, 326 N.W.2d 519 (Mich. Ct. App. 1982)]

Can a dress code ban employees from wearing union insignia?

As a general rule, the National Labor Relations Act (NLRA) gives employees the right to wear union insignia without fear of retaliation. Companies have implemented dress codes that restrict buttons or union insignia when (1) the ban is needed to ensure productivity, (2) the ban is needed to reduce conflict in the workplace and maintain discipline, (3) the ban is needed to ensure the safety of the workers by preventing accidents or avoiding violence, and (4) the ban is needed to ensure good employee customer relations or other business goals. Courts have upheld some of these dress codes. Some courts have looked at whether the ban is specific to prohibit union items, or is a general ban such as a "no pin" policy. There is a balancing between labor laws that allow insignia showing support of the union and business goals that may necessitate limits on certain types of dress, buttons, or insignia.

In a recent district court case, a carpenter who worked at a hospital which had a "no pin" policy except for professional pins or hospital service awards wore a button to work that said "union yes." He was asked to remove the button as violating company policy. He refused and continued to wear the button. When the issue went to court, the district court determined that wearing the button was permissible free speech. On appeal, the circuit court reversed the decision, finding that the hospital had an interest in promoting efficient service and the uniform nonadornment policy outweighed the employee's right to free speech. The court found that the button was not protected speech and the hospital policy was neutral. [*Communications Workers of Am. v. Ector County Hosp. Dist.*, 241 F. Supp. 2d 617 (W.D. Tex. 2002), *aff'd*, 392 F.3d 733 (5th Cir. 2004), *rev'd*, 467 F.3d 427 (5th Cir. 2006)] Because this area of the law is evolving and varies from state to state it is important to consult with legal counsel in establishing a policy.

Refusal to Treat Patients

Can a hospital discharge an ED employee who refuses to treat a patient with HIV or AIDS?

In most cases, if the ED is following proper infection control techniques and properly educates the employee, but the employee continues to refuse to care for an HIV-positive patient, the hospital can impose discipline, including termination. In one case, for example, a pregnant home care nurse sued for pregnancy discrimination under Title VII after she was discharged for her refusal to treat an AIDS-infected patient. The nurse declined to care for the patient, even with universal precautions, because she feared the accompanying opportunistic infections often present in AIDS patients (in this case, cryptococcal meningitis) would harm the fetus. The court noted that the hospital had a policy requiring all nurses to treat AIDS patients or be subject to termination and that this policy applied to nonpregnant as well as pregnant nurses. The court therefore dismissed the suit, reasoning that the nurse could not establish that the hospital's policy affected pregnant employees more harshly than other classifications of employees. Although the primary focus of the court's analysis was on the standard for establishing a valid claim of pregnancy discrimination, the case also reflects the court's tacit approval of a hospital policy allowing termination of employees who refuse to treat patients with HIV or AIDS. [*Armstrong v. Flowers Hosp.*, 812 F. Supp. 1183 (M.D. Ala. 1993), *aff'd*, 33 F.3d 1308 (11th Cir. 1994)]

Under certain circumstances, however, the health care employer cannot discharge an employee for refusing to care for HIV-infected patients. For example, if an employee has a reasonable good-faith belief that a hospital's failure to follow proper infection control procedures poses an immediate and grave danger to his or her health, the employee falls within the protection of the Occupational Safety and Health Act. [29 U.S.C. §§ 651 through 678] Occupational Safety and Health Administration (OSHA) regulations allow an employee in this situation to refuse to work, and they also provide that the employee cannot be discharged for such refusal. [29 C.F.R. § 1977.12]

Hospitals also may not have the option to discharge employees for refusal to care for patients with HIV or AIDS in circumstances in which the employment relationship is governed by a collective bargaining agreement. If there is such an agreement, the hospital must follow any contract requirements and procedures for discipline, which may or may not preclude employee discharge for certain charges. In addition, employees may be protected under provisions of the National Labor Relations Act (NLRA), which protect employees engaged in concerted activity for material aid and protection. [29 U.S.C. §§ 141 through 187]

What should an ED do upon learning that an employee refuses to treat a patient with HIV or AIDS?

If proper infection control procedures are being enforced in the ED and an employee refuses to treat a patient with HIV or AIDS, a supervisor or other ED staff member should first ensure that the employee is properly educated about how the virus is transmitted and how employees can protect themselves using universal precautions. The employee may also benefit from education about any professional ethical obligations that may be relevant to providing medical care to patients infected with HIV or AIDS, as well as legal liability issues arising under disability discrimination statutes such as the ADA. For a more detailed discussion, see "Can hospitals and health care providers be liable for refusing to treat patients with HIV or AIDS?" under Antidiscrimination Laws.

The hospital or other health care employer should not discipline an ED employee for refusing to care for patients with HIV or AIDS before investigating whether the employee has legitimate reasons for such refusal. An employee who is undergoing chemotherapy, for example, may have a diminished immune system that would make the employee more susceptible to the secondary infections an HIV-positive patient may be experiencing. Reasons for refusing to care for patients with HIV or AIDS should be evaluated on a case-by-case basis in light of the most current medical information, and if such an evaluation indicates that the employee's health concern is legitimate, the employer should try to reasonably accommodate the health care worker.

Can a health care provider refuse to treat a patient on moral or religious grounds?

Refusal to treat on moral or religious grounds often arises when a procedure such as abortion or sterilization is anticipated or in the context of prescriptions such as contraception where the health care provider may have strong moral views. There has been increasing movement among state legislatures to pass what are known as "conscience clauses" that give health care providers the right to refuse to participate in care because of their moral or ethical values. For example, Missouri law focuses specifically on abortion and gives physicians, nurses, midwives, and hospitals the right to refuse to provide abortions and prevents an employer from discriminating against the employee for refusal to participate unless the refusal creates an undue hardship for the employer. [Mo. Rev. Stat. §§ 188.105, 197.032] Similarly, federal law would require a facility to make reasonable accommodation when an employee objects to treatment on religious grounds as long as the accommodation is not an undue burden to the organization.

Pharmacy refusals to fill prescriptions have risen as more pharmacists have relied on conscience clauses to refuse to fill prescriptions on moral grounds. The American Pharmacy Association has supported policies that allow pharmacists the right to choose not to fill prescriptions they find morally or ethically objectionable, but supports systems to ensure that patient needs are met. The American Medical Association (AMA) passed a resolution in June 2005 restating patient's right to access medical care and noting the need for pharmacists to fill valid prescriptions or refer to a pharmacy that would dispense the medication prescribed. Some states have responded by passing laws requiring pharmacists to fill prescriptions in good faith. [*See, for example,* 225 I.L.C.S. 85/30 or Cal. Bus. & Prof. Code § 4052 that requires pharmacists to dispense emergency contraception drug therapy.]

Staff Substance Abuse

What are some legal concerns for hospital EDs arising from staff substance abuse?

The problem of employee substance abuse among health care professionals may give rise to a number of legal concerns for the ED. If a patient is harmed by an impaired health care provider, both the hospital and the provider may be held liable for the patient's injuries because the physician's negligence may be imputed to the hospital. The hospital may also be subject to direct liability for negligent monitoring of its medical staff member and failing to protect the patient.

What should an ED do when it becomes aware of a staff member with a substance abuse problem?

A first step for the ED would be to informally persuade the impaired practitioner to seek help and to refer him or her to the hospital's employee assistance program or in-house rehabilitation program, if one exists. In the absence of such a program, the ED should refer the employee to an external professional treatment program. Next, the ED should report the impaired practitioner to the chief of the appropriate clinical service, the chief of staff, or a supervisor. Then, if required, the hospital must report that practitioner to the appropriate state licensing body. In some states, state law may insulate impaired practitioners from disciplinary action, including peer review and medical board reporting, unless the impairment becomes habitual or poses a danger to patients.

Participating in a rehabilitation program should be required of any employee or medical staff member who voluntarily admits to having a substance abuse problem or whose substance test results are positive. Employees and medical staff members who successfully complete treatment should be provided with an opportunity to continue working in the ED under an agreement that provides for unannounced testing for a reasonable period after return to work. If an employee is unable or unwilling to rehabilitate, the hospital may have no other option than termination. [*See, e.g.,* American Hospital Association, *Management Advisory, Substance Abuse Policies of Health Care Institutions* (Jan. 1992)]

All communications should be kept strictly confidential to comply with the ADA and with state laws governing medical information and peer review because impaired physicians may have protected status under these statutes. As soon as a potentially impaired practitioner is discovered, ED managers should consult with the hospital's human resources department and medical staff committee for assistance in complying with disability discrimination, confidentiality, and other federal and state laws.

Discrimination and Harassment

What are an ED's legal duties regarding disabled workers?

Under Title I of the Americans with Disabilities Act (ADA), the disabled hospital employee can request reasonable accommodation. The manager should first determine whether the employee has a disability that interferes with a major life function. A doctor's report may be requested in order to confirm the disability, but should be kept confidential. If a disability exists, then the employer determines what constitutes a reasonable accommodation, but this does not mean the employee gets everything he or she asks for. Further, if the accommodation creates an undue burden on the company because of time, money, expense, scheduling, etc., then the manager should document this and can refuse the accommodation.

When the disabled worker is a physician or nurse contracting to provide services, the court may still allow a disability claim under Title III protections for the general public. At least one appeals court has found that a contracted medical doctor was an individual who could sue under the public accommodation law. [*Menkowitz v. Pottstown Mem'l Med. Ctr.*, 154 F.3d 113 (3d Cir. 1998)]

What are an ED's legal duties regarding workers with HIV or other bloodborne infections?

The Supreme Court has held that a disabled worker can be denied a position that would pose a direct threat to the worker's health and safety or pose a significant risk to others. In this case, a worker with a serious chronic illness (hepatitis C) was denied a position in an oil refinery that would harm his health. Similarly, a business may deny employment to a worker who would pose a direct threat to the health and safety of others. [*Chevron USA v. Echazabal*, 122 S. Ct. 2045 (2002)] When a dental hygienist posed a threat of safety to patients, it was not discriminatory to offer her a desk job at half pay. [*Waddell v. Valley Forge Dental*, 276 F.3d 1275 (11th Cir. 2001)] When an emergency room physician was exposed to hepatitis C and subsequently tested positive, she took a two-year break from work but continued to attend staff meetings. The virus went into remission and she requested to return to work. She was given three conditions to return to work: (1) obtain a physician's medical release, (2) attend a refresher in emergency medicine, and (3) submit to weekly blood samples. She was assigned to the emergency room schedule but declined to return to work and sued, claiming disability discrimination and harassment. The court found that the requirements to return to work were reasonable and that subsequent failure of the hospital to offer her an interim contract related to the fact that she had not come in to work, so there was no basis for a disability discrimination or harassment claim. [*Gowesky v. Singing River Hosp.*, 321 F.3d 503 (5th Cir. 2003)]

A policy statement by the American College of Emergency Physicians (ACEP) focuses on ensuring access to emergency care while preventing exposure and transmission of bloodborne infections. The general principles it adopts are that

- appropriate care should be given to all patients who seek emergency care regardless of risk of HIV or other bloodborne infections,
- mandatory testing for HIV, HBV, or HCV should not be required prior to receiving emergency services,
- infection control guidelines should be followed in the emergency room,
- health care workers with potential exposure should have immediate evaluation and prophylaxis,
- when health care workers are infected and cannot perform their duties they should be eligible for disability insurance coverage. [*ACEP Policy Compendium: Bloodborne Infections in Emergency Medicine* (2004)]

What is the ED legal duty under Title VII?

Title VII prohibits discrimination based on race, color, national origin, sex, and religion. The ED should focus all hiring, promotion, and employment decisions on legitimate qualifications for the job. Documentation of employment decisions based on poor productivity, performance, etc., is invaluable if claims of discrimination arise later.

What does the ADEA require?

The Age Discrimination in Employment Act (ADEA) protects employees 40 and over from discrimination based on age. The department can make decisions based on business necessity including establishing bona fide seniority systems. [29 C.F.R. § 1625.8] It is best to focus on employee ability to do the job and avoid age-related comments. In a claim for age discrimination by the nursing director of an ED who was fired after management made comments that she was "burned out" and "unable to change her old ways," the court found that this did not create an inference of discrimination. The employee must demonstrate the management action was discriminatory or that the reason for discharge was a pretext for discrimination. [*Perry v. St. Joseph Regional Medical Center*, No. 03-6120 (10th Cir. 2004)]

What is the ED responsibility in regard to sexual harassment claims?

Sexual harassment occurs in the workplace when an employee is asked to exchange sexual favors in order to keep a job, receive a promotion, etc. It can also occur when there is a hostile work environment that is severe and pervasive such as an atmosphere of regular jokes, remarks, or pictures. A one-time comment will not be sufficient. The Supreme Court has found employers vicariously liable for the unlawful sexual harassment of their supervisors when it results in a tangible employment action such as discharge. If there was no tangible employment act, liability can be avoided by taking reasonable care to prevent and correct harassment and demonstrating that the employee did not take advantage of opportunities to prevent or correct harassment. [*Burlington Industries, Inc. v. Ellerth,* 118 S. Ct. 2257 (1998) and *Faragher v. City of Boca Raton,* 118 S. Ct. 2275 (1998)]

The ED should participate with the hospital in having a sexual harassment policy in place, conducting regular training and education so that all employees know the policy and standards, setting up a reporting process to file complaints of harassment, and promptly and confidentially investigating allegations of harassment. Prompt action should be taken when employees breach the harassment policy. At least one court has found a hospital liable for the sexual harassment of an employed female nurse by a physician with staff privileges who was not an employee. [*Dunn v. Washington County Hosp.,* 429 F.3d 689 (7th Cir. 2005)]

What standard determines if an action against an employee is retaliatory?

In a 2006 case, the Supreme Court clarified the standard to determine if employment actions taken against an employee after a claim of discrimination has been filed constitute retaliation. This case involved the reassignment of a worker to less desirable duties within the same job description and suspension without pay. The court adopted a broad view of retaliation and found that these actions could be retaliatory. Actions outside the workplace and employment environment can be retaliatory and harm the employee, but the plaintiff must show that a reasonable person would have rethought filing a claim after the action took place. [*Burlington Northern Santa Fe Railway Co. v. White,* Docket No. 05-520 (U.S. June 22, 2006)] To avoid retaliation claims, the ED should keep good records of decisions made regarding employees to demonstrate that actions were based on employee performance, not in response to the filing of a claim of discrimination.

OCCUPATIONAL SAFETY

There are occupational safety concerns in all areas of the hospital, including the ED. The bloodborne pathogens standard is of particular concern in the ED because of the likelihood of exposure to blood and other body fluids. Other occupational safety concerns include airborne hazards, smoking, ergonomic hazards, emergency response planning, and clearance in aisles and passageways. Each of these areas is discussed in the following section. For sample documentation, see **Part 4**.

The Occupational Safety and Health Administration (OSHA) and the Joint Commission have formed a successful partnership to promote safety and health for health care workers. The joint program, initiated in 1996, was originally developed as a three-year venture, but has recently been extended in recognition of the benefits gained from the partnership. OSHA and the Joint Commission have worked together to help hospitals and other health care facilities understand how to meet the requirements of both the federal agency and the accreditation organization. As part of that effort, OSHA and the Joint Commission have jointly developed training materials and publications for health care facilities, and provided specific examples in Joint Commission accreditation manuals to illustrate how compliance with OSHA standards also satisfies Joint Commission standards. In addition, the partnership has enabled OSHA and the Joint Commission to minimize duplicative compliance activities.

Bloodborne Pathogens

What is OSHA's bloodborne pathogens standard?

The OSHA bloodborne pathogens standard applies primarily (although not exclusively) to the health care industry and is particularly applicable to the ED, where health care workers are exposed to potentially contaminated body fluids. The standard's requirements extend to anyone who may come into contact with blood or potentially infectious material in performing his or her job duties; in essence, this means reasonably anticipated skin, eye membrane, or other parenteral contact with blood or other infectious materials. The standard requires employers to implement an exposure control plan to minimize employees' exposure to bloodborne pathogens. The plan must contain the following key provisions:

- engineering and work practice controls,
- personal protective equipment (PPE),
- disposal of waste and cleaning of workplace,
- employer-provided hepatitis B vaccinations,
- postexposure evaluation,
- notice of hazards to employees, and
- recordkeeping. [29 C.F.R. § 1910.1030]

In November 2000, Congress passed the Needlestick Safety and Prevention Act, which revised the bloodborne pathogens standard, requiring employers to select safer needle devices as they become available and to involve employees in identifying and choosing the devices. The updated standard also requires employers to maintain a log of injuries from contaminated sharps.

Hospital EDs must participate in hospital-wide efforts to develop and implement policies and procedures aimed at satisfying these requirements.

What is an exposure control plan, and does it apply to the ED?

Hospitals must develop written exposure control plans that identify employees at risk of exposure to blood and the methods to be used to protect and train these workers. This exposure control plan must be accessible to employees and must be updated annually or whenever job task additions or changes affect employee exposure to bloodborne pathogens. The new revisions to the bloodborne pathogens standard require that hospitals review their exposure control plans annually to reflect changes in technology that will help eliminate or reduce exposure to bloodborne pathogens. That review must include documentation of the hospital's consideration and implementation of appropriate and effective safer medical devices. In doing so, the hospital must solicit input from nonmanagerial health care workers in identifying, evaluating, and selecting safer devices and must document that solicitation in the exposure control plan. Because ED employees are considered to be at risk of exposure to blood, the exposure control plan applies to ED employees. [29 C.F.R. § 1910.1030(c)].

What kinds of equipment or engineering controls must be used in the ED to help prevent the spread of bloodborne pathogens?

Hospitals must implement engineering controls, such as puncture-resistant containers for used needles, self-sheathing needles, protective shields, biosafety cabinets, and safer medical devices such as sharps with engineered sharps injury protections and needleless systems. The standard requires employers to regularly inspect and repair engineering controls. [29 C.F.R. §§ 1910.1030(b) & (d)]

What are the handwashing requirements?

Handwashing must be performed as soon as feasible after exposure to blood or other potentially infectious materials and after removal of gloves or other personal protective equipment. [29 C.F.R. §§ 1910.1030(d)(2)(iii) through (vi)] For more information, see Centers for Disease Control and Prevention, *Guideline for Infection Control in Health Care Personnel* (1998), and Centers for Disease Control and Prevention, *Guidelines for Isolation Precautions: Preventing Transmission of Infectious Agents in Health Care Settings* (2007)] The new guideline focuses on health care associated infections (HAI), respiratory hygiene and safe injection practices, protective environment controls, administrative support of infection control, and focus on multidrug-resistant organisms (MDROs).

What kinds of work practices are prohibited in the ED to prevent the spread of bloodborne pathogens?

Employees are prohibited from eating, drinking, and storing food in areas where there is potential for exposure to bloodborne pathogens or where blood, body fluids, or both are stored (e.g., refrigerators and cabinets, medication carts, etc.). [29 C.F.R. §§ 1910.1030(d)(2)(ix) & (x)] Employees are also prohibited from suctioning blood or other body fluids by mouth. [29 C.F.R. § 1910.1030(d)(2)(xii)] For more information, see Centers for Disease Control and Prevention, *Guideline for Infection Control in Health Care Personnel (1998)*.

What are ACEP recommendations in regard to bloodborne infections?

The American College of Emergency Physicians (ACEP) has made recommendations in regard to HIV, hepatitis B, and hepatitis C.

The HIV recommendations are to

- Recommend an HIV test for patients at risk for the disease.
- If clinically appropriate, discuss HIV testing and prophylaxis with victims of sexual assault.
- Use sound physician judgment to inform about HIV risk, balancing the patient need for confidentiality and privacy with the need for a third party to know they may be at risk for HIV.

- Use rapid HIV tests on a patient when health care workers are exposed to blood/body fluids.
- Mandatory HIV testing should not be a condition of employment for health care workers, and disclosure is only recommended when HIV status impacts job performance.
- Health care workers who are HIV-positive should not be precluded from medical service based on HIV status, should not required to inform patients of HIV status unless the patient is at risk of exposure because of contact with the health care worker's blood or body fluids, and are not required to obtained special consent before delivery of emergency services.
- Unless the practitioner has been implicated in provider-to-patient HIV transmission, the health care worker who is HIV positive should not be banned from patient care activities including invasive procedures.
- Decisions to restrict the practice of a HIV-positive worker should be based on objective standards and not HIV status.

The hepatitis B recommendations are

- All emergency health care workers who may be exposed to blood should receive a hepatitis B vaccine unless contraindicated and should be tested to ensure positive immunity after the vaccine.
- The CDC recommendations for health care workers who are HBsAg and/or HbeAg should be followed. HbeAg workers should routinely double glove and should not perform activities that would risk HBV transmission despite use of appropriate infection control techniques.
- If clinically appropriate, hepatitis B testing and prophylaxis should be discussed with victims of sexual assault.

The hepatitis C recommendations are

- Mandatory HCV testing should not be a condition of employment for workers.
- HCV infection should not bar the worker from patient care, including invasive procedures, unless the practitioner has been implicated in a provider-to-patient HCV transmission.
- Decisions to restrict the practice of a HCV-infected health care worker should be based on objective standards and not on HCV status. [*ACEP Policy Compendium: HIV Recommendations, Hepatitis B Recommendations, Hepatitis C Recommendations* (2004)]

What are the OSHA requirements for handling sharps in the ED?

Employees are prohibited from shearing, breaking, recapping, removing, or bending contaminated needles and other sharps; from picking up potentially contaminated glassware by hand; and from reaching by hand into a container that may contain contaminated reusable sharps. [29 C.F.R. §§ 1910.1030(d)(2)(vii), d(4)(ii)(D) & (E)] For related information, see U.S. Department of Health and Human Services, *Selecting, Evaluating, and Using Sharps Disposal Containers*, NIOSH Pub. No. 97-111 (1998).

Do any other federal agencies address infection control practices in hospitals?

Detailed recommendations on work-practice infection controls relevant to hospital are also specified in guidelines issued by the Centers for Disease Control and Prevention (CDC). [*See* CDC, *Guidelines for Isolation Precautions: Preventing Transmission of Infectious Agents in Health Care Settings* (2007)]

Do any state laws address bloodborne pathogen exposure through needle safety?

States have begun to enact additional requirements in an effort to reduce health care worker exposure to bloodborne pathogens. Legislation in California, for example, requires the state Occupational Safety and Health Standards Board to revise the state's bloodborne pathogen standard by adopting an emergency regulation aimed at compelling health care facilities to use safer needles and syringes. The statute provides that sharps prevention technology is required in all cases except where the employer or other appropriate party can demonstrate circumstances in which the technology interferes with a medical procedure or does not promote employee or patient safety. The statute requires the revised standard to specifically delineate the circumstances falling within the exception, and to include circumstances where the technology is medically contraindicated or not more effective than alternative measures used by the employer to prevent exposure incidents.

The statute also provides that the new standard contain the following requirements: Written exposure control plans must include an effective procedure for identifying and selecting sharps prevention technology. Written exposure control plans must be updated when necessary to reflect progress in implementing the sharps prevention technology. Information concerning exposure incidents must be recorded in a sharps injury log, including, but not limited to, the type and brand of device involved in the incident. [Cal. Lab. Code § 144.7. *See also* Tenn. Code Ann. § 50-3-203 (requiring state departments of labor and health to jointly develop standards nearly identical to those required by the California legislation).]

OSHA required states that operate their own OSHA-approved state programs to adopt the new federal bloodborne pathogens standard, or a more stringent amendment to their existing standards, by October 18, 2001. [OSHA National News Release, *"Prevention is the Best Medicine"—OSHA Announces Outreach Effort on Needlestick Prevention* (May 9, 2001), available on the Internet at *www.osha.gov*]

Is the hospital required to provide personal protective equipment in the ED?

The OSHA final rule clarifies the policy: employers are required to pay for PPE that is required for the employee to safely perform the job. The rule requires the employer to pay for the minimum level of PPE required by safety standards as well as replacement PPE required to meet OSHA standards. An employer is not required to pay for employee-owned PPE that meets standards as long as the employee voluntarily chooses to purchase the PPE. The rule clarifies exceptions to employer payment and indicates that an employer is also not required to pay for everyday work clothing. Nor does the employer need to pay for ordinary safety toewear, prescription safety eyewear, weather protective jackets, or gloves. The deadline for compliance with the final rule is May 15, 2008. [72 Fed. Reg. 64,341 (Nov. 15, 2007); 29 C.F.R. §§ 1910.1030(d)(2)(i), (d)(3)(iv)–(viii)]

What kinds of items are considered personal protective equipment?

The OSHA standard contains a comprehensive list of such equipment, which includes gloves, gowns, laboratory coats, masks, eyeglasses, surgical caps, shoe covers, and resuscitation devices. The type and characteristics of the PPE that must be offered to the employee will depend on the task and degree of exposure anticipated. The standard also contains specific details regarding the adequacy of certain items of protective equipment; for example, it specifically requires the disposal of torn, cracked, or punctured gloves because their function as a barrier may be compromised. [29 C.F.R. § 1910.1030(d)(3)(i)] Hands must be washed after the removal of gloves used as PPE, whether or not the gloves are visibly contaminated. [29 C.F.R. § 1910.1030(d)(3)(ix)(C)]

Do employees always have to wear personal protective equipment?

A limited exemption applies when the employee refuses to wear the equipment because its use "would have prevented the delivery of health care or public safety services or would have posed an increased hazard to the safety of the worker or a co-worker." An example of such an occasion would be an unanticipated emergency in which a patient suddenly begins bleeding and workers lack time to delay treatment to put on gloves, masks, or gowns. OSHA may determine that an employee's decision not to wear PPE does not fall within this limited exemption, however, and fine the employer for violating the standard. [29 C.F.R. § 1910.1030(d)(3)(ii)]

Are there any guidelines on latex sensitivity?

Sensitivity to latex products, or latex allergy, develops in some individuals exposed to natural rubber latex—a plant substance that is used extensively to manufacture latex gloves. Allergic reactions to latex range from skin disease to asthma and anaphylaxis that can result in chronic illness and other disabilities; there is no treatment for these problems other than complete avoidance of latex.

OSHA's sister agency, the National Institute for Occupational Safety and Health (NIOSH) has issued guidance regarding prevention of latex-related health problems in the workplace. [National Institute for Occupational Health and Safety, *NIOSH Alert: Preventing Allergic Reactions to Natural Rubber Latex in the Workplace*, DHHS Pub. No. 97-135 (June 1997), available on the Internet at *www.cdc.gov/niosh/latexalt.html*] NIOSH recommends that hospitals implement policies and procedures to require, or at least encourage, appropriate engineering and work practice controls to reduce the risk of allergic reactions to latex. Such controls include the use of nonlatex gloves for activities that are not likely to involve contact with infectious materials, and where latex gloves are necessary for handling infectious materials, use of reduced protein, powder-free gloves to minimize worker exposure to allergy-causing proteins. Other controls include good housekeeping practice to remove latex-containing dust in latex-contaminated areas, and training materials/education programs about latex sensitivity.

What measures must be taken to clean the work site and dispose of contaminated waste?

Requirements for cleaning the work site and disposing of contaminated waste include

- implementing a written plan that describes the method and frequency of cleaning ensuring regular inspection and decontamination of reusable garbage bins, pails, and laundry carts that hold potentially contaminated medical waste;
- ensuring that blood specimens and other potentially infectious materials are placed in properly labeled containers that will prevent leakage during handling, storage, and transport; and
- requiring employees who have contact with potentially contaminated laundry to wear appropriate personal protective equipment such as gloves and gowns [29 C.F.R. § 1910.1030(d)(4)].

How should disposal of contaminated needles and blood tube holders for phlebotomy take place?

In a Safety and Health Information Bulletin (SHIB), OSHA sets forth advisory guidelines with the best practice for disposal of contaminated needles and blood tube holders. The best practice is to use a share with engineered sharps injury protection (SESIP) such as a safety needle attached to the blood tube holder. After a single use, the blood tube holder and needle assembly should be disposed of in a sharps container. Re-use of the needle will seldom be appropriate. [*Disposal of Contaminated Needles and Blood Tube Holders Used for Phlebotomy*, SHIB 10-15-03]

Must hospitals give employees free hepatitis B vaccines?

Employers must give all employees who have occupational exposure the option to receive a free hepatitis B vaccine and must educate them about the benefits of obtaining a vaccination. The vaccination must be made available to the employee within 10 days after initial assignment to a job task with potential exposure to bloodborne pathogens. It is the employee's choice whether to receive the hepatitis B vaccine, but an employee who chooses not to be vaccinated must sign a waiver form. [29 C.F.R. § 1910.1030(f)]

Employers are allowed to delay offering the vaccine to collateral first-aid providers, defined as employees whose primary jobs are not the rendering of first aid, until after these employees have rendered assistance in a situation presenting a risk of exposure to blood or another potentially infectious body fluid.

If the employee must travel to another location to obtain the vaccination, the employer must pay for the entire travel cost. The employer cannot require the employee to pay for the vaccine and later be reimbursed if reimbursement is contingent on the employee remaining employed at the employer for a specific length of time. Nor can the employer require that the employee's health insurer pay for the vaccine unless the employer pays the entire premium for the coverage and there is no deductible, copayment, or other expense to the employee.

Must hospitals provide an employee post-exposure evaluation following an exposure incident?

Employers must conduct post-exposure evaluations of employees who are exposed on the job. As part of that evaluation, which is to be provided at no cost to the employee, the employer must make available to the employee a confidential medical examination, including a blood test if the employee consents; post-exposure preventive treatment; and counseling. For more information, see Centers for Disease Control and Prevention, *Guideline for Infection Control in Health Care Personnel (1998)*.

The employer must also document the circumstances surrounding the employee's exposure and, if possible, identify the source individual. If an identifiable source individual exists, the employer must test that individual's blood for hepatitis B and HIV, provided that the individual consents. The employer must inform the exposed employee of the source individual's test results but also must be careful not to violate state or local AIDS confidentiality laws by disclosing the identity of the source individual along with those results.

The employer must provide the employee with a copy of the written medical evaluation within 15 days after completion of the evaluation. Aside from information regarding whether the employee should receive a hepatitis B vaccine, all other information (including blood test results) in this report must be kept confidential, even from the employer, to encourage the employee to participate in the medical examination process and to obtain follow-up care. [29 C.F.R. § 1910.1030(f)]

What must employers do to communicate the hazards of bloodborne pathogens to employees?

Employers are required to communicate the hazards of bloodborne pathogens to employees through employee training and education and proper placement of written warnings and labels. Employers must provide training when the employee is first assigned to a job in which there is occupational exposure and then provide additional training on an annual basis, or any time changes in work tasks affect the employee's risk of exposure.

Employers must affix labels to containers of regulated waste. Employers either must affix a biohazard symbol on all transport, storage, and waste containers that hold substances contaminated with blood or other potentially infected body fluids or must place such materials in red bags or containers. In addition, employers are required to appropriately label all contaminated equipment or partially contaminated equipment. [29 C.F.R. § 1910.1030(g)]

What kinds of records must employers keep regarding occupational exposure?

Employers must maintain medical records for each employee with occupational exposure for the duration of the employee's employment plus 30 years. The records must be kept confidential by the employer during this period, and the employer may not disclose contents of the records without the employee's express written consent. The standard also requires employers to maintain training records for a period of three years from the date of training but does not require that they be kept confidential. [29 C.F.R. § 1910.1030(h)]

Additionally, under the new bloodborne pathogens standard employers must also maintain a sharps injury log. The log must be maintained in a way to ensure employee privacy and will contain, at a minimum, information regarding the type and brand of device involved in the incident, if known; the location of the incident; and a description of the incident.

What will OSHA compliance officers look for with respect to bloodborne pathogens?

OSHA compliance officers likely follow an OSHA instruction document developed specifically for their use in enforcing OSHA's bloodborne pathogens standard. [U.S. Department of Labor, OSHA Instruction CPL 2-2.69, Enforcement Procedures for the Occupational Exposure to Bloodborne Pathogens (2001), available on the Internet at *www.osha.gov*] Although the OSHA standard has not been revised since 1991, the Instruction replaces and updates some of OSHA's practical recommendations and sample documentation pertinent to compliance with the standard. For example, appendices to the guidance document provide an Internet resource list, as well as references to current CDC guidelines and updated sample policies and procedures. The new enforcement procedures do not carry the force of law or regulation, but EDs are nonetheless well advised to become familiar with the Instruction, because it will direct compliance officers during hospital inspections.

Airborne Hazards

Are airborne pathogens a concern in the ED?

The risk of tuberculosis (TB) infection, which is an airborne transmissible disease, is the major airborne pathogen transmission concern in the ED. OSHA has shown active interest in the area of TB prevention in health care settings, emphasizing this in introductory comments to both its proposed TB prevention standard (discussed next) and an updated respiratory protection standard [29 C.F.R. § 1910.134] that TB remains a serious health risk, particularly because some outbreaks have involved drug-resistant strains of the disease.

What are the OSHA requirements regarding prevention of the spread of TB in the health care workplace?

For several years, OSHA has relied on the Centers for Disease Control and Prevention (CDC) for guidance on how to respond to the threat of TB transmission in the workplace. In 2005, the CDC updated its guidelines for tuberculosis prevention. The updated guidelines focus on a TB infection control program that includes risk assessment, tuberculin testing with screening of health care workers based on risk, airborne precautions, respiratory training, and respirator fit. For the ED recommendations include prompt evaluation and separation of TB patients and having a room with air cleaning technology available. [*Guidelines for Preventing the Transmission of Mycobacterium Tuberculosis in Health Care Settings* (Dec. 30, 2005) 54 RR17, pp. 1-141]

In 2003, OSHA terminated rulemaking in regard to tuberculosis based on the reduced number of tuberculosis cases nationwide, steps that had already been taken to prevent transmission of the disease, and the difficulty of identifying those infected. OSHA noted that the greatest risk of transmission was for those with undiagnosed and unsuspected tuberculosis and the rule could do little to eliminate this risk. OSHA will continue to use the general-duty clause or other respiratory protection standards for enforcement. [*Occupational Exposure to Tuberculosis, proposed rule; Termination of rulemaking respiratory protection for M. Tuberculosis; Final Rule; Revocation*, 68 Fed. Reg. 75,767 (Dec. 31, 2003)] New enforcement policy under the code focuses on detailed medical evaluation, fit testing, written program, training, and recordkeeping. [*Tuberculosis and respiratory protection, Enforcement Policy Memorandum* (July 30, 2004) effective July 2, 2004) and 29 C.F.R. § 1910.134]

Ergonomic Hazards

Why should ED leaders consider the impact of ergonomic hazards?

Ergonomic hazards are of particular relevance to hospital EDs where health care workers may be repeatedly lifting patients. Where there is a mismatch between the physical requirements of the job and the physical capacity of the worker, musculoskeletal disorders can result. In a controversial study on musculoskeletal disorders, NIOSH found evidence that work-related lifting and awkward postures are associated with low back disorders. Such disorders are very common in the health care industry overall, where workers' job duties include lifting patients.

Is there an OSHA standard addressing ergonomic hazards at the workplace?

In April 2002, however, OSHA announced a comprehensive plan designed to reduce ergonomic injuries through a combination of industry-targeted guidelines, enforcement measures, workplace outreach, and research. OSHA has begun to develop industry- and task-specific guidelines to reduce and prevent musculoskeletal disorders, starting with guidelines applicable to nursing homes.

In 2003, nursing home guidelines were released that focus on processes to protect employees, identification of problems and solutions in lifting and repositioning, solutions for other high-risk activities, and employee training. OSHA identified risks and solutions related to patient transfer and repositions as well as other activities such as bending to make a bed, collecting waste, pushing heavy carts, removing items from deep carts, and lifting and carrying supplies. While written with the nursing home industry in mind, the guidelines include many activities that take place within the ED and can serve as a reference for solutions to prevent injuries for the identified activities.

It is important to note that even in the absence of a general ergonomics standard, the Department of Labor can issue citations in this area under the general duty clause of the OSH Act. [*See, e.g., Secretary of Labor v. Pepperidge Farm Inc.*, OSHRC Dkt. No. 89-0265 (Apr. 26, 1997) (upholding OSHA's issuance of lifting-hazard violations under the general duty clause); *Secretary of Labor v. Beverly Enterprises, Inc.*, OSHRC Dkt. Nos. 91-3344, 92-0238, 92-0819, 92-1257, 93-724 (Oct. 27, 2000)]. That clause provides that any hazardous working condition not covered by a specific regulation or standard may be cited as a violation and a penalty issued. [29 U.S.C. § 654(a)(1)] OSHA has cautioned that it will vigorously enforce the general-duty clause and will prosecute violators.

Smoking

Does federal law require hospitals to ban smoking in the ED?

There is no federal law that specifically provides the legal authority to ban smoking in the ED. It may be argued, however, that the Occupational Safety and Health Act's general-duty clause, which requires employers to provide a safe working environment, provides support for a smoking ban.

Do state laws address smoking in EDs?

Many state laws do provide such authority. Maryland state law, for example, states that there will be no smoking in any area of the hospital. The exceptions to this broad prohibition do not apply to the ED. [Md. Code Ann., Health-Gen. § 24-205] Virginia law specifies that smoking is prohibited in hospital EDs. [Va. Code Ann. § 15.2-2801]

Passageways and Exits

What are OSHA's requirements regarding aisles and passageways?

OSHA regulations mandate that aisles and passageways must be kept clear, in good repair, and free from obstruction across or in aisles. In addition, permanent aisles and passageways must be appropriately marked. [29 C.F.R. § 1910.22(b)] In the ED, these regulations prohibit the blockage of passageways by, for example, supplies or patient gurneys.

Are there regulatory requirements for exits?

Regulatory rules effective December 2002 require the hospital to comply with either OSHA exit, emergency action plan, and fire prevention plans or the National Fire Protection Association's Standard (NFPA) 101, Life Safety Code, 2000 Edition. Companies that comply with NFPA 101 are deemed to be OSHA compliant. This approach is intended to increase flexibility of compliance while protecting the safety and health of employees through performance-oriented objectives. Compliance standards focus on design and construction, maintenance and operational safety requirements, and employee warning of the need to escape. For example, OSHA allows fire doors to remain open as long as they can close in an emergency. Exit heights and widths are set forth and any objects projecting into the exit route must allow the exit to meet minimum width requirements. Exits must not require employees to travel toward high hazard areas and exit signs should have "exit" written overhead, while nonexit doors should have a sign such as "not an exit." [67 Fed. Reg. 67,950 (Nov. 7, 2002)]

What are the 2006 Life Safety Code requirements that impact the ED?

The 2006 Life Safety Code spells out compliance requirements for new and existing hospitals and focuses on further methods to reduce fire risk. The code clarifies the speed at which people must be able to exit the health care facility; requires aisles, corridors, and ramps to be clear; establishes minimum door widths; and requires effective notification of employees of the emergency. Sprinkler systems should be in place as spelled out by the guidelines. Waiting areas must have access to an exit corridor with walls sufficiently thick to form a barrier to limit smoke. Every facility should have written copies of a fire protection plan, conduct fire drills, and train employees for emergency response. Smoking should be prohibited when combustible gases or oxygen are in use or stored. [Life Safety Code, NFPA 101 (2006 ed.)]

SECURITY IN THE ED

Security in the ED is a growing concern due to increased incidents of violence in EDs. The factors contributing to increased violence are many and include increased gang activity, drug abuse, alcohol abuse, and mental illness. Circumstances of hospital violence differ from circumstances of workplace violence in general, often resulting from patients and occasionally from their family members who feel frustrated, vulnerable, and out of control. Several studies indicate that violence against hospital workers often takes place during times of high activity and interaction with patients, such as at meal times and during visiting hours and patient transportation. Assaults may occur when service is denied, when a patient is involuntarily admitted, or when hospital personnel attempt to set limits on eating, drinking, or tobacco or alcohol use. (DHHS (NIOSH) Publication No. 2002-101 (Apr. 2002), available on the Internet at *www.cdc.gov/niosh/2002-101.html*).

Although anyone working in a hospital may become a victim of violence, nurses and aides who have the most direct contact with patients are at higher risk. Emergency response personnel and health care providers are also at increased risk of violence, which may occur anywhere in a hospital, but is most frequent in the ED and in waiting rooms, as well as psychiatric wards and geriatric units. It is the responsibility of the hospital to ensure the safety of employees, patients, and visitors to the ED. Other factors which increase the risk of violence include working directly with volatile people such as those under the influence of drugs and alcohol or with psychotic diagnosis, working when understaffed, transporting patients, working in a situation where patients wait a long time for service in crowded waiting rooms, working in situations where staff are alone or with inadequate security, staff training that is inadequate in crisis intervention, working areas where there is access to firearms, failing to restrict public movement through the area, and working in poorly lit areas such as parking lots, rooms, or corridors.

Major areas of concern addressed in this section include legal consequences of violence in the ED, security measures the hospital must undertake, training for ED and security personnel, the use of restraints, reporting of crimes that occur outside the ED, handling of criminal evidence, and administering tests at the request of law enforcement officers.

Legal Consequences of Violence

Can a hospital be liable for violence that occurs in the ED?

A hospital may be liable to employees, patients, and visitors for assaults that occur in the ED. As an employer, a hospital has a duty to provide a safe working environment for its employees. Like all facilities open to the public, the hospital has a duty to provide a safe environment to those it invites onto its premises.

Hospital liability will depend on whether the hospital reasonably could have anticipated (foreseen, in legal terms) the assault on the employee, patient, or visitor, yet failed to take action to prevent the assault. Proper planning, security policies, and staff training should substantially reduce the risks of liability and provide a safer environment for employees, patients, and visitors.

Foreseeability of a risk may depend to some extent on the location of the ED. In high-crime areas, for example, where gang violence is commonplace, a hospital may be negligent for failing to recognize and take precautions against the possibility of violence stemming from retribution against a gang member who is being treated in the ED.

What are some of the potential legal consequences if there is an episode of violence in the workplace?

Depending on the circumstances, ED violence could lead to

- OSHA citations,
- penalties for violation of state law,
- workers' compensation claims by injured employees,
- negligence claims by injured patients or visitors,
- assault and battery or false imprisonment claims by persons who are wrongfully restrained.

Federal Law Regarding Violence in the ED

Has OSHA issued any regulations regarding prevention of workplace violence against health care workers?

OSHA has issued voluntary guidelines for preventing workplace violence against health care workers. While the guidelines do not carry the legal effect of regulations, health care employers can expect agency investigators to look to the guidelines to determine whether the employer's violence prevention program meets OSHA standards. [*Guidelines for Preventing Workplace Violence for Health Care and Social Service Workers*, OSHA 3148 (2004), available on the Internet at *www.osha.gov*]

How can OSHA use the general-duty clause to issue citations for workplace violence?

Although there are no OSHA regulations regarding workplace violence, OSHA can invoke the general-duty clause in issuing citations. The general-duty clause is a "catch-all" provision that provides that any hazardous working condition not covered by a specific regulation or standard may be cited as a violation and a penalty may be issued. [29 U.S.C. § 654(a)(1)] According to OSHA instructions to field offices, a general-duty clause citation should be issued only in the absence of a specific standard if a hazard is recognized that poses a serious threat to worker safety or health and is capable of being corrected. Four elements are necessary to use the general-duty clause in an enforcement action for workplace violence in the ED.

1. The ED failed to keep the premises free of a hazard.
2. It was a recognized hazard.
3. The hazard caused death or serious harm.
4. There was a feasible and useful method to correct the hazard.

What do OSHA's voluntary guidelines for preventing workplace violence against health care workers say?

The guidelines contain detailed recommendations for developing an effective violence prevention program, identifying the four main components of a program as

1. management commitment and employee involvement,
2. worksite analysis,
3. hazard prevention and control,
4. safety and health training.

Minimum requirements for an effective workplace violence prevention plan include a zero-tolerance policy for workplace violence, assurance that employees reporting violence will not suffer reprisal, and a comprehensive plan for maintaining security. The guidelines outline specific methods of preventing violence in the health care workplace, such as arranging furniture to prevent entrapment of staff, instituting visitor sign-in procedures, and establishing a system to identify patients with a history of assaultive behavior. [*Guidelines for Preventing Workplace Violence for Health Care and Social Service Workers*, OSHA 3148 (2004), available on the Internet at *www.osha.gov*]

What can ED staff do to prevent violence?

ED staff can be trained to watch for signals that warn of potential violence such as verbal anger or frustration, body language such as threatening gestures, signs of drug or alcohol use, or the presence of a weapon. Each encounter should be evaluated for the potential for violence and staff should avoid being isolated with a potentially violent person and keep an open path to exit from the room for safety reasons. Staff should be familiar with the warning signs of potential violence: pacing and restlessness, clenched fists, increasingly loud speech, and excessive insistence, threats, or cursing. Staff members may be able to diffuse anger and potential violence by remaining calm and caring, by acknowledging the person's feelings, by avoiding aggressive behavior such as rapid movement, moving close to the person, touching the person, or speaking loudly. Staff should avoid making threats or giving orders to a potentially volatile person. If the situation cannot be diffused, then the staff should remove themselves from the situation, call security for help, and report any incidents to management. Training slides and handouts are available on the OSHA Internet site at *http://www.osha.gov.* [DHHS (NIOSH) Pub. No. 2002-101 (Apr. 2002), available on the Internet at *www.cdc.gov/niosh/2002-101.html.* OSHA E-Tools Emergency Department]

The ED should have a violence checklist in place that includes the following:

- A workplace violence prevention plan to train staff to recognize and diffuse violent situations,
- ED doors that exit out, so that people from the street can only access the ED through the waiting area,
- ED access that is controlled by a receptionist who buzzes people in through a secure door.

Why should EDs follow OSHA's voluntary guidelines?

There are several reasons to follow OSHA's voluntary workplace violence prevention guidelines for health care workers, including

- protection of employees, patients, visitors, and vendors,
- reduction in workers' compensation and insurance claims,
- insurance premium savings,
- compliance with Joint Commission standards,
- proof of compliance with OSHA's general-duty clause (and avoidance of OSHA fines and litigation),
- increased employee attendance,
- increased employee morale.

Are there OSHA reporting obligations when violence occurs in the ED?

OSHA regulations require the entry on the Injury and Illness Log (OSHA 300) of any injury that requires more than first aid, is a lost-time injury, requires modified duty, or causes loss of consciousness. [29 C.F.R. § 1904.9] Injuries resulting from assaults, which are otherwise recordable, must also be entered on the log. (This applies to establishments required to keep OSHA logs.) A fatality or catastrophe resulting in the hospitalization of three or more employees must be reported to OSHA within eight hours. [29 C.F.R. § 1904.39]

Are there other federal guidelines for preventing violence in hospitals?

The National Institute for Occupational Safety and Health (NIOSH) has also issued voluntary guidelines outlining prevention strategies for hospitals. NIOSH recommends that employers develop a safety and health program that includes management commitment, employee participation, hazard identification, safety and health training, and hazard prevention, control, and reporting, and that employers evaluate their program periodically. Although risk factors for violence are specific for each hospital and its work scenarios, employers can follow general prevention strategies:

1. Environmental designs
   - Develop emergency signaling, alarms, and monitoring systems.
   - Install security devices such as metal detectors to prevent armed persons from entering the hospital.
   - Install other security devices such as cameras and good lighting in hallways.
   - Provide security escorts to the parking lots at night.
   - Design waiting areas to accommodate and assist visitors and patients who may have a delay in service.
   - Design the triage area and other public areas to minimize the risk of assault.
     —Provide staff restrooms and emergency exits.
     —Install enclosed nurses' stations.
     —Install deep service counters or bullet-resistant and shatterproof glass enclosures in reception areas.
     —Arrange furniture and other objects to minimize their use as weapons.
2. Administrative controls
   - Design staffing patterns to prevent personnel from working alone and to minimize patient waiting time.
   - Restrict the movement of the public in hospitals by card-controlled access.
   - Develop a system for alerting security personnel when violence is threatened.
3. Behavior modifications
   - Provide all workers with training in recognizing and managing assaults, resolving conflicts, and maintaining hazard awareness. [*Violence: Occupational Hazards in Hospitals*, DHHS (NIOSH) Pub. No. 2002-101 (Apr. 2002), available on the Internet at *www.cdc.gov/niosh/2002-101.html*]

State Law Regarding Violence in the ED

Do state laws address violence in the ED?

Several state laws addressing violence in the ED have been enacted as legislative responses to the perceived increase of violence in hospital EDs. Hospital administrators should be familiar with laws in their state. ED managers should ensure that individuals responsible for hospital-wide violence prevention are familiar with the unique problems and risks of the ED.

What is an example of a state law governing violence in hospitals?

California law provides an example. In that state, hospitals are required to "conduct a security and safety assessment and to develop a security plan with measures to protect personnel, patients, and visitors from aggressive or violent behavior. The security and safety assessment must examine trends of aggressive or violent behavior at the facility. . . . Hospitals are required to track incidents of aggressive or violent behavior as part of the quality assessment and improvement program and for the purpose of developing a security plan to deter and manage further aggressive or violent acts of a similar nature."

By law, the security plan must include (but is not limited to) security considerations relating to the following:

- physical layout
- staffing
- security personnel availability
- policy and training related to appropriate responses to violent acts

California law also specifies that the person or hospital committee members who develop the security plan must be familiar with all of the following:

- "the role of security in hospital operations
- hospital organization
- protective measures, including alarms and access control
- the handling of disturbed patients, visitors, and employees
- identification of factors predicting aggressive and violent behavior
- hospital safety and emergency preparedness
- the rudiments of documenting and reporting crimes, including not disturbing a crime scene" [Cal. Health & Safety Code § 1257.7]

Are there state law reporting obligations when violence occurs in the ED?

State law may also require reporting of violent incidents in the ED. Under California law, for example, any act of assault or battery that results in injury or involves the use of a firearm or other dangerous weapon against any on-duty hospital personnel must be reported to the local law enforcement agency within 72 hours of the incident. [Cal. Health & Safety Code § 1257.7]

Security Measures

What security measures are required in the ED?

Necessary security measures vary from facility to facility and also vary as the social and environmental circumstances around the facility change. Ongoing data regarding violent incidents in the ED, the hospital, and the surrounding areas should be monitored to ensure proper response to changing circumstances. Proper security measures may range from adequate lighting and proper personnel identification to armed security guards and metal detectors.

State law may mandate certain security measures in hospital EDs. For example, Massachusetts law requires that proper identification be worn by all persons, including ED personnel, who observe or treat hospital patients. [Mass. Gen. Laws ch. 111, § 70E] California law requires adequate security personnel. [Cal. Health & Safety Code § 1257.7] State law varies widely and should be consulted to discover particular requirements in each jurisdiction. ACEP policy recommends that each ED have adequate security personnel, barriers, surveillance equipment; coordinate with local law enforcement; have written protocols for violent situations; and educate staff about violence. [*ACEP Policy Compendium: Protection from Physical Violence in the Emergency Department* (2007)]

How much authority can a hospital security guard assume?

The three basic types of private security officers and their scopes of authority are as follows:

1. *Private citizens* are hired to perform as security officers at the hospital. They have no more authority than a private citizen.
2. *Security officers* have special police or special deputy commissions that grant them more authority than a private citizen but less than that of regular police or deputies. Because these officers generally do not have good-faith immunity, they may be liable for false arrest if they arrest a person who did not commit an offense.
3. *Off-duty police officers or deputies* may moonlight as hospital security guards. State law governs whether these officers retain their authority, powers, and protections while privately employed. In some states these officers retain their authority, while in others they do not. In some states off-duty police officers are required to be armed.

Hospitals should be aware that the scope of authority varies from jurisdiction to jurisdiction. Hospital policies should clearly delineate the security guard's scope of authority. Security guards should also receive adequate training to allow them to perform their duties.

Can hospitals prohibit weapons in the ED?

The hospital can prohibit weapons, dangerous devices, and contraband in the ED and should post a notice to that effect in a conspicuous place. Patients and visitors can be instructed to check all weapons with hospital security. Those not complying can be denied access to the ED. If visitors become disruptive, local authorities may be contacted. Patients admitted through the ED may have weapons confiscated and stored in the hospital security department until they are discharged.

A number of states have passed concealed carry weapons laws that allow a gunowner to obtain a permit to carry a concealed weapon. States differ in terms of where a concealed weapon may be carried. Some allow the weapon anywhere once the person has a permit, while others prohibit concealed weapons in certain locations such as a school, hospital, or government building. For example, in Missouri, a person must be 23 years old to obtain the permit and submit to fingerprinting and background checks as well as safety training to carry the concealed weapon. Missouri prohibits concealed weapons in certain public locations including hospitals accessible to the public. [Mo. Rev. Stat. § 571.101] Some local cities and counties also have weapons laws that may impact whether weapons can be prohibited in the ED. It is important to check local laws for the specific jurisdiction.

Are there legal ramifications regarding the use of metal detectors?

The hospital is responsible for the safety of staff, patients, and visitors to the ED. As part of an effort to provide a safe environment, metal detectors may be used to protect against weapons being brought into the ED. All persons entering the ED can be subjected to a metal detector search as a condition of entering the property. Those refusing the search can be denied entry to the ED.

What should security do in response to an unruly visitor?

Unruly visitors or visitors who refuse to cooperate or follow hospital policies can be escorted from the premises. If the visitor refuses to leave, he or she should be informed that the hospital is private property and he or she may be subject to arrest.

What kind of security training should ED staff receive?

Necessary training may be mandated by state law, which should be incorporated into hospital and ED policies. In California, for example, the law requires all hospital employees who are regularly assigned to the ED to receive "security education and training related to the following topics:

- general safety measures
- personal safety measures
- the assault cycle
- factors predicting aggression and violence
- obtaining patient history from a patient with violent behavior
- characteristics of aggressive and violent patients and victims
- verbal and physical maneuvers to diffuse and avoid violent behavior
- strategies to avoid physical harm
- restraining techniques
- appropriate use of medications as chemical restraints
- any resources available to employees for coping with incidents of violence, for example, critical incident stress debriefing or employee assistance programs."

The law also requires members of the medical staff of hospitals and all other practitioners, including nurse practitioners, PAs, and other personnel who are regularly assigned to the ED, to receive the same training as hospital employees, or at least training identified in the security plan as sufficient. [Cal. Health & Safety Code § 1257.8]

Are there staffing and training requirements for security personnel?

State law may determine staffing and training requirements. California law, for example, states that hospitals must have sufficient personnel to provide security pursuant to the security plan. Persons regularly assigned to provide hospital security must be trained regarding the role of security in hospital operations, including the identification of factors predicting aggressive and violent behavior and management of violent disturbances. [Cal. Health & Safety Code § 1257.7]

What security considerations apply when a patient is in custody?

When an ED patient is a prisoner, the hospital and staff must balance the need to provide quality care and protect the patient's safety against the security of staff members and other patients. The care of patients in custody should be provided in accordance with written procedures, by properly trained staff, and in cooperation with law enforcement officials. Considerations include whether

- the patient is permitted to have a family member present;
- knowing the details of the patient's criminal record or circumstances of custody would influence the staff's ability to provide care;
- staff members are permitted to refuse to participate in the care of the prisoner;
- handcuffs and other restraining devices are consistent with or can be removed for needed treatment;
- law enforcement officers may be present during emergency treatment;
- compliance with life safety precautions is followed; and
- forensic personnel (i.e., the custodial officer) is oriented to life safety requirements.

Responsibilities Relating to Crimes Outside the ED

What types of crimes are EDs responsible for reporting?

State law governs reporting requirements, and, thus, what must be reported varies. However, most states require reporting of sexual abuse, child abuse and/or neglect, abuse of disabled and elderly adults, and other violent crimes, such as gunshot wounds.

What is the ED's responsibility regarding child abuse?

Every state has a mandatory reporting law that obliges health care providers who have reason to believe that a child has been abused to report their findings to a designated state agency, such as a child welfare bureau. If the provider making the diagnosis is a member of a hospital staff, the report may be channeled through the administrator's office.

Many states also authorize hospitals or, alternatively, attending physicians to retain a child in their custody without parental consent irrespective of whether the child requires further medical attention. A decision to take a child into protective custody must be based on a determination that returning the child to the custody of the parents or guardian would present an imminent danger to the child's health or life. Procedures set forth in these statutes require prompt notification of appropriate state officials. Certain states also impose a time limitation on protective custody. Provision must be made for a hearing to determine whether the child should be permanently or temporarily removed from the parents or guardian.

In addition, some states have enacted legislation calling for the creation of multidisciplinary teams in the community and in hospitals to identify and assist victims of child abuse.

What are the consequences of failing to diagnose or report child abuse?

A failure to exercise reasonable care in diagnosing child abuse or laxity in complying with the mandatory reporting laws may result in liability for an errant physician or hospital. This was illustrated in a California case in which a physician in the ED of a hospital treated an 11-month-old child with a fractured leg, a fractured skull, and multiple bruises about the body. The child's mother gave no explanation for the injuries. Three months later the child was taken by her mother to another hospital with puncture wounds on her leg and back, severe bites on her face, and a mutilated hand. A physician at the second hospital diagnosed the child's condition as battered child syndrome, and the child was placed in foster care. A suit was brought on behalf of the child against the first physician and hospital for negligently failing to diagnose the child abuse syndrome and to report the child battery pursuant to California's mandatory reporting laws. The California Supreme Court held that the health care providers would be liable if the child's most recent injuries were a proximate result of the first physician's failure to diagnose child abuse and to report the matter to appropriate officials. [*Landeros v. Flood*, 551 P.2d 389 (Cal. 1976)]

What are the consequences of reporting child abuse when it later turns out there was no child abuse?

Many state laws provide immunity from liability for individuals who report suspected child abuse in good faith. In a 1985 Michigan case, a court reviewed a physician's liability for reporting child abuse when it was later proven that the charges were not true. The child instead had a disease that caused the bones to be brittle and easily broken. The court held that the parents could not recover for erroneous abuse charges because the physician was acting in good faith and was therefore entitled to statutory immunity. [*Awkermann v. Tri County Ortho*, 373 N.W.2d 204 (Mich. Ct. App. 1985); *see also, Howe v. Andereck*, 882 So. 2d 240 (Miss. Ct. App. 2004) and *Casbohm v. Metrohealth Med. Ctr.*, 746 N.E.2d 661 (Ohio Ct. App. 2000)]

What is the ED's responsibility regarding sexual abuse?

State law, particularly hospital licensing provisions, may require hospitals to provide treatment for persons who have been sexually abused. Hospital licensure acts that do not specify that care must be provided to victims of sexual assault might imply that facilities with EDs are obliged to care for such individuals. In the absence of explicit or implicit statutory requirements, hospitals that maintain emergency care facilities should have clearly established procedures for managing a person who has been sexually abused. Further, because of the potential for liability, it would be inadvisable to deny hospitalization or medical services to an individual on the grounds that the person's complaint involved a sexual assault.

It is not uncommon to find local hospital consortia cooperating in the development of guidelines for treating victims of sexual assault. Some hospitals have rape crisis units staffed by specially trained physicians, nurses, psychologists, and social workers who provide the medical and psychosocial support a patient needs following an assault.

The American College of Emergency Physicians (ACEP) policy statement on sexual assault recommends that the ED work with local government authorities and establish a plan to address the needs of the sexually assaulted patient including medical, psychological, safety, and legal needs. This would include psychological counseling, pregnancy testing and counseling, treatment for sexually transmitted diseases, and evidentiary exams to collect criminal evidence. The department can establish patient care criteria and prepare staff through ongoing training and education. [*ACEP Policy Compendium: Management of the Patient with the Complaint of Sexual Assault* (2007)]

What are examples of state laws requiring treatment of sexually abused patients?

Hospital administrators in states with specific statutory requirements regarding the treatment of persons who have been sexually abused should review these provisions carefully in drafting hospital policy. Florida, for example, has a statute that sets forth the types of services that hospitals with EDs should have available in treating victims of sexual assault. These include gynecological and psychological care as well as medical examinations and procedures required by police officials for the collection of evidence necessary in the prosecution of assailants. [Fla. Stat. ch. 395.1021]

Illinois also has legislation requiring hospitals to provide emergency care for victims of rape. Under that law, hospitals must provide appropriate medical examinations; laboratory tests; medication; blood tests; oral and written information concerning the possibility of infection, sexually transmitted disease, and pregnancy; oral and written information concerning medications and medical procedures; and counseling. [410 Ill. Comp. Stat. Ann. § 70/5]

Are there concerns about evidence in sexual abuse cases?

Physical evidence relating to the sexual abuse is important in pursuing criminal charges against the perpetrator. To ensure that the evidence is preserved in a legally proper manner, the ED must follow certain procedures, which should be specified in ED policies for treating persons who have been sexually abused. A number of groups, including many local prosecutors' offices, willingly provide rape evidence kits along with instructions and training programs on their use.

What is the ED's responsibility for reporting abuse of disabled or elderly patients?

Many states have enacted laws mandating the reporting of abuse, neglect, or exploitation of disabled adults or elderly persons. The laws vary widely. Some laws define "elderly" and "disabled" as well as the terms "abuse" and "neglect," while others do not. The laws also vary regarding who has a reporting obligation and to whom the abuse must be reported. It is therefore important that ED personnel be familiar with the requirements of their own jurisdictions. ACEP recommends written protocols to recognize and treat elder abuse, staff education regarding agencies that oversee abuse, and immunity from liability for those reporting abuse in good faith, as well as further research on the issues. [*ACEP Policy Compendium: Management of Elder Abuse and Neglect* (2007)]

What is an example of an abuse reporting law that applies to disabled and elderly patients?

Florida has a broad reporting law. In that state, a health professional who knows, or has reasonable cause to suspect, that a vulnerable adult has been or is being abused, neglected, or exploited must immediately report that knowledge or suspicion to the central abuse registry and tracking system on the statewide toll-free number.

A report of abuse in Florida must contain, to the extent possible, specific information regarding the vulnerable adult, the person's family members, the alleged perpetrator, the caregiver, and the person reporting. The report must also contain a description of the injuries; actions taken by the reporter, if any, such as notification of the criminal justice agency; and any other information that might establish abuse, neglect, or exploitation. [Fla. Stat. ch. 415.1034]

Does the ED have responsibility for reporting special types of wounds?

States generally require the reporting of gunshot wounds. Texas, for example, has a mandatory reporting law that requires that such a case be reported immediately to the law enforcement authority of the municipality or county by the hospital administration or by a physician who treats, or is requested to treat, a bullet or gunshot wound. [Tex. Health & Safety Code § 161.041]

In Florida, the reporting obligation applies to, among others, physicians, nurses, and any employee of a hospital who knowingly treats, or receives a request to treat, a person suffering from a gunshot wound or life-threatening injury indicating an act of violence. The health care provider is required to report to the sheriff's department of the county. Anyone willfully failing to report the treatment or treatment request is guilty of a misdemeanor. [Fla. Stat. ch. 790.24]

A Colorado law obligating physicians to report gunshot wounds to law enforcement officials was interpreted by that state's highest court. In a case where a sheriff's officer asked a female physician assistant to photograph a female victim's bullet wounds to the buttock and thighs, the victim's husband, on trial for the incident, claimed that the photographs violated his wife's physician-patient privilege. The Colorado Supreme Court found that the reporting statute nullified that privilege. The statute clearly stated that in cases where the physician has a reporting obligation, the physician-patient privilege is abrogated with regard to testimony about the information received from the physician's observations of the patient. Because the incident involved gunshot wounds, and the photographs were obtained through the PA's observation of the wounds, rather than through communication with the patient, the court found the privilege did not apply. [*People v. Covington,* 19 P.3d 15 (Colo. 2001), *cert. denied,* 2002 Colo. LEXIS 226 (Colo. March 18, 2002)]

Because state laws vary, it is important that ED personnel know the scope of the reporting requirements in their particular jurisdiction. Failure to report could lead to penalties. On the other hand, disclosure of conditions that are not required by law might violate the patient's privacy rights. Strict adherence to state reporting requirements is therefore necessary and should be incorporated into ED policies and procedures.

What does "maintaining the chain of custody" mean?

When a person is arrested and tried for a crime, various types of evidence are presented in an effort to prove the person's guilt or innocence. Maintaining the chain of custody means that there is continual tracking and documentation of evidence from the time it is collected until it is presented in the courtroom. The goal of maintaining the chain of custody is to prevent tampering with evidence, which would deprive the accused of a fair trial.

In the ED, the issue of chain of custody arises when physical evidence is gathered from, for example, a rape victim. The protocol to be followed must have the prior approval of the police, district attorney, public defender, courts, medical examiner, hospital, and laboratory. That protocol should be reviewed before the evidence is collected to prevent invalidating specimens by inappropriate handling. The protocol should be followed and documented. All specimens must be appropriately labeled and should be signed for by each person handling the specimen thereafter.

The chain of custody issue may also arise with various types of contraband brought into the ED, such as a weapon or illegal drugs. There should be an established policy for handling contraband, which should include maintaining the chain of custody in the event that there is future prosecution in which the contraband will be used as evidence. For example, if a patient presents at the ED with gunshot wounds and is in possession of a gun, the ED staff should follow the established policy in handling the weapon. This generally involves contacting security and releasing the gun to a security officer who locks the weapon in a safe. All steps are documented. It could be that the person is properly licensed to carry a gun and is in fact a police officer. It could be that the person was committing armed robbery and the weapon will be used in prosecuting the case.

Abandonment in the ED

What considerations surround elderly abandonment at the ED?

Policies and procedures that direct the staff how to act in the event of elderly patient abandonment at the ED should be carefully reviewed because these vulnerable individuals trigger special concerns.

According to the American College of Emergency Physicians (ACEP), EDs are used as a safety net not only for medical emergencies, but also for social emergencies faced by individuals and institutions responsible for the care of elderly individuals. ACEP cites a number of factors contributing to the problem of elderly abandonment, including rising health care costs, two career families, cutbacks in government support, and lack of coverage for long-term services needed by the elderly population.

If an elderly patient is brought to the ED for emergency care, but does not have an emergency medical condition, the hospital is not obligated to admit that individual. Where the patient cannot care for him or herself, however, and the person who brought the patient to the hospital will not assume responsibility, the hospital must attempt to make alternate arrangements, by contacting the patient's relatives and social services, for example. In addition, because elderly abandonment constitutes abuse or neglect under many state laws, ED staff will be required by law to file a report with the appropriate authorities to trigger an investigation, likely Adult Protective Services.

Transfer agreements with long-term care facilities will reduce the possibility that a patient transferred to the hospital for emergency care may not be readmitted to the long-term care facility when the emergency medical condition is stabilized. If the long-term care facility should refuse to readmit a stable patient, because the facility can no longer provide the level of care now needed by the resident, hospital and long-term care facility administration should be consulted as to how to develop a safe discharge plan.

Insurance coverage is a significant issue for abandoned patients, as payers will not likely cover the cost of acute care where it is not medically necessary, simply because the patient has been abandoned at an acute care facility. Insurers may prove helpful in these cases, however, as case managers or care coordinators may have the necessary resources to arrange for alternate site care at an appropriate level.

Practical considerations include identifying how and when hospital administration must be notified, what information (if any) may be released to the media and whether staff is properly trained to handle these patients.

What should hospitals consider when designing policies regarding the treatment and custody of abandoned infants?

In the last few years, in the wake of publicity surrounding high profile cases of infants who were abandoned in public places, a number of state legislatures proposed legislation aimed at discouraging abandonment by allowing unwanted newborns to be safely left at hospitals. Where this legislation has been enacted, hospitals must review newborn abandonment policies and revise them to comply with these new laws. In Florida, for example, hospitals with emergency services must admit and provide all necessary services and care to any infant who appears three days old or younger. The hospital has implied consent to perform necessary services and care. The parent who expresses the intent to leave a newborn and not return has "the absolute right to remain anonymous and leave at any time." The parent may not be pursued or followed, unless the parent seeks to reclaim the newborn. After receiving the infant, the hospital must immediately contact a local licensed child placement agency or the statewide central abuse hotline to transfer custody. [Fla. Stat. § 383.50.]

Whether hospitals are required by law to accept abandoned infants, or seek to do so voluntarily, the policies and procedures for treatment and custody of these infants must be carefully outlined. The following should be considered:

- Where may infants be "abandoned"?
- How will individuals know where to leave an unwanted infant?
- What steps will the hospital take to prevent abandoned infants from going unnoticed, or from being harmed or abducted?
- When the infant is discovered, who will be notified?
- Who will assume responsibility for notifying authorities?
- What age children will the hospital accept?
- If the parent brings the child into the hospital, what steps are taken to protect the parent's anonymity? To ascertain the parent's identity?
- What staff training is necessary?
- Does voluntarily accepting abandoned babies create an increased risk of liability for the hospital or for treating staff? Is additional insurance necessary?

- What happens if the parent returns and seeks custody of the child?
- What if another individual arrives and claims custody?
- What information may be released to the media?
- How and when must administration be notified?
- May hospital employees attempt to adopt babies abandoned at the facility?

Administering Tests at Request of Law Enforcement Without Patient Consent

If ED personnel perform test procedures on criminal suspects at a police officer's request, can the suspect later sue?

A successful lawsuit against medical personnel for performing a police ordered test would be a rarity. Some states have statutes providing immunity to physicians, nurses, and employers in such situations. Under an Illinois statute, for example, a hospital and its staff were judged immune from civil liability in connection with a patient's lawsuit alleging that hospital staff grabbed her arm and forcibly drew her blood without her consent after she was arrested on hospital premises for driving under the influence of alcohol. The patient arrived at the hospital following a traffic accident in which another driver had been injured, although the patient had sustained no injuries. Although she declined any treatment, she was detained by emergency room staff until a police officer arrived, placed the patient under arrest, and in accordance with the state vehicle code, advised her that she must submit to a blood alcohol test. Despite the patient's refusal, a hospital physician and nurse grabbed the patient's arm and drew blood from her against her will. The court found that the actions of the hospital and its staff were authorized under another state vehicle code provision which provides that persons authorized to withdraw blood or collect urine cannot be sued civilly for damages, unless they act in a "willful or wanton manner." Grabbing the patient's arm to withdraw blood simply did not rise to the level of "willful and wanton" conduct, the court concluded. [*Ruppel v. Ramseyer*, 33 F. Supp. 2d 720 (C.D. Ill. 1999)]

Note that the Illinois statute, as well as many others, refers only to drawing blood and collecting urine, leaving unanswered the question of what liability might attend more risky, more seriously invasive, or inherently unpleasant tests or procedures such as the pumping out of the subject's stomach or the surgical removal of a bullet for the purpose of ballistics tests.

Can the police order a blood test without the subject's consent?

This situation most often arises when the police want to know the subject's blood alcohol level. The blood must be drawn and tested quickly or the evidence will be destroyed. If the police want the subject's blood tested for another reason, for example, to discover the subject's blood type while in the course of a rape investigation, they can wait until a search warrant is issued, as the evidence will not be destroyed.

The United States Supreme Court has ruled that police may legally order a blood test without the subject's consent if five conditions are satisfied.

1. The suspect has been formally arrested.
2. The blood test is reasonably likely to produce evidence in the forthcoming criminal prosecution.

3. The delay involved in obtaining a search warrant would lead to destruction of the evidence.
4. The test chosen is a reasonable one (e.g., there are no medical or religious reasons for not carrying out the test).
5. The test is performed in a reasonable manner (e.g., the blood is taken by a qualified health care professional using accepted medical techniques in a hospital environment). [*Schmerber v. California*, 384 U.S. 757 (1966)]

Courts continue to define when a police officer can seek a blood test without a warrant. In reviewing the basis for obtaining a blood test, the Tenth Circuit noted that the officer should obtain a warrant for a blood test since a blood test is considered a search protected by the Fourth Amendment unless the officer has probable cause for the blood test and exigent circumstances exist. Exigent circumstances are determined by looking at state law and the importance of the evidence and severity of the offense. Preservation of evidence alone would not necessarily justify a warrantless blood test. [*Marshall v. Columbia Lea Reg'l Hosp.*, 345 F.3d 1157 (10th Cir. 2003); *see also State v. Cormier,* 928 A.2d 753 (Me. 2007)]

Assuming these conditions are met and that the police are therefore acting within their authority, any hospital or health professional could conduct the blood test under police request without fear of liability for battery. In a New Hampshire case, a person refused to have an alcohol blood test administered by the state trooper. When he came into the hospital, the doctor ordered a routine blood test and the results were subsequently given to the trooper. The court found the test admissible in court. While state law prohibited a trooper from administering a test upon refusal, it did not preclude obtaining other blood test results. [*State v. Nickerson*, 780 A.2d 1257 (N.H. 2001)]

What should ED staff do when a police officer asks for a blood test on a patient?

To ensure that the procedure is performed within the parameters discussed in the previous question and answer, ED staff should require the police officer to sign a form attesting that the first three conditions are met. For maximum protection, the provider can supply his or her own determination about the final two conditions. The subject should be asked to sign a consent form, even when it appears that the five conditions for police authority have been met.

Two additional points should be noted. First, the test should not be performed if the subject offers physical resistance because this would tend to make the test procedure unreasonable, defeating the fourth of the listed conditions. Second, the hospital or health professional has no legal duty to obey the police request to perform the test. Thus, cooperation can be withheld if it is not clear that the five conditions are met or if the provider wishes not to participate for any other reason.

What about other kinds of tests to which the suspect does not consent?

In cases in which the invasion of the body is significant and in which time would allow the police to obtain a search warrant, the provider should insist that this be done before acceding to the police request. Although the pressure may be strong to follow police orders without question, there is no reason why health professionals or institutions should be subjected to even a slight risk of tort liability when a court order that would avoid this could be secured. In no event should hospital personnel use physical force to compel a subject to undergo a test.

For example, a state hospital set up a program to test maternity patients' urine for evidence of cocaine use. The Supreme Court found that this was an unreasonable search in violation of the Fourth Amendment if the patient did not consent to the urine test. Even though the goal of the program was to reduce drug use, the immediate outcome of the program was to provide evidence for law enforcement. The interest in deterring drug use did not justify a search without a warrant or without consent. Law enforcement did not demonstrate a special need to justify the tests. [*Ferguson v. City of Charleston*, 532 U.S. 67 (2001)]

DNA testing capabilities have led to an increased focus on using DNA databases as a tool in solving crimes. In analyzing whether DNA collection can be obtained without consent, courts have looked at Fourth Amendment rights requiring probable cause for a search balanced against government interests in supervising probations, preventing recidivism, and developing a DNA database to resolve crimes. A number of courts have upheld DNA collection without a search warrant as a special need when the collection is from a convicted felon, or as a condition of parole or probation for a convicted felon. [*U.S. v. Weikert,* 2007 U.S. App. LEXIS 18845 (1st Cir. Sept. 21, 2007); *U.S. v. Amerson,* 483 F.3d 73 (2d Cir. 2007) upholding testing under the federal DNA Analysis Backlog Elimination Act of 2000 and *U.S. v. Conley,* 453 F.3d 674 (6th Cir. 2006); *Nicolas v. Goord,* 430 F.3d 652 (2d Cir. 2005) upholding state statutes that require DNA sampling] Some state statutes extend testing to those arrested for a felony. For example, Virginia requires everyone convicted and arrested for a felony to provide a DNA sample [Va. Code Ann. § 19.2-310.2:1 (2006), upheld by *Anderson v. Commonwealth,* 634 S.E.2d 372 (2006)], and Louisiana requires testing of certain arrestees including juveniles arrested for a felony. [La. Rev. Stat. Ann. 15:690 (2006)]

DUTY TO TREAT PATIENTS REGARDLESS OF ABILITY TO PAY

Legal complications may arise when a hospital conditions admission on a patient's ability to pay for medical services, especially when a patient seeks emergency care. Federal legislation not only precludes such restrictive admission policies but also sets forth specific circumstances when a hospital must provide care without regard to ability to pay. Failure to provide uncompensated care can also lead to the loss of tax-exempt status.

State statutes and judicial decisions also limit the use of a patient's ability to pay as a criterion for denying hospitalization and medical services. Some legislation includes criminal sanctions for those who prohibit admission to a hospital when patients are unable to demonstrate an ability to pay for their care.

EMTALA

What are COBRA and EMTALA?

These two acronyms refer to the same federal law. Hospitals that participate in the Medicare program are subject to the emergency care requirements enacted in the Emergency Medical Treatment and Active Labor Act (EMTALA), as part of the Consolidated Omnibus Budget Reconciliation Act of 1986 (COBRA). [42 U.S.C. § 1395dd] An amendment to the Medicare statute, the law sets forth parameters regarding the treatment and transfer of all emergency patients, whether or not they are eligible for Medicare. EMTALA, sometimes called the "antidumping" law, was enacted largely out of legislative concern that hospital emergency departments (EDs) were turning away or transferring patients who could not pay for treatment but needed emergency medical care. Because EMTALA has detailed requirements, and because violations may lead to serious administrative consequences as well as liability, hospitals should review their ED procedures for compliance with this important federal law. For sample documentation relating to EMTALA, see **Part 4** under Continuum of Care.

What does EMTALA require hospitals to do?

Under EMTALA, a hospital must examine all individuals who come to the ED seeking treatment. The hospital must provide an appropriate medical screening examination (MSE) to determine if an emergency medical condition exists or if the patient is in active labor. If the patient does have an emergency medical condition or is in active labor, the hospital must stabilize the patient before discharge. The hospital may transfer the patient only upon the signed certification of a physician that the benefits of transfer outweigh the risks. [42 U.S.C. § 1395dd] Each of these requirements is discussed in detail in the questions and answers that follow.

To which patients does EMTALA apply?

Although EMTALA is a Medicare law, it is not limited to Medicare patients. Every patient who comes to the hospital for acute care is protected by EMTALA. The courts have interpreted the wording "any individual" to mean that EMTALA can apply to any patient who comes to the ED, whether they are denied treatment or not and whether they pay for care or not. EMTALA was designed to remedy economic discrimination by hospitals that deny care or transfer indigent and uninsured patients in unstable medical conditions and to extend protection to any individual who enters a hospital's ED. Most federal appeals courts have applied EMTALA's language to allow any patient to challenge his or her emergency treatment under EMTALA, whether alleging economic discrimination or not. The U.S. Supreme Court settled the question when it ruled that a charge of financial discrimination is immaterial to an EMTALA lawsuit. [*Roberts v. Galen of Virginia*, 525 U.S. 249 (1999)]. "Any individual," then, includes not only the indigent, but also all patients, including minors, illegal aliens, private patients, managed care patients, and psychiatric patients.

Note that when an individual comes to the dedicated ED requesting examination and treatment but the condition is clearly not an emergency, the hospital is only required to perform sufficient screening to determine that the condition is not an emergency. [42 C.F.R. § 489.24(c)]

What does "comes to the emergency department" mean?

EMTALA's provisions apply to patients who "come to the emergency department" and request examination or treatment for a medical condition. The Centers for Medicare and Medicaid Services' final regulations on EMTALA take a broad view of the meaning of this phrase—beyond its common sense meaning. The patient does not have to formally enter the ED. According to final regulations, "comes to" the ED means one of the following has occurred.

A person comes to the hospital's "dedicated emergency department" and requests examination or treatment. A dedicated ED is defined as "any department or facility of the hospital" whether on- or off-campus, which meets one of the following requirements:

- state licensure as an emergency room or ED,
- advertising or holding out to the public as a place that provides emergency care on an urgent basis without a prior appointment, or
- a patient sample demonstrates that one-third of outpatient visits for the treatment of emergency medical conditions took place on an urgent basis without prior appointment.

In the absence of a request, a request will be presumed if a reasonable layperson observer would believe that based on the person's appearance or behavior, the person needs a medical exam or treatment for a medical condition.

A person presents to hospital property and requests an exam or treatment for what may be an emergency medical condition. When no request is made, the reasonable layperson observer standard would apply to presume a request. Hospital property refers to the hospital main campus defined in 42 C.F.R. § 413.65(b), including the parking lot, sidewalks, and driveway, but excludes other buildings not part of the hospital such as physician offices, rural health centers, skilled nursing facilities, or non-medical facilities such as a restaurant or shop.

When a person is in a ground or air ambulance enroute to the hospital, i.e., not on hospital grounds, the hospital owns the ambulance, and transport is to examine and treat the person in the hospital's ED, then the person is considered to have come to the dedicated ED. However, if a hospital-owned ambulance is operated under community protocols that require transport to the nearest facility, the person is considered to have come to the facility to which he or she is transported. If the hospital-owned ambulance is under the direction of a non-employed or non-affiliated physician, the person being transported is not presumed to have come to the hospital.

When a person is in a ground or air ambulance on hospital property for treatment at the hospital's dedicated ED, then the person is considered to have come to the dedicated ED. Even if the ED indicates it is on diversionary status and does not have the staff or facilities to accept any further emergency patients, the person will be considered to have come to the ED if the ambulance staff ignores the comments and brings the person to hospital property. However, if the ambulance transports the person elsewhere because of the diversionary status, then the person is considered to have come to the facility to which he or she transported. [42 C.F.R. § 489.24]

Thus, the final rule excludes off-campus hospital departments that do not routinely provide emergency care from the scope of "coming to the emergency room," and clarifies that a hospital would not have an EMTALA obligation with respect to persons presenting to those departments. A hospital should, however, have appropriate protocols in place for dealing with persons who come to off-campus non-emergency facilities to seek emergency care. [*EMTALA Final Rule*, 68 Fed. Reg. 53,222 (Sept. 9, 2003)]

Does this also apply to a hospital's helipad?

Where a local EMS system or private ambulance uses the hospital's helipad for the sole purpose of meeting a helicopter not owned by the hospital for transport to another facility,

CMS will not apply the "comes to" rule to require EMTALA compliance by the hospital that owns the helipad.

If the ambulance or flight crew, however, requests assistance in the medical management of the patient, the hospital with the helipad becomes obligated to initiate EMTALA procedures for MSE and for any further transfer compliance. [42 C.F.R. § 413.65, 42 C.F.R. § 489.24]

What happens when a patient is close to the ED, but off hospital property, and needs emergency care?

Under the final regulations, property means the entire main hospital campus including the parking lot, sidewalk, and driveway. The hospital campus is defined as the physical area immediately adjacent to the main buildings, as well as other areas and structures that are not contiguous but are within 250 yards of the main buildings. The final regulations clarify that an EMTALA obligation arises when someone presents elsewhere on hospital property, not the dedicated ED, and requests treatment for an *emergency* medical condition. Hospital property specifically excluded other buildings such as physician offices, rural health centers, skilled nursing facilities, or non-medical areas like a restaurant or shop. No EMTALA obligation arises for treatment requests in these other areas. [*EMTALA Final Rule*, 68 Fed. Reg. 53,222 (Sept. 9, 2003)]

As a practical matter, those in areas not designated as hospital property can determine whether emergency care can be provided in that location or whether the person should be referred to the ED. Hospital planning should consider the following issues:

- establishing the geographical boundaries of hospital responsibility,
- under what circumstances EMS will be called,
- under what circumstances hospital personnel will transport the patient,
- what personnel will be contacted and called to assist with transport,
- who will cover for those personnel if they are called away from patient care areas,
- what equipment must be kept available for patient transfer,
- to what part of the hospital will the patient be transported, and
- whether additional insurance is necessary.

Are there any limits on when patients in ambulances have "come to" the ED?

As stated above, an individual in an ambulance that is owned and operated by the hospital is normally considered to have "come to" the emergency room of that hospital. Final rules issued by CMS in 2003, however, make an exception in the case of hospital-owned ambulances operating under community-wide EMS protocols. Under the proposed rules, the rule on hospital-owned ambulances does not apply if the ambulance is operating under a community-wide EMS protocol that requires it to transport the individual to a hospital other than the hospital that owns the ambulance. In such a case, the individual is considered to have come to the ED of the hospital to which the individual is transported. [68 Fed. Reg. 53,222 (codified at 42 C.F.R. Part 489)]

An individual in a non-hospital-owned ambulance off hospital property is not normally considered to have come to the ED, even if a member of the ambulance staff contacts the hospital asking to transport a patient to the facility. The hospital may deny access if it is in diversionary status, i.e., it does not have the staff or facilities to accept any additional emergency patients. The capacity of a facility to receive emergency care patients means the ability of the hospital to accommodate the individual patient, including numbers and availability of qualified staff, beds, and equipment, as well as the hospital's past practices of accommodating patients beyond its occupancy limits. [42 C.F.R. § 489.24(b)] However, if the ambulance staff disregards the hospital's instructions, and brings the patient to the facility, the patient has come to the ED and EMTALA applies.

One federal appeals court has ruled, however, that a hospital may not divert a non-hospital-owned ambulance that has contacted the hospital's ED and is en route to that hospital with a patient unless the hospital is in diversionary status. While transporting a heart attack victim to a Honolulu hospital, ambulance personnel radioed the hospital to advise of their imminent arrival. The ED physician redirected the ambulance to another hospital that was farther away, and the patient died soon after arrival at the other hospital. The trial court dismissed an EMTALA suit because the patient had never "come to" the hospital's emergency room as required by EMTALA, but the appeals court disagreed, finding that "comes to" could mean either physical arrival or the act of traveling to the hospital. Although the patient was in a non-hospital-owned ambulance, the court cited HHS regulations providing that if non-hospital-owned ambulance personnel contact a hospital to advise of their approach with a patient, the hospital may deny access if it is on diversionary status. The court concluded that a hospital may not prevent a non-hospital-owned ambulance from coming to the hospital unless it has a valid treatment-related reason for doing so. [*Arrington v. Wong*, 237 F.3d 1066 (9th Cir. 2001)]

Does EMTALA extend to telephone requests for emergency treatment?

Not ordinarily, unless the patient is on hospital property; however, a telephone call requesting emergency treatment may trigger EMTALA if the call is from a medical facility requesting specialized care from the hospital, such as those provided in a burn unit or trauma unit. Under federal regulations, a hospital with specialized services cannot refuse a telephone request for a transfer. Specifically, the regulations provide that a hospital that has specialized capabilities or facilities may not refuse to accept from a referring hospital an appropriate transfer of an individual who requires such capabilities or facilities if the receiving hospital has the capacity to treat the individual. [42 C.F.R. §§ 489.24(e) & (f)] Even a hospital that does not hold itself out as having specialized units may be subject to these regulations; CMS's application of the rule makes it clear that if the requested destination hospital has services and physicians available that are better able to meet a patient's medical needs than the transferring facility, the requested hospital is considered to have specialized capabilities and must accept the transfer.

One federal appeals court has ruled that a telephone request for admission to the ED does not trigger EMTALA. In that case, a seriously injured child was brought to a hospital ED. The general practitioner on duty called an orthopedist at another hospital to request transfer. The orthopedist agreed to treat the patient, but an administrator at the second hospital determined that the patient was not insured and refused the transfer. The patient was treated at a third facility, after a delay of approximately seven hours. The patient's parents sued the second hospital under EMTALA. The hospital defended that EMTALA did not apply because the patient had not come to its facility requesting care. The federal appeals court agreed that the patient was not entitled to sue. Although the patient did request treatment from the second hospital, the patient did not come to that facility, the court emphasized. Equating a telephonic request for treatment with the "comes to" clause would render the clause meaningless, according to the court. [*Miller v. Medical Ctr.*, 22 F.3d 626 (5th Cir. 1994)] This decision, however, did not consider the application of the provisions of EMTALA that require hospitals with specialized capabilities to accept transfers. As such, it is not a reliable indicator of how the law will be enforced, either by CMS or by the courts.

What should a hospital do if a patient will not consent to care?

EMTALA requires not only that a patient come to the ED but also that the patient, or someone acting on the patient's behalf, request an examination or treatment for a medical condition. If a patient withdraws his or her request for treatment, the hospital will not be liable under EMTALA. A hospital satisfies EMTALA if it offers medical examination or treatment and informs the patient of the risks and benefits of the examination or treatment but the patient refuses to consent.

The statute does require hospitals to take "all reasonable steps" to obtain written informed consent to refuse the examination or treatment, however. The medical record should document the exam and treatment refused, and the refusal should outline the risks and benefits of treatment. [42 U.S.C. § 1395dd(b)(2), 42 C.F.R. § 489.24(d)] HCFA explained in its November 1999 Special Advisory Bulletin:

> If an individual chooses to withdraw his or her request for examination or treatment at the presenting hospital, and if the hospital is aware that the individual intends to leave prior to the screening examination, a hospital should take the following steps: (1) Offer the individual further medical examination and treatment within the staff and facilities available at the hospital as may be required to identify and stabilize an emergency medical condition; (2) Inform the individual of the benefits of such examination and treatment, and of the risks of withdrawal prior to receiving such examination and treatment; and (3) Take all reasonable steps to secure the individual's written informed consent to refuse such examination and treatment.

The medical record should indicate that the person was informed of the risks and benefits of the examination or treatment or both, if applicable, that was refused, and should contain a specific description of the risks and benefits discussed. It is not sufficient to merely state "risks and benefits explained to patient," or to simply note that the family consented. The record should contain the signature of the refusing individual or person acting on the individual's behalf, or should reflect the reasonable efforts made by the hospital to obtain a written refusal. Adequate documentation is vital because there must be no indication that a patient was coerced into refusing care. Numerous hospitals have been cited for failure to obtain written refusals of care when patients leave the ED prior to screening. "If an individual leaves without notifying hospital personnel, the hospital should, at a minimum, document the fact that the person had been there, what time the hospital discovered that the patient had left, and should retain all triage notes and additional records, if any. However, the burden rests with the hospital to show that it has taken appropriate steps to discourage an individual from leaving the hospital without evaluation." [OIG/HCFA Special Advisory Bulletin on the Patient Anti-Dumping Statute, OIG and HCFA, HHS, 64 Fed. Reg. 61,353, 61,359 (Nov. 10, 1999)]

May hospital staff seek authorization for payment from a patient's managed care organization (MCO) or insurer before the patient has received a medical screening evaluation (MSE)?

The CMS final rule in 2003 that clarified that hospitals may not seek prior authorization for payment before screening a patient for an emergency medical condition and stabilizing the patient was subsequently adopted in the final rule. However, an emergency physician may contact a patient's regular-care physician for advice based on patient medical history, provided the consultation does not delay screening and stabilization services. Once stabilizing treatment has begun, the hospital may then contact the plan for payment authorization. [68 Fed. Reg. 53,222 (codified at 42 C.F.R. § 489.24)]

How should ED staff respond to patient inquiries regarding the cost of care or eligibility for insurance coverage?

An HCFA (now CMS) advisory bulletin outlines suggested practices to minimize the likelihood that a hospital will violate EMTALA. The advisory suggests that when a patient inquires about financial liability for emergency services, the question should be answered by a staff member who has been well trained in EMTALA compliance. The staff member must clearly inform the patient that, notwithstanding the patient's ability to pay, the hospital stands ready and willing to provide a medical screening examination and stabilizing treatment, if necessary. Any patient with a potentially emergency medical condition should be encouraged by hospital staff to remain until after screening. Staff efforts must be fully documented, because "the burden rests with the hospital to show that it has taken appropriate steps to discourage an individual from leaving the hospital without evaluation." [OIG/HCFA Special Advisory Bulletin on the Patient Anti-Dumping Statute, OIG and HCFA, HHS, 64 Fed. Reg. 61,353, 61,359 (Nov. 10, 1999)]

What is an MSE under EMTALA?

Under EMTALA, if a patient comes to the ED and the patient or someone acting on his or her behalf requests an examination or treatment for a medical condition, the hospital must provide for an appropriate MSE within the capability of its ED, including ancillary services routinely available to the ED, to determine whether an emergency medical condition exists. A hospital cannot delay an MSE, further medical examination, or treatment to inquire about the individual's method of payment or insurance status. [42 U.S.C. §§ 1395dd(a) & (h)]

ACEP recommends that a standard process be in place to ensure that those presenting to the ED receive a medical screening exam by a qualified medical person as required under EMTALA. The examiner should be delineated in the hospital bylaws. ACEP also indicates that caution should be in place in implementing processes that refer non-emergent patients away from the emergency room. Physicians should be involved in any such process development and keep the opportunity to evaluate and further treat patients who present to the ED. [*Medical Screening of Emergency Department Patients,* ACEP, April 2006]

Where can the MSE take place?

According to guidelines for CMS investigators, the MSE may take place in an area of the hospital other than the ED as long as the MSE takes place in a contiguous part of the facility or on part of the hospital campus operating under the hospital's provider number. Specifically, the MSE may be provided in another hospital department or in a hospital-owned physician office on hospital grounds. Hospitals are cautioned that patients with similar conditions must be provided an MSE in the same manner. That is, patients should not be directed to different parts on the hospital campus based on who their physician is or what managed care plan they are enrolled in. Referring a patient to a managed care physician's office, even if the office is on campus, violates EMTALA because the referral is for insurance purposes rather than for medical benefit. If the MSE is not conducted in the ED, a valid medical reason should support the movement of the patient. Further, qualified medical personnel should accompany the patient on any movements between areas on the hospital campus. [CMS State Operations Manual, Appendix V, A406]

Regulations issued in 2003 clarify that EMTALA does not apply to hospital outpatient facilities except the dedicated ED. Therefore, the movement of patients between these locations and the ED does not constitute a transfer under the statute. Movement of a patient to a satellite that is not a hospital department, however, qualifies as a transfer, which triggers a host of regulatory requirements, discussed later in this section. Thus, ED staff must be familiar with the status of each location to which a patient might be moved, to determine whether the movement is a transfer to which EMTALA restrictions and requirements apply. [68 Fed. Reg. 53,222 (Sept. 9, 2003), codified at 42 C.F.R. §§ 409 through 413, 419, 424, 489, 498, & 1003]

How does a court decide whether an MSE meets EMTALA's standards?

Courts have generally held that EMTALA does not allow patients to sue for negligent screening or screening that fails to properly identify an emergency condition. Instead, courts defining "appropriate screening" have typically required hospitals to follow the same screening procedures for similarly situated patients. In other words, courts will examine whether a patient received an MSE consistent with that provided to other individuals with the same complaints or symptoms as well as whether the MSE was consistent with hospital protocols. [*See, e.g., Correa v. Hospital San Francisco*, 69 F.3d 1184 (1st Cir. 1995), *cert. denied sub nom. Hospital San Francisco v. Gonzalez*, 517 U.S. 1136 (1996) (hospital liable for delaying screening exam in violation if its own procedures); *Bloomer v. Norman Reg. Hosp.*, No. 99-6074 (10th Cir. July 12, 2000) (adequacy of MSE will be judged by hospital compliance with its own screening procedures); *Nolen v. Boca Raton Cmty. Hosp.*, 373 F.3d 1151 (11th Cir. 2004) (hospital provided the same screening it would with another other patient and was not required to have written screening procedures in place)]

What happens if hospital personnel mistakenly overlook a patient's symptoms?

The courts have generally held that, if the MSE performed on a particular patient is consistent with MSEs performed on similar patients and complied with hospital standards, the hospital will only face EMTALA liability for failure to stabilize if staff discovered an emergency medical condition. In other words, the negligent failure to diagnose an emergency condition does not generally constitute an EMTALA violation; the patient must sue under state malpractice law instead. The Eighth Circuit, for example, has held that what constitutes an appropriate MSE depends on the patient's condition as perceived by the treating ED providers, even if that perception is negligent. A patient came to an ED after a fall, complaining of chest pain and a popping noise in his chest. After physicians ordered a spinal X-ray, but no chest X-rays, the patient was discharged. Two days later, the patient went to another hospital where it was discovered that he had a broken vertebra, sternum, and rib. The patient sued the first hospital under COBRA, charging that it did not provide an appropriate MSE. The hospital acknowledged that a chest X-ray should be ordered for patients complaining of popping noises in the chest but defended that the patient stated a negligence claim, not an EMTALA claim. The court ruled in favor of the hospital because EMTALA does not create a malpractice cause of action. The court ruled that a patient arguing that an MSE was not appropriate must show that the screening constituted disparate treatment.

In this case, the patient argued that he received nonuniform treatment because the hospital admitted that a patient complaining of popping noises in the chest would be X-rayed. The court rejected this argument, explaining that a physician is required to screen patients only for the conditions that the physician perceives the patient to have. Finding that the physician, either through inadvertence or inattention, did not perceive the patient to have popping noises in the chest or chest pain, the court ruled that the patient was treated no differently from any other patient perceived to have the same condition. [*Summers v. Baptist Med. Ctr. Arkadelphia*, 91 F.3d 1132 (8th Cir. 1996)] Allegations of failure to diagnose or treat a person are actionable under state medical malpractice law, not EMTALA. EMTALA does not create a federal cause of action for medical malpractice in emergency rooms. [*Vickers v. Nash Gen. Hosp.*, 78 F.3d 139 (4th Cir. 1996); *Reynolds v. Maine General Health*, 218 F.3d 78 (1st Cir. 2000)]

The Ninth Circuit joined the Eighth Circuit and several others in a recent ruling that a hospital does not violate EMTALA when it fails to diagnose the cause of a patient's emergency condition, but treats the symptoms it identifies and concludes that the patient has been stabilized. In that case, the patient presented in the ER and was diagnosed with acute psychosis, but was not found to have an emergency medical (as opposed to a psychiatric) condition. After his discharge he died of a heart attack caused by psychotic delirium, which was in turn caused by drug toxicity. The patient's family sued for the hospital's failure to provide adequate screening under EMTALA. The appeals court agreed with the trial court that the hospital followed its own screening guidelines, and there was no evidence that the screening was so substandard that it violated EMTALA, or that the patient was treated differently from any other patient presenting similar symptoms in the ED. [*Jackson v. East Bay Hosp.*, 246 F.3d 1248 (9th Cir. 2001); *see also, Bryant v. Adventis Health Sys. West*, 289 F.3d 1162 (9th Cir. 2002); *Hunt v. Lincoln County Mem'l Hosp.*, 317 F.3d 891 (8th Cir. 2003)]

Is triage an appropriate MSE?

Many hospital EDs have instituted a triage system, in which patients are screened to determine the order in which they should be examined. Because the purpose of triage differs from the purpose of an MSE under EMTALA (that is, to determine whether an emergency medical condition exists), triage screening does not necessarily satisfy EMTALA requirements. Note, however, that a federal appeals circuit found that the failure of an ED to follow its triage classifications may give rise to a cause of action for EMTALA. This case involved patient who presented to the ED with chest pain, arm, and wrist pain. The hospital triage classification system required a Level 2 triage with a complaint of chest pain, but the doctor triaged the patient at a lower level. The case was to go to trial to determine if the patient had complained of chest pain in the ED. [*Cruz-Queipoetal, et al. v. Hospital Espanol Auxilio Mutuo De Puerto Rico*, 417 F.3d 67 (1st Cir. July 27, 2005)]

Hospitals must not, after triage, delay an appropriate MSE to obtain financial information from the patient. Hospitals that seek health maintenance organization (HMO) authorization for payment immediately after triage, for example, are in violation of COBRA if the authorization process delays the MSE. Further, triage is often performed by a nurse or physician assistant rather than by a physician, which also raises EMTALA concerns, as discussed below in "Who must perform the MSE?"

Why is dual staffing a problem with respect to the MSE requirement?

As noted above, courts in a variety of jurisdictions have ruled that an "appropriate MSE" is one that is uniformly performed on patients with similar conditions. In a dual staffing system, staff members are assigned to patients depending on the mode of reimbursement, for example, whether the patient is covered by Medicaid or by an HMO. Some managed care companies have "hospitalists," physicians who work solely in the hospital to attend patients under the managed care plan. The managed care plan may dictate that its physician be the only physician to attend to the ED patient. This staffing approach seems inconsistent with the "uniform screening" standard established by the courts and may expose the hospital to possible EMTALA violations. HCFA (now CMS) has expressed concerns regarding whether dual staffing systems can provide truly consistent treatment of patients in different tracks. A special advisory bulletin stated that dual staffing would not "necessarily constitute a per se violation" of EMTALA, but cautions that certain practices would constitute a violation. For example, a violation would occur if either the managed care or nonmanaged care track were understaffed or overcrowded and patients on one "side" experienced a delay in screening or stabilizing treatment, even though a physician in the alternative track was available to see the patients; if quality oversight plans differ between the two "sides;" or if the protocols for transfer differ between the two sides. [*OIG/HCFA Special Advisory Bulletin on the Patient Anti-Dumping Statute*, OIG and HCFA, HHS, 64 Fed. Reg. 61,353 (Nov. 10, 1999)] Because dual staffing may inherently create a discrimination in treatment among patients with similar conditions by providing a "separate but equal" track, it is essential that clear and well-detailed criteria and operational practices be enacted in the ED in order to minimize, if not eliminate, any discrepancies between the two tracks. [M.M. Moy, *The EMTALA Answer Book, 2008 Edition* (Aspen Publishers 2008)]

How do EMTALA MSE requirements apply to patients in managed care plans?

In its guidance for COBRA investigators, HCFA (now CMS) has specifically stated, "A managed health care plan (e.g., HMO, PPO) cannot deny a hospital permission to treat its enrollees. It may only state what it will or will not pay for. Regardless of whether a hospital will be paid, it is obligated to provide the services specified in [COBRA]."[CMS State Operations Manual, Appendix V, A407]

In addition, the Office of Inspector General (OIG) and HCFA (now CMS) have issued a Special Advisory Bulletin addressing hospitals' responsibility to provide emergency treatment to patients enrolled in managed care, Medicare, and Medicaid plans. The bulletin notes that hospitals routinely seek prior authorization for care for patients in managed care plans, cites the "inherent problems" in seeking prior authorization, and cautions that this practice may improperly influence patients to leave the hospital without receiving an appropriate medical screening examination. The bulletin advises that, "no contract between a hospital and a managed care plan can excuse the hospital from its anti-dumping statute obligations. Once a managed care enrollee comes to a hospital that offers emergency services, the hospital must provide the services . . . without regard for the patient's insurance status or any prior authorization requirement." With regard to Medicare and Medicaid managed care plans, the advisory bulletin notes that the Balanced Budget Act of 1997 requires the federal health plans to pay for emergency services based on a prudent layperson standard. That law also prohibits Medicare and Medicaid from requiring prior authorization for emergency services, including those needed to evaluate or stabilize an emergency medical condition.

Finally, the bulletin outlines suggested practices to minimize the likelihood that a hospital will violate EMTALA. The advisory suggests that hospitals not request prior authorization before screening or stabilization. Nor should staff members ask patients to complete a financial responsibility form or advanced beneficiary notification form before screening. Hospitals should ensure that only qualified medical personnel perform medical screening examinations. Either a physician or a hospital staff member approved by the facility's governing body to perform certain medical functions constitutes qualified medical personnel. When a patient inquires about financial liability for emergency services, the question should be answered by a staff member who has been well trained in EMTALA compliance. The staff member must clearly inform the patient that "notwithstanding the patient's ability to pay, the hospital stands ready and willing to provide a medical screening examination and stabilizing treatment, if necessary." Any patient with a potentially emergency medical condition should be encouraged by hospital staff to remain until after screening. Finally, when a patient chooses to withdraw a request for examination or treatment, a staff member must offer further medical examination and treatment necessary to identify and stabilize an emergency medical condition, inform the patient of the risks and benefits of leaving prior to treatment, and take all reasonable steps to secure the patient's written informed consent to refuse treatment, with full documentation in the medial record. [*OIG/HCFA Special Advisory Bulletin on the Patient Anti-Dumping Statute*, OIG and HCFA, HHS, 64 Fed. Reg. 61,353]

Does a hospital have to provide an MSE to patients who use the ED for routine follow-up?

Some EDs see patients for routine suture removal, follow-up vaccinations, lab work, series of injections, and the like. A hospital could argue that such a patient has not come to the ED seeking examination or treatment and so does not come within EMTALA's medical screening requirement. Hospitals may also decide that an appropriate screening examination satisfying EMTALA requirements for these patients constitutes a cursory visual inspection of the patient and asking whether the patient has any complaints. This issue has not been resolved in the courts. Consideration should be given to how these patients should be entered in the central log, how their status and disposition will be documented, and whether it would be appropriate for them to sign a waiver stating that they are not seeking care for an emergency medical condition.

Who must perform the MSE?

The qualifications for who may perform an MSE are not outlined in the federal regulations. Under EMTALA's regulations, the MSE must be conducted by qualified individuals. Hospital bylaws or rules and regulations must identify which individuals are qualified to perform screening examinations. The decision may not be made on an informal or ad hoc basis [42 C.F.R. §§ 489.24(a) & 482.55] In many hospitals, for example, MSEs of women in labor are performed by experienced registered nurses, advanced practice nurses, or nurse midwives. Where nonphysicians perform the MSE, these individuals must be properly trained, acting under a protocol that clearly delineates the circumstances under which they must consult a physician, and within their permissible scope of practice under both state law and facility privileges. While the MSE should never be referred to as "triage," this is particularly important where nurses or other nonphysicians are performing the MSE.

It is not likely that CMS will completely defer to hospitals to determine who may perform the MSE. Rather, the issue of who is a qualified individual may be questioned under EMTALA, even if a hospital follows its own bylaws and rules. For example, HCFA (now CMS) has cited hospitals that allow nurses to perform MSEs for violating EMTALA. When looking at a hospital's policies on non-physician screening, however, CMS most often finds that a hospital policy has not been complied with, such as instances where nonphysicians have exceeded their permissible scope of practice or licensure. CMS has, for example, cited a hospital for a physician assistant who was licensed under state law to see persons over the age of 12, but saw babies and young children in the ED. CMS looks closely at the ED's written policies and may request personnel files to document that all criteria for personnel are met and documented. Lapsed certifications, lack of current copies of licenses, or lack of privileges have resulted in citations on this basis. [M.M. Moy, *The EMTALA Answer Book, 2008 Edition* (Aspen Publishers 2008)]

Requiring physicians, rather than nurses or physician assistants, to screen patients for emergency medical conditions provides the greatest assurance that the person conducting the MSE possesses sufficient training and expertise to be qualified under EMTALA.

Have any courts addressed personnel requirements for MSEs?

At least one federal appeals court has refused to evaluate whether a hospital's policy for allowing nurses to conduct MSEs violates EMTALA. The Tenth Circuit has ruled that a hospital that discharged a patient with chest pain after being examined and treated by a nurse did not violate EMTALA's screening requirement. The patient went to the ED at the instruction of her personal physician, who had called ahead to prescribe a pain shot for her chest pains. A nurse examined the patient, determined that the patient did not suffer an emergency medical condition, administered the prescribed pain shot, and discharged the patient. The patient died that night after a heart attack. The patient's husband sued, claiming that the hospital violated EMTALA by failing to comply with its own policy that requires a physician to examine patients with "life-threatening symptoms of chest pain." The hospital countered that the policy did not apply because the nurse determined that the patient's symptoms were not life-threatening. Rather, the facility complied with a second applicable policy, which allows nursing personnel to evaluate patients with conditions with low complexity and low possibility of morbidity, the hospital argued. Reading the two policies in combination, the court determined that hospital policy requires evaluation by a physician for a patient complaining of chest pain only if nursing personnel determines the patient has life-threatening symptoms. The court refused to assess the adequacy of the hospital's policies under EMTALA. Courts may determine only whether a hospital followed its own policies, the Tenth Circuit concluded, not whether the policies themselves constitute an appropriate screening policy under EMTALA. [*Cunningham v. Fredonia Reg'l Hosp.*, No. 95-3350 (10th Cir. Oct. 11, 1996) (unpublished)]

Unlike the courts, CMS has not been reluctant to subjectively evaluate a hospital's policies and its relative adequacy in individual cases, and has issued citations to hospitals on non-physician screening issues. Thus, it is probably more valuable to look to CMS standards than to court decisions in guiding ED practices regarding personnel requirements for MSEs. CMS standards for EMTALA investigations allow nonphysicians to conduct EMTALA screening as qualified medical persons, but require those practitioners who will perform MSEs to be identified in hospital bylaws or medical staff rules and to be approved by the governing board. It is not sufficient for the ED Medical Director to make personnel assignment changes in regard to screening. [CMS State Operations Manual, Appendix V, A406] Labor screening can be conducted by nonphysicians as defined in the hospital bylaws, within the state scope of practice and with policies and procedures in place. [*CMS Final Rule on Inpatient PPS and FY 2007 Rates,* 41 Fed. Reg. 47,870 (Aug. 18, 2006)]

How should hospitals meet the MSE requirements when a community protocol to perform screening of exposed individuals exists?

As a result of the widespread fears in the fall of 2001 about potential bioterrorism, and in particular, the exposure of numerous individuals to anthrax, CMS issued a program memorandum to its regional administrators, clarifying hospitals' EMTALA obligations when staff encounter situations related to the actual or potential exposure to a biological agent. CMS acknowledged that in certain circumstances, referral of a potentially exposed patient prior to the actual MSE would be appropriate. Specifically, there could be cases in which state or local governments have developed community response plans that designate specific entities, such as hospitals or public health facilities, with responsibility for handling certain categories of patient in bioterrorism situations. The transfer or referral of these patients in accordance with such a community plan would not violate the hospital's EMTALA obligations. If, for example, a potentially exposed patient presented at an undesignated hospital, after questioning the patient and determining that the patient falls into the category for which the community has a specified screening site, that hospital could refer the patient to the designated community facility without violating EMTALA. [CMS Memorandum to Regional Administrators, *Question and Answer Relating to Bioterrorism and EMTALA*, Ref. S&C-02-04, Nov. 8, 2001] The 2003 final rule clarified that EMTALA does not apply to a dedicated ED located in an emergency area during a national emergency. [68 Fed. Reg. 53,222 (Sept. 9, 2003), codified at 42 C.F.R. § 489.24]

What is an emergency medical condition under EMTALA?

Under the regulations, an emergency medical condition is a "medical condition manifesting itself by acute symptoms (including severe pain, psychiatric disturbances, and/or symptoms of substance abuse)" of sufficient severity such that the absence of immediate medical attention could reasonably be expected to result in

- "placing the health of the individual (or, with respect to a pregnant woman, the health of the woman or her unborn child) in serious jeopardy"
- "serious impairment to bodily functions"
- "serious dysfunction of any bodily organ or part"

In the case of a woman having contractions, an emergency also exists when there is "inadequate time to effect a safe transfer to another hospital" before she delivers or when "that transfer may pose a threat to the health or safety of the woman or the unborn child."[42 C.F.R. § 489.24(b)] Final rules clarify that a woman in contractions is considered to be in true labor, but false labor can be certified by the physician or qualified medical person. Once false labor is certified, an emergency medical condition no longer exists and there is no further EMTALA obligation. [*CMS Final Rule on Inpatient PPS and FY 2007 Rates*, 71 Fed. Reg. 47,870 (Aug. 18, 2006)]

When does a patient with psychiatric symptoms have an emergency medical condition under EMTALA?

Under COBRA interpretive guidance, a patient is considered to have an emergency medical condition if he or she expresses suicidal or homicidal thoughts or gestures, or is determined to be dangerous to self or others. [CMS State Operations Manual, Appendix V, A406]

What must a hospital do when a patient has an emergency medical condition?

If the MSE reveals an emergency medical condition, the hospital must either stabilize the patient or arrange for an appropriate transfer in accordance with EMTALA. The requirements for stabilization and transfer are discussed below.

What if the hospital does not discover an emergency medical condition?

The requirements of EMTALA do not apply unless an emergency medical condition exists. Therefore, hospitals are not obligated to provide screening services beyond those needed to determine that there is no emergency. Once an appropriate medical screening examination has been performed, if no emergency medical condition is revealed, the hospital may properly refer an individual to an outpatient clinic for nonemergency care. This was illustrated by a Tenth Circuit case in which a hospital was not liable for discharging a high-risk pregnancy patient after a nonreactive stress test. A nurse at a hospital's obstetrics department administered the test, which indicated no fetal movement, and consulted with a physician. The nurse then instructed the patient, expecting twins, to return to the hospital the next morning for another stress test. When the patient returned the next morning, test results indicated no movement or breathing in either fetus. One twin was stillborn, and the other was born with brain damage. The patient and her family sued the hospital, arguing that discharging her after the first stress test in an unstabilized, emergency condition violated EMTALA. The hospital asserted that EMTALA does not impose liability if a hospital lacks actual knowledge that an emergency exists.

The court agreed that the hospital was not liable. Following the Fourth, Sixth, and D.C. Circuits, the court ruled that the stabilization requirement of EMTALA is triggered only if a hospital determines that a patient has an emergency medical condition. In this case, the patient did not meet the statute's definition of emergency because she did not exhibit severe "acute symptoms." Because the hospital did not have actual knowledge of an emergency condition, the court ruled in favor of the hospital. [*Urban v. King*, 43 F.3d 523 (10th Cir. 1994)]

Similarly, when a family claimed that EMTALA screening and stabilization was violated when a man died from deep vein thrombosis after release from the hospital, the court disagreed. The man had come into the ED for leg and foot fractures, had two surgeries for the fractures and was released from the hospital where he then died. The family contended that a family history of coagulation problems required evaluation of deep vein thrombosis prior to hospital discharge. The court found that EMTALA focused on emergency room stabilization and treatment which the man received before being transferred to the hospital as an inpatient for the surgeries. His admission to the hospital demonstrated adequate EMTALA screening and stabilization. A failure to diagnose the DVT might be actionable as a state medical malpractice claim, but the EMTALA claim was dismissed. [*Reynolds v. Maine General Health*, 218 F.3d 78 (1st Cir. 2000)]

What if no emergency psychiatric condition is discovered upon screening but the patient later harms himself or herself?

Just as with patients who present with medical conditions, a hospital's duty under EMTALA to a patient with a psychiatric condition is to provide an appropriate medical screening, which generally means that the MSE is performed uniformly for patients with identical symptoms, and in accordance with hospital standards. If that MSE nonetheless fails to identify an emergency medical condition and the patient who is discharged later harms himself or herself, the likelihood of hospital liability under EMTALA is low. A medical malpractice claim remains a possibility, however.

A federal district court in North Carolina illustrated this when it held that a hospital's duty to provide stabilizing treatment under EMTALA does not arise unless the hospital has actual knowledge of the emergency medical condition. A patient came to a hospital emergency room suffering from depression and anxiety, and after a physical exam, blood tests, review of his medical history, and a psychiatric evaluation which resulted in a seven-page report by a psychiatric social worker, it was determined he had bipolar disorder and had not been taking his medication. Because it was determined that the patient did not present a threat to himself or others, he was discharged with instructions to go to a mental health facility and return to the hospital if he felt worse. Three days later, unable to obtain an appointment at the mental health facility, the patient committed suicide, and his survivors sued the hospital under EMTALA, claiming the hospital failed to stabilize the patient before discharging him. The federal district court held that the hospital had no duty to provide stabilizing treatment, because the plain language of EMTALA requires that the hospital staff have actual knowledge of the emergency medical condition in order to trigger a duty to stabilize. Even assuming that the patient had an emergency medical condition, there was no evidence that the hospital had actual knowledge of it; to the contrary, hospital records indicated that the patient was not suffering from an emergency medical condition and was stable. The court pointed to case law holding that EMTALA does not impose any duty on a hospital requiring that screening result in a correct diagnosis. Therefore, whether this diagnosis was correct was not an issue in a suit under EMTALA, although it might be addressed in a suit for malpractice under state law. [*Pettyjohn v. Mission St. Joseph's Health Sys.*, No. 1:99cv171-C (W.D.N.C. Jan. 8, 2001 (unpublished), *aff'd*, 21 Fed. Appx. 193 (4th Cir. 2001); *Thomas v. Christ Hosp. and Med. Ctr.*, 328 F.3d 890 (7th Cir. 2003), in which the court said that whether the person, who subsequently harmed herself, was stabilized as required under EMTALA was a question of fact]

What does "stabilize" mean under EMTALA?

According to the regulations, "to stabilize" means to provide such medical treatment of the emergency medical "condition necessary to assure, within reasonable medical probability, that no material deterioration of the condition is likely to result from or occur during the transfer of the individual from a facility or that . . . (in the case of a woman in labor) the woman has delivered the child and the placenta."[42 C.F.R. § 489.24(b)]

CMS guidance to COBRA investigators has elaborated on this definition, distinguishing between patients stable for discharge and patients stable for transfer.

A patient is stable for discharge "when, within reasonable clinical confidence, it is determined that the patient has reached the point when his/her continued care, including diagnostic work-up and/or treatment, could be reasonably performed as an outpatient or later as an inpatient, provided the patient is given a plan for appropriate follow-up care with the discharge instructions."

A patient is stable for transfer when the treating physician has determined with reasonable clinical confidence, that the patient is expected to leave the hospital and be received at the second facility, with no material deterioration in his/her medical condition; and the treating physician reasonably believes the receiving facility has the capability to manage the patient's medical condition and any reasonably foreseeable complication of that condition. [CMS State Operations Manual, Appendix V, A407]

When is a psychiatric patient stable under COBRA?

A patient may only be transferred to another facility without following COBRA procedures or discharged for follow-up care if he or she is stable. HCFA (now CMS) has developed a two-part definition of "stable" for patients with psychiatric conditions, which has one meaning that applies to transfer eligibility, and another for discharge eligibility. For purposes of *transferring* a psychiatric patient from one facility to a second facility, the patient is considered to be stable "when he/she is protected and prevented from injuring himself/

herself or others." Chemical or physical restraints may stabilize a psychiatric patient for a period of time so that the presenting emergency medical condition is removed; however, the underlying medical condition may persist and if left untreated may exacerbate the emergency medical condition. Thus, care should be taken in determining whether a patient is truly stable. [CMS State Operations Manual, Appendix V, A407]

It must be noted, however, that the use of both chemical and physical restraints are limited by the Medicare Conditions of Participation, as described under Patient Rights, above.

How does the stabilization requirement apply when treatment is medically futile?

A controversial case has addressed the tension between the duty to stabilize and physician reluctance to provide medically futile treatment. EMTALA requires a hospital to resuscitate an anencephalic infant, according to a federal appeals court in Virginia. Shortly after an infant was born missing a substantial portion of her brain, a hospital recommended that the infant's mother authorize a do not resuscitate (DNR) order because aggressive treatment would serve no therapeutic or palliative purpose. The mother refused to authorize a DNR order and transferred the infant to a nearby nursing home. The infant was subsequently readmitted to the hospital three times for respiratory assistance. The hospital sought a court declaration that it was not required to provide treatment other than warmth, nutrition, and hydration should the infant be hospitalized for respiratory distress again. The hospital argued that EMTALA did not require treatment beyond this standard of care and that Virginia physicians could refuse to administer medically and ethically inappropriate treatment.

The court rejected those arguments and ruled that the hospital's refusal to resuscitate the infant would violate EMTALA. The court noted that the statute plainly requires the hospital to prevent the infant's condition from deteriorating. Respiratory distress, not anencephaly, was the condition requiring emergency treatment, the court ruled, reasoning that the hospital must resuscitate the infant as it would any other patient in respiratory distress. Neither the statute nor its legislative history created an exception for treatment beyond the standard of care, the court held. The court also concluded that EMTALA overrides state law regarding a physician's right to refuse to administer treatment and ruled that the hospital would violate the statute if it refused to resuscitate the infant in the future. [*In re Baby "K,"* 16 F.3d 590 (4th Cir. 1994), *cert. denied*, 513 U.S. 825 (1994)]

Does the stabilization requirement apply to areas of the hospital other than the ED?

This has been one of the most hotly debated issues related to EMTALA. While at least one early court case found that EMTALA applied to patients admitted to the hospital, the final rule has taken an opposing position. The final rule clarifies that when a person is admitted to the hospital for stabilization of an emergency medical condition, then the ED EMTALA responsibility has been fulfilled. Inpatient admission means the person is received for inpatient care and occupies a bed, even if the person is subsequently discharged or transferred before occupying a bed overnight. When individuals are already patients of the hospital, with an established relationship that includes previously arranged medical appointments, they are not considered to have "come to the hospital" for reasons that would be covered under EMTALA. [68 Fed. Reg. 53,222 (codified at 42 C.F.R. § 489.24)]

When may a hospital transfer a patient in an emergency medical condition?

An individual in an emergency medical condition who has not been stabilized can be transferred only if one of the following conditions is met.

- The transfer is appropriate as outlined below.
- The individual (or a legally responsible person acting on the individual's behalf), after being informed of the hospital's obligations and of the risk of transfer, requests transfer in writing, indicating the reasons for the request and that risks of transfer are known, may then transfer to another facility.
- A physician (or other qualified person in consultation with a physician when a physician is not physically present) "has signed a certification that, based on the information available at the time of transfer, the medical benefits reasonably expected from the provision of medical treatment at another medical facility outweigh the increased risks to the individual or, in the case of labor, to the woman or unborn child, from effecting the transfer." The certification should include a summary or risks and benefits of the transfer.
- If a physician is not physically present in the ED, a qualified medical person has signed a certification after consultation with a physician who subsequently countersigns the certification. [42 C.F.R. § 489.24(e)]

A transfer is appropriate if:

- The transferring hospital provides medical treatment within its capacity that minimizes the risks to the individual's health or the health of the unborn child, in case of labor.
- The receiving facility has available space and qualified personnel to treat the individual and has agreed to accept the transfer and to provide treatment.
- The transferring hospital sends to the receiving facility all medical records (or copies) related to the emergency condition, available at transfer, including observations of signs or symptoms, preliminary diagnosis, and treatment provided; results of any tests and the informed consent to transfer or the physician's certification; and the name and address of any on-call physician who has refused or failed to appear within a reasonable time to provide necessary stabilizing treatment.
- The transfer is effected through qualified personnel and transportation equipment, including the use of necessary and medically appropriate life support measures.
- The transfer meets any other requirements the Secretary of DHHS finds necessary to the health and safety of the individual. [42 C.F.R. § 489.24(e)]

What considerations apply when a hospital seeks to transfer or discharge a psychiatric patient?

As with all patients, EMTALA procedures must be followed when a patient with a psychiatric condition is transferred (i.e., either the patient is stable or a physician has certified that the benefits of transfer outweigh the risks, the patient has consented to transfer, the receiving hospital has agreed, etc.). (See the previous questions and answers.) The level of medical support necessary for transfer must also be considered. Use of ambulance transport and escort by qualified medical personnel may protect the patient from harm during transport, as well as shield the transferring hospital from EMTALA exposure. Transport via police car does not likely satisfy EMTALA requirements. Likewise, transport of a patient with suicidal or homicidal ideations by private car is not advised.

What if a patient refuses to consent to a transfer?

If a hospital offers to transfer the individual and informs the individual of the risks and benefits of the transfer but the individual refuses to consent, the hospital will have fulfilled its obligation under EMTALA. The hospital chart must indicate that the patient has been informed of the risks and benefits of the transfer and state the reasons for the person's refusal. The chart must also contain a description of the proposed transfer that was refused by or on behalf of the patient, the risks and benefits of the transfer, and the reasons for the refusal of the transfer. [42 C.F.R. § 489.24(c)(4)]

How do state civil commitment statutes affect a hospital's duty to psychiatric patients?

State civil commitment procedures generally apply when a patient poses a threat to himself or herself, or others, and refuses needed treatment or transfer. Civil commitment statutes vary by state. However, most laws provide

- criteria for involuntary detention or commitment;
- a brief initial period of emergency detention for treatment or evaluation;
- an opportunity to petition for longer periods of detention; and
- a procedure for release when the symptoms of mental illness and dangerousness have been alleviated.

Because state civil commitment laws and procedures vary, it is important for ED personnel to be aware of the particular requirements in their jurisdiction and be prepared to carry out whatever the law requires.

May hospitals refuse to accept a patient transfer?

A hospital that has specialized capabilities (such as burn units or neonatal intensive care units) cannot refuse to accept an appropriate transfer of an individual who requires such specialized capabilities if the hospital has the capacity to treat the individual. [42 C.F.R. § 489.24(e)] However, EMTALA does not address lateral transfers between hospitals of equal capabilities. Thus, a hospital without specialized units may refuse a transfer without violating EMTALA. This was illustrated by a Sixth Circuit case that held that the mother of a patient who died of injuries resulting from an accidental gunshot wound could not sue the multiple hospitals that refused to accept the patient because the patient had not "come to" any of those hospitals under the meaning of EMTALA. The patient sought treatment at a hospital ED that did not have a surgeon available. The ED physician contacted five other hospitals, all of which refused the patient's transfer. The patient died two hours after he arrived at the ED. His mother sued the hospitals that refused to accept the patient, alleging that they had breached their duty to provide emergency treatment under EMTALA. The appeals court dismissed the claims. The EMTALA duty to provide screening for and stabilization of emergency conditions is triggered only when a patient comes to the ED, the court explained. In this case, the patient was not physically presented to any of the hospitals that refused transfer. Acknowledging that EMTALA requires hospitals with specialized capabilities to accept a transfer if they have the capacity to treat a patient, the court ruled that the lawsuit failed to state this type of claim because the suit did not directly or indirectly allege that any of the hospitals had specialized capabilities or that they had the capacity to treat the patient. [*Fingers v. Jackson-Madison County Gen. Hosp. Dist.*, 101 F.3d 702 (6th Cir. Nov. 21, 1996) (unpublished)]

The incident that gave rise to this case occurred prior to CMS regulations issued in 1994 that focused on the availability of specific equipment, specialties, services, or levels of care that are not available at the sending hospital to constitute "specialty capabilities" of the receiving hospital. The case did not follow the later regulations in coming to a decision. Thus, if there is a mechanical failure of equipment, no ICU beds available, or an on-call physician is not available due to being currently in surgery or if the hospital does not have a specialist in the needed area of practice, CMS has found that the requested receiving facility must accept the transfer. [M.M. Moy, *The EMTALA Answer Book, 2008 Edition* (Aspen Publishers 2008) citing CMS, State Operations Manual, Appendix V, A411]. Under federal law, courts are required to defer to the interpretation of the regulatory agency unless patently in controvention of the law. Using CMS's standards, the availability of the specialist in the above case created an obligation to accept the patient.

What is "reverse dumping" under EMTALA?

Reverse dumping occurs when a hospital emergency room refuses to accept an appropriate transfer of a patient that requires the specialized capabilities the hospital offers. The refusal by a physician to receive a patient needing the care the hospital is equipped to provide is binding on the hospital and can expose the hospital to liability for reverse dumping. In order for a transferring hospital to make a transfer, the consent of the receiving hospital is required when the patient is unstable.

A person was involved in an automobile accident on a highway outside the city and was taken to a small regional hospital outside the city. The man was diagnosed with a life-threatening injury to his abdominal aorta which required surgery the small hospital was not capable of performing. The doctor at the small hospital called to arrange transfer to a city hospital. Doctors at the city hospital refused to accept the transfer even though the city hospital had the capacity and capability of performing the surgery. The court found that the city hospital was bound by the actions of the ED physicians who declined the transfer. [*St. Anthony Hosp. v. United States Dep't of Health & Human Servs.*, 309 F.3d 680 (10th Cir. 2002)]

What is EMTALA's transfer certificate requirement?

EMTALA requires an express written certification for all unstabilized transfers. Physician certification cannot simply be implied from the findings in the medical record and the fact that the patient was transferred. The transfer certificate must meet EMTALA requirements. Although technically, EMTALA requires certification only if a patient has an emergency medical condition that has not been stabilized, the most prudent policy would be for ED staff to fill out certificates for every transfer. The important elements that the certificate must include are: patient condition, risks and benefits of transfer, receiving hospital, mode of transportation, signed consent by the patient or legally responsible person, and certification by the transferring physician.

How has CMS interpreted the transfer certification requirement?

The statement of risks and benefits is often the source of EMTALA citations. CMS does not permit a purely "check in the box" form; at least one handwritten risk and benefit should be entered. ED physicians must be aware that the reason for transfer is not the same as the benefit of transfer. HCFA has cited hospitals for listing benefits merely as "higher level of care," "to PICU," "Trauma Center," and "equipment not available here." CMS expects the statement of benefits to explain specifically what the destination hospital can provide that the transferring hospital cannot. Unlike the examples above, the statement of benefits should identify the exact service, specialty care, level of care, or equipment that the patient needs that is not currently available at the transferring hospital. For example, if the transfer is for an MRI and the transferring hospital has an MRI, the statement of benefits should explain, "Our MRI is down."

CMS also expects the possible risks to be expressly stated if they include death or disability. Failure to list known risks in sufficient detail for the patient to understand may result in citation, possible fines, and potential civil liability for the hospital and the physician. Often physicians simply enter "none" in this section, but CMS has cited this as not entered in good faith. Again, the statement of risks should be handwritten; preprinted risks such as traffic accidents are helpful, but are not sufficient. At the very least, all transfers pose a risk of increased pain from the vibration and jolting involved in a routine ambulance transport, and the best procedure is to note this.

How have courts interpreted physicians' duty to certify transfers?

At least two federal appeals courts interpreting EMTALA have examined whether a physician actually deliberated the risks and benefits of transfer. EMTALA certification must be a true assessment, not merely a signature, according to one of the first cases to arise under the law. The Fifth Circuit ruled that a physician's failure to weigh the medical risks and benefits before transferring a severely hypertensive woman in active labor violated the law. Although the physician had signed the "Physician's Certificate Authorizing Transfer," the court concluded that he had not engaged in a meaningful weighing of the risks and benefits. [*Burditt v. United States Dep't of Health & Human Servs.*, 934 F.2d 1362 (5th Cir. 1991)]

On the other hand, the Ninth Circuit has ruled that a hospital did not violate EMTALA by failing to enumerate the risks and benefits of a patient's transfer on a form if the hospital could show that a physician actually considered the medical risks and benefits. An infant arrived at a hospital ED having seizures. Unable to control the seizures, a physician decided to transfer the infant to a larger hospital with a pediatric intensive care unit. Before transfer, the physician filled out a certification form, checking a box to confirm that the benefits of transfer outweighed the risks to the patient. The physician did not summarize the medical risks and benefits as the form required, however. The infant was transferred but became quadriplegic as a result of the seizures. Her guardian sued the first hospital under EMTALA, relying on the section of the statute requiring the transferring physician to include a written summary of the risks and benefits to the patient. The federal appeals court refused to impose EMTALA liability. Although the hospital violated a "recordkeeping" provision of the law, the court acknowledged, the purpose of the statute was satisfied, as evidence demonstrated that the physician deliberated over the risks and benefits before signing the transfer certification form. [*Vargas ex rel. Gallardo v. Del Puerto Hosp.*, 98 F.3d 1202 (9th Cir. 1996)]

What is the obligation of specialty hospitals with no ED in regard to transfers?

In 2006 the EMTALA Technical Advisory Group (TAG) met and recommended that specialty hospitals with no emergency department should be subject to EMTALA requirements to accept patients needing transfer. The CMS final ruling in 2006 did not finalize this recommendation, but will wait for further suggestions from the TAG that is continuing to review this issue. [*CMS Final Rule on Inpatient PPS and FY 2007 Rates*, 71 Fed. Reg. 47,870 (Aug. 18, 2006)]

What is the hospital's duty under EMTALA with regard to posting signs?

The law requires a hospital to conspicuously post signs specifying the rights of individuals under EMTALA with respect to examination and treatment for emergency medical conditions and women in labor, and to indicate whether or not the hospital participates in the Medicaid program. [42 C.F.R. § 489.20(q)] The signs should be posted in a place likely to be noticed by all persons entering the ED, as well as persons waiting for examination and treatment, and must be clearly readable from the patient's perspective. Signs in general waiting areas must be readable from a distance of 20 feet. Signs must also be posted in all other areas covered by EMTALA, such as obstetrics, psych assessment, and out-patient clinic areas.

CMS has required hospitals investigated for EMTALA violations to post signs advising the public that the hospital is obligated to provide screening for emergency medical conditions without regard to their ability to pay. CMS has also found an EMTALA violation in a hospital that posted signs stating that if an ED visit turned out not to be a true emergency, the patient would be responsible for the bill. This was despite state Medicaid rules that required such posting. CMS surveyors have also cautioned hospitals that signs similar to those stating "Payment for services due at discharge" may violate EMTALA. The rationale is that these signs may discourage patients from remaining in the ED until they have undergone an MSE. While it is not certain that a citation for this type of sign would be upheld, administrators should consider how the usefulness of the sign balances against CMS's concern.

Can managed care organizations be held responsible for EMTALA violations?

Generally, the hospital alone will be fined for violating EMTALA, even where the transfer or referral was at the behest of a patient's managed care plan. A federal trial court in Illinois, for example, refused to apply EMTALA to a utilization review company. The court held that the EMTALA provision creating a patient's right to sue specifically limits its application to instances in which a Medicare-participating hospital violated EMTALA. [*Bangert v. Christian Health Servs.*, No. 92-613 (S.D. Ill. Dec. 17, 1992) (unpublished)] Similarly, HMOs are not subject to liability for failing to satisfy EMTALA's requirements. [*Dearmas v. Av-Med, Inc.*, 814 F. Supp. 1103 (S.D. Fla. 1993)] Managed care organizations may be subject to liability, however, under other federal or state laws, such as the Social Security Act [42 U.S.C. §§ 1395f, 1395mm], for failing to provide medically necessary services, including emergency services, to enrollees.

What are on-call requirements under EMTALA?

EMTALA requires a hospital to provide emergency screening or treatment. The hospital should have a list of physicians who are on call after the initial exam to stabilize an individual with an emergency medical condition. The capability of a hospital to provide services is based on the skills of specialists who have staff privileges and who are required to provide on-call services. The hospital has discretion to maintain the on-call list in a manner to best meet patient needs. A hospital is not required to have a specialist on call at all times, but should have policies and procedures to follow when a certain specialty is not available. When a specialist is not available, the hospital will lack the capacity to treat patients requiring that specialty and can appropriately transfer the patient. Hospitals are expected to provide services based on the availability of physicians on call. However, if a physician is on call and does not respond as required, there could be EMTALA liability.

In determining whether a hospital has established reasonable on-call coverage, CMS will look at all relevant factors such as the number of physicians on staff, other demands of the physicians, the frequency of patients requiring certain on-call physicians, and provisions the hospital has made when someone of a certain specialty is not available. CMS requirements do not preclude a hospital from exempting senior medical staff from on-call duties based on years of service or age or both as long as patient care is not adversely affected. The hospital must list individual physicians on its on-call list; the name of a physician group is not sufficient. CMS leaves the hospital flexibility to implement an on-call schedule that works well with its community and medical staff. [*CMS Program Memorandum on On-Call Requirements-EMTALA*, S & C 02-34 (June 13, 2002)] Final regulations give hospitals discretion in contracting for on-call specialists. [*EMTALA Final Rule*, 68 Fed. Reg. 53,222 (Sept. 9, 2003)]

Under EMTALA, can a physician be on call at more than one hospital simultaneously?

EMTALA requires an on-call list to be maintained in a manner that best meets the needs of patients. This may include allowing physicians to be on call at more than one hospital simultaneously. Each hospital involved should be aware of the on-call schedule. Medical staff bylaws or policies and procedures should define the requirement of an on-call physician to respond, examine, and treat patients. The policies and procedures should also clarify how it will handle the situation when the primary specialist is not available or the on-call physician can't respond because of unavoidable conditions. This may include a backup call schedule or transfer of the patient. Allowing physicians simultaneous call does not relieve the hospital of its EMTALA obligation.

In determining whether the on-call list meets the needs of patients, CMS will look at all relevant factors such as physicians on staff, other demands on the physicians, frequency of services needed, and provisions the hospital has made for situations in which specialty is not available. Thus, a reasonable approach is taken to review of on-call scheduling. [*EMTALA Final Rule*, 68 Fed. Reg. 53,222 (Sept. 9, 2003) and *CMS Program Memorandum on Simultaneous On-Call Responsibilities*, S & C 02-35 (June 13, 2002)]

Can physicians be liable for EMTALA violations?

Courts have ruled that physicians cannot be found liable under EMTALA. However, EMTALA's administrative civil money penalties do apply to physicians. A physician responsible for the examination, treatment, or transfer of an individual (including a physician on call) who negligently violates the law is subject to a civil money penalty of up to $50,000 per violation. If the violation is gross and flagrant or repeated, the physician is subject to exclusion from Medicare and Medicaid. [42 U.S.C. § 1395dd(d)(1)]

Physicians and other individuals should also note that state laws may provide for individual liability. Further, hospitals found liable for EMTALA violations may be able to recover from the individuals who actually committed the violations, including physicians. A federal trial court in Louisiana has held that a hospital may recover damages from the independent staff physician directly responsible for its EMTALA violation. [*McDougal v. Lafourche Hosp. Serv. Dist. No. 3*, No. 92-2006 (E.D. La. May 25, 1993) (unpublished)] However, a federal trial court in Kansas ruled that a jury award could not be apportioned between a hospital and a physician in an EMTALA suit, even though the jury attributed specific percentages of fault to each party. The court did note that the hospital could bring a separate indemnity claim against the physician to recover the damages attributable to his negligence. [*Griffith v. Mt. Carmel Med. Ctr.*, 842 F. Supp. 1359 (D. Kan. 1994)] Another federal court dismissed claims against the physicians and only allowed hospital EMTALA claims to proceed. [*Binkley v. Edward Hosp.*, 2004 U.S. Dist. LEXIS 18838 (N.D. Ill. 2004)]

What are the penalties for a hospital that violates EMTALA?

The government may fine a hospital that negligently violates EMTALA up to $50,000 (or up to $25,000 for hospitals with less than 100 beds) for each violation. Hospitals that fail to substantially meet the EMTALA requirements are also subject to suspension or termination of their Medicare provider agreements. [42 U.S.C. § 1395dd(d)(1), 42 C.F.R. § 489.53] Although many hospitals have been fined, few have been terminated.

In calculating the penalty amount for EMTALA violations, HHS/OIG will also consider "other instances" of patient dumping. In a final rule issued in March 2002, penalties imposed for a violation of EMTALA may reflect other, unrelated instances where an ED failed to provide appropriate emergency medical screening, stabilization, and treatment of persons coming to the ED or to effect an appropriate transfer. [67 Fed. Reg. 11,928 (2002) (codified in 42 C.F.R. Parts 1001, 1003, 1005, and 1008)] The "other instances" that may be considered include anything that is relevant to the hospital's culpability, regardless of whether they resulted in convictions or judicial or administrative decisions, and also regardless of when they occurred, so that HHS/OIG can consider prior events as well as those that occurred after the incident for which penalties are being assessed. Thus, the method of determining civil monetary penalties will impose greater fines on hospitals with multiple abuses rather than treating them like those with a single violation.

Liability is another potential consequence of EMTALA violations, as illustrated by the cases discussed earlier. An individual who suffers personal harm as a direct result of a hospital's violation of the law can sue the hospital for damages. A medical facility that suffers a financial loss as a direct result of a hospital's violation of EMTALA (a transferee hospital, for example) can also sue the hospital for damages. [42 U.S.C. § 1395dd(d)(2)] EMTALA does not, however, permit private parties to sue to terminate a hospital's provider agreement. [*Deberry v. Sherman Hosp. Ass'n*, 775 F. Supp. 1159 (N.D. Ill. 1991)] EMTALA violations may also lead to investigations under Hill-Burton (described below), state laws regarding patient admissions, and Joint Commission on Accreditation of Healthcare Organizations (Joint Commission) accreditation.

How likely is a CMS investigation?

CMS has dedicated significant resources to investigate EMTALA violations. Between 1986 and 1996, $1.45 million in settlements and judgments were levied. In fiscal year 1999 by contrast, 61 settlements resulted in penalties of more than $1.7 million. ED administrators should note that CMS investigation or citation may trigger lawsuits by patients who, after reading press reports of the CMS investigation, believe their care violated EMTALA.

In 2004, Interpretive Guidelines were released by CMS explaining the current approach to EMTALA investigation. CMS will investigate based on complaints of EMTALA violations. The investigation will focus on the initial allegation as well as whether other EMTALA infractions have taken place. The investigation is unannounced and will include the following steps:

- entrance conference,
- case selection,
- record review,
- interviews,
- exit conference,
- professional team review (M.D. peer review), and
- assessment of compliance or deficiency.

The CMS process provides for sharing information on the findings and giving the hospital a chance to share information on its compliance. [CMS State Operations Manual, Appendix V (May 21, 2004)]

Hill-Burton

What is Hill-Burton?

The Hospital Survey and Construction Act of 1944, commonly known as the Hill-Burton Act, requires facilities receiving financial assistance under the Act to provide a reasonable volume of services to patients who cannot pay for such care. Under the regulations, a facility must provide uncompensated services at a certain level to comply with Hill-Burton. [42 U.S.C. §§ 291 through 291c-1] The duty to provide uncompensated care lasts 20 years for hospitals that received funds under Title VI. Many hospitals have now satisfied their uncompensated care obligation. Receiving Hill-Burton funds also triggers a community service assurance, which does not expire.

What does Hill-Burton require EDs to do?

The Hill-Burton regulations require facilities under an uncompensated care obligation to provide notice that uncompensated services are available. This is accomplished by notices published in newspapers with a general circulation; notices posted in the admissions area, ED, and business office of the hospital; and notices given to individuals. The posted notices, furnished by DHHS, must be printed in English and Spanish, as well as any other language spoken by more than 10 percent of the population in the hospital's service area. Before care is initiated, individual notice must be given to each person who seeks service, except in the case of an emergency. In an emergency, it should be given to the next of kin or to the patient as soon as it is practical to do so. Notice must be provided before the bill for services is presented. Once the notice is given, the patient must actually request that care be provided. The notice must clearly indicate the eligibility standards and the procedure to follow to apply for care. It should also indicate that providing uncompensated care is a legal obligation of the hospital and that the hospital will make a written determination on a patient's request by a specific date. [42 C.F.R. § 124.504]

What are the consequences of failing to provide Hill-Burton notice?

The ramifications of failing to provide notice can be severe. At least one court has ruled that a hospital's failure to notify a medically indigent ED patient of the potential availability of free or reduced-cost health care under the Hill-Burton Act bars that hospital from later suing to collect its bill. [*Hospital Ctr. v. Cook*, 426 A.2d 526 (N.J. Super. Ct. App. Div. 1981), *see also Cooper Med. Ctr. v. Boyd*, 430 A.2d 261 (N.J. Super. Ct. App. Div. 1981) and *Yale New Haven Hosp. v. Mitchell*, 683 A.2d 1362 (Conn. 1995)] At least one court has limited private action to those who applied for and were improperly denied funds while the uncompensated service fund was in operation, thereby limiting recovery by a widow whose application was denied because the hospital did not have a compensation program in operation believing it had met its quota under the statute. The hospital's failure to operate the program was remedied by prospective program implementation, not by privately compensating the widow. [*White v. Moses Taylor Hosp.*, 841 F. Supp. 629 (M.D. Pa. 1992)] Another court ruled, however, that the U.S. government violated the 1979 Hill-Burton regulations when it refused to give a hospital credit toward its uncompensated care obligation on the grounds that the hospital was in technical violation of the Hill-Burton notice requirements. [*Douglas County d/b/a Douglas County Hosp. v. Bowen*, No. 6-85-1078 (D. Minn. Aug. 3, 1988) (unpublished), *see also Flagstaff Med. Ctr. v. Sullivan*, 962 F.2d 879 (9th Cir. 1992) noting new era of "substantial compliance" rather than "technical violations"]

HHS may disallow all uncompensated services claimed in a year when it finds that the facility was in substantial noncompliance with its assurance. Even if a hospital substantially complies, HHS may disallow claims for uncompensated services that are not documented as uncompensated services. [42 C.F.R. § 124.512(d)] Further, if HHS dismisses a complaint or if there has been no action on the part of the attorney general to ensure compliance within six months from the time the complaint is filed, the individual who filed the complaint may bring an action to effect compliance. [42 C.F.R. § 124.511(a)(4)]

What is the community service assurance?

Hospitals that have received Hill-Burton funds must also satisfy a community service assurance. Unlike the uncompensated care obligation, which expires after a period of years, the community service assurance lasts indefinitely and applies specifically to emergency services. The community service assurance requires the hospital to serve all patients in the "facility's service area without discrimination on the basis of race, color, national origin, creed, or any other grounds unrelated to either the individual's need for the service or the availability of the service in the facility." [42 C.F.R. § 124.603] Thus, failure to treat patients based on inability to pay violates Hill-Burton as well as COBRA.

What are a hospital's duties under the community service assurance?

The Department of Health and Human Services Office for Civil Rights has outlined the community service assurance to include the following duties:

- Hill-Burton facilities may not deny emergency services to any person residing in their service area on the grounds that the person is unable to pay for those services.
- Hill-Burton facilities may not adopt patient admissions policies that have the effect of excluding persons on grounds of race, color, national origin, creed, or any other grounds unrelated to the patient's need for the service or the availability of the needed service.
- Hill-Burton facilities must post notices informing the public of their community service obligations in English and Spanish as well as any other language that 10 percent or more of the households in their service area usually speak. [Office of Civil Rights Fact Sheet, *Community Service Assurance under the Hill-Burton Act*, available on the Internet at *http://www.hhs.gov/ocr/hburton.html*]

How does Hill-Burton affect a hospital's emergency admissions policies?

The regulations prohibit a facility from denying a person emergency care because of an inability to pay for care rendered if that person resides in the area (or works in the area according to Title XVI). However, a patient accepted for care under this provision may be discharged or transferred to another facility when doing so would not carry a substantial risk of deterioration in the patient's medical condition. [42 C.F.R. § 124.603(b)]

If a hospital requires preadmission deposits and this policy effectively denies or substantially delays hospitalization or care because the individual cannot pay the deposit, the hospital has violated Hill-Burton's community service obligation. The facility need not eliminate the deposit requirement in all cases. Rather, the hospital must establish alternative arrangements so that individuals who do not have the necessary cash when the services are requested, but who are likely to be able to pay at a later date, are not denied care. [42 C.F.R. § 124.603(d)(3)]

State Law Duties

Have courts interpreted a hospital's duty to provide emergency care to nonpaying patients?

In nearly every state, a hospital can be liable for refusing to provide emergency treatment to a patient who cannot pay. The extent of a hospital's duty to provide either treatment or admission for care is not unlimited, however. Several states still follow the legal principle that a hospital does not have a responsibility to admit or treat a person in a *nonemergency* situation. Yet, differentiating emergency from nonemergency matters is not a simple task. There is a common point in many court decisions considering this issue: To deny a person treatment or admission solely because he or she cannot pay for services has been seen by some courts as an unlawful, arbitrary action by an institution charged with the responsibility of serving the community. Courts may draw upon a facility's charter, incorporation papers, licensure application, or the state indigency laws in determining a hospital's duty to look beyond a person's ability to pay when it decides whether to treat or admit that individual. [*See, e.g., Williams v. Hospital Auth.*, 168 S.E.2d 336 (Ga. Ct. App. 1969)]

How have state legislatures addressed the duty to provide emergency treatment to indigent patients?

Many states have enacted statutes to address the relationship between a hospital's obligation to provide care and patients' inability to pay for care. Many of the medical indigency statutes establish administrative bodies that promulgate rules and regulations to determine individuals' eligibility for state-funded care. These rules apply to publicly operated facilities as well as to private hospitals that have contracted with Medicaid. [Va. Code Ann. § 32.1-11, Cal. Welf. & Inst. Code § 14000, 35 Pa. Cons. Stat. 449.8]

The duty to provide care without regard to the ability to pay may appear in state hospital licensure laws or implicate licensing status as a penalty. In New York, for example, a hospital's operating certificate can be revoked for failing to provide emergency care. [N.Y. Pub. Health Law § 2806]

Legislative enactments may be similar to EMTALA, specifically stating that no one in need of emergency medical care may be denied hospitalization or treatment on the grounds of an inability to pay for necessary services. ED administrators must be familiar with these types of state statutes, as they may impose duties beyond those created by EMTALA. In Florida, for example, the legislature has enacted a statute similar to EMTALA but with no "comes to the ED" provision, triggering a screening requirement upon a mere request for emergency services. In Florida, hospitals not operating at capacity have a duty to accept and treat patients en route to the hospital for whom ambulance personnel request care. [Fla. Stat. ch. 395.1041]

REIMBURSEMENT

This section addresses several reimbursement issues of concern to EDs. EDs have had difficulty obtaining payment from managed care organizations, and this section discusses federal and state laws intended to remedy this problem as well as a series of studies examining the impact of the laws. This section also addresses those Medicare reimbursement issues of particular importance to EDs such as the outpatient prospective payment system, provisions contained in the Balanced Budget Act (BBA) of 1997, teaching physician regulations, reimbursement for interpreting X-rays and electrocardiograms (EKGs), and CMS guidance concerning the use of physician staffing companies. It is important for EDs to understand the legal issues surrounding these reimbursement issues so they can obtain adequate revenue to meet their financial requirements and avoid fraud and abuse allegations.

Payment by Managed Care Organizations

Have state legislatures addressed the tension between managed care plans' restrictive payment policies and the duty to treat under COBRA?

In response to retrospective denials that occur when a managed care payer refuses to pay for treatment because the condition is later revealed to be a nonemergency, more than half of state legislatures have enacted laws requiring payers to cover ED treatment for nonemergency medical conditions under certain circumstances. Maryland was the first state to enact such a law. The Maryland statute requires HMOs to reimburse hospital emergency facilities and providers for medically necessary services rendered to meet federal emergency treatment requirements. The law also prohibits retrospective denials, requiring HMOs to reimburse facilities and providers if the HMO "authorized, directed, referred, or otherwise allowed" an HMO member to use the ED. The law also prohibits preauthorization requirements and defines "emergency services" under a prudent layperson standard. Emergency services are services provided after the sudden onset of sufficiently severe symptoms that a prudent layperson could reasonably expect to result in serious jeopardy of health, serious impairment of bodily function, or serious dysfunction of any bodily organ or part in the absence of immediate medical attention. Other states, such as Arizona, have responded to retrospective denials with a requirement that initial ED screening and stabilizing treatment be covered. [Md. Code Ann., Health-Gen. § 19-712.5; Ariz. Rev. Stat. § 20-2803] A recent study indicated that 47 states have adopted the prudent layperson law and that this standard has not led to increased costs, nor increased ED use. However, disputes still arise between managed care organizations and hospitals over the amount that will be paid. [Hall, Mark. *The Impact and Enforcement of Prudent Layperson Laws*, 43 Annals of Emergency Medicine, 5 (May 2004)]

Has the federal government adopted the prudent layperson standard?

The prudent layperson standard for payment of ED services has also been adopted at the federal level, in certain contexts. The BBA of 1997 adopted prudent layperson language for both Medicare+Choice enrollees and Medicaid managed care participants. Specifically, Medicare+Choice organizations and Medicaid managed care plans must cover emergency services that are needed to evaluate or stabilize an emergency medical condition, defined as a medical condition manifesting itself by acute symptoms of sufficient severity (including severe pain) such that a "prudent layperson, who possesses an average knowledge of health and medicine, could reasonably expect the absence of immediate medical attention to result in (1) placing the health of the individual (or, with respect to a pregnant woman, the health of the woman or her unborn child) in serious jeopardy, (2) serious impairment to bodily functions, or (3) serious dysfunction of any bodily organ or part." [42 U.S.C. §§ 1395w-22 & 1396u-2]

To implement the BBA, the Medicaid program has specifically prohibited Medicaid managed care plans from requiring preauthorization for screening and treatment of conditions that meet the prudent layperson standard for emergencies. The agency has eliminated any confusion regarding whether managed care organizations operating under a Medicaid "waiver" were subject to COBRA by clarifying that all Medicaid beneficiaries should have access to emergency services whether in a managed care program or not. [*Final Rule*, 67 Fed. Reg. 40,989 (June 12, 2002)]

CMS has clarified coverage of emergency services by Medicaid managed care organizations. In a letter to state Medicaid directors, the agency stated that, "The BBA requires that a Medicaid beneficiary be permitted to obtain emergency services immediately at the nearest provider when the need arises. When the prudent layperson standard is met, no restriction may be placed on access to emergency care. Limits on the number of visits are not allowed."[Timothy M. Westmoreland, Director, Center for Medicaid and State Operations, Letter to State Medicaid Directors, Apr. 18, 2000] These actions were an outgrowth of the Patient Bill of Rights set forth that included coverage of emergency services in situations where a prudent layperson could reasonably expect the absence of care to place their health in serious jeopardy.

Are EDs having difficulty obtaining reimbursement from managed care organizations for emergency services in spite of the enactment of these federal and state laws?

According to several studies published in the March 2000 *Annals of Emergency Medicine*, managed care organizations (MCOs) in many states are not providing reimbursement for emergency procedures and some MCOs are violating laws designed to ensure payment for emergency services. In one study that looked at the impact of two laws in Florida designed to prevent denial of claims for emergency services, the study's authors found that the laws did reduce the number of denied claims but that inappropriate denials persisted. In addition, claims denied due to lack of a medical emergency increased since the laws were enacted. The study's authors concluded that even with the passage of legislation, auditing of emergency claim denials remains necessary. In an analysis of payment claim denials due to lack of a medical emergency in North Carolina by two

MCOs, the study's authors found many of the denials met the state's prudent layperson standard. The study again illustrates the need to monitor compliance with the law. [Effect of State Legislation Prohibiting Denial of Emergency Department Patient Claims, *Annals of Emergency Medicine* (Feb. 2000)]

A 2004 study reviewed coverage of ED services in two health plans and found that there was a wide variety of interpretation of the prudent layperson standard. The ED post-service denials comprised one-half of appeals in one plan and one-third in the other. Ninety percent of the claims were overturned and paid on appeal. The appeals typically had the following characteristics: one in five claims related to services for children; a common reason for dispute was diagnosing illness; typical signs and symptoms bringing people to the ED were abdominal pain, cramps, and spasms; and the average cost for services appealed was $1,107.00.

Several state health regulators, including Florida and Washington, have fined MCOs for denying claims for emergency services. Florida has fined at least five HMOs for denying emergency room claims. In Washington, an HMO paid a $10,000 fine for violating the state's prudent layperson law.

Hospitals should note that enforcement of prudent layperson laws is more likely now than it was a few years ago. Hospitals should ascertain whether their billing procedures can track claims in a way that will reveal a pattern of denials for emergency services by a particular payer. If a pattern of inappropriate denials is detected, the hospital should complain to the state attorney general, the state insurance commissioner, or to the state authority that enforces the prudent layperson statute. Hospitals may also want to seek advice from their state or national hospital association. Exchanges of reimbursement information with other hospitals may raise antitrust concerns; accordingly hospitals should be careful not to share reimbursement information with other hospitals. [Disputes over Coverage of Emergency Department Services: A Study of Two Health Maintenance Organizations, *Annals of Emergency Medicine* (Mar. 2004)]

Billing Medicare for ED Services

What is the prospective payment system for hospital outpatient services?

The outpatient prospective payment system is a payment system for hospital outpatient services, including emergency services and urgent care. Payment for hospital outpatient services is made under rates for Ambulatory Payment Classification (APC) groups. CMS has classified outpatient services and procedures into 451 groups that are comparable clinically and use similar resource amounts. CMS has assigned each APC a weight based on the median costs for the services within the APC group. The payment rate is the product of a conversion factor and the APC rate. The prospective payment system applies to nearly all hospitals, including those hospitals that are excluded from the inpatient prospective payment system and community mental health centers, but it does not apply to critical access hospitals and Maryland hospitals. Outpatient PPS went into effect on August 1, 2000, except for the provisions that apply to provider-based facilities owned by hospitals, such as physician office practices; these provisions became effective on October 10, 2000. [65 Fed. Reg. 18,434 (2000), codified at 42 C.F.R. §§ 409 through 413, 419, 424, 489, 498, & 1003]

What services are excluded from the outpatient PPS?

The following services are not paid for under the outpatient prospective payment system:

- services provided by certain providers, including: physicians, nurse practitioners, physician assistants, certified nurse midwives, psychologists, anesthetists, and clinical social workers, which will continue to be paid for under the Medicare fee schedule;
- rehabilitation services;
- ambulance services;
- prosthetics, prosthetic supplies, devices, and implants (except for intraocular lenses), and orthotic devices;
- durable medical equipment, except implantable durable medical equipment;
- clinical diagnostic laboratory services;
- services provided to patients with ESRD that are paid under the ESRD composite; rate and drugs and supplies furnished during dialysis;
- services and procedures that cannot be safely furnished in an outpatient setting or that require inpatient care;
- services provided to persons who are inpatients of a skilled nursing facility and which are covered under the SNF prospective payment system;
- services not covered by Medicare, including services that are not medically necessary; and
- screening and diagnostic mammography. [42 C.F.R. § 419.22]

How does CMS reimburse physician visits in the ED?

The physician provider manual sets forth use of the ED billing codes 99281 through 99288. The ED billing codes can only be used from the ED, but they can be used by any physician who evaluates someone there. The ED codes should be used even if it is determined that the person did not present with an emergency condition. A lower level billing code will simply be used. The ED will typically bill a 99281 to 99288 code, with the code level based on how extensive the evaluation and management services are. If a critical care emergency occurs in the ED, the critical care billing codes (99291 and 99292) can be billed. If trauma activation occurs, as defined by the National Uniform Billing Committee (NUBC) guidelines, and the hospital is licensed as a designated trauma center, then revenue codes 68X can be billed. The hospital may also bill for one unit of code G0390 for trauma activation with critical care. Revenue codes 68X and G0390 must be billed for the same date of service. [*Medicare Processing Manual, Ch. 4 Part B Hospital,* 160.1 Critical Care Services (effective 01-01-07)]

If the patient's regular treating physician is asked to come in and evaluate the patient, the regular physician can bill an initial hospital visit (code 99211 or 99223) if the patient is subsequently admitted to the hospital. If the patient is subsequently discharged, the physician will bill using an ED visit code. If the treating physician is contacted by telephone only, there will be no service billing.

Similarly, if another physician is asked to consult, i.e., an on-call specialist is contacted, the specialist or consulting physician can bill for a consultation if the patient is admitted and treatment continues. If the patient is discharged, the evaluation will be billed using an

ED code. [*Medicare Processing Manual: Ch. 12 Physician and Non-physician Services,* 30.6.11 Emergency Department Visits (revised 10-1-03)]

How does CMS reimburse hospital services in the ED?

Hospital ED services are billing using codes 99218 through 99285 depending upon the severity of service. The bill should include the site of the visit and level of intensity. If someone comes to the ED for services, then seen again the same day for a different problem; the bill should be submitted with a GO code. [*Medicare Processing Manual: Ch. 4 Hospital (Including Impatient Hospital Part B and OPPS)*, 160 Payment for Hospital Emergency Services (revised 10-03-03)] Providers should apply their hospital's internal guidelines and follow the intent of the CPT code descriptors based on the intensity of resources related to the visit. Hospital guidelines should distinguish between the five levels of codes.

A Type A hospital emergency department is open 24/7 and either state-licensed or held out as a location where emergency care is provided on an urgent basis. Type A hospitals will bill using CPT emergency department E/M codes. A Type B emergency department is a dedicated emergency department to which EMTALA applies as defined in 42 C.F.R. § 489.24. The dedicated emergency department must either (1) be licensed as an emergency department, (2) be held out as a site of treatment for emergency medical conditions, or (3) provide one-third of outpatient visits for emergency medical services without an appointment. The Type B hospital emergency department will bill using emergency department G codes. [*Medicare Processing Manual: Ch. 4 Part B Hospital,* 160 Clinic and Emergency Visits (effective 1-1-07)]

How does CMS reimburse physician observation services?

CMS reimburses physicians' services for observation to the physician who admits the person for hospital observation using codes 99217 through 99220. The physician does not need to have hospital admitting privileges, but does need to have privileges for observation. A medical observation record should be kept that includes the date and time of admission, nursing notes, and progress notes made by the physician while the patient is in observation. This record should be in addition to the ED or outpatient record. If another physician is called in to consult, then the other physician will bill an outpatient consultation code.

If the patient is discharged the same day as the observation, then the initial observation will be billed. On the other hand, if the observation patient is subsequently admitted to the hospital and discharged the second day, the second day will be billed as 99217 hospital observation discharge. It will seldom be necessary to bill for more than two days of observation, but should this situation arise, days more than two days before discharge will be billed with an outpatient visit code.

If the patient is admitted as an inpatient after observation, the physician will bill an initial hospital visit code and cannot bill 99217 hospital observation discharge or an outpatient visit on the date of admission. [*Medicare Processing Manual: Ch. 12 Physician and Non-physician Services,* 30.6.8 Payment for Hospital Observation Services (revised 10-1-03)]

How does CMS reimburse hospital observation services?

Observation services are outpatient services that are usually included in the APC reimbursement for the ED service or procedure. CMS has clarified that observation services must be billed one of two ways: (1) as packaged services or (2) as a separate APC under APC 339 for the diagnosis of chest pain, asthma, or congestive heart failure that warrant observation. Thus, packaged service billing can take place when observation services are ordered by a physician or approved by an appropriate authority and last less than 48 hours, then CMS will reimburse the observation when billed as revenue code 762. If other ancillary services are provided in connection with the observation, the code 760 for treatment/observation can be billed in connection with ancillary laboratory services. If observation is for a non-covered service and notice of non-coverage has been given to the beneficiary, then the facility can bill for only the services that are covered. On the other hand, separate APC billing (APC 339) for observation can take place when the patient has a diagnosis of chest pain, asthma, or congestive heart failure for a stay of 8-48 hours. Observation time begins at the time (as rounded to the nearest hour) indicated on the patient record that the patient was placed in a bed for observation. Observation ends when the patient is discharged from the hospital or admitted as an inpatient. It can include services provided after discharge orders are written that are medically necessary, but should not include wait time for transport home.

Prior to January 1, 2006, observation services could be billed using codes G0244, G0263, and G0264, as well as evaluation and management codes 99217 through 99220 and 99234 through 99236. However, effective January 1, 2006, these codes have been discontinued for billing of observation services. Observation services should be billed with codes G0378 (hospital observation per hour) or G0379 (direct admission of patient for hospital observation). Code G0378 should be used for any patient being observed regardless of the condition and can be packaged with 0339 if appropriate. The units are the number of hours the patient is in observation. Code G0379 should be used when a patient is admitted directly to the hospital without a prior emergency, outpatient, or critical care visit.

In order to receive a separate payment for APC 0600 (separate payment for direct admission to observation), the claim must show that G0378 and G0379 were billed on the same date of service, have no T or V status indicators or critical care (Code 0620) on the same date or service, and that observation does not qualify for separate payment under APC 0339. The direct admission considered for separate payment must be submitted on a 13x bill. If the hospital provides non-covered care such as custodial services, it cannot bill for these non-covered services. [*Medicare Processing Manual: Ch. 4 Hospital,* 290, 290.1-290.5 (revised 12-16-05)]

How is a hospital reimbursed if an ED patient is admitted to the hospital?

Medicare patients who are seen in the emergency room and then admitted to the hospital will have the cost of emergency care bundled into the payment for their inpatient care. The diagnosis-related group (DRG)-based prospective payment made to the hospital under Part A of Medicare is calculated to include many of the costs of services provided to hospital patients, including the cost of emergency services.

How does Medicare pay for the services of nonphysician providers?

Medicare will cover the services of some nonphysician providers at a percentage of the physician fee schedule rate. PA services are reimbursed at 80 percent of the lesser of either the actual charge or 85 percent of the physician fee schedule amount. [42 U.S.C. § 1395l(a)(1)(0)] Payment for PA services is only made to the PA's employer, regardless of whether the PA is an employee or independent contractor. A PA's employer must accept assignment, that is, accept the Medicare rate as payment in full, when a PA treats beneficiaries. Medicare will reimburse nurse practitioners and clinical nurse specialists for the services they provide in any geographic area at 80 percent of the lesser of either the actual charge or 85 percent of the physician fee schedule amount. [42 U.S.C. §§ 1395x(s)(2)(K) & 1395l(a)(1)] In addition, Medicare covers payment for certified nurse-midwives' services at no greater than 65 percent of the physician fee schedule amount and pays for the services of certified registered nurse anesthetists. [42 C.F.R. §§ 414.54 & 414.60] CMS will reimburse nurse practitioners (NPs), certified nurse specialists (CNSs), certified nurse midwives (CNMs), and physician assistants (PAs) for evaluation and management services as long as the service is medically necessary and within the scope of services in the state for that practitioner. CMS will not independently reimburse for occupational therapy or physical therapy services. [*Medicare Processing Manual: Ch. 12 Physician and Non-physician Services*, 30.6.1 Selection of E & M Service (revised 5-14-04)]

How are shared ED visits billed?

If the nonphysician provider provides the face-to-face portion of the evaluation and management visit and the physician does not have a face-to-face encounter with the patient but reviewed the medical record, then the nonphysician provider should bill for the service. If the physician and nonphysician provider both had a face-to-face encounter with the patient, then the evaluation and management service can be billed under either the physician or nonphysician provider UPIN/PIN number. [*Medicare Processing Manual: Ch. 12 Physician and Non-physician Services*, 30.6.1 Selection of E & M Service (revised 5-14-04)]

Can physicians bill Medicare for services provided to hospital patients by members of their staff who cannot bill Medicare directly, such as nurses or therapists?

Unlike its coverage in the outpatient setting, Medicare coverage in a hospital setting does not include services and supplies provided "incident to" a physician's services. In addition, a physician cannot bill Medicare for the supervision of his or her staff. Medicare will only pay for physician services provided in a hospital if the services are personally furnished for an individual beneficiary by a physician; the services contribute directly to the diagnosis or treatment of the patient; and the services ordinarily require performance by a physician. When a physician's staff provides services in a hospital setting, Medicare includes payment for these services in the payment it makes to the hospital. Although a physician cannot seek payment from Medicare or the beneficiary for services provided by his or her staff, a physician may seek payment from the hospital. [42 C.F.R. § 415.102]

However, if the physician assumes the operating costs of the department, for example, through a contractual agreement, then the reimbursement includes:

- payment for physician services, and
- payment for reasonable cost basis for costs such as overhead, supplies, equipment costs, and non-medical personnel, as long as the books are made available as requested to verify costs.

The physician will be treated as being related to the hospital under this kind of agreement. [42 C.F.R. § 415.102(d)]

Can an ED physician bill Medicare for the assistance of a physician assistant (PA) performing an evaluation and management service when the PA is employed by the emergency physician group and not by the hospital?

The physician can bill for the services of the employed PA. The PA should have his or her own provider information number, and claims should be submitted on an assignment basis. When the PA conducts the evaluation and management visit, the service should be billed under the PA provider number. However, if the physician also evaluates the patient in person, then either the physician or PA number may be used for billing. A physician billing for services of an employee should use code 99211. [*Medicare Processing Manual: Ch. 12 Physician and Non-physician Services*, 30.6, 30.6.1 Selection of E & M Service (revised 5-14-04) & 110.3 (10-01-03)]

Can a physician staffing company receive Medicare payment for services provided by physicians who have contracted with the company?

CMS has indicated that physician practice management companies, including ED staffing companies, cannot receive payment from Medicare for the services provided by physicians who have contracted with the practice management companies. Direct payments cannot be made to companies that staff hospitals with physicians who have an independent contractor relationship with the companies. Because these physicians are not employees, they do not fit into an existing exception that allows a hospital or clinic to receive payment for the services of a physician employee. In addition, an independent contractor physician who purchases stock in an ED staffing company is not able to reassign his or her Medicare benefits to the company. Shareholders of a corporation are not necessarily employees. Finally, physician practice management companies generally do not qualify under the agency exception because of the method of calculating the physician practice management company's fee. However, a physician may bill for physician he/she employs or for another doctor with whom he has a reciprocal arrangement. [42 U.S.C. § 1395u(b)(6)]

How can physicians in a group practice bill?

Physicians in a group practice can bill as if they were one physician. If they are of the same specialty, only one evaluation and management service should be billed in a day. If the physicians are of different specialties and see the patient for different reasons, more than one evaluation and management code may be billed in a day. [*Medicare Processing Manual: Ch. 12 Physician and Non-physician Services*, 30.6.5 Physicians in Group Practice (10-01-03)]

How does CMS reimburse telehealth services?

Telehealth services are reimbursable when an expert physician, nurse practitioner, physician assistant, nurse midwife, certified nurse specialist, clinical psychologist, or clinical social worker is needed for consultation, an office visit, individual psychotherapy, or pharmacologic management from a distant site. The initiating site will be eligible if it is in a professional shortage area or demonstration project and not classified as a metropolitan statistical area (MSA). The telehealth services must be interactive unless the services are in Alaska or Hawaii. Reimbursement is at the same rate as if the service were provided in person. [*Medicare Processing Manual: Ch. 12 Physician and Non-physician Services*, 190 Medicare payment for telehealth services (10-01-03)]

What billing risks can impact claims integrity?

Billing risks that can impact claims integrity and compliance with procedure coding requirements include outpatient coding, admissions and discharge coding, supplemental payments, and use of information technology. Outpatient coding risks include:

- billing an outpatient service code for a service that is considered an inpatient only service,
- billing for medically unnecessary services,
- failure to follow the National Correct Coding Initiative (NCCI)
- using outdated charge description masters (CDMs) resulting in improper claims for ancillary services,
- failure to follow multiple procedure discount rules,
- improper E & M coding and observation service coding.

Admission and discharge coding risks include the need to comply with the "same day rule" to bill services rendered on the same day together unless an exception is met, monitoring of partial hospital payments, abuses with same day discharge and readmissions, the need to keep an up-to-date list of DRGs impacted by Medicare post-acute transfer policy, and excessive transfers between hospitals and adjacent long-term care hospitals.

Supplemental payment risks include improper pass-through costs, non-compliance with DRG outlier rules, improper designation and claims for provider-based entities, and improper claims for clinical trials, organ acquisition, and cardiac rehab. Providers should also ensure that information technology is used to protect data privacy, security, and accuracy of claims. [Department of Health and Human Services, Office of Inspector General, Supplemental

Compliance Guidance for Hospitals, Jan. 27, 2005 (70 Fed. Reg. 4858)] As of October 1, 2005, CMS no longer processed non-HIPAA compliant electronic Medicare claims.

What is the Medicare claims appeal process?

The Medicare appeal process has been standardized so that there is a similar appeal process for eligibility, enrollment or claims decisions for all Medicare claims (Part D prescription drug appeals began January 1, 2006). The Medicare beneficiary or their representative (such as a medical provider) can file the claims appeals. The initial claim determination will be made by the fiscal intermediary or carrier. If there is disagreement with the initial decision, then a request for reconsideration can be filed and a Qualified Independent Contractor (QIC) will review the case. The third level of appeal requires filing the appeal with an Administrative Law Judge (ALJ) within 60 days of the notice of reconsideration. The ALJ in the Health and Human Services Office of Medicare Hearings and Appeals (OMHA) will then review and decide the claim. The fourth and last level of appeal is to district court.

Interpreting X-Rays and EKGs

Can only board-certified radiologists provide X-ray interpretations and board-certified cardiologists furnish EKG interpretations?

CMS has stated that nothing in the Medicare Act indicates that special qualifications are needed to interpret an X-ray or EKG. Thus, an ED physician can interpret an X-ray or EKG and bill Medicare for this service. [*Medicare Claims Processing Manual: Ch. 13 Radiology Serves & Other Diagnostic Procedures*, 100.1 (revised 10-02-03)]

Will Medicare pay both ED physicians and specialist physicians to interpret X-rays and EKGs furnished to ED patients?

Generally, Medicare will pay for only one interpretation of an EKG or X-ray furnished to an ED patient. Under unusual circumstances, Medicare will pay for a second interpretation. For example, Medicare will pay for a second interpretation if the first interpretation results in a questionable finding for which the physician performing the initial interpretation believes another physician's expertise is needed. In addition, a second interpretation may be justified when a second interpretation of the results of the procedure results in a changed diagnosis. Medicare will not pay for a second interpretation made for quality control purposes. Medicare requires documentation of the unusual circumstances before it will pay for a second interpretation.

CMS has stated that if a radiologist or cardiologist furnishes a contemporaneous interpretation (a written interpretation or an oral interpretation that will be written later), the emergency physician should not bill for the service. The Medicare carrier should pay only the cardiologist or radiologist. A "contemporaneous" interpretation is an interpretation that occurs at the same time as the diagnosis and treatment of the patient in the ED, not hours or days after the patient is sent home. Medicare has also stated that it will pay for an interpretation furnished by teleradiology as long as the interpretation is used in the diagnosis and treatment of the patient. [*Medicare Claims*

Processing Manual: Ch. 13 Radiology Serves & Other Diagnostic Procedures, 100.1 (revised 10-01-03)]

What conditions must an ED meet to receive payment for interpretation of an X-ray or EKG?

Medicare will pay for an interpretation of an X-ray or EKG only if there is a written report prepared for inclusion in the patient's medical record maintained by the hospital. A review of the findings of the procedure without a written report similar to a written report that a specialist in the field would prepare does not qualify for separate payment because it is included in the ED visit payment. For example, notations such as "fx-tibia" or "EKG-normal" would be considered a review of the findings that is included as part of the ED payment and does not qualify for separate payment. According to CMS, an interpretation and report should address the findings, relevant clinical issues, and comparative data (when available). [*Medicare Claims Processing Manual: Ch. 13 Radiology Serves & Other Diagnostic Procedures,* 100.1 (revised 10-01-03)]

Who will Medicare reimburse if both the ED physician and a radiologist or cardiologist submit a claim for the interpretation of an X-ray or EKG?

The Medicare Carrier's Manual instructs carriers to pay the first bill they receive when the carrier receives multiple claims for the same interpretation. Carriers will no longer use physician specialty as the primary factor in deciding which claim to pay. In some cases, Medicare carriers will be required to institute recovery action. For example, if the first claim is from a radiologist, the carrier will pay the radiologist's claim because the carrier does not know that a second claim is forthcoming. However, if a second claim comes from an ED physician and the carrier can determine that this was the interpretation that contributed to the diagnosis and treatment of the patient, the carrier will pay that claim. If the radiologist's claim was for quality control purposes and not because the ED physician required a second interpretation, the Medicare carrier will institute recovery action against the radiologist. [*Medicare Claims Processing Manual: Ch. 13 Radiology Serves & Other Diagnostic Procedures,* 100.1 (revised 10-01-03)]

Services Provided by Teaching Physicians and Residents

When will Medicare reimburse physician services under the physician fee schedule for services furnished in teaching settings?

Regulations revised on October 1, 2004, set Medicare reimbursement for services provided by teaching physicians working with residents. Teaching physicians are physicians, other than another resident, who involve residents in the care of their patients. The regulations require that teaching physicians provide more than general direction to interns and residents to obtain Medicare reimbursement. Teaching physicians must be "present during the key portion of any service or procedure for which payment is sought." [42 C.F.R. § 415.172(a)]

Are there special requirements concerning a physician's presence during high-risk or other complex medical procedures?

For surgery and high-risk or other complex medical procedures, the teaching physician must be present during all critical portions of the procedure and must be immediately available to provide services during the entire service or procedure. Complex and high-risk procedures include interventional radiologic and cardiologic supervision and interpretation, cardiac catheterization, cardiovascular stress test, and transesophageal echocardiography. The regulation does not define the terms "all critical portions" or "immediately available." For endoscopic procedures, the teaching physician must be present during the entire procedure. However, teaching physicians do not need to be present during other diagnostic tests and may bill for test interpretations if they document that they personally performed the tests or reviewed a resident's interpretation with the resident. Minor procedures taking less than five minutes require the teaching physician's presence during the entire procedure in order to bill. [42 C.F.R. § 415.172; *Medicare Claims Processing Manual: Ch. 12 Physician/Nonphysician Practitioners*, 100.1.2 (revised 01-01-06) & 100.1.5 (revised 10-01-03)]

What special requirements must a teaching physician meet to receive Medicare reimbursement for evaluation and management services?

Except for services provided in certain primary care centers, the teaching physician must be physically present during the portion of the service that determines the level of service that will be billed (the "key portion"). The teaching physician must personally document the patient's medical record, either in writing or by a dictated note, indicating his or her presence and participation in the service. CMS has indicated that some reliance on resident documentation is permissible, although the degree of reliance on resident documentation remains somewhat confusing. CMS has stated that if the teaching physician is repeating the key elements of the service previously obtained and documented by the resident, the teaching physician does not need to repeat the documentation. The teaching physician can make brief summary comments that tie into the resident's entry and confirm or revise the key elements. The key elements include the following:

- services performed,
- physical presence,
- participation of the teaching physician in management of the patient, and
- plan of care. [*Medicare Claims Processing Manual: Ch. 12 Physician/Nonphysician Practitioner*, 100.1 (revised 01-13-06)]

What are the special rules applicable to diagnostic radiology and other diagnostic tests provided by teaching physicians?

Teaching physicians receive full payment for the interpretation of diagnostic radiology and other diagnostic tests if the teaching physician performs the interpretation or reviews the resident's interpretation. CMS has indicated that it will not pay for an interpretation if the documentation is only a countersignature of the resident's interpretation. The teaching physician must document that he or she performed the interpretation or reviewed the resident's interpretation. [42 C.F.R. § 415.180; *Medicare Claims Processing Manual: Ch. 12 Physician/Nonphysician Practitioner*, 100.1.2 (revised 01-13-06)]

EMERGENCY RESPONSE PLANNING

What federal laws require hospitals to implement emergency response plans?

The Homeland Security Act of 2002 established the Department of Homeland Security (DHS) with the intent to coordinate emergency management between a variety of government agencies. It also provides for emergency preparedness and response. [6 U.S.C. § 101] The DHS has released a national response plan focused on a comprehensive approach to manage domestic incidents that integrates best practices from a variety of first responders such as EMS, law enforcement, fire, and health professionals. It focuses on both private citizen and public organization involvement and is available at the DHS website at *www.dhs.gov*. OSHA has also issued a National Emergency Management Plan (NEMP). [OSHA Directive HSO-01-00-001 (Dec. 18, 2003)]

Under Title III of the Superfund Amendments and Reauthorization Act of 1986 (SARA), every state is required to coordinate emergency response activities by establishing local emergency planning committees (LEPCs) responsible for developing community response or contingency plans that contain emergency response procedures and programs for hospitals, police, emergency medical personnel, and other first-responders to emergency circumstances. [42 U.S.C. §§ 11001 through 11050] A hospital designated by an LEPC to handle emergency victims suffering from exposure to hazardous substances must have an Emergency Response Plan as well as decontamination equipment, personal protective equipment (PPE), and trained personnel. As directed by SARA, OSHA established a comprehensive rule to protect employee health and safety during hazardous waste operations, including emergency responses to the release of hazardous substances. [29 C.F.R. § 1910.120] This regulation requires hospitals to plan for emergencies if they expect to use their employees to handle emergencies involving hazardous substances and to ensure that employees are trained by an Emergency Response Plan that is approved by the Joint Commission and meets criteria set out in the regulations.

According to an OSHA informational booklet released in 1997, hospitals in many localities have not been effectively integrated into the community disaster response system required under SARA. The booklet describes in detail the steps that hospitals should take to implement a comprehensive Emergency Response Plan that complies with OSHA regulations. [*Hospitals and Community Emergency Response—What You Need To Know*, OSHA 3152 (Dec. 12, 1997)] OSHA has also set forth investigative procedures when fatalities and catastrophes occur. [*Fatality/Catastrophe Investigation Procedures*, CPL 02-00-137 (Apr. 14, 2005)]

Has the Joint Commission issued standards for disaster preparedness?

For over 30 years the Joint Commission has required its accredited health care organizations to meet established disaster preparedness standards, but failed to specifically address what should be included. The standards were significantly changed in 2001 to introduce the concept of multijurisdictional and community involvement into the disaster preparedness process. This new emphasis was prophetic of the terrible reality of terrorism and mass destruction of September 11, 2001. The focus of the standards shifted from a very basic approach to emergency preparedness to the concept of integrated emergency management. The Joint Commission now expects that health care organizations will address the four specific phases of disaster planning: (1) mitigation, (2) preparedness, (3) response, and (4) recovery. In addition, health care organizations must take an "all-hazards approach" to planning and develop a chain-of-command approach that is common to all hazards determined to pose credible threats to the community. Hospitals need to conduct a hazard vulnerability assessment (HVA) and identify potential hazards, threats, and adverse events and their impact on care and services. This information is then used to develop emergency operation plans (EOPs) that are regularly tested.

What constitutes an "emergency" according to the Joint Commission?

An emergency is a natural or manmade event that suddenly and significantly

- disrupts the environment of care,
- disrupts care and treatment, and
- changes or increases demands for the organization's services.

What are the management activities that must be addressed?

"*Mitigation activities* lessen the severity and impact of a potential emergency." Mitigation begins by identifying potential emergencies (hazards) that may affect the "hospital's operations or the demand for its services, followed by implementing a strategy that supports the perceived areas of vulnerability within the organization."

"*Preparedness activities* build hospital capacity to manage the effects of emergencies, should one occur." Some of the important preparedness steps include

- creating an inventory of resources, including supplies and equipment, that may be needed in an emergency, including prearranged agreements with vendors and health care networks;
- maintaining an ongoing planning process;
- holding staff orientation and training on basic response actions; and
- implementing hospital wide rehearsals or drills.

"*Response activities* control the negative effects of emergency situations." These activities are best divided into two categories. The first category includes actions that all staff must take when confronted by an emergency, such as reporting to prearranged locations. The second category includes actions taken by management, such as initiating the plan, assessing the situation, issuing warning and notification announcements, setting objectives and priorities, and serving as a liaison with external groups, such as federal and state agencies of emergency management and public health departments.

"Recovery actions begin almost concurrently with response activities and are directed at restoring essential services and resuming normal operations." Depending on the emergency's impact on the organization, this phase may require a large amount of resources and time to complete. Recovery not only includes activities related to the facility, but also loss of revenues, support of staff, dealing with community reaction, and so forth. [JCAHO Comprehensive Accreditation Manual for Hospitals, EC 4.1 (2007)]

What are the applicable Joint Commission standards?

The standards are found in the Environment of Care standards 4.10 et seq. and focus on six critical areas of emergency management:

1. Communication: In the event that usual communication paths fail, the hospital is required to have a plan to maintain communication pathways within the hospital and to critical community resources.
2. Resources and Assets: The scope and availability of hospital resources and assets during an emergency need to be determined in order to ensure patient safety and care. Assets and resources may include materials and supplies, vendor and community services, and other resources that would be available in a time of crisis.
3. Safety and security: This focuses on the strategies the hospital will take to keep patients safe and secure during an emergency.
4. Staff responsibilities: An emergency will create new demands on staff to care for patients and should be anticipated.
5. Utilities management: The hospital should have a plan for uninterrupted function of utilities such as power, water, ventilation, and fuel during an emergency.
6. Patient clinical and support activities: The hospital should have a clear plan to address the clinical needs of patients during an emergency, including extreme conditions. The hospital goal is to protect life and prevent disability.

A planned response in all six areas allows the hospital to take an "all hazards" approach to being prepared. The hospital should conduct a hazard vulnerability analysis (HVA) and prepare an emergency operation plan (EOP) that addresses these six critical areas. [JCAHO Comprehensive Accreditation Manual for Hospitals, ED 4.10 (2007)]

What should a hazard vulnerability analysis (HVA) include?

The HVA requires the hospital to identify potential hazards, threats, and adverse events and assess their impact on care and services during an emergency. Medical staff should actively participate in emergency management planning. These emergency events should be prioritized and evaluated at least annually. For each emergency event identified in the HVA, the hospital should identify mitigation activities to reduce the risk and damage from the emergency, establish preparedness activities to use essential resources, identify response strategies that will be activated during the emergency, plan recovery actions to help restore the systems vital to resuming normal services, keep a written inventory of assets and resources available on site that would be needed in an emergency, and establish a system to monitor assets and resources during an emergency. [JCAHO Comprehensive Accreditation Manual for Hospitals, EC 4.11 (2007)]

What should an emergency operation plan (EOP) include?

The hospital should have a written EOP with an all-hazards command structure to coordinate the six critical areas within the hospital during an emergency. This would require an incident command structure that is integrated into the community command structure, that identifies whom staff report to in the command structure, who has authority to activate and terminate response and recovery phases and the process involved, and that identifies hospital capabilities and response efforts when the hospital cannot be supported by the local community for at least 96 hours. The EOP will also designate alternative sites for care, treatment, or services that meet the needs of patients during emergencies. [JCAHO Comprehensive Accreditation Manual for Hospitals, EC 4.12 (2007)]

What emergency communication strategies does the Joint Commission require?

The Joint Commission requires a plan to notify and communicate with staff when emergency response measures begin, to notify and communicate with external authorities of emergency response measures that have begun, to communicate with patients and their families during emergencies including family notice of patient relocation, to communicate with the community and the media during emergencies, and to communicate with providers of supplies, services, and equipment during an emergency. It also requires plans to communicate with other health care organizations that provide services. Communication plans should include information about command and control centers, resources, names of patients and deceased individuals, circumstances in which and plans to communicate with others such as police or state health departments, and alternative care sites. The hospital should have a back-up communication system and technology to complete the required communications. [JCAHO Comprehensive Accreditation Manual for Hospitals, EC 4.13 (2007)]

What are the resource and asset strategies the Joint Commission requires?

The emergency operation plan (EOP) should identify how resources and assets will be obtained in order to continue to provide treatment and care in an emergency, including emergencies of long duration or broad geographic scope. This should also include contingency plans if necessary critical supplies are not available from planned sources. Planning should focus on maintaining the facility but also consider evacuation of the facility if it is no longer safe. Specifically, these plans should address obtaining and replenishing medical, pharmaceutical, and non-medical supplies; managing staff support activities such as housing, transportation, and stress debriefing; potential sharing of resources and assets such as personnel, beds, linens, and equipment with other health care organizations in or outside the community; evacuation when required; transporting patients to alternative care sites; and relaying information such as necessary patient clinical and medication data to alternative care sites. This should include identification of alternative means for provision of utility services such as electricity, water, fuel, and ventilation and gas systems during an emergency. [JCAHO Comprehensive Accreditation Manual for Hospitals, EC4.14, EC 4.17 (2007)]

What are the safety and security strategies the Joint Commission requires?

The hospital should establish a plan to keep patients safe and critical supplies and equipment secure. This includes establishing the type of access and movement allowed by staff, patients, visitors, emergency volunteers, vendors, and others during emergency situations. Access may depend upon the type of emergency and local conditions. The plan should include coordination with the community command structure and direct contact with agencies charged with community security. Specifically, this includes internal security and safety operations during an emergency; identification of the roles of community security agencies and how the hospital will coordinate with these agencies; a process to manage hazardous materials and waste during an emergency; and ways to isolate and decontaminate radioactive, biological, and other toxic chemicals. The hospital will have emergency processes to control entrance to and exit from the health care facility, movement of individuals within the facility, and traffic accessing the facility. [JCAHO Comprehensive Accreditation Manual for Hospitals, EC 4.15 (2007)]

What are the staff responsibility strategies the Joint Commission requires?

The emergency operation plan (EOP) defines staff roles and responsibilities in the six critical areas, staff are trained for their assigned roles during emergencies, and the hospital communicates to licensed independent practitioners their roles during the emergency and establishes a process to identify care providers assigned to particular areas during an emergency. [JCAHO Comprehensive Accreditation Manual for Hospitals, ED 4.16 (2007)]

The hospital may grant disaster privileges to volunteer health care professionals through modified credentialing and privileging processes during an emergency once the emergency management plan is activated. The hospital must still ensure that there is proper license verification and proper oversight of the care, treatment, and services provided by volunteer staff. The privileging process should be described in the bylaws and include a written process to oversee professional volunteers. At a minimum, the volunteer would need to provide photo identification and one of the following: a current picture hospital ID card with the professional designation; a current license to practice; primary source verification of license or membership with an organization such as the Disaster Medical Assistance Team (DMAT), Medical Reserve Corps (MRC), or Emergency System for Advance Registration of Volunteer Health Professionals (ESAR-VHP); identification indicating authority to render disaster care; or identification by a hospital staff member who knows of the volunteer's ability to act as a licensed professional. Primary source verification should begin as soon as the situation is under control and within 72 hours of the time the volunteer presents to the organization. Medical staff should observe the practice of the volunteer. [JCAHO Comprehensive Accreditation Manual for Hospitals, MS 4.110 (2007)]

What patient clinical and support activities does the Joint Commission require?

The hospital should have a plan to manage a patient's clinical conditions during severe emergencies. This will include emergency triage and discharge of those whose needs can be met outside the hospital. Thus, the hospital plan should include strategies to manage patient scheduling, triage, assessment, treatment, admission, transfer, discharge, and evacuation; clinical services for vulnerable populations; personal hygiene and sanitation needs of patients; mental health service needs; mortuary services; and plans to document and track clinical information. [JCAHO Comprehensive Accreditation Manual for Hospitals, ED 4.18 (2007)]

What types of problems need to be considered?

Risks vary by type and intensity at each location, but some of the issues that must be considered include the following:

- Security
  - —bomb threats and the resulting need for investigation and evacuation
  - —civil disturbances in the ED
  - —gang-related activity in the ED or involving a patient
  - —community panic that may result in ED patients attempting to leave the hospital at a time or under circumstances that are unadvisable
  - —hostage incidents involving staff or patients
  - —terrorist attacks, including nuclear, biological, chemical, and traditional explosives and arms
  - —VIP patients or visitors
  - —employee violence against self, other employees, or patients
  - —domestic violence involving a patient or employee
  - —theft of drugs, chemicals, or radiological materials
- Weather
  - —snowstorms or ice storms
  - —earthquakes that may involve damage to the physical structure of the hospital
  - —hail or high winds that may involve damage to the physical structure of the hospital
  - —hurricanes or tornadoes that may involve damage to the physical structure of the hospital
  - —severe cold or heat/humidity
  - —severe rainfall or floods that may involve damage to the physical structure of the hospital
  - —sinkholes

Any of the above weather events may prevent oncoming staff from getting to work and require on-duty staff to shelter in place, and may result in the disruption of vital services to the hospital.

- Utility system failures
  - —central medical vacuum
  - —electrical
  - —emergency power

—fuel for heat
—heating/air conditioning
—communications systems, internal or external
—fuel for reserve power
—water supply
—water contamination
—sewage
—fire suppression systems
—oxygen systems
—internal gas leaks

- Other

—structural compromise
—internal or external fires or explosions
—air system contamination
—internal biohazard spill
—internal nuclear material incident
—natural epidemics
—mass casualty transportation accidents
—mass casualty external structural incident
—bioterrorism threat
—external hazardous material incident
—external chemical attack
—internal chemical contamination
—refugees from metropolitan area disasters
—transfer patients from another hospital evacuation or disaster
—need for immediate evacuation

Has the Joint Commission issued any interpretive guidelines to help hospitals in complying with the disaster preparedness standards?

Since 2001, the Joint Commission has focused on guiding health care organizations in preparing for terrorist attacks that may involve nuclear, biological, or chemical incidents. [JCAHO *Perspectives*: Special Edition on Emergency Management Planning (Dec. 2001)] The guidance outlines how to use Joint Commission standards as a starting point to prepare for an emergency, and recommends development of practical emergency management education programs and recognition of common elements among mass casualty emergencies that can help an organization better prepare for such emergencies.

The Joint Commission has also issued a policy statement focusing on strategies for community-wide emergency preparedness systems. The Joint Commission recommends that the entire community become involved in preparing for a local response. Key aspects of preparedness should focus on the community health resources that are available to care in the event of an emergency. Community should evaluate their "surge capacity" or ability to care for large numbers of patients at a given time as well as their ability to stand alone providing services for the 48 to 76 hours it may take for back up assistance to arrive. Each system should have strong leadership in preparing the community for an emergency situation. [*Health Care at the Crossroads: Strategies for Creating and Sustaining Community-Wide Emergency Preparedness System*, JCAHO (Mar. 12, 2003) available on the Internet at *http://www.jointcommission.org/PublicPolicy/Emergency_Preparedness.htm*. Recent experience with Hurricane Katrina has led to a focus on "surge hospitals" which are temporary facilities set up to triage and treat the increased numbers of people needing immediate care. Emergency planning should include evaluation of ways to create surge hospitals to expand the organization's ability to handle increased numbers of patients. Integrated planning should include review of ways to handle staffing, equipment, available pharmaceutical reserves, and coordination with community-based systems. [*Surge Hospitals: Providing Safe Care in Emergencies* (Dec. 2005) available on the Internet at *http://www.jointcommission.org/PublicPolicy/surge_hospitals.htm. See also, Standing Together: An Emergency Planning Guide for America's Communities* (Sept. 2005) also available on the JCAHO Internet site.] A guide to Emergency Preparedness Competencies outlining core skills for hospital leaders and workers is available on the Internet at *http://images.main.uab.edu/isoph/SCCPHP/documents/compbroch.pdf.*

What kind of testing of Emergency Medical Plans is required by the Joint Commission?

The 2007 standards revise testing of Emergency Medical Plans under standard EC 4.2 with the goal of accessing preparation and capabilities for an actual emergency. Tests should include plausible scenarios based on hazard vulnerability analysis (HVA) and demonstrate effectiveness of capabilities and identify areas of improvement in the emergency operations plan (EOP). Measurable performance expectations should be set to work with data analysis and strategies for improvement. Emergency services should be tested twice a year; once a year with simulated patients. The hospital should participate in a community-wide emergency exercise once a year. [JCAHO Comprehensive Accreditation Manual for Hospitals, ED 4.2 (2007)]

What other state or federal resources provide guidance for emergency management?

As the medical community learned on September 11, 2001, a large-scale disaster can strike without warning. The attacks on the World Trade Center and the Pentagon, as well as subsequent incidents of anthrax exposure, placed hospitals on the front lines in triaging the injured and diagnosing those infected. In the event of a future mass casualty event, hospital administrators and staff will play a vital role as responders and as sources of accurate information for patients, the public and the medical community. Because of this it is essential that administrators have access to current information on preparing for a variety of disaster related emergencies.

The Federal Emergency Management Agency (FEMA) provides a variety of information on preventing and preparing for disasters, as well as disaster assistance. FEMA has also compiled a list of state emergency managers, available on the Internet at *http://www.fema.gov*. Another educational resource for disaster preparedness is the American Hospital Association (AHA), which has compiled an overview of the needs of the nation's hospitals related to future mass casualty events and a list of resources for hospital readiness, response and recovery activities (available on the Internet at *www.aha.org*). The AHA has also prepared a Chemical and Bioterrorism Preparedness Checklist that is designed to help hospitals describe and assess their preparedness for chemical and biological incidents. The American Medical Association (AMA) also offers extensive information on disaster preparedness and medical response to bioterrorism (available on the Internet at *http://www.ama-assn.org*). The AMA publishes the journal *Disaster Medicine and Public Health Preparedness,* which focuses on public health preparedness. The Department of Homeland Security (DHS) established effective March 1, 2003, plans and prepares for and coordinates emergency response that occurs on a national level (available on the Internet at *http://www.dhs.gov*). Should an incident occur emergency response will be under the direction of the medical director for the emergency medical services (EMS) system and the incident command system (ICS). ACEP recommends that volunteer medical personal work within the established systems as requested by the ICS and that preparation is made to develop a better surge capacity. It also recommends national credentialing and an up-to-date database of physicians and health care volunteers who are qualified to assist in the event of a national emergency. [*ACEP Policy Compendium: Unsolicited Medical Personnel Volunteering at Disaster Scenes* (2002), *Disaster Medical Response* (2006), *and Health Care System Surge Capacity Recognition, Preparedness, and Response* (2004)] ACEP has a hospital survey form to assess community health care disaster preparation. It is available on the Internet at *http://www.acep.org.* The Centers for Disease Control and Prevention (CDC) coordinates emergency preparedness and planning in regards to chemical agents and bioterrorism (available on the Internet at *http://www.bt.cdc.gov*). [*See also In a Moment's Notice: Surge Capacity in Terrorist Bombings,* on the Internet at *http://www.bt.cdc.gov/masscasualties/surgecapacity.asp.*] Agency for Healthcare Research and Quality (AHRQ) has a mass casualty event (MCE) planning guide, emergency department triage tools, and other tools for disaster planning available on the Internet at *http://www.ahrq.gov/prep/.*

PATIENT SAFETY

Patient safety is an important component of any hospital unit. The Joint Commission national patient safety goals for 2008 are: (1) improve the accuracy of patient identification, (2) improve the effectiveness of communication among caregivers, (3) improve the safety of using high alert medications, (7) reduce the risk of health care associated infections, (8) accurately and completely reconcile medications across the continuum of care, (9) reduce the risk of patient harm from falls, (13) encourage patients' active involvement in their own care as a patient safety strategy, (15) identify safety risks inherent in the patient population including suicide risk, (16) improve recognition and response to changes in a patient's condition. [Note that other goals and numbers omitted are not applicable] [*2008 National Patient Safety Goals* available at *http://www.jcaho.org*]

How can the requirement to improve the accuracy of patient identification be met?

This goal involves two components. First, use at least two patient identifiers when taking blood samples, administering medication or blood products, taking blood and other specimens for clinical testing, or providing any other treatment or procedures. A patient identifier may be the patient's name, assigned identification number, telephone number, or other patient specific identifier. Bar coding that includes two or more patient specific identifiers is acceptable, but room number is not. The term "identifier" refers to methods of identifying the patient, not sources of information. Thus, comparing the name of the patient with the name on a record would be one identifier found in two places. A second identifier might be date of birth, social security number, address, phone number, etc. The two-identifier requirement applies to order entry and providers are encouraged to use computerized prescriber order entry. The second component incorporated in the Universal Protocol is to confirm the correct patient, procedure, and site prior to any surgical or invasive procedure. This requires active communication through an affirmative statement or action that the patient, procedure, and site are correct.

What is required to improve effectiveness of communication among caregivers?

Ineffective communication is the most common cause of sentinel events, while effective communication improves patient safety. The following actions should be taken to ensure effective communication within the organization:

- verify verbal or telephone orders and test results by having the person receiving the order "read-back" the complete order or test result, (In an emergency it is acceptable for the physician to call out the order, have the nurse repeat it back, and have the recorder document the time, dose, drug, route, and rate),
- standardize a list of abbreviations that should not be used in the organization,
- measure timeliness of reporting of critical test results and values,
- report all critical test results within time frames and collect data to measure reporting timeliness.
- implement a standard approach to "hand-off" communication which includes the opportunity to ask and answer questions.

What are recommendations for telephone orders in the ED?

Telephone orders involve good communication between health care providers. First, there should be a process for taking verbal or telephone orders that require verification of the order by having the person receiving the order read the entire order back to the person giving the order. This involves writing down the complete order, reading it back, and then receiving confirmation that the order is correct. Second, standard abbreviations, acronyms and symbols should be used throughout the organization including a list of abbreviations not to use. A standard list of dangerous abbreviations is available at the Institute for Safe Medication Practices (ISMP) available at their web site at *http://www.ismp.org.* ACEP recommends that the hospital have a policy in place regarding criteria for dictating and accepting telephone orders and that telephone orders given to ED personnel should be subject to the review and approval of the emergency room physician on duty. Drug Enforcement Administration (DEA) regulations prohibit dispensing controlled substances from ED stocks of patients by telephone order. [*ACEP Policy Compendium* (2007): *Telephone Orders in the Emergency Department* (rev. 2002)]

Other recommendations to reduce error with verbal orders include limiting verbal orders to urgent situations where immediate written or electronic communication is not feasible; establishing policies and procedures that limit use of verbal orders; define the parameters of who may send and receive such orders and how they will be documented; creating a culture where it is acceptable to question verbal orders; defining elements to be included in the verbal order such as name, age, weight, drug name, drug form, strength, dose frequency, route of administration, quantity and duration, indication; verifying the content of the orders by confirming drug names and spelling or providing brand and generic names and indications for use; repeating the entire verbal order to the prescriber; and documenting orders in the medical record where they are cosigned by the prescriber as soon as possible. [Recommendations to Reduce Medication Errors Associated with Verbal Medication Orders and Prescriptions, National Coordinating Council for Medication Error Reporting and Prevention (adopted Feb. 20, 2001)]

What can be done to avoid medication errors?

Medical error occurs when the wrong medication, wrong dose, or wrong patient occur during medication administration. The Institute of Medicine (IOM) identified medical error as prevalent in its 1999 report titled "To Err Is Human" [*To Err Is Human*, Institute of Medicine (1999)] JCAHO has also noted that medical error is one of the top reasons for sentinel events in JCAHO audits. Medication errors can be caused by a number of factors including poor handwriting, similar sounding or looking drug names, drug abbreviations, misinterpretation of labeling or packaging, miscalculations, lack of knowledge or skill, or incorrect administration. Ways to address specific problems leading to medication errors are listed below.

Sound-alike drugs—Sound-alike drugs such as Celebrex and Celexa and Cerebrex; Xanax and Zantac; or Cytotec and Cytoxan can lead to error. Clear handwriting, exact spelling, and reading back of verbal orders can reduce medical error.

Inadequate patient history—Inadequate patient history can lead to drugs that are contraindicated for comorbid conditions, drug allergies, or wrong form or dose of the medication.

Dose error calculations—To verify dose calculations, the physician can include the clinical pharmacologist in prescription preparation or take drug levels prior to determining dose.

Decimal points—Misplaced decimal points can lead to confusion. A whole number should not have a zero after the decimal point (2 mg NOT 2.0 mg) and a zero should be placed before any number less than 1 mg (0.2 mg. NOT .2 mg).

Inappropriate abbreviations—Abbreviations can be easily misinterpreted and should not be used unless approved by the hospital for use.

Illegal and incomplete orders—Unclear handwriting can lead to confusion. Printing can make things more clear or use of a computer system. All components of the complete medication order should be verified including the name of the drug, dose, route, and frequency of administration.

In July 2006, the Institute of Medicine (IOM) issued recommendations for preventing medical error. The focus is on establishing a patient-centered, integrated medication system. Providers and patients should partner to ensure that medications are appropriate. Patients should keep a list of medications they are taking as should the provider. Improved communication between medical practitioners and patients will help establish a patient-centered system. The next step is for each organization to take steps to improve safety. Things like electronic prescribing, appropriate drug labeling and packaging, and other organization-specific strategies can reduce medical error. [*Preventing Medical Error* Institute of Medicine (2006)]

What are Joint Commission standards for medication use?

JCAHO Medication Management Standards focus on reducing process variation, error and misuse through uniform medication processes and practices based on sound medical evidence. These standards require the following:

- Access to patient and medication information such as age, weight, diagnosis, comorbidities, pregnancy status, medication allergies and sensitivities, and current medications;
- Medication availability, selection, storage, and safe management in the hospital setting including management of medications brought into the hospital by families;
- Clear ordering and transcribing policies and processes;
- Safe preparation and dispensing of medications through review of medication orders and correct labeling, including processes to provide medications when the pharmacy is closed and to retrieve recalled or discontinued drugs;
- Safe administration of medication including self-administered medications;
- Monitoring the effects of medications on patients including action and reporting of adverse drug events or medication errors;
- A process to manage high-risk or high-alert medications; and
- Regular evaluation of medication management systems.

[JCAHO Comprehensive Accreditation Manual for Hospitals, MM 1.10–MM 8.10 (2007)]

JCAHO requires evaluation of drugs that look and sound alike. For example, do not store the problem medications by name but in alternative locations. Ensure both the generic and brand name of the drug are included on orders to avoid duplication, and determine the purpose for which the medication is prescribed. [*Look-alike, sound-alike drug names*, JCAHO Sentinel Event Alert, Issue 19 (May 2001)] The 2007 safety goal to improve medication safety requires an annual review and list of look-alike/sound-alike drugs with actions to prevent errors in use of these drugs. If the facility does not use look-alike/sound-alike drugs from the JCAHO list, it can use the lists available from the Institute for Safe Medication Practices (ISMP) or U.S. Pharmacopoeia (USP). [JCAHO Comprehensive Accreditation Manual for Hospitals, NPSG 3C (2007)]

Proper labeling of medications and solutions requires labeling all medications, including labeling medication transferred from the original package to another container. The label should contain the drug name, strength, amount, and expiration date of the mixture, including time if expiration is less than 24 hours. For intravenous solutions, the date prepared and dilutent should be included. Prelabeling a syringe or basin for use for a certain mixture is not acceptable since a different mixture could be used and result in error. If two or more people participate in mixing and administering the medication, then two people are required to verify the label, but if the same person mixes then administers the medication, the same person can verify the label. Only one medication should be labeled at one time and any unlabeled medication should be discarded. [JCAHO Comprehensive Accreditation Manual for Hospitals, NPSG 3D (2007)]

Patient safety goals for 2008 also include a requirement to reduce the likelihood of harm when using anticoagulation therapy. Implementation milestones during 2008 require assignment of responsibility for the goal by April 1, an implementation workplan by July 1, pilot testing by October 1, and full implementation by January 1, 2009. Full implementation requires an organization-wide anticoagulant management program to individualize the care of each patient receiving coagulation therapy. This should include using only oral medications and premixed infusions when available, dispensing warfarin in accordance with monitoring procedures, using approved protocols for anticoagulation therapy to ensure proper medication for the patient condition and to evaluate possible drug interactions, obtaining and having available a baseline international normalized ratio (INR) during warfarin treatment, coordination with dietary services to coordinate a food/drug interaction program, using programmable infusion pumps for I.V. heparin administration, and establishing a policy to address baseline and ongoing lab tests required during herapin use. [JCAHO Comprehensive Accreditation Manual for Hospitals, NPSG 3E (2007)]

Medications with the highest risk of injury include insulin, opiates and narcotics, potassium chloride concentrate, anticoagulants, and sodium chloride solutions above 0.9 percent. For medications that require a high concern for safety, the standard focuses on first, removing concentrated electrolytes such as potassium phosphate, sodium chloride above 0.9 percent from patient care areas. This is to avoid inadvertent use in an undiluted form. Second, standardizing and limiting the number of drug concentrations available in the organization. When multiple concentrations of a drug are necessary, such as for infants, special precautions should be taken to avoid dosing errors by specifying actual drug dose, not volume and writing out the dose calculation as part of the order.

The patient safety goals require hospitals to reconcile medications across the continuum of care through a process to obtain and document a complete list of the patient's current medications upon admission so that medications the organization provides can be compared to the list. A complete list of the patient's medications should be communicated to the next provider of service when the patient is transferred inside or outside the organization. The next service provider also reconciles the list. The patient should receive a complete list of medications on discharge from the facility. [JCAHO Comprehensive Accreditation Manual for Hospitals, NPSG 8 (2007)]

There are two exceptions to the requirement that all prescriptions or medication orders be reviewed for appropriateness by a pharmacist prior to administration. The first is when an independent practitioner controls the ordering, preparation, and administration of the medication. This includes preparation by a registered nurse or other licensed staff when a physician is present. In urgent situations, patient care takes precedence, and if a delay in care would harm the patient or if there is a sudden change in the clinical status of the patient, then care should be provided first and a process should be in place to obtain the information as soon as possible. Adequate documentation of this standard would allow someone to ask and answer "How do I know the comparison process is consistently happening in my organization?" [JCAHO Urgent Bulletin—Update on Standard MM 4.10, Perspectives (2007)]

What medications are on the hospital look-alike/sound-alike drug list?

JCAHO has a list of common look-alike/sound-alike drugs for different care settings. Each organization must select at least ten drug combinations on which to focus safety strategies. The hospital list includes the following medications:

- Concentrate morphine vs. conventional morphine—It is recommended that concentrated morphine only be dispensed as needed for specific patients.
- Epinephrine and ephedrine—Follow general recommendations for safety.
- Hydromorphone and morphine—Follow general safety recommendations.
- Hydroxyzine and hydralazine—Differentiate with tall letters to distinguish drugs, i.e., hydrOXYzine and hydrALAzine.
- Insulin products—Limit insulin 70/30 mixtures to a single product. Limit insulin stored in patient care areas. Use labeling to differentiate products.
- Lipid based vs. conventional formulation of products, i.e., daunorubicin and doxorubicin or amphotericin (lipid or conventional)—Train staff to be aware of differences and to refer to lipid-based products by their brand names.
- Metronidazole (flagyl) and metformin (glocophage)—Set computer to display all medications with word root "met," use tall unique letters to differentiate, and order metronidazol in 250 mg tablets only since metformin is not available in 250 mg tablets. OxyContin and oxycodone—Do not store together, try to dispense oxycodone for specific patients only, and educate staff.
- Vinblastine (velban) and vincristine (oncovin)—Include maximum dose in the computer to alert staff to name mix-up during order entry. Use brand names or brand and generic names when prescribing.

Other things that can be done to avoid drug mix-ups include:

- Encourage awareness of look-alike/sound-alike drugs,
- Include the purpose of the drug with the prescription,
- Use verbal and telephone orders only when necessary,
- Encourage computer prescribing,
- Include both brand and generic names in the patient record,
- Change the appearance of the drug names on the computer screen by using large letters, colors, etc.
- Use name alert stickers to alert staff of drugs with potential for mix-up,
- Consider name confusion when new drugs are used,
- Set up a system to double check drugs, and
- Have a process for reporting errors that may occur.

[*Look-alike/Sound-alike Drug List* 2006-2007 available on the Internet at *http://www.jcaho.org*]

How can medication reconciliation prevent errors?

Medication reconciliation involves comparing the patient's medication orders to all the medications the patient has been taking. This can prevent omissions, duplications, dosing errors, and prevent drug interactions. The comparison should be completed whenever there is a transition of care such as when the orders change, the provider of care or service changes. For example, hospital admission, transfer, or discharge would require reconciliation. Medication reconciliation involves (1) obtaining a current list of medications, (2) making a list of medications to be prescribed, (3) comparing the two lists, (4) making clinical decisions based on the comparison, and (5) establishing a new list. JCAHO requires that medications be reconciled across the continuum of care. Those assigned to reconciliation should have the expertise to make appropriate decisions and all reconciliation should take place within a specified time frame such as 24 hours after admission or sooner for high-risk drugs. Hospitals should use a standard form to document reconciliation and establish policies and procedures for the process. [*Using Medication Reconciliation to Prevent Errors,* JCAHO Sentinel Event Alert, Issue 35 (Jan. 25, 2006)]

What potentially dangerous abbreviations can lead to medication errors?

A major cause of medication error is the use of abbreviations and dose expressions. For example, when using "U" for units, the U may be interpreted as a zero. Similarly the use of a zero after a decimal point such as 2.0 may be misinterpreted as 20 or failing to put a zero before a decimal point such as .2 may be interpreted as 2.

Other examples of confusing abbreviations are:

- **D/C** which could stand for discharge or discontinue,
- **DPT** which could stand for demoral, phenergan, thorazine or the diphtheria, pertussis, tetanus vaccine,
- **MgSO4** or **MSO4** which could be magnesium sulfate or morphine sulphate,
- **Qhs** which could be read every evening or every hour,
- **Sub q** which could be read as subcutaneous or every so often.

JCAHO has recommended the following risk reductions strategies: (1) develop a list of unacceptable abbreviations that is shared with all prescribers, (2) develop a policy requiring medical staff to refer to the list, and (3) establish a policy that if an unacceptable abbreviation is used, the prescription order is verified with the prescriber before being filled. [*Medication Errors Related to Potentially Dangerous Abbreviations,* JCAHO Sentinel Event Alert, Issue 23 (Sept. 2001); *Please Don't Sleep Through This Wake Up Call,* ISMP Medication Safety Alert, (May 2, 2001); *Eliminating Dangerous Abbreviations and Dose Expressions in the Print and Electronic World,* ISMP Medication Safety Alert, (Feb. 20, 2002) with table of dangerous abbreviations linked to the article. Available on the Internet at *www.ismp.org*]

Creative ways to communicate the list of dangerous abbreviations to staff include:

- distribution of pocket cards to staff with the printed list,
- stickers or magnets with the list near computer or patient care areas,
- laminated list on the back of the physician order divider in patient chart,
- the list printed on pens or displayed on mousepads, or
- by providing regular information on the list through newsletters, intranet, or other staff communication.

A complete list of implementation tips is available at *http://www.jcaho.org.*

What abbreviations are on the JCAHO "do not use" list?

The following abbreviations are on the JCAHO "do not use" list because of the possibility of confusion.

- **U**—write out the word *unit* to avoid confusion with 0 or cc,
- **IU**—write out "*international unit*" to avoid confusion with I.V. or 10,
- **QD** or **QOD**—write out "*daily*" or "*every other day,*"
- **.X**—avoid missing decimal points by writing zero before the decimal, but not after (i.e., do write 0.X or X, but do *not* write .X or X.0),
- **MS** or **MSO4** or **MgSO4**—write out "*morphine sulfate*" or "*magnesium sulfate*" to avoid confusion.

Other abbreviations under consideration for future "do not use" list include: > or < which can be confused with a 7 or L, drug names and apothecary units, @ which can be confused with 2, cc which can be mistaken for u, or ug which can be mistaken for mg.

What can be done to prevent nosocomial infections?

Nosocomial infections can be reduced through infection control strategies in the department. These include things like adequate orientation and training, sound equipment cleaning, good handwashing, use of single-use intravenous flush vials, use of waterless handrubs, raising expectations, and regular training on infection control. The organization must comply with World Health Organization (WHO) hand hygiene guidelines or Centers for Disease Control and Prevention (CDC) hand hygiene guidelines and manage unanticipated death or loss of body function as a result of infection as a sentinel event. [JCAHO Comprehensive Accreditation Manual for Hospitals, NPSG 7 (2007); *see also CDC Hand Hygiene Guideline* available on the Internet at *http://www.cdc.gov/handhygiene/*]

What are Joint Commission standards for fall reduction?

JCAHO requires a fall reduction program. A fall reduction program should include assessment of the patient population served, the services provided, and the environment of care to determine the risk of falls. Risk factors that make someone more likely to fall include a history of falls, a person over 65 years of age, function and mobility, cognitive impairment, confusion, equipment, incontinence or urinary frequency, hypotension or vertigo, medication, depression, reduced hearing or visual ability, and reduced peripheral sensation. Steps that can be taken to reduce falls include impacting the physical abilities of the person through exercise, adequate caring for toileting needs, medical evaluation, pain management, and good sleep patterns. Psychological steps that can be taken to reduce falls include reorientation to the environment, communication of the fall risk, relaxation, and diversion. Environmental factors that can be impacted include things such as orientation, adequate light, bed alarms and monitoring, assistive devices, placing needed objects nearby, using side rails, and other equipment. Finally, education of staff and family about fall risks can also prevent falls. [JCAHO Comprehensive Accreditation Manual for Hospitals, NPSG 9 (2007). *See also http://www.guideline.gov* for fall reduction information.]

How can patient safety be protected in emergency situations?

In an emergency situation such as during a code in the ED, the "repeat back" method is an acceptable way to verify an order. For example, during a code the physician calls out the medication order and the nurse repeats it back before administering the drug. The code recorder documents the name of the drug, dose, time, route, and rate. This is an acceptable method of documenting and verifying the order.

Since the risk of making a mistake is higher during an emergency, it is recommended that medications be stored in the emergency department in ready to use forms or that other protections against misuse be put in place. If a procedure is performed emergently, then the practitioner should verify the site and location and if possible, take a "time out" to verify that the appropriate site has been selected for the procedure. JCAHO has a protocol to avoid wrong site, wrong procedure, and wrong person surgery through preoperative verification, site identification and marking prior to the procedure, and use of "time out" to verify the appropriateness of the site, procedure, and person. [*Universal Protocol for Wrong Site, Wrong Procedure, and Wrong Person Surgery*, JCAHO (July 1, 2004)]

What are ways to encourage medical error reporting?

Medical error reporting is vital to obtain the information to determine risks of error, knowledge about actual errors and their causes, and to develop ways to prevent errors. Processes to encourage reporting will make it possible to manage the risk of error. Each organization can create a culture that encourages reporting by setting up processes that instill trust by focusing on ways to improve the system rather than punishing the individual who made the error. All reporting should be kept confidential to protect the reporting employee. The reporting form should be clear and easy to use. Once a report has been submitted, the reporting employee should receive a reward or recognition for reporting and feedback on how the information was used. Finally, all new staff should be trained on the importance of reporting and the process to use to report errors and concerns. [*Pump Up the Volume—Tips for Increasing Error Reporting,* ISMP Safety Alert (Feb. 9, 2006); *Harmful Errors: How Will Your Facility Respond?* ISMP Safety Alert (Oct. 5, 2006)]

What is the impact of patient safety legislation?

Federal patient safety legislation was signed into law on July 29, 2005, and encourages voluntary reporting of patient safety data to approved provider or patient safety organizations (PSO). Patient safety data is defined broadly to include data, reports, records, memoranda, analysis, deliberations, work statements, root cause analysis, and quality improvement processes. The law prohibits accrediting bodies from taking action based on patient safety data nor can providers be required to reveal communications with a PSO.

The PSO can only disclose patient safety data when the data is non-identifiable, when there is evidence of wanton or criminal actions that lead to patient harm, as needed to carry out PSO or research activities, and voluntary disclosures can be made for public health surveillance. The Department of Health and Human Services (DHHS) will maintain a patient safety network of databases based on voluntary reporting, develop voluntary national standards to encourage electronic exchange of health care information, and contract with research organizations to study the impact of medical technology on health care. [Patient Safety and Quality Improvement Act (PSQIA), Pub. L. No. 109-41 (July 29, 2005)]

APPENDIX 1-A

State Regulation of Consent to Treatment in an Emergency

The following state-by-state analysis provides a detailed summary of state laws and regulations regarding exceptions to patient consent under emergency circumstances. The state laws and regulations are divided into the following three categories:

- **Emergency:** Under this heading laws and regulations are noted that waive or modify the general requirement for patient consent in the event of an emergency. Some states waive consent in an emergency altogether, while others establish that consent in an emergency is implied. Other variations include whether a second opinion is necessary before proceeding with treatment, and whether and when relatives or other individuals must be located and informed.
- **Incapacity:** This analysis addresses statutes and regulations that give general direction to health care providers seeking to treat patients who lack the capacity to consent. Because this concept overlaps with consent in an emergency, the Emergency section also should be consulted.
- **Minors:** This analysis addresses state laws and regulations that contain exceptions allowing physicians to treat minor patients under emergency circumstances without parental consent. Not included in this analysis, however, are emergency exceptions to parental notification/consent under special circumstances such as abortion, suspected child abuse, treatment for venereal disease, HIV testing, and mental health or substance abuse treatment.

Where a category has not been included within the summary for a particular state, the issues covered in that category are not presently governed by statute or regulation. State case law should be consulted in these areas as well as for assistance in interpreting the summarized statutes and regulations. This analysis should not be construed as legal advice, but as a research tool.

ALABAMA

- **Emergency:** Consent is not required if a person is physically or mentally unable to consent to services and there are no known relatives or legal guardian. Two or more physicians must decide that a delay would increase the risk to the person's life or health. [Ala. Code § 22-8-1]
- **Incapacity:** Consent is not required if a person is physically or mentally unable to consent to services and there are no known relatives or legal guardian. Two or more physicians must decide that a delay would increase the risk to the person's life or health. [Ala. Code § 22-8-1]
- **Minors:** Services may be rendered without parental consent when, in a physician's judgment, an attempt to secure consent would result in a delay that would increase the risk to the minor's life or health. [Ala. Code § 22-8-3]

ALASKA

- **Emergency:** It is a defense that consent by or on behalf of the patient was not possible under the circumstances. [Alaska Stat. § 09.55.556(b)(3)]
- **Incapacity:** Capacity to give informed consent is present when the patient is competent as demonstrated by the ability to assimilate relevant facts, understand any mental limitations, can rationally think about treatment decisions, and can state reasons to object to offered medications. [Alaska Stat. § 47.30.837] A person is considered competent to make decisions, but can authorize an agent to make health decisions for the person if the person later lacks capacity through an advanced directive or can appoint a surrogate decision maker. [Alaska Stat. §§ 13.52.010, 13.52.030, and 13.52.100]
- **Minors:** Minors can consent to their own medical or dental treatment when the minor is living alone and managing his/her own affairs, when the parent or guardian cannot be reached or is unwilling to give or withhold consent, when the minor is the parent of child, or when the care is for pregnancy or venereal disease. The consent is valid if the representations of the minor were relied on in good faith. [Alaska Stat. § 25.20.025] A minor can reach majority at the age of 18 or when married. [Alaska Stat. §§ 25.20.010, 25.20.020]

ARIZONA

- **Emergency:** In a medical emergency where surgical or medical is necessary to save the "life, physical health, eyesight, hearing or member of the person" then the Medical Director of the agency may consent to the treatment if time does not permit obtaining a court order. Upon rendering of treatment, the patient's guardian will be immediately notified. [Ariz. Rev. Stat. § 36-512]
- **Incapacity:** A person with serious mental illness shall be determined to be in need of guardianship or conservatorship if the person's ability to make important decisions is so limited that absence of a person with legal authority to make such decisions creates a serious risk to the person's health, welfare, or safety. [Ariz. Admin. Code § 9-21-206(C)(1)]

- **Minors:** A surgical procedure cannot be performed upon a minor without the written consent of a parent, except when an emergency exists and treatment is necessary, or if the parent cannot be located or contacted after reasonable effort. [Ariz. Rev. Stat. § 36-2271] Any person acting in loco parentis can consent for treatment for a minor when an emergency exists and the parents cannot be located. [Ariz. Rev. Stat. § 44-133]

ARKANSAS

- **Emergency:** When an emergency exists and no one is immediately available who is authorized or capable of consent, consent is implied. Consent may be given by a court where an emergency exists, there has been a protest or refusal of consent, and there is no other person immediately available who is authorized or capable of consent. [Ark. Code Ann. §§ 20-9-603 & 20-9-604] Specific consent for surgery shall be documented prior to the procedure, except in case of emergency. [Ark. Reg. DHFS 603]
- **Incapacity:** A person has an "unsound mind" and is incompetent to consent to treatment where the person is unable to perceive all facts relevant to the condition and proposed treatment in order to make an intelligent decision. An unsound mind may be temporary or intermittent. Whether a person has an unsound mind does not depend on the cause of the incapacity (i.e., whether from natural state, age, shock, anxiety, illness, injury, drugs, sedation, intoxication, or other cause). [Ark. Code Ann. § 20-9-601]
- **Minors:** Consent is not required when the attending physician certifies an emergency and there is not sufficient time to obtain consent from a pregnant minor or incompetent woman. [Ark. Code Ann. 20-16-805]

CALIFORNIA

- **Emergency:** A provider is not liable for damages for injury or death in an emergency situation for failure to inform the patient of the possible consequences of a medical procedure. This applies when the patient is unconscious, the provider reasonably believes that there is insufficient time to fully inform the patient, or the patient is legally incapable of consenting and the provider reasonably believes that the procedure should be begun immediately and there is insufficient time to obtain the consent of an authorized person. [Cal. Bus. & Prof. Code § 2397] A provider may give treatment without informed consent in an emergency if it is documented in the patient's record that immediate action is necessary to preserve life, prevent serious bodily harm to the patient or others, or alleviate severe pain. To act without consent, it must be impractical to obtain the required consent and the action taken must be customary among physicians of good standing in similar circumstances. [Cal. Code Regs. tit. 22, §§ 73524(e) (intermediate care facilities), 72528(e) (skilled nursing facilities)]
- **Incapacity:** If the attending physician in a skilled nursing or intermediate care facility orders treatment that requires informed consent, but is unable to obtain consent because the resident lacks capacity and there is no person with legal authority

to make decisions for the resident, the physician shall inform the facility, and an interdisciplinary team will oversee the resident's care. [Cal. Health & Safety Code § 1418.8]

- **Minors:** A minor can consent to medical care if 15 or older, is living separately, and manages his/her own finances. The physician can advise the parents or guardian of medical treatment with or without the minor's consent. [Cal. Fam. Code § 6922] A minor is considered emancipated upon turning 18, when married, or when serving in the military. [Cal. Fam. Code § 7002] A minor can consent to treatment for pregnancy, treatment for a communicable disease, or drug and alcohol counseling if over 12. [Cal. Fam. Code §§ 6925, 6926, 6929]

COLORADO

- **Incapacity:** If a patient's attending physician or the court has determined that the patient lacks the capacity to give informed consent to medical treatment and there is no guardian with medical decision-making authority, agent appointed in a medical power of attorney, or other person with legal authority to consent for the patient, the physician or his or her designee must attempt to locate as many interested persons as practicable (i.e., the patient's spouse, parent, adult child, sibling, or grandchild, or any close friend), and inform them that a proxy decision maker should be selected, and the person selected shall make medical treatment decisions on behalf of the patient. [Colo. Rev. Stat. § 15-18.5-103]
- **Minors:** A minor can consent to drug and alcohol treatment. A minor 15 years or older who is emancipated or married can consent to medical treatment. [Colo. Rev. Stat. §§ 13-22-102 & 13-22-103]

CONNECTICUT

- **Incapacity:** Informed consent must be received from a patient prior to receiving medication for the treatment of psychiatric disabilities. No medical procedure may be performed without the patient's written informed consent or, if the patient has been declared incapable, the written consent of a conservator. [Conn. Gen. Stat. § 17a-543] By statute, a person can create a document designating a health care agent, attorney-in-fact, or conservator to act in the event of future incapacity or in regards to an anatomical gift. The document must be put in place by someone over 18 and signed and witnessed. [Conn. Gen. Stat. § 19a-575a]
- **Minors:** Parental consent is generally required for treatment of a mentally ill child unless the physician believes treatment is needed to avoid serious harm to the child in which case treatment can be administered while waiting for parental consent. An involuntary patient may receive medications or treatment without consent, but written consent is required for a medical or surgical procedure by the parent, next of kin, or court-appointed doctor. However, if the head of the hospital and physician determine that the child is in a critical emergency measures to protect the child's well-being may be taken without consent. [Conn. Gen. Stat. § 17a-81]

DELAWARE

- **Emergency:** A health care provider is not liable for damages for negligence for lack of an informed consent (*State Regulation of Consent to Treatment in an Emergency* App 1-A:3) in an emergency situation. In a negligence claim for lack of informed consent, health care providers can also raise the defense that a person of ordinary intelligence would understand the hazards of the treatment, the injured person indicated that he wanted treatment regardless of the risk or was not interested in receiving information about the risk, or it was reasonable for the health care provider to limit disclosure because it might have an adverse outcome on the person. [Del. Code Ann. tit. 18, § 6852]
- **Incapacity:** Capacity to consent to medical care or treatment includes the ability to understand and make choices, the information upon which consent is based, and the voluntariness of the decision. Consent is not required for emergency treatment defined as action required to preserve the life or bodily integrity of the person. [Code of Del. Regs. 40-601-401]
- **Minors:** A minor age 12 or older who is or may be pregnant or suffering from an infectious disease may give written consent for any diagnostic, preventive, or therapeutic procedure, except abortion. The minor's consent is valid regardless of whether the pregnancy or disease is later confirmed. The physician has the discretion to provide or withhold information concerning treatment from the minor's parents or spouse. If the minor consents to an operation, however, notice of intent to perform the operation shall be given to the minor's parents by telegram sent at the time of diagnosis by the surgeon. The surgeon may proceed without notice if delay would endanger the minor's life or if there is a reasonable probability of irreparable injury. [Del. Code Ann. tit. 13, §§ 708 & 710] The following individuals may consent to any diagnostic or therapeutic procedure for a minor by a health care provider: a parent, a married minor, a spouse (if the minor is unable to consent due to physical disability), a minor 18 or older, or a minor parent for his or her child. In the case of a traumatic injury that, if untreated, might reasonably threaten the minor's health or life, a temporary custodian may consent, after reasonable efforts are made to obtain parental consent. [Del. Code Ann. tit. 13, § 707]

DISTRICT OF COLUMBIA

- **Emergency:** In an emergency in which delay in obtaining consent for surgery would create a risk or harm as indicated by the judgment of two physicians, the surgery may be performed without consent of the person if information is provided to the person's parent, guardian, spouse or next of kin to allow them to make a knowing consent prior to the surgical procedure. If there is no person who can be reasonably contacted then the surgery may be performed with the approval of the chief medical officer of the facility. [D.C. Code Ann. § 7-1305.07]
- **Incapacity:** Mental incapacity to make health care decisions shall be certified by two physicians, one a psychiatrist, with a written opinion to be included in the patient's record regarding the cause and nature of the incapacity and its extent and probable

duration. The record must show that the patient is incapable of understanding the health care choice, making a decision concerning the particular treatment, or communicating a decision even if capable of making it. A provision also specifies which individuals are authorized to consent for an incapacitated person, in order of authority. [D.C. Code Ann. §§ 21-2204, 21-2210 & 21-2211]

- **Minors:** A health care provider may treat a minor without parental consent when the provider believes that delay would substantially increase the risk to the minor's health or life, or would unduly prolong suffering. A health care provider may render emergency services to any injured minor when the provider believes that giving aid is the only alternative to probable death or serious physical or mental damage. In an emergency where major surgery or any dangerous procedures will be performed, concurrence of another physician shall, if practical, be obtained. [22 D.C. Code Mun. Regs. § 600] No health care professional is compelled to treat a minor based on the minor's own consent, but may refer the minor. A health care provider may rely upon a minor's representations if the provider acts in good faith. The health care provider has discretion whether to inform the parents of any treatment given or needed in the following situations: (1) severe complications, major surgery, or prolonged hospitalization; (2) the safety and health of the minor patient is in jeopardy; or (3) the minor's physical and mental health and family harmony would benefit. [22 D.C. Code Mun. Regs. § 602]

FLORIDA

- **Emergency:** Any hospital or employee working within a clinical area of the facility and providing patient care, who renders good faith medical care because of an emergency, will not be liable for damages for the medical care except when care is given with reckless disregard for the consequences to the life or health of another. Reckless disregard for consequences is conduct of the health care provider that the health care provider knew or should have known would result in injury to life or health. Factors to consider in determining whether there was reckless disregard include: seriousness of the situation, lack of time to obtain consultation, lack of a prior patient-physician relationship, inability to obtain a proper medical history, and time constraints of co-existing emergencies. [Fla. Stat. § 768.13]
- **Incapacity:** A facility administrator may petition the court to appoint a guardian based upon the opinion of a psychiatrist that a patient is incompetent to consent to treatment. The facility must provide sufficient information so that the guardian can decide whether to consent to treatment, including information that the treatment is essential to the care of the patient and does not present an unreasonable risk of serious, hazardous, or irreversible side effects. [Fla. Stat. § 394.4598] If the patient has not named a surrogate decision maker, the following persons are authorized to consent to health care for the patient, in order of priority: court-appointed guardian; spouse; adult child; parent; adult sibling; adult relative having regular contact with the patient; close friend. [Fla. Stat. § 765.401]
- **Minors:** A physician may render emergency medical care to a minor without parental consent when delay would endanger the health or well-being of the minor and care is rendered in a licensed hospital or college health service. Treatment without parental

consent is only permissible when parental consent can not be immediately obtained because the minor's condition renders him incapable or revealing the identity of the parents or guardian or the parents or legal guardian cannot be immediately located at their residence or business. The parents should be given notice of the medical care as soon as possible after care is rendered and the reason for treatment without consent should be documented in the medical record. There is no liability for medical care provided within accepted standards of medical practice. [Fla. Stat. § 743.064]

GEORGIA

- **Emergency:** Consent to medical care is implied in an emergency. An emergency arises when competent medical judgment dictates that treatment is necessary, a person authorized to consent is not readily available, and delay in treatment is reasonably expected to jeopardize the patient's life or health, including potential disfigurement or impaired faculties. [Ga. Code Ann. § 31-9-3; Ga. Comp. R. & Regs. § 360-14-02] A patient is presumed to consent to CPR unless a do not resuscitate order is in place and nothing limits the right of an adult to refuse medical care. [Ga. Code Ann. §§ 31-39-7 & 31-39-9] Detailed consent procedures relating to cardiopulmonary resuscitation. [Ga. Code Ann. §§ 31-39-3 through 31-39-9]
- **Incapacity:** The inability of any adult to consent to treatment must be documented in the medical record by a physician who has personally examined the adult and found that the adult either lacks sufficient understanding or capacity to make a responsible decision regarding medical treatment, or lacks the ability to communicate consent decisions. When a person has been found unable to consent to treatment, the following persons may consent on the person's behalf, in order of priority: spouse; guardian; adult child; parent; adult sibling; grandparent. [Ga. Code Ann. § 31-9-2]
- **Minors:** A parent may consent to treatment for a minor, even if the parent is a minor. A married person may consent to treatment even if a minor. A person acting in loco parentis may consent for a minor under his care. Any female may consent to treatment for childbirth, pregnancy, or prevention of pregnancy regardless of age. [Ga. Code Ann. § 31-9-2]

HAWAII

- **Emergency:** Informed consent is not required when obtaining consent for an emergency treatment or surgical procedure is not feasible under the circumstances without adversely affecting the patient's condition. [Haw. Rev. Stat. § 671-3(d)]
- **Incapacity:** Informed consent must be obtained from the patient's guardian if the patient is not competent to give informed consent, before any non-emergency treatment for mental illness. This consent shall be a part of the patient's record. [Haw. Rev. Stat. § 334E-1]
- **Minors:** The consent for medical care by a minor is valid when it is for pregnancy, venereal disease, or family planning. The consent is binding as if the minor was of the age of majority and cannot be later disaffirmed. [Haw. Rev. Stat. § 577A-2]

IDAHO

- **Emergency:** When a medical emergency exists that would endanger the life or health of the person if treatment is delayed or withheld, then the attending physician or dentist may authorize and provide for the care and treatment or procedure as if consent had been given. [Idaho Code § 39-4504(g)]
- **Incapacity:** Any person of ordinary intelligence can consent to his or her own health care. If a person does not have the capacity to consent for medical care for himself, then the law presumes the following may consent in the order of priority listed: legal guardian, living will and durable power of attorney for health care, spouse, parent, relative, competent person responsible for the care of the person. [Idaho Code §§ 39-4502 & 39-4504]
- **Minors:** The following may consent to care for a minor in the order of priority listed: legal guardian, living will and durable power of attorney for health care, spouse, parent, relative, competent person responsible for the care of the person. [Idaho Code § 39-4504] A court may authorize medical or surgical care for a child when the parents or legal guardian are not immediately available and cannot be found after reasonable effort and a physician indicates that it is his professional opinion that the life of the child would be greatly endangered without treatment and the parent or guardian refuses or fails consent. The court will make every effort to grant the parents or guardian an immediate informal hearing as long as the hearing does not jeopardize the child's life. Oral authorization by the court is sufficient to allow for treatment of the child. [Idaho Code § 16-1627]

ILLINOIS

- **Emergency:** The mental health code specifies that when a medical or dental emergency exists and the person is evaluated and determined unable to give consent, then essential treatment can be rendered without consent. [405 Ill. Comp. Stat. 5/2-111]
- **Incapacity:** Declaration form for mental health treatment. [755 Ill. Comp. Stat. 43/75] Providers may rely on the decision by a surrogate decision maker to the same extent as if the decision had been made by a patient with capacity. [755 Ill. Comp. Stat. 40/30]
- **Minors**: A physician may render services without parental consent when the physician believes that an attempt to obtain consent would result in delay that would increase the risk to the minor's life or health. [410 Ill. Comp. Stat. 210/3(a)]

INDIANA

- **Emergency:** Consent to health care is not required in an emergency. [Ind. Code § 34-18-12-9]
- **Incapacity:** Before providing mental health services, a provider must obtain consent. A patient's legal guardian or other court-appointed representative, health care representative, or attorney-in-fact for health care are authorized to consent on behalf of a mentally incompetent person. [Ind. Code §§ 16-36-1-4 through 16-36-1-6]

Whenever a provider believes that a patient may lack capacity to give informed consent, the provider shall consult with the attorney-in-fact who has the power to act for the patient. [Ind. Code § 30-5-7-3] Consent to medical treatment of an incompetent person is not required in an emergency. A superintendent of a health care facility may consent to treatment of an incompetent patient. If the superintendent and the treating physician determine that a patient is incompetent to consent to treatment that is medically necessary, the superintendent shall obtain a second opinion from a physician independent of the facility. [Ind. Code §§ 16-36-3-3, 16-36-3-4 & 16-36-3-5]

- **Minors:** The following persons may consent to health care for a minor: (1) a guardian; (2) a parent or person in loco parentis, if there is no guardian or the guardian is unavailable or fails to act; (3) an adult sibling, if there is no guardian, or if a parent is not available or declines to act. [Ind. Code § 16-36-1-5]

IOWA

- **Emergency:** A provider may render emergency care without consent when the patient is unable to consent for any reason and there is no legally authorized person reasonably available to consent. [Iowa Code § 147A.10]
- **Incapacity:** A person may prepare a durable power of attorney for another to make health care decisions in their behalf in the event the person is incapable. A health care provider caring for the person or the provider's employee cannot serve as the attorney in fact. [Iowa Code §§ 144B.1 *et seq.*]
- **Minors:** A minor can consent to treatment for a sexually transmitted disease (STD). [Iowa Code § 139A.35]

KANSAS

- **Minors:** A health care provider may render emergency care in good faith to a minor without first obtaining parental consent. [Kan. Stat. Ann. § 65-2891] A minor 16 years of age or over may consent to hospital, surgical, or medical treatment procedures when no parent or guardian is immediately available and the consent may not be disaffirmed by the minor. [Kan. Stat. Ann. § 38-123b] A pregnant minor can consent to medical care. A minor can also consent to treatment for venereal disease, drug abuse or addiction. [Kan. Stat. Ann. §§ 38-123, 65-2892 & 65-2892a]

KENTUCKY

- **Emergency:** A provider is not required to obtain consent prior to providing care in an emergency situation. [Ky. Rev. Stat. Ann. § 304.40-320(3)]
- **Minors:** A minor may receive emergency medical services without parental consent when the provider believes that delaying treatment to obtain consent would risk the minor's life or health. [Ky. Rev. Stat. Ann. § 214.185(4)]

LOUISIANA

- **Emergency:** Consent to treatment is implied where an emergency exists, a person authorized to consent is not reasonably available, and a delay in treatment could jeopardize the patient's life or health or result in disfigurement or impaired faculties. [La. Rev. Stat. Ann. § 40:1299.54]
- **Incapacity:** The following may consent, in order of priority, to medical treatment for an adult who is not competent to act: a judicially appointed tutor or curator; an authorized agent for health care; a spouse not judicially separated; an adult child; a parent; a sibling; other relatives. [La. Rev. Stat. Ann. § 40:1299.53]
- **Minors:** Minors may consent to diagnosis and treatment of an illness or disease. Parental or spousal consent is not necessary, but a provider has discretion as to whether to inform a spouse or parent as to treatment given or needed. [La. Rev. Stat. Ann. § 40:1095]

MAINE

- **Incapacity:** A surrogate may make a decision to withhold or withdraw life sustaining treatment for a person who lacks capacity when there is no guardian and the person has a terminal illness or is in a persistent vegetative state (PVS). The priority of family members who can act as surrogate is spelled out. No judicial approval is needed for the surrogate decision to be binding. [Me. Rev. Stat. Ann. tit. 18A, § 5-805]
- **Minors:** A children's home may consent to emergency treatment for a state ward residing in the home. [Me. Rev. Stat. Ann. tit. 22, § 3-B] Treatment for venereal disease, drug and alcohol abuse, or sexual assault evidence can take place without the consent of a parent or guardian. [Me. Rev. Stat. Ann. tit. 32, § 3292]

MARYLAND

- **Emergency:** In an emergency, a health care provider may treat a patient who is incapable of making an informed decision without consent if no person authorized to consent is immediately available, there is a substantial risk of death or serious harm to the patient, and delaying treatment to obtain consent would adversely affect the patient's condition. [Md. Code Ann., Health-Gen. § 5-607]
- **Incapacity:** If a person has been certified to be incapable of making an informed decision and has not appointed a health care agent, a provider may obtain consent for the person's health care from the following, in order of priority: an appointed guardian; a spouse; an adult child; a parent; an adult sibling; a friend or relative who has had regular contact with the person and is familiar with the person's activities, health, and beliefs. [Md. Code Ann., Health-Gen. § 5-605]
- **Minors:** A minor may consent to medical treatment if the minor is married or is a parent, or if the provider believes that the minor's life or health would be adversely affected by delaying treatment to obtain the requisite consent. [Md. Code Ann., Health-Gen. § 20-102]

MASSACHUSETTS

- **Emergency:** No consent is required for medical care in an emergency. A medical emergency includes a condition that is immediately life threatening including severe bleeding, blocked airway, unconsciousness, cardiac arrest, cardiovascular accident, a fracture, extensive burns, severe cuts, severe injury, or any condition where delay in treatment would harm the life, limb, or mental well-being of the patient. [110 Mass. Code Regs. 11.01 & 11.03]
- **Incapacity:** When an attending physician determines that a patient lacks capacity because of mental illness or developmental disability, based upon training or experience in diagnosing or treating similar conditions, the authority of a health care agent, if one has been named, shall begin, and the agent has authority to make any health care decision that the patient could make after receiving all medical information necessary to make informed decisions about his or her health care. [Mass. Gen. Laws ch. 201D, §§ 5 & 6] If there is no health care proxy, a provider may rely upon the informed consent of responsible parties on behalf of incompetent or incapacitated patients. [Mass. Gen. Laws ch. 201D, § 16]
- **Minors:** A physician or hospital may provide emergency treatment to a minor without parental consent when delay in treatment will endanger the minor's life, limb, or mental well-being. [Mass. Gen. Laws ch. 112, § 12F] A provider may treat a minor in the custody or care of the Department of Social Services (DSS) in an emergency without anyone's Consent. [110 Mass. Code Regs. 11.01 & 11.03; *see* 110 Mass. Code Regs. 11.11 through 11.23 for consent requirements applicable to specific extraordinary medical treatment] A provider may treat a minor in the custody of the Department of Youth Services (Medicaid recipient) in an emergency without anyone's consent. [109 Mass. Code Regs. 11.04; *see* 109 Mass. Code Regs. 11.13 through 11.17 & 11.30 for consent requirements applicable to specific extraordinary treatment]

MICHIGAN

- **Emergency:** Emergency medical services personnel may provide treatment to a person who objects to the treatment if they determine that the person's condition makes him or her incapable of competently objecting, unless the objection is expressly based on the person's religious beliefs. [Mich. Comp. Laws § 333.20969]
- **Incapacity:** Written consent of the nearest relative, legal guardian, or person in loco parentis is required for a person needing surgical or medical treatment who is not of sound mind or not in a condition to make his or her own decisions. [Mich. Comp. Laws § 400.66H]
- **Minors:** A court may order that medical services be provided to a child whose health requires it and whose parent has not provided treatment because of legitimate religious beliefs. [Mich. Comp. Laws § 722.634] A minor can consent to substance abuse treatment and the health professional may inform the spouse, parent, guardian or person in loco parentis of treatment given for medical reasons. [Mich. Comp. Laws § 333.6121]

MINNESOTA

- **Incapacity:** A health care facility must attempt to notify the family or designated emergency contact of a patient who enters the facility unconscious, comatose, or unable to communicate, so that the family member may participate in treatment planning, unless the patient has an advance directive to the contrary or has previously named a health care agent. [Minn. Stat. § 144.651, sub. 10(b)] Unless the person specifies otherwise, the appointment of the health care agent is considered a nomination of a guardian of the person. [Minn. Stat. § 145C.07]
- **Minors:** Any minor may receive health services without parental consent when delaying treatment to obtain consent would risk the minor's life or health. [Minn. Stat. § 144.344]

MISSISSIPPI

- **Emergency:** Consent to medical treatment is implied in an emergency if a person authorized to consent has not refused to consent or, if so, there has been a subsequent material and morbid change in the patient's condition and no authorized person is immediately available to consent. An emergency is defined as a situation where any delay caused by an attempt to obtain consent would jeopardize the patient's life or health or would reasonably result in disfigurement or impairment. [Miss. Code Ann. § 41-41-7]
- **Incapacity:** An adult or emancipated minor may execute a power of attorney for health care, which may authorize the agent to make any health care decision the principal could have made while having capacity. Unless otherwise specified, the agent's authority becomes effective upon a determination that the principal lacks capacity and ceases to be effective when the principal has recovered capacity. [Miss. Code Ann. §§ 41-41-205 & 41-41-215]
- **Minors:** The following, in order of priority, may consent to surgical or medical treatment of an unemancipated minor: the minor's guardian; a parent; an adult sibling; a grandparent. If none of the above is reasonably available, an adult who has shown special care and concern for the minor and who is reasonably available may act. [Miss. Code Ann. § 41-41-3]

MISSOURI

- **Emergency:** Consent is implied in an emergency if an authorized person has not refused to consent or, if so, there has been a subsequent material and morbid change in the patient's condition and no authorized person is immediately available and willing to consent. A situation is an emergency if medical treatment is immediately necessary and any delay caused by an attempt to obtain consent would jeopardize the patient's life or health or result in disfigurement or impairment. [Mo. Rev. Stat. § 431.063]
- **Incapacity:** An adult who is incapable of giving informed consent for treatment with any experimental treatment, test, or drug at a teaching hospital for a medical school may be treated with the consent of the following persons, in order of priority: spouse; adult child; parent; sibling; relative by blood or marriage. [Mo. Rev. Stat. § 431.064]

- **Minors:** Any parent may consent to medical treatment for his or her minor child in his or her legal custody. In the absence of an authorized parent at a time when delay may jeopardize the minor's life or health or result in disfigurement or impairment, any adult sibling, grandparent, or any adult standing in loco parentis for a minor may consent. A minor may consent to his own care when legally married, for pregnancy, venereal disease, or drug or substance abuse. [Mo. Rev. Stat. § 431.061] A physician, nurse, or emergency medical technician may render emergency care without compensation to a minor at the scene of an accident without obtaining parental consent. [Mo. Rev. Stat. § 537.037]

MONTANA

- **Emergency:** A health professional can render emergency care, without compensation, when it is believed that the care is the only alternative to death or serious physical or mental damage. [Mont. Code Ann. § 41-1-405]
- **Incapacity:** Anyone 18 years of age or older may have a written declaration to withhold or withdraw life sustaining treatment. [Mont. Code Ann. § 50-9-103]
- **Minors:** Any minor may consent to emergency care without which the minor's health would be jeopardized. [Mont. Code Ann. § 41-1-402] A minor may consent to emergency psychiatric counseling without parental or spousal consent when that consent cannot be obtained within a reasonable time and there is danger to the life, safety, or property of the minor or others. [Mont. Code Ann. § 41-1-406] A health professional does not need parental or spousal consent to provide non-emergency services to a minor for a condition that will endanger the minor's life or health if obtaining consent would delay services. If a minor is mentally or physically incapable of giving consent and has no known relatives or guardian, consent is not required for necessary health services. [Mont. Code Ann. § 41-1-405]

NEBRASKA

- **Emergency:** There is no liability for medical care rendered at the scene of the accident. [Neb. Rev. Stat. § 25-21,186] Emergency care is not required when the person objects to treatment on religious or other grounds. Out-of-hospital care providers are not liable for rendering treatment when the person is unable to give consent. [Neb. Rev. Stat. §§ 71-5193, 71-5195] Signing of written information is not required prior to an initial telehealth consultation in an emergency in which the patient is unable to sign and the legal representative is unavailable. [Neb. Rev. Stat. § 71-8505]
- **Incapacity:** Incapacity means that the person is unable to understand the health care decision and its alternatives or is unable to communicate an informed health care decision. [Neb. Rev. Stat. § 30-3402(7)] A person can designate another competent adult with power of attorney to make health care decisions. [Neb. Rev. Stat. § 30-3403]

NEVADA

- **Emergency:** Consent will be implied if the proposed procedure is reasonably necessary and any delay could reasonably be expected to result in death, disfigurement, impairment, or serious bodily harm, and no authorized person is available to consent. [Nev. Rev. Stat. § 41A.120]

- **Incapacity:** The legal guardian of a person who has been adjudicated mentally incompetent must give written informed consent to a plan of care, treatment or training, or necessary surgical procedure at a mental health facility. [Nev. Rev. Stat. § 433.484]
- **Minors:** A minor may consent to treatment for him or herself or his or her child if the minor is in danger of a serious health hazard if treatment is not provided. Parental consent is not necessary if a minor described above understands the nature and purpose of the treatment and its probable outcome and voluntarily requests it. Before initiating treatment, the provider must attempt to obtain the minor's consent to communicate with a parent and note such efforts in the record, but may omit such efforts if it would jeopardize necessary treatment. [Nev. Rev. Stat. § 129.030] Any person standing in loco parentis to a minor may consent to emergency treatment of a minor who needs immediate hospitalization or medical attention if a parent cannot be located. [Nev. Rev. Stat. § 129.040]

NEW HAMPSHIRE

- **Emergency:** A health care professional need not obtain consent in rendering emergency treatment to any person who is unable to give consent for any reason, including minority where there is no person available who is legally authorized to consent to the treatment. [N.H. Rev. Stat. Ann. § 153-A:18]
- **Incapacity:** A person may appoint a health care agent who can make decisions on behalf of the person when the person lacks the capacity to do so himself. [N.H. Rev. Stat. Ann. § 137-J:14] A guardian can consent or withhold consent to medical treatment. [N.H. Rev. Stat. Ann. § 464-A:25]
- **Minors:** Any minor 12 years of age or older may consent to treatment for drug dependency. [N.H. Rev. Stat. Ann. § 318-B:12-a]

NEW JERSEY

- **Emergency:** No consent is required for an emergency. [N.J. Stat. Ann. § 26:2H-12.8] If a patient does not give informed consent, the physician will explain the reasons in the medical record. [N.J. Admin. Code § 8:43-G-4.1(a)(7)]
- **Incapacity:** Executive officers of state or county mental or correctional institutions or juvenile facilities may consent to essential medical treatment of incompetent persons confined in or placed by those facilities if there is no known parent or guardian competent to consent to the treatment or if after reasonable notice the parent or guardian refuses or fails to execute written consent or denial to the treatment. [N.J. Stat. Ann. § 30:4-7.2] If the patient is unable to give informed consent, then the consent of the next of kin, or guardian, or by advanced directive should be sought. [N.J. Admin. Code § 8:43G-4.1(a)(7)] If a person lacks capacity the health care representative can make decisions on behalf of the person, even if a legal guardian is appointed, unless the terms of the legal guardian appointment or court decree indicate otherwise. [N.J. Stat. Ann. § 26:2H-61]

- **Minors:** Parental notice is required for treatment of a minor who appears to have been sexually assaulted, unless it is not in the minor's best interests, but emergency care may be provided if the parents cannot be located. [N.J. Stat. Ann. § 9:17A-4]

NEW MEXICO

- **Emergency:** A person who renders care in good faith at the scene of an emergency is immune from liability. [N.M. Stat. Ann. § 24-10-3] A physician may administer a psychotropic medication in order to protect the client from serious harm on an emergency basis. The medical record should include a report explaining the emergency and the reason other less drastic treatment without consent would not work. [N.M. Stat. Ann. § 43-1-15]
- **Incapacity:** Any person regardless of age can consent to care for a sexually transmitted disease or her own pregnancy. [N.M. Stat. Ann. §§ 24-1-9, 24-1-13] If a person is not competent, consent can be obtained from the legal guardian or other person authorized by law. [N.M. Stat. Ann. §§ 24-2B-3, 45-5-209] A surrogate may make a health care decision on behalf of a person who lacks capacity when there is no agent or guardian. Family members are listed as potential surrogates followed by someone with special care for the person. If there is a disagreement among surrogates, the health provider may follow the decision of the majority. N.M. Stat. Ann. § 24-7A-5]
- **Minors:** Anyone standing in loco parentis to a minor may consent to emergency medical attention for the minor if a parent cannot be located with reasonable efforts. [N.M. Stat. Ann. § 24-10-2] An emancipated minor or minor who is married may render consent to medical care which cannot later by disaffirmed. [N.M. Stat. Ann. §§ 24-10-1 & 24-10-2] A minor can consent to an HIV test on himself. [N.M. Stat. Ann. § 24-2B-3]

NEW YORK

- **Emergency:** Informed consent is only required before non-emergency procedures. [N.Y. Comp. Code R. & Regs. tit. 10, § 405.7(b)(9)]
- **Incapacity:** Generally, a person who is not capable of providing informed consent may receive treatment with the consent of close relatives (a parent, spouse, or adult child) or a judicially appointed surrogate (a guardian, conservator, or committee), or by court order. In the absence of one of those surrogates or where those surrogates are willing, a surrogate decision-making committee may consent. [N.Y. Comp. Codes R. & Regs. tit. 14, § 710.1]
- **Minors:** A medical practitioner may render emergency medical attention to a minor without parental consent when an attempt to obtain consent would delay treatment that would increase the risk to the minor's life or health. [N.Y. Pub. Health Law § 2504] A person who is married or pregnant can consent to medical care for herself. [N.Y. Pub. Health Law § 2504]

NORTH CAROLINA

- **Emergency:** Informed consent is only required before non-emergency procedures or treatments. [10A N.C. Admin. Code 13B.3302]
- **Incapacity:** Any adult of sound mind may make an advance instruction regarding mental health treatment, which may include consent to or refusal of mental health treatment when the principal has been determined to be incapable. Such an advance instruction may be combined with a health care power of attorney. [N.C. Gen. Stat. §§ 122C-72 & 122C-77, 32A-16]
- **Minors:** A physician may provide emergency treatment to a minor where: (1) a parent cannot be located or contacted after reasonable effort when the minor needs the treatment; (2) an effort to contact a parent would cause a delay that would seriously worsen the minor's condition or endanger his or her life; (3) the minor's identity is unknown; or (4) the parents refuse to consent, and the need for immediate treatment is so apparent that the delay involved in obtaining a court order would endanger the minor's life or seriously worsen his or her condition, in which case a second medical opinion shall be obtained. [N.C. Gen. Stat. § 90-21.1]

NORTH DAKOTA

- **Incapacity:** Persons who may consent to health care for an incapacitated person are, in the following order of priority: (1) a person to whom the patient has given a durable power of attorney that includes the authority to make health care decisions, unless the court has authorized a guardian to make medical decisions; (2) the appointed guardian; or (3) any persons from the following classes who have maintained significant contacts with the patient: (a) the patient's spouse; (b) children older than age 18; (c) parents, including a stepparent; (d) adult siblings; (e) grandparents; (f) grandchildren older than age 18; (g) close relative or friend older than age 18. [N.D. Cent. Code § 23-12-13]
- **Minors:** Persons who may consent to health care for a minor are, in order of priority, the same as those listed under the Incapacity category. [N.D. Cent. Code 23-12-13] A minor may consent to emergency treatment in a life-threatening situation without parental consent. [N.D. Cent. Code § 14-10-17.1]

OHIO

- **Emergency:** No person is liable for rendering care at the scene of an emergency outside the doctor's office or hospital unless there is willful or wanton misconduct. [Ohio Rev. Code Ann. § 2305.23] No physician or registered nurse advising emergency medical services through communication device or telemetering will be liable unless there is willful or wanton misconduct. [Ohio Rev. Code Ann. § 4765.49]
- **Incapacity:** An adult of sound mind may create a durable power of attorney for health care. The attorney-in-fact can make health care decisions for the principal. [Ohio Rev. Code Ann. §§ 1337.12, 1337.13]
- **Minors:** A minor can consent to an HIV test. [Ohio Rev. Code Ann. § 3701.242]

OKLAHOMA

- **Emergency:** No informed consent required in an emergency. [Okla. Stat. tit. 36 § 6804]
- **Incapacity:** An attorney-in-fact previously designated by a person may make mental health treatment decisions for the person in the event that the person is certified as incapable of giving informed consent to mental health treatment that is necessary. [Okla. Stat. tit. 43A, §§ 11-104 through 11-107]
- **Minors:** A minor may consent to emergency medical treatment if delaying treatment to obtain parental or spousal consent would endanger his or her life or health; the provider must, however, make a reasonable attempt to inform the minor's parent or spouse. Any spouse of a minor may consent to treatment when the minor is unable to consent because of physical or mental incapacity. When a minor is incapacitated and has no known relatives, two physicians may agree on the treatment. [Okla. Stat. tit. 63, § 2602]

OREGON

- **Incapacity:** A person of sound mind may appoint a representative to make decisions regarding mental health treatment on his or her behalf in the event that he or she becomes unable to evaluate information or communicate, to the extent that he or she lacks capacity to consent to mental health treatment. [Or. Rev. Stat. §§ 127.700 through 127.705 & 127.712] A health care representative can be appointed to make decisions on behalf of a person who lacks capacity, or the person may set forth advance directives in advance regarding the medical choices he would like made. [Or. Rev. Stat. §§ 127.535, 127.550] A physician may withdraw life sustaining procedures if no surrogate decision maker is available and if certain conditions are met, i.e., a terminal illness, unconsciousness, when no benefit would come from the procedures, etc. [Or. Rev. Stat. § 127.535]
- **Minors:** A minor age 15 or older may consent to medical or surgical treatment without parental consent. [Or. Rev. Stat. § 109.640] When a parent is not available to consent to the emergency medical care for a minor, a judge of the juvenile court can authorize care. [Or. Rev. Stat. § 419B.110]

PENNSYLVANIA

- **Emergency:** In an emergency there is no duty to obtain informed consent. [40 Pa. Stat. § 1303.504]
- **Incapacity:** A person may set forth a durable power of attorney authorizing someone to act on their behalf making medical decisions if needed, or a person can be declared incapacitated and a guardian established. [20 Pa. Cons. Stat. § 5604, 20 Pa. Cons. Stat. § 5512.1]
- **Minors:** Parental consent is not needed for treatment of a minor when an attempt to obtain consent would cause a delay of treatment that would increase the risk to the minor's life or health. [35 Pa. Stat. § 10104] A parent or legal guardian may confer

the power to consent to health care to an adult friend or family member. [11 Pa. Stat. § 2513]

RHODE ISLAND

- **Emergency:** Informed consent is impliedly waived in connection with emergency services rendered outside a hospital or in connection with EMS training, unless the treatment is inconsistent with the level of the person's training and experience and unless it involved gross negligence or willful misconduct. [R.I. Gen. Laws § 23-17.6-5]
- **Incapacity:** The individual durable power of attorney allows a health care agent to consent when the individual lacks capacity. [R.I. Gen. Laws § 23-4.10-2]
- **Minors:** Any person age 16 or older or who is married may consent to routine emergency or surgical care. [R.I. Gen. Laws § 23-4.6-1]

SOUTH CAROLINA

- **Emergency:** No consent is necessary for treatment of a patient unable to consent if no representative of the patient is available immediately and the delay of trying to locate an authorized person presents a substantial risk of death, serious permanent disfigurement, loss or impairment of a bodily member or organ, or other serious threat to the patient's health. No consent is needed for treatment to relieve suffering if an authorized person is unavailable. [S.C. Code Ann. § 44-66-40]
- **Incapacity:** Health care decisions regarding an adult, or a married or emancipated minor, who is unable to consent, may be made by the following, in order of priority: court-appointed guardian; person named in a durable power of attorney; person given priority to make health care decisions for the patient under another statute; spouse, unless legally separated; parent or adult child; adult sibling, grandparent or adult grandchild; any other relative with a close personal relationship with the patient; person with authority to make health care decisions for the patient under another statute. [S.C. Code Ann. §§ 44-66-20 & 44-66-30] No consent is needed for treatment that is necessary to relieve suffering; restore bodily function; or preserve the life, health, or bodily integrity of a patient unable to consent, where no one authorized to make health care decisions for the patient is available. [S.C. Code Ann. § 44-66-50] The preceding does not apply where the physician knows that the health care is contrary to the patient's religious beliefs. [S.C. Code Ann. § 44-66-60]
- **Minors:** A health care provider may render any necessary health services to a minor without parental consent, with the exception of an operation. An operation may be performed without consent if essential to the child's health or life. [S.C. Code Ann. § 20-7-290] A minor age 16 or older may consent to any health services other than an operation. [S.C. Code Ann. § 20-7-280] A minor parent can consent for care of his/her child. [S.C. Code Ann. § 20-7-300] Non-emergency health care decisions for minors can be made by others in the following order of priority: legal guardian, parent, grandparent or adult sibling, other relatives with a close relationship to the person, authorized designee of the department. [S.C. Code Ann. § 44-26-60]

SOUTH DAKOTA

- **Emergency:** Consent is not required in an emergency. [S.D. Codified Laws § 34-12C-8]
- **Incapacity:** A health care decision may be made by another person for a person who (1) has been declared legally incompetent, (2) has had a guardian appointed, or (3) whose physician has determined that he or she is incapable of giving informed consent. Such a determination by a physician is effective until either the physician or a court later determines that the person is capable of giving informed consent or that the diagnosis is no longer valid. An attending physician may decline to determine a person's capacity for informed consent and a health care provider may, but need not, rely on any such determination. [S.D. Codified Laws § 34-12C-2] The family members of an incapacitated person who has no legal guardian or attorney-in-fact may consent to medical treatment for the person, in the following order of priority: spouse; adult child; parent; adult sibling; grandparent or adult grandchild; aunt or uncle, or adult niece or nephew. [S.D. Codified Laws §§ 34-12C-3 & 34-12C-6]
- **Minors:** A minor may receive emergency medical treatment without parental consent if a parent is not immediately available and delaying treatment to obtain consent would threaten the minor's life or health. [S.D. Codified Laws § 20-9-4.2]

TENNESSEE

- **Minors:** Parental consent is not necessary for emergency medical treatment of a minor in order to save the minor's life or prevent worsening of his or her medical condition, but a reasonable effort must be made to notify the minor's parents before treatment begins. [Tenn. Code Ann. § 63-6-222]

TEXAS

- **Emergency:** Consent for emergency medical care is not required when a person can not communicate because of injury, accident, illness, or when unconscious and suffers from a life-threatening injury or illness. A court may order treatment for a person in an emergency when the person is unable to consent to prevent serious bodily injury or loss of life. [Tex. Health & Safety Code § 773.008] A health care provider's failure to disclose the risks of treatment may not be considered negligent in the case of an emergency. [Tex. Civ. Prac. & Rem. Code § 74.106] In the case of emergency care, there is no obligation to obtain consent from a surrogate decision maker. [Tex. Health & Safety Code Ann. § 313.003]
- **Incapacity:** The following persons, in order of priority, may consent to treatment of a hospital or nursing home patient who is mentally or physically incapable of communicating: the patient's spouse; adult child (with waiver and consent of other adult children); a majority of available adult children; parents; the person the patient identified to act for him or her before becoming incapacitated; nearest living relative; or clergy member. [Tex. Health & Safety Code Ann. § 313.004]

- **Minors:** Consent for emergency care for a minor is not required when there is a life-threatening injury of illness, and the parents or guardian are not present. [Tex. Health & Safety Code § 773.008] When a parent is unable to consent for a minor, the following may consent: a grandparent, adult sibling, adult aunt or uncle, an educational institution or adult that has written authority to consent, the court, an adult responsible under juvenile court proceedings, a peace officer who has a minor in custody, and the Texas Youth Commission for a child who has been committed. [Tex. Fam. Code § 32.001]

UTAH

- **Emergency:** Health care providers who render emergency medical care in good faith to a patient have implied consent of the patient where the patient is unable to give his or her consent and where there is no legal representative available to consent to emergency treatment. [Utah Code Ann. § 26-8a-601] A person who is terminally ill may establish an advance directive to withhold life sustaining measures, but an emergency provider is not bound by the directive unless the person who is ill is identified as a person with a directive such as through an identifying bracelet. [Utah Code Ann. § 75-2-1105.5]
- **Incapacity:** A guardian may be appointed to make decisions on behalf of a person who is incapacitated. [Utah Code Ann. § 75-5-303] The following can consent to health care: a parent for a minor child, a married person for a spouse, a person acting in loco parentis for a minor, a person 18 or over for a parent, any person 18 years of age or older, a female of any age in connection with pregnancy and childbirth, or an adult sibling or grandparent in the absence of a parent. [Utah Code Ann. § 78-14-5] When a person has a terminal illness and lacks the capacity to consent, life-sustaining procedures may be withdrawn when the physician has the written concurrence of another physician and the spouse, parent, or adult child. If the family member making the decision is not the legal guardian, the document must have two witnesses as well. [Utah Code Ann. § 75-2-1107]
- **Minors:** Consent for medical treatment for a minor as indicated in the section on incapacity. [Utah Code Ann. § 78-14-5]

VERMONT

- **Emergency:** There is no right of action to recover for medical malpractice based on lack of informed consent in the case of an emergency. Further, in an informed consent suit, it is a defense that consent was not reasonably possible. [Vt. Stat. Ann. tit. 12, § 1909(b) & (c); Vt. Stat. Ann. tit. 18, § 1852]
- **Incapacity:** Adults can designate someone with a durable power of attorney for health care in the event of later incapacity through an advanced directive. [Vt. Stat. Ann. tit. 18, § 5263]
- **Minors:** A minor 12 years of age and over can consent for treatment for drug dependence, venereal disease, or alcoholism. [Vt. Stat. Ann. tit. 18, § 4226]

VIRGINIA

- **Emergency:** Consent is not required in an emergency for mental health or drug abuse treatment. Consent for continued treatment that lasts more than 24 hours for care rendered in an emergency should be obtained. If capacity of the person to consent is in question, an independent evaluation should be performed by a qualified professional not participating the person's care. [12 Va. Admin. Code § 35-115-70].
- **Incapacity:** Advanced directives can be put in place including physician procedure when advance directive is lacking. [Va. Health Care Decisions Act, Va. Code Ann. § 54.1-2981 through 54.1-2993]
- **Minors:** Where a minor has been separated from parental custody, a judge, superintendent of social services, director, or principal executive officer of the agency or institution that has control of the minor's custody, or any person in loco parentis, may authorize necessary surgical or medical treatment. Where that person's consent cannot be obtained within a reasonable time and delay may adversely affect the minor's recovery, consent is impliedly waived, but the minor's own consent is needed if he or she is at least age 14 and physically able to consent. [Va. Code Ann. § 54.1-2969]

WASHINGTON

- **Emergency:** Consent to treatment is implied in a recognized health care emergency if the patient is not competent to give informed consent and a person authorized to consent on his or her behalf is not available. [Wash. Rev. Code § 7.70.050]
- **Incapacity:** Informed consent for an incompetent person may be obtained from, in order of priority: the patient's appointed guardian; the person to whom the patient has given a power of attorney for health care decisions; the patient's spouse; the patient's adult children; the patient's parents; the patient's adult siblings. [Wash. Rev. Code § 7.70.065]
- **Minors:** Health care providers are immune from liability for failure of informed consent if a parent consents to treatment of the minor regardless of whether the parents are married or separated, whether the consenting parent is the custodial parent, and whether or not the parents agree about the issue of consent. [Wash. Rev. Code § 26.09.310]

WEST VIRGINIA

- **Emergency:** No consent is needed for emergency medical services when the person is unable to consent and there is no person reasonably available to consent; however, this does not contravene objections to treatment on the grounds of religion, in a living will, or in a do not resuscitate order when the treating physician is aware of the will or order. [W. Va. Code § 16-4C-17]
- **Incapacity:** When a person is or becomes incapacitated and has no legal guardian or representative under a medical power of attorney, the attending physician shall select

a surrogate decision maker who is authorized to make health care decisions for the incapacitated person without a court order. [W. Va. Code § 16-30-7]

- **Minors:** If there is a substantial possibility that a minor will suffer death or serious disability, disfigurement, or suffering as a result of the refusal of a parent to consent to necessary medical treatment, a court may appoint a special guardian to consent to necessary treatment. [W. Va. Code § 49-6B-1]

WISCONSIN

- **Incapacity:** A person age 18 or older and of sound mind may voluntarily execute a power of attorney for health care, which will take effect upon a finding of incapacity by two physicians or by a physician and a psychologist. [Wis. Stat. 155.05]

WYOMING

- **Emergency:** Consent is not required for emergency surgery. [Wyo. Stat. § 35-2-115] Consent is implied/waived where volunteer ambulances or emergency vehicles furnish emergency medical services, unless grossly negligent. [Wyo. Stat. § 1-1-120]
- **Incapacity:** When a person is suspected by a law enforcement officer or examiner to be mentally ill, treatment may be given during an emergency detention period if the incompetent person's guardian consents, but that consent is not necessary where treatment is limited to diagnosis or evaluation or where treatment is necessary to prevent immediate serious physical harm. [Wyo. Stat. Ann. § 25-10-109]
- **Minors:** The court may consent to emergency medical or surgical examination or treatment of a minor taken into custody under the Juvenile Justice Act if a qualified physician believes that the minor has a serious physical condition or illness that requires prompt treatment. [Wyo. Stat. Ann. § 14-6-220]

PART 2

Joint Commission Survey Questions and Answers

INTRODUCTION

This section presents first-person accounts of the Joint Commission accreditation process from the point of view of the emergency department. The following interviews with emergency department managers and hospital accreditation officers describe the staff preparation activities demonstrated by recently surveyed hospitals, their methods of sharing information about critical performance improvement initiatives, and their overall 2007 survey experience. In addition, several hospitals share tips on how best to prepare for a Joint Commission visit.

SURVEY FOCUS

Question: What was the Joint Commission survey team focus when it visited your emergency department in 2007?

Answers:

Amber Styles
Director of Quality Services
Lawrence Memorial Hospital
Lawrence, Kansas

They focused on security and suicide—security of the department, like being able to lock it down, security of the physical environment, and then our procedures and protocols for dealing with suicide. They also focused on medication safety. They didn't focus on medication reconciliation in the emergency department. It was more on identification and labeling. The other thing they focused on was patient flow.

Debbie Wingate, ASN
Emergency Room Director
Lake City Medical Center
Lake City, Florida

They focused on a lot of topics, but for the emergency department specifically the focus was on medicine reconciliation and eMAR (Electronic Medication Administration Record). They looked at the process as far as how we were doing in getting the medicine reconciliation completed.

Laura Giles, BS
Nurse Manager
The New York Hospital Medical Center of Queens
Flushing, New York

They focused on hand washing in the emergency department, completion of documentation, and medication reconciliation.

Lorrie Mortensen, RN
Chief Nursing Officer
Alta Vista Regional Hospital
Las Vegas, New Mexico

They looked at reporting structure for any quality or safety concerns and how we notify patients of that requirement.

Patricia Erbst, RN
Emergency Department Director
Community Hospital of Los Gatos, Inc.
Los Gatos, California

They really focused on suicidal documentation and what we do with the psychiatric patients—that was a big focus—and also how we store drugs.

Debbie Fleischmann, MPA, RN, CNAA-DC
Administrative Director of Emergency Services
Howard County General Hospital
Columbia, Maryland

They focused on safety, but one of the big things they focused on was safety for psychiatric patients. That got a lot of attention. They were looking at how we processed those patients. They were looking at the safety of the environment—looking at what kind of facilities we had to care for these patients, what safeguards we provided; and also construction design. If an emergency department has a dedicated psychiatric area, like we do, they were very much looking at that; looking at it architecturally.

Rita Garner, RN
Emergency Department Manager
Delta Medical Center
Memphis, Tennessee

They actually focused on our Broselow cart—making sure the correct modules were in each drawer.

STAFF EDUCATION AND TRAINING

Question: Have you changed your staff education and training in response to the Joint Commission's focus on continuous readiness, unannounced surveys, and tracer methodology?

Answers:

Amber Styles
Director of Quality Services
Lawrence Memorial Hospital
Lawrence, Kansas

Yes. We do ongoing education and continual monthly tracers, whereas in the past we did not. We started it right before the Joint Commission visit.

Debbie Wingate, ASN
Emergency Room Director
Lake City Medical Center
Lake City, Florida

This is our second go around for using the tracer methodology, so we are pretty well up to date. We have continuous education every month with regard to the Joint Commission.

Laura Giles, BS
Nurse Manager
The New York Hospital Medical Center of Queens
Flushing, New York

Yes. In this hospital, we do a mock survey at least every month. It's a much more aggressive program.

Lorrie Mortensen, RN
Chief Nursing Officer
Alta Vista Regional Hospital
Las Vegas, New Mexico

We have not since their visit, but we have in general for the entire hospital—not just the emergency room. We've done so through education, through posters, through executive rounding, and manager oversight.

Patricia Erbst, RN
Emergency Department Director
Community Hospital of Los Gatos, Inc.
Los Gatos, California

We were doing that before, in preparation of the visit, and it's still the same.

Debbie Fleischmann, MPA, RN, CNAA-DC
Administrative Director of Emergency Services
Howard County General Hospital
Columbia, Maryland

Yes. We do mock tracers as part of our preparation for site visits. The tracer methodology is incorporated into the mock surveys we conduct as well as discussed in staff meetings. As we were approaching the window of opportunity where we thought they would be coming, we did three hospital-wide mocks, but we are now doing monthly mock tracers on two units, which means each month two units get a mock tracer.

Rita Garner, RN
Emergency Department Manager
Delta Medical Center
Memphis, Tennessee

Our charge nurse is taking care of that. She is doing additional education and training, which just started on January 1.

Question: Do you think your staff feels better prepared and less anxious when called upon by the surveyors during a visit?

Answers:

Amber Styles
Director of Quality Services
Lawrence Memorial Hospital
Lawrence, Kansas

Yes.

Debbie Wingate, ASN
Emergency Room Director
Lake City Medical Center
Lake City, Florida

Yes, because we have continuous education all year long regardless of whether we know they are coming or not.

Laura Giles, BS
Nurse Manager
The New York Hospital Medical Center of Queens
Flushing, New York

No.

Lorrie Mortensen, RN
Chief Nursing Officer
Alta Vista Regional Hospital
Las Vegas, New Mexico

Yes, I do.

Patricia Erbst, RN
Emergency Department Director
Community Hospital of Los Gatos, Inc.
Los Gatos, California

Yes.

Debbie Fleischmann, MPA, RN, CNAA-DC
Administrative Director of Emergency Services
Howard County General Hospital
Columbia, Maryland

I think they always feel anxious, but the preparation does help. So, they are well prepared but still anxious.

Rita Garner, RN
Emergency Department Manager
Delta Medical Center
Memphis, Tennessee

Yes.

PERFORMANCE IMPROVEMENT

Question: How did you demonstrate performance improvement for the surveyors? What areas did you focus on this year?

Answers:

Amber Styles
Director of Quality Services
Lawrence Memorial Hospital
Lawrence, Kansas

We focused on medication reconciliation. We had a big revamp of how we did our radiology orders.

Debbie Wingate, ASN
Emergency Room Director
Lake City Medical Center
Lake City, Florida

We focused on the emergency department dashboard and turnaround times. It's all on the computer, so we just have to print it off for them.

Laura Giles, BS
Nurse Manager
The New York Hospital Medical Center of Queens
Flushing, New York

We focused on the Joint Commission Core Measures that everyone in the country is measured against. The cath lab for MI, treatment of pneumonia—that's the big focus, and we've made very significant inroads on that over the past year.

Lorrie Mortensen, RN
Chief Nursing Officer
Alta Vista Regional Hospital
Las Vegas, New Mexico

Our primary area of focus has been in the area of Core Measures.

Patricia Erbst, RN
Emergency Department Director
Community Hospital of Los Gatos, Inc.
Los Gatos, California

We focused on emergency preparedness, and we focused on all the Core Measures and following through with CORE Measures. We monitor this monthly through quality and risk management. We have graphs. We do customer satisfaction with scoring. We interview patients.

Debbie Fleischmann, MPA, RN, CNAA-DC
Administrative Director of Emergency Services
Howard County General Hospital
Columbia, Maryland

We focused on medication reconciliation. As part of our performance improvement, we also looked at fall safety and safe management of psychiatric patient belongings.

Rita Garner, RN
Emergency Department Manager
Delta Medical Center
Memphis, Tennessee

We focused on EMTALA and triaging categories. We provided education on going from the three-level triage classification system to the five-level system. We have not gone to the five categories yet, but we plan to as of April 2008.

PATIENT SAFETY

Question: Was there an apparent emphasis on the National Patient Safety Goals (NPSGs) and patient safety in general? How did the focus on the NPSGs affect your ED policies and procedures; e.g., improve communications; improve medication safety; decrease infection rate?

Answers:

Amber Styles
Director of Quality Services
Lawrence Memorial Hospital
Lawrence, Kansas

Yes, there was a focus on it, but I don't really think it changed much for the emergency department. On the medication labeling, we really had to focus on that and on the medication reconciliation, and even to this day, we continue to focus on that.

Debbie Wingate, ASN
Emergency Room Director
Lake City Medical Center
Lake City, Florida

Yes, there was an emphasis. The biggest effects we felt were in the areas of improved communication and patient safety with the medicine reconciliation process.

Laura Giles, BS
Nurse Manager
The New York Hospital Medical Center of Queens
Flushing, New York

I don't have an answer for this one specifically, but I will say that our policies are constantly being reviewed.

Lorrie Mortensen, RN
Chief Nursing Officer
Alta Vista Regional Hospital
Las Vegas, New Mexico

Yes, but I can't say that I saw it specifically just for the emergency department, at least not with the survey we had in October. It was more hospital-wide. And I can't really say that it affected anything in the emergency department.

Patricia Erbst, RN
Emergency Department Director
Community Hospital of Los Gatos, Inc.
Los Gatos, California

We have a whole book dedicated to National Patient Safety Goals—a whole binder—and we closely monitor each National Patient Safety Goal and turn that in monthly. Then we do graphs so we can see where we need to improve.

We did it pre-survey; we did it for a year. We knew that was going to be a big focus, so we created the binder, and we educated the staff. As I mentioned before, we monitored each goal in the binder monthly. This was turned in to risk management/quality, and they collated it and then prepared it. They did graphs on who was doing better and who was doing worse. It was all posted—each department—and we presented it at our safety meetings.

Debbie Fleischmann, MPA, RN, CNAA-DC
Administrative Director of Emergency Services
Howard County General Hospital
Columbia, Maryland

There was absolutely a focus on the National Patient Safety Goals, and one of the big things that we've been looking at is hand off—hand off of the patient when it comes time to transport the patient to another department, such as diagnostic imaging. We worked on communication between departments. We developed a hand-off report form that we call the "ticket to ride" for patients who are being transported to ancillary services for CAT scans, X-rays, and things like that so that the receiving departments would have basic information related to patient safety when they received that patient in their department.

Rita Garner, RN
Emergency Department Manager
Delta Medical Center
Memphis, Tennessee

Yes, it improved both communications and safety.

Question: The 2007 National Patient Safety Goals include a new goal for hospitals:
Goal 13: **Encourage patients' active involvement in their own care as a patient safety strategy.**
13A: **Define and communicate the means for patients and families to report concerns about patient safety and encourage them to do so.**
Given that this was a new goal for 2007, how did you approach this? What, if anything, did you do differently to achieve this goal? Also, do you feel the surveyors focused on that goal?

Answers:

Amber Styles
Director of Quality Services
Lawrence Memorial Hospital
Lawrence, Kansas

We have the director's name, phone number, and a picture posted in every single patient room, and then we also have the number to the quality department, in case they want to talk to someone outside of the department. We also have patient safety numbers throughout. Staff members are also trained to use scripting to prompt patients to voice any questions or concerns that they may have.

The surveyors did focus on it in the beginning, and then as they realized that patients have a lot of channels to voice their concerns, they stopped.

Debbie Wingate, ASN
Emergency Room Director
Lake City Medical Center
Lake City, Florida

I don't really have an answer for this.

Laura Giles, BS
Nurse Manager
The New York Hospital Medical Center of Queens
Flushing, New York

We have signs up that direct the patients to participate in their care.

Lorrie Mortensen, RN
Chief Nursing Officer
Alta Vista Regional Hospital
Las Vegas, New Mexico

To answer the last question, no, as far as our survey from October 2007. I didn't see the Joint Commission surveyors focusing on that at all. We have just done that through education. We've changed a couple of forms, documentation requirements in our electronic medical record, to make sure that the patient was involved in their decision making and knew what their plan of care was—how their plan of care was being directed.

Patricia Erbst, RN
Emergency Department Director
Community Hospital of Los Gatos, Inc.
Los Gatos, California

We made sure we were telling the patients we were washing our hands before we would take care of them. We were checking identification when we went into the room. We were checking it for their safety—making sure it was for the right patient, the right medication, the right dose—all those things. And if the patients had any questions about their medicines or they saw anything that they thought was unsafe, we told them to let us know.

Debbie Fleischmann, MPA, RN, CNAA-DC
Administrative Director of Emergency Services
Howard County General Hospital
Columbia, Maryland

They did not focus on it—at least not in the emergency department. They did not focus on direct patient involvement, but in terms of the safety aspect of that goal, what we have done is, we've combined that with the issue of medication reconciliation, which includes a focus on increasing the patient's involvement in verifying that the information we've put down about their medications is indeed accurate. It's not just enough for the nurse to record it in the computer. We want the patient, with a family member if the patient can't speak for him/herself, to sit down with the nurse at the computer and do a verification of the information. Our goal is to do this with every patient or a patient's family member, if that is more appropriate.

Rita Garner, RN
Emergency Department Manager
Delta Medical Center
Memphis, Tennessee

Yes, they did focus on this goal. As far as the emergency room was concerned, the nurses did a lot more patient education—encouraging the patients to be more involved, making sure the patients understood why we wanted them to participate in their own safety. They also encouraged patients to report anything they were concerned about.

ORGAN DONATION

Question: The Joint Commission has stepped up its emphasis on increasing organ donations. Are you doing anything differently in response to this? For example, have you changed any policies and procedures as a result of this increased emphasis?

Answers:

Amber Styles
Director of Quality Services
Lawrence Memorial Hospital
Lawrence, Kansas

No, not at this time. But we won an award for highest tissue conversion rate in May of last year.

Debbie Wingate, ASN
Emergency Room Director
Lake City Medical Center
Lake City, Florida

Other than what we are required to do, no. We speak to each family as that incident occurs, but we haven't changed any of our policies and procedures.

Laura Giles, BS
Nurse Manager
The New York Hospital Medical Center of Queens
Flushing, New York

We aren't really doing anything differently. We are primarily using the policies and procedures we already had in place.

Lorrie Mortensen, RN
Chief Nursing Officer
Alta Vista Regional Hospital
Las Vegas, New Mexico

We already had an organ donation plan here and have worked with our statewide organ procurement agency, and our stats for either tissue or organ donation have been at 100 percent for the last, I think it has been two, almost three years, now. So we didn't change anything.

Patricia Erbst, RN
Emergency Department Director
Community Hospital of Los Gatos, Inc.
Los Gatos, California

No, because we always have to call the transplant bank and tell them of any deaths in the emergency room. The donor network—that's who we call.

Debbie Fleischmann, MPA, RN, CNAA-DC
Administrative Director of Emergency Services
Howard County General Hospital
Columbia, Maryland

No. We have not changed any policies. Maryland is one of the states where the legislature has taken action concerning organ donation and extends authority to the Living Legacy Foundation, which is our statewide organ and tissue donation group. So we had a pretty solid process in place for staff needing to call and make referrals when they know that a patient is expiring or there is a withdrawal of life support. There's a requirement for them to call as soon as that is evident. It's a very solid program, and we haven't changed anything other than to focus a little more on staff education, but our policies and procedures haven't changed.

Rita Garner, RN
Emergency Department Manager
Delta Medical Center
Memphis, Tennessee

No, because we were compliant with this before they came here this year.

SURVEY PREPARATION ADVICE

Question: What advice can you share with other emergency departments that would help them prepare for a Joint Commission site visit?

Answers:

Amber Styles
Director of Quality Services
Lawrence Memorial Hospital
Lawrence, Kansas

My advice would be to have pharmacists in the emergency department. I wish we had a pharmacist in the emergency department for medication safety.

Debbie Wingate, ASN
Emergency Room Director
Lake City Medical Center
Lake City, Florida

I don't know if every facility is going to eMARs. This is kind of an HCA thing, but certainly if they can do anything as far as their medicine reconciliation, that seems to be the big emphasis for the emergency departments, or at least for our facility. Also, have good policies and procedures for bed holds in the ED.

Laura Giles, BS
Nurse Manager
The New York Hospital Medical Center of Queens
Flushing, New York

Constant drilling, reviews, and morning huddles to prepare people.

Lorrie Mortensen, RN
Chief Nursing Officer
Alta Vista Regional Hospital
Las Vegas, New Mexico

They were in and out so fast, so it was really a focus on how we are notifying our patients that they can report any safety or quality of concerns and issues to the Joint Commission; that's what they primarily focused on.

Patricia Erbst, RN
Emergency Department Director
Community Hospital of Los Gatos, Inc.
Los Gatos, California

I would say just to make sure they have current record keeping. Also, they love to see improvement, and they like to see graphs, so make sure they have it posted on a wall and can actually go to the wall and read it without having to dig through a bunch of papers.

We have a big bulletin board dedicated to quality and risk management and JCAHO, and it shows your progress. They liked all that because they knew we were paying attention to it.

Debbie Fleischmann, MPA, RN, CNAA-DC
Administrative Director of Emergency Services
Howard County General Hospital
Columbia, Maryland

Really prepare the staff. They don't really want to talk to the managers. Make sure the staff knows the information; also, if the staff gets stumped by a question, make sure they are able to verbalize who they would seek out to get the information they need.

Rita Garner, RN
Emergency Department Manager
Delta Medical Center
Memphis, Tennessee

You're never ready. Keep preparing!

Part 3

Hospital Accreditation Standards Analysis

INTRODUCTION

Part 3 of the *Emergency Department Compliance Manual* analyzes the standards in the *Comprehensive Manual for Hospitals: The Official Handbook* (CAMH) published by the Joint Commission on Accreditation of Healthcare Organizations (Joint Commission) and updated quarterly. Part 3 was prepared based on the new standards published on the Joint Commission's website, *www.jointcommission.org,* effective January 1, 2007 and July 1, 2007. The website contains a cross reference for readers to compare the 2005 to the 2006 standards.

The information in Part 3 is presented in a chart format for easy reference. The chart format contains four columns: Standard, Comments, Evidence, and Staff Questions.

- The **Standard** column designates those particular Joint Commission standards and Elements of Performance that uniquely apply to the Emergency Department.
- The **Comments** column provides a brief explanation of each standard and special consideration for the Emergency Department.
- The **Evidence** column outlines specific types of evidence that may be used to show Emergency Department compliance with the standard. The types of evidence suggested include both written documentation review and physical inspection.
- The **Staff Questions** column lists detailed questions to use in preparing staff for the Joint Commission survey.

ETHICS, RIGHTS, AND RESPONSIBILITIES

Standard	Comments	Evidence	Staff Questions
RI.1.10 RI.1.20 RI.1.30	**Ethical Issues** **Conflicts of Interest** ED policy and procedures, and performance must be in compliance with the hospital's ethics code. Staff members must be well informed about the content and application of the code to ensure business is conducted in an ethical manner. Any relationship between a staff member including physicians that could impact care, treatment, or services should be disclosed to the patient. Care and treatment of patients must be delivered based on patient need, regardless of the hospital's financial implication. Areas of particular impact in the ED include admission, transfer, and discharge of patients. Staff needs to be prepared to discuss the circumstances and the hospital's policy and procedure when a staff member requests not to perform patient care, while still ensuring that the patient's needs will be met. Excuses from patient care include cultural, ethical, and/or religious reasons. *Note:* In an emergency situation, when other accommodations cannot be made, the staff member may need to perform assigned duties so that the patient is not negatively affected by the delivery of care.	• Patient, staff, and physician interviews • Open medical records will be reviewed during the ED tour but closed records may also be reviewed. On the day(s) of the survey ED management and the charge nurse should be familiar with all patient medical records. You may be allowed to pick the medical record used for the surveyor to review • Hospital policy and procedures: - supporting ethical business and patient care practices (e.g., code of ethics, governing body and medical staff bylaws, hospital compliance, conflict of interest, staff rights/exclusion from patient care plan for provision of patient care specific to ED). Staff does not need to know the medical staff bylaws and rules and regulations or the entire governing body bylaws. They only need to know the pertinent applicable components related to ED care, services, and treatments • Marketing materials that accurately represent the hospital. Read the marketing pamphlets, documents, or other material that describes the care in the ED. If the documents state you are a Level I Trauma Center and do not offer those services, then this would be considered a conflict • Ability to demonstrate decisions are based on identified patient care needs per hospital policy and procedure. For example, do you ask for insurance information prior to the patient receiving a Medical Screening Examination (MSE) or is the initial MSE based on the patient's ability to pay? • Pre-employment processes re: staff rights to assess whether the job duties would conflict with the person's cultural values or religious beliefs	• How does your ED ensure adherence to ethical care and business practices? • What is an example of an ethical business practice that is discouraged in the ED? • Does your hospital have a written ethics code? Describe how you were informed about this. What does this code mean in the ED? Can you show me a copy? What is the purpose of the ethics code? • What ethical issues pertain to admission, transfer, discharge, billing and marketing in the ED? • Have you had any of these issues arise in the last year? If so, can you describe them? How were they handled? What was the final outcome? • What is your policy and procedure if a staff member has a relationship with another organization such as a nursing home, home care, hospice, ambulance company, or payer (e.g., ownership, contractual arrangement)? • Does the ED allow staff to refer patients and/or their family members to businesses that family members/friends may own or where they work? • How do you define a conflict of interest in the ED? • Can you give me an example of one that has occurred in the ED and what steps were taken? • How and when do you inform patients about the cost of care? How do you know the dollar amount to quote the patient? • When do you ask for insurance information? Do you ask prior to deciding what care, treatment, or services need to be delivered to the patient who requires an emergency procedure? • Do any of your physicians or staff own or have financial interest in a service such as an MRI, CT, or other diagnostic test where your patients are referred when they leave the ED? • What happens when a staff member refuses to

Standard	Comments	Evidence	Staff Questions
			participate in an aspect of patient care such as blood administration for religious or cultural reasons? What do you do to ensure that the patient's care is not impacted? • Does the hospital/ED ask applicants during the interview process if there are any areas of care they cannot participate in prior to employment in the ED?

Standard	Comments	Evidence	Staff Questions
RI.1.40	**External Insurance/HMO Reviews** Care is based on the patient's needs and not on any insurance payment. Policy and procedures must address how to resolve denial-of-care conflicts over care, services, or payment. Needs of patients should take precedence over denial-of-care conflicts: when care or services are subject to internal or external review that results in a denial of care or payment, treatment, and discharge decisions must be made in response to the care needed by the patient, regardless of the recommendations of the review entity. ED leaders and staff should be aware of special utilization review issues pertinent to the ED.	• Patient, staff, and physician interviews • Interviews with ED leaders and staff regarding utilization review criteria that are likely to affect care decisions in the ED • Hospital policy and procedures: - addressing resolution of denial-of-care conflicts re: payment - When to notify the insurance/HMO company that one of its patients is in the ED and pre-authorization is needed • Description of the hospitals' relationship to external entities conducting the utilization review of ED policy and procedures addressing potential disagreement with external organizations' recommendations for treatment and/or discharge • Process for what happens when the ED contacts the insurance/HMO company for pre-authorization and the request for treatment is denied • Case management practices in the ED if any • Documentation of data collected for external utilization review process relevant to the ED • ED PI activities that incorporate information from external utilization review, managed care issues • ED denials for care, treatment, or services data	• How has managed care impacted the ED? • Does the hospital or insurance companies require you to deny care in certain situations? • Describe an instance when care was denied to a patient and explain why. What happened to the patient? • Do you ever deny emergent care to a patient based on what their insurance/HMO says? Do you inform the patient that their insurance company/HMO will not pay for the care? • How does the ED staff interact with the patient's insurance company, HMO, etc., while in the ED? • When does the conversation occur related to charges the patient will incur for this visit?

Standard	Comments	Evidence	Staff Questions
RI.2.10 RI.2.20 RI.2.40 RI.2.50 RI.2.60	**Patient Rights** **Informed Consent** **Consent for Filming** **ED Caregiver ID** These standards require hospitals to address the rights of patients while in the care of the ED. Patients' rights to treatment or service are protected, in compliance with applicable law and regulation. Patients/surrogate decision makers must be involved in all aspects of care and informed of the following rights: privacy, effective communication with hospital caregivers, informed consent, consent for recordings/filming that is not related to patient care, knowledge of professionals providing care, ability to refuse care/treatment, access to protective/advocacy services, confidentiality, security, pain management, end of life care, complaint resolution, personal dignity and a positive image, possible outcomes of care, cultural, spiritual, psychosocial, and personal values, beliefs, and preferences, accommodation to pastoral and other spiritual care, name of the physician or other practitioners delivering care, name of physician primarily responsible of their care. Patients must be informed of the hospital's advance directive policy and procedure. Patients or authorized family members also have the right to access, amend, and receive an accounting of disclosures regarding their health information. The surveyor will use the tracer methodology where care is traced through the hospital and ED to evaluate how different departments and disciplines work together to provide optimal patient care and outcomes. Patients are encouraged to become active in their own care (Joint Commission NPSG 13)	• Patient, staff, and physician interviews • Medical record documentation • The patient/surrogate decision maker is informed within a timeframe specified by the hospital of the name of the Licensed Independent Practitioner (LIP) (physician) primarily responsible for care, as well as the name of any LIPs performing care, treatment, and services • Hospital policy and procedures: - copy of patient rights and responsibilities handouts. This may also be posted in the ED waiting room. - hospital's informed consent policy and procedures, and forms - accessing pastoral care services - pastoral care telephone number readily accessible - hospital's HIPAA policy and procedures - hospital's consent policy and procedure, and form for recording or filming for purposes other than the identification, care, and treatment of the patient • A separate consent is needed if the intent is to use the recording/filming externally. If the recording/filming is used internally, the consent may be part of a general consent to treat or another form if a statement is included in the form regarding the use of the recording/filming. Be prepared for the surveyor to ask numerous questions if you are videotaping care in the ED • Staff orientation materials on patient rights, hospital ethics, and training records • Hospital ethics committee or functioning of ethics resolution process. You may also have a telephone number posted for staff to use for this process • Patient and family education committee or process • Evidence of how the ED communicates information to patients on their rights and responsibilities • List of procedures that require informed consent • Hospital consent forms for patient care designed and written in terms and language the patient can understand	• Does the patient know the name of the physician treating them in the ED? What about the names of other physicians or practitioners, performed procedures, or consults on them in the ED? • Describe how staff learns about patient rights and responsibilities. Is this documented? • Have you participated in any in-service or education on this topic? • How do you communicate to other care givers that the patient has an advance directive? How do you communicate to the Radiology Department or wherever the patient is going for a procedure? • What types of procedures do you obtain informed consent for? Is there a policy and procedure that lists these? What about moderate sedation and blood and blood product administration? • Where and how is patient understanding of the informed consent documented? • What components are included in the informed consent process? • Is informed consent obtained before or after the procedure is performed? • Who obtains informed consent? • What is the role of the nurse re: informed consent? • What is the role of the physician re: informed consent? • Can medical students obtain informed consent? • Show me your consent forms for various procedures, tests, treatments, or patient types. • Who obtains informed consent for invasive radiology procedures off-hours and weekends? • When would you not obtain informed consent for these situations? • What mechanism do you have in place for obtaining informed consent from patients with limited English proficiency? How do you know that the patients understand?

Standard	Comments	Evidence	Staff Questions
		• Examples of executed consent forms • Evidence that the hospital informed consent process for high-risk medications, procedures, blood administration, and moderate sedation includes the *following elements:* nature of the proposed procedure along with the potential benefits, risks, or side effects, including potential problems that might occur during recuperation, the likelihood of achieving goals, reasonable alternatives, the relevant risks, benefits, and side effects related to alternatives, including the possible results of not receiving care, treatment, and services and when indicated, any limitations on the confidentiality of information learned from or about the patient • Documentation of pastoral care in the medical record • Hospital written copy of patients' rights and responsibilities appropriate to patient's language, age, and understanding for common patient populations available/posted in the ED	• Do you have a consent form for recording or filming patients or their care when the purpose is not for medical care, treatment or services (e.g., use for PI or education)? • In the event videotaping is allowed, what policy and procedure are followed? • Describe your policy and procedure for using surrogate decision makers for consent. • What is the procedure staff follow when the hospital cannot provide the care a patient requests? Can you discuss an example of such an incident and how staff responded? • Do you have a medical review process? • Are medical records reviewed for compliance with patient rights policy and procedures? Who performs the review? How often? Where is this data reported? • Who or what resources can staff access if there is an ethical issue regarding a patient's care? • Do you use pastoral care services? When would you access pastoral care services? • How would you access these services? Would this service be documented in the medical record? • Describe your policy and procedure for informing patients of their rights • Are these rights posted? If yes, are these rights in each of the patient rooms in a font that can be read form the stretcher/bed at all times? • What happens if the patient requests a written copy of the rights? • How do you communicate patient rights if the patient speaks another language, cannot read, or is hearing or sight impaired? • Describe your process for allowing patients to access, request amendment, and receive an accounting of disclosure regarding his/her health information • How do you encourage the patient's active involvement in their own care? (Joint Commission NPSG 13)

Standard	Comments	Evidence	Staff Questions
RI.2.30 RI.2.70	**Patient Involvement** **Refusal of Treatment** This standard addresses patients being actively involved in making all decisions about their care, and resolving any dilemmas that may arise (e.g., controversy over end-of-life decision making and pain management). If the patient cannot make health care decisions, a surrogate or representative decision maker (next of kin) is identified, as allowed by law and regulations. The legally responsible representative would then approve care decisions. The family should be as involved in the care as permitted by law and with the permission of the patient/surrogate decision maker. ED staff must know how to determine the appropriate surrogate decision maker. Durable power of attorney, living wills/advance directives, and information supplied by extended care facilities, are often sources of this information.	• Patient, staff, and physician interviews • Medical record documentation • Hospital policy and procedures related to the following: - guardianship - family/surrogate decision makers' involvement in care decisions - access to legal counsel regarding care decisions - patient and family education (e.g., brochure or handouts on ethics process) - specifically resolving conflicts in care decisions/ethical dilemmas • ED staff orientation	• When authorized, does the family or surrogate engage in the patient's care decisions? Where is this documented? • How do you include the patient in the decision regarding his/her care? Where is this documented? • What is the policy and procedure when the patient does not have the mental or physical capacity to make care decisions? • How do you determine who is the next of kin? • How do you determine who the legal surrogate decision maker is? • How are conflicts in care (e.g., end-of-life decisions) resolved? • Can you recall a situation that required an ethics consultation? How/who do you contact for an ethics consultation? • Where would this conflict and resolution be documented? • Is there a hospital or ED-specific committee and/or individual responsible for coordinating the ethics consultation process? • How do you inform patients, families, and staff about your ethics resolution process? • Give me an example of an ethical dilemma re: patient care that occurred in the last 12 months • Do you receive education on ethical issues that may occur in the ED and who to call if an issue arises?

Standard	Comments	Evidence	Staff Questions
RI.2.80	**End-of-Life** The hospital has a mechanism to address end-of-life decision making, specifically related to advance directives, organ donation, and resuscitative services. For example, when a patient comes to the ED with an advanced directive, staff know the process to care for the patient. Adults are given written information about their rights to accept or refuse care, including resuscitative services and life-sustaining treatment. Patients are asked if they have an advance directive which is then documented in the medical record. The patient has the right to modify his/her advance directive at any time. In the absence of an actual advance directive, and in accord with applicable state law, the patient's wishes may be documented within the patient's medical record, when feasible. Evidence of a written advance directive does not hamper his/her ability to receive care. Procedures should ensure thorough communication of the patient's wishes, and there should be a mechanism to assist or refer the patient for help with formulating advance directives upon his/her request. In the ED, processes are implemented for clinicians and the patient's surrogate decision maker to honor the patient's advance directive according to policy and procedure and meeting applicable laws and regulations. In addition, the hospital documents and follows the patient's wishes with respect to organ and tissue donation, to meet the intent of the law. If the hospital cannot meet the patient's wishes regarding end-of-life measures, the patient is notified. For example, the hospital may have religious affiliations that may not support the patient's wishes related to advance directive and end-of-life.	• Patient, staff, and physician interviews • Demonstration that staff caring for a patient is aware of the existence of an advance directive. • Process for when the patient with an advance directive travels to the Radiology Department for a procedure • Medical record documentation • Hospital policy and procedure, including: - advance directives - forgoing or withdrawing life-sustaining treatment - Do Not Resuscitate (DNR) - care at the end of life - patient and family educational handouts related to patient rights (e.g., patient rights and responsibilities, advance directives) • Staff education regarding patient and family sensitivity to end-of-life issues. Usually performed in general clinical orientation	• Describe how you inquire about patients' advance directive status. • Do you perform "slow-codes"? • What are the legal requirements for your hospital related to advance directives? • What is your policy and procedure if the patient comes into the ED with an advance directive? • Are patient armbands used in this community to signify the patient is a DNR? • How is a patient's advance directive information communicated to members of the care team? To other departments? • What happens if the patient travels to the Radiology Department for a procedure and he/she is a DNR? How is that communicated? • Are advance directive educational materials distributed to patients? • Describe your policy and procedure for assisting patients who do not have an advance directive but wish to create one. How is one created? • If the advance directive is not with the patient, for example, it has been left at home, do you attempt to document its substance in the patient's medical record and notify all patient caregivers? Where is this documented? Do you document the patient's wishes concerning organ and tissue donation? How is this communicated with the inpatient care providers when the patient is admitted? How often do you ask the patient of their advance directive that was left at home? • Describe your policy and procedure for resuscitative services • What training is provided to staff regarding end-of-life care ethical and legal issues?

Standard	Comments	Evidence	Staff Questions
RI.2.90	**Unanticipated Outcomes** It is essential that the patient is informed regarding the outcomes of care, including unanticipated outcomes. The LIP or his/her designee must inform the patient, and when appropriate, family regarding any unanticipated outcome related to a Joint Commission Sentinel Event if the patient does not already know of the event or if further discussion is warranted. The LIP must advise the patient if he or she has been harmed by the care provided, i.e., if medical errors were made, and what treatment is being administered to manage the patient's condition.	• Staff and physician interviews • Hospital policy and procedure for communicating outcomes to patients • Medical record documentation • Staff knowledge of process for informing patient of unanticipated outcome	• What is the ED policy and procedure and/or practice regarding communications with patients and/or authorized family members regarding unanticipated outcomes of care? • Do you inform the patient/ authorized family member about unanticipated outcomes of care that relate to Joint Commission Sentinel Events considered reviewable by the Joint Commission? • Can you name examples of Joint Commission Sentinel Events? • What information is given to patients or their families regarding outcomes of treatments or procedures when those outcomes differ significantly from the anticipated outcomes? • Who informs the patient of the unanticipated outcome? • How is this documented? • Are these events trended for the hospital? Whose role is it to trend this data? • Is this information linked to a committee charged with overseeing patient safety?

Standard	Comments	Evidence	Staff Questions
RI.2.100	**Patient Communication/ Translation** The hospital must demonstrate how it ensures effective communication with its patients.	• Patient, staff, and physician interviews • Hospital policy and procedure on communicating with patients • Hospital mechanisms/resources exist for ensuring patients receive information in an understandable format regarding care and services • ED signage or information notifying patients that communication assistance is available if needed • ED call list for interpreters/ translators • Hospital advocacy services or patient care service representatives available to assist with meeting patients' special communication needs • Hospital resources to overcome communication barriers for vision, speech, hearing, language, and cognitive impairments • Patient access to areas where they can have private telephone conversations based on their needs and care provided	• Do you assess patients for barriers related to communication with ED staff? • What barriers have you had regarding communication to patients in the ED? • How have you overcome these barriers to communication with the patients you serve in the ED? • How do you communicate with patients who are deaf or have limited English proficiency? • What services can you access for patients who have hearing difficulties? Is there a telephone number posted? • When do you access interpretive services? How do you know if the interpretive service person is competent to translate? • What are the prominent languages spoken in the ED other than English? • Approximately what percentage of the patients seen have limited English proficiency? Has the hospital offered classes in that language for staff? • Have there been issues related to limited English proficiency in the ED? What PI activities have occurred in regards to this?

Standard	Comments	Evidence	Staff Questions
RI.2.120	**Patient Complaints** The hospital has a mechanism to resolve patient and family complaints.	• Staff and physician interviews • Policy and procedure: - complaint resolution including a statement that patients are free to complain and make suggestions for improvement without retaliation (i.e., coercion, discrimination, reprisal, or unreasonable interruption of care) • Example of complaint resolution form • Any complaint signage required by the state • Education material informing patients, families, and staff about the hospital's complaint resolution process, including a patient's right to file a complaint with the state • Complaint resolution process demonstrating how complaints are received, reviewed, and when feasible, resolved • Examples of how the hospital has responded to complaints, incorporating suggestions into its PI program • Process for reporting complaints to committees, the governing body (mandated per the CMS Conditions of Participation) and any state-required reporting • Patient satisfaction data, surveys, results (e.g., complaint tracking)	• How are patients and families made aware of their right to make a complaint or grievance? • What type and volume of complaints do you receive in the ED? • What type of complaints do you receive? Are these fed into the PI process? • What is your role in resolving complaints? • What is your mechanism to resolve patient and family complaints? • Which complaints require a written or verbal response from the hospital? For example, do you respond to all complaints or just complaints that are considered significant or a grievance per your complaint policy and procedure? • What do you do if you cannot resolve a patient complaint? • How does this link to the patient grievance process? • What improvements have been made based on complaints in the ED?

Standard	Comments	Evidence	Staff Questions
RI.2.130 RI.2.140	**Patient Privacy, Security & Confidentiality** The hospital is responsible for establishing and maintaining methods of ensuring patient rights to privacy (auditory and visual), security, and confidentiality of information. The environment of care safeguards patient dignity and promotes a positive self image.	• Patient, staff, and physician interviews • Medical record documentation. • Relevant hospital and ED-specific policy and procedure, to include those related to HIPAA and safety • Safety and security programs and strategies implemented • Reviewing ED operations for compliance with hospital policy and procedure • Ensuring proper security regarding patient valuables including when patients are transferred within and out of the ED • Physical design of the environment • Staff orientation • PI studies concerning privacy, confidentiality, security • Patient and family education materials distributed on patient rights, including patient safety, privacy, security, and confidentiality • Patient satisfaction data *Surveyor tour of ED* • Inappropriate placement of stretchers and chairs in interview areas and examination areas where others may hear private patient/hospital communication • Use of curtains and partitions without compromising monitoring of patient condition and safety • Patient covered during treatment or care • Patient names do not have clinical information, treatments, or diagnostic tests ordered displayed on patient tracking boards (white boards) • Patient surveys/comment boxes • Patient medical records secure with no visible information to other patients/family • Registration/triage area conducive to confidential communication	• Describe the mechanisms you use to ensure privacy for patients during triage, registration, medical screening examination, assessment, examinations, treatments, and discharge. • How do you keep written patient information confidential? • Are all areas where patients receive care private? How are they private? • If hallways are used as treatment areas, how do you minimize the privacy and confidentiality issues? • What are you doing to minimize or eliminate your space constraints (numbering treatment areas, use of curtains, staff education, etc.)? • Are renovations planned to increase the space to treat patients? • What policy and procedure do you follow to secure patient valuables and other possessions? What happens when the patient is transferred? • What is your policy and procedure for allowing family members to accompany patients in the ED? • Do you measure compliance with protecting the privacy and confidentiality of patient sensitive information?
RI.2.150	**Protection From Abuse** Hospitals must ensure patients are free from mental, physical, verbal, and sexual abuse; neglect; and exploitation. Policy and procedure is in place in the event a patient states someone touched her/him inappropriately.	• Patient, staff, and physician interviews • Mechanism to protect patients from abuse, neglect, and exploitation from an individual (e.g., staff, students, volunteers, patients' visitors, family) • Hospital policy and procedure • Medical record documentation • Education records of staff attending in-services on abuse and neglect. This education is required upon hire by the Joint Commission and annually by CMS [§ 482.13(c)(3)].	• How are allegations of observed or suspected cases of abuse that occur in the hospital managed? • How do you protect patients from abuse in the ED? • What do you do to protect the patient in restraints from possible abuse? • What resources are available to staff in assisting with suspected or actual cases of abuse?

Standard	Comments	Evidence	Staff Questions
RI.2.160	**Pain Management** Policy and procedure should address the care of ED patients to define when pain should be screened, assessed, and reassessed, and to provide education to patients about effective pain relief.	• Patient, staff, and physician interviews • Hospital and ED-specific policy and procedure: - pain assessment, reassessment, and management • Examples of pain scales used (e.g., 0–10) for patients who are verbal, as well as nonresponsive/ nononverbal and pediatric pain scales • Medical record documentation • Clinical staff education related to pain assessment and management including nurses, respiratory therapist, EKG technicians, patient care assistants, nurse's aides, etc. • Patient education on pain management using medications and other pain management techniques including patient controlled analgesia pumps when used • PI data related to pain management	• Describe how the patients' pain is screened/assessed upon arrival in the ED, and whether and how it is. reassessed at any other time • What is the difference between screening for pain and assessing for pain in the ED? • What are the components of the pain screening and then pain assessment? When should this be completed? Who can complete? • How do you screen/assess pain in the patient who is nonverbal? • How do you screen/assess pain in the pediatric pr infant? • How often do you reassess for pain in the ED? • How do you reassess for the effectiveness for pain management interventions such as medication administration? Oral medication? IV medication? • How do you ensure effective management of pain for patients? • In what time frame do you reassess post-medication intervention? • What are the primary medications you administer for pain management? What is their drug half life? • How are you competent to administer and monitor the effects of these medications? • Where is this documented? • Are there any educational programs for clinical staff regarding pain assessment and treatment? • Describe how the patient is educated about pain management in the ED.

Standard	Comments	Evidence	Staff Questions
RI.2.170	**Protective and Advocacy Services** The ED is responsible for implementing the hospital's policy and procedure for the patient population needing protective services (e.g., guardianship, advocacy services, conservatorship, and child/adult protective services). Policy and procedures exist to help patients' families and courts determine a patient's need for special protective services due to the following evidence.	• Patient, staff, and physician interviews • Hospital policy and procedure, forms (see sample documentation section) • Medical record documentation • Staff orientation and continuing education documentation • Hospital educational material supplied to patients/families on protective services/resources (e.g., lists of state client advocacy groups, posting of legal patient rights, etc.) • Signage	• Describe how you protect the rights of victims of aggravated assault, domestic, child, geriatric abuse or neglect • What training have you had to determine a patient's special needs for protective services? Have you had this for elder abuse, domestic abuse, child abuse, and aggravated assault? • What resources are available to certain patient populations needing protective services? Can you show me examples? • What steps do you take to ensure safety of patients while they are in the ED? • What are some of the signs and symptoms for child, elder, domestic abuse, and aggravated assault? How do you screen for these? • How do you contact social services worker if needed? What about off-hours and weekends? • Do you have a list of community resources available to patients/family? Is this available in a handout for patients?

Standard	Comments	Evidence	Staff Questions
RI.2.180	**Research** These standards assess how the rights of patients asked to participate in any research/investigational study/clinical trial are protected. The ED is a key area in which to initiate research projects, trials, and studies. ED staff must ensure that the patient and family receive all information necessary for full understanding of the research project. There is a requirement added to address confidentiality and inclusion of research information in the medical record. All research projects are reviewed per policy and procedure prior to being used in the hospital.	• Patient, staff, and physician interviews • Hospital policy and procedure: - investigational medications, clinical trials, research • Medical record documentation • Copies of all information given to the research participant are contained within the medical record or research file, along with evidence of informed consent • Evidence that the research protocol was reviewed and approved per the hospital's policy and procedure prior to implementing the study • Patients are informed of any risks, benefits, and alternatives associated with the research to assist with their decision to participate or refuse • Patients are given information related to other treatment options and may refuse the research without any ramification • Executed hospital consent forms and relevant discussions include the following documentation: the name of the person providing the information to the participant, his/her right to privacy, confidentiality, safety, and the date the form was signed • List of current research projects in the ED • Staff education to research projects as warranted • Involvement of Pharmacy and Therapeutics Committee when an investigational drug is used • Approval by ED medical staff of educational materials distributed to patients on investigational medications • Patients are told the extent of how their personal health information will be kept in confidence • Staff membership or input on Institutional Review Board (IRB) or body assigned to approve research projects	• How do you know what research is being conducted in the ED? How are you educated to this research? • What committee or body reviews investigational medications, protocols? • Does the ED medical staff have knowledge of this research? • Who obtains consent for patients participating in research projects? Where will this be documented? What is the physician involvement? • What information is given to patients participating in investigational studies or clinical trials? • What happens when a patient refuses to participate in a research project/clinical trial? Where is this documented? • If investigational medications are administered or dispensed in the ED, how is staff educated on the medications? How is pharmacy involved? Is there literature on the research available to staff? • How is the principal investigator involved? • Give me an example of research that has occurred in the ED within the last 12 months. What was your role? • What would happen if there were a research-related injury?

Standard	Comments	Evidence	Staff Questions
RI.3.10	**Patient Responsibilities** Patients and authorized families are informed on their responsibilities and role in the treatment process, specifically, their role in helping to facilitate the safe delivery of care. The Joint Commission outlines the essential responsibilities, such as: • providing information to assist the staff in gathering a complete medical information (e.g., history, indicating changes in health status, perceived risks in care, indicating care expectations) • asking questions to staff, clarifying information provided (including expressing concerns, and understanding expectations) • following instructions/treatment plan, working with staff to adjust their plan of care to meet specific needs/limitations, accepting outcomes if not following treatment plan • acting according to the hospital's regulations—with consideration and respect for others in the ED, other care areas, meeting financial obligations, etc.	• Patient, staff, and physician interviews • Hospital policy and procedure: - process for reviewing responsibilities • Documentation of patient education to responsibilities in care/treatment • Hospital handout, brochure, and postings of patient responsibilities in treatment and waiting areas • Evidence of medical staff involvement in pre-printed handouts or education protocols • Evidence of involving patients/ authorized family in patient safety (e.g., implementation of the SpeakUP program sponsored by the Joint Commission)	• Are patients informed of their role and responsibilities in the treatment process? How do you inform patients of their responsibilities? • Do you have any booklet or handout indicating patient responsibilities to orient your patient/authorized family to the ED? Is this documented anywhere? • Describe your procedure for informing patients and their families, when appropriate, on their responsibilities for care (e.g., their role in patient safety, the assessment process, use of medications, medical equipment, pain management, use of SpeakUP campaign). Can you show me this? • How do you know the patient understands information given to him/her?

PROVISION OF CARE

Standard	Comments	Evidence	Staff Questions
PC.1.10	**Patient Access** This standard concerns the hospital evaluating the needs of its patients and accepting only those patients when it can provide the appropriate level of care to meet those needs.	• Staff and physician interviews • Policy and procedures - plan for provision of patient care and services specific to the ED - triage screening/assessment - triage protocols - patient assessment and reassessment - assessment requirements - admitting - transfer internal and external - referral process - accessing other services, providers, staff, as needed for appropriate level of patients' care • On-call physician list • Evidence of the application of the criteria that define the information needed to match the patient to the appropriate care setting (e.g., intensive care unit admission, and discharge criteria) • Admission criteria defined, including exclusionary statements indicating information needed for referral to a more appropriate service or setting; defining patient populations not served by the hospital • Criteria for discharge, transfer of patients from the ED • Criteria for placement on established Clinical Practice Guidelines (CPG) or protocols • Referrals to outside clinics • Referral and transfer agreements • Observation of patient entry to ED, flow-through waiting, triage area, and transfer internal and external • Medical record documentation. • PI studies on appropriateness of admissions, transfers, and discharges	• What type of patients do you treat in this ED? • How do you know patients receive the right care in the ED? Is this in policy and procedure? • Describe the patient's initial experience on entering the ED. • What information do you obtain during patient triage and screening to determine what care and services the patient needs? • What is the range of care you provide? What is your patient volume per day/annually? • Is this a trauma, burn etc. referral center? • Do you treat OB patients in the ED or do they go straight to the OB department for screening? How many weeks before they go to the OB area for medical screening or treatment? • Do you treat pediatrics in the ED? What about infants? • Do you have sufficient staff and equipment to provide services to meet the needs of your patient population including pediatrics? • Do you have a pediatric crash cart in the ED? Can you open the cart and describe the supplies? • Where are patients referred when needed care cannot be provided? How do you access these services? What about off-hours and weekends? • How are patients transported to another hospital? • How do you access the services of other departments within your hospital? • What types of patients do you accept from other hospitals? What is this process? • What criteria determine whether a patient is admitted for treatment? • How are patients selected for transfer or referral to another setting?

Standard	Comments	Evidence	Staff Questions
PC.2.20 PC.2.120 PC.2.130	**Initial Assessment** ED assessment and reassessment policy and procedures must be defined in writing. These standards concern performing a thorough initial assessment and reassessment in specified timeframes of the patient's care needs. The information collected on patient's entry into the ED may indicate the need for further assessments. Triage, used to determine the order in which patients will be treated, does not meet the criteria of patient assessment. Assessment includes physical, psychological, social assessments, including patients' age-specific needs/ information (infant, child, adolescent, and geriatric). Data and information is also gathered during the initial screening. As appropriate, an assessment is required if the screening indicator(s) are positive. Screening indicators are: • Pain • Nutrition • Functional • Abuse • Discharge planning There are usually three to four indicators for each of the above screens. Patients requiring further assessments for rehabilitation and/or nutritional services are referred to the appropriate care provider and/or setting, as needed.	• Staff interviews • Medical record documentation indicating patient screening (pain, nutrition, functional, abuse, and discharge planning) and further assessments for physical, psychological status when indicated • Policy and procedures: - triage - scope of assessment, reassessment, and care for the ED patient approved by a LIP with appropriate ED clinical privileges - assessment and reassessment specific to type, age of patient, and condition - scope of assessment/ reassessment by each discipline, criteria defined for when an additional assessment is needed • Medical staff bylaws, rules, and regulations defining the medical staff's documentation requirements for ED physicians • CPGs, algorithms for assessment • Hospital communication (hearing impaired) and translation (limited English proficiency) services available for performing assessments • Observation of staff screening, assessing, reassessing within their scope of practice: - nutrition screen - pain screen - functional screen - abuse screen - discharge planning screen • Evidence that initial assessments are performed as defined by the hospital • Evidence a nursing assessment is performed by a registered nurse, if applicable • Initial ED and inpatient assessment tool • Medical record PI data • Evidence of ED physician examination. Inpatient history and physical when appropriate, nursing assessment, and other ancillary screens and assessments such as respiratory therapy	• Describe how you developed the triage protocols and the scope of assessment and care for patients in need of emergency care. Who approved these for the ED? Did you have input? Did the medical staff have input and approval? • Do L&D nurses perform medical screening exams? Do they have documented competencies? Did medical staff approve the competencies? • How long does it take to perform the triage screen from the time the patient enters the ED? • How long until each patient is triaged? • How long from the time of the triage until the initial screening and assessment is completed? What about reassessment? • Have you implemented any improvements to decrease throughput time? If so, what are these? Did the ED collaborate with other departments? • What objective screening indicators do you use for pain, abuse, functional, nutrition, and discharge planning? Who developed these? • What is the difference between a "screening" and an "assessment"? • Is there an emphasis to involve authorized family members in gathering this information? • Describe the assessment processes for infants, children, adolescent, and geriatric patients. Show me the forms used for pediatrics. • Where do you have in writing the data and information collected in the ED? Please show me the form. • When would you reassess the patient? • When would you document developmental age, length or height, head circumference, weight, and immunization status for patients? Do you collect these for all pediatrics? • How do you ensure that staff are properly trained in

Standard	Comments	Evidence	Staff Questions
			performing population (age-specific, trauma, OB, etc.) assessments? • What is the process for responding to a pediatric code? • How are you competent to care for neonate, infants, pediatrics, adolescents, and geriatrics? • What information do you assess regarding end-of-life, spiritual, and cultural variables? • Do ED physicians perform inpatient history & physical in the ED? How are the initial screens (nutrition, pain, abuse, discharge planning, and functional) reported to the physician if needed? • What happens when a patient is admitted as an inpatient but stays in the ED because there is no bed? Do you perform an inpatient initial nursing assessment?

Standard	Comments	Evidence	Staff Questions
PC.2.150	**Reassessment** The standards concern reassessment intervals and criteria for the ED, depending on the type of patient, condition, care received, and procedure performed. Reassessment determines the continuing care needs of the ED patient.	• Staff interviews. • ED policy and procedure: - assessment and reassessment practices - clinical care for certain patient types - significant changes in patient condition - care given, procedures performed - CPGs • Assessment/reassessment forms • Compliance with hospital medical staff bylaws, rules, and regulations for assessment and reassessment • Medical record documentation demonstrating follow-up care that is arranged for further assessments of patient's care needs (e.g., referral to primary care physician, community resource)	• When are patients reassessed? • What are the timeframes per level of care? • What is the scope of the reassessment? • Please show me the assessment and reassessment for the respiratory therapist who works in the ED. • Who can reassess the patient? RN, LVN/LPN, aide? • What data/information is included in a reassessment? • What procedures do you follow if there is a significant change in patient's condition and care needs? • How often does respiratory therapy reassess patients in the ED?
PC.3.10	**Identifying Victims of Abuse** This standard concerns the identification of victims of abuse or neglect using established criteria set by the hospital. Examples of abuse or neglect include: - physical assault - domestic abuse - abuse/neglect of children and elders - aggravated assault/rape or other sexual molestation Staff must be educated on how to screen patients for abuse and neglect and how to treat and/or refer these cases appropriately.	• Staff interviews • Hospital and ED-specific policy and procedures: - abuse and neglect screening, use of criteria - reporting mechanisms - assigning responsibilities for collecting, safeguarding, and releasing evidentiary material(s) • PI studies re: victim of abuse • Medical record documentation • ED assessment tools designed to document domestic, child, elder, physical abuse, aggravated assault. • List of community agencies that provide assistance for victims of abuse • Staff knowledge of criteria for screening abuse or neglect; ability to discuss reporting mechanisms, time frames for reporting as per policy and procedure • Staff records indicating attendance at mandatory orientation, continuing education sessions • Evidence that all cases of abuse or neglect are immediately reported in compliance with the hospital's policy and procedure and federal, state, and local legal requirements	• What types of abuse do you care for in this ED? • What training have you received to assist you in identifying victims of abuse and neglect? • Can you describe your screening mechanism for identifying victims of abuse (e.g., elder, child, physical, domestic, aggravated assault)? • Who performs further assessments, if needed? • If a child is a potential victim of abuse, who do you report this to? How soon? Who reports? Where is this documented? • What are examples of criteria used to assess elder abuse? Adult violence? Child abuse? • Have you cared for a patient who you have suspected of being a victim of abuse? • What did you do after you suspected the abuse? • How was medical staff involved? • Where are the telephone numbers for reporting abuse as mandated by local and state laws? • How do you safeguard any evidence collected in the assessment process? • Do you perform sexual assault nurse examinations? • How often do you receive education on abuse? • What do you do if the patient states he/she was abused while in the ED? Is there a policy and procedure for this?

Standard	Comments	Evidence	Staff Questions
PC.3.120- PC.3.130	**Addiction Treatment** **Behavioral Health Disorders** These standards (PC.3.120) are required for hospitals that have programs for alcohol and/or addiction to substance abuse. Standards (PC.3.130) apply to hospitals treating patients for behavioral or emotional issues. The ED must ensure its patient population includes appropriate assessments for this population in order to optimize the care to patients with these high-risk needs.	• Staff and physician interviews • Medical staff bylaws or rules and regulations	• Do you offer substance abuse or behavioral health treatment in this hospital? • How is the ED linked to this inpatient treatment program? • What communication process is in place? • What is the process for transferring these patients? • Can I speak with the person responsible for these programs?
PC.3.230	**Diagnostic Testing** These standards concern performing tests in a timely manner to determine patient's clinical needs while in the ED. Clinical information regarding the reason for the test is submitted with the order based on hospital policy and procedure and applicable law and regulation. Testing that requires clinical interpretation must have appropriate information supplied with the order.	• Interviews with staff, physicians, radiology, laboratory, and EKG department employees • Hospital and ED-specific policy and procedure: - list of procedures that can be performed - testing and reporting procedures - protocols including critical results (Joint Commission NPSG 2C) - pertinent information included in order as appropriate • Access to testing time frames • Laboratory and radiology reports • Medical record documentation indicating diagnostic tests and procedures were performed as ordered within the time frame established by the hospital • Diagnostic study request filled out completely. • Radiology "overread" data • Diagnostic testing turnaround time, PI data, and activities	• How does the ED ensure that required clinical information is submitted with requests for diagnostic tests? • What information would you give to the Radiology Department when ordering a radiograph for a long bone fracture? What about for a patient who may have pulmonary infiltrates, head MRI, or CT scan? • What is the most common laboratory procedure that you perform in the ED? What is the turnaround time for this test both routine and stat? • If there is 24-hour radiologist coverage, how do the residents, when applicable, learn to read radiographs? Do you have an overread or discordance program? • What are main radiographs taken in the ED? Do the ED physicians read these test results? What happens if they are overread the next day by radiologist and the reading is not the same as the ED physicians?

Standard	Comments	Evidence	Staff Questions
PC.4.10 PC.5.10 PC.5.50	**Plan of Care** **Interdisciplinary Team** These standards concern the integration of assessments to assign priorities to the patient's needs and develop a plan of care. There must be evidence that care is planned with patient participation, and with the clinical staff working together as a team. The plan of care for a patient must be monitored and modified, as needed, to ensure that clinicians are achieving established goals/outcomes. The patient's plan of care is typically not in the format that most inpatient settings use. In the ED, the focus is on meeting patients' emergent and urgent care needs, while also planning for any continuous needs. ED clinicians often participate in planning for a patient's continuous care needs by admitting, transferring, or discharging a patient to another care provider in the community.	• Staff interviews • Policy and procedures: - documentation forms - assessment - triage - care planning - admission, transfer, discharge - ED scope of services • Criteria for requests for consultation of specialists • Evidence that care decisions are based on the assessment of patient needs • Use of at least two patient identifiers (neither being the patient room number) whenever taking blood samples, administering medications, blood products, or performing procedures or treatments (Joint Commission NPSG 1A) • Process for identifying the "John Doe" patient who comes in via ambulance and time does not permit registration in the computer • When applicable, the patient's plan of care incorporates mechanisms to limit the use of restraints • Medical record documentation • Assignment of severity categories, triage classifications to patients (e.g., level 1—acute to level 5—non-acute) • CPGs for assessment and care of different types of patients and patients with specific conditions, disorders, injuries, for example: - geriatric - adult - pediatric - infant - pregnant - patient with cognitive impairment - patient with disabilities - patient with infectious disease (e.g., tuberculosis) - victims of abuse (pediatric, adult female, adult male); domestic, child, elder abuse, aggravated assault - behavioral health, substance abuse disorders - care protocols - decision algorithms - clinical practice guidelines, criteria for implementation - preprinted orders - moderate sedation - trauma resuscitation forms - emergency (stat) operating room case - observation bed patients	• Describe how various disciplines in the ED collaborate to prioritize specific patient care needs. Can you give me an example of this? • How are patients and, when appropriate, families, involved with planning for care? • Have appropriate resources been allocated to the ED to meet its patient care goals? • What is your process when the patient's care needs cannot be handled in the ED? • Do you develop a plan of care for each patient? If so, where is this documented? • When is this plan evaluated for success? • Are other disciplines involved in the plan? • Are these needs prioritized? • How do you evaluate if the patients care goals have been met? • What practice standards, protocols, and CPGs do you use? How were you educated about these guidelines? • If a patient has been placed in restraints do you include this in their place of care? Is the patient educated to the behaviors required to remove the restraint? • Do you include fall and skin precautions in your care planning? • Do you use an objective scale for this assessment? • How do you assess for risk of suicide? (Joint Commission NPSG 15A) • Who is involved in this assessment? • Do you use psychiatric evaluation teams? • How do you access chaplain services, social services, and rehabilitation services? • How do you arrange for equipment to be sent home with the patient? • If a patient cannot ambulate upon discharge and has no family to transport him or her, what do you do? • How do you reach a social worker after hours and on weekends? • What do you do when the patient has not met a goal that was initiated for his/her care and he/she is being discharged home?

Standard	Comments	Evidence	Staff Questions
		- behavioral health transfers - care of prisoners (forensic patients) • Job descriptions, competencies of staff, continuing education outlining responsibilities for assessments and care planning	• What PI activities have you conducted to ensure patient care was delivered in the appropriate timeframe?

Standard	Comments	Evidence	Staff Questions
PC.5.60	**Coordination of Care** The continuum of care is essential to the provision of optimal care and services to patients. Providers in the ED must coordinate care with others in the continuum to ensure a smooth transition through the continuum to meet patient needs.	• Staff and physician interviews • Referral and transfer agreements • Medical record documentation (plan of care, progress notes, and related sections) • ED policy and procedures including timeframes to meet patient needs: - internal and external patient transfers to the hospital - referral - discharge process - follow-up process - call-back system - ancillary studies (e.g., laboratory turnaround times, radiology recalls, and rereads) • Communication, documentation with other departments, services, external resources (e.g., home care, social work, primary care physician, case managers) • Information management (e.g., computer, software) support for continuous care processes • Meeting minutes reflecting discussions of continuum of care issues, review of cases/medical record reviews/focus on timely provision of services to meet patient needs • Minutes contain the topic, findings, conclusions, actions, and responsibility • PI projects involving admission, care planning, transfer, referrals, discharge processes • Process to resolve any issues involving internal/external resources (duplication/conflicts)	• Describe how you provide patients seamless, coordinated care. • What processes ensure effective communication by care providers in various settings? • When is this documented? • Describe the procedure for transferring a patient to another department or another hospital. • Describe the process for discharging a patient home or to a nursing home. • Does the ED nurse go with the critical patient to radiology or other areas of the hospital? • How is the patient transported to Radiology, OR, MRI? • Who is responsible for responding to resuscitation codes in the ED, MRI, and Radiology? What about pediatric resuscitation codes in these areas? • Who oversees the patient's care in the ED? • How do you communicate the patient's status (hand-off) treatments, and medications to a receiving unit when the patient is transferred? (Joint Commission NPSG 2E) Where is this documented? • Describe your procedure for notifying and recalling patients who need additional studies (i.e., radiology, laboratory, or EKG). Do you document this in the patient's medical record? • How do you obtain any needed external resources? • What timeframe expectations have you defined in the department to ensure you meet patient needs (triage, turnaround for studies, reassessing vitals, etc.)? • Do you have any contracted services that deliver care in the ED? If yes, how are these evaluated annually and reported to the governing body?

Standard	Comments	Evidence	Staff Questions
PC.6.10	**Patient Education** Assessing the patient and family, when appropriate, educational needs is critical to ensure a favorable outcome. Staff should consider cultural, religious, emotional, and language barriers, readiness to learn (motivation level), physical and cognitive limitations. Patient education varies depending on the patient's diagnosis, condition, assessed needs, as well as the hospital's services that it provides. When appropriate to the needs of the patient, educational topics include: the plan of care, safety measures, safe and correct use of medications, diets, nutritional care, medical equipment or supplies and pain management.	• Patient and staff interviews • Observation of patients • Policy and procedures: - patient education - self-care upon discharge from the ED - assessments of educational needs • Evidence of barriers to learning being identified • Evidence of patient and family involvement in care, and the education being provided to the patient/authorized family to meet patient needs • Hospitals may want to show evidence of the implementation of the Joint Commission's SPEAK UP campaign. Signage and/or brochures will demonstrate a hospital's commitment to educating patients/families about important patient safety topics • Medical record documentation that the patient was educated regarding topics: - pain management options offered during treatment/ method for treating pain - risk for pain - use of pain scales - importance of effective pain management - understanding pain - how to assess/reassess pain - follow-up for management of pain at home - when to contact a physician or health care provider in the event pain symptoms worsen or fever or nausea occur - medication usage (e.g., medication handouts) - nutrition counseling, oral health and drug-food interactions (e.g., evidence of literature/brochures regarding diet) as warranted - medical equipment (e.g., crutches) - rehabilitative techniques - continuing care needs, plan of care	• How do you get the patient involved in his/her care before being discharged so that continuing care needs are met? • How do you know the patient understands the education staff provides? Where is this documented? • What actions do you take if you know there are barriers preventing understanding? How do you make accommodations for any limitations identified? • Can you describe a challenging case involving communicating with the patient that was successfully managed? • Show me a medical record that demonstrates you have assessed for barriers to learning • What provisions do you make if the patient is deaf or has a communication barrier other than limited English proficiency? • Show me evidence that you educated patients on the safe and effective use of medications prescribed for the patient. • Who performs the patient's education? • Who educates the patient on a multi-dose inhaler if the physician orders for use at home? • In reviewing a medical record, indicate evidence of instructions provided regarding medical equipment, special diet needs, pain management, self-care, and/or any rehabilitative techniques offered to the patient/family (if applicable). How do you know the patient understood the instructions?

Standard	Comments	Evidence	Staff Questions
PC.6.30	**Comprehension of Patient Education** There are methods to educate and train patients that are based on their abilities, and as appropriate to the care and services provided by the hospital. EDs must assess a patient's preferred method of learning (e.g., verbal, demonstration, written) and readiness to learn. The ED must demonstrate education is provided using strategies to meet patient's identified needs, preferences, abilities, attempting to overcome any identified barriers, when feasible. Understanding a patient's comprehension of education provided is essential.	• Patient and staff interviews • Hospital policy and procedures: - related to the patient education process • Medical records documentation demonstrating education provided based on patient's abilities • CPGs incorporating patient and family education and other preprinted education handouts • Evidence that the content of teaching material is understandable • Staff education and instructional material regarding teaching methods based on various ages, learning styles, evaluating if patients understand education being provided, etc. • Demonstration of medical staff involvement in the development of patient education material	• What role does the ED staff play in developing and implementing patient and family education material? Is the medical staff involved? • What grade level do you use for patient education material? • What patient education material is available in the ED? • How is the patient's education communicated to the appropriate caregivers? • Who approves patient education material? • Can you describe a case that would depict how you would demonstrate compliance with providing collaborative, interdisciplinary education? • How do you determine a patient's preference for learning? • How do you adopt teaching methods based on a patient's assessed educational needs? • Has the hospital supported any programs to assist clinical staff in learning patient teaching techniques? • How do you know a patient understands the education delivered? • How is teaching different for the adolescent than for the adult?
PC.7.10	**Food** **Dietary** **Nutrition** There should be a process to provide appropriate food and nutrition products to meet any patients' nutritional needs while in the ED. Physician diet orders may need to be modified based on the patient's diagnosis, condition, and any special cultural, religious, ethnic preferences. Food and nutrition products must be stored and prepared under appropriate conditions in the ED. All meals must be ordered by a physician.	• Staff interviews • Hospital and ED policy and procedure: - provision of food and nutrition products - meeting special preferences for food • Medical record documentation • Ordering food and nutrition • Nutritional Services Department policy and procedures re: the ED • Provision of food products in an efficient, effective manner • Monitoring of response to nutrition care. • Inspection of refrigerators: - temperature logs - cleanliness - separation of food from non-food and patient food from staff food - expiration dates on food • Inspection of ice machines for calcium, rust, and lime deposits. • Inspection of ED nutrition room, drawers, sink, and cabinets.	• What is the ED policy on providing meals for patients? • What do you do if the patient is in the ED long enough for a meal and has a special diet based on cultural or religious preferences? • How does the ED oversee management of food and nutritional issues? • How are food and nutrition supplements ordered or prescribed, stored, and distributed in the ED or observation bed patients? Are diet orders required for patients to receive a meal? • Who monitors the refrigerators where patient food is stored? What is the correct temperature to store patient meals/snacks? • Who cleans the patient refrigerators?

Standard	Comments	Evidence	Staff Questions
PC.8.10	**Pain Assessment** The ED must screen patients for signs and symptoms of pain, conduct further assessments (e.g., use pain scale, assess quality of pain), as needed, and implement treatment interventions with the goal of obtaining maximum pain relief. If the patient's pain cannot be managed, the patient is referred for further treatment to meet his or her ongoing care needs.	• Hospital and ED-specific policy and procedures: - regarding pain assessment that includes criteria for following-up on pain • Staff interviews: - evidence of staff knowledge regarding pain management - indications that staff encourage patients to self-report their pain • Documentation of a further comprehensive assessment if pain is identified, appropriate to the patient's condition, diagnosis, and scope of services provided • Pain signage, if any • Medical record documentation of pain management—assessing pain on admission, reassessments, pain consults/referrals, flow sheets • CPGs or protocols • Documentation of staff education to pain management • Patient and family education materials, when appropriate • Pain assessment system or tools allowing documentation of each pain site • Pain surveys, including assessing patient satisfaction with pain management within the ED • Use of pain management procedures, interventions • Pain scales (for use with verbal, nonverbal, age appropriate, for cognitively impaired) available for staff to use to assess pain • Neonatal and pediatric pain scales • Evidence of medical staff involvement in pain policy and scale	• Describe your pain screening/assessment protocol (for pediatrics, adults, geriatrics, and cognitively impaired patients). • How were you educated in pain management? • How do you record pain screening/assessment and reassessment findings? • How do you educate the patient to pain management? • How do you measure a patient's response to pain management interventions? Where is this documented? • What do you do if a patient is not responding to pain management interventions during their stay? At discharge? • How do other disciplines participate in the pain management process? • Where do other disciplines document their treatments given when pain is a factor? • How is pain assessed for cognitively impaired individuals? • How do you assess pain in children?

Standard	Comments	Evidence	Staff Questions
PC.8.70	**End-of-Life Interventions** This standard applies to all dying patients, ensuring that appropriate and palliative measures are implemented for patients to receive optimal care and treatment at the end of their life. Patients' end-of-life care needs must be met in an environment supporting patient comfort and dignity.	• Staff and physician interviews • Hospital policy and procedure: - caring for patients end-of-life care needs • Staff education programs implemented on end-of-life care • Medical record documentation • Examples of physical and psychological measures used to provide patient comfort (e.g., bereavement group, ethics consult, palliative measures, visits with clergy, spiritual advisers) • Discussions with staff regarding cases that provide evidence of their meeting patient/family end-of-life care needs (e.g., cultural, psychosocial, religious, ethnic)	• How have you (clinical staff) been educated to meet the end-of-life care needs of your patients? • How has non-licensed staff been educated? • When appropriate, how have you supported families of dying patients? • How do you ensure that patients die comfortably, privately, and with dignity? • Is there any patient in the ED that is dying right now? Can you show me evidence of how you have met their end-of-life care needs? • What are examples of measures you implement to meet a patient's end of life care needs? • How do you ensure that the patient's and family's psychosocial, emotional, and spiritual needs are identified and addressed?
PC.9.30	**Resuscitation** This standard addresses a hospital system for resuscitation services. The ED should not only have sufficient ED appropriate equipment and processes, but also demonstrate compliance with hospital standards. The hospital uses evidence-based training programs for staff to recognize and intervene including the use of life-saving equipment during resuscitation.	• Staff interviews • Staff training and orientation documentation • CPR, BLS, ACLS, PAL, NAL, NRP cards • PI documentation and data • Policy and procedures, processes, and protocols • Equipment to meet needs of patient population in the ED (pediatric vs adult) • Evidence of medical staff approval of emergency medication, supplies and location of crash carts • Site inspection • Medical record documentation • Crash cart logs	• What is the ED's role in the hospital's resuscitation services? • What is the procedure for responding to a resuscitation code? • How is staff trained? • What is required for the ED: NRP, NALS, BLS, and ACLS? • What indicators have been developed to monitor resuscitation activities for PI? • Are these indicators both process and outcome driven? • Can you show me the pediatric dosing sheet/tool, etc. used to calculate emergency medications? • Are the criteria approved by the medical staff? • Do you respond to codes outside of the ED? • Do you participate in hospital PI for CPRs? • Have you been educated in the crash cart in the ED? Where is this documented? • What CPR requirements are in place to assure licensed staff members are educated to find medications and supplies as well as operate the defibrillators? • What have you improved related to resuscitations in the ED?

Standard	Comments	Evidence	Staff Questions
PC.11.10 through PC.11.100	**Restraint & Seclusion** Restraint and Seclusion standards. These standards apply to ED patients where restraints are used for medical/ surgical purposes; primary reason for use is to support and promote medical healing.		
PC.11.30 PC.12.60 PC.12.70 PC.12.90 PC.12.100 PC.12.110 PC.12.130 PC.12.140	**Restraint & Seclusion** These standards are for ED patients in a non-behavioral health care setting in which restraint or seclusion is used for behavioral health reasons—due to emotional or behavioral disorders that may lead to injury against the patient or others. These patients are often in the ED to be stabilized, and may be awaiting admission to an inpatient psychiatric unit or to be transferred to a psychiatric facility.		

Standard	Comments	Evidence	Staff Questions
PC.11.10 through PC.11.100	**Restraint & Seclusion** These standards address the use of restraints and seclusion in the ED for other than behavioral health care reasons (e.g., used to promote healing).	• Staff interviews • Hospital policy and procedures in compliance with applicable laws and regulations approved by the hospital leaders including physicians • Medical record documentation, with particular emphasis on dated and timed, patient-specific orders and qualification of the practitioner entering the order, clinical justifications, attempts at less restrictive alternatives, and assessment and monitoring of patients • Observation of patient care • Staff education materials, inservice/orientation records, and observable competencies • Awareness of staffing needs in relationship to restraint alternatives • Orders written, renewed according to policy and procedure regarding assessing the patient, applying restraints, criteria for monitoring/ reassessing needs, criteria for discontinuing the use • Regulatory requirements met per the Joint Commission standards include: - restraints used with an order from the LIP which must be in the record within 24 hours of the initiation of restraints (immediately to meet CMS requirements) - restraint use may be initiated by an RN if the LIP is not available and he/she has completed an appropriate assessment, used alternatives, and least-restrictive measures - the LIP must be immediately notified if restraints use is because of a significant change in the patient's condition, otherwise the Joint Commission standards allow for the LIP to be notified within 12 hours of use (hospitals must be in compliance with the most stringent of their applicable laws/regulations—CMS requires notification within 1 hour of use) - continued use of restraints beyond 24 hours is authorized by an LIP renewal or new order if clinically justified and after a qualified person (e.g., LIP, RN, NP) has examined the patient - the LIP must examine the patient at least every 24 hours	• What is the hospital's philosophy regarding restraining patients? • What is the difference between a non-behavioral and a behavioral restraint? • Can you give me an example? • What are some examples of restraint alternatives used in the ED? • What are the criteria for placing a patient in restraints? • What are the criteria for removing restraints? • How is this communicated to the patient? • Who may order restraints? • May restraints be initiated before an order is given, and if so, how soon after, restraints are initiated must an order be obtained? • What staff members may participate in the application/ use of restraints and/or in assessing or monitoring patients in restraints or seclusion? How were they trained? Were they trained on each type of restraint device used in the ED? • Do you have annual observable competency assessments related to restraint use for employees? • How long is an order for restraints valid? • How often is a patient in restraints monitored? • What do you monitor for the patient in restraints? • What steps do you take to try to avoid restraint use for a particular patient? • How do you protect the safety and dignity of patients in restraints in the ED? • How do you document restraint use? • How do you identify those patients who may be at risk for needing restraints during your assessment process? • Due to the potential risks in this setting, what strategies have been implemented to prevent the use of restraints, when feasible? Do you perform a trial release for patients in restraints? • When would you communicate with the patient and/or, when appropriate, family regarding the potential for restraint use or if restraints have been applied?

Standard	Comments	Evidence	Staff Questions
		to re-evaluate the need (clinical justification) for restraints/order - evidence of when restraints have been applied, removed, or reapplied - no standing orders or PRN allowed - when feasible, patient and, when appropriate, family, are informed as soon as possible regarding restraint use • PI data and resulting improvements - Hospitals should have aggregate, baseline performance measures established prior to instituting targeted monitoring of restraint and seclusion usage • External benchmarks for restraint use, if available	• What restraint education is given to the patient and family when appropriate? • Do you use PRN orders for restraints? (Not allowed by CMS or Joint Commission) • Do you have a PI process for reviewing restraint usage in the ED? What does your PI data reflect? What preventive approaches, new alternatives, and process improvements have been attempted? Have your efforts resulted in improvements?

Standard	Comments	Evidence	Staff Questions
PC.11.30 PC.12.30 PC.12.60 PC.12.70 PC.12.90 PC.12.100 PC.12.110 PC.12.130 PC.12.140	**Restraint & Seclusion** Joint Commission standards used for restraint use in the non-behavioral health care settings where restraints are applied for behavioral health reasons. Hospitals that use the Joint Commission for CMS Deemed status must have an LIP or trained RN or physician assistant evaluate the patient within one hour of the initiation of the restraint. *(CMS Final Rule for Patient Rights, effective January 8, 2007).* ED staff should be familiar with these standards, as well as applicable laws and regulations pertinent to this patient population. Those standards apply to the ED when the patient is assessing, stabilizing, treating or awaiting transfer to a psychiatric hospital or unit.	• Staff interviews • Hospital policy and procedure: - requirements for patients restrained for behavioral reasons in non-behavioral health care settings; use must be for managing a patient's emergent needs, when non-physical alternatives are ineffective • Documentation forms • Medical record documentation indicating the following: - reason for use indicates the patient's behavior may result in harm to the patient, staff, or others - restraint order (written or verbal) required by an LIP within 1 hour of restraint initiation if the LIP determines restraints should be continued - the LIP must come to the unit within the following time frames to physically evaluate the patient's emergent needs: within 4 hours of restraint use for patients 18 years or older; within 2 hours for all others under the age of 17 (within 1 hour for hospitals with Medicare-Deemed status—CMS requirement) - when the LIP agrees with the use of restraints, evidence of time-limited orders and renewals according to policy and procedure: - 4-hour order for patients 18 years or older - 2-hour order ages 9 to 17 - 1 hour under 9 years - if restraints were applied urgently, and removed prior to an order by an LIP, the LIP must evaluate the patient in person within 24 hours of the initiation of the restraint/ seclusion • Interviews with staff and physicians to indicate the following procedures are followed: - informing patients of the behaviors necessary to allow for the discontinuation of restraints - discontinued restraints prior to the order expiring if the patient meets the discontinuation criteria - providing continued monitoring by a trained staff member during restraint use. For the first hour of restraint usage, continuous in-person	• Describe how procedures are different for those patients restrained for behavioral health or emotional disorders as opposed to restraints for medical purposes. • How are you trained in the ED to differentiate the restraint procedures for medical surgical patients versus patients with medical surgical needs? • What are your criteria used to discontinue a behavioral health patient from restraints? • For patients restrained emergently due to behavioral health reasons, how soon is an order from the LIP obtained? • How soon does the LIP need to physically evaluate the patient from the time restraints were initiated? What are the time limits for orders for this population? For monitoring requirements initiated?

Standard	Comments	Evidence	Staff Questions
		monitoring is required. Following that hour, continuous monitoring through audio and video is allowed if the patient's condition permits, and the patient/authorized family member agrees	

Standard	Comments	Evidence	Staff Questions
PC.13.20	**Planning for Moderate Sedation** The following standard focuses on planning for operative or other procedures, and/or the administration of moderate sedation. This includes general, spinal or other major regional and sedation (with or without analgesia) where you would normally expect for the patient to have a loss of protective reflexes. Generally, moderate sedation is the only type of anesthesia that is delivered in the ED. The Joint Commission standards related to operative/other procedures would include any procedure (e.g., MRI, CAT scan) where moderate sedation is being administered. The ED's provision of moderate sedation should be consistent with hospital policy and procedures. The hospital/ED needs to demonstrate that clinicians have the skills and available resources to recover patients who have the potential of reaching various stages of moderate sedation to reduce the potential for any adverse events. A "time-out" is performed prior to the initiation of a procedure as outlined in the Universal Protocol (Joint Commission NPSG Universal Protocol)	• Staff interviews • Scope of care in the ED with evidence of qualified staff available to manage patients at whatever level of sedation the patient reaches • Access to privileges for all medical staff who may administer moderate sedation prior to the procedure • Staff monitoring moderate sedation are not involved in the procedure, such as assisting the physician with the procedure • Compliance with the following policy and procedures, if applicable to your ED: - moderate sedation - deep sedation (It is important to note that deep sedation is rarely, if ever, used in the ED unless administered by an anesthesiologist) - limitations on surgery/ procedures and general anesthesia in the ED • ED policy and procedures: - assessment, - guidelines for emergency procedures (e.g., physical status (ASA), risk assessment, diagnostic data) - patient classification levels concerning specific operative or other procedures performed in ED - airway assessment • Job descriptions, competencies of team members involved with administering moderate demonstrate appropriate qualifications for position/ services performed • Evidence of a registered nurse that oversees perioperative nursing care • Resuscitation materials, crash carts (age-appropriate, if applicable) and other necessary equipment for moderate sedation indicating up-to-date preventive maintenance, and accessible for staff involved with procedures/ sedation • Equipment to meet the scope of services in the ED (e.g., cardiac monitor, pulse oximeter, blood pressure cuff, crash cart, to monitor the patient's physiological status) • Implementation of hospital patient safety measures, such as the use of two patient-specific identifiers when identifying patients prior to administering a medication, or performing a procedure	• What types of sedation do you give in the ED? • How do you know the physician is privileged to administer moderate sedation in the ED? • Do you administer moderate sedation? If so, who oversees the care of the patient? Describe your policy and procedures. • Does the patient receive pre-procedural education? If yes, where is this documented? • Who decides when to administer moderate sedation for each patient? Does your state nurse practice act allow you to administer deep sedation? • Describe your staffing arrangement when providing moderate sedation in the ED. • Who completes/is responsible for the pre-anesthesia (moderate sedation) risk assessment? (This should be the LIP or CRNA per federal, state requirements) • What steps are involved in the pre-anesthesia (moderate sedation) risk assessment? • Do you have separate policy and procedures for pediatric assessment prior to moderate sedation? • How is the pediatric pre-anesthesia (moderate sedation) risk assessment different? • Who performs the immediate anesthesia (moderate sedation) reassessment? What does this include? Does it include heart rate, blood pressure, respirations, level of consciousness, and airway? • How are you competent to perform or assist with moderate sedation in the ED? • Who approves moderate sedation policy and procedures for the ED? • Do you provide obstetric or emergency operative services? If so, how long does it take to initiate anesthesia once the need for it has been identified? More than 30 minutes? • Show me in an applicable record, where moderate sedation was planned. • Do you perform a "time out" prior to an invasive procedure in the ED? What

Standard	Comments	Evidence	Staff Questions
		• Evidence of the use of moderate sedation risk assessment guidelines according to patient type (e.g., pediatric, diabetic) • A determination that the planned moderate sedation is suitable for the patient based on a pre-anesthesia (moderate sedation) risk assessment performed by LIP • PI studies showing an effort to monitor practice versus policy and procedure regarding operative and other procedures and a focus on optimizing patient outcomes (e.g., minimizing complications resulting from sedation, assessing the appropriateness of moderate sedation plans, monitoring activities, etc.) • Medical records demonstrating implementation of policy and procedure for moderate sedation • These processes must occur as indicated in the Joint Commission's elements of performance: - determining patient acuity (e.g., assignment of ASA class) - providing education to patient/family (when appropriate) on the procedure, services to be rendered - evidence of implementing the Joint Commission's National Patient Safety Goals: (1) marking the surgical site and involving the patient (2) use of time-out procedure to verify/confirm the correct patient, procedure, and site - pre-sedation/pre-anesthesia (moderate sedation) assessment completed (Joint Commission NPSG Universal Protocol) - plan of care completed by LIP or LIP confirms agreement with a plan for services being rendered - re-evaluation/assessment is conducted by an LIP with appropriate qualifications, immediately prior to the induction of moderate sedation. Re-evaluation should include pulse, respirations, blood pressure, and airway	does "time out" mean in the ED? • How do you care for a patient who has just received moderate sedation? What do you document? • How do you know which physicians have the credentials to perform procedures in your area? How is this list updated? • When and how is the "time out" conducted? • What PI data is collected in the hospital/ED regarding assessment and planning procedures involving moderate sedation?

Standard	Comments	Evidence	Staff Questions
PC.13.30	**Moderate Sedation Monitoring Intraprocedure** This standard concerns demonstrating that appropriate policy and procedures, and processes exist for monitoring patients during operative and other procedures. Appropriate processes to ensure patient safety must be in place whenever moderate sedation is being administered.	• Staff interviews • Hospital policy and procedures: - protocols for administration, monitoring, and documenting for moderate sedation - number and qualifications of staff needed to perform and monitor • Medical record review of monitoring processes • Documentation in the medical record indicating compliance with the procedure and/or administration of moderate sedation for each patient, evidence of appropriate monitoring procedures (e.g., flow sheets) • Required equipment necessary for monitoring patients • Evidence of appropriate methods/techniques implemented to monitor patients • Evidence of staff competencies, training to monitor patients appropriately, based on service rendered	• Who is responsible for monitoring the patient during moderate sedation? • What do you monitor during the procedure where moderate sedation is used? • What equipment is used during the monitoring phase? • Where are the policy and procedures, guidelines or protocols for moderate sedation)? • What forms do you use to document the monitoring? • If applicable, what methods are used to continuously monitor patients' oxygenation, ventilation, heart rate, blood pressure, level of consciousness? • How are you competent to monitor the patient who is receiving moderate sedation? • What is your role vs. the physician's role in the care of the patient receiving moderate sedation? • How do you know a LIP can administer moderate sedation or perform an invasive procedure in the ED? • Do you ever get pulled away from the bedside while monitoring intraprocedure?

Standard	Comments	Evidence	Staff Questions
PC.13.40	**Moderate Sedation Monitoring Post Procedure** This standard concerns post procedure monitoring of patients including physiological and mental status, pathological conditions, IV fluids and medications administered, impairments and functional status, pain intensity and quality and response to treatment, and unusual events or complications and their management. An LIP must discharge the patient from the area using criteria approved by the hospital's medical staff leaders. If criteria are used, the LIP must still write an order to use the criteria for discharge.	• Staff interviews regarding proficiency in evaluating the patient, performing the procedure, monitoring and recovering the patient from moderate sedation based on the standards, and hospital policy and procedure • Hospital policy and procedures: - post-operative/procedure monitoring - criteria for post-anesthesia discharge including documentation guidelines (to include monitoring for physiological, mental status, pain level) - procedures for ensuring patient safety at discharge post-procedure, moderate sedation (e.g., discharged by LIP in the care of a responsible adult) - RN is responsible to monitor the patient during moderate sedation • Preprinted physician orders that include discharging the patient from the ED • Medical record documentation evidence of appropriate post-procedure monitoring and discharge from ED • Staff personnel records/medical staff files indicating staff qualifications, documentation of competencies • Medical staff bylaws regarding the qualifications for the LIP that can deliver moderate sedation • Immediate access to physician delineation of privileges for procedures including moderate sedation • Patient care checklists, assessment/monitoring tools, flow sheets, scoring sheets, risk assessment/patient classifications • Patient discharge instructions that include where to return in the event of nausea, pain, or respiratory distress • PI studies, medical record review data, and any corrective action plans	• Describe your process for monitoring patients following a procedure performed in the ED. • Who is allowed to monitor the patient post moderate sedation administration? • What do you monitor? (Pulse, heart rate, oxygenation, level of consciousness, pain, level of consciousness?) • Where is this documented? • What are the criteria for discharging patients who have received moderate sedation from this area? • Do you use a protocol or criteria to discharge a patient who has had moderate sedation? If so, did medical staff approve this process? • Can the patient who receives moderate sedation in the ED be discharged home alone? Can he/she drive an automobile home? • Does the physician write a post-procedure note?

Standard	Comments	Evidence	Staff Questions
PC.15.10	**Discharge & Transfers** This standard requires that the hospital's follow-up process provide for continuing care to meet patients' needs. Follow-up planning should identify the patient's physical, emotional, symptom management, and social needs following discharge or transfer.	• Staff, physician, and ED leader interviews • Hospital policy and procedures: - external transfers including reason for transfer - who is responsible for the patient during transfer - conditions under which transfer can occur - mechanism for transfer accountability, and responsibility for the patient's safety during the transfer - discharge planning - patient and family education, discharge instructions, handouts - patient call-back • Lists of private and community resources given to patients/ families • Medical record documentation of the patient's continuing care needs following discharge	• What comprises the discharge screen in the ED? • When does discharge planning occur? • What is your role in the discharge planning process? What is the physician's role? • How do you ensure that the patient receives necessary follow-up care or diagnostic testing? • When do you inform the patient they are being transferred either out of the hospital or to an inpatient room? • Can you show me the procedure? • Describe the procedure you follow if the patient lacks a primary caregiver or social support services. • Do you phone patients following discharges to assess their clinical needs and satisfaction with care? • If yes, do you use a survey tool? Who makes the calls? How long after discharge are the calls made? Is this conducted seven days a week? How do you use the data collected? • How do you reassess and evaluate the services used by patients after they move to another level of care? • What do you do if a patient cannot read discharge instructions? • Do you ever need to access a social worker for patient care needs in the ED? What is the process for accessing the social worker? • Can you give me an example of an instance where you contacted the social worker for a patient's care need?

Standard	Comments	Evidence	Staff Questions
PC.15.20	**Discharge & Transfer Assessment** This standard requires that referral, transfer, discontinuation of services, or discharge of a patient to another level of care, health professional, or setting is based on the patient's needs and the hospital's capability to provide the care needed. The hospital must inform the patient/authorized family member in a timely manner about the discharge plan and/or transfer to another facility or level of care. All patients must receive education about other available resources, and how to obtain further care, services and treatment to meet his/her identified needs. Under the federal "Emergency Medical Treatment and Active Labor Act" (EMTALA), hospitals are prohibited from discharging or transferring a patient in an emergency condition for financial reasons (42 U.S.C. § 1395dd). This standard also concerns discharge planning. Discharge planning should be initiated early in the treatment process, based on the outcomes of the initial screen and assessment. Improved discharge planning within a hospital may assist the ED in facilitating the flow of patients to appropriate care settings. The goal is to reduce ED waiting times and improve patient satisfaction.	• Patient, staff, physician and ED leader interviews • Policy and procedures: - triage protocols - assessment (continuing physical and psychosocial care needs identified) - criteria for admission, referral, transfer to the inpatient setting, transfer to another facility, discontinuation of services, discharge - transfer - referral - discharge planning - follow-up - call back • Medical record documentation (including triage assessment, reassessments, ongoing charting, necessary documentation such as discharge instructions, transfer forms, etc.) • Referral and transfer agreements • Evidence of patient/authorized family education regarding the reason for transfer or discharge, including: - alternatives to transfer, if applicable - anticipated need for continuing care following discharge, and how to obtain these services, if applicable • Evidence of arrangements made to meet a patient's needs following discharge • Evidence of referrals to private and community groups, consultation notes • Case management program, if applicable, to facilitate patient flow through the hospital and ED • List of Medicare-certified home health agencies and other external resource agencies • PI projects (re: discharge planning) demonstrating ED participation	• What are the ED criteria for referral? Transfer? Discontinuation of services? Discharge? • Describe when a transfer can take place. Under what circumstances? • During transfer, how do you know who is responsible for the patient? • What information must be documented in the medical record prior to transfer? • What information must be provided to patients/authorized family members? • What is the hospital's mechanism for referrals to other care institutions and providers? • Do you ever transfer ICU patients to the ED when it is very busy? Are standards in place for this practice? How are staff competent to take care of these patients when this happens? • What happens when the patient activity increases in the ED but nurse staffing remains the same? • When ED staff anticipates some level of continuing care after a patient's discharge, what is the procedure for keeping the patient informed of the care process? • Describe the types of information that is provided to the patient regarding continuing care • What community resources do you promote prior to discharge and include in your discharge instructions? Where is this documented? • How are you trained to identify and assist patients for whom discharge planning is essential? • Describe the discharge planning for this patient • Do you have a social worker you work with? How are they contacted after hours and on weekends? • What is the role of the social worker in the ED? • What are the components of an ED discharge plan? • What patient care instructions does the patient leave the ED with prior to being discharged? • Do you collect data to measure improvement in the hospital's internal transfer process?

Standard	Comments	Evidence	Staff Questions
PC.15.30	**Discharge & Transfer Medical Record Documentation** This standard requires that appropriate information be communicated when patients are transferred or discharged.	• Staff and physician interviews • List of documents or forms that follow both internal and external transfers • Medical record documentation (e.g., review of transfer forms) • Medical record review results • Use of fax machines, networked personal computers to assist with the flow of patient information among providers and various health care settings	• Describe the flow of clinical information when patients are transferred or discharged. • What type of information management support do you have for the exchange of clinical patient information? • Describe how treatment records are made available to providers performing follow-up care. • How do you document that you have notified and communicated information to other areas transferring or receiving patients? • Is there evidence demonstrating the following information is shared with other providers to meet a patient's continuing care needs: reason for transfer or discharge; physical and psychosocial status; summary of care, treatment, services, progress towards goals, and community resources or referrals provided to the patient? • Do you communicate directly when handling after-care from the ED to another area in the hospital or an external facility? • Where do you document the "hand-off" communication to the next provider? (Joint Commission NPSG 2E)

Standard	Comments	Evidence	Staff Questions
PC.16.10 PC.16.20 PC.16.30 PC.16.40 PC.16.50 PC.16.60	**Waived Testing** Hospital and ED policy and procedure concerning waived testing. These policy and procedures must be consistent throughout the hospital. The policy and procedure must review the following topics: - how the results of each waived test are to be used in patient care areas, that is definitively or only as a screen - identification of the staff members to perform the test, and supervise the testing - that staff performing the tests are oriented and trained with the hospital policy and procedure, and pass a competency regarding the testing process on a regular basis defined by the hospital The standards pertain to CLIA '88 legislation. The Food and Drug Administration (FDA) allows certain tests to be performed by individuals other than laboratory staff as long as manufacturer instructions are followed.	• Physician interviews • Staff interviews, knowledge regarding how the hospital defines the use of waived tests, who performs the test, training, education, and competency completed, QC • Policy and procedures related to waived testing: - list of waived tests performed in the ED - specimen procedures (collecting, identifying, labeling, preserving) - how waived testing results are used (screening, diagnoses, making care decisions) - current test instructions - system for ensuring quality of testing equipment, supplies (e.g., instrument calibration) - scope of staff responsibilities in ED for waived testing - up-to-date checklist of waived testing/laboratory testing - documentation of waived testing results - quality control methodologies • PI activities • Staff records supplying the following information: - job descriptions identifying staff assigned waived testing responsibilities - competencies evaluating staff proficiency in test methodologies - attendance records for orientation, continuing education training for staff performing tests - role of the pathology/ laboratory in the development and approval of all waived tests and procedures • Site inspection • Examination of storage areas for waived testing supplies • Observation of staff performing quality control checks as indicated by policy and procedure • Evidence that waived tests are being used according to hospital policy and procedure (e.g., as a screen or definitively) • Logs or audits of quality control records, instrument problems, waived test results	• What waived testing is performed in the ED? • How do you use the results of waived testing? • Can you define how waived testing is evaluated (definitive or for screening purposes only)? • How are you trained to perform particular waived testing (e.g., use of glucometers)? • Are you trained on each test in the ED? • How often are your waived testing competencies evaluated? • Who monitors your performance? • Can you demonstrate quality control activities for the test? • Who is responsible for performing waived testing? • Do you have more than one waived testing CLIA license for the hospital? • Who is responsible for overseeing waived testing for the hospital? What is their role? • Describe the procedures you follow when performing waived testing activities. • If the waive test is used for screening purposes, do you complete a confirmatory test? • Where are your policy and procedures for point of care or waived testing? • Where are your quality control and test records stored? • Do physicians perform their own waived testing? Is care based on these test results? Do the physicians go though the same waived testing competencies training as the nurses go through? • Where are the reference ranges for each specific waived test in the medical record (conducted in ED)?

MEDICATION MANAGEMENT

Standard	Comments	Evidence	Staff Questions
MM.1.10	**Patient Specific Information** This standard relates to using patient information to safely prepare and dispense medications. To assist with the safe provision of medications, the hospital defines in policy and procedure the health care providers that must have access to *a minimum amount of patient-specific information* that includes: age, sex, current medications, diagnoses, co-morbidities, concurrently occurring conditions, relevant laboratory values, allergies, and past sensitivities. When applicable to the patient, the health care providers also have height, weight, pregnancy/lactation status, and any other information defined by the hospital.	• Staff, physician, and pharmacy interviews • Policy and procedure: - gathering and using patient information for ensuring safe medication practices • Medical records, medication administration records • Information support systems • Automated dispensing machines if used	• What patient-specific health information is available for those health care professionals involved with medication usage processes in the hospital? ED? Who collects this data? • What is the minimal information required to process a medication order? • Who determines if the patient is pregnant or lactating and what medications can be administered? • Who has access to this information? • How do you assess the patient for herbal, vitamin and over-the-counter drug use? • When and where do you need to document the following: weight and height? pregnancy and lactation?

Standard	Comments	Evidence	Staff Questions
MM.2.10 MM.2.20 MM.2.30 MM.2.40	**Formulary** **Medication Storage & Security** **Patient Self-Medicating** ED Policy and procedures need to be consistent with the hospital's regarding selecting, procuring, storing, and securing all medications, including those medications brought in by patients/authorized family. There is an emphasis on medication orders being legible and transcribed correctly. This standard also concerns improving the safety of using sound-alike/look-alike, high-alert medications as indicated in the Joint Commission's National Patient Safety Goals. (Joint Commission NPSG 3C) The Joint Commission expects hospitals to implement the following actions to improve patient safety when using high-alert medications: (1) remove concentrated electrolytes from patient care units; (2) standardize and minimize the number of drug concentrations available. The Joint Commission defines medication as any substance (excluding food and devices) used to diagnose, treat, or prevent an abnormal condition.	• Staff, physician, ED leaders, pharmacy staff interviews • Medications are appropriately labeled • Medications are in the most ready-to-use form/unit dose • Approved locations of medication storage areas in the ED • The ED must be aware of the hospital's medication policy and procedures: - selecting - procuring - storing medications based on applicable law and regulations from the time the ED receives the medication to the time the care provider receives the medication to the time the medication is administered - list of sound-alike and look-alike medications, and policy of special precautions (Joint Commission NPSG 3C) - physician input ED for selecting medications used in the hospital formulary - list of medical staff approved medications, criteria used (minimum criteria includes indications for use, effectiveness, risk, cost, patient response) - annual review of this list and quantities of ED floor stock by medical staff - communicating medication shortages to physicians and staff - obtaining medications during disasters - restocking medications and supplies as soon as they are used - using patient medications brought into the ED from home • Using approved medications properly and safely storing/ stocking medications in the ED under appropriate conditions (e.g., temperature control) and in compliance with applicable laws/ regulations - will observe if only hospital licensed staff has access to medications within their professional capacity - regular 30-day inspections of medication storage areas by pharmacy staff to ensure laws, regulations, policy and procedures are enforced. The ED is also reviewed for patient safety concerns (e.g., separating look-alike/sound-alike medications) (Joint Commission NPSG 3C)	• Where are medications stored in the ED, and who is responsible for them? • What medications in the ED are on the look-alike and sound-alike list? What special precautions are taken with these medications? (Joint Commission NPSG 3C) • Are medications provided to the ED using a unit dose system? If not, what system is used? • Are all medications dispensed in a ready-to-use form to minimize medication errors (e.g., use of unit-dose distribution system vs. having to pour or crush medications)? • What about liquid (P.O.) acetaminophen for children? Is this provided to the ED in a unit-dose form? • How do you ensure that unlicensed individuals cannot obtain them? Does this include IV fluids? • How are medications selected for the hospital? For the ED? What criteria are used? Where is your formulary or the hospital's list of approved medications? • Describe the procedure for procuring medications that are not on the formulary/ drug list if ordered by an LIP? • When you add a new drug in the ED, do you monitor to see if the drug is safe? • How do you ensure that emergency medications are always available, controlled, and secured? • What medications are kept in the ED? Did the ED medical director approve of this list? • Are crash carts checked per policy and procedure? • Who decides what is contained in the crash carts? • What is the process for replenishing crash carts? How soon is the crash cart replenished after use? • Are crash carts in the ED stocked the same as in other areas of the hospital? Are crash cart locks kept in the ED? • Who inspects for location of security locks to see if they are kept secure and how emergency medications and supplies are restocked after use? • Who examines crash cart to determine enforcement of

Standard	Comments	Evidence	Staff Questions
		• Medical record documentation ED surveyor tour • Tour of medication areas • Tour of medication preparation areas • Inspection of ED logs, medical records, accurate inventory, and storage of approved medications, security mechanisms in effect • Prescriptive and non-prescriptive medications stored in locked containers in a room or on a cart • Procedures involving controlled substances to meet applicable state and federal laws, hospital policy and procedure; practices enforced to prevent misuse of medications, proper storage and replacement of inventory after use • Standardized drug concentrations limited • ED inventory accurate—evidence of no expired, damaged, contaminated medications, or storing of concentrated electrolytes such as concentrated potassium	policy and procedure on emergency medications/ crash carts? • If applicable, will check to see if daily inspections or per policy and procedure are performed on crash carts in the ED; will want to see no missing shifts/days; keep only one month's checklists on the crash cart. File the others in the manager's office and available as requested • Are all emergency travel boxes secured with a sequentially numbered lock? How often are these checked? • Does pharmacy check the crash carts on a monthly basis? • Do you keep extra crash cart locks in the ED? • How often does the pharmacy inspect your medications and stock levels in the ED? • How do staff in the ED know the medications are within date? • Where are syringes stored? Are these locked? • Where are concentrated electrolytes kept? • Does the process for maintaining concentrated electrolytes in the ED have approval from the Joint Commission? • Has pharmacy approved concentrated electrolytes being kept in the ED? • What special precautions have been taken to prevent accidental rapid IV infusion? How does staff obtain them when needed? • What procedures are in place for minimizing the diversion of controlled substances? How often do you count narcotics? Where are the narcotic keys kept? Do you ever keep these keys in a drawer? Do you have an automated dispensing machine? If yes, when do you run the discrepancy and reconciliation report? • What is your procedure if a patient brings medications in from home? • How has the ED prepared for emergencies/disasters re: medication replenishment?

Standard	Comments	Evidence	Staff Questions
MM.3.10 MM.3.20	**Patient Self Medicating Medication Orders** These standards concern the processes for ordering or prescribing medications based on the patient's diagnosis or condition, and assesses if orders are legible and transcribed correctly.	• Staff, physician and pharmacy interviews • Applicable medications orders • Special precautions when ordering for specific patient populations • Actions to take for managing incomplete or unclear orders (includes legibility issues, range orders, rewrites) • Use of an approved "Do Not Use" list of abbreviations, symbols, and acronyms (Joint Commission NPSG 2B) • Evidence of a "read-back" process for verbal/telephone orders (Joint Commission NPSG 2A) • Steps to minimize use of verbal/ telephone orders • Data demonstrating a decrease in verbal/telephone order use in the ED • Processes implemented for the following type of orders: PRN, standing, hold, automatic stop, resume, titrating, taper, range, use of compounded drug, drug mixtures, use for medication-related devices, investigational medications, herbal products, medications at discharge, standardized orders • An indication for each PRN medication is documented in the physician order • Medical record documentation indicating physician orders are written according to policy and procedures, required elements of order documented, justification for order documented, transcribed correctly. • Evidence of weight-based dosing for pediatric patients	• Do you use "resume" or "continue" medication orders in the ED? • What are the requirements for a complete medication order? • What abbreviations or symbols cannot be used in the ED? (Joint Commission NPSG 2B) • What is your procedure if you cannot read a medication order? • Describe your process for rewriting previous orders • Do you have standard medication order sets, protocols or guidelines? Who updates these? • Do you use verbal orders in non-urgent situations or non-emergencies? • How do you know the verbal/ telephone order given by the physician is what you have correctly transcribed? • Have you minimized the use of verbal orders in the ED? • Do you use generic or brand names when ordering medications in the ED? • Where do you store your floor stock? Are there any medications that sound alike or look alike that are stored next to each other? • Tell me about weight-based dosing for pediatrics seen in the ED • Do you have any PI projects or activities related to improving the medication ordering/transcribing process over the past year (e.g., limiting verbal/ telephone orders, improving legibility, implementing Joint Commission National Patient Safety Goals, improving completeness of orders, etc.)?

Standard	Comments	Evidence	Staff Questions
MM.4.10 MM.4.20 MM.4.30 MM.4.40	**Medication Preparation, Dispensing & Labeling** These standards address the control of preparing and dispensing of medications, medication dose system, and process for reviewing medication/ prescription orders.	• Staff, physician, and pharmacy staff interviews • Policy and procedures: - process for preparation and dispensing medications in the ED - process for preparing and mixing medications (process for compounding additive mixing sterile medications, intravenous admixtures, or other medications) in the ED when the pharmacy may be closed, when there is an emergency, or the stability of the product is limited - process to review all medications for appropriate drug dose frequency, route, therapeutic duplication, real or potential allergies, sensitivities, real or potential interactions between the prescription and other food or medications, current potential impact per diagnostic test values, other contraindications, variance from hospital policy and procedure, other pertinent medication issues or concerns - labeling procedures for meeting applicable law, regulation, including the elements of performance in standard • Any concerns or questions are clarified with the prescribing physician • Employee files indicating appropriate staff were trained to use the proper procedures for preparing hazardous medications as indicated by policy and procedure • PI studies involving medication usage related to preparing and dispensing medications *Site inspection* • Medications in the ED are appropriately labeled, including prepared medications that are not being used immediately for patient care • When preparing hazardous medications: - observation of staff using procedures, appropriate equipment, and materials to comply with the hospital's policy and procedure, and relevant laws/regulations - preparation area(s) that is clean, organized, and functional to ensure patient, and staff safety • Appropriate dispensing procedures to meet law, regulation, hospital policy and procedure that ensures timeliness, use of unit-dose or ready-to-administer format when dispensing	• What medications do you label when you prepare them? What if you are preparing them for more than one patient? What does the label include: Drug name, strength name/amount if not already on the product, expiration date, time if not used within 24 hours, date prepared, and dilutent? • Do you label IV bags in the ED? • Do you use a unit dose system? • How are you trained to prepare hazardous medications used in the ED? • What techniques do you use when preparing medications? Can you demonstrate how you prepare and administer a medication? • Describe how you control medication preparation and dispensing processes • Do you have a 24-hour pharmacy? • Do you compound medications in the ED? • Do you mix IV fluids in the ED? Where do you mix these? How have you been educated to perform this function? • Who reviews medications for drug-food or drug-drug interactions? • When the medication is removed from floor stock and administered to the patient without a pharmacy review, who checks the medication for appropriate drug dose frequency, route, therapeutic duplication, real or potential allergies, sensitivities, real or potential interactions between the prescription and other food or medications, current potential impact per diagnostic test values, other contraindications, variance from hospital policy and procedure, and other pertinent medication issues or concerns? • What do you do when the narcotic count does not match at the end?

Standard	Comments	Evidence	Staff Questions
MM.4.50	**Medication Access** This standard is applicable to hospitals with pharmacy services that do not have 24-hour coverage. The hospital must ensure there is a mechanism in place to obtain medications to meet patient needs when the pharmacy is closed.	• Staff, physician, and pharmacy interviews • Policy and procedure: - after-hours access by qualified, trained, non-pharmacy health care professionals to limited approved medications within the pharmacy • Medical staff must approve the removal process from the pharmacy after hours, if applicable - use of night cabinets, closets, automated medication storage/distribution systems, and after-hours drug carts used to decrease the need for non-pharmacy staff to enter areas where medications are stored when the pharmacy is closed • Storage inspection schedules and documentation logs • Use of work process controls (e.g., bar coding, verification checks by a second individual, pharmacy oversight of logs) that would prevent possible errors during after-hour access • Evidence that only trained, competent designated health professionals (may be dependent based on state law) are able to perform this function • Evidence that the hospital arranges for a qualified pharmacist to be available on-call or at another location to support staff questions, or provide those medications not available within the limited, approved supply • Quality Control and PI studies, outcomes, and action plans to reduce the incidence of non-pharmacy staff entering the pharmacy; and to reduce possible errors from allowing after-hour access. Pharmacy and Therapeutics Committee must review and approve the data and actions to improve	• Do you have a 24-hour staffed pharmacy? • How do you obtain medications that need to be administered when the pharmacy is closed? • Do you use a night cabinet or automated dispenser for obtaining medications after the pharmacy is closed? • What are the main medications you access after the pharmacy has closed? • Who has access to these medications? • Do these individuals have access to the entire pharmacy or a limited inventory of medications in a night cabinet or lock box? • Is agency staff allowed to remove medications from the night cabinet after-hours storage area? • If a non-pharmacy clinician enters areas where pharmacy stock is stored for after-hours use, does pharmacy check the order against the patient's medication profile the next morning? • Does the ED RN leave a sample of the medication he/she removed from the pharmacy after-hours stock? • Is data related to after-hours pharmacy access reported to the multidisciplinary group overseeing medication management in the hospital (P&T Committee)? • Have you been successful in limiting the use of accessing the pharmacy after hours?

Standard	Comments	Evidence	Staff Questions
MM.4.70 MM.4.80	**Medication Dispensing & Recalls** These standards concern the hospital having a mechanism to manage medication recalls, the discontinuation of medications, and the process for managing unused or expired medications. The hospital must comply with applicable laws and regulations with regard to these processes.	• Staff, physician and pharmacy interviews • Policy and procedure: - hospital medication recall/ discontinuation procedures, including the notification process - management of all unused, discontinued, recalled, and/or expired medications; process for controlling and accounting for all unused medications returned to pharmacy • Examples of incidence when the hospital has informed health care professionals ordering, dispensing, and/or administering recalled or discontinued medications; the process also includes notifying patients who may have received the medications	• How are you informed if a medication is recalled or discontinued by the manufacturer or the FDA for safety reasons? • Describe how the ED manages unused, expired or returned medications. What is the pharmacy's involvement? • What do you do with unused or expired medications?

Standard	Comments	Evidence	Staff Questions
MM.5.10 MM.5.20	**Medication Administration** These standards concern ensuring that hospitals have mechanisms for the safe and accurate administration of medications. This includes patient self-administering medications in the ED.	• Patient, staff, physician and pharmacy interviews • Policy and procedure: - defining the staff members' qualifications to administer based on the following parameters: medication, medication class, or route of administration - mechanisms for patient self-administration of medications - medication administration - patient identification procedures • Verifying staff using the following mechanisms prior to administration of the selected medication via observation: - washing hands - identifying patients prior to drug administration - ensuring the patient receives the correct medication by comparing the medication order/prescription with two patient-specific identifiers (e.g., name, medical record number, birth date), excluding patient location such as room number. The two patient-specific identifiers selected should be consistently used throughout the ED. (Joint Commission NPSG 1A). Have in place a process for the above for the patient in isolation. - validating that the correct patient receives their intended medication as ordered/prescribed by verifying the medication order/label - visually confirming the medication has not expired - observing the medication for any visual evidence that the medication is stable - checking that there are no contra-indications for administering the medication - validating that the medication is being given accurately according to the order (re: proper time, dosage, and route) - instructing the patient/authorized family member regarding any potentially significant adverse reactions or concerns about administering a new medication - communicating any medication usage concerns with the ordering physician or other prescriber, and appropriate clinical staff - wash hands per policy and procedure during the medication preparation and administration process	• How do you validate the medication orders and identify patients prior to giving medications? • What is your procedure if you cannot read the physician's handwriting or you are unclear of the elements of an order such as dose, route, and frequency? • Do you allow a patient to self-administer his/her own medications in the hospital? If yes, describe the procedure you follow for this process to occur. • How do you validate that the patient can safely self-administer medication? • How is this documented in the medical record? • Can you describe safety measures that you implement prior to administering a patient's medication(s). - verify correct medicine based on product label and MD order - visual exam of no particles, discoloration, and within date - verify no contraindication - verify proper time, dose, and route - patient education - address concerns with proscribing/ordering medical order

Standard	Comments	Evidence	Staff Questions
MM.6.10 MM.6.20	**Monitoring the Effects of Medications** Hospitals must have mechanisms to monitor the effects of medication(s) on patients to assess the appropriateness of the medication, ensure patient safety, and decrease the potential for adverse events and medication errors.	• Patient, staff, physician and pharmacy interviews • Policy and procedures: - food-drug interaction reporting - ADR follow-up reporting - medication error reporting process - monitoring of medication effects • Medical records (i.e., flow sheets, progress notes, areas in the medical record to demonstrate evidence of medications monitored by members of the clinical team) • Evidence that clinicians gather information regarding a patient's own perception about the effects of the medication, including side effects, outcomes, use of diagnostic test results, medication profile • Documentation of the hospital monitoring the patient's initial response to the first dose(s) of a medication new to a patient while he or she is being cared for prior to discharge • Discharge instructions to teach patients/authorized family members regarding side effects, food-drug interactions	• What is your process for monitoring the effects of the medication on the patient? • Where do you document patient's response to their prescribed medication, including any issues? Do you document a patient's response to a new medication administered prior to discharge? Give me an example. • When assessing the effects of medication, do you evaluate the patient's perception of effectiveness, comparison with diagnostic test results, clinical response to the intervention, and the medication profile? • When do you reassess the patient post-PRN pain medication administration? • When do you assess the patient for a PRN medication other than for pain?

Standard	Comments	Evidence	Staff Questions
MM.7.10 MM.7.40	**High-Risk/High-Alert Medications** The ED needs a process that has identified the management of high-risk or high-alert medications and investigational medications.	• Staff, physician, and pharmacy interviews • Policy and procedures: - ADEs - medication errors - investigational medications - Joint Commission Sentinel Event • List of high-risk or high-alert medications defined by the hospital/ED based on trends external literature, etc. (e.g., investigational medications, controlled medications, concentrated electrolytes, new medications or non-FDA-approved medications, psychotherapeutic medications, look-alike/sound-alike medications, etc.) (Joint Commission NPSG 3C) • Segregation of look-alike/sound-alike (Joint Commission NPSG 3C) medications • Evidence of use of Joint Commission Sentinel Event Alerts, other external databases (ISMP, USP) to minimize risks related to the administration of high-risk/high-alert medications • Documentation of safe control and administration of investigational medications • Evidence of action taken when an actual or potential ADE or medication error occurs • Compliance with internal and external reporting requirements for actual or potential ADE • Inspection of medication refrigerators, crash carts, and other storage locations. • Evidence of PI studies, strategies to reduce the risk of medication errors, adverse events, enhance patient safety	• What is the process for an ADR and medication error reporting? • How do you minimize the incidence of adverse events? • How and who in the hospital would you report medication errors or ADRs? • What are your high-risk high-alert medications used in the ED? • What safety mechanisms do you implement for patients receiving investigational medications? • Describe the process for the management of high-alert high-risk medications in the ED specific to procuring storing, ordering, preparing, dispensing, administering, and monitoring. • Do you segregate look-alike/ sound-alike medications? (Joint Commission NPSG 3C) • Do you handle insulin and heparin in the ED as a high-risk high-alert medication? (Joint Commission NPSG 3C) • When an investigational drug is used, does the pharmacy control storage, dispensing, labeling, and distribution of the investigational medication? • Who reviews and approves any investigational medication used in the ED? • Who supervises and monitors investigational medications being used in the ED?

Standard	Comments	Evidence	Staff Questions
MM.8.10	**Evaluation of Hospital Medication Management Processes** The hospital oversees and evaluates its performance of medication usage for the following practices such as: ordering (LIP order), procuring (how the medications get to the ED from the pharmacy), dispensing, and preparing, administering, monitoring effects of medications.	• Patient, staff, physician, and pharmacy interviews • ED and/or hospital PI activities concerning medication usage (i.e., ADR, medication errors, Drug Utilization Effectiveness (DUE) studies, pain management, etc.) • Medical record documentation: - monitoring after medications are administered (e.g., IV fluid for low blood pressure, pain medication) - contra-indications, adverse effects noted - weight, height, allergies, etc. - effectiveness of pain medication evaluated post-administration • Observation of medication pass • Evidence of staff inservices on medication safety • Minutes that reflect ED participation in collecting and reporting data related to ADR, ADE, medication errors, pain management, etc. • FMEA for high-risk medication processes • P&T minutes available re: ED data	• What safety mechanisms have been implemented to improve the management of medications in the hospital? ED? • What is your role in medication safety? • How are you competent to administer medications new to the hospital? • What are the risk points in the medication management process in the ED? Has the pharmacy performed a Failure Mode Effects Analysis (FMEA)? If so can you describe the outcome of the FMEA? How have you worked on processes to reduce risks? • What type of literature do you read as an ED manager to keep abreast of medication safety initiatives? • What type of data is collected internally to track and trend performance to oversee medication management? • Can you demonstrate improvement over time following PI strategies you have implemented? • What external reference databases have been used to assist with improving the hospital's performance with medication management?

IMPROVING ORGANIZATIONAL PERFORMANCE

Standard	Comments	Evidence	Staff Questions
PI.1.10	**Data Collection** The hospital is responsible for collecting data to monitor its performance with important processes. The ED must demonstrate compliance with specific data collection activities for high priority and required areas, where applicable. Data collection assists with determining priorities, if strategies implemented have led to improvement, and with monitoring the stability of existing processes. ED leaders and staff need to demonstrate their ongoing efforts to continuously improve performance within the ED and the hospital. The PI focus is on high-risk, low volume, problem-prone processes and functions, and sentinel events. Data collection must also include areas targeted for further study and PI efforts. The hospital must consider collecting data in the following areas: staff opinions and needs; staff perceptions of risks to patients and suggestions for improving patient safety; staff willingness to report unanticipated adverse events; and perceptions of care, treatment and services delivered to patients. The hospital must also consider collecting data on patient perception of care/services rendered. Data must be collected to determine patient needs and expectations, how well their needs/expectations are being met, how the hospital can improve safety, and the effectiveness of pain management, when pertinent.	• Patient, staff, and physician interviews • Plans, strategies for data collection • Data collection tools used (e.g., surveys, flow sheets) • Measurement and improvement committee reports, minutes (e.g., aggregate, comparative data collected, dwell time, throughput data, left without being seen (LWBS), absent without leave (AWOL), and against medical advice (AMA)) • Participation in a reference database • Hospital and ED PI plans, reports based on data collected, meeting minutes • Graphs interpreting ED data collected, other trend analysis • Documentation illustrating the periodic evaluation of common ED procedures including patient throughput • Use of data collection tools to measure the functions of important processes and services such as: - operative and invasive procedures - medication management - quality controls - incident reports - reports of unanticipated adverse events and/or outcomes - IC indicators and mandatory local and state required reporting - Joint Commission Sentinel Events - patient wait times - appropriateness of procedures - appropriateness/ effectiveness of pain management - blood and blood products - restraint use - seclusion use and seclusion - resuscitation and outcomes - utilization management - autopsies and organ procurement organization (OPO) data: notification to OPO and conversion rate for the hospital - patient's perception of the care received meet their needs, expectations, how the ED can improve patient safety, effectiveness of pain management-research, when applicable	• What are you measuring as part of ED improvement activities? • How have you used the data to make improvements, and enhance care, services, and outcomes? • Are your improvement efforts consistent with the priorities established by hospital leaders? • Is PI an ongoing activity in your hospital? In the ED? • How do you select and prioritize PI processes? Are there criteria to guide this prioritization process? • Who is responsible for collecting data? Where are the data reported and how will data be used? • Do you use external comparative data (e.g., state, peer review hospital, comparisons)? • Is the ED included in the aggregated hospital data? • Describe a disease process/ chief complaint for which data has been measured. What did you do with the data? • How do you measure the quality of invasive and noninvasive procedures performed in the ED that place the patient at risk? • What sampling methodology do you use for studies? • Can you demonstrate if PI is sustained over time? • What have you done with patient satisfaction/ perception data? • Do you collect moderate sedation data? Medication management, blood and blood products, restraint, resuscitation, risk management, UM, QC, IC surveillance, autopsies, and/or OPO? What improvements have you made based on the data? • How are you measuring compliance with the national patient safety goals? - Have you had education about the hospital's influenza vaccine program?

Standard	Comments	Evidence	Staff Questions
		- staff and patient opinions and needs, views on perceived risks to patients and opportunities for improving patient safety - staff willingness to report medical/health care errors - staffing effectiveness if applicable • Patient safety initiatives	

Standard	Comments	Evidence	Staff Questions
PI.2.10 PI.2.20	**Data Aggregation** **Undesirable Trends** These standards focus on the hospital's assessment, aggregation, and analysis of data. Data is aggregated at established intervals based on the ED process being assessed. ED leaders, in collaboration with staff, need to be prepared to discuss the analysis and use of data collected, especially where undesirable trends are identified. It is important to demonstrate that the ED assesses its performance over time and when available, with external sources that gather comparative information. Statistical analysis is helpful in comparing the ED's performance with historical data trends, as well as against other EDs used as benchmarks. These can assist the ED in assessing common or special cause variations. • Show current, historical and benchmark data on graphs when presenting to groups or committee for analysis and actions. • Further analysis of the following incidents is mandated per Joint Commission: - confirmed transfusion reactions, - serious Adverse Drug Events, sometimes referred to as ADEs) - significant medication errors, - major discrepancies between preoperative and post operative diagnoses, - adverse events or patterns of adverse events during moderate sedation, - hazardous conditions, - Joint Commission ORYX core measures when initiated in the ED, Joint Commission Sentinel Events, - staffing effectiveness issues (if applicable to the ED), and - staff influenza vaccine program data.	• Patient, staff and physician interviews • ED and hospital PI plan • Policy and procedures: - error reporting procedures - risk reduction plans - strategies, and the management of Joint Commission Sentinel Events • Data collected, aggregated, and analyzed to demonstrate current performance levels, patterns, and trends compared against benchmarks • Use of statistical analysis, assessment techniques, e.g., run charts, control charts, and other graphic displays of data. • Use of external comparative data, when available • Follow-up action concerning opportunities for improvement for data that reflect poor performance, major discrepancies, undesirable patterns, and other problematic issues (e.g., use of medication reversal agents after administering moderate sedation, patients leaving without being seen, patients return to the ED for the same condition within 72 hours of their initial ED visit, medication usage and medication errors, and hazardous conditions, transfusion practices, staffing effectiveness) • Documentation of data collected regarding radiology misreads, electrocardiogram (EKG) wait time, and other variances, and their follow-up • Use of information from external sources such as recent scientific, clinical and management literature, including relevant Joint Commission *Sentinel Event Alerts* and ED professional associations	• How is data transformed into meaningful information used by the hospital? • Can you tell me about something you have measured in the ED and the steps used to aggregate and analyze the data? Who performed the analysis? • Can you describe techniques you use to analyze data collected for established PI priorities? Do you present data using graphs? • How is statistical analysis applied? What statistical quality control methods do you use to analyze data collected? How do you identify a need for a more intensive assessment? • Have you seen any trends in the data? • When trends are unfavorable, what have you done to correct them? • How do priorities change based on data collection activities? • Does the hospital participate in a reference database (e.g., trauma registry)? • How do you obtain information to use as benchmarking data? • How does the ED partner with other departments regarding PI projects? • How are PI activities communicated to staff? How is staff involved in PI activities? • What is the staff's role in ED PI activities? • Are you measuring staffing effectiveness in the ED?

Standard	Comments	Evidence	Staff Questions
PI.2.30 PI.3.10 PI.3.20	**Joint Commission Sentinel Events Adverse Events** These standards require hospital leaders to implement a patient safety program that includes processes for identifying, reporting, reducing, and managing risks to patient safety, including Joint Commission Sentinel Events. The ED does not need to have its own patient safety committee; however it does need to participate in the hospital's patient safety plan and activities. The hospital must use data collected to identify changes that will improve performance, outcomes, and promote patient safety. The goal of the program is to proactively identify potential patient safety risks, prevent adverse occurrences, and Joint Commission Sentinel Events. The ED team needs to demonstrate their role in prioritizing patient safety, and implementing strategies to reduce risks. Modifications made to improve patient safety related care processes, services, outcomes are assessed to confirm they accomplish expected results and maintain improvements. The ED modifies an improvement priority if the data collected and analyzed do not reflect improvement. Each hospital (not specifically the ED) must demonstrate that at least one high-risk process is analyzed via an FMEA (Failure Mode Effects Analysis) annually with the implementation of a corresponding strategy and action plan. The process selected must be described, indicating failure modes in the process, and how the failure modes or breakdowns could result in impacting patient care and services. The potential failure modes are then prioritized and analyzed for causes. The hospital then redesigns the processes with the greatest risk for adversely influencing care and services. Pilot testing and/or implementing the redesigned process, and monitoring its effectiveness is essential.	• Patient, staff, and physician interviews • Plans, policy and procedures: - risk management - patient safety - environment of care - Joint Commission Sentinel Event management - hospital patient safety improvement activities that include ED representation • Documentation of patient safety program education attended by ED leaders (e.g., seminars, visits to other hospitals, consultants, training programs) • hospital evaluations of patient safety programs • Specific ED education—allocation of human and other resources to patient safety improvement activities • The hospital conducts a FMEA at least annually for a high-risk process. The ED is not specifically required to conduct a FMEA. • Evidence of implementation of the hospital's Joint Commission Sentinel Event policy and procedure and reporting process • Documentation of procedures for immediate response to unanticipated adverse events/ health care errors • Documented mechanisms for responding to various occurrences (e.g., Root Cause Analysis (RCA) of a Joint Commission Sentinel Event) • Reporting of medical/health care errors, and actions taken to improve patient safety	• What risks are involved with your job? What have you done to minimize those risks and prevent health care errors? • Do you feel comfortable reporting incidents? Has the hospital worked to create a blame-free environment? • What do you do when you discover that a medical/ health care error has been made in the ED? • What is a Joint Commission Sentinel Event? Does your definition of a Joint Commission Sentinel Event include "near misses" or "close calls"? • How would you report a Joint Commission Sentinel Event? • Is a root cause analysis performed when an incident is defined as a Joint Commission Sentinel Event? • Have you participated in a Root Cause Analysis (RCA)? • What was your role? • What were your findings, actions, and improvements? • What is your role in conducting a root cause analysis? • How do you review and respond to information and recommendations the Joint Commission provides about Joint Commission Sentinel Events? • What risk-reduction strategy has the hospital implemented within the past year to promote patient safety, and reduce risk? How are you measuring your efforts to reduce risk in care processes?

LEADERSHIP

Standard	Comments	Evidence	Staff Questions
LD.1.10 LD.1.20 LD.1.30 LD.2.10	**Hospital's Governing Body** The following standards are related to the hospital identifying how it is governed. This is typically not a focus of the ED surveyor's tour of the ED. The governing body of the hospital has the following responsibilities: • Establishing how it is governed, membership, and defining its responsibilities in writing via bylaws • Overseeing the hospital's reporting structure for planning, operations, quality, and management with clear lines of responsibility and accountability within the ED and between departments and administration • Ensuring the medical staff is involved with the governing body • Making sure the hospital complies with law and regulation such as Joint Commission, CMS, and state regulations • Appointing the CEO to be responsible for operating the hospital according to the authority granted by governing body • Providing mechanisms for conflict resolution between the governing body and the medical staff/medical executive committee • Promoting PI throughout the hospital	• Staff and physician interviews • Access to governing body bylaws, rules, and regulations. These are not expected to be available in the ED • Access to minutes of hospital leaders and governing body meetings. These are not expected to be available in the ED. • Access to evidence of hospital licensure, inspection results. These are not expected to be available in the ED. • Hospital medical records(s) with specific mention of the ED • Recruitment activities for staff • ED Management understanding of budget issues related other ED	• How is the medical staff in the ED involved with the hospital's governing body? • How do hospital leaders (vice presidents) and governing body support PI in the hospital and ED? • Does ED nursing report to the CNO? • Have you reported throughput or patient wait times to the governing body this year? • Does AWOL/AMA data go to the governing body? • Is there any feedback to the ED from the governing body re: these reports? If so, what type of information do you hear back from them? • Do you use agency staff in the ED? • What is your vacancy/turnover rate in the ED? • What has been done to recruit staff? • Do you recruit from outside of the state/USA?
LD.2.20	**Effective Leadership** The ED must demonstrate effective leadership ultimately responsible for care, service, and meeting or exceeding its goals in assisting the hospital to meet its mission.	• Staff, physician, and ED leader interviews • An organizational chart indicating leaders oversee the operations of the ED program, service, site/location • Evidence the ED is operating effectively, efficiently, and coordinating care and services • ED is directed or managed by one or more individuals with appropriate education and experience and/or is an LIP with appropriate clinical privileges • Evidence of the responsibilities of ED director/manager defined in job description • ED scope of services/goals defined • ED director/manager personnel file, credentialing file (if physician) • Medical staff bylaws, rules, and regulations regarding ED	*To ED staff* • How do hospital and ED leaders support you and include you in improving the processes and jobs you perform in the hospital? • How is patient care integrated throughout the hospital? *To ED directors/managers* • Do you have your qualifications and responsibilities defined in writing? • How do you coordinate and integrate the ED's services with other departments, services, and with the hospital's primary function? • How do you get the staff involved improving care and processes? • How do you report ED issues to the governing body?

Standard	Comments	Evidence	Staff Questions
LD.2.50 LD.3.10	**Budget** **Goal Planning** The hospital must show evidence of short-term and long-term planning, including its annual operating budget, and long-term capital expenditure plan approved by the governing body. The ED leaders must show participation in these activities.	• Physician and ED leader interviews • Meeting minutes demonstrating ED leaders' participation in hospital planning activities • Documents indicating that ED planning issues, such as space allocation, equipment needs, are addressed at the hospital level (such as at budget meetings) • ED budgets approved by hospital leaders • Plans demonstrating that ED leaders have planned for the provision of care, services, and treatment needs of the population served either directly or through contracts, consultations, or other agreements • PI data	*To ED leaders/medical director* • Describe how the ED is represented in strategic and operational hospital planning. What is your role in this process? • What is the process for requesting additional resources and capital, such as space or staff? • What resources have been allocated to recruiting and retaining staff in the ED? • How does the ED participate in the hospital's budget process? • How is staff involved when developing your budget? • Describe the hospital's process for overseeing the ED budget. • What types of care and services are provided in the ED? • How have you planned for providing patient care and services? • Are anesthesia services available if surgery or obstetrical services are provided? • What new services are you planning to implement—short-term (less than 1 year), long-term (more than 1 year)? Have you developed indicators to determine if the project was a success? • What data have you collected on measuring patient outcomes?

Standard	Comments	Evidence	Staff Questions
LD.3.15	**Patient Flow** An important responsibility for ED leaders is planning for situations where there is an excessive number of patients to manage in the ED. ED leaders must recognize the causes for ED overcrowding (e.g., limited beds, increased demands on ancillary services, staffing shortages, increased patient demands due to limited availability of other EDs and alternative providers) and take action to better serve its community and improve outcomes. This means ED and hospital leaders must assess and improve patient flow issues in the ED and all applicable hospital departments.	• Staff and physician interviews • Plans for assessing and managing patient care volumes and demands in the ED to reduce overcrowding, and to prevent adverse outcomes. The plans must address the following elements of performance: - hospital medical staff share responsibility with developing strategies to improve patient flow - delivering care to patients ("holds") in the ED - collecting PI data to monitor the capacity of support services, and patient care areas receiving ED patients - specific data includes supply of patient beds, efficiency of care processes, patient safety, ancillary support services that support these patients and services - inefficient processes that are related to patient safety are identified and reported to ED and hospital leaders - criteria to address the initiation of ED diversion - gathering PI data to assess the effectiveness of the plan to reduce the effects of overcrowding - incorporating strategies to improve the flow of patient care in the ED, enhance throughput, and incorporate these activities in the hospital PI program/activities - implementing mechanisms to reduce or eliminate ED diversions by working with community resources such as the EMS, air ambulances, fire department, etc. - reporting of these activities to the hospital PI committee, medical staff, and the governing body • Patient flow process charts, data: temporary beds, transfers internally • Minutes reflecting hospital leaders participation in patient flow activities • PI indicators: (1) Supply of bed space (2) Patient care process data (3) Patient safety data (4) Support/ancillary services data Criteria for initiating diversion (5) Time on diversion	• How have ED and hospital leaders planned for excessive patient volumes in the ED? • Has the hospital evaluated the plan for its effectiveness? • Is the plan incorporated in the hospital PI activities? • What strategies have been implemented to mitigate situations resulting in ED overcrowding? • Have you included external entities? Is the hospital medical staff involved? • Where do you care for patients requiring admission when there are no available inpatient beds available? • Describe how you have overcome any treatment delays. What disciplines are on your PI team that is addressing overcrowding? • Has the data been reported to the hospital PI Committee? • Has this been reported to the governing body? • How is the governing body involved in this process? • What have you done to identify and improve patient flow processes? • What departments have been involved in identifying those processes? • What data is collected re: patient flow processes? • Where is this data reported? • Does staff participate in analyzing this data? • On what schedule is this data reported? • What criteria guide the decision to place the ED and hospital on diversion?

Standard	Comments	Evidence	Staff Questions
LD.3.20	**Same Standard of Care** This standard measures uniformity of care across services. The hospital must demonstrate that care, services and treatment delivered in the ED is of the same quality as that of an inpatient. Examples of issues surveyed during the surveyor's tour of the ED and then compared with the inpatient setting include: - staff and equipment for moderate sedation - pediatric crash carts - defibrillators - waived testing - respiratory therapy staff coverage - pain management	• Staff and physician interviews • ED knowledge and enforcement of hospital policy and procedures (e.g., restraint and seclusion, moderate sedation, pain reassessment, fire drill response, staff meeting attendance, advance directives) • ED implementation and support for hospital plans (e.g., PI, HR, IC) consistent with the mission, values, and goals of the hospital • Application of the hospital's quality control policy and procedures approved by administration (e.g., glucometers, crash carts checks, medication storage, semi-annual EC, and IC tours) • Clinical treatment protocols consistent with those implemented in other departments of the hospital • Enforcement of preprocedure verification of physician privileges is consistent with the ICU and OR • ED participation in hospital PI projects, committees (e.g., patient and family education, ethics, P&T, IC, patient safety) to ensure uniform care • Staffing plans related to staff qualifications • Evidence that all sites providing emergency services in a hospital provide a comparable level of care and services	• How do ED, hospital leaders and staff ensure one standard level of patient care across the hospital? • Where do you keep your ED and hospital policy manuals? • What happens if a patient is admitted but they have no inpatient bed where they can be transferred? Do you initiate inpatient documentation forms for those patients awaiting admission? • Are all medical specialties such as orthopedics, internal medicine, ophthalmology, etc., available to the ED 24 hours per day? • Do all RNs providing care in the ED have the same type orientation, certifications (e.g., ACLS, PALS, NRP, and trauma care)? • Does the ED provide the same level of care as other hospital services with respect to: - restraints - moderate sedation - patient education - waived testing • Describe how you know a consulting physician has the credentials to provide the care that your patient may need

Standard	Comments	Evidence	Staff Questions
LD.3.30 LD.3.50	**Timeliness of Services Including Contracts** This standard evaluates: • Timeliness and availability of services needed in relationship to the ED • Whether the services meet patient needs	• Staff and physician interviews Policy and procedures: - ED scope of services - timeliness of services provided such as delivery of medications, EKG, stat portable radiology films, respiratory therapy inhalation treatments • Evidence of essential services (e.g., radiology, dietetic, nuclear medicine, nursing care, lab, pharmaceutical, rehab, respiratory) being provided as stated in intent of standard, as well as at least one acute clinical service (e.g., Medicine; OB/GYN; pediatrics; surgery; child, adolescent, or adult psychiatry; substance abuse) • Services provided directly by the ED or through referral, agreement, consultation or contractual arrangements are provided safely and effectively • Contractual agreements for care rendered in the ED must have an annual evaluation submitted to the governing body addressing the quality of care provided by the vendor • Evidence of a plan approved by ED leaders defining the care or appropriate referral of patients with behavioral health and/or substance abuse issues when a hospital does not provide these services. This plan must be approved by the hospital's medical staff leaders • Patient and family satisfaction surveys • Patient flow documentation, time studies, data, CPGs • Medical records indicating that services are provided within time frame established by hospital • Tools used to measure patient wait time *For laboratory services* • Evidence the hospital has access to pathology, clinical laboratory services, and consultations to meet patients' health care needs • Meeting minutes on discussion of laboratory services, staff satisfaction with diagnostic test selection, results, reporting mechanisms, approval of reference laboratory • CPGs that include time frames for required testing • Listing of available diagnostic tests performed in the hospital and those performed by a reference laboratory	• Describe how you ensure patients' clinical needs are met in a timely fashion. Have you measured this process? If yes, what were the results? Did you make improvements? What were these? • What aspects of timely care do you measure to improve services in the ED? • Do you measure any of the following waiting times? - triage - the patient to be seen by a physician - obtaining a consult from another service - admitting a patient - diagnostic studies • How have you used patient satisfaction data to improve patient services in the ED? • How do you request a consult from another service area? How do you know a physician has privileges to perform a specific procedure in the ED? • How does the ED coordinate services with other hospitals and departments? • How do you coordinate services within the ED? • Who interprets radiology tests after hours and on weekends? How is the interpretation documented? Who follows up on unexpected results? • Describe your relationship with the emergency medical service (EMS). Are you satisfied with its services? • How do you ensure that patients with abnormal lab results receive appropriate follow-up? *To the ED director* • What services are contracted in the ED? • Regarding contracts, contractual relationships or consultative arrangements: - Do hospital and ED leaders approve services provided to patients by consultation or contractual arrangements or any other type of agreement? - Did the medical staff have feedback in the selection process? - Are the agreements or contracts defined in writing?

Standard	Comments	Evidence	Staff Questions
		• Process for laboratory or radiology testing on off-shifts and weekends • Procedure for requesting diagnostic tests *Site inspection* • Design of waiting areas, triage, treatment rooms • Observation of patient flow through the ED at time the surveyor tour. This includes the transfer of patients to radiology, OR, MRI, inpatient bed, and other areas	- Do the services provided meet Joint Commission standards? Do these contracts contain the verbiage stating adherence to Joint Commission standards is required? - Does the hospital evaluate that the terms of the contract or agreement and that performance expectation are met? - Where is this recorded? - Is there evidence that the hospital assumes ultimate responsibility for the services provided? • Has the governing board approved these contracts? • How do you educate contract staff and measure their competency? Where is this documented? • If the hospital does not provide inpatient care to patients with behavioral health and/or substance abuse issues, does the hospital have a plan for patient care or the appropriate patient referral? Is there evidence that the plan is followed? • Do the laboratory services provided by your hospital meet the needs of your ED? • Are laboratory services/ pathology results sent on a timely basis? Are you confident in the results?

Standard	Comments	Evidence	Staff Questions
LD.3.60	**Leadership Communication** ED leaders must communicate effectively throughout the hospital.	• Staff and physician interviews • Evidence of communicating and educating staff such via documentation materials, memos etc. • Staff orientation materials on mission of the hospital, staff orientation attendance records • Educational bulletin boards posting examples of activities supporting the hospital's mission and strategic plans • Observation of ED management interfacing with staff	*To staff* • How do you communicate with other departments, programs and with hospital leaders? • How does the hospital foster communication with staff? With patients and families, as appropriate? • Describe how ED leaders communicate the hospital's mission, goals, plans, policy and procedures, etc. • How does your ED's performance contribute to the hospital's mission and strategic plan? • What information has been communicated to you regarding patient safety activities within the ED and hospital?

Standard	Comments	Evidence	Staff Questions
LD.3.70 LD.3.80 LD.3.90	**Staff Competencies** **Equipment** **Policy Implementation** ED leaders have the following responsibilities: • Ensuring all staff hired to deliver care, treatment, and services have the required credentials, experience, and skill based on the scope of services of the ED, equipment used, and the health status of staff as required by external regulatory bodies • Implementing an effective staffing plan to provide for patient safety, positive outcomes, and to meet the mission, goals of the ED • Developing and enforcing hospital and ED policy and procedures • Providing adequate resources for the ED to operate (e.g., space, equipment, technology) • Hospitals should work closely with their organ procurement organization (OPO) to agree on a decision related to asystolic organ and tissue recovery. If an agreement can not be made, justification must be in writing and addressed in the hospital's organ and tissue donation policy. Hospital medical staff should approve this policy then forward to the governing body.	• Staff, leaders and physician interviews • Evidence that LIPs, Physician Assistants (PAs), and Advance Practice Registered Nurses (APRNs) have the privileges according to the medical staff bylaws and rules and regulations approved by the governing body • Updated policy and procedures developed, reviewed, and approved by ED leaders • Documents demonstrating request for resources (e.g., staff, equipment, supplies, budget) • Job descriptions and competencies for nurses, technicians, and other care providers including contracted staff • Staff orientation materials and attendance records • Ongoing education and competency validation materials • Staffing plans • HR file review - Organ and tissue donation policy and procedure	*To staff* • Is this ED adequately staffed? If not, what has been communicated to hospital leaders? What safety-related issues that could impact patient care are in the ED? • Are the facilities, equipment, and supplies in the ED adequate for you to do your job? *To ED leaders* • How do you create an environment to help the staff meet the established ED goals? • What are the job functions of a RN (or other non-LIP)? • How do you know if he or she is competent? • Who trains the licensed staff? • Can staff work prior to completing the initial hospital orientation? • Can you show me an orientation checklist of a newly hire employee? • What competencies are required for RNs in this ED? • How do you define competencies? • How do you know if the agency nurses are competent to take care of patients in this ED? *To the medical director* • Can you demonstrate there is adequate physician coverage in the ED? • How many physicians (i.e., attending and residents) are in the ED at any time? • Are all medical specialties available in the ED 24 hours away? • How do you know what privileges medical staff members practicing in the ED have? • Who defines the qualifications? • How is the clinical competency of ED staff physicians documented? Where could I find this? • If applicable, what can a medical student do in the ED? • How do you know a medical student is competent? • How do you communicate with the Graduate Medical Education program director re: medical students and residents?

Standard	Comments	Evidence	Staff Questions
			• If applicable, who supervises residents? • What are your policy and procedures on staff supervision? • What is the policy and procedure for systolic donation in the ED/hospital?

Standard	Comments	Evidence	Staff Questions
LD.3.110	**Organ & Tissue Procurement** The ED follows the hospital's policy and procedure for procuring and donating organs and other tissues. Hospitals involved with organ donation must have an affiliation agreement with an appropriate organ procurement organization (OPO) for tissue and solid organ procurement.	• Staff and physician interviews • Organ and tissue procurement and donation policy and procedure naming the OPO affiliation, indicating important processes such as determining medical suitability, potential donor notification, consent process and asystolic donation • Documentation indicating timely notification of the OPO of patients who have died or whose death is imminent • An organ procurement representative, or a designated hospital requester (employee trained in the notification process) must complete the notification process. Documentation indicates if the patient or authorized family accepts or declines the opportunity to donate • Patient names that have been communicated to the OPO when death is imminent • Collaboration with the OPO and/or tissue/eye bank for the following: - gathering and reviewing PI data/projects regarding the identification of potential donors - education to OPO policy and procedures (see HR files) - educating staff who interact with the family re: being sensitive to the psychosocial and cultural issues of families of potential donors - maintaining the potential donor through the donation process • Hospital conversion rate data - percent OPO notification of impending or actual deaths	• Discuss the hospital's mechanism to address procurement and donation of organs and tissues • Who is responsible for determining medical suitability for donation? • Who is involved in the family approach? Where is the family approach documented? • What type of education did you receive about organ and tissue donations? Who is your OPO? • Are any members of the ED staff trained to perform the role of the designated "regulator"? • Who educated the staff? • Who do you notify when organs or tissue become available? • What steps do you take to procure organs and tissues from potential donors? • What steps do you take to ensure sensitivity of donation, religious, spiritual, and psychosocial needs at the time of donation for the family? • How do you collaborate with the OPO regarding improving the organ and tissue donation process? • What data do you have that reflects the number of deaths vs. number of telephone calls to the OPO? • What data do you have re: the donors who met criteria for donation versus number of donations? • What PI data do you collect to track, trend and improve OPO notification and conversion rates? • Do any of the nurses or other staff in the ED approach the family re: donation? If yes, were they trained by the OPO as a designated "requestor"?

Standard	Comments	Evidence	Staff Questions
LD.3.120	**Support for Patient Education** **These standards address how the hospital plans, coordinates, and provides resources for patient education activities in all settings including the ED.** **Education must be relevant to the patient's unique set of circumstances and characteristics consider any potential barriers to learning.** **Validation that the patient understood the material taught is by verbal or return demonstration.**	• Patient, staff, physician, and ED leader interviews • Hospital patient education plan supporting coordinated patient education activities, establishing educational objectives • Review of flow sheets, progress notes, discharge instructions, handouts, etc. • Direct observation of patient education occurring in the ED • Evidence of education material for patients and families (e.g., brochures, handouts, videos, closed circuit television education channel, education display rack, bulletin boards, poster projects) • Physician involvement in educating • Committee minutes, budgets • Evidence of ED participation in the patient and family education process	*To ED leaders* • Does the hospital have a plan for the provision of patient education activities? • How has the hospital improved its processes to achieve educational objectives? • How are medical staff involved in the development and approval of patient educational literature? *To staff* • Has the ED developed or implemented any innovative patient teaching materials or programs? • What type of patient and family education activities do you provide to improve outcomes, promote self-care? • What information is assessed on admission concerning patient education needs? • How do you assess the patient's readiness, ability, motivation, and preferences to learning? Do you assess patient barriers to education? • What do you do with this information? • What education have you received about teaching techniques? Have you had a competency in educating patients? • How do you assess and address cultural or language barriers to learning? • Where is this documented? • Who do you share this information with? • How are your patients educated on medication? Food and drug interactions? Medical equipment? How to obtain further treatment? Where is this documented? *To patient* • What education have you received or do you expect to receive regarding your care? • Was your family included in the education process if authorized? • Based on your condition, were you referred to any community education resources? • Were you informed where to seek additional treatment if needed? • What were you told about your medications? • Were you asked about your pain? Were you instructed on the importance of reporting your pain?

Standard	Comments	Evidence	Staff Questions
LD.3.140	**Psychiatric Services/Behavioral Health** Hospitals including EDs that do not offer psychiatric or substance abuse services must have a written plan process for providing the appropriate service or referral.	• Staff and physician interviews • Policy and procedures: - the provision of patient care for psychiatric and substance abuse services for the hospital and ED or referral process. This policy and procedure is approved by the hospital's medical staff leaders	• What happens when a patient enters the ED and needs psychiatric care? • Are these patients referred? Where do they go? What is the process? • Who provides the care? Are they competent to do so? What makes them competent to provide emergency psychiatric/substance abuse nursing care? • How do you stabilize the patient with a psychiatric condition? • Do you assess patients with a primary psychiatric diagnosis for the risk of suicide? (Joint Commission NPSG 15A) • How do you ensure the treatment room for a patient with a psychiatric condition is safe? • Do you ever use psychiatric evaluation teams? • Who performs the medical screening examination for a patient with a psychiatric condition? • Where do you place patients with a psychiatric condition awaiting transfer to another hospital?
LD.3.150	**Forensic Patients** The ED staff complies with hospital requirements when patients are in custody or other legal restrictions. The prisoner/patient's plan of care and clinical decisions are coordinated for the following topics: use of restraint and seclusion for non-clinical purposes, disciplinary restrictions, length of stay, restriction of rights, and discharge planning.	• Staff, physician, forensics staff interviews • Policy and procedures: - treating prisoners and other restricted patients • Documentation of treatment of patients in custody or under other restriction • Orientation material (on important hospital policy) provided to guards monitoring prisoners that enter the hospital • Staff have education on additional security measures to take when caring for prisoners or patients with legal restrictions.	• Describe training staff receive in caring for prisoners or for patients with legal restrictions • What is the procedure you follow if a patient is brought in wearing handcuffs? When can you remove handcuffs? How do you know that thc handcuffs are not impairing blood circulation? • How would you respond if a police officer asked you to restrain a patient or put a patient in seclusion? • How do you address the restrictions on the rights of the patient in police custody? • How do you ensure the patient in custody receives discharge and follow-up care? • Do you share follow-up appointments with the patient? • Do you separate a prisoner from other patients? • How do you communicate the plan for follow-up care for a prisoner? • Who is authorized to remove handcuffs and ankle cuffs from patients? • What is the difference between handcuffs and restraints? • Do you inform the prisoner of his/her follow-up care?

Standard	Comments	Evidence	Staff Questions
LD.4.10	**Leadership Expectations** ED leadership implement a PI plan that defines quality, sets minimum thresholds for action, and involves staff in the process. Reports are shared with the hospital's governing body.	• Plan for improvement, evidence of its implementation and that ED leaders understand the approach to and method of PI used in the hospital • Performance expectations for improving care and processes established • Minutes of meetings, strategic plans, goals indicating ED leaders participates in PI, and that processes are managed using PI • Examples of PI projects indicating the appropriate individuals from relevant departments collaborate in hospital and ED PI activities • Documentation of PI and patient safety education attended by ED leaders (e.g., seminars, visits to other hospitals, consultants, training programs, focus groups) • Evidence of collaboration between nursing, physician, and other staff in the ED • Allocation of human and other resources to performance and patient safety improvement activities	• Can you name examples of PI objectives established by the hospital and in the ED? • Does the hospital have a PI plan? If yes, describe the plan and how it relates to the ED. • Do you have any PI activities related to patient flow? • How have the ED leaders participated in PI priorities for the department? • Is PI an ongoing activity in your hospital? ED? How are appropriate individuals involved in the PI process? Is PI a collaborative process involving various disciplines, fostering interdisciplinary/ interdepartmental PI activities? • Do you include other disciplines in these activities? • Do you report your PI activities to a hospital PI Committee?

Standard	Comments	Evidence	Staff Questions
LD.4.20	**New or Modified Processes** ED leaders plan new or modified services by having staff work together to design or redesign them. The design of the ED care and services is appropriate to the population served, their expectations, and considers the following topics: needs and expectations of population served and staff; any results of PI studies; potential risks to patients; use of current knowledge/best practices; information about sentinel events, when available; testing (pilot) and analysis to determine proposed design or redesign is an improvement.	• Staff and ED leader interviews • Use of data collected concerning ED patients' needs (e.g., patient and staff satisfaction surveys, community focus group sessions), as well as data and results from PI activities, including risks to patients • Planning documents involving the ED demonstrating process or service design based on patient needs and consideration of the mission, human resources, best practices, practice guidelines, material (Joint Commission Sentinel Event Alerts, when applicable) resources, and pilot testing/analysis • PI projects showing participation of various departments in planning and improving patient care in the ED • Data collected prior to and after implementing process changes	• How do you know the services provided in the ED are suitable for the hospital? • How were community needs determined and considered in your planning process? • What have you done to make improvements based on patient satisfaction, patient safety, staff opinion surveys, and/or results of PI activities? • Describe how the ED participates in hospital planning. How has staff been involved in the design or redesign of services/processes? • Does the ED have representatives participating in hospital committees or projects (e.g., ethics, strategic planning, PI, patient and family education, etc.)? • Do you pilot a project prior to implementing throughout the ED? • What is your improvement model?

Standard	Comments	Evidence	Staff Questions
LD.4.40	**Patient Safety Program** ED leaders are responsible for implementing an effective patient safety program with the goal of ensuring coordinated patient care, where system risks, and failures are eliminated or reduced. The patient safety processes must be integrated across the hospital proactively and in response to any identified risks or failures, including Joint Commission Sentinel Events.	• Staff and ED leader interviews • Evidence of a hospital, integrated patient safety program led by one or more qualified individuals or an interdisciplinary team, with ED participation in patient safety activities • Plans, policy, and procedures: - developed in collaboration with various disciplines - scope of the patient safety program, the range of incidents reported - reviewed and response to unanticipated adverse events, including Joint Commission Sentinel Events, process for implementing proactive strategies to reduce risks • Staff participation in orientation and continuing education programs that include patient safety topics • Staff knowledgeable about reporting mechanism for system or process failures • Internal communication and education regarding the patient safety program using bulletin boards, suggestion boxes, flyers, posters, staff meetings, communication logs • Participation in interdepartmental patient safety PI projects - Patient care flow charts and other documents illustrating how patient safety is coordinated among departments • Implementation of CPGs, clinical protocols, etc. that include processes to reduce risk/errors • Documentation of measurement and analysis of performance of high-risk processes that affect patient safety • Evidence of a hospital's annual report to the governing body on system/process failures and measures taken to improve patient safety is required that notes the ED patient safety status	• Can you name the Joint Commission's National Patient Safety Goals and what you have implemented in the ED to make these a success? • What do you do if you observe or hear of a system failure that impacts patient safety? • Who is your patient safety officer? What is his/her role? • How has the ED participated in the hospital patient safety program? • Was the ED addressed in the evaluation? • Have you implemented a process to eliminate or reduce risks associated with the medications? • Walk me through the process of notifying the physician of a critical test result • What has been the most challenging Joint Commission National Patient Safety Goal to implement? • What strategies did you use to overcome this challenge? • Do you collect data on the Joint Commission's National Patient Safety Goals? • When is this reported? • How do you identify patients who come to the ED and are unable to give their name or birthdate? • Have ED leaders evaluated the patient safety program over the past year and reported efforts made to reduce or eliminate risks and failures to hospital leaders and governing body leaders?

Standard	Comments	Evidence	Staff Questions
LD.4.50 LD.4.60 LD.4.70	**Performance Improvement Priorities** These standards require hospital leaders to establish PI priorities for improving systems and processes that are low volume, high risk, or problem prone, and that would lead to improved outcomes. ED leaders must indicate how they alter priorities based on internal/external events. There must be evidence of resources provided for PI and patient safety. ED leadership evaluates the PI and patient safety program to monitor its effectiveness.	• Staff and ED leader interviews • PI initiatives, priority planning, matrixes, lists, assessment tools • Orientation, continuing ED leaders/staff education (e.g., seminars, visits to other hospitals, consultations with specialists, training programs, fairs, focus groups) related to PI and patient safety • ED, leaders, and hospital evaluations of PI and patient safety improvement programs, staffing effectiveness; staff surveys on opportunities for improvement with the adjustment of priorities, as indicated • Evidence of sufficient resources (e.g., staff, information technology, software, time) allocated for PI and patient safety in the hospital and in the ED • Hospital performance and patient safety improvement activities that include ED participation	• What resources are committed to improving the performance of care, services and patient safety? • How do ED leaders prioritize PI projects? When are priorities adjusted? • Are the ED priorities consistent with the mission of the hospital? • What have you improved in the ED over the past year? • How is staff involved in PI projects and ideas? How do you ensure the ED staff has sufficient time to participate in PI and safety improvement? • How do you communicate the data from PI activities to staff? • How do you involve staff in PI activities? • What education is provided to staff regarding the hospital PI and patient safety program? What were you taught? • What activities have led to improvement in performance and patient safety? • How do ED leaders assess the effectiveness of the PI and patient safety program? • How often do you evaluate the PI Plan?
LD.5.10 LD.5.20 LD.5.30 LD.5.40	**Clinical Practice Guidelines (CPG)** ED leaders consider the use of CPGs for improving processes. It is important not to confuse preprinted physician order forms with the term "clinical practicc guideline." If a preprinted order sheet is used to increase compliance with documentation and/or optional for the physician to use, it is not considered a CPG. When used, ED leaders identify criteria for their CPG selection and implementation. The ED leaders review and approve the guidelines selected. The hospital evaluates the use of the CPGs as part of its PI program.	• Staff and ED leader interviews • Minutes of meetings documenting ED participation in discussions of CPG evaluation and use • Policy and procedure: - development, approval, and monitoring process for CPGs or protocols • Examples of CPGs used in the ED and modifications based on PI results • Protocols or CPGs developed based on sources such as the Agency for Healthcare Research and Quality, National Guideline Clearinghouse, and organizations • Staff training materials	• What is an example of a CPG used in the ED? If none are used, have you considered using any to design or improve processes? *For hospitals choosing to use a CPG* • Was a literature search completed prior to initiation? • Why was it adopted? • How was it selected? • Who reviewed and approved the use of the CPG? • What data do you collect re: the CPG? • Is the data physician specific? • Have any modifications been made to improve its effectiveness? • What have you learned from any variations in care identified? • How are staff trained regarding this CPG? • Have outcomes improved as a result of its use? • What criteria are used to prioritize future CPGs?

MANAGEMENT OF THE ENVIRONMENT OF CARE

Standard	Comments	Evidence	Staff Questions
EC.1.10 EC.1.20	**Safety Management** These standards relate to the hospital developing, implementing, and monitoring a safety management plan for the protection of patients, staff, and others visiting on the facility's property. This includes the inside of the hospital as well as on the grounds, parking garages, etc. It is important to note the term "safety" in these standards relates to safety of the environment vs. patient safety. It can be confusing for leaders and staff to differentiate between the two terms. You may want to consider referring to these standards as "environmental safety" and the standards addressing clinical safety as "patient safety" to decrease any confusion. The safety management program includes proactive risk reduction strategies. The hospital appoints a person(s)/committee to oversee the overall safety management program as well as an individual(s) to intervene under conditions that endanger life, health, or that may damage equipment, grounds, or facilities. Safety tours or environmental inspections are performed in the ED at least every six months to comply with the standards. The surveyor will tour the ED to assess ongoing proactive risk reduction monitoring and strategies to detect environmental hazards, unsafe practices, and other deficiencies.	• Staff and physician interviews. The surveyor may ask specific emergency management questions to the physicians working in the ED as well as the ED medical director • Evidence of a written plan and its implementation to manage a safe environment of care for patients, staff, and others • Hospital and ED-specific safety policy and procedures accessible to staff that are enforced, reviewed as needed, minimally every three years. ED-specific safety policy and procedures should be reviewed by an oversight body (e.g., the hospital's environment of care committee, or group in charge of the safety function, safety officer) • ED participation in the hospital's safety committee or function • Examples of involvement with safety/environment of care: PI projects, meeting minutes, agendas, action plan, attendance lists, response to ED safety surveillance rounds • Communication with local law enforcement to gather data specific to the geographic area the hospital serves • Notification and response to product safety recalls, when applicable • Communication/reporting of trends in occupational illness, personnel injuries to the IC Department • Documentation that environmental tours are completed every 6 months in the ED *Surveyor tour of ED* • Tour of ED, surrounding grounds, and equipment free of hazards, such as exposed electrical wiring • Exit signs visible and operational • Outdoor lighting functional with no dead zone areas • Panic button at nurse triage • Ability to lock-down the ED in the event of a threat • Key pad access to treatment areas • Radiograph machine without key left in ignition • Housekeeping closets locked • Oxygen cylinders appropriately secured • Locked linen chutes • No electrical cords hanging in pediatric and psychiatric treatment areas • No electric hospital beds in psych • Helicopter pad secure. Staff competent to access helicopter pad	• Does your hospital have a safety committee or function overseeing the environment of care and patient safety? Is there a person(s) in charge of the committee/function? How does the ED participate in the safety program? • How do you ensure that the environment is safe to take care of patients? • What is the frequency of any surveillance rounds in the ED? What data is collected? What is done with this data? Where is this data? Where is this data repeated? What are the trends with the data? • How do you contribute to eliminating and minimizing safety risks? • What is the procedure for reporting an incident or threat involving a patient, staff, or visitor? • How do you prevent patient falls? (Joint Commission NPSG 9B) • What is the policy and procedure on allowing equipment (e.g., stretchers, portable radiology equipment) in hallways? • How do you know the equipment in the ED is safe to use? • Describe the safety risks you encounter during your job and how you minimize them to protect yourself, reduce or prevent errors, and/or improve outcomes of care. • What activities have been implemented to increase worker safety? • What incident trends have been noted in the ED? • How are you notified of product safety recalls? • Describe the process for distribution, enforcement, monitoring, and review of the ED and hospital safety policy and procedures.

Standard	Comments	Evidence	Staff Questions
EC.1.30	**Smoking** The standard concerns enforcement of the hospital's policy and procedure to prohibit smoking in the ED. There are no medical exceptions that can be made in the ED. The ED should monitor compliance with the policy and procedure and ensure strategies are implemented to reduce violations.	• Staff interviews • Policy on smoking in all building(s) under the hospital's control with the requirement that smoking is strictly prohibited in all hospital-based ambulatory programs which includes the ED • Process enforced to monitor compliance with the hospital's smoking policy and procedure. Results discussed in environment of care committee/ group • Orientation and continuing education material on efforts to communicate, enforce the nonsmoking policy and procedure • Patient and family education materials on smoking cessation including its harmful affects on care, passive smoke inhalation, potential fire risks, smoking cessation programs, etc. • No smoking signs posted, as appropriate	• Describe how patients, families, visitors, and staff learn about the hospital's smoking policy and procedure. • What do you do if an ED patient violates the no smoking policy and procedure? • If you observe someone smoking in the building, what is the procedure to follow? • Take me to where your ED staff smoke. • Can patients go to the designated smoking area with IV pumps? If so, how do you monitor the alarms on the IV pumps?

Standard	Comments	Evidence	Staff Questions
EC.2.10	**Security Management** The standard relates to monitoring and compliance with the hospital security plan. This will be assessed by the surveyor during the ED tour. The ED is not specifically required to monitor each of the seven management plans found in the Environment of Care chapter. There is an individual assigned by hospital leaders to oversee the performance of the security management program.	• Staff and physician interviews • Implementation of hospital security plan and related policy and procedure • Proactive risk assessment of the hospital including the ED for security issues (consider the influence of environmental factors and services rendered). This is usually done by partnering with local law enforcement agencies • Mechanisms implemented to reduce and prevent security threats or incidents to patients, staff, visitors, etc. • Policy and procedures: - security incidents - civil disturbances - Very important people (VIP) patients that could generate media attention - where to place media trucks, control of media staff - communication with media - staffing during disasters - visitor identification, - managing patient property - responding to an infant and pediatric abduction or drill - workplace violence - patients with weapons - metal detector use, if applicable - care of prisoner - vehicular access to ED - access to and egress from sensitive areas secured - method for reporting security incidents - method for reporting missing patient/family property • Security orientation, continuing education materials, education schedules, staff files • Hospital PI projects, measurement of performance standards, action plans in response to security trends *ED surveyor tour* • Evidence of the security of the ED environment, equipment, supplies, information • Staff wearing ID badges • Patients with identification bands • Panic buttons for staff at triage • Locked doors in ED to prevent public access to appropriate areas • ED accessible to emergency vehicles; unauthorized cars addressed • Staff entrance doors locked at night • Panic alarms at triage • ED well lit • Telephone numbers for security and police posted	• How do you ensure the physical and personal security of patients, visitors, and staff in the ED? • Explain the security coverage for the ED. It this sufficient? • Did you receive security orientation? • Do you receive continuing education on security? • Whom do you call if a patient or visitor threatens violence? • Describe what you do if a patient has a weapon • Who is responsible for the metal detector, and how was that person trained? • How do you identify a staff member in the ED? • What do you do when you see someone without an ID badge? • How do you file a security incident report? • What are your most common security incidents? • Can you describe a security improvement in the ED? • Give me an example of a process for reducing security risks • How responsive is security when you call? Where is their number posted? • Describe the procedure you use when a patient's belongings are missing • How would you manage the care of a VIP? What about the media inquiring about the VIP? Where would the media park? Who would speak to the media for the hospital? What patient information would you disclose to the media? • How would you respond if there was an abduction announcement called for an infant or pediatric patient? How many infant abduction drills do you have in a year? Has the "infant" ever made it outside the door? • What training have you had for the management of a patient exhibiting physically aggressive behaviors?

Standard	Comments	Evidence	Staff Questions
EC.3.10	**Hazardous Waste** The standard addresses the hospital's ongoing monitoring of risk and compliance with the hazardous waste plan. Because the ED is a high-volume area for certain hazardous materials, staff should pay particular attention to policy and procedures related to hospital and any ED-specific requirement minimizing risks related to their use and disposal.	• Staff and physician interviews Policy and procedures: - when and how to empty hazardous waste disposal containers - hospital hazardous materials and waste plan • ED material safety data sheets (MSDS) inventory list identifying hazardous materials and waste used, stored, and/or generated based on criteria that meets applicable law and regulation such as the EPA, OSHA. Evidence of ED inventory continuously updated. If an electronic MSDS inventory is used staff may be asked to access • Approved processes implemented concerning the following aspects of hazardous materials and waste (includes chemicals, chemotherapeutic materials, radioactive materials, infectious, and regulated medical wastes, sharps): - selecting - handling (including precautions to take, protective gear used, and the management of spills, exposures) - storing (adequate space and equipment for safe management of waste; separation of hazardous waste storage and processing areas from other areas of the facility) - transporting - using - disposing (includes monitoring the disposing of hazardous gases, and vapors) • Staff knowledge of emergency procedures to manage spills and exposures • Evidence of permits, licenses, manifests for handling • Proper labeling of hazardous materials and waste • Hospital compliance with reporting procedures for hazardous material spills • Hospital PI projects, measurement of performance standards, action plans in response to hazardous material trends (e.g., ED staff knowledge of what to do in the event of a hazardous material spill, etc.) *ED surveyor tour* • Inspection showing proper use, disposal of hazardous materials • Space for safe handling and	• Where do you store hazardous materials? • What does MSDS stand for? • Where is MSDS information located? (Usually asked of a clinician and a housekeeper.) • What information is contained in an MSDS? • What procedure is followed when a hazardous material is spilled? • What would you do for a mercury spill? What would you do for a blood spill? Do you have mercury thermometers in the ED? Do you have cleaning chemicals in the ED? • How is a hazardous material or waste spill reported? • Do you have hazardous material spill kits in the ED? If so, where are these kept? • What procedure is followed if someone becomes covered with hazardous material? • What procedure do you follow if you encounter an unknown chemical? • How do you dispose of contaminated sharps or gauze contaminated with body fluids? Are these kept in a place that is not accessible to children in exam rooms/areas? • Do you lock your dirty utility room to keep patients and family members from exposing themselves to hazardous waste? Are these rooms negatively vented? • How often is regular trash and biohazardous waste picked up from the dirty utility room? Can you show me the schedule? • Do you store gloves underneath wall-mounted sharps containers? Is there a chance that blood or body fluids could fall onto the clean gloves used for patient care? • What do you do if a patient comes into the ED with chemical contamination? Has this happened? • How have you been trained to care for these patients specific to the hazardous waste? • Can you show me your Personal Protective Equipment (PPE)? Who replenishes this equipment? How often is it checked?

Standard	Comments	Evidence	Staff Questions
		storage of hazardous materials and waste • Hazardous materials labeled in accordance with federal, state, and local regulation, in a manner adequate to protect patient, visitor, and staff safety • Hazardous waste containers appropriate to minimize potential harm to patients, staff, and visitors • Hazardous waste containers located appropriately throughout the ED (off the floor) • Flammable liquids stored in fire-resistant cabinets; toxic, corrosive materials segregated, and appropriately stored • Poison control number accessible to staff	• What exam gloves would I use if I had a latex allergy? • What are some examples of hazardous wastes in the ED? Mercury? Disinfection supplies? • Do you have a decontamination shower? If so please explain how this works. • Are all hazardous waste storage areas locked? • Are chemicals secured on the cleaning carts? • Is the dirty utility room negatively ventilated to prevent the aerosolize of hazardous waste placed in the room while waiting for transfer out of the ED?

Standard	Comments	Evidence	Staff Questions
EC.4.10 EC.4.11 through EC.4.18 EC.4.20	**Emergency Management Implementation** The hospital's emergency preparedness plan needs to include the role of the ED. Emergency planning uses a four-phase, "all-hazards" approach that should address mitigation, preparedness, response, and recovery. The Joint Commission requires the hospital to participate in two emergency preparedness exercises per year (the exercise may be in response to an actual emergency or be planned). One exercise involves the community. The exercise involving the community should include an influx of simulated patients into the ED and should assess communication, coordination, and the effectiveness of the hospital's command structure. Of the two required exercises, one exercise is evaluated to determine performance when the communities cannot support or offer resources to the hospital. The type of exercise selected is relevant to the priority emergencies identified in the hospital's hazard vulnerability analysis (HVA). As part of its PI program, the hospital needs to critique all exercises to identify opportunities for improvement.	• Staff and physician interviews • Copy of Emergency Management Plan • Evidence of an emergency preparedness plan demonstrating ED leaders and medical staff's involvement with disaster readiness and emergency management. The plan is implemented when deemed appropriate, and indicates the following: • Hospital policy and procedures for each type of emergency identified. These include mitigation, preparedness, response, recovery strategies, actions, and responsibilities • Hospital process for activating the emergency response and recovery phase that includes a description of how, when, and by whom the phases are to be activated - how staff and external authorities are notified of the emergency response activation - process for identifying and assigning staff to perform essential staff functions under emergency conditions process for physicians to have emergency privileges - processes for managing the following under emergency conditions: provision of care, treatment, services, staff and family support activities, having necessary supplies, security, and communicating with the media. - evacuation procedures - arrangements of an alternate site identified for patient care which includes preparing for transportation issues, tracking patients, communication between the original care site and alternate facility - procedures for the identification of care providers, and other staff during a disaster - cooperative planning with other health care hospitals for sharing of information regarding command structures and control centers, resources, assets that could be shared in an emergency, and the names of patients and the deceased for identifying and locating victims - procedure for communicating in the ED during an emergency, with	• How does the ED manage demands in emergency situations (e.g., assigning staff, making space accommodations, ensuring supplies and security)? • How many emergency management exercises do you have a year? • When was the last emergency preparedness exercise? • Describe community involvement in the exercise. Did you have an influx of patients? • What did you learn from the exercise? • Describe any backup communication systems and alternatives to utilities. Do you include the threat of nuclear, biological and terrorism in your disaster exercises? • How would you manage patients in need of radioactive or chemical isolation, and decontamination? • Describe your evacuation routes • Describe your role in an evacuation • Are there alternate sites to take patients in the event the ED becomes overcrowded during an emergency? • How are you notified after hours that the emergency plan has been activated? • Who authorizes an evacuation? • What equipment is available for transporting patients in emergencies? • Where do the medical records go during an evacuation? • What is your procedure for notifying authorities when emergency measures are initiated? • How do you know which physicians have privileges during a disaster? • How do you know that a licensed individual/ professional such as an RN, can volunteer? What is the process for placing these individuals in areas of the ED where registered/ certified individuals can volunteer in an emergency?

Standard	Comments	Evidence	Staff Questions
		backup internal and external communication systems established - defined roles and responsibility of staff during an emergency, including who they should report to in the hospital command center and/ or community's command structure - identification of radioactive, biological, and chemical isolation and decontamination • Examples of the ED's contribution to the hospital's emergency management plan, policy and procedures, role of staff • Evidence of participation in community emergency management planning • ED participation in safety and/or emergency (disaster) preparedness committee, minutes of meetings • Updated disaster call list • On-call list • Inventory of emergency supplies • List of duties to be performed in an emergency • Reports on emergency preparedness exercise performance. • Emergency supplies accessible, stocked; supplies (including electrical) in working condition • Posting education/procedures for managing emergencies, if available (e.g., Utility Systems Failure Guide, bomb threat procedures, roles and responsibilities of staff in a disaster) • PI projects, measurement of performance standards, action plans in response to emergency preparedness (e.g., indicator might be using disaster critiques to prepare for future disasters)	• What is the hospital's alternative care site if evacuation is necessary? • Where would you place patients in the event of a surge of patients?

Standard	Comments	Evidence	Staff Questions
EC.5.10 EC.5.20 EC.5.30 EC.5.40 EC.5.50	**Life (Fire) Safety** The hospital has a fire prevention plan addressing fire response, evacuation routes, roles and responsibilities of staff, LIPs, volunteers with respect to the fire's point of origin and with evacuation procedures. Surveyors will look for monitoring and compliance in the ED to determine if the area is fire safe. They will inspect to determine if the fire safety plan is implemented to prevent fire, smoke, and other related hazards, protecting patients, visitors, staff, and property. Fire drills are conducted on a quarterly basis on all shifts and are critiqued for the hospital to use for PI purposes. The hospital oversees the development and maintenance of a Statement of Conditions (SOC).	• Staff and physician interviews • Hospital fire safety plan and evaluation of the plan through fire drills to improve the performance of staff and equipment. Includes an annual assessment of the effectiveness of fire response training • Implementation of fire response plan and the ED's role in supporting the plan • PI projects, at least one hospital PI measurement (not specific to the ED), action plans in response to life safety issues, staff knowledge with drills (e.g., responding to fire alarm and duties, containment of smoke and fire, transferring patients to safety, use of the fire extinguisher, and evacuation procedures) • Purchase and use of nonflammable products in the ED (e.g., bedding, draperies, curtains) • Compliance with life safety codes, reporting of fire protection deficiencies, failures, and user errors • Evidence of staff participation in quarterly fire drills on all shifts in the ED with at least 50% of the drills being unannounced • The hospital should insure the fire safety system, equipment and components in the ED meet the prescriptive requirements as stated in standard EC.5.40 • Implementation of interim life safety measures (ILSMs) when indicated by policy and procedure. ILSMs are implemented as outlined in hospital policy and procedure during ED construction, and when life safety deficiencies exist. This process is overseen by those in charge of overseeing the environment of care function within the hospital to ensure the elements of performance (e.g., ensuring unobstructed exits, access to emergency services, the operation of the fire alarm system, construction site safe, use of additional fire safety equipment, additional staff training, extra fire drills, etc.) in standard EC.5.50 are met *Surveyor tour of ED* • ED compliance (e.g., hallways unobstructed, fire/smoke doors working properly) • Portable fire extinguishers properly identified, mounted, and	• What training did you receive during orientation on life safety issues? Give an example of what you learned. • What life safety measures take effect if a construction project causes blocked exits or entrances? • How often do you have fire drills? Are these drills conducted without notice? How often? • How do you know if the fire drill was a success? • Is staff performance and knowledge during drills evaluated? • How do you know all staff in the ED have participated in a fire drill at least annually? • Do you receive feedback from the drill? • What do you do if there is a fire? • Where is the closest fire exit? • How do you evacuate the area during a fire? • Where is the closest fire extinguisher? • What type of extinguisher is it? • What procedures do you follow to contain smoke and fire? • How would I know what to do during a fire if I were a contract worker here only for the day? • Who is responsible for turning off mechanical gasses including oxygen valves in the event of a fire? Are these gas valves labeled? • Where is the nearest fire alarm? How do you operate it? • How do you know when the alarm is being tested? • What expectations do you have for the ED medical staff, students, contracted workers and volunteers in learning about fire safety? • What is your role and responsibility if you are at the fire's point of origin (away from the fire's point of origin)? • What do you do if you see a ceiling tile that is broken, not correctly in place or missing completely? • Show me in this patient care area two illuminated exit signs. • Do you have ongoing education and training on fire safety?

Standard	Comments	Evidence	Staff Questions
		inspected at least monthly, and maintained at least annually • Storage is less than 18" from sprinkler heads • Fire/smoke doors are not propped open	• Do you educate agency staff to the fire safety plan prior to the start of their shift? • Are the stairwells lighted? • Can you show me there is no dust in the electrical closets and mechanical closets? • Do all fire doors positively latch? • Do you prop open fire or smoke doors? • What can be placed in a hallway? • What can block a hallway? • How do you ensure fire extinguishers are not blocked by equipment? • How do you ensure emergency shut off valves for mechanical gasses are not blocked? • Have you had any construction in the ED in the last 3 years? Did you implement ILSM? If not, why not? If so, then show me the documentation for ILSM in the ED.

Standard	Comments	Evidence	Staff Questions
EC.6.10 EC.6.20	**Medical Equipment** The hospital demonstrates the monitoring of risk and compliance with the medical equipment management plan. Medical equipment is maintained, tested, and inspected per policy and procedure. Any specific ED policy and procedures are consistent with the hospital's. The hospital demonstrates compliance with the Joint Commission's National Patient Safety Goals as they relate to several equipment management topics—improving the safety of using infusion pumps, and improving the effectiveness of clinical alarm systems. Clinical staff are familiar with these goals, including what mechanisms the hospital has implemented to comply with the goals. Hospitals demonstrate the following strategies have been implemented to promote patient safety: (1) making sure there is free-flow protection on all general-use and Patient Controlled Analgesia (PCA) intravenous infusion pumps; (2) conduct preventive maintenance and testing of alarm systems according to a schedule; and (3) staff ensure that alarms can be heard and that they are set correctly.	• Staff, physician, and ED leader interviews • Hospital medical equipment plan • Policy and procedures - equipment disruption or failure - availability of backup equipment - how to obtain repair services - safety testing of equipment prior to use - testing of clinical alarms in all areas • ED's role in supporting and implementing the equipment management plan • Staff orientation, continuing education materials, and attendance records • Current, accurate and separate hospital inventory of medical equipment (regardless of ownership) based on criteria (function, physical risks, incident history). This is kept in the Engineering Department • Medical equipment properly maintained, carries inspection tags for preventative maintenance or a system where staff can articulate service logs are completed per policy and procedure • Documentation of a hospital's process for medical equipment recalls, medical device alerts, Joint Commission Sentinel Events • Hospital compliance with the Safe Medical Device Act of 1990 that requires processes for identifying, implementing, monitoring and reporting incidents where a medical device is suspected or attributed to the death, serious injury, or serious illness • Hospital PI projects, measurement of performance standards, action plans in response to medical equipment management (e.g., staff knowledge of response to medical equipment failure, preventive maintenance) • Hospital inventory (specific to ED) of clinical alarms and evidence alarms are tested according to preventive maintenance schedules • Evidence that the ED can ensure free-flow protection on all general-use and PCA intravenous infusion pumps used in the hospital	• Who uses this piece of equipment? How do you know it is safe to use? How do you operate it? What do you do if it malfunctions? • Who trains staff on using the medical equipment? Where is this documented? • Who trains staff, medical students, nursing students, and physicians to medical equipment? • What is the process for bringing new equipment into the ED? Can LIPs bring their own medical equipment into the ED? • What is the training process when new equipment is introduced? How are LIPs trained on medical equipment they use? • How is staff competent to use medical equipment assessed? • What do you do if this piece of medical equipment malfunctions? Whom do you inform? How do you document this? • How often is this medical equipment serviced? How do you know? • What is your policy on safety testing of medical equipment prior to initial use? • What is your policy on safety testing for contracted medical equipment? • What is your procedure for checking infusion pumps? Defibrillator? • Who trained you? • Do you lend medical equipment to other hospitals? What is the process?

Standard	Comments	Evidence	Staff Questions
EC.7.10 EC.7.20 EC.7.30 EC.7.40 EC.7.50	**Utility Management** These standards include critical components of life support, IC systems for high-risk patients, and non-life support utility systems and equipment. Examples are electrical outlets for crash carts and ED cardiac monitors, oxygen and vacuum systems. The hospital has a utility system plan that promotes a highly functioning, adequately monitored, operational utility system by reducing the risks associated with utility failure.	• Staff and ED leader interviews • Hospital utility management plan, policy and procedures (e.g., emergency procedures for responding to utility disruptions or failures); ED's role in implementing plan • Hospital inspection and testing records of preventive maintenance, testing of utilities, and their critical components (usually not kept in ED) • A hospital utility management program that has a current, accurate, and separate inventory of utility equipment, assigns risk using selected criteria, implements strategies to test, and maintain equipment to reduce clinical and physical risks • Evidence the hospital's plant operations conducts maintenance, testing, and inspections on emergency power systems • ED staff education, continuing education materials, attendance records for instructional programs on utilities • Hospital documentation in meeting minutes of any utility management issues within the ED • Hospital documentation of performance and safety testing of critical components of utility system prior to initial use *Surveyor ED tour* • Unobstructed and appropriately labeled mechanical gas shutoff controls in the ED • Appropriate negative and/or positive ventilation systems/ equipment to control air-borne contaminants, when applicable • Appropriate emergency telephone numbers posted for utility failures or disruptions • Proper installation of emergency power source adequate to the hospital as required by the Life Safety Code (LSC). Electricity supplied to essential areas (emergency areas, elevators, areas providing life support, etc.) and equipment (e.g., life support systems, air compressors, alarm systems, exit lighting for signs/ routes, communication systems) when normal electricity is interrupted • Hospital PI projects, measurement of performance standards, action plans in response to utilities (e.g., staff knowledge of actions to take in a utility system failure)	• What orientation and continuing education have you received on utility management? • What do you do if the power goes out? • Do you perform moderate sedation in the ED? Are there battery-powered lights where moderate sedation occurs in the ED? • How do you report a utility problem, failure, or user error? • Who do you call after-hours for utility problems? • Who examines, maintains, and tests critical operating components in the ED? • Describe clinical interventions that care providers may need to perform if there is a complete power outage. • Who would turn off the main utility (electricity, water, gas, medical gasses) sources on weekends and after-hours? • Do you have elevators in the ED? Who checks them for safety?

Standard	Comments	Evidence	Staff Questions
EC.8.10 EC.8.30	**Environment Promotes Healing** The survey will assess ED compliance with hospital policy and procedure on environmental considerations related to care.	• Staff, physician, and ED leader interviews • Policy and procedures with respect to patients rights and ethics, specific to environmental factors such as privacy, security, confidentiality • Hospital policy and procedures: - construction - door locking policy and procedures (for observation units, bathrooms, forensic patients, etc.) • Documentation of an ED risk assessment related to planned construction or renovation that might compromise patient care in the ED (consider air quality, IC, utility requirements, noise, vibration, and emergency procedures) *Surveyor ED tour* • Appropriate space for emergency services relative to patient population (age, and characteristics) • Area for care is safe, clean, functional to meet the needs of the patients served • Ventilation appropriate with respect to air quality considering temperature, humidity, odor • Any locked doors or occupied spaces have mechanisms to provide emergency access • Reducing or eliminating ED overcrowding and use of equipment, stretchers in hallway • Patient privacy not violated on overhead paging system • Doors closed, curtains used where appropriate • Emergency access to locked rooms, such as bathrooms • Adequate lighting for patient care activities • Rooms for patient/religious advisor discussions available • Environment is safe, clean, and attractive • Auditory privacy • Environmental IC risk assessment completed prior to renovation	• Is there enough space in the ED exam rooms to provide services? Manage a code? • Where does triage occur? How is patient confidentiality protected? • How are you sensitive to patients' needs for privacy, respect, and dignity in the triage environment? In the waiting area and treatment rooms? • How are conversations at registration, triage, and other areas kept confidential? • Describe any projects or initiatives that have been implemented to improve the environment of care in the ED. • Did you have renovations in the ED in the last year? If so, what changes if any to fire exits did you make? • How were IC practices impacted during the renovation?

Standard	Comments	Evidence	Staff Questions
EC.9.10 EC.9.20 EC.9.30	**Environmental PI** The hospital and ED seek to monitor and improve environmental conditions. Data is collected, aggregated, assessed, and used to improve the environment of care and patient safety program within the hospital. A multidisciplinary hospital process exists to improve the hospital's environment of care in the hospital.	• Staff and ED leader interviews • Staff are aware of the reporting and data collection mechanism for patients and visitors. • Staff can speak to reporting and actions to take for security and property incidents, occupational health illness and injuries, hazardous materials and waste spills, exposures, medical equipment and utility management deficiencies, failures, or user errors related to fire safety • The ED participates in data collection activities to identify deficiencies, opportunities for improvement, and to monitor the overall environment of care. • The ED leaders and staff are aware that an individual(s) is assigned to oversee the major functions of the hospital's environment of care • Evidence of hospital meetings, reports, evidence of a multidisciplinary PI team or group analyzing environment of care findings, plans for improvement to resolve any identified issues • Hospital outcomes, improvement reports, including annual reports of the objectives, scope, performance, and effectiveness for each of the seven required Environment of Care plans. Reports demonstrate that recommendations based on PI activities and monitoring of the environment of care plans have been communicated at least annually to hospital leaders for consideration • Hospital environment of care data, environmental safety issues, recommendations for improvement, and measurable outcomes are integrated into the hospital's patient safety program as indicated in the Leadership chapter.	• Have you participated in any data collection to measure the effectiveness of the environment of care plans in the ED? • What strategies have you implemented to improve the environment of care in your unit? • What communication do you receive from the hospital re: EOC monitoring, improvements, actions needed? • How do you monitor the effectiveness of any new environment of care recommendations implemented? • Where do you report this monitoring data? • Describe how you resolve environment of care issues identified in your system and in your service area. What other disciplines have you worked with to improve the environment of care? • Does your hospital have a committee or process for measuring performance, outcomes, resolving environment of care issues in a timely manner? How is the ED represented in the process? • How does IC and engineering work together in the ED? • How are environment of care issues and measurable outcomes integrated with the hospital's patient safety program? Communicated to hospital leaders and/or the individual(s) responsible for patient safety, and PI? • Explain how you implemented your disaster plan, measured and reported findings. Did you make improvements?

MANAGEMENT OF HUMAN RESOURCES

Standard	Comments	Evidence	Staff Questions
HR.1.10 HR.1.20	**Adequate Staffing & Qualifications** The ED ensures there are sufficient staff within the ED who have education, training, licensure, and knowledge consistent with legal requirements to meet the needs of the population served. Employee, contract worker, student*, volunteer* personnel files demonstrate evidence that his/her qualifications correspond with assigned job responsibilities. **Note:* the requirements pertain to students and volunteers working in the same capacity as staff who provide care and treatment.	• Staff and ED leader interviews • ED staffing plan and evidence of its implementation • Access to personnel files that indicate the following (files may be kept in the HR Department): - job descriptions/clinical privileges reflecting state law requirements for licensure, scope of practice - staff orientation (hospital and ED) - performance evaluations corresponding with job descriptions - defined qualifications and competence of staff making decisions about the use and implementation of restraint and seclusion use - verification of observable competencies • The hospital demonstrates the following according to the hospital's policy and procedure, and in accord with laws and regulations for applicable individuals providing health care, treatment, and services in the hospital: - Current licensure (e.g., LVN/LPN), certification (e.g., CPR/CEN), registration, (e.g., RN) if required by state law or per the job description - Training, experience, and competency for the job assignment - Criminal background check - Compliance with employee health policy and procedures of the hospital for health screening requirements (e.g., TB, Hepatitis) - Staff supervision of students providing patient care/ treatment/services • Hospital ensures that individuals hired who do not have a license, registration, and/or certification are not providing care that would require licensure/registration/ certification by law or regulation. • ED and hospital organizational chart • Meeting minutes, reports on PI studies regarding appropriate staffing levels and skills • Contracts, if the ED uses contracted staff	*To staff* • What knowledge and abilities do you need to work in this ED? • How did you gain that knowledge? • How is your performance evaluated in measurable terms? • What qualifications or competencies do you have related to the use of restraint and/or seclusion? How was your competency for restraints evaluated? • How are you competent to assist with moderate sedation in the ED? • Do you ever need to use a reversal agent after moderate sedation is administered? • Describe your staffing process and how ED leaders ensure an adequate number of staff is available for patient care. • Do you use non-hospital nurses (e.g., agency, travelers, etc) in the ED? If so, how do you know they are competent? • Is there an RN in the ED on all shifts? • How many nurses are certified by the Emergency Nurses Association (ENA)? • Have nurses here attended the Trauma Nurse Care Course (TNCC)? *To ED leaders* • What is your process for defining staff qualifications and responsibilities? • Do all your staff meet the requirements you have for any specialized training for the ED RN (e.g., ACLS, PALS, TNCC, NALS, and CEN)? • How do you match staffing needs with the education level and experience of staff? • How do you monitor and adjust staffing based on patient need? • What process do you use for assigning staff to triage based on their education and experience? • How do you ensure that each staff member has a job description that meets essential job requirements? • What happens if the number of staff is on a particular shift is less than planned? • Tell me about how staff are oriented. How long does this last? Is there a checklist you could show me?

Standard	Comments	Evidence	Staff Questions
HR.1.25	**Emergency Management/Disaster Responsibilities** Prior to activating the Emergency Management/Disaster plan, the hospital is required to make a decision whether they are going to use or not use volunteer practitioners. This decision must be known by leadership and a policy/process developed and tested with one of the two required emergency management exercises.	• ED leader interviews • HR Emergency Management/ Disaster Volunteer policy • Emergency Management/ Disaster Plan • Emergency Management Disaster exercise where the volunteer practitioner policy was tested • ED participation in safety and/or emergency (disaster) preparedness committee, minutes of meetings	• How do you know that a licensed individual/ professional, such as an RN, can volunteer? • What is the process for placing these individuals in areas of the ED where registered/certified individuals can volunteer in an emergency? • How are these individuals supervised?
HR.1.30	**Staffing Effectiveness** The hospital evaluates Joint Commission staffing effectiveness indicators. It is no longer specifically required that this be conducted in every department of the hospital. If the ED does participate in this standard, data from at least four indicators—two clinical/service screening indicators and two Human Resource (HR) screening indicators are selected. At least one clinical/ service indicator and one HR indicator are selected from the Joint Commission's recommended list of indicators. The hospital clearly demonstrates its reasoning for selecting its indicators, as well as if direct and indirect caregivers are included in the HR screening indicators. ED leaders should collaborate with the HR Department to determine participation.	• Staff, physician, and ED leader interviews • Data collected from HR screening indicators such as: - overtime - staff vacancy rate, turnover rate - staff satisfaction - understaffing as compared to hospital's staffing plan - nursing care hours per patient day - staff injuries on the job - on-call or per diem use - sick time • Data collected from clinical/ service indicators such as: - patient or family complaints - adverse drug events - patient falls or other injuries (Joint Commission NPSG 9B) - post-operative infections - shock/cardiac arrest - skin breakdown - urinary track infections • Hospital leaders report at least annually on the analysis of data (relative to expected targets, goals, desired performance, external comparisons) related to staffing effectiveness and any actions taken to improve staffing. Line graphs, run and/or control charts are used to determine the stability of the process. All indicators are analyzed in combination using statistical techniques to determine if outcomes may be influenced by staffing	• Are you participating in any staffing effectiveness data collection? If yes, what is your process for using screening indicators to determine staffing effectiveness? • How many screening indicators are analyzed to assess the effectiveness of staff? • What is the rationale for selecting those particular screening indicators? • What caregivers are included in the human resource screening indicators? Is there a process to analyze screening indicator data over time per measure (e.g., target ranges, trends over time, external comparison data) and then in combination with other screening indicators (i.e., statistical correlation)? • How have staff been involved in the review of data from the screening indicators? • What changes have been made based on the staffing effectiveness data? • What has been shared with the governing body re: staffing effectiveness?

Standard	Comments	Evidence	Staff Questions
HR.2.10	**Initial Orientation** The standard addresses the hospital and ED staff orientation programs. Staff members, students, and volunteers receive initial job training and information on their responsibilities and their workplace prior to providing care or performing services.	• Staff and ED leader interviews • Job description, staff orientation program, verification policy and procedures, etc. • Evidence that new hires received orientation for the hospital and ED: - attendance records - training material presented - participation in preceptor program • Does the training material presented at staff orientation include the following topics: - review of mission, strategic goals - hospital, program specific and/or ED policy and procedures - overview of hospital policy and procedures relative to environment of care, IC - specific job duties and responsibilities unit specific responsibilities related to safety and IC - cultural diversity and sensitivity - patient rights and hospital ethics - pain management for clinical staff - abuse and neglect - moderate sedation, if applicable - error reporting (patient safety) - team dynamics - organ and tissue procurement - sensitivity toward the dying patient - restraints (if applicable, requires a competency) - patient safety, hospital and unit specific • Following staff orientation, evidence that the hospital assesses and documents each person's ability to carry out assigned responsibilities safely, proficiently, and in a timely manner upon completion of staff orientation (initial competency and/or orientation performance evaluation) • Policy and procedure: - caring for prisoners - educating forensic staff (e.g., correctional officers, guards, and others) with no clinical training or experience on how to interact with patients; procedures for responding to incidents/unusual clinical events; channels for	• How were you trained to perform this procedure? • What specialized training do you have as an ED LPN, LVN, RN, or CNA? • How are non-hospital employees/agency nurses oriented to the ED? • Describe how a new staff member of your ED would receive the following: - orientation to the hospital and ED (e.g., specific equipment, procedures, patient safety, environment of care, IC) - evaluation determining that he or she is ready to perform responsibilities • Do you have volunteers, residents, agency, contract staff or students working in the ED? If yes, what type of orientation do they receive to the hospital and ED? • How do you orient forensic staff? • How do you educate ED staff to care for forensic patients? • Describe the staff orientation topics. • Who do you approach to discuss issues about the prisoner/patient you are overseeing? • How are students and volunteers educated on patient safety in the ED? • Have you been educated to the hospital's influenza vaccine program? • Have you been educated on how you can contact the Joint Commission to report any quality or safety concerns without reprisal? Were you provided the contact information such as telephone number and address? *Questions for forensic staff:* • What is your role with regard to the care of this patient? • How are you educated in performing your role? • How does the hospital know you are competent to perform your role in the ED? • Describe any training the hospital provided to you (e.g., fire safety, restraint, chain of command, safety procedures, etc.) • What is the difference between use of administrative (i.e., for law enforcement

Standard	Comments	Evidence	Staff Questions
		communicating with clinicians, security and administration; and the difference between administrative and clinical restraint and seclusion	purposes) and clinical restraint, and seclusion? • How do you manage restraint and seclusion issues?

Standard	Comments	Evidence	Staff Questions
HR.2.20	**Error Reporting Education** Staff members, LIPs, students, and volunteers (as appropriate) can convey their specific job duties or responsibilities pertaining to safety. Staff need to understand who, when, how, and what clinical and environmental issues to report related to safety.	• Staff and ED leader interviews • Safety and HR department plans policy, and procedures: - error reporting education - ongoing error reporting education, inservices, training to enhance staff competencies/performance in risk management, and/or the environment of care • Continuing education for staff relative to risk management and safety • Evidence that LIPs, students, and volunteers can describe and demonstrate their roles and responsibilities pertaining to safety management • Ongoing error reporting education • PI related to patient safety and environmental safety	• What are the risks associated with your job? What actions do you do to eliminate or reduce risks? • How do you report risks associated with your job? • Describe your error or incident reporting mechanism. Do you report "close calls" or "near misses" where no harm occurred to the patient but could have? • What is your mechanism to report problems, failures, and user errors? • How does the hospital train you about safety topics, precautions to take, the environment of care, and patient safety? • What emergency procedures should be instituted should an incident or failure occur in the environment?

Standard	Comments	Evidence	Staff Questions
HR.2.30	**Ongoing Staff Education** The ED must show evidence of staff that focus on self-improvement and self-learning to improve their competence. The hospital must provide ongoing education and training to staff, students and volunteers who render patient care, treatment and services. Staff participates in education and training programs to stay current, confirm with law and regulations, to promote patient safety, and when there are changes in job responsibilities. Education and training provided is documented.	• Staff and ED leader interviews • Policy and procedures specific to education and training • Submitting and responding to data collected on ED staff's education and learning needs • Schedule of hospital training programs and evidence of topics covered • Documentation of ED specific training programs • Training tools (journals, Internet, self-study guides, audiotapes, videotapes, teleconferences, product demonstration, access to school credits, self-tests, cross-training program descriptions, etc.) • Meeting minutes (e.g., medical staff, PI, ED, or governing body) on improving competencies, staff proficiency, through staff development/training • Education attendance records indicating staff, student, volunteer (when providing patient care, treatment and/or services) participation in outside seminars, internal classes, and/or other continuing education programs • Examples of how data was assessed and used to design education program and activities for staff, volunteers, and students • Ongoing: - ED-role specific education - ED-role specific population/age-related competency - ED-role specific patient and environmental safety - ED-role specific IC - hospital team training - hospital training re: reporting unanticipated - continuing education records, evidence of meeting requirements for any specialized training and education as per hospital and/or ED policy and procedure	*To ED leaders* • How do you ensure staff have the skills needed for their jobs? • Describe how you identify staff learning needs • How do you prioritize and monitor staff education requirements? • What training have you planned for your ED within the past year? How do you select training topics? • What internal education programs do you have? • How do you educate the night shift? • Do staff pursue higher education and training? • How do you enhance team building and improve the training to staff? • How does the hospital assist you in training to improve your skills and knowledge? *To staff* • What type of staff educational activities are available? How often? • Do education programs have continuing education unit (CEU) credits? • If yes, how many CEU programs are provided annually? • What resources does your hospital devote to continuing education (e.g., journals, books, videos, seminars, college credits, etc.)? • What was the last training session you attended? Has it helped you to improve patient care? • How are you competent to screen and treat different patient groups (e.g., pediatric, domestic, geriatric abuse, and aggregated assault victims)? • Are you meeting the continuing education requirements for your job based on your hospital's policy and procedures? • What training have you received relative to team building, team dynamics, and team? Communication? Patient safety? IC? • Describe training programs designed for your job classification and patient population/programs (e.g., behavioral health, dialysis, etc.) • Were you taught to report unanticipated outcomes or medical errors?

Standard	Comments	Evidence	Staff Questions
HR.3.10 HR.3.20	**Competency & Evaluations** Competence to perform job duties is assessed, evaluated, and maintained. The staff performance evaluations must be completed at least once in the three-year accreditation cycle, unless applicable law/regulation requires a shorter timeframe.	• Staff and ED leader interviews • HR and ED policy and procedures: competency and the performance evaluation process • Competence assessments exist for students, and volunteers who work in the same capacity as staff providing patient care/services • Competencies are designed and implemented based on: - population served, (trauma, OB, geriatric, pediatric) - required by job responsibilities - at orientation - on an ongoing basis relative to techniques, procedures, technology, equipment or skills needed to provide care or services • The hospital must define the timeframe for frequency of competency assessments for each job, and indicate the assessment methods. • Individuals who assess competencies must be qualified to conduct the evaluation. • Hospitals must demonstrate evidence of implementation of the competency assessment program, as well as periodic performance evaluations conducted at timeframes identified by the hospital's policy and procedure • Performance evaluations are based on the performance expectations identified in the corresponding job descriptions • Meeting minutes (e.g., medical staff, PI, ED, or governing body) on improving competencies, staff proficiency, staffing levels • Employee, contracted staff, volunteer records include: - job description, signed - staff orientation - performance evaluations (blank examples) - competency program, orientation for specific age groups, as applicable - continuing education, training - job and age-specific (if direct care provider) competencies • PI studies, reports, minutes on age-specific competency issues	• What competencies are required to meet the specific population served in the ED, for example, Level 1 trauma, burn center, infants, pediatrics, geriatrics, and other groups? • How often are competencies assessed? Where is this documented? • Who assess competencies? How are they competent to do so? Does the competency assessment include observing the individual staff member performing the skills while using critical thinking? • If improvement activities determine that a person with performance problems is unable/unwilling to improve, what action will the hospital take? Will the hospital modify the person's job assignment? • How often do you receive a performance evaluation? • What are the competencies of an ED nurse? Technician? • Who assesses your competencies? • How are your competencies assessed? • What mechanism is used to evaluate how staff meet their defined responsibilities? • Do you have age-specific competencies? • Do you have population-specific competencies?

MANAGEMENT OF INFORMATION

Standard	Comments	Evidence	Staff Questions
IM.1.10	**Information Management Plan** This standard concerns the hospital having an information management plan created by assessing the hospital's internal and external information needs. Representatives from the ED must demonstrate their participation in having their information management needs assessed so that they are incorporated within the overall panning process. Surveyors may focus on how ED leaders make their ED's information management needs known to hospital leaders.	• Staff and ED leader interviews • Evidence of a hospital Information Management Steering Committee, group, or process that prioritizes projects, requests, needs for the hospital, including the ED (based on the hospital's mission, goals, scope and complexity of services, patient safety, staffing, performance, method of service delivery, resources, availability of technology, and communication barriers evident among caregivers) • Hospital information management plan includes planning for ED services • ED participation in ongoing information management planning documents, strategic plans, needs assessment surveys, requests to administration • Meeting minutes indicating hospital information management planning • PI projects in the ED or hospital displaying plans, outcomes to improve the flow of patient information (e.g., plans for or observation of new computer system, charting, scheduling system, information storage and feedback mechanisms) • Evidence that staff have their need for knowledge-based information met by the hospital	*To ED leaders* • How do you participate in information management planning? Are physicians and other clinicians involved in the process? • How has the hospital assessed your information management needs? • Can you give an example of how you had an information management need met? • Has the hospital performed an assessment of the needs of the ED for knowledge-based information to assist with information management planning? • While not required products, has the ED considered automated medication dispensing machines, computerized physicians order entry, electronic medical record documentation? • Do you document against medical advice (AMA) and left without being seen (LWBS) in the patient's medical record?

Standard	Comments	Evidence	Staff Questions
IM.2.10 IM.2.20 IM.2.30	**Privacy & Confidentiality of Patient Information** The ED should ensure that privacy and confidentiality policy and procedures are enforced. Information security practices comply with hospital policy and procedures while allowing access to data and information in a timely fashion. To protect confidentiality, staff should limit access to patient information that is needed to care for the patient. Systems are implemented to protect the integrity of the data (e.g., active medical record, computer system, stored medical records). Maintaining the continuity of information is essential for patient care and outcomes.	• Staff, physician, and ED leader interviews • Hospital policy and procedures consistent with applicable federal, state, and local law regarding: - privacy, confidentiality, and security of information— - monitoring and enforcing compliance - obtaining access to information - release of information - preservation of the medical record - removal of medical records - destroying records and copies - falsification of medical records - protecting the integrity of data (e.g., operation of back-up systems) - contingency plans - down-time procedures - data retrieval - measures for protection against emergencies - security systems that include passwords, codes - HIPAA requirements: disclosure, authentication, nonrepudiation, encryption, when warranted, and auditability for patient billing - removal of personal identifiers when releasing health data and information whenever feasible • Evidence of staff education regarding information management policy and procedures, and further communication when modifications are made • Technology used to assist with limiting access of the information to authorized individuals delivering care, services, treatment, research, education, and proper management of the patient • Examples of preserving information considered "sensitive" and that requires extraordinary means to preserve patient privacy and confidentiality • Security of any clinical information identifying the patient evidence that protected health information, is used for purposes identified or as required by law and not further disclosed without patient authorization	• How do you preserve the confidentiality and security of data/information? • Who has access to a patient's medical record? To the computer terminal? • What information do you have access to on the computer? • What do you do if a family member asks to look at a patient's record? • What is your policy and procedure on releasing clinical information, copies of the record? Can ambulance personnel review ED patient information? • Do you get a consent for the release of information? • How do you manage inquiries regarding patients? • What do you do if the media calls for patient information? • How are you trained on confidentiality and security of information issues? • What special procedures do you have to protect patient information (e.g., staff sign confidentiality statements on hire or when using computer system)? • What measures does the hospital take to protect information being revealed to individuals who do not have permission? What processes protect the data or information from security breaches, harm, or being altered? • Who can you give your computer access code to? • When using and disclosing health information, does the hospital remove the personal identifiers as much as possible? • Describe your disclosure of information practices. • How do you ensure that staff with legitimate needs have access to data and information without compromising its integrity? • Do you have communication/white boards in the ED? How do you protect the patient's confidentiality if you use these?

Standard	Comments	Evidence	Staff Questions
		• Security of active and inactive medical records • Computer terminals logged off when not in use • Patient names and diagnoses not recorded on a board visible to visitors and other patients • Protective measures implemented to prevent distribution of sensitive information to public (e.g., limiting access to operating room or procedural schedules, special sign-in logs protecting patient name and information that could be viewed by others, and use of technology to provide additional security measures) • Confidential, sensitive patient information not discussed in areas where it may be overheard by individuals other than the patient • Measures to protect medical records from damage (e.g., sprinklers, fireproof cabinets)	

Standard	Comments	Evidence	Staff Questions
IM.3.10	**Medical Record Entries** This standard covers expectation of the use of standard terminology, definitions, and abbreviations, as well as uniform data collection methodologies. (Joint Commission NPSG 2B) Policy and procedures for retaining data and information must comply with law and regulations. The hospital must ensure all medical record entries are dated, timed, signed by the author, precise, and that there is a uniform method of disseminating complete data among users. These entries must be written in a manner so data can be extracted and interpreted in meaningful information to be used by leaders to make decisions. The hospital must have mechanisms to ensure that information management policy and procedures are enforced (e.g., read-back, signing verbal orders, dating and timing of entries). This standard also concerns ensuring hospital has a "do not use" list of those abbreviations, acronyms, and symbols that are not to be used by staff, LIP, etc. (Joint Commission NPSG 2B)	• Staff and ED leader interviews • Staff knowledge of a policy and procedure and/or list of abbreviations not to be used that are considered risky and problematic (Joint Commission NPSG 2B) • Hospital medical and clinical policy and procedures: terminology, minimum data sets, data definitions, classification, vocabulary, standardized nomenclature, collection, storage, and retrieval of data, unscheduled downtime, data transformation and dissemination • Medical record accuracy, use of "do not use" unapproved terminology and abbreviations, timeliness and accuracy of data collection and dissemination into usable information (Joint Commission NPSG 2B) • QC systems to oversee data collection activities that includes consideration for timeliness, accuracy of content, completeness, and discrimination necessary for intended use • Hospital policy and procedure outlining the time frame for retention of data to comply with law accrediting and regulatory bodies • Hospital mechanism for ensuring systems are compatible for accurate transmission and assimilation of data for analysis and reporting: - diagnostic study turnaround time - medical record entry accuracy • PI data, medical record reviews, practices that ensure the accuracy of data and information (e.g., use of standard abbreviations, codes, definitions, turnaround time, medical record completion rates) • Improving diagnostic test turnaround time for test results to become available to practitioners • Education, lecture outlines on information management - confidentiality, security, access - use of computers, software - documenting in medical records - data collection techniques, ensuring accuracy of collecting data	• What abbreviations have you defined as problematic that staff should not use? Is the use of an unapproved abbreviation in a medical record entry considered an incomplete order? (Joint Commission NPSG 2B) • Can you show me in this medical record any abbreviations that should not be used based on your hospital's policy and procedure? What do you do when you find these? What does this data reflect? Where is this data reported? (Joint Commission NPSG 2B) • How do you ensure that data is collected in a uniform manner? • How long are your ED medical records retained? Where are they stored? • Describe any mechanisms you use to ensure that data is collected in a timely and precise manner. • How long does it take the medical record to get from the triage area to the treatment area? • What is the expected turnaround time for the following: - radiology reports? - lab tests? - blood tests? • Describe your process for notifying physicians of discrepancies in radiology, laboratory, or other diagnostic test results • What is your procedure for notifying patients of the results of diagnostic studies after they have left the ED? • What type of information management (e.g., medical record entries, software) training have clinical staff received? What elements does the education include? From the ED viewpoint, has there been any specialized education? Have you added any information management systems or support specific to your area? • Are medical staff and students trained in information management? • How do you assess staff knowledge of information management?

Standard	Comments	Evidence	Staff Questions
		- using data, exchanging information, interpreting data - tools available - PI techniques on using data to support decisions, statistical and nonstatistical analysis methods - access to literature, library services - HIPAA • Personnel files showing information management training provided based on the individual's job requirements, information needs	• What ED indicators are collected to improve systems and processes? How do you ensure consistency when gathering the data? Have you trended your data? Do you use statistical techniques to interpret the data?

Standard	Comments	Evidence	Staff Questions
IM.4.10	**Use Information Management Software** Information management planning allows for the sharing and exchange of data and information from different resources such as the ED, OR, Lab, etc. to support decision making. The following are examples of data being used and aggregated to support important functions: individual care, decision making, management, operations, PI, benchmarking with other hospitals, research, IC, patient safety, educating, and analyzing trends.	• Interviews with staff members that collect and/or use data to support decision making • Information management system structure that collects, organizes, analyzes, and assists with interpreting data • Evidence that systems and processes support easy access to the record (by authorized users) to assist with clinical decision making balancing privacy, security, and confidentiality concerns • Documentation illustrating that the ED uses data to make patient care decisions and management decisions, to reduce risks to patients, to look for trends over time, to compare with other hospitals, and for PI • PI data reports, use of aggregate data in system • Minutes of meetings indicating use of data and information • Standardization of the medical record • Medical records demonstrating the following regarding data and information: recorded accurately, timely, completely, and organized for efficient retrieval of needed data • In the ED, surveyors may focus on the maintenance of the control register that gathers the following information from each ED patient: - ID—name, age, gender - date, time, means of arrival - nature of complaint - disposition - time of departure • Evidence of participation with reference or external databases • Reports demonstrating the integration of data from various sources (e.g., clinical with non-clinical information) • Examples of how data was used for - decision making - management - analysis over time - PI - IC - patient safety	• How are ED clinical systems linked (e.g., food and nutrition with laboratory)? • Do you trend reports on volumes, staffing patterns, billing records and throughput times? • How do you use ED data and compare comparative data and information in the hospital and ED? • Is your medical record standardized? • Do you have any performance measures that you are collecting to ensure data is complete, accurate, timely and/or readily available? • How do you handle verbal/telephone orders in the ED? • Can you describe your maintenance of the ED control register? What are the items included in the content? • How do you collect information on patient demographics? • Where do you record that required reports have been made to authorities? • Show me a sample of a report where you aggregate the data and use it for decision making. • Do you have an electronic documentation process? • Do you have plans of going to an electronics format? • Do you have computerized physician order entry? Have you thought of going to this order entry process? • What is considered a complete ED record?

Standard	Comments	Evidence	Staff Questions
IM.5.10	**Medical/Nursing Literature References** The standard concerns knowledge-based ("literature") information management needs and access of staff. Hospital's must meet staff's needs for resources in print, electronic, on the Internet, audio, and/or in another appropriate format. When the Internet or other electronic reference systems are unavailable, the hospital must have a plan to provide access to knowledge-based information. There must be a mechanism to provide resources to staff at all times, through automation, after-hours access, etc. A hospital is not required to have an on-site library, but must demonstrate that information may be obtained in a timely manner by sharing services with another hospital or resource.	• Staff and ED leader interviews Hospital systems, resources, literature searches, use of library services • Listing of library literature, periodicals, CPGs, texts, indexes, abstracts, on-line services, satellite services, research data, audio resources, etc. • On-site library services, cooperative or contractual arrangement with another hospital	• Describe resources available to meet your knowledge-based ("literature") information management needs. • Do you have access to the Internet? An intranet? Have you had training on this? • Does you staff have access to the latest resources available in ED services (e.g., latest standards of care, care planning books, medication references, reference literature, articles, etc.) on all shifts? • How would you access these resources? • How have you used knowledge-based information to support clinical, management decisions, PI, patient safety, staff and patient/family education and/or for research needs? • What procedures do you follow when the hospital's electronic system is unavailable: - MSDS - laboratory - a medication ordering

Standard	Comments	Evidence	Staff Questions
IM.6.10 IM.6.20	**Accuracy of Medical Record Entries** Each patient must have a medical record to document treatment rendered in inpatient and outpatient settings being surveyed by the Joint Commission. The following elements of performance must be met in the ED and hospital: • Only authorized staff and individuals make medical record entries. Each entry indicates the author, date and time. • The hospital requires authentication for at least the following elements: history and physical, operative report, consultations, and discharge summary. • The hospital must indicate which entries made by non-independent practitioners require countersigning. • There are uniform procedures and formats implemented to document patient care and services within the medical record. • The medical record contains a variety of patient specific data and information to address the following: patient identification, reasoning for diagnosis/treatment, plan of care, progress of case, prognosis, and outcomes from care delivered, and that supports the continuity of care. • A concise discharge summary (for admissions) or final progress note (for individuals with minor problems or interventions defined by the medical staff) includes at least the following topics: reason for hospitalization, significant findings, procedures performed, condition at discharge, and instructions to patient/authorized family. • Hospital policy and procedure and/ or bylaws indicate required medical record entries and corresponding timeframes for completion of entries. The timeframes for these processes (history and physicals, verbal/ telephone orders) vary from state to state. • This standard requires hospitals to define when a medical record is considered complete, including the timeframe for completeness. Hospital's leaders can report statistics on the medical record delinquency rate at least every three months and include inpatient/ outpatient medical records. • There is a defined process for ongoing, open, medical record review based on indicators selected by the hospital such as: timeliness, legibility/readability, quality, consistency, clarity, accuracy,	• Staff, physician, and ED leader interviews • Compliance with the hospital's medical staff bylaws, rules, regulations, policy and procedures (e.g., authenticating medical records, verbal orders, transfer of information, release of information, discharge instructions, medical record completion) • ED policy and procedures enforced • Medical record documentation • Meeting minutes discussing AMA and LWBS (any potential EMTALA issues), risk management issues, PI activities, strategies to improve documentation deficiencies identified, outcomes, etc. • Medical staff office profiling of physician medical record completion statistics as one element of the recredentialing process • Ongoing medical record review results of defined ED indicators (e.g., evidence of patient identification, legibility, appropriate orders, countersigning as indicated, consents, consultations, verbal orders, conclusion at termination of treatment, final disposition, and discharge instructions, etc.) • Evidence of discharge handouts containing instructions for self-care, follow-up care, what to do if symptoms worsen • Referrals to community resources both private and non-private • PI studies to improve documentation	*Medical record review questions* • Describe the hospital policy and procedure on authenticating a medical record entry. What elements of the medical record must be authenticated? • How does the hospital define authentication of a medical record entry? • Who can document in the medical record? How are you sure that only authorized individuals chart within the medical record? When must entries be countersigned? For nursing students? For residents, midlevel practitioners, midwives, nurse practitioners, physician assistants? • Where is it noted that a physician order has been implemented or completed by nursing? • Where in the medical record do you document: - time and means of arrival, triage documentation including emergency care provided prior to arrival? - identification data (e.g., name, sex, age, date of birth, race, and authorized representative)? - evidence if patient left without being seen? - assessment, diagnosis, and chief complaint? - informed consent, if applicable? - orders, including medications, tests/results? - response to care? - consultations with internal, external care providers? - advance directives? - use of standards of care, CPGs, standardized charting formats? - conclusions at treatment? - final disposition? - documentation for follow-up care? • What is the ED's policy and procedure on honoring advance directives? What procedure do you follow if the patient does not have an advance directive? What if the patient has an advance directive and it is not in the record?

Standard	Comments	Evidence	Staff Questions
	completeness, and authentication, scanning/indexing of images. • Medical records must be retained based on applicable state law and regulations, and according to use. Patient care, research, PI, legal requirements, and educational endeavors may also bear on the length of time a record is retained. • Original medical records are not released unless mandated by federal or state laws, court orders, or subpoenas. • The following information must be documented for patients seeking emergency care: Time and means of arrival, if the patient left against medical advice (AMA) or left without being seen (LWBS), conclusion at termination of treatment, including final disposition, condition, and instructions for follow-up care, instructions that a copy of the record is available to the practitioner or medical hospital providing follow-up care. IM.6.20 needs to be reviewed in detail regarding the list of items that must be included in a medical record, when applicable.		• Where is there evidence that you provided information for a patient's continuous care needs (e.g., discharge instruction, transfer summary, transfer to another unit within the hospital, progress notes)? • How long are your medical records maintained? • Does each entry in the record indicate an author, time and date? • How does the ED participate in the ongoing medical record review process? How often? What clinicians participate in reviewing medical records? What are examples of indicators reviewed? • Describe any improvements or plans for improvement based on data collected from medical record reviews • Have you identified further needs for education, skills reviews based on the record review? *Other Questions* • What education did the patient receive? • Do you have a patient callback program? Has it helped with the continuity of care? • Describe your policy and procedure on releasing emergency medical records to other practitioners providing follow-up care. • If an ED patient goes to another facility, how do you release the patient's record to that facility? • How long does a record stay in the ED prior to going to medical records? • Describe your policy and procedure for when a patient leaves AMA. Where this would be documented? • What steps have been taken to reduce the number of patients leaving AMA or LWBS?

Standard	Comments	Evidence	Staff Questions
IM.6.30	**Operative and High-Risk Procedure Documentation** The standard requires complete documentation of pre, intra, and postoperative procedures, including those other procedures placing the patient at risk. Included in this standard is any procedure using moderate sedation.	• Documentation for operative procedures contains the following: - provisional diagnosis prior to procedure by the LIP - immediate operative progress note recorded immediately after the procedure while the patient is still in the ED.	• Tell me about the process for moderate sedation: - is an H&P required? - is an anesthesia assessment needed prior to administering moderate sedation? - plan for moderate sedation? - ASA completed prior to moderate sedation? • Are your discharge criteria from post moderate sedation approved by the medical staff? • How do you determine the patient's readiness for discharge? Is an order needed by the physician to discharge? • Do physicians in the ED document post procedure notes? What are the elements of this note?
IM.6.50	**Telephone/Verbal Orders** It is imperative that clinicians comply with their medical staff bylaws, rules, and regulations stating the hospital's verbal order requirements. Approved ED staff that accept and record verbal/telephone orders or receive critical test results, must also be familiar with the requirements of the Joint Commission's National Patient Safety Goals regarding improving communication among caregivers. (Joint Commission NPSG 2C) The expectation is that staff use a process to ensure the accuracy of the transcription of verbal/telephone orders or critical test results that require a verification "read-back" of the complete order or test result by the person receiving the order or test result. (Joint Commission NPSG 2A & 2C)	• Compliance with the following: - medical staff bylaws, rules, and regulations - hospital verbal order policy and procedure - state and federal law • Record review of the verbal order indicating the following: date, time of the order, name of the individual who gave it, received it, implemented it, and authorized it within time specified (timeframe is based on the requirements of the hospital, and in compliance with state and federal rules and regulations). • Trended verbal/telephone order data with improvements if a problem was identified • Observation of authorized staff accepting verbal orders according to hospital policy and procedure, and the Joint Commission's National Patient Safety Goals	• Describe your verbal order policy and procedure. Is it different for telephone orders? What are the elements for a valid verbal/ telephone order? • How do you know that a physician order has been completed? • Who is authorized to accept verbal/telephone orders in the ED? • Who may transcribe a verbal/telephone order? Who may transcribe a verbal/ telephone order? • Do you review verbal/ telephone orders during the patients ED visit via a medical record check process? • Describe your process for verifying the accuracy of verbal/telephone orders • Do you perform "read-backs" in the ED? (Joint Commission NPSG 2A) • Have you minimized verbal/ telephone orders in the ED? • What does your data reflect?

Standard	Comments	Evidence	Staff Questions
IM.6.60	**Availability of the Medical Record** This standard refers not only to ED access to patient medical records, but also to ED contribution to the record in a manner that makes information accessible to staff providing follow-up care. The hospital must ensure that all relevant data/information from a patient's record is available when needed for patient care.	• ED policy and procedures • Use of a computer patient information system • Manual or automated systems exist to track the location of all data and information within the medical record. There is a mechanism to gather required information, or a synopsis of information within the record to have available for follow-up care • Interviews with staff, ED leaders • Observation of accessing medical records (e.g., access to fax machines, computer records)	• Describe your medical record system for assembling clinical information for patient care. • Can you show me how to access this patient's record that is in the ED and the one in medical records? What if the medical records on a patient exist in more than one location? • How quickly can you assemble a record from different settings (e.g., hard copy or screen display)? • Who has access to medical records after hours? • What is the process for obtaining them? • Does the record system alert users when components are stored in other location? • How long are the medical records kept in the ED after a patient has been discharged, admitted, or transferred? • How long does it take to retrieve medical records?

SURVEILLANCE, PREVENTION, AND CONTROL OF INFECTION

Standard	Comments	Evidence	Staff Questions
IC.1.10	**Infection Control (IC) Program** This standard refers to the hospital's IC program and the selection of a surveillance process based on specific criteria. When creating the IC plan/program, the hospital must consider its demographics, patient population, patient care demands/volumes, staffing, priority initiatives, research data available, and data that can be gathered hospital and ED-specific. Those concerns considered to be epidemiologically important are targeted for improvement by staff. The aim of the IC program is to reduce risks of infections among LIPs, patients, staff, contracted workers, volunteers, students, and visitors, using epidemiological principles. Activities of the IC program must be planned with in conjunction with applicable agencies (e.g., the local health department, external support systems) to prevent/limit IC issues/outbreaks when applicable. Consideration must be made to also decrease the risk of infection from the environment (contamination through food and water). Hospitals should be familiar with the sentinel event alert regarding IC and prevention, and consider implementing strategies to reduce infection risks as outlined in the alert.	• Interviews with staff • Implementation of hospital IC plan • Policy and procedures • Implementation of ED specific IC policy and procedures in which the ED participates • Committee minutes demonstrating ED membership and/or contributions to the IC committee/function • Minutes from ED decision-making body meetings relating to IC issues • Staff education materials • Attendee list for IC training • The use of evidence-based information on reducing nosocomial infections, use of Joint Commission Sentinel Event Alert on IC and prevention	• What is the hospital's process for prevention, surveillance, and control of infection? • How do you treat a patient who presents a risk of epidemiologically important nosocomial infection? • Describe the hospital's IC training program. How was this implemented in the ED? • Where are the IC policy and procedures kept within the ED? • Where is the Personal Protection Equipment (PPE) kept? • Do minutes from hospital IC meetings reflect a continuous IC system that uses data to improve services (clinical), an epidemiological process, and partnering with the hospital IC program? • Who collects IC data? How is it used? • What information do you submit to the local health department? • What types of infections are you working on reducing (e.g., device-related, surgical site, communicable diseases, nosocomial TB, vaccine preventable)? • What is the biggest IC risk in the ED? What have you done to mitigate this risk? • How does the IC practitioner communicate to you as a staff member re: IC issues? • Have you conducted a bioterrorism drill using an infectious disease as the threat? • What IC components do you orient the new employee to in the ED?

Standard	Comments	Evidence	Staff Questions
IC.2.10	**Infection Control Data** This standard addresses hospital data collection and surveillance of IC and employee health issues.	• Observation and interviews with staff to review IC strategies • Consistent implementation of hospital and ED IC and employee health policy and procedures • Records of IC and/or safety team surveillance rounds, and follow-up activities • ED data collection compliance with hospital requirements • Case findings of nosocomial infections, employee health issues, and any corresponding action plan • Process of capturing data for employees who have contracted significant infections • Ability to demonstrate that surveillance activities are selected based on the hospital's demographics and services • ED management representation on hospital IC committees • IC risk assessment for all construction	• Describe your process for collecting data on nosocomial infections and employee health issues • What is a nosocomial infection? • What is a bloodborne pathogen? • How do you monitor compliance with IC procedures? • What IC issues have you encountered this year? • What IC risk assessment was conducted this year? • How does the IC coordinator know that there are several ED staff calling in sick for the same reason? What does the IC coordinator do with this information?
IC.3.10	**Infection Control Priorities & Reports** Hospitals have a responsibility to report relevant nosocomial infections through appropriate internal and external reporting mechanisms (e.g., public health agencies, as appropriate).	• Hospital policy and procedures: - reporting nosocomial infections internally and to public health agencies, as appropriate specific to the ED - reporting employee illness of epidemiological significance to public health agencies specific to the ED • Evidence of reporting of case findings of demographically significant nosocomial infections within committee minutes/PI reports	• Describe the procedure for reporting information about nosocomial infections • Describe the procedure for reporting employee health problems. Whom do you contact within the hospital? • Who is responsible for informing public health agencies of pertinent cases involving nosocomial infections? • What is the process for reporting a patient with a communicable disease? • Does management support reporting nosocomial infections to local health departments, as appropriate? • How does the hospital manage any incidence of unanticipated death or major permanent loss of function associated with health care acquired infection?

Standard	Comments	Evidence	Staff Questions
IC.4.10 IC.4.15 IC.5.10	**Infection Control (IC) Compliance & Handwashing** (Joint Commission NPSG 7A) Hospitals must implement strategies to prevent, minimize, and contain the risk of nosocomial infections throughout the hospital, particularly in patient care settings such as the ED. The IC program must include both patient care and employee health services. The ED is in compliance with the World Health Organization (WHO) hand hygiene guidelines or Centers for Disease Control and Prevention (CDC) hand hygiene guidelines. Education of healthcare workers to the benefits of an influenza vaccine is now required along with monitoring for compliance.	• Observation and interviews with staff • Hospital policy and procedures for IC and employee health • Staff orientation, continuing education material, attendance records for IC training • Any PI projects to reduce risks/control the identified outbreaks of infections where the ED staff participated • Minutes of IC discussions, activities displaying evidence that the hospital takes action to prevent or reduce the risk of nosocomial infections in patients, staff, and visitors • Evidence the hospital uses strategies from knowledge-based resources such as through published in scientific research, accrediting and regulatory standards, Association for Professionals in Infection Control and Epidemiology (APIC), and acceptable practice guidelines (e.g., use of the CDC guidelines for hand hygiene) *Surveyor Tour of ED* • Alcohol-based hand sanitizers and/or sinks in readily available locations for patients, visitors, and staff • Proper disposal of waste that may transmit infection • Gloves, gowns, goggles, shields, and other protective gear worn when contacting blood or body fluid • Protective gear stored appropriately and not on side rails • Staff demonstrating proper handwashing/hand hygiene techniques • Separation of soiled and clean linen • Clean room not contaminated • Open solution bottles dated as per hospital policy and procedure • Linen hampers not overfilled • Bagged linen not on floors • Food refrigerators - free of outdated containers - patient food containers dated - patient and employee food separated - food and non-food items separated - thermometer in medication - medication refrigerator free from food, clean refrigerator • Food/beverages away from possible contamination • Needle boxes not more than two-thirds full, off floor in ED • ED staff influenza vaccine plan and compliance data	• Have you had any outbreak of nosocomial infection identified within the past year? If yes, how did you respond to control the outbreak? • Have you implemented the CDC recommendations for handwashing/hygiene techniques? • Where are your hand degermers located? How much solution do you use in a month? • What strategies are used to reduce nosocomial infections? • Describe IC/employee health orientation and continuing education programs • Are there any patients who should be immediately removed from the waiting room? Which patients? • What precautions do you take when a patient may have TB? • Name two work practice controls in the ED • What is the single most important way to prevent the spread of infection? • Where does the triage person wash his or her hands? • What is the procedure to follow in the event of a sharps exposure? • Have you been involved in any PI projects targeted at reducing and controlling the risks associated with nosocomial infections? • Does anyone from the ED attend the IC Committee meeting? How do you receive information from this committee re: IC issues? • What have you done to promote handwashing in the ED? • Can you tell me about how you were educated to the hospital's influenza vaccine program?

Standard	Comments	Evidence	Staff Questions
IC.6.10	**Influx of Infectious Patients** These standards deal with the hospital responding to the potential or actual influx of patients who are infectious.	• Evidence - plan for influx of patients due to infectious disease • Minutes from ED committee meetings where influx of patients are discussed/addressed • Literature search used to develop policy and procedures • Risk assessment for the ED related to the potential or actual influx of infectious patients	• How have you planned for an influx of infectious patients? • How would you take care of these patients over time? • What resources in the community are available to you in the event of this influx?
IC.7.10	**Infection Control Management** This standard refers to hospital management of IC by a qualified individual.	• Hospital IC plan, policy, and procedures • Meeting minutes, plans reflecting qualifications of those overseeing IC/employee health program • Personnel records of IC/ employee health professionals indicating their qualifications, such as training, experience, and certification or licensure	• What data are provided to you by the IC Department? • Who oversees IC and employee health? • How do you find out about the activities of the IC Committee? • Who would you notify if staff were exposed to an infectious disease? How would you do this?
IC.7.10 IC.8.10 IC.9.10	**Infection Control Strategies & Resources** These standards concern hospital efforts to reduce the risk of significant nosocomial infection transmission. The emphasis is on automating IC data collection, analysis, and improvement efforts (e.g., computer and software resources). The ED must be aware of at least one strategy used to prevent the spread of infections between patients and staff.	• Evidence of the plan for influx of patients due to infectious disease • Staff knowledge of objectives of IC program, link to PI • Management systems support for the IC program through staff and data systems • Employee health lists of staff immunizations, staff needing immunization • ED process for participating in IC program • Knowledge of data collection efforts, PI studies, monitoring, trending of nosocomial infection rates, endemic verses epidemic • Evidence of a system that is used to improve IC processes hospital improving rates/trends of epidemiologically significant infections • Management support for IC (e.g., computers, software, data analysis, interpretation, presenting findings)	• How have you planned for an influx of infectious patients? • How would you take care of these patients over time? • What resources in the community are available to you in the event of this influx? • What resources support IC practices? Management staff? Data systems? • Describe at least one activity in the ED performed to reduce infections between patients and staff. • How are employee health programs integrated with IC practices? How is the ED linked to this? • How is your ED IC program designed to lower the risks and improve the rates/trends of epidemiologically significant infections?

Part 4

Reference Materials for Emergency Department Compliance

The following forms serve as examples. Hospitals could consult with appropriate advisors before adapting the forms in this Part to suit their particular purposes.

ETHICS, RIGHTS, AND RESPONSIBILITIES

4-1 Consent to Treatment in the Emergency Department

PURPOSE

To set guidelines for obtaining appropriate consent for treatment. Every patient in the ED will receive a Medical Screening Exam (MSE) by the ED physician.

POLICY

Consent for treatment will be obtained, in writing if possible, from all competent adult patients and from parents or appropriate guardians for children and non-competent adults, prior to initiating evaluation and/or treatment in the ED. When immediate treatment is imperative to preserve the life of the patient, or to prevent a serious impairment of the patient's health and the patient's state of competency is such that the patient cannot rationally consent, or where delay in obtaining the consent of the parent or guardian when otherwise appropriate involves grave risk to the patient, then evaluation and treatment required may be undertaken without obtaining consent. If the patient refuses treatment, the emergency physician will perform sufficient evaluation to determine if the patient is competent. If the emergency physician feels the patient is competent to refuse care, the benefits and risks of the proposed treatment, and the possible consequences of refusing treatment, will be explained to the patient and he/she will be asked to sign out Against Medical Advice. If the patient has a medical emergency as defined above, refuses treatment, and is felt by the emergency physician to be incompetent to refuse treatment, necessary therapy will be undertaken while attempting to convince the patient of the need. The patient will not leave the ED until the medical emergency no longer exists or until the physician feels the patient is competent to refuse therapy.

In the event of a minor (under age 18) presenting to the ED without a parent or guardian for treatment, the following are acceptable means of obtaining consent:

1. Parent(s) or guardians will be contacted by phone for permission to treat.
2. Telephone consents shall be witnessed by two (2) persons and shall be documented on the consent form.
3. Another adult blood relative may be contacted for consent if unable to contact the parents; this may be a grandparent, adult sibling, aunt, or uncle.
4. Designated guardian of the minor may give consent.
5. Social Services will be contacted to take custody or to obtain a court order for treatment.
6. The patient will be considered emancipated if the patient is married; merely having a child while unwed does not imply emancipation.
7. However, the unwed minor mother of a child has the right to give permission for her child to be treated.
8. A patient is considered emancipated when he/she is living separate and apart from his/her parents or legal guardian and is managing his/her own financial affairs.

9. A minor greater than age 14 years does not require parental permission for psychiatric evaluation or treatment.

If treatment is initiated without written consent, the circumstance surrounding the event and the steps taken to obtain consent will be documented in the ED record.

Source: Parkview Medical Center, Pueblo, Colorado. Reprinted with permission.

4-2 Informed Consent for Thrombolytics

Your doctors have determined that your chest pain is caused by a heart attack. Heart attacks are usually due to blood clots in one or more of the arteries in the heart, which blocks the supply of oxygen-rich blood to the heart muscle. This blockage causes pain and may result in permanent damage to your heart, or death. Such heart damage may or may not cause a noticeable impairment in your future ability to perform exertional activities.

There are medications available, called **thrombolytics,** that are sometimes able to dissolve the clot in your artery if administered soon after the onset of symptoms. This stops the heart attack process and reduces the extent of heart muscle damage.

In clinical trials involving many patients in both the United States and Europe, some patients receiving thrombolytics have shown a significant improvement in both heart function and in survival from their heart attacks (as compared to similar groups of patients treated in the same manner but without thrombolytics).

Like any medication, thrombolytics have side effects, usually in the form of **bleeding disturbances,** which may require blood transfusions. More serious adverse reactions, some even resulting in stroke and death, have been uncommon but can occur.

The particular thrombolytic drug will be administered through an intravenous catheter in your arm. It will be necessary to have 2 or 3 sites available for other medications as well. During and following the infusion you will otherwise receive standard and conventional heart attack therapy. If you select not to receive thrombolytic therapy you will still be afforded this same standard medical and nursing care.

PATIENT STATEMENT

By signing below I acknowledge that I have read and understand the nature and consequences of my medical condition and the treatment about to be rendered unto me. I have had the opportunity to ask questions. I understand that there may be untoward side effects ranging from bleeding to stroke to death.

I accept these risks in the hopes that this medication will dissolve the blood clot in the artery of my heart, improve performance of my heart, and reduce the extent of heart damage.

I understand that all standard medical care for the treatment of heart attacks will be afforded me whether I accept or refuse this medication. I further certify that I have no known tumor or growth inside my body and that I have no history of abnormal bleeding in the past.

PATIENT SIGNATURE ____________________

DATE ____________________

TIME ____________________

WITNESS SIGNATURE ____________________

Source: Twin Cities Community Hospital, Templeton, California.

4-3 Psychiatry Emergency Department: Involuntary Patient Rights

PURPOSE

To define the process of explanation of patient rights.

POLICY

All involuntary patients will be informed of their legal rights.

PROCEDURE

1. The registered nurse (RN) or psychiatric assistant assigned in the psychiatry emergency department will verbally inform the involuntary patient of the following rights:
   - A physician at the psychiatric emergency department has decided to initiate an order of protective custody because of a concern for your mental well-being.
   - This may lead to further hospitalization.
   - You have the right to a reasonable opportunity to contact your attorney.
   - After further evaluation you may be sent home if any of the following apply to you:
     —You are not mentally ill.
     —You are not going to harm yourself or someone else.
     —Emergency detention is not the least-restrictive means by which the necessary restraint may be affected.
   - Anything you say here or during hospitalization may be used in further proceedings.
   - A report of your examination may be forwarded to the court.
2. The RN will be responsible for documenting in the nurses' notes that the patient has been informed of his or her rights.

Source: Rusty McNew, RN, MA, CPHQ, Dallas, Texas.

4-4 Policy on Emergency Treatment Involving Investigational Drugs, Devices, or Biologics

A. Emergency Treatment Is Not Included in "Research" Data

Federal regulations for the protection of human subjects do not permit research activities to be started without prior IBRA review and approval. These regulations, however, do not limit or interfere with the authority of a physician to provide **emergency medical treatment** for patients, subject to FDA requirements for release and emergency use of an unapproved drug, biologic, or device on a single patient.

When emergency treatment is initiated without prior IBRA review and approval, the patient data **may not be** included as research data in a prior or subsequent IBRA-approved project.

B. FDA Regulation of Emergency Use

The emergency use provision in the FDA regulations is an exemption from prior review and approval by the IBRA of a *single* patient use of a drug, device, or biologic considered to be investigational. The emergency use exemption of an investigational drug, biologic or device is permitted ***only*** if each of the following conditions exist:

- A life-threatening or severely debilitating situation exists necessitating the use of the investigational drug, biologic or device.
- No standard acceptable alternative treatment is available.
- Because of the immediate need to use the drug, biologic or device, there is not sufficient time to use existing procedures to obtain IRBA approval for the use.

For purposes of this section, the following terms have the following meanings:
"Emergency use" of an investigational drug, biologic or device is defined as the use of an investigational article with a human subject in a life-threatening situation in which no standard acceptable treatment is available and in which there is not sufficient time to obtain approval from the IBRA.

"Life-threatening" means diseases or conditions where the likelihood of death is high unless the course of the disease is interrupted and diseases or conditions with potentially fatal outcomes, where the end point of clinical trial analysis is survival. The criteria for life threatening do not require the condition to be immediately life threatening or to immediately result in death. Rather, the subjects must be in a life-threatening situation requiring intervention before review at a convened meeting of the IBRA is feasible.

"Severely debilitating," means diseases or conditions that cause major irreversible morbidity. Examples of severely debilitating conditions include blindness, loss of arm, leg, hand or foot, loss of hearing, paralysis or stroke.

The FDA regulations do not provide for expedited IRB approval in emergency situations. An IRB must either convene and give "full board" approval of the emergency use or, if the conditions of 21 C.F.R. 56.102(d) are met and it is not possible to convene a quorum within the time available, the use may proceed without any IRB approval.

Some manufacturers will agree to allow the use of the test article, but their policy requires "an IRB approval letter" before the test article will be shipped. If it is not possible to convene a quorum of the IRB within the time available, the IRB may send the sponsor a written statement with the IRB is aware of the proposed use and considers the use to meet the requirements of 21 C.F.R. 56.104I. Although this is not an "IRB approval," the acknowledgement letter has been acceptable to manufacturers and has allowed the shipment to proceed.

C. Patient Consent in an Emergency

Even in an emergency use situation, the Principal Investigator is required to obtain informed consent to the treatment from the patient or the patient's legally authorized representative (as specified under State law) **unless** both the Principal Investigator and an independent physician certify in writing that ***all*** of the following conditions exist:

- The patient is confronted by a life-threatening situation necessitating the use of the investigational drug, biologic or device.
- Informed consent cannot be obtained because of an inability to communicate with, or obtain legally effective consent from, the patient.
- Time is not sufficient to obtain consent from the patient's legal representative.
- No alternative method of approved or generally recognized therapy is available that provides an equal or greater likelihood of saving the life of the patient.

If time is not sufficient to obtain the determination by an independent physician, the determination should be obtained within five (5) days after the use of the investigational article. *See* "Model Emergency Use Consent Form."

D. Informing the IBRA of Emergency Use

Principal Investigators are required to submit a written report on the emergency use to the IBRA and to the applicable hospital administration within five (5) working days. However, this notification should not be construed as an IRB approval. If the subject's consent was not obtained to the emergency use, the written report must include a written determination by a non-participating staff physician that the four conditions specified in Section C above are met. The report is reviewed by the Chair to ensure that the emergency use meets the applicable regulations. The Principal Investigator is informed that if he/she anticipates the need to use the investigational article in additional subjects, prior review and approval by the IBRA is required. *See* "Notification of Emergency Use of Investigational Product."

In addition, if an IDE for the device exists, the Principal Investigator must notify the sponsor of the emergency use. If an IDE did not exist, the Principal Investigator must notify the FDA of the emergency use and provide the FDA, with a copy to the IBRA, of a written summary of the conditions constituting the emergency, subject protection measures and results. Subsequent emergency use of the device may not occur unless the physician obtains approval of an IDE for the device and its use, as well as IBRA approval.

Source: New York University Cancer Institute, New York, New York.

4-5 Model Consent Form for Emergency Use of Investigational Drugs, Devices, or Biologics

Physician Name: ______________________ Dept.: ______________________

Phone: ______________ Fax: ______________ E-Mail: ______________

Name of investigational drug/biologic/device:

Your consent is requested to use the above-named product in

☐ your care

☐ the care of your child

☐ the care of someone for whom you are the legal representative.

Patient Name: ____

Patient at the following facility: ______________________________

This product has not been approved by the Food and Drug Administration. If you agree to the use of this product, this is what we will do:

The most likely risks of using this drug/biologic/device are

There may be other significant or even life-threatening risks that we do not know about. The possible benefits are

If you do not consent to the use of this product, the alternatives are

If this study involves medications or devices regulated by the Food and Drug Administration (FDA), the FDA and other regulatory agencies, the sponsor of the study and Hospital staff working under the direction of the IBRA may inspect records identifying you as a subject in this investigation. In addition, if your participation in this research is for treatment or diagnostic purposes, the facility in which you are treated may ask you to sign a separate informed consent document for specific procedures or treatment, and that informed consent form may be included in the medical record of that facility. The medical record is maintained by your treating physician or hospital, as applicable, and will be subject to state and federal laws and regulations concerning confidentiality of medical records.

This Hospital and any government agency or sponsor providing the drug will *not* provide special services, free care, or compensation for any injuries resulting from the use of this drug/biologic/device. Treatment for such injuries will be provided under the same financial arrangements as those under which treatment is usually provided.

If you consent to this treatment and later believe that you have suffered any injury as a result of this emergency care, you may contact Dr. _____ at _____ or the IBRA administrative office at ___-___-___. They can review the matter with you, identify other resources that may be available to you, and provide information as to how to proceed.
This emergency treatment **will not** be claimed as research and you **will not** be considered a research subject. Any data regarding your treatment **will not** be included in any report of a research activity.

If you have any questions about the drug/biologic/device or about the rights of those agreeing to have an experimental article used in their medical care, you may contact Dr. ________ at ________ or the IBRA at ___-___-___.

I have read the above explanations and have received answers to any questions I have about treatment with this product. I consent voluntarily to the emergency use of this drug/biologic/device.

Patient's Signature (as applicable)	Date
Legal Representative's Signature (as applicable)	Date
Parent's Signature (as applicable)	Date
Signature of Person Obtaining Consent	Date

4-6 Transfer Decision Matrix

	Incoming for a Higher Level of Care	Incoming for the Same Level of Care	Outgoing to a Higher Level of Care	Outgoing to the Same Level of Care
Definition	Patients who have Emergency Medical Conditions **OR** are **IN** Active Labor. Capability &/or Capacity are not available at referring facility.	Patients who do not have Emergency Medical Conditions **OR** are **Not** in Active Labor.	Patients who have Emergency Medical Conditions **OR** are **IN** Active Labor. Capability &/or Capacity are not available.	Patients who do not have Emergency Medical Conditions **OR** are **Not** in Active Labor.
Memorandum of Transfer (MOT)	YES, except for patients transferred from Veterans Administration Hospitals and other federal facilities, and nursing homes.	YES, except for patients transferred from Veterans Administration Hospitals and other federal facilities, and nursing homes.	YES, except for patients transferred to Veterans Administration Hospitals and other federal facilities, and nursing homes.	YES, except for patients transferred to Veterans Administration Hospitals and other federal facilities, and nursing homes.
Admission Eligibility	Criteria Does Not Apply	Criteria Applies	Criteria Does Not Apply	Criteria Applies—the transfer of a patient may not be predicated upon arbitrary, capricious, or unreasonable discrimination based upon race, religion, national origin, age, sex, physical condition, or economic status.
Consent	YES	YES	YES	YES
Role of Physician	Determine clinical capability	Determine clinical capability	Determine clinical capability and patient's stability for transfer. Contact the Transfer Hotline. Arrange for duplication of patient's medical record which shall include: Medical history & physical exam; provisional diagnosis, recorded observation of physical assessment of patient's condition at the time of transfer & treatment provided; results of all diagnostic tests, i.e., X-ray films & reports, laboratory tests; reason for transfer; and any other pertinent information.	Determine clinical capability and patient's stability for transfer. Contact the Transfer Hotline. Arrange for duplication of patient's medical record which shall include: Medical history & physical exam; provisional diagnosis, recorded observation of physical assessment of patient's condition at the time of transfer & treatment provided; results of all diagnostic tests, i.e., X-ray films & reports, laboratory tests; reason for transfer; and any other pertinent information.
Role of Administrator	Determine capacity	Determine capacity and admission eligibility	Determine capacity	Determine capacity and admission eligibility
Hotline	YES	YES	YES	YES

Source: Rusty McNew, RN, MA, CPHQ, Dallas, Texas.

4-7 ED Rape Trauma Syndrome Standard of Care

PURPOSE

To provide quality physical and emotional care to the patient who has been sexually victimized.

STANDARD OF CARE

All patients who present to the ED with rape trauma syndrome will be considered a priority and treated with sensitivity and adherence to Public Health Law, section 2805.

STANDARD I

The nurse will provide the following interventions during the immediate phase of management of a rape trauma victim.

Immediate Phase

All patients presented to the Emergency Department with complaints of sexual abuse will be accompanied to a private room and a Rape Crisis Counselor from VIBES will be called pending patient approval.

- Police will be notified only when consent is given by the patient or when there is a legal obligation on the part of the hospital to do so (see ED Policy Treatment of Victims of Sexual Assault).
- The appropriate physician will be called (see ED Policy Treatment of Victims of Sexual Assault).

STANDARD II

A sensitive interview will be conducted with the patient regarding the sexual assault.

Intermediate Phase

A. Perform physical assessment of patient as follows:
   1. History of present condition
      a. Time, place, and circumstances of assault
      b. For sexual assault or incest involving child; same as adult, plus interview child and parent/significant other separately
   2. Past medical history
      a. date of LMP
      b. date and time of last consensual intercourse
   3. Physical examination
      a. Assess for physiological stability related to physical injury
      b. Prior to physical exam:
         — establish trust relationship
         — explain all procedures
         — obtain consents for procedures and/or photographs

c. Assist with collection of evidence and physical examination—see guidelines for use of NYSDOH Sexual Offense Evidence Kit
d. For sexual assault or incest involving child, assess for signs and symptoms of child abuse (see child abuse)
e. Assist with diagnostic procedures

B. Psychosocial Intervention
Consider that the patient is going through a traumatic acute phase or may experience a delayed or long-term phase. The possibility of these reactions needs to be discussed with the patient so he/she is prepared.
There may also be feelings of powerlessness related to inability to prevent or control the situation.

C. Interventions
- Offer immediate assistance.
- Develop trust relationship.
- Focus on facts and immediate problem solving.
- Accept all types of responses.
- Assist with problem solving and decision making.
- Offer assistance in calling friends or support.
- Encourage patient to make decisions (e.g., now or in 30 minutes).
- Discuss usual post-traumatic reactions.
- Discuss reactions of significant others.
- Provide available resources for unresolved anger and rejection.
- Arrange for transportation to safe environment.
- Refer to mental health counselor if patient unable to progress with direct problem solving assistance.

For pediatric victims of sexual assault or incest:

1. Notify parent if not with child; consider if child is incest victim.
2. Adult interventions are all applicable but must be modified to accommodate development level of child.
3. Notify proper authorities which may include police and child protective services.
4. Refer family for counseling.

STANDARD III

Evaluation

The victimized patient has just undergone a most traumatic event. The sensitive care that has been provided should result in a positive outcome for the patient at time of discharge.

The patient

- exhibits decreased anxiety with relaxed body posture and acceptance of help
- cooperates and participates in verbal dialogue
- makes decisions and follows through with plan
- demonstrates coping reactions that are appropriate for event and is aware of own responses

- accepts offer to call supportive person
- relates appropriate telephone numbers
- accepts and understands reason for referral
- comprehends and repeats types of reactions that may occur
- decides to inform others based on usual coping behaviors and cites available referral resources
- leaves ED with escort

For children: as for adult, plus

- child is emotionally secure; parent, significant other or adult advocate is present
- authorities are notified
- child leaves ED to return to safe environment

Source: Adapted from Huntington Hospital, Huntington, New York.

4-8 Consent for Donation of Organs and Tissues

I, ______________________________, being the legal next-of-kin and/or
NAME OF NEXT-OF-KIN OR AGENT

______________ of ______________,
RELATIONSHIP NAME OF DONOR

(1) In the hope and with the expectation that this contribution will be used for transplantation, or for therapy, medical research or education, I, a person authorized by State law to make this contribution, do hereby authorize, as the Donor or on behalf of the Donor, the transplantation, retention, preservation or donation of the organs and parts described below.

A) ☐ Any needed organs or tissues
B) ☐ Only the following organs and/or tissues. Check below.
☐ Kidney ☐ Heart ☐ Lungs ☐ Liver ☐ Pancreas ☐ Eyes ☐ Corneas
☐ Heart valves ☐ Skin ☐ Bone ☐ Other______________
C) ☐ Limitations, if any ______________
D) ☐ The removal of organs and/or tissues for medical research, if not accepted for transplant.

(2) I understand that this authorization includes any examination, test, and review of medical history, including but not limited to, the removal of blood, spleen and lymph nodes, which may be necessary to assure medical acceptability of the organ and/or tissue I am donating. It also includes the transfer to the transplant facility of medical information or records pertaining to the Donor.

(3) This authorization is voluntarily made, without obligation on the part of the donee, the Hospital, or any person authorized by law to receive this gift, and is motivated solely by humanitarian instincts without hope of compensation of any kind. I therefore release any claims that I or my legal representative may have now or in the future against my physician, his or her associates, the Hospital, its agents or employees, and any donee or authorized person or organization.

______________ ______________
SIGNATURE, LEGAL NEXT-OF-KIN OR AGENT SIGNATURE OF WITNESS

______________ ______________
ADDRESS SIGNATURE OF WITNESS

______________ ______________
CITY, STATE, ZIP, COUNTRY DATE TIME

Source: Aspen Publishers.

4-9 Consent Form for Emergency Contraception

I have requested and wish to be treated with medication containing synthetic progestin in order to attempt to prevent a possible pregnancy.

I have given an accurate medical and sexual history to my health care provider, and have been evaluated by her or him.

It has been explained to me that this medication reduces the risk of pregnancy following a single act of unprotected intercourse. Depending on the exact time in the menstrual cycle, the pregnancy rate following a single act of unprotected intercourse may be 0 to 33 percent. (On average, it is 8 percent.) After taking emergency contraception, the pregnancy rate is 0 to 8 percent. (On average, it is 1 percent.) This represents a 75 to 80 percent reduction in risk of pregnancy for this single act of unprotected intercourse. I understand this medication is not 100 percent effective. It has been explained to me that this medication is thought to work in most cases by preventing or delaying ovulation. If ovulation does occur, the medication may prevent implantation of a fertilized ovum into the uterine lining. This medication will not prevent pregnancies resulting from sexual intercourse occurring after I have taken it. My risk of pregnancy may actually be increased if I have unprotected intercourse in the week following emergency contraception.

I understand that this is not a method of birth control that can be used repeatedly or long-term. My health care provider has explained to me how I can obtain information about and access to methods that can be used for pregnancy prevention from now on. My health care provider has explained to me that there may be some side effects from this medication. These may include nausea, abdominal pain, fatigue, headache, breast tenderness, and dizziness. It is very unlikely that I would have any serious side effects, but I have been told to contact the health clinic if I have severe abdominal, chest or leg pain, or severe headache, or problems with my vision.

If this method fails and I do become pregnant, I understand that there is a theoretical risk that this or any medication I may have taken since conception could harm the developing fetus.

I have agreed to return to the health clinic in three weeks for follow-up.

Signed: ______________________________

Clinician: ______________________________

Date: ______________________________

Source: University of Virginia Student Health, Charlottesville, Virginia.

4-10 Emergency Induced Abortion Certification Form

Name of physician performing the procedure: ______________________________
State License Number: ______________________________
Information on facility where procedure performed:
Name ______________________________
Address ______________________________
Telephone Number ______________________________
Date of Procedure ______________________________

> "The patient whom this certification concerns is an unemancipated minor. Based on my good faith clinical judgment, I hereby affirm that the following medical condition(s) necessitated the immediate abortion of my patient's pregnancy without prior parental notice otherwise required by Family Code § 33.002 to avert her death or to avoid a serious risk of substantial and irreversible impairment of a major bodily function. I understand this certification is confidential and may not contain personal or identifying information about my patient, including her name, address, or social security number. I have included a copy of this certification in my patient's medical record as required by law."

List the medical indications supporting the physician's judgment:

____
____
____
____

______________________________ ________
Physician's Signature Date

____
Physician's Printed Name

Please mail the completed form to the following: ______________________________

Any person other than the intended recipient who receives this document in error is hereby notified that any disclosure, copying, distribution, use or taking of any action in reliance on the contents of this document is strictly prohibited. Please notify the state Department of Health at ______________ immediately to arrange for return of this document to the department.

Source: Texas Department of Health, Austin, Texas.

4-11 Organ/Tissue Donation: Identification of Donors and Procedures

APPROVED BY THE DIRECTOR OF NURSING

SIGNATURE: ______________________________

DATE: ______________________________

PURPOSE STATEMENT

The purpose of this Nursing policy is to ensure that the appropriate organ procurement organization is notified for identification of potential organ and tissue donors.

STATEMENT OF RESPONSIBILITIES

Performed by: Unit Coordinator, Nurse Managers
Physician's Order: Not required
Special Education: Not required

POLICY STATEMENT

In order to comply with legislative requirements, all deaths will be considered potential donors. All deaths are reported to the appropriate agencies for the purpose of identifying potential organ/tissue donors. Documentation in the medical record reflects this contact and determination of donor suitability.

GUIDELINES PROCEDURE

A. Supporting statements regarding compliance with legislative and legal regulations.
   1. Uniform anatomical gift act. California Health and Safety Code, Section 7150: Any person of sound mind and 18 years of age or older may give all or any part of his body for any purpose specified. The gift to take effect upon death.
   2. Required Request Act. California Health and Safety Code. Section 7184: Each general acute care hospital shall develop a protocol for identifying potential organ and tissue donors. The protocol shall require that any deceased individual next of kin, at or near the time of notification of death, be asked whether the deceased was an organ donor or if the family is a donor family. If not, the family shall be notified of the option to donate organs and tissues.
   3. Omnibus Budget Reconciliation Act, November 1987: This federal law made Medicare and Medicaid reimbursement to acute care hospitals contingent on (1) establishment of written protocol for the identification of potential donors (2) notification of the potential donor's family of the option to approve or decline donation and (3) notification of the organ procurement agency.
   4. California Health and Safety Code, Section 7151.5: Any of the following persons, in order of priority stated, when persons in prior classes are not available at the time of death, and in the absence of actual notice of opposition by a member of

the same or a prior class, may give all or any part of the decedent's body for any purpose specified.
   a. Durable Power of Attorney
   b. Spouse
   c. Either parent
   d. An adult son or daughter
   e. Either grandparent
   f. A guardian or conservator of the person of the decedent at the time of the decedent's death.
   g. Any other person authorized or under obligation to dispose of the body.
5. California Uniform Determination of Death Act (1992) California Health and Safety Code, Section 7180: An individual who has sustained either (1) irreversible cessation of circulatory and respiratory functions, or (2) irreversible cessation of all function of the entire brain, including the brain stem. A determination of death must be made in accordance with accepted medical standards.
6. California Health and Safety Code, Section 7181: When an individual is pronounced dead by determining that the individual has sustained an irreversible cessation of all functions of the entire brain, including the brain stem, there shall be independent confirmation by another physician.
7. California Health and Safety Code, Section 7182 (as refers to above): Neither the physician making the independent confirmation shall participate in the procedures for removing or transplanting a part.

B. Definitions
   1. Brain death
      a. A patient who has suffered complete and irreversible cessation of all functions of the brain, including the brain stem. To be a donor, this patient must be maintained on a ventilator and have an intact circulation. This patient may be an organ and/or tissue donor.
   2. Biological death
      a. A patient who has suffered complete and irreversible cessation of the circulatory system. This patient could not be an organ donor but can still donate some tissues for up to 24 hours after biologic death.
   3. Tissue donation
      a. A biologically dead patient is only able to donate tissues. This may include corneas, bone, skin, ligaments, tendons, duramater, heart valves, and veins.

C. All cardiopulmonary deaths will be reported to the Inland Eye and Tissue Bank (IETB) at 800-555-6555, Extension 15.

D. All brain deaths will be reported to the Southern California Organ Procurement Center (SCOPC) at 800-555-6112.

E. Consult the organ donation manual for:
   1. Supporting statements regarding compliance with legislative and legal regulations
   2. Definitions
   3. Criteria for identification of potential donor
   4. Consent
   5. Confidentiality

PROCEDURE

1.0 In order to comply with legislation, all deaths, both cardiopulmonary and brain deaths, shall be considered potential donors.

1.1 Call SCOPC (800-555-6112) if the patient has brain death (on ventilator).

1.2 Call IBID (800-555-6555, extension 15) if patient has cardiopulmonary death (off ventilator).

1.2.1 Call within one (1) hour of death.

1.2.2 Have the patient's chart available.

1.2.3 Do not notify a funeral home until patient is dismissed as a potential donor.

1.2.4 Send the body to the hospital morgue.

1.2.5 Notify the Coroner whenever applicable.

2.0 The Potential Organ/Tissue Donor Notification Form is to be completed and attached to all death reports. It should state when the appropriate agency was contacted, and the result. If the donor did not meet requirements due to absolute contraindications, then this will be documented. Do not speak with the family until SCOPC has been contacted and advised.

3.0 Review suitability and discuss potential organ donation with primary physician. SCOPC will not approach family without the physician's knowledge.

4.0 Ascertain that brain death declaration has or will be made. Documentation of brain death declaration must be made by two physicians independently of each other. These declarations must be written in the progress notes with date and time included. It is a legal requirement that these physicians cannot be involved in the procurement or transplant procedures.

5.0 Physician is then to notify family of patient's death. (Please advise, if necessary, that the subject of organ donation is not discussed at the same time they are informed of loved one's death. The family usually cannot assimilate thoughts of organ donation at this time.) Social Services may be contacted at this point, if not already, to support the family in their grieving process.

6.0 ALLOW UNDERSTANDING AND ACCEPTANCE OF DEATH (brain death) BEFORE APPROACHING FAMILY ABOUT ORGAN DONATION.

7.0 Only those trained to perform this kind of conversation should be utilized in approaching the family about donation.

7.1 There is specific information that must be told to the family to comply with informed consent for organ donation.

7.2 The goal in talking with a family is not to achieve consent. Organ donation is not for everyone. The family has a legal right to be given the information to make an informed decision, whether it is yes or no.

8.0 SCOPC/IETB will ensure that there is legal consent.

8.1 Report any case in which brain death appears imminent, such as the following catastrophic head injuries:

8.1.1 Head trauma

8.1.2 Intracranial bleed

8.1.3 Metabolic or primary brain tumor.

8.2 Have the patient's chart available.

9.0 SCOPC/IETB will obtain Coroner's consent, if applicable.

10.0 SCOPC/IETB Coordinator will order lab and donor maintenance orders. SCOPC/IETB will contact transplant centers to coordinate surgery schedule. SCOPC will contact the Division of Nursing or the Surgery Department to facilitate Bakersfield Memorial's surgery schedule and availability of Anesthesiologist and support staff.

11.0 It should be determined by the primary nurse or the SCOPC Coordinator what the family intends to do prior to the surgery. Some families make plans for a final goodbye to their loved one. Occasionally, some families want to see the body after the surgery. If the case is a Coroner's case SCOPC will contact the Coroner after the case to inform them of the clamp time, as well as notify them that they may pick up the body.

12.0 All other hospital policies and procedures regarding the care of the body should be followed.

13.0 If the donor is a tissue donor, the following will need to occur:

13.1 The body will need to be cooled in the morgue within approximately four (4) hours after biologic death. For cornea donations, the eyes may be instilled with sterile saline and eyelids closed (may need to tape them shut in some circumstances).

Source: Adapted from Bakersfield Memorial Hospital, Bakersfield, California.

4-12 Emergency Judicial Consent to Treatment for Minors Documentation Form

Date of Treatment: ______________________ Name of Judge: ______________________

Note: For the purpose of this form only, a minor is defined as a patient less than 18 years old.

DOCUMENTATION RECORD

Please provide the following information regarding juvenile.

Patient's Last Name: ______________________

Patient's First Name: ______________________

Patient's Date of Birth: ______________________

Patient's Address: ______________________

Please provide the following information concerning patient's parent, guardian, or legal custodian.

Parent/Guardian/Custodian's Relationship to Patient: ______________________

Parent/Guardian/Custodian's Name: ______________________

Parent/Guardian/Custodian's Address: ______________________

Consent of parent/guardian/legal custodian or other person standing in loco parentis is unobtainable because:

Such person is not a resident of this state.	____ Yes	____ No
His or her whereabouts are unknown.	____ Yes	____ No
He or she cannot be consulted with promptness reasonable under the circumstances.	____ Yes	____ No
He or she refuses to give consent after the recommended care and risks associated with treatment or refusal to authorize treatment have been explained.	____ Yes	____ No

Please state the diagnosis of the patient's physical condition and nature of the emergency.

____

____

____

____

____

Please state the recommended medical, surgical, and nursing care needed.

____
____
____
____
____

Please provide name of nearest known relative if no parent or guardian can be found.

Relative's Relationship to Patient: ____

Relative's Name: ____

Relative's Residence: ____

Please provide name and address of physician petitioning the court for authorization of surgical or medical treatment for the patient.

Physician's Name: ____

Physician's Address: ____

Please provide name and address of the hospital or medical facility petitioning for authorization of surgical or medical treatment for the patient.

Hospital's Name: ____

Hospital's Address: ____

Has patient ever been married? ___ Yes ___ No

PLEASE RETURN TO THE RISK MANAGEMENT DEPARTMENT WITHIN 24 HOURS OF OBTAINING EMERGENCY JUDICIAL CONSENT

Source: Aspen Publishers.

4-13 National Standards for Culturally and Linguistically Appropriate Services (CLAS)

The U.S. Department of Health and Human Services Office of Minority Health (OMH) has developed a set of 14 standards intended to assure cultural competence in health care; i.e., "that all people entering the health care system receive equitable and effective treatment in a culturally and linguistically appropriate manner."

The standards are intended to be inclusive of all cultures and not limited to any particular population group or sets of groups; however, they are especially designed to address the needs of racial, ethnic, and linguistic population groups that experience unequal access to health services. Ultimately, the aim of the standards is to contribute to the elimination of racial and ethnic health disparities and to improve the health of all Americans.

The CLAS standards are primarily directed at health care organizations; however, individual providers are also encouraged to use the standards to make their practices more culturally and linguistically accessible. The principles and activities of culturally and linguistically appropriate services should be integrated throughout an organization and undertaken in partnership with the communities being served.

HOW ARE THE STANDARDS ORGANIZED?

The 14 standards are organized by themes: Culturally Competent Care (Standards 1–3), Language Access Services (Standards 4–7), and Organizational Supports for Cultural Competence (Standards 8–14). Within this framework, there are three types of standards of varying stringency: mandates, guidelines, and recommendations as follows:

- CLAS mandates are current federal requirements for all recipients of federal funds (Standards 4, 5, 6, and 7).
- CLAS guidelines are activities recommended by OMH for adoption as mandates by federal, state, and national accrediting agencies (Standards 1, 2, 3, 8, 9, 10, 11, 12, and 13).
- CLAS recommendations are suggested by OMH for voluntary adoption by health care organizations (Standard 14).

THE 14 STANDARDS

1. Health care organizations should ensure that patients/consumers receive from all staff members effective, understandable, and respectful care that is provided in a manner compatible with their cultural health beliefs and practices and preferred language.
2. Health care organizations should implement strategies to recruit, retain, and promote at all levels of the organization a diverse staff and leadership that are representative of the demographic characteristics of the service area.
3. Health care organizations should ensure that staff at all levels and across all departments receive ongoing education and training in culturally and linguistically appropriate service delivery.
4. Health care organizations must offer and provide language assistance services, including bilingual staff and interpreter services, at no cost to each patient/

consumer with limited English proficiency at all points of contact, in a timely manner during all hours of operation.

5. Health care organizations must provide to patients/consumers in their preferred language both verbal offers and written notices informing them of their right to receive language assistance services.
6. Health care organizations must assure the competence of language assistance provided to limited English proficient patients/consumers by interpreters and bilingual staff. Family and friends should not be used to provide interpretation services (except on request by the patient/consumer).
7. Health care organizations must make available easily understood patient-related materials and post signage in the languages of the commonly encountered groups and/or groups represented in the service area.
8. Health care organizations should develop, implement, and promote a written strategic plan that outlines clear goals, policies, operational plans, and management accountability/oversight mechanisms to provide culturally and linguistically appropriate services.
9. Health care organizations should conduct initial and ongoing organizational self-assessments of CLAS-related activities and are encouraged to integrate cultural and linguistic competence-related measures into their internal audits, performance improvement programs, patient satisfaction assessments, and outcomes-based evaluations.
10. Health care organizations should ensure that data on the individual patient's/consumer's race, ethnicity, and spoken and written language are collected in health records, integrated into the organization's management information systems, and periodically updated.
11. Health care organizations should maintain a current demographic, cultural, and epidemiological profile of the community as well as a needs assessment to accurately plan for and implement services that respond to the cultural and linguistic characteristics of the service area.
12. Health care organizations should develop participatory, collaborative partnerships with communities and utilize a variety of formal and informal mechanisms to facilitate community and patient/consumer involvement in designing and implementing CLAS-related activities.
13. Health care organizations should ensure that conflict and grievance resolution processes are culturally and linguistically sensitive and capable of identifying, preventing, and resolving cross-cultural conflicts or complaints by patients/consumers.
14. Health care organizations are encouraged to regularly make available to the public information about their progress and successful innovations in implementing the CLAS Standards and to provide public notice in their communities about the availability of this information.

The complete report, along with supporting material, is available online at *www.OMHRC.gov/CLAS*.

Source: U.S. Department of Health and Human Services' (HHS) Office of Minority Health (OMH) Web site: *www.omhrc.gov/clas/finalculturalla.htm*.

4-14 Patient Identification Policy

POLICY

Each patient will be properly identified before receiving patient care.

PURPOSE

To define the process of patient identification.

PROCEDURE

A. Patient Identification Requirement

1. Patient Identification using 2 patient identifiers is required prior to the following:
   a. Transportation to Surgery or to any Invasive Procedure area
   b. Surgery or Procedure, in the procedure area
   c. Each time medication is administered and/or IV fluids administered
   d. Blood or Blood Product Administration
   e. Blood or specimen collection for any Lab Testing
   f. Any procedure or care for which the patient is new to the care provider (except life-threatening emergencies)
2. The Patient's Identification is compared to a written source relevant to the care provided, such as, the MAR or written physician order compared to the Identification band for each medication administration. (Positive patient identification is never possible from memory.)

B. Identification Band Placement

1. All inpatients, outpatient observations patients, outpatients receiving invasive procedures with sedation or anesthesia, and ECC patients will have an Identification band applied upon arrival.
2. **A temporary identification band is to be applied upon the patient's arrival if a computer generated ID band is not available. The patient's name and date of birth are to be present on the identification band. The computer generated identification band is to be applied as soon as it is available.**
3. The Identification band shall be applied to the patient's wrists unless clinical reason prevents this location. Alternate location is ankles. Identification band placement is not acceptable on patient's clothing.
4. Accuracy of the Identification band at time of placement shall be confirmed by the patient and staff member applying the band. If the patient is unable, confirmation shall be with the person consenting to the care of the patient. If there is no one, a picture ID (e.g., Driver's License) may be used for correct identification with verification by two staff members. (If unable to verify identity, refer to Unknown Patient Policy.)
5. If a patient Identification band is removed for any reason, it must be immediately replaced using the above guidelines to assure the band is correct.
6. Refer to CBU policies on identification of infants born at _____.
7. For select NICU patients who may not be able to have the patient identification band on their person for clinical reasons, the patient's crib may be labeled with

the patient's identification. If the child is removed from the crib for any reason, the child must be identified or have a staff member present at all times to verify the identity of the child. In this situation, the staff member must not have responsibility for any other child at the same time.

C. **Checking Patient Identification for patients with Identification Bands**

1. The acceptable 2 patient identifiers are Patient Name and Date of Birth except:
    a. When Bar Coding technology is provided, the 1st patient identifier is the written review of the Patient Name and the second is the Bar Coded review of the Patient's Financial (FIN) Number (Account Number) to the written source.
    b. _________ Hospital staff will use Patient Name and Medical Record Number if Date of Birth is not present on their data source.
    c. In CBU, NICU, and Nursery, in situations of multiple births when patients have the same last Name and Date of Birth, the two Identifiers will be Patient Name and Medical Record Number or Infant Identification Number.
2. Checking the Patient's Identification is required even when the patient is known by the staff member as a repeat patient.
3. Patients who have had their identification band removed are to be re-identified and a new name band applied.

D. **Checking Patient Identification for patients in areas not using Identification Bands**

a. The patient shall be asked to give Name (first and last) and Date of Birth. The patient's response shall be compared to the written source of information, i.e., patient chart, etc.
b. Minor children and adults unable to identify themselves, or for any reason unable to consent to their own treatment, shall be identified by the parent, guardian or other consenting person present with the patient.

E. **Emergency Situation**

Emergency situations (i.e. a code blue) may require treatment without the patient having a name band.

Non-Compliance

Any staff member not adhering to this policy will be subject to disciplinary action, up to and including discharge from _____ Hospital.

Original Approval By:	Original Date:
Revision Number:	Replaces Policy Last Dated:
Last Revised/Reviewed By:	Review/Revised Date:
Signed Document Held By:	

SIGNATURES OF APPROVAL:

Date Signed	Signature	Name	Title
__________	__________	__________	__________
__________	__________	__________	__________
__________	__________	__________	__________

Source: Memorial Hospital & Health System, South Bend, Indiana.

4-15 Identification and Labeling of Patient Specimens Policy

POLICY

It is the policy of _____ to properly and accurately identify all patient specimens (blood, urine and tissue).

PURPOSE

To provide a system for accurate identification and labeling of all patient specimens.

PROCEDURE

1. Collect specimens according to the policy and procedure outlined for specific specimen collection.
2. Obtain a sufficient number of patient labels to affix one label to each specimen.
3. The initials of the person collecting the specimen, the date, time, and source of the specimen i.e., throat, cervix, etc., are to be placed on each label. For Urine Specimens the method of collection will also be written on the label, i.e., voided, CCMS, cath.
4. The patient label will be checked against the patient's arm band, or the staff person will ask the patient to state their name and date of birth while reading the patient label to be placed on the specimen.
5. The specimen will be transported to the lab via designated, approved means.
6. Specimens are to remain with the patient until labeled.
7. The individual drawing/collecting the specimen is expected to label the specimen. Lab personnel may label a specimen they witness the nursing staff draw.
8. Patients admitted and their identity is unknown will be given a number (i.e., trauma patient) until their identity is known. Once name and date of birth are known, those become the identifiers to use.

Original Approval By:
Revision Number:
Last Revised/Reviewed By:
Signed Document Held By:

Original Date:
Replaces Policy Last Dated:
Review/Revised Date:

SIGNATURES OF APPROVAL:

Date Signed	Signature	Name	Title
___________	___________	___________	___________
___________	___________	___________	___________
___________	___________	___________	___________

Source: Memorial Hospital & Health System, South Bend, Indiana.

4-16 Unanticipated Outcomes and Adverse Events—Responding, Disclosure, and Action Policy

POLICY

It is the policy of _____ Hospital to maintain honesty and integrity in all organizational functions. Consistent with this policy it is appropriate to disclose events or unanticipated outcomes that might adversely affect a patient's health. Our framework for discussing unanticipated outcomes is premised on strong communication processes, both before and after treatment or procedures.

PURPOSE

The purpose of this policy is to provide guidance for physicians and care givers when a procedural or judgmental decision made during the course of care resulted in an adverse patient outcome.

PROCEDURE

Definition

1. Adverse event—an unintended negative result stemming from a diagnostic test or medical/surgical treatment.
2. Disclosure—communications of information regarding the results of a diagnostic test, medical treatment or surgical intervention.
3. Unanticipated Outcomes—a result that differs significantly from what was anticipated to be the result of a treatment or procedure.

General Principles

1. Events to be disclosed—occurrences where patients are significantly harmed or have the potential to be significantly harmcd.
2. To whom disclosure will be made—disclosure should be made (when appropriate) to the patient and the patient's family, significant other, or patient advocate.
3. The timing of disclosure of adverse events should occur as soon as possible after the recognition that an adverse event has occurred. If the patient is not able to comprehend the information, disclosure to the patient advocate should occur depending on the severity of the occurrence and their need to know the information.
4. Disclosing adverse events is primarily a physician responsibility. When there are situations in which it is impractical or unreasonable for the physician to do so, the use of a designee is in order. If the physician is out of town or unavailable, the physician covering will be responsible. If the covering physician is unavailable, the ED Medical Director will be contacted. If the physician that is not available is the director, the Chief of Staff will be contacted. The Vice President of Medical Affairs and Risk Manager will have the responsibility to ensure disclosure of information regarding an adverse event (to a patient) if a physician cannot or does not inform the patient in a timely manner.

Responding

1. First and foremost, attend to the patient's medical needs. Obtain medical consultation and make arrangements for follow-up care as may be necessary.
2. If the adverse event is of serious nature, notify the unit manager, risk manager, and the physician as soon as possible.
3. Patient outcomes, including poor outcomes, must be explained to the patient by the physician most knowledgeable of the incident, in substantially the same manner that the physician is expected to explain and then obtain informed consent before medical care is rendered.
4. Determine how the details of the event, the outcome, and the treatment plan occurred and explain to the patient and family. Designate a family contact person.
5. Be accessible for questions. Repeated requests for an explanation of the event is a common reaction when patients and family members are informed of an adverse outcome.
6. If the physician is unable to respond, the case will be directed to a physician partner, covering physician, or consulting physician knowledgeable of the case. The Chief of the Department, the Chief of Staff, the Vice President of Medical Affairs and/or the Administrator-on-call may also be consulted by the Administrative Supervisor, as appropriate.
7. Contact/consult with Risk Management and/or the Vice President of Medical Affairs to collaborate and complete reporting requirements as soon as possible.
8. Share information as soon as possible after the test, treatment, or intervention. NOTE: Sometimes the information can put a patient at risk of harm either due to psychological trauma or exposure to physical harm. (Example—physical abuse) If in the professional judgment of the physician, information should be withheld, the reasons for such should be documented in the medical record by the physician.

A. Information to Be Disclosed

The information provided to the patient and authorized immediate family members/decision makers shall be true and should contain these elements where appropriate. As many of these elements as possible should be in the communications:

1. Describe the incident that happened.
2. Who was involved (by job function, not by name).
3. What the reasonable potential short term and long term consequences are.
4. What we have done to reduce or manage the consequences to the patient.
5. Signs and symptoms that may indicate complication.
6. Appropriate actions the patient or decision-maker shall take if complications occur.
7. What plans are there to prevent the same type of incident from recurring.

B. What to Do in Disclosing an Adverse Event

1. Honesty—Be honest with the patient and family. Organize a family meeting if several relatives are involved in the patient's care or if treatment decisions are complicated.
2. Empathy—Empathize with the patient and family; offer emotional support. Show compassion for the patient's distress and accept responsibility for follow-up and action but do not assign blame, or criticize the care or response of other providers.
3. Apologizing—Saying you're sorry to a patient when an adverse event occurs can be appropriate and can be done without placing blame or criticizing yourself or others.

Start by describing the event and the medical response in brief, factual terms. Avoid guessing or contemplating out loud about what happened or why, if unknown. An appropriately, worded show of concern can increase the rapport between the patient and provider.

4. Disclosure regarding the event/outcome does not require an admission of liability or error. It takes time to analyze and determine what occurred. Avoid giving misinformation before all the facts are known. To avoid the appearance of contradictory information, it is important to provide an explanation in a context that allows for further elaboration, as details become available. Until all facts are known about what occurred, what systems are involved, etc., it is advisable to do no more than furnish an explanation regarding the unanticipated outcome.

Documenting Action in the Medical Record by the Physician

1. Documentation should be factual stating that there was a discussion of the unanticipated event. It must also be objective and completed immediately after the discussion occurred.
2. Documentation should be dated, timed, and signed at the time of the entry.
3. Avoid writing in the record any information unrelated to the care of the patient (e.g., "incident report filed" or "notified Risk Management").
4. Do not use the medical record to speculate or air grievances about other care givers, about equipment issues, or administrative processes.
5. Record factual statements of the event in the patient's record and any follow-up needed or done as a result of the event.
6. Do not alter any prior documentation.
7. While an addendum to the record can be made, consider carefully whether this information is relevant to the patient's clinical management. Accepted rationale for an addendum would be for the correction of facts (i.e., persons involved, time of event, sequence of events) and for the addition of facts or clarifying information. If you participated in the care, but were unable to access the record until a later date, you may provide added information. An addendum should not be used to state your opinions, perceptions, or defenses.

Equipment and Medical Device Preservation

When an adverse event involves equipment or medical device, preserve these materials for investigation, do not clean or alter them in any way and contact the Risk Manager. The equipment involved needs to be bagged, tagged, and sequestered by biomedical staff or the Administrative Supervisor or designated RN. (Do not return any involved devices to a manufacturer.)

Related Policies and Procedures

1. Patient complaint management.
2. Sentinel event.

Original Approval By:	Original Date:
Revision Number:	Replaces Policy Last Dated:
Last Revised/Reviewed By:	Review/Revised Date:
Signed Document Held By:	

SIGNATURES OF APPROVAL:

Date Signed	Signature	Name	Title
________	____________	________	________
________	____________	________	________
________	____________	________	________

Source: Memorial Hospital & Health System, South Bend, Indiana.

4-17 Against Medical Advice Policy and Form

POLICY

________ Hospital and Health System respects an individual's right to consent and refuse any or all medical treatment. A person refusing a part of treatment may consent to other aspects of medical treatment.

PURPOSE

To outline the process when a patient refuses medical treatment. To make the patient aware of risks when refusing treatment against medical advice.

PROCEDURE

Refusal of Treatment/Leaving the Hospital Against Medical Advice

1. An adult patient or emancipated minor who is conscious and mentally competent has the right to refuse treatment against medical advice.
2. Upon identification of the patient's desire to refuse medical treatment or to leave the hospital without a physician's order, advise the patient of the need to discuss the situation with the attending physician.
3. Ask the patient the reason for his/her refusal. (Appreciate that action can be taken in response to resolve the patient's reason for refusal). Notify the physician of the patient's refusal of medical treatment or his/her desire to leave against medical advice.
4. Inform the patient of the potential risks associated with his/her refusal as provided by the physician. This information may be provided by the physician and/or hospital staff.
5. Have the patient sign the Refusal of Treatment/Against Medical Advice form.
6. If the patient refuses to sign the Refusal of Treatment/Against Medical Advice form, document the refusal to sign on the form. Two witnesses are necessary.
7. Provide the patient with discharge instructions. Prescriptions may also be provided by the physician. Encourage the patient to obtain medical care.
8. If the patient returns to _____ Hospital for inpatient care, no matter how long he/she is absent the patient is to be re-admitted.
9. If an inpatient or an outpatient changes his/her mind, documentation regarding his/her consent to treatment is to be contained in the patient's medical record.

10. An incompetent or unconscious patient or minor is not legally capable of executing an order to refuse medical treatment against medical advice.
11. In the case of an incompetent patient or minor, and if the patient does not have guardian, or the Health System or Hospital personnel believe that the patient's guardian is not acting in the patient's best interest, a social worker and the Risk Manager should be contacted and substitute guardianship should be sought. This would necessitate a referral either to Adult Protective Services or Child Protective Services.
12. If there is a question as to whether or not the patient is competent the physician should be informed of the concern. A psychiatric evaluation may assist in determining competency. A physician is to determine competency.
13. If the health care professionals have any doubt as to the competency of the patient and the potentiality of the patient doing harm to third parties or self as a result of refusal of medical care/treatment, the patient is delayed/restrained until the physician determines the patient's current competency. The need for a 72-hour detention may need to be determined by a licensed physician and initiated if indicated.
14. If a homicide threat is voiced, a health care worker will notify the police. Efforts will then be made to notify the identified person(s) against whom the threat is voiced. (Refer to the Duty to Warn policy.)
15. If the situation is such that personnel are unable to physically restrain the patient, and the patient is considered to be a danger to themselves or others and the patient leaves, the police are to be notified of the situation.

Original Approval By:
Revision Number:
Last Revised/Reviewed By:
Signed Document Held By:

Original Date:
Replaces Policy Last Dated:
Review/Revised Date:

SIGNATURES OF APPROVAL:

Date Signed	Signature	Name	Title
______	______	______	______
______	______	______	______
______	______	______	______

Refusal of Treatment/Against Medical Advice

I have been advised by Dr. _____ of my need for the following treatment: ______________________________

____

____

____

____

I have been advised that the possible consequences of refusing the advice are ______________________________

____

____

I refuse this advice and accept total responsibility for the consequences. I release and hold harmless __________ Hospital, its Directors, Officers, Agents, Employees, Physicians, and successors from any liability resulting from my refusal of recommended medical care.

If not signed by patient, why: ____

____

____

*Signature of Patient or Individual Authorized to Consent for Health Care for the Patient

*	Time:	Date:
Signature of Witness	Time:	Date:
Signature of Witness	Time:	Date:

Source: Memorial Hospital & Health System, South Bend, Indiana.

4-18 Communication Disabilities Policy

INTENT

To efficiently serve patients with communication disabilities. Language Assistance is provided through Patient Relations Services. Representatives are assigned to areas within the hospital. In-house resources are used whenever possible. Interpretations may be provided in person or via telephone.

PROCEDURE

1. **Request for Language Assistance,** Monday through Friday 8:30 AM to 5:00 PM. Contact area language assistance representative. Beeper numbers should be available from unit or area manager. OR After hours or weekends and holidays, contact Telecommunications or Page Operator at ext. XXXX.
2. **Information required when placing request for Language Assistance**

- patient name, unit location
- specific language, dialect, or communication disability
- circumstances (needed to determine urgency of request)
- estimated length of time service needed
- requesting staff name and telephone number or beeper to contact

For language or dialects not covered, a volunteer (from Employee Volunteer Interpreters) may be available via telephone OR AT&T Language Assistance line telephone service may be available.
To access this service:

- Dial 0 (zero) hospital operator
- Request AT&T Language Assistance line

For **Hearing Impaired Assistance** contact Patient Relations Services OR _____ Interpreting Agency at (XXX) XXX-XXXX after hours.
3. Additional Information

- Physician or staff member must be present for the translation process.
- Volunteer Language Assistance time is limited, please expedite the service.
- Employee volunteers must have permission from their supervisor before interpreting.
- Employee must wear ID badge (Volunteer Language Assistance) when interpreting. Patient Relations will provide the ID badge.
- Patient Relations will rotate use of employee volunteers to avoid overutilization of any one volunteer.
- Patient Relations will maintain records of language assistance requests and current list of employee volunteer language assistants.
- Any concerns regarding language assistance should be directed to the Manager of Patient Relations or Director of Patient Services.

Source: Reprinted with permission from Rusty McNew, RN, MA, CPHQ, Dallas, Texas.

4-19 Communication with Persons with Limited English Proficiency

PURPOSE

To efficiently and effectively serve patients with Limited English Proficiency and/or communication needs.

POLICY

No patient shall be denied effective access to health and social services based on their ability to communicate.

Limited English Proficiency (LEP) shall be defined as patients who cannot speak, read, write or understand the English language at a level that permits them to interact effectively with health care providers and social service agencies.

Language Assistance services shall be offered 24 hours per day, 7 days per week.

Onsite interpreters and/or telephone interpreting services shall offer Language Assistance services throughout the PHHS system.

Persons with Limited English Proficiency shall be offered interpreting services free of charge via onsite interpreters and/or telephone interpreting services.

Persons with hearing impairments shall be offered sign language interpreting services and/or use of a TTD/TTY machine free of charge.

Family members, friends, visitors shall not be used to assist with language assistance services unless specifically requested by the patient.

Children under 18 years of age shall not be used to provide/assist with language assistance.

Validation of competency shall be completed for all Language Assistant personnel throughout the hospital system via competency testing prior to employment.

PROCEDURE

Requesting Language Assistance

- Information required when making request for onsite interpreter (*regardless of location*):
  - Patient name
  - Patient location
  - Specific language, dialect or other communication need
  - Service required (*i.e., consent, history and physical, psychosocial interview, etc.*)
  - Estimated length of time required
  - Requesting staff to contact and phone/pager number.

Availability

- Language Assistants are assigned to areas in the hospital and can be reached by their individual pagers or by calling the Patient Relations department.
- Onsite Spanish interpreters are available 24 hours a day, 7 days a week.
- Onsite Vietnamese, Chinese, Cambodian, Laotian interpreters are available Monday-Friday, day shift only.
- Telephone interpreting services are available 24 hours a day, 7 days a week.
- Verbal and written interpreting services are available.
- Onsite interpreting services for Women's & Children's Services (*except L&D*) are provided by Language Assistance staff in the Women's & Children's Division.
- Onsite interpreting for all other areas (*ESO, Medicine, Surgery, OPC, L&D, etc.*) are provided by Language Assistance staff in the Patient Relations department.
- TTD/TTY machines are available through the Patient Relations department.

Telephone Interpreting Services

- Available 24 hours a day, 7 days a week throughout the hospital.
- Language Line can be accessed from any telephone. Reference the specific unit, HUC or call Patient Relations for directions on how to access.
- Cordless interpreter phones are available in designated areas; services through these phones are available 24 hours a day, 7 days a week; service is accessed by pressing the appropriate button on the hand-held speaker.
- Concerns regarding telephone interpreting services will be communicated to the Manager of Patient Relations and/or the Director of Social Services.

Documentation

- Language assistance services provided shall be documented in the patient's medical record
- Information to be documented shall include:
  - Date and time of services
  - Language
  - Health Care Provider involved (*i.e., name of physician, nurse, social worker, etc.*)
  - Type of service provided (*i.e., consent, H&P, patient teaching, etc.*)
  - Signature, title and ID# of Language Assistant providing interpreting services.

Use of Non-Language Assistant Staff for Interpreting

- Family members, friends, visitors or other patients shall not be utilized to provide interpreting services unless the patient has specifically been offered free interpreting services and refused them as well as specifically requested a family member or friend be utilized to interpret.
- Children shall not be utilized to provide interpreting services.
- Incentive Pay staff shall be utilized for general, non-clinical, non-technical interpreting only (*i.e., directions, non-medical questions such as address, phone #, etc.*).
- Bilingual Providers (*i.e., physician, nurse, dietitian, etc.*) may provide medical/health care services to patients in the patient's primary language providing they:
  - Are fluent in the patient's primary language including medical terminology
  - Document in the patient's medical record the services they provided were provided in the patient's primary language

- Bilingual Providers who have limited fluency or no medical terminology in the patient's primary language shall use Language Assistance staff. (i.e., is provider is fluent conversationally but has no medical terminology training)
- Do not act as interpreters for other staff.

Competency

- Competency for all Language Assistance (Language Assistant/Patient Representative L100 & L101) staff shall be validated prior to employment.
- On-going continuing education is the responsibility of each employee.
- Continuing education opportunities shall be offered jointly by Patient Relations, WCS and COPC.

Source: Rusty McNew, RN, MA, CPHQ, Dallas, Texas.

4-20 Patients with Limited English Proficiency, Civil Rights VI

The U.S. Department if Health & Human Services (HHS) has released new regulations for organizations that receive federal financial assistance regarding Language Assistance to Persons with Limited English Proficiency (LEP). We are obligated to follow these regulations just as we are for TDH, HCFA & JCAHO.

1. **Reason for New Regulations:**
   a. To ensure that persons with limited English skills (Spanish, Chinese, etc.) can effectively access health & social services. The regulations are part of Title VI of the Civil Rights Act of 1964 (Title VI).
   b. Title VI & its implementing regulations provide that no person shall be subjected to discrimination based on language. Title VI prohibits recipients of Federal financial assistance from denying LEP persons access to programs, on the basis of their national origin (language).
2. **Examples of LEP Violations:**
   a. Providing services to LEP persons that are more limited in scope or are lower in quality than those provided to other persons
   b. Subjecting LEP persons to unreasonable delays in the delivery of services
   c. Limiting participation in a program or activity on the basis of English proficiency
   d. Providing services to LEP persons that are not as effective as those provided to those who are proficient in English.
3. **What This Means & Steps to Comply:**
   a. Assess Current Practice:

      —Identify the non-English languages that are likely to be encountered in its program and by estimating the number of LEP persons that are eligible for services. (Determine non-English speaking languages & the approximate number of patients that speak that specific language)

      —Identify the language needs of each LEP patient & document this information in the medical record. (Directors to determine if this is performed in their assigned areas for non-English speaking patients.)

      —Identify the points of contact in the organization or activity where language assistance is likely to be needed. (All areas of the organization including business/registration staff shall be educated & have the capability to access translation services as needed.)

—Identify the resources that will be needed to provide effective language assistance.

—Identify the location and availability of these resources.

—Identify the arrangements that must be made to access these resources in a timely fashion.

b. Development of Comprehensive Written Policy on Language Access.
c. Training of Staff:
Performed by Translation Services. Directors to ensure staff attendance.
d. Monitoring:
(Patient Satisfaction Surveys, Patient Complaint/Grievance Data, Risk Identification Reports & other internal documents used for Performance Improvement.)

Source: Rusty McNew, RN, MA, CPHQ, Dallas, Texas.

4-21 Guidelines for DNR, AND, and CPR Directives

POLICY

All patients have the right to accept or reject treatment. Every effort will be made to respect the preference of patients. Patients and their families will be involved in decisions concerning care and treatment. The appropriate type and level of care consistent with good medical practice and the resources of the medical staff and hospital will be rendered to each patient in the hospital.

DEFINITIONS

1. Do Not Resuscitate (DNR)/Allow Natural Death (AND): Is a written order to suspend the otherwise automatic initiation of cardiopulmonary resuscitation.
2. Cardiopulmonary Resuscitation (CPR): Refers to any means used to restore circulatory and/or ventilatory function until these functions are spontaneously resumed by the patient or until artificial maintenance is established or until the patient is pronounced dead.
3. CPR Directive: Means an advanced medical directive pertaining to the administration or withholding of cardiopulmonary resuscitation executed and signed by the patient's physician prior to admission.
4. Decision-making capacity: A patient has decision-making capacity when:
   a. The patient understands the nature and purpose of CPR treatment and procedures; and
   b. The patient understands the consequences and risk of accepting or refusing CPR; and
   c. The patient is able to make an informed choice to refuse CPR.
5. Futility of Treatment: Treatment is futile when it will not, with reasonable medical certainty, preserve a physiological function necessary to maintain life, with the result that the patient's death is proximate.

6. Medical Treatment: Any health care medical procedure, including artificially provided nourishment and hydration, surgery, cardiopulmonary resuscitation, or service to maintain, diagnose, treat or provide for a patient's physical or mental health.

Standard of Care:

The establishment and management of DNR/AND orders and CPR directives will reflect medical, nursing, nationally accepted guidelines, and state laws.

Standard of Practice:

A. **General**

1. When a patient or legal representative presents a CPR directive, the directive will be honored. The attending physician will be notified immediately of the CPR directive. If the physician does not wish to honor the directive, s/he must discuss the disagreement with the patient or legal representative, if appropriate. The directive may only be suspended after the physician obtains proper informed consent to do so and an order is written.
2. The physician should initiate a dialogue about CPR and the option of a DNR/AND order whenever there is reason to question the usual presumption of consent to CPR. Such occasions may include:
   a. When the patient or the patient's family, surrogate, or friend initiates discussion about CPR and/or DNR/AND.
   b. When cardiopulmonary arrest is likely to occur during the current hospitalization; for example, when:
      i. death is imminent and expected, or
      ii. the patient has suffered a severe and irreversible loss of consciousness; or
      iii. the patient has a severe and irreversible illness.
   c. When the burden of CPR and its sequelae may reasonably be expected to exceed its benefits; e.g., when the patient:
      i. is terminal;
      ii. has suffered a severe and irreversible loss of consciousness;
      iii. has a severe and irreversible illness.
3. In all cases, as in other health care decisions, the decision whether or not to write a DNR/AND order should emerge from the process of a discussion and interaction between the physician and the patient and/or legal representative. Of course, if the patient wishes, others such as family members or concerned friends may become involved. When a patient or legal representative requests a family member not be involved in or informed of the decision regarding a DNR/AND order, the patient's or legal representative's decision and request for confidentiality will be honored and documented in the medical record by the physician.
4. The physician is responsible for providing the DNR/AND order. However, it is beneficial for the physician to recognize that many disciplines contribute to the total care and welfare of the patient and, as such, nursing, social service, pastoral care, and other health care providers may be utilized as support personnel throughout the decision-making process. The physician has the responsibility to ensure that all parties receive full disclosure of the nature,

purpose, risks, and benefits of CPR and the option of a DNR/AND order. If the diagnosis or prognosis is unclear, participation of various consultants or the Bioethics Committee might be helpful. The purpose of the various consultants and support personnel is to aid the physician and the family and/or decision makers in the decision-making process. Once the decision is made to enter a DNR/AND order, the attending physician must document in the chart the circumstances surrounding the order, including the following:

a. Medical situation,
b. Opinion of the attending physician and any consultants,
c. Discussion and review with the patient, and
d. Opinion of the patient, family, and other pertinent discussions.

5. Emergency Department physicians may write DNR/AND orders if the patient is transferred from a nursing home with a copy of the DNR/AND orders or if the DNR/AND orders are faxed to the ED.
6. Except as provided in Section D, Paragraph 2, a physician may not write a DNR/AND order without permission of the patient and/or other appropriate decision makers. A DNR/AND order may be given as a verbal or telephone order to an RN, must be witnessed by another staff member, and must be co-signed within 24 hours or it will become invalid after 24 hours has lapsed. The physician ordering the DNR/AND will be contacted to re-establish or cancel the order. If re-established, then it must be co-signed within 24 hours or the patient will again have full code status. DNR/AND orders will be reviewed by the physician as changes in the patient's condition warrant such review, when requested by the patient or other decision maker, or if the patient is transferred to another physician.
7. "Limited Codes," "Show Codes," and "Slow Codes," by definition, are emergency interventions with stated limitations such as no drugs, no intubation, or no compressions. This type of code is not permitted unless there is documentation of a decision by the patient or decision maker to the contrary, such as an advance directive. All "Limited Codes" must be called as a full code but limited interventions must be controlled at the scene. Specific limitations on CPR, such as "no intubation" or "no defibrillation" make successful resuscitation much less likely. Such limitations should therefore be exceedingly rare and should be used only if explicitly requested by a fully informed patient or surrogate decision maker.

B. Patient Has Decision-Making Capacity

1. If a patient is conscious and has the decision-making capacity, the patient may refuse or direct care according to their wishes. If the patient is pregnant or has minor children, the Hospital Attorney should be consulted prior to withholding or withdrawing treatment.
2. In the case of a patient with a CPR directive who is about to receive conscious sedation, anesthesia, or contrast media, undergo surgery or procedures including those with contrast media that could potentiate an arrest situation, the surgeon, anesthesiologist, or physician performing the procedure must review with the patient or legal representative that the CPR directive will be suspended during the procedure. This will be documented in the surgical/procedure consent form.

C. Patient Lacks Decision-Making Capacity

1. In any case where the decision-making capacity of the patient is unclear, participation of psychiatric consultant may be necessary. In some cases a lack of decision-making capacity may have a reversible cause such as medication, pain,

dehydration, or another metabolic abnormality. Under such circumstances, the health care team should attempt to restore the patient's decision-making capacity if at all possible.

2. Check to see if there is a CPR directive. Pursuant to state law, any person over age 18 who has decisional capacity to provide an informed consent may execute a CPR directive. All physicians and hospital staff shall comply with the CPR directive that is apparent and immediately available. A CPR directive for any patient admitted to the hospital shall be implemented as a physician's order until suspended by the patient or family after informed consent.
3. In the case of a patient with a CPR directive who is about to receive conscious sedation, anesthesia, or contrast media, undergo surgery or procedures including those with contrast media that could potentiate an arrest situation, the surgeon, anesthesiologist, or physician performing the procedure must review with the legal representative that the CPR directive will be suspended during the procedure. This will be documented in the surgical/procedure consent form.
4. If there is no CPR directive, then a check should be made to see if the patient has a durable medical power of attorney. If the patient has a durable medical power of attorney, then the person named in the power of attorney should be contacted. Thereafter, the same rules apply as if the patient were competent; that is, the person named in the power of attorney may make all decisions the patient could have made if competent, including affirming or revoking a CPR directive, unless there are limitations in the power of attorney consenting to the entry of a DNR/AND order.
5. If the patient does not have a durable medical power of attorney, then a check should be made to see if the patient has a court-appointed guardian or a legal representative. Thereafter, the same rules apply as if the patient were competent; that is, the guardian may make all decisions the patient could have made including affirming or revoking a CPR directive, or consenting to the entry of a DNR/AND order unless there are limitations in the guardianship.
6. If the patient has a valid living will or if the conditions that activate the living will are present, i.e., the patient is terminal and unable to communicate, then the physician must write a DNR/AND order in compliance with the patient's or legal representative's designated wishes.
7. If the patient has no CPR directive, guardian, or person with evidence of durable medical power of attorney, but has known relatives, then the physician must make a reasonable effort to locate all interested parties (i.e., spouse, parents, children, grandchildren, siblings, or close friends). The family or, in the absence of a family decision, a physician may designate one family member to contact and may rely upon such family member to notify others. After interested parties are located, the physician advises them of the patient's incompetency and that a proxy decision maker should be selected. Interested parties should then choose a person with the closest relationship to and knowledge of the patient's wishes. If there is any disagreement of the selection of the proxy or the treatment of the patient, any interested party may seek a court guardianship. In the meantime, CPR will be administered.
8. If the patient has no CPR directive, durable medical power of attorney, guardian, or any known relative, contact the Hospital Attorney for further advice.

D. _____ **(state)** law requires that physicians comply with a CPR directive that is apparent and immediately available or a DNR/AND order. In an emergency situation, however, where in the judgment of a physician acting in good faith, there are exceptional circumstances such as, but not limited to, foul play, the CPR directive or DNR/AND order may be suspended by the physician at the physician's discretion. In any such case, every attempt should be made to contact the attending physician. Such a resuscitative order and the reasons therefore shall be documented in the chart in the physician orders and progress note sections.

1. When it is clear to the physician that CPR would be futile because of the patient's physical condition or because the patient would not respond to CPR, the physician must review the reasons for declaring futility and must discuss these issues with the patient, legal representative, proxy decision maker, or family. The reasons must be documented in a summary on the chart. **Before** proceeding to write a DNR/AND order, the physician must obtain a second opinion that a DNR/AND order is appropriate. When a patient, legal representative (or proxy decision maker) disagrees with the physician's judgment on medical futility and would like to receive CPR, the physician should not write a DNR/AND order until there is resolution of the disagreement.
2. The attending physician must inform the patient or other appropriate decision makers if he/she cannot ethically agree with the decision not to resuscitate the patient and that he or she has decided to remove him/herself from the care of the patient and transfer care to another physician. In such event, the physician will stay on the case until another physician is found.

E. Nursing Documentation of DNR/AND Status

1. A change in code status is considered a STAT order and implementation and documentation must proceed immediately.
2. A red DNR/AND sticker is placed on the outside of the chart. Notation may also be found on the patient census board, kardex, daily plan of care, or at the head of the patient bed, depending on the nursing unit.
3. A DNR/AND order may be taken by telephone by a Registered Nurse by having another staff member witness the telephone call. The RN and the witness shall sign the telephone order.

F. DNR/AND Status for Patients on Telemetry

It is the responsibility of the admitting unit to inform telemetry of the patient's DNR/AND status. When the DNR/AND status changes, the individual transcribing the orders will call telemetry to change the order.

TO OUR PATIENTS

YOUR RIGHT TO MAKE HEALTH CARE DECISIONS

________'s policy is to honor your health care decisions as long as it is legal and reasonable. *You are not required to have* a *medical directive to receive care at* _____ *or any other health care facility.*

WHAT YOU NEED TO KNOW ABOUT MEDICAL DIRECTIVES

Federal law requires us to give this information to every patient we admit to the hospital. It is about *your right* to make health care decisions. By making such decisions, you can let your doctor and family know what kind of medical treatment you do or do not want to receive. It can also let them know what kind of medical treatment you want stopped. It also allows you to name a person to make health care decisions for you when you can't make them yourself. Medical directives can only be put into action if the conditions you list are met by your medical condition. Having the forms *does not* mean you will stop receiving care or medical treatment. If you already have a Living Will, Medical Durable Power of Attorney, or a CPR Directive, please tell your doctor and your nurse. We must have a copy of the document(s) for your hospital chart in order to assure that your wishes are honored. Here are three examples of medical directive forms:

1. DURABLE MEDICAL POWER OF ATTORNEY FOR HEALTH CARE

(**Please note:** a Medical Durable Power of Attorney is not a Power of Attorney for business or personal financial matters.)
In this kind of document you can state what types of medical treatment you want to have or don't want to have. For example, do you want surgery, dialysis, blood transfusion, or cancer treatment? You can also name someone to make decisions for you when you can no longer make them yourself. That person can **only** make health care decisions for you when you are no longer able to make them for yourself.

2. LIVING WILL

(**Please note:** A "Living Will" is not the same as a "Last Will & Testament." It has nothing to do with what happens to your personal property or your estate after death.)
You can let us know in advance how long you want life support treatment to be provided for you if you ever have to be put on life support machines. This is often called a "Living Will." It tells your doctor and family how long you want treatment provided and when you want it stopped.

3. CPR DIRECTIVE—ALSO KNOWN AS A "NO COR" OR "NO CODE"

A CPR (<u>C</u>ardio-<u>P</u>ulmonary <u>R</u>esuscitation) directive tells your doctor and family what to do <u>if your heart stops beating or you stop breathing.</u> If you <u>do not</u> want CPR, a physician's order must be written in your chart each time you are admitted. If you <u>do</u> want CPR, it will be automatically given to you, if necessary, while you are a patient.

PHYSICIAN ORDER FOR DNR/AND
Do Not Resuscitate/Allow Natural Death

☐ **DO NOT RESUSCITATE/ALLOW NATURAL DEATH (DNR/AND)**

☐ **DNR/AND order discussed with patient and/or legal representative** ☐ Yes ☐ No If discussed with legal representative/family: ________________________ (Name and relationship)

☐ **Does patient have capacity to make health care decisions?** Yes ☐ No ☐
If no, DNR/AND order based on: (check one only)

☐ Living Will

☐ Discussion with next of kin

☐ Consent from legal guardian or Medical Durable Power of Attorney
(Name: ______________________)

☐ Futility of resuscitation is of discretion of the health care team
(Name of second concurring physician(s) or ethics consult:
__________)

____
Printed name

____
Signature of attending physician

____
Date

____
Time

Source: Parkview Medical Center, Pueblo, Colorado. Reprinted with permission.

PROVISION OF CARE

4-22 Assessment of the Emergency Department Patient

PURPOSE

Establish assessment criteria for all Emergency Department patients.

POLICY

1. All patients presenting to the Emergency Department will be triaged and categorized as either Emergent, Urgent or Non-Urgent.
2. All patients admitted to the Emergency Department will have the following documentation:
   - Chief complaint:
     - Subjective data;
     - Objective data.
   - Physical assessment
   - Assessment of psychological status
   - Vital signs:
     - Initial vital signs shall be obtained on arrival to the ED
     - Additional vital signs shall be obtained depending on patient's condition
     - Patients with unstable vital signs are placed on propack cardiac monitoring machine. Vital signs monitored every 30 minutes.

- Comfort goal and pain scale upon arrival to treatment room
- Level I & Level II trauma patients will have vital signs recorded every hour
- Abnormal vitals will be repeated prior to discharge
- All other patients every 2 hours

- Pain will be managed per the nursing policy—Pain Management
- Allergies and medications
- Interventions performed and response to interventions
- History of present illness
- Pertinent past medical history
- Response to medication
- Tetanus status
- Patient education
- Reassessment and/or evaluation of expected outcomes prior to discharge
- Nutritional assessment if clinically indicated

3. In addition, the pediatric patient (<16 years old) shall have the following information documented:
   - Weight
   - Head circumference if clinically indicated for infants 24 months and younger.
   - Activity for age
   - Developmental assessment (DASA)
   - Behavior or LOC
   - Referral to pediatrician or specialist as indicated
   - Height if clinically indicated
   - A complete set of vitals will be taken on arrival to ER to include BP, pulse, respiratory rate, and temperature. Repeat vital signs will be taken per ER vital sign protocol.

Source: Parkview Medical Center, Pueblo, Colorado.

4-23 Assessment of the Trauma Patient

POLICY

The trauma patient shall be assessed and treated according to Emergency Nursing Association/Trauma Nurse Care Course criteria.

OBJECTIVES

Upon completion of this chapter/lecture, the learner should be able to:

1. Describe the components of the primary assessment.
2. Correlate life-threatening conditions with the specific component of the primary assessment.
3. Identify interventions to manage life-threatening conditions assessed during the initial assessment.
4. Identify the components of the secondary assessment.
5. Describe how to conduct a complete head-to-toe assessment.

Use the ENA/TNCC criteria to assist the nurse with the complete initial assessment of a trauma patient.

A systematic process or initial assessment of the trauma patient is essential for recognizing life-threatening conditions, identifying injuries, and for determining priorities of care based on assessment findings. The initial assessment is divided into two phases, primary and secondary assessments. Both phases can be completed within several minutes unless resuscitative measures are required. Within an organized team approach to trauma care, this first step of the nursing process (assessment) is often simultaneously conducted with the identification of nursing diagnoses that require immediate intervention. Utilizing an organized, systematic approach when assessing each trauma patient also helps to ensure that injuries will not be missed and that priorities can be set for each intervention based on the life-threatening potential of each injury.

Adherence to "Standard Precautions" (precautions for care of all patients in hospitals) and "transmission-Based Precautions" for care of patients who are known or suspected of being infected or colonized by certain pathogens transmitted by contact with skin, airborne, or droplet are indicated for use by the trauma team. The team "Standard Precautions" encompasses "Universal Precautions" used to protect against transmission of pathogens from moist body surfaces. Use of lead aprons by the trauma team during radiologic procedures is necessary and can often be initiated prior to the patient's arrival. Initial assessment provides the nurse with subjective and objective data that are analyzed, interpreted, and documented. During this initial encounter with the patient, initiate the health care team's protocol for informing family members of the patient's arrival and condition.

A GUIDE TO INITIAL ASSESSMENT

The following mnemonic may assist nurses during the initial assessment of a trauma patient:

- Primary Assessment
  - A—Airway with simultaneous cervical spine stabilization and/or immobilization
  - B—Breathing
  - C—Circulation
  - D—Disability (neurologic status)
- Secondary Assessment
  - E—Expose/environmental control (remove clothing and keep patient warm)
  - F—Full set of vital signs/five interventions (electrocardiographic monitor, pulse oximeter, urinary catheter, gastric tube, and laboratory studies)/facilitate family presence
  - G—Give comfort measures (verbal reassurance, touch)
  - H—History and Head-to-toe assessment
  - I—Inspect posterior surfaces

PRIMARY ASSESSMENT AND RESUSCITATION

Airway, with simultaneous cervical spine stabilization and/or immobilization, breathing, circulation, and disability (neurologic status) are the A-B-C-Ds of the primary assessment.

Remove only those clothes necessary to expose the patient in order to conduct the primary assessment. If any life-threatening compromises or injuries are determined, implement interventions to correct them immediately. Additional assessment steps are not taken until measures to ensure an adequate airway, effective breathing, and effective circulation have been instituted.

In the presence of potentially life-threatening injuries, begin assessment immediately on the patient's arrival to collect objective assessment information. The extent and timing of obtaining information related to both the injury event and the patient's past medical history depend on the severity of the patient's condition. Subjective information from pre-hospital personnel, family, or the patient at this point of the assessment process is limited to a brief statement composed of the patient's major injuries or chief complaints and the mechanism of injury. A more detailed history is obtained during the secondary assessment.

AIRWAY

Assessment

Inspect the patient's airway while maintaining cervical spine stabilization and/or immobilization. Since partial or total airway obstruction may threaten the patency of the upper airway, observe for the following:

- Vocalization
- Tongue obstructing airway in an unresponsive patient
- Loose teeth or foreign objects
- Bleeding
- Vomitus or other secretions
- Edema

INTERVENTIONS

Airway Patent

- Maintain cervical spine stabilization and/or immobilization
- Any patient whose mechanism of injury, symptoms, or physical findings suggest a spinal injury should be stabilized or remain immobilized.
- If the patient is awake and breathing, he or she may have assumed a position that maximizes the ability to breathe. Before proceeding with cervical spine stabilization, be sure interventions do NOT compromise the patient's breathing status.

Airway Totally Obstructed or Partially Obstructed

- Position the patient
  Position the patient in a supine position. If the patient is not already supine, logroll the patient onto his or her back while maintaining cervical spine stabilization. Remove any head gear, if necessary, to allow access to the airway and cervical spine; removal of such gear should be done carefully and gently to prevent any manipulation of the spine.

- Stabilize the cervical spine
  - If the patient has not been stabilized, manually stabilize the head. Stabilization includes holding the head in a neutral position.
  - If the patient is already in a rigid cervical collar and strapped to a backboard, do NOT remove any devices. Check that the devices are placed appropriately.
- Complete spinal immobilization with a backboard and straps should be done at the completion of the secondary assessment, depending on the degree of resuscitation required and the availability of team members.
  - Open and clear the airway.
- Techniques to open or clear an obstructed airway during the primary assessment include:
  - Jaw thrust
  - Chin lift
  - Removal of loose objects or foreign debris
  - Suctioning
- Maintain the cervical spine in a neutral position. Do not hyperextend, flex, or rotate the neck during these maneuvers.
- Suctioning and other manipulation of the oropharynx must be done gently to prevent stimulation of the gag reflex and subsequent vomiting and/or aspiration.
- Insert an oropharyngeal or nasopharyngeal airway.
- Consider endotracheal intubation (oral or nasal route).

Ventilate the patient with a bag-valve-mask device prior to endotracheal intubation. For patients requiring control of the airway with an endotracheal tube, the decision must be made to use the oral versus the nasal route.

- Oral endotracheal intubation is done with the patient's cervical spine in a neutral position and without any extension or flexion of the cervical spine. This requires a second person to hold the patient's head in this position.
- Blind nasotracheal intubation is NOT indicated when the patient is apneic or when there are signs of major midface fractures (e.g., maxillary fractures [LeFort II or III]). Basilar skull fractures or fractures of the frontal sinus or cribriform plate are considered relative contraindications.
- The use of neuromuscular blocking agents along or in combination with other drugs administered before intubation is usually dictated by institutional protocols.
- Consider needle or surgical cricothyroidotomy.
- Ventilate the patient with a bag-valve-mask device prior to these procedures. In rare circumstances, the patient's condition may restrict passage of an endotracheal tube. To establish an airway, a needle cricothyroidotomy may be performed with an over-the-needle catheter placed into the trachea through the cricothyroid membrane. Another method is a surgical cricothyroidotomy. An incision is made in the cricothyroid membrane, and a tube is placed into the trachea. Both of these approaches to a cricothyroidotomy should be performed by skilled physicians. In some settings, advanced life support (ALS) personnel (e.g., flight nurses or advanced practice nurses) may also be trained and qualified to perform cricothyroidotomies.

If there are any life-threatening compromises in airway status, stop and intervene to correct the problem before proceeding to breathing assessment. Examples of life-threatening airway conditions are partial or complete obstruction of the airway from foreign bodies or debris (blood, mucus, vomitus) and/or obstruction by the tongue. Penetrating wounds may cause disruption of the integrity of the airway, and blunt trauma may lead to injury of the larynx and/or other upper airway structures.

Breathing

ASSESSMENT

Life-threatening compromises in breathing may occur with a history of any of the following:

- Blunt or penetrating injuries of the thorax
- Patient striking the steering column or wheel
- Acceleration, deceleration, or a combination of both types of forces (e.g., motor vehicle crashes, falls, crash injuries)

Once the patency of the airway is assured, assess for the following:

- Spontaneous breathing
- Chest rise and fall (depth and symmetry)
- Skin color
- General respiratory rate
    - Normal
    - Slow
    - Fast
- Pattern of breathing
    - Regular
    - Irregular
    - Cheyne Stokes
- Integrity of the soft tissue and bony structures of the chest wall
- Use of accessory and/or abdominal muscles
- Bilateral breath sounds
    - Auscultate the lungs bilaterally at the second intercostal space midclavicular line and at the fifth intercostal space at the anterior axillary line.
- Jugular veins and position of trachea

INTERVENTIONS

Breathing Present: Effective

Administer oxygen via a *nonrebreather mask* at a flow rate sufficient to keep the reservoir bag inflated; during inspiration, usually requires a flow rate of at least 12 liters/minute and may require 15 liters/minute or more.

Breathing Present: Ineffective

When spontaneous breathing is present but ineffective, the following may indicate a life-threatening condition related to breathing:

- Altered mental status (i.e., restless, agitated)
- Cyanosis, especially around the mouth
- Asymmetrical expansion of the chest wall

- Use of accessory and/or abdominal muscles
- Sucking chest wounds
- *Paradoxical* movement of chest wall during inspiration and expiration
- Tracheal shift from the midline position

To inspect and palpate the anterior neck region (i.e., jugular veins and trachea), remove the anterior portion of the cervical collar. Another team member must hold the patient's head while the collar is being removed and replaced.

- Distended external jugular veins
- Absent or diminished breath sounds
- Auscultate breath sounds to determine if present, diminished, or absent
- Administer oxygen via a nonrebreather mask or assist ventilations with a bag-valve-mask device, as indicated
- Assist with endotracheal intubation as previously described

Breathing Absent

- Ventilate the patient via a bag-valve-mask device with an attached oxygen reservoir system
- Assist with endotracheal intubation; ventilate with oxygen via a bag-valve device attached to an oxygen reservoir system

If there are any life-threatening injuries that compromise breathing, stop and intervene before proceeding to circulation assessment. Examples of life-threatening injuries that may compromise breathing are tension pneumothorax, open pneumothorax, flail chest with pulmonary contusion, and hemothorax. These conditions may require simultaneous assessment and immediate intervention (*e.g., needle thoracentesis* or covering an open chest wound).

Circulation

ASSESSMENT

- Palpate a central pulse (e.g., femoral or carotid) initially if there is any question as to whether the patient has adequate circulation.
- Palpate the pulse for quality (i.e., normal, weak, or strong); and rate (i.e., normal, slow, or fast).
- Inspect and palpate the skin for color, temperature, and degree of diaphoresis
- Inspect for any obvious signs of external bleeding
- Auscultate *blood pressure*
- If there are other members of the trauma team available, auscultate the blood pressure. If not, proceed with the primary assessment and auscultate the blood pressure at the beginning of the secondary assessment.

INTERVENTIONS

Circulation: Effective

If the circulation is effective, proceed with assessment and intervene according to interventions for ineffective circulation, as indicated.

Circulation Present: Ineffective

Although the pulse is present, other signs may indicate inadequacy of the circulation such as:

- Tachycardia
- Altered level of consciousness or mental status (e.g., agitated, confused, decreased arousability)
- Uncontrolled external bleeding
- Distended or abnormally flattened external jugular veins
- Pale, cool, diaphoretic skin
- Distant heart sounds

Circulation: Effective or Ineffective

- Control any uncontrolled external bleeding by:
  - Applying direct pressure over the bleeding site
  - Elevating the bleeding extremity
  - Applying pressure over arterial pressure points
  - The use of a tourniquet is rarely indicated; however, if the above interventions do not control the bleeding and operative bleeding control is not readily available, a tourniquet may be the last resort.
- Cannulate two veins with large-bore 14- or 16-gauge catheters, and initiate infusions of *lactated Ringer's solution* or normal saline
  - Use warmed solutions
  - Use plastic bags to facilitate pressurized infusion
  - Use "Y" tubing for possible administration of blood
  - Use rapid infusion device, as indicated
  - Use normal saline (0.9%) in intravenous tubing through which blood is administered
  - Venous cannulation may require a surgical cutdown and/or central venipuncture
  - Consider use of a *pneumatic antishock garment* (PASG) for intra-abdominal and/or pelvic bleeding with hypotension
  - Obtain a blood sample for typing to determine the ABO and Rh group
  - Administer blood, as prescribed

Circulation: Absent

If a patient does not have a pulse, cardiopulmonary resuscitation (CPR) is indicated. However, it is possible to have electrocardiographic activity even when the pulse and blood pressure cannot be auscultated. The term *electromechanical dissociation* (EMD) refers to one example of pulseless electrical activity (PEA), whereby the patient has no pulse but has narrow complexes indicating depolarization of the myocardium with no mechanical contraction. *Pseudo-EMD*, a newer term, describes a patient who has no blood pressure by auscultation, but may have some degree of myocardial muscle contraction, albeit too weak to generate a blood pressure. If there is no palpable carotid pulse:

- Initiate cardiopulmonary resuscitation (CPR)
- Initiate advanced life support measures
- Administer blood, as prescribed

- Prepare for and assist with an emergency thoracotomy, as indicated, in the emergency department or resuscitation area; open thoracotomies should only be done in facilities with the resources to manage post-thoracotomy patients.
- Prepare patient for definitive operative care after thoracotomy, if indicated

If there are any life-threatening conditions compromising circulation, stop and intervene before proceeding to the neurologic assessment. Examples of life-threatening conditions that may compromise circulation are uncontrolled external bleeding, shock because of hemorrhage or massive burns, pericardial tamponade, or direct cardiac injury.

Disability—Brief Neurologic Assessment
ASSESSMENT
After the primary assessment of airway, breathing, and circulation, conduct a brief neurologic assessment to determine the degree of disability (D) as measured by the patient's level f consciousness.

- Determine the patient's level of consciousness by assessing the patient's response to verbal and/or painful stimuli using the ***AVPU*** mnemonic as follows:
  A—Speak to the patient. The patient who is alert and responsive is considered **A** for **Alert**.
  V—The patient who responds to verbal stimuli is considered **V** for **Verbal**.
  P—Apply a painful stimulus. The patient who does not respond to verbal stimuli, but does respond to a painful stimulus is considered **P** for **Pain**.
  U—The patient who does not respond to painful stimulus is considered **U** for **Unresponsive**.
- Assess pupils for size, shape, equality, and reactivity to light

Interventions

- If the disability assessment indicated a decreased level of consciousness, conduct further investigation during the secondary focused assessments.
- If the patient is not alert or verbal, continue to monitor for any compromise to airway, breathing, or circulation.
- If the patient demonstrates signs of herniation or neurologic deterioration (e.g. unilateral or bilateral [pupillary] dilation, asymmetric pupillary reactivity, or motor posturing) consider hyperventilation.

SECONDARY ASSESSMENT
After each component of the A-B-C-D of the primary assessment has been addressed and life-saving interventions initiated, start the *secondary assessment.* This assessment is a brief, systematic process to identify **ALL** injuries. **Exposure/environmental control (E)** is necessary to assess the patient adequately. It may be necessary to cut away clothing in certain circumstances. Timing of the removal of clothing will depend on the number of trauma team members available. Once clothing has been removed, it is important to prevent heat loss by using overhead warmers, warming blankets, and warmed intravenous fluids.

The **F** of the assessment mnemonic stands for a **full set of vital signs/five interventions/ facilitate family presence**.

Prior to initiating the head-to-toe assessment to identify other injuries, obtain a full set of vital signs, including blood pressure, pulse rate, respiratory rate, and temperature. If chest trauma is suspected, auscultate the blood pressure in both arms.
After completing the A-B-C-D-E of the assessment, intervening for life-threatening conditions, and obtaining a complete set of vital signs (F), critical decision-making will determine whether to continue with the secondary assessment or to perform additional interventions. The availability of other trauma members to perform these **five** interventions will influence the decision. If the patient sustained significant trauma and required life-saving interventions during the primary assessment, perform the following interventions before proceeding with the secondary assessment:

- Assign another trauma team member to attach leads and monitor the patient's cardiac rate and rhythm.
- Assign another trauma team member to attach a *pulse oximeter*, if available, to monitor the patient's arterial *oxygen saturation* (SpO_2). The normal SpO_2 is greater than 95%, meaning hemoglobin is 95% saturated with oxygen. SpO_2 readings may not be accurate if the patient has inconsistent blood flow, vasoconstriction, or altered hemoglobins such as *carboxy-hemoglobin*. Even if the patient has only a slight change in SpO_2 readings, the change in arterial *partial pressure of oxygen* (PaO_2) is significant, especially if the PaO_2 changes between 100 and 60 mm Hg. The percent of hemoglobin saturated with oxygen has a relationship to the partial pressure of oxygen as demonstrated by the oxygen-hemoglobin dissociation curve. The curve plateaus when PaO_2 levels are high but the SpO_2 will not significantly change at these higher ranges since essentially the hemoglobin is 100% saturated; however, at lower ranges of PaO_2 where the curve is more sigmoidal-shaped, the changes in SpO_2 are extremely significant. For example, a 10 mm Hg drop in PaO_2 from 90 to 80 represents only a drop in SpO_2 from 96.5% to 94.5%. However, if the PaO_2 drops from 50 mm Hg to 40, the drop in SpO_2 is from 83.5% to 75%. The clinical significance is that patients who have pulse oximetry readings above 90% could have varying levels of PaO_2, and, therefore, pulse oximetry alone should not be used to predict PaO_2. Oxygen saturation measurements can also be calculated from an arterial blood sample (SaO_2).
- Insert an indwelling urinary catheter to monitor urinary output. Suspected injury to the urethra is a contraindication to catheterization through the urethra. Indications of possible urethral injury are:
  - Blood at the urethral meatus
  - Palpation of a displaced prostate gland during a rectal examination
  - Blood in the scrotum
  - Suspicion of an anterior pelvic fracture
- Insert a gastric tube. In the presence of severe facial fractures, insert the gastric tube through the patient's mouth. Gastric decompression and emptying of gastric contents will reduce the risk of aspiration, reduce the risk of respiratory compromise, reduce the risk of vagal stimulation and bradycardia, and prepare the patient for possible operative intervention. Test gastric contents for blood. The tube must be passed carefully while:
  - Maintaining cervical spine stabilization and/or immobilization
  - Minimizing the stimulation of the patient's gag reflex
  - Having suction equipment available

- Facilitate laboratory studies
- Blood typing the highest priority. Depending on the severity of the patient's condition, blood typing studies may also include screening and crossmatching.
- Frequently ordered studies are blood typing, hematocrit (Hct), hemoglobin (Hgb), *blood urea nitrogen* (BUN), creatinine, blood alcohol, toxicology screen, arterial partial pressure of oxygen (PaO_2), arterial *partial pressure of carbon dioxide* ($PaCO_2$), pH, base deficit, lactate, electrolytes, glucose and clotting profile (platelets, *prothrobin time* [PT], partial thromboplastin time [PTT]), and beta human chorionic gonadotropin or urine test for pregnancy.

The **F** of the mnemonic also represents family presence. Facilitate the presence of the family in the treatment area and their involvement in the patient's care.

- Assess the family's desires and needs
- Facilitate and support the family's involvement in the care
- Assign a health care professional to provide explanations about procedures and to be with the family in the emergency department
- Utilize resources to support the family's emotional and spiritual needs, such as a social worker or chaplain

The **G** of the mnemonic is a reminder to the trauma team to give comfort measures. Such measures may include, but are not limited to, consideration of pain management (e.g., pharmacologic analgesia); alternative pain control such as touch, positioning, distraction, relaxation techniques; and general comfort measures such as verbal reassurance, stimuli reduction, listening to the patient, and developing a trusting nurse/patient relationship.

History

The **H** of the mnemonic stands for history which can be obtained from the following:

- Pre-hospital information
  Obtain information from pre-hospital personnel as indicated by the circumstances of the injury event. The mnemonic ***MIVT***—which stands for Mechanism of injury, Injuries sustained, Vital signs, and Treatment—can be used as a guide to obtaining pre-hospital information.
  - Mechanism and pattern of injury
    Knowledge of the mechanism of injury and specific injury patterns (e.g., type of motor vehicle impact) will help to predict certain injuries. If the patient was transported by pre-hospital personnel, have them describe pertinent on-scene information to the trauma team. Such information includes the location of the patient on their arrival, length of time since the injury event, and extent of extrication or reasons for extended on-scene time.
  - Injuries suspected
    Ask pre-hospital personnel to describe the patient's general condition, level of consciousness, and apparent injuries.
  - Vital signs
  - Treatment initiated and patient responses
- Patient-generated information
  - If the patient is responsive, ask questions in order to evaluate the patient's level of consciousness and for the patient to describe discomforts or other complaints. Elicit patient's description of pain (i.e., location, duration, intensity, and character).

If domestic violence is suspected, as appropriate question while providing comfort and a sense of security. Talking to the patient provides reassurance and emotional support and provides the patient with information regarding upcoming procedures.

- Past medical history
  Gather information from the patient or family regarding:
  - Age
  - Pre-existing medical conditions
  - Current medications
  - Allergies
  - Tetanus immunization history
  - Previous hospitalizations and surgeries
  - Recent use of drugs or alcohol
  - Smoking history
  - Last menstrual period

Head-to-Toe Assessment

The **H** stands for head-to-toe assessment. Information from this assessment is collected primarily through inspection, auscultation, and palpation. In specific circumstances, percussion may be indicated. The patient may focus on the more obvious distracting injury and have a decreased response to other injuries. While systematically moving from the patient's head to the lower extremities and the posterior surface, complete the assessment as described on the following pages.

General Appearance

Note the patient's body position, posture, and any guarding or self-protection movements. Observe for stiffness, rigidity, or flaccidity of muscles. Characteristic positions of limbs (flexion or extension), trunk, or head may indicate specific injuries. Note and document any unusual odors such as alcohol, gasoline, chemicals, vomitus, urine, or feces.

Head and Face

- Soft tissue injuries
  - Inspect for lacerations, abrasions, contusions, avulsions, puncture wounds, impaled objects, *ecchymosis*, and edema
  - Palpate for crackling association with subcutaneous emphysema
  - Palpate for areas of tenderness
- Bony deformities
  - Inspect for exposed bone
  - Inspect for loose teeth or other material in the mouth that may compromise the airway
  - Inspect and palpate for depressions, angulation, or areas of tenderness
  - Inspect and palpate for facial fractures resulting in loss maxillary and/or mandibular or structural integrity
- Observe for asymmetry of facial expressions. Also inspect the area for any exposed tissue that may indicate disruption of the central nervous system (CNS) (i.e., CNS tissue from open wounds).
- Eyes
  - Determine gross visual acuity by asking the patient to identify how many of your fingers you are holding up

- Inspect for periorbital ecchymosis (*raccoon's eyes*), subconjunctival hemorrhage, and/or edema. Determine whether the patient is wearing contact lenses.
- Assess pupils for size, shape, equality, and reactivity to light
- Assess eye muscles by asking the patient to follow your moving finger in six directions to determine *extraocular eye movements* (EOMs)
- Ears
  - *Inspect* for ecchymosis behind the ear (*Battle's sign*)
  - Inspect for skin avulsion
  - Inspect for unusual drainage, such as blood or clear fluid from the external ear canal. Do **NOT** pack the ear to stop drainage as it may be cerebrospinal fluid (CFS).
- Nose
  - Inspect for any unusual drainage, such as flood or clear fluid. Do **NOT** pack the nose to stop clear fluid drainage as it may be CSF. If CSF or drainage is present, notify the physician and do not insert a gastric tube through the nose.
  - Inspect position of nasal septum
- Neck
  - Inspect for signs of penetrating or surface trauma, including presence of impaled objects, ecchymosis, edema, or any open wounds
  - Observe position of trachea and appearance of external jugular veins
  - Palpate trachea to determine position (i.e., midline, deviated)
  - Palpate neck area for signs of subcutaneous emphysema and/or areas of tenderness

Chest

- Inspection
  - Observe breathing for rate, depth, degree of effort required, use of accessory and/or abdominal muscles, and any paradoxical chest wall movement
  - Inspect the anterior and lateral chest walls, including the axillae for lacerations, abrasions, contusions, avulsions, puncture wounds, impaled objects, ecchymosis, edema, and scars
  - Inspect the expansion of the chest and excursion during ventilation
  - Observe for expressions or reactions that may indicate the presence of pain (e.g., facial grimace)
- Auscultation
  - Auscultate lungs for breath sounds and note presence of any adventitious sounds, such as wheezes, rales, or rhonchi
  - Auscultate heart sounds for presence of murmurs, friction rubs, and/or muffled sounds
- Palpation
  - Palpate for signs of subcutaneous emphysema
  - Palpate the clavicles, sternum, and the ribs for bony *crepitus* or deformities (e.g., step-off, areas of tenderness)

Abdomen/Flanks

- Inspection
  - Inspect for lacerations, abrasions, contusions, avulsions, puncture wounds, impaled objects, ecchymosis, edema, and scars
  - Observe for evisceration, distension, and scars

- Auscultation
  - Auscultate for presence or absence of bowel sounds. Auscultate before palpating because palpation may change the frequency of bowel sounds.
- Palpation
  - Gently palpate all four quadrants for rigidity, guarding, masses, and areas of tenderness; begin palpating in an area where a patient has not complained of pain or where there is no obvious injury.

Pelvis/Perineum

- Inspect for lacerations, abrasions, contusions, avulsions, puncture wounds, impaled objects, ecchymosis, edema, and scars
- Bony deformities
  - Inspect for exposed bone
  - Palpate for instability and tenderness over the iliac crests and the symphysis pubis
- Inspect for blood at the urethral meatus (more common in males than females because of length of urethra), vagina, and rectum
- Altered neurologic function
  - Inspect penis for *priapism* (persistent abnormal erection)
  - Palpate anal sphincter for presence or absence of tone
- Ensure that an appropriate trauma team member has performed a rectal examination to determine if there is any displacement of the prostate gland in males (this may also be done in the posterior assessment)
- Note pain and/or the urge, but inability, to void

Extremities

- Inspect previously applied splints and to **NOT** remove if applied appropriately and if neurovascular function is intact
- Circulation
  - Inspect color
  - Palpate skin temperature
  - Palpate pulses (In lower extremities, palpate femoral, popliteal, dorsalis pedis; in upper extremities, palpate the brachial and radial pulses.)
- Soft tissue injuries
  - Inspect for bleeding
  - Inspect for lacerations, abrasions, contusions, avulsions, puncture wounds, impaled objects, ecchymosis, edema, angulations, deformity, and any open wounds
- Bony injuries
  - Inspect for angulation, deformity, open wounds with evidence of protruding bone fragments, edema, and ecchymosis
  - Note bony crepitus
  - Palpate for deformity and areas of tenderness
- Motor function
  - Inspect for spontaneous movement of extremities
  - Determine motor strength and range of motion in all four extremities; use range of motion (ROM)/muscle strength scale 0-5.
  - 5 = complete ROM or active movement against gravity and full resistance
  - 4 = complete ROM or active movement against gravity and some resistance
  - 3 = complete ROM or active movement against gravity
  - 2 = complete ROM or active body part movement with gravity eliminated

  - 1 = barely detectable contraction
  - 0 = no detectable contraction
- Sensation
  - Determine patient's ability to sense touch in all four extremities

Inspect Posterior Surfaces
The I of the mnemonic stands for inspection of the patient's posterior surfaces.

- Maintain cervical spine stabilization
- Support extremities with suspected injuries
- *Logroll* patient with the assistance of members of the trauma team. This maneuver keeps the vertebral column in alignment during the turning process. Do not logroll the patient onto his or her side with an injured extremity. Logroll away from you (if possible) to inspect the back, flanks, buttocks, and posterior thighs for lacerations, abrasions, contusions, avulsions, puncture wounds, impaled objects, ecchymosis, edema, or scars.
- Palpate the vertebral column including the costovertebral angles (CVA) for deformity and areas of tenderness
- Palpate all posterior surfaces for deformity and areas of tenderness
- Palpate anal sphincter for presence or absence of tone, if not already done during the assessment of the pelvis and perineum

FOCUSED SURVEY
After the primary and secondary assessments and any simultaneous interventions are completed, a more detailed, focused assessment will be necessary for each area or system injured. This will further direct the priorities of care.
Frequently ordered radiographic studies are of the chest, pelvis, and cervical spine (C-1 through T-1 must be visualized). Follow cervical spine clearance procedures as indicated by individual hospital protocols. These radiographic studies may be performed during any phase of the primary or secondary assessment, depending on the patient's condition and the availability of resources.

PAIN MANAGEMENT
The patient's perception of pain may originate from a number of sources because of injury (e.g., the actual injury, procedures, the environment). Trauma patients will have their pain managed per the nursing policy P-005—Pain Management.

TETANUS PROPHYLAXIS
Determination of the need for *tetanus prophylaxis* following trauma depends on:

- Condition of the wound
- Patient's past vaccination history
- First determine whether the patient has ever received primary vaccination.

SEVERITY INDICES
The *Glasgow Coma Scale score* and the *Revised Trauma Score* are two scoring systems that measure the acuity and severity of the patient's physiologic response to injury. The Revised Trauma Score may be used by pre-hospital personnel and emergency

staff as a triage tool. Changes in both scores will reflect the patient's ongoing response to the injury event. Scores can be calculated using a preprinted source indicating the points for each area. Data from the primary and secondary assessments can be used to determine the severity of the patient's condition and provide a baseline for ongoing evaluation of the patient's responses to the injury event and treatment.

Glasgow Coma Scale

The Glasgow Coma Scale (GCS) score ranges from 3 to 15 and is a measure of the patient's level of consciousness. It is not a measure of total neurologic function. Points on the scale correspond with specific responses in three areas; eye opening, verbal response, and motor response. The patient's **BEST** response in each of three areas if noted. For example, if a patient presents with paralysis of the lower extremities but can move an upper extremity, the BEST motor based on the patient's ability to move the upper extremity.

The patient's eye opening response cannot be measured if the eyes are so swollen that the patient cannot open them. Patients who have been given a drug for neuromuscular blockade cannot be evaluated. Patients who have been intubated or who cannot speak because of maxillofacial trauma cannot be evaluated for verbal response.

Source: Parkview Medical Center, Pueblo, Colorado.

4-24 Triage System Policy and Procedure

POLICY

It is the policy of Parkview Emergency Department that all patients be seen by the ER physician as soon as possible. Under no circumstances will a medical screening exam be delayed on the basis of insurance or ability to pay.

PURPOSE

To increase the quality of patient care by quickly and accurately prioritizing patients' care needs. All patients will be triaged on arrival (within 5 minutes) and registration will occur after triage is completed.

PROCEDURE

1. Triage Assessment

   All patients presenting to the ED will have a routine triage assessment performed, including a primary and focused secondary assessment.

   The following will be accurately documented:

   - Patient name
   - Date and time of arrival
   - Time of initial contact with triage nurse

- Age
- Chief complaint—usually 2 to 3 quoted words from the patient
- Brief triage history
- Allergies
- Immunization status if less than 18 years old
- Vital signs: blood pressure does not need to be taken in triage unless:
  1. the patient has more than a 15-minute wait in triage holding/waiting room, or;
  2. the triage nurse needs it to help determine appropriate placement
- Glasgow Coma Scale per protocol
- The triage assist will escort patient to room and undress patient and take vital signs. If the triage assist is busy with another patient then the ER tech or nurse will take vital signs.
- Triage acuity assessment
- Signature of triage nurse
- Weight if less than 16 years old
- Pain will be managed per the nursing pain policy—Pain Management

2. Bed Assignment
   a. Bed assignments of triaged patients are dependent on:
      - Acuity of patient
      - Availability of ER beds
   b. When an ER patient is "Emergent," but no beds are currently available, communication between the ER triage nurse and the ER charge nurse to quickly reassign a lower acuity patient to another site so that "emergent" patients will immediately have a monitored bed to be treated on.
   c. "Urgent and Non-Urgent" patients may be asked to wait in the ER Triage holding area until a bed becomes available. All "holding" patients will be reassessed and monitored by the triage nurse or designated RN.
   d. The nurse will be notified by the charge nurse whenever an emergent patient is placed in the nurse pod.
3. Tracker Board (Electronic tracking system cannot identify the patient with any confidential information.) When the triaged patient is assigned a room and bed, the charge nurse or designee will write the patient's location on the EDM Tracker Board. In addition, the following will be recorded on the board:
   a. Patient's last name
   b. Time of placement in treatment room
   c. Initials of nurse assigned to patient
   d. Acuity assignment—assigned by charge nurse

Source: Parkview Medical Center, Pueblo, Colorado.

4-25 Suicide Precautions/Constant Precautions/Attempted Suicide

PURPOSE:
To prevent injury to patient by maximizing environmental safety.

LEVEL:
This procedure is instituted by the RN. The LPN and NA may monitor and observe the patient if qualified.

SUPPORTIVE DATA:
Suicide Precautions are ordered for patients who have either harmed themselves, verbalized intent to do so, or indicated, in an overt or covert manner, a wish to do so. If the nurse is concerned about the patient's potential for suicide, institute Suicide Precautions then contact the patient's physician for an order and a psychiatric consult. If a psychiatric consult is ordered it should be completed the same day as the request. The psychiatrist will evaluate the patient for suicide potential and may recommend Suicide Precautions or Constant Precautions. **If this procedure is implemented, then the Self Harm Behavior protocol must also be implemented.**

Constant Precautions are ordered for patients whose suicide potential appears extremely high (any patient who has just made an attempt or who is believed to be planning an attempt). Outside of the Psychiatry Service and Critical Care units Constant Precautions must be instituted for all patients who are placed on Suicide Precautions (with the exception of forensic patients wherein the guard provides continuous 1:1 safety monitoring).

The nurse will institute Constant Precautions following a suicide attempt or gesture regardless of the severity. The nurse will immediately notify the patient's physician and request an urgent psychiatric consult. The patient's physician must write the order for Suicide or Constant Precautions.

On a psychiatric unit if the RN believes the gesture to be a self-mutilating or self-injurious behavior, Constant Precautions may not be appropriate. In this case, the patient's physician or on call psychiatric resident should be notified immediately and asked to evaluate and/or recommend the appropriate level of observation.

Patients who are at increased risk of suicide are those who:

- are experiencing severe anxiety or agitation
- are depressed and/or psychotic
- have a history of previous suicide attempt
- are experiencing intense feelings of hopelessness or abandonment
- have sleep disturbance
- are actively abusing alcohol or substances
- verbally express suicidal thoughts
- have a family history of suicide
- have a suicide plan, with the intent and means to carry out the plan

- have sustained a recent loss (including death of a loved one, divorce, separation, loss of a job, or financial loss)
- say goodbye with finality (e.g., tell staff "I won't be here when you return")
- are unwilling to make a no-harm/no-suicide contract with staff (i.e., patient is not willing to inform staff if he feels like harming himself).

Times of increased risk of a patient attempting suicide are: at change of shift, early morning hours, night time, weekends, holidays, after visitors leave, after phone calls, after disturbing/distressing news, either shortly after admission, and near or at discharge from the hospital.

CONTENT:

STEPS: Suicide Precautions:	KEY POINTS: **NOTE: With the exception of forensic patients, *all* patients on Suicide Precautions who are not in a Psychiatric or Critical Care unit must be on Constant Precautions.**
1. Place the patient in a room, which affords the best observation and protection.	1. On non-psychiatric units, if possible, move the patient to a private room close to the nurses' station.
2. Search the patient's belongings, clothing, luggage, and packages at the time precautions are instituted. Tell the patient of your concern for safety and the reason for the search. Remove all medications and other items considered unsafe, including glass or sharp items, nail polish remover or other alcohol-containing solutions, matches or lighter, and any aerosol spray cans (i.e., hairspray). Similar items belonging to the patient's roommate must also be removed.	2. The patient may be allowed to keep eyeglasses, non-breakable toiletry items, or a cordless electric razor. Patient's belongings not in daily use should be sent home or to the Motel Unit. (Document disposition of belongings on the Valuables/Belongings Inventory and place this in patient's chart.) NOTE: Outside of Psychiatry if Suicide Precautions are instituted at anytime after the admission process, a room search must be ordered by the physician. (See Room Search Procedure.) NOTE: Be aware that cleaning agents used by housekeepers are a potential means of self-harm if ingested and should not be accessible to the patient.
3. Monitor items brought onto the unit by visitors. Remove any item considered unsafe (as above) and return it to the visitor when they leave the unit.	3. Check all bags and packages upon entry to the unit. NOTE: Outside of the Psychiatry Service this pertains to only those items brought to the patient who is on precautions, or to the patient's roommate.
4. Supervise patient when he is using sharp/glass articles, toxic solutions, aerosol sprays, lighter, or razor.	4. Neither the patient nor his roommate may keep these articles in the room. These items must be secured at the nurses' station.
5. Restrict patients on Suicide Precautions to the unit unless it's absolutely necessary to leave the unit for testing or procedures that cannot be delayed.	5. Maintain a *minimum* staff ratio of 1 to 1 when off the unit.
6. Stay with the patient while he is taking prescribed medication to make sure he/she swallows the medication.	6. Check to see that patient has swallowed medication. If you have reason to believe the patient may be "cheeking" the medication, ask patient to open his mouth, stick out his tongue, and to touch his tongue to the roof of his mouth while you check for "cheeked" medication.
7. Assess the patient's physical/emotional condition and suicide potential every eight hours. NOTE: The attending psychiatrist and the patient's attending physician must document the patient's suicide potential in the Progress Notes of the patient's medical record, at least every 24 hours.	7. Refer to **Self Harm Behavior protocol.** Ask the patient if he is having thoughts of suicide. If yes, ask him if he has a plan as to how he would do it and ask him to share that plan with you. Ask if he can agree to tell a staff member if he is thinking of harming himself, rather than acting on it. Place on **"Constant Precautions,"** if patient is unable or unwilling to agree to this. **NOTE: The patient's willingness to contract in this way *does not* mean the patient can be trusted not to attempt suicide. An unwillingness to make such an agreement may indicate the patient is at risk of suicide.**

STEPS **Suicide Precautions**:	KEY POINTS **NOTE: With the exception of forensic patients, *all* patients on Suicide Precautions who are not in a Psychiatric or Critical Care unit must be on Constant Precautions.**
8. Make a visual observation of the patient every 15 minutes throughout all shifts and document. Observe for any potentially unsafe behavior.	8. Stagger the 15-minute checks so that they are not made at predictable times. Checks may not exceed 15-minute intervals. **Observation frequency and supervision of the patient may be intensified at the discretion of the charge nurse. Notify the physician of intensified observations.**
CONSTANT PRECAUTIONS:	**NOTE: With the exception of forensic patients, *all* patients on Suicide Precautions who are not in a Psychiatric or Critical Care unit must be on Constant Precautions.**

STEPS **Follow Steps 1 through 7 as above.**	KEY POINTS
9. Keep the patient within sight and within reach at *all times.*	9. Patients are observed at all times, which include: bathroom and bathing times, procedures, tests off the unit, and when visitors are present.
10. Instruct Nutrition and Food Services to use disposable products on trays including plastic flatware. No cans or glassware are permitted.	10. Count flatware before and after use. If anything is found missing from the tray the patient and immediate surroundings must be searched until lost item is accounted for.
11. Obtain sitter if need exists for supplemental personnel. Have sitter read these procedures and verbalize to the charge nurse his understanding of the meaning and requirements of Constant Precautions.	11. On non-psychiatric units a sitter is ***required***, with the exception of the Critical Care Units. Within the ICUs, patient safety checks will be completed and documented at least every 15 minutes, beginning as soon as the patient is responsive. See below, "Obtaining Sitter for Suicidal Patient on Constant Precautions."
12. Obtain a physician's order to take the patient off the unit if the patient wishes to smoke (required only on non-psychiatric units).	12. The physician must write an order allowing the patient to be escorted by staff to the courtyard that adjoins the ICU Waiting Room to smoke. When off the unit, maintain a ***minimum*** staff ratio of 1 to 1.
13. Make every attempt to verbally convince the patient to stay if the patient tries to leave the unit or hospital without physician authorization. (Psychiatry Staff see "Elopement" policy and procedure in the *UNC Hospitals/ NC Neurosciences Hospital Inpatient Psychiatry Policy and Procedure Manual*).	13. Contact Hospital Police immediately at X-XXXX if assistance is needed to prevent patient from leaving. If the patient leaves without authorization, immediately do the following: • call Hospital Police with a description of the patient and instructions to return patient to the unit • search for the patient and attempt to verbally convince the patient to return to the unit • notify the patient's physician • notify nursing supervisor

Obtaining Sitter for Suicidal Patient on Constant Precautions

1. Notify the covering house supervisor that a sitter is needed.	1. When possible, Constant Precautions observations are provided by hospital staff. When the nursing staff cannot provide sufficient hours of care, the charge nurse notifies the covering House Supervisor. Supplemental personnel will be employed only when other options for coverage are exhausted.
2. Complete the Sitter Request form and send to the Nursing Supervisor.	2. If the patient has not yet been admitted the admitting unit is responsible for completing the request form.
3. Instruct supplemental personnel of their duties and responsibilities as described in this procedure.	3. The assigned sitter should be made aware of why the patient requires constant supervision, have read this procedure, and they must verbalize their understanding of these responsibilities to the charge nurse.

ATTEMPTED SUICIDE:

1. Initiate "Constant Precautions" (see above).	1. Remain with the patient while calling for assistance via emergency call light. Provide any emergency care, as situation requires. Initiate constant 1-to-1 supervision assuring patient safety.
2. Notify the patient's physician, the covering nursing supervisor, Risk Management.	2. The covering nursing supervisor will notify the hospital director on call.
3. Document incident in the patient's chart and complete an incident report.	

DOCUMENTATION: Document every 15-minute checks of the patient on Suicide Precautions on the Safety Precaution Checklist (obtained from Psychiatry). This should include the specific location (patient room, nursing station, etc.) and the behavior of the patient. For patients on Constant Precautions, document the block of time the patient was observed on the Safety Precaution Checklist.
Document RN assessment of physical/emotional condition and suicide potential of patient on Suicide or Constant Precautions each shift in the Progress Notes or Patient Care Record.
Document attempted suicide in Progress Notes.

REFERENCES:
Busch, KA; Fawcet, J; Jacobs, DG. Clinical correlates of inpatient suicide. **Journal of Clinical Psychiatry** 2003; 64: 14-19.
Cardell, R; Horton-Deutch, S. A model for assessment of inpatient suicide potential. **Archives of Psychiatric Nursing** 1994; 8 (6), 366-372.
Goodwin, FK. Preventing inpatient suicide. **Journal of Clinical Psychiatry** 2003; 64: 12-13.
Shea, SC. **The Practical Art of Suicide Assessment.** 2002. John Wiley & Sons, Inc., Hoboken, New Jersey.

APPROVAL: __________ By: Nursing Procedure Committee

REVISED: ______________________________ (Date)

Source: UNC Health Care, Chapel Hill, North Carolina.

4-26 Thrombolytic Guidelines Screen

Date of Service ______________________ Reviewer ______________________

Pt Name ______________________ Data Source ______________________

Medical Record # ______________________ Physician #s ______________________

ASPECT OF CARE: Thrombolytic Therapy in Acute MI

1. Indicator: **Appropriate Patient Selection for Thrombolytic Therapy during MI**

Yes	No	Data Elements (At least one of the following):
__	__	1. Chest pain or symptoms of AMI of at least 30 minutes duration and beginning within 12 hours of presentation to the ED
__	__	2. Patient beyond the 12-hour window with ongoing or recurrent symptoms or if patient presented in cardiogenic shock
__	__	3. EKG changes consistent with AMI (ST elevation > 1 mv in 2 contiguous leads) or the presence of a LBBB or RBBB pattern on EKG
__	__	4. Chest pain and EKG changes persist after administration of SL NTG
__	__	5. Age < 75 yrs—decision to administer thrombolytic therapy made on a case-by-case basis

2. Indicator: **The management is in compliance with the standard of care:**

__	__	1. Internist arrival to ED within 30 minutes of patient arrival and/or notification
__	__	2. Thrombo Panel—Chem 19 (Lytes, BUN, Glucose, Creatinine, liver panel), Cardiac Panel—CBC, PT/PTT, Type & Screen, Time from Admission ____ (mins)
__	__	3. EKG—12 lead (Time from ____ admission)
__	__	4. ASA 160 mg at the onset of thrombolytic administration
__	__	5. Two large bore Peripheral IV lines (18 G if possible)
__	__	6. Time infusion started after patient arrival to hospital
__	__	7. Heparin infusion—Start at 1000 units/hr (**SK—No bolus;** TPA—Bolus of 5000 u and then infusion) Note: For TPA pts > 80 kg—Bolus of 70 u/kg and infusion at 1200 units/hr

3. Indicator: **Exclusion Criteria—Absolute Contraindications:**

__	__	1. Active internal bleeding
__	__	2. Hx of hemorrhagic CVA, esp within the previous 6 months
__	__	3. Recent (within 2 months) neurosurgery or trauma to head or spine
__	__	4. Intracranial neoplasm, AV malformation or aneurism
__	__	5. Known bleeding diathesis
__	__	6. Severe, persistent uncontrolled HTN (> 200 mm Hg systolic or > 120 mm Hg diastolic) despite analgesics, nitrates and/or beta blockers

4. Indicator: **Exclusion Criteria—Relative Contraindications:**

__	__	1. Recent major surgery or organ bx (within 10 days)
__	__	2. Recent (within 10 days) GI or GU bleeding (excluding menses)
__	__	3. Recent trauma to chest or abdomen (within 10 days)
__	__	4. Acute pericarditis
__	__	5. Bacterial endocarditis
__	__	6. Severe renal or hepatic disease
__	__	7. Pregnancy
__	__	8. Diabetic or other hemorrhagic retinopathy
__	__	9. Septic thrombophlebitis or occluded AV cannula at seriously infected site
__	__	10. Pts already on oral anticoagulants with a PT of > 15 seconds
__	__	11. Prolonged CPR (> 5 minutes) or traumatic ED intubation < 10 days
__	__	12. Puncture of a noncompressible vessel (e.g., Subclavian catheterization)
__	__	13. Any other reason that would result in a significant bleeding hazard

5. Indicator: **Follow-Up Care**

__	__	1. Continue patient on oral aspirin—160 mg/day
__	__	2. CK/ISOS, CBC and PTT 6 hrs after infusion complete
__	__	3. PTT q hrs for duration of Heparin infusion
__	__	4. EKG every 30 minutes during 2 hours of infusion and in one hour after infusion
__	__	5. Begin patient on an H2 blocker
__	__	6. Admission to TCGH
__	__	7. Transfer to another facility (Timing in hours after ED _______ presentation)

6. Indicator:		**Adverse Events**
Yes	**No**	**Data Elements (At least one of the following):**
__	__	1. Bleeding Complications
__	__	2. Reocclusion
__	__	3. Other

Source: Tillamook County General Hospital, Tillamook, Oregon.

4-27 Asthma Screening Tool

Who is your asthma doctor? ______________________________

SIGNS AND SYMPTOMS	NO	YES	COMMENTS
How long have you/your child had asthma?			Number of Years ______________
Do you smoke or are you exposed to smoke often?	☐	☐	
Do you/your child have pets or are you/your child around pets often?	☐	☐	☐ Dog ☐ Cat ☐ Hamster/Rat ☐ Other: ______________
Do you/your child cough or wheeze or does your/ your child's chest feel tight during the day?	☐	☐	How often does this happen? ☐ Once a week ☐ Once a day ☐ 2-3 times a day ☐ All day long
Do you/your child cough or wheeze or does your/ your child's chest feel tight when you exercise or play?	☐	☐	How often does this happen? ☐ Once a month ☐ Once a week ☐ Once a day ☐ Every time I exercise/play
Do you/your child cough or wheeze or does your/ your child's chest feel tight during the night that wakes you up?	☐	☐	How often does this happen? ☐ Once a week ☐ Once a night ☐ 2-3 times per night ☐ All night long
What do you/your child think makes your asthma worse?			☐ Do Not Know ☐ Air pollution ☐ Dust ☐ Molds ☐ Pollen ☐ Pets ☐ Strong Smells ☐ Exercise ☐ Foods ☐ Weather Change ☐ Other: ___________
Do you/your child know what to do if you have trouble breathing?	☐	☐	☐ If No, instructions were given to patient ☐ If Yes, instructions were reviewed with patient
MONITORING			
Do you/your child have a peak flow meter?	☐	☐	How often do you use it? ☐ Every Day ☐ Weekly ☐ Monthly ☐ Never ☐ Only when sick
What was your/your child's highest reading over the past week?			
FUNCTIONALITY			
Have you/your child missed any school or work because of your asthma over the past month?	☐	☐	How much school or work was missed? ☐ 1 day ☐ 2-3 days ☐ 4-5 days ☐ Over a week
Is there anything you/your child can not do because of your asthma?	☐	☐	If Yes, explain:
Have you/your child seen a doctor or been to a clinic during the past month for your asthma?	☐	☐	How many times during the past month? ☐ Once a month ☐ Twice a month ☐ More than 3 times a month

FUNCTIONALITY			
Have you/your child needed to go to the Emergency Room because of your asthma in the past year?	☐	☐	How many times during the past year? ☐ Once ☐ 2-3 times ☐ 4-5 times ☐ More than 5 times
Have you/your child had to spend the night in the hospital because of your asthma in the past year? (other than the Emergency Room)	☐	☐	How many times during the past year? ☐ Once ☐ 2-3 times ☐ 4-5 times ☐ More than 5 times
MEDICATIONS			
What medication(s) do you/your child take for your asthma and how often do you take them?	☐	☐	List:
Do you/your child use a spacer when you take your medications?	☐	☐	
Do you/your child need medication(s) refill(s)?	☐	☐	If Yes, which medication(s)?
Do you/your child have problems taking your medications?	☐	☐	What type of problems? ☐ Side Effects ☐ Trouble getting child to take the medications ☐ Not taking medications as ordered
Has the cost of your medical care kept you/ your child from getting medical care for asthma?	☐	☐	If Yes, explain: ☐ Medicine cost too high ☐ Medical visit cost too high ☐ Other
EDUCATION			
Have you/your child ever attended classes on asthma?	☐	☐	When was the last time you took an asthma class? ☐ Within 6 months ☐ Within 1 year ☐ More than 1 year ago

RECOMMENDATIONS TO THE PROVIDER:

☐ Appointment requested within: ____ days/ weeks
☐ Referral to Asthma Education Program
☐ Referral to Social Services
☐ Referral to Child Life Specialist
☐ Referral to Smoking Cessation Program
☐ Other:

Signature/Title of person performing the screening: ______________________

ID# ______________________ Date: ______________________

Source: Rusty McNew, RN, MA, CPHQ, Dallas, Texas.

4-28 Pediatric Asthma Continuity Flow Sheet

Chronic Medications: ______________ ______________ ______________ ______________

Severity Code: (1) Mild Intermittent (2) Mild Persistent (3) Moderate Persistent (4) Severe Persistent

	+ −	Comments	+ −	Comments	+ −	Comments
Date of Visit						
Severity Level Code						
Basic Assessment						
Vital Signs (t/r/p/bp)						
Height/Weight						
Predicted Peak Flow						
Current Peak Flow %						
Personal Best Peak Flow						
O_2 Sat Level						
Signs & Symptoms						
Coughing, wheezing, SOB or chest tightness during the day? (freq.)						
Awakened at night due to asthma symptoms? (freq.)						
How long does your quick relief inhaler last?						
Symptoms while exercising or playing?						
Episodes when asthma symptoms were a lot worse than usual?						
What does pt think caused the symptoms to get worse? (pets/weather change/cig. smoke/molds/pollens/wood stoves/fireplaces/chemicals/roaches)						
Monitoring						
Has peak flow dropped below 80% of personal best since last visit?						
If yes, what did pt do when this occurred?						
When does pt usually measure peak flow?						
Functionality (Since Last Visit)						
Missed work or school? (freq)						
Reduced your activities? (amt)						
Change in caregiver's work/school due to child's asthma? (amt)						

	+ –	**Comments**	+ –	**Comments**	+ –	**Comments**
Any emergency room visits? (Include dates and location)						
Any hospitalizations? (Dates/location)						
Medications						
Has pt missed/stopped taking any regular doses of meds for any reason?						
Has pt had trouble filling prescriptions?						
Has asthma medicine caused you any problems? (shakiness, nervousness, bad taste, sore throat, cough, upset stomach)						
Other Medications Being Taken/Alternative Treatments or Remedies (List)						

Examination/ Meds/Procedures/ Follow-Up	Date:	Examination/ Meds/Procedures/ Follow-Up	Date:	Examination/ Meds/Procedures/ Follow-Up	Date:

	+ –	**Comments**	+ –	**Comments**	+ –	**Comments**
Education						
Learning Style Evaluated/Documented						
Signs & Symptoms of Asthma						
Inflammatory nature of asthma						
Avoiding asthma/environmental triggers						
Patient compliance using tools (MDI, Spacer, Nebulizer)						
Can patient demonstrate use of peak flow meter and inhaler with spacer?						
Role of Medications						
Smoking avoidance						
Action Plan						
Written Action Plan revised						
Written Action Plan reviewed with Pt						
Date of Last Flu Vaccination						
Referrals						
Referral to Asthma Education						

	+ –	Comments	+ –	Comments	+ –	Comments
Referral to Psychosocial Services						
Referral to Other (list)						
Signatures:						
Nurse/Initials:						
Provider:						

Source: Rusty McNew, RN, MA, CPHQ, Dallas, Texas.

4-29 Child Abuse Assessment

POLICY

In accordance with State law, physicians or any other persons having reason to suspect that a child has been abused or neglected are required to report directly to the Division of Youth and Family Services (DYFS), the name and age of the child, address of the parent or guardian, description of the child's condition, type of abuse or neglect to which the child has been subjected, an indication of the seriousness of the situation and whether the child appears in immediate or imminent danger, any other information concerning the circumstances of the abuse or neglect, including any evidence of past abuse or maltreatment. The law also requires that such reports be made only to the DYFS, and not to the County Prosecutor.

The entire _____ Health System will comply fully with the State reporting laws, and will cooperate with the Division of Youth and Family Services in its effort to provide for proper child care. All children under age 18 admitted to _____ Health System will be assessed for abuse and neglect (Assessment Criteria). Any person knowingly violating the provisions of this act, including the failure to report an act of child abuse, having reasonable cause to believe that an act of child abuse has been committed, is subject to criminal liability as a disorderly person.

DEFINITIONS

State Law defines an "abused child" as a child under the age of 18 whose parent, guardian, or other person having custody and control:

1. inflicts or allows to be inflicted upon such child physical injury by other than accidental means that causes or creates a substantial risk of death, serious or protracted disfigurement, protracted impairment of physical or emotional health, or protracted loss or impairment of the function of any bodily organ
2. creates or allows to be created a substantial or ongoing risk of physical injury to such child by other than accidental means that would be likely to cause death or serious protracted disfigurement or protracted loss or impairment of the function of any bodily organ
3. commits or allows to be committed an act of sexual abuse against the child
4. a child whose physical, mental or emotional condition has been impaired or is in imminent danger of becoming impaired as the result of the failure of his parent or guardian, or such other person having his custody and control, to exercise a minimum degree of care (1) in supplying the child with adequate food, clothing, shelter, education, or medical or surgical care though financially able to do so, or through offered financial aid or other reasonable means to do so, or (2) in providing the child with proper supervision or guardianship by unreasonably inflicting or allowing to be inflicted harm, or substantial risk thereof, including the infliction of excessive corporal punishment, or using excessive physical restraint under circumstances that do not indicate that the child's behavior is harmful to himself, others, or property, or by any other act of a similar nature requiring the aid of a court
5. a child who has been willfully abandoned by his parent or guardian or such other person having his custody and control

6. a child who is in an institution and (1) has been so placed inappropriately for a continued period of time with the knowledge that the placement has resulted and may continue to result in harm to the child's mental or physical well being, or (2) has been willfully isolated from ordinary social contact under circumstances which indicate emotional or social deprivation. A child shall not be considered abused pursuant to this subsection if the acts of omissions described occur in a day school.

PROCEDURE

Reporting

1. Any person who has reasonable cause to believe that a child has been abused is legally obligated to immediately report that belief to the Division of Youth and Family Services (DYFS) appropriate for that county. DYFS will request the following information: the name and phone number of the person making the report; the name and address of the child; the name and address of the parent, guardian, or other person having custody and control of the child; the child's age; the nature and possible extent of the child's injuries; and any other information that DYFS believes may be helpful with respect to the child abuse and identity of the abuser.
2. In compliance with the legal obligations to report, ________ Health System has established a procedure for notifying DYFS of suspected cases of child abuse. The assigned designee, i.e., social worker, nurse manager, charge nurse, clinician, or program director shall be the coordinating and liaison department with DYFS during normal hours of operation. After hours, weekends and holidays, the administrator-on-call, the attending physician or nursing supervisor will carry out these functions with DYFS.
3. The parent or guardian of the child must be advised of the report to DYFS. All patients five (5) years of age and older must be informed that the allegation(s) will be reported to DYFS. If this creates a problem for either the child or parent/guardian, associates will explain mandatory reporting. Concerns will be given serious consideration and attention.
4. Upon receipt of such a report, DYFS is obligated to respond and take such action as it believes is necessary to ensure the safety of the child. DYFS may request appropriate assistance from local or state law enforcement officials.

Allegations Regarding Health System Associates (Institutional Abuse)

1. Under no circumstances will any form of physical or verbal abuse by any ____________ associate to a patient be tolerated. This includes: hitting, slapping, use of excessive force, verbal put-downs, sarcasm, or belittling comments, etc. Such behavior, or allegations of such behavior, will be investigated thoroughly and may lead to disciplinary action if substantiated.
2. Neglectful behavior occurs whenever an associate is engaged in any behavior other than their current assignment as outlined by the supervisor. Associates will monitor and observe patients at all times during their assigned shift. Taking care of personal business must be done outside of the workplace or while on assigned break. Any

report of neglectful behavior by staff will be investigated thoroughly and may lead to disciplinary action if substantiated.

3. Allegations made during the day shift, Monday through Friday, should be reported to the program director, nurse manager or designee. An Incident Report must immediately be initiated. The patient, any witnesses and the alleged perpetrator will be interviewed by the program director, nurse manager or designee. A determination for further action will then be made after consultation.
4. Allegations made evenings, nights, weekends or holidays will be managed consistently by the nursing supervisor. An Incident Report must immediately be initiated. Whenever physical abuse allegations are made, the appropriate physician(s) will be contacted in order to examine the alleged abuse. The nursing supervisor, in conjunction with the administrator-on-call will make a decision regarding the status of the associate.
5. DYFS Institutional Abuse must be notified immediately of the abuse allegation. DYFS will request the name, address, and other data pertaining to the allegation for all involved, as well as a brief description of the alleged incident. In cases involving allegations made by a patient against another patient, information on all parties involved may be shared with DYFS specific to the present allegation and investigation. DYFS may decide to come to the location to begin the investigation. Note: DYFS may request a medical examination by a physician of its own choice. This will need to be cleared through Administration.

Immunity

Anyone acting pursuant to this act in the making of a report under this act shall have immunity from any liability, civil or criminal, that might otherwise be incurred or imposed. Any such person shall have the same immunity with respect to testimony given in any judicial proceeding resulting from such report. (state law)

Hospital Hold/Protective Custody

The Protective Custody Law allows for the hospital administrator or any physician examining and/or treating a child suspected of being abused or neglected to invoke protective custody, without the consent of parents or guardian, for up to three (3) court days (excludes weekends and holidays), during which time DYFS, upon notification of the custody action, will investigate the circumstances in the home environment leading to the suspected abuse or neglect.

Hospital Hold should be considered as a last resort, due to the restriction of time in which DYFS has to work (3 court days). When necessary to protect the child, DYFS will take steps through the court and/or request an extension of the period of custody.

1. The appropriate DYFS must be notified immediately of the child taken into protective custody.
2. If the hold is invoked by a physician, the hospital administrator or designee, and guest relations must be notified within twenty-four (24) hours.
3. DYFS must serve or attempt to serve written notice upon the parent or guardian that said child has been taken into protective custody. The notice will contain information about the duration and location of the protective custody.

4. The initiation of a Hospital Hold means that a child is in the protective custody of the hospital administrator or examining physician as the protem legal guardian of the child. In a situation where the life or health of a child is in danger, treatment may be provided by the hospital without consent of parent(s) or guardian.
5. Visitation by the parents or guardian of a child in protective custody may occur upon request and in the reasonable discretion of the physician, administrator, or designate from DYFS, provided that the life or health of the child will not be endangered. In some instances, visits will be supervised or suspended pending recommendations from DYFS.
6. Differences between the hospital and DYFS regarding visitation and termination of a Hospital Hold should be resolved by collaboration.

Discharge Disposition

1. The child should be discharged to the parents only upon the approval of DYFS. The parents may arrive alone or accompanied by a DYFS worker.
2. The child may be directed to a foster home or other institution if so ordered by the court or if so arranged between DYFS and the parents.
3. If the child is to be picked up by the parents, DYFS or other court-appointed person, this will be documented in the progress notes of the chart. The child should be released only after proper identification has been seen by the nursing staff and documented in the chart.
4. The discharge instruction sheet will be given to the person to whom the child is released.

Release of Medical Record Information

Medical records resulting from the examination of a child may be released to DYFS upon their request for the purpose of aiding in the determination of whether or not the child has been abused or neglected. Such requests should be referred to the Medical Records Department. If the Medical Records Department is not open, the hospital administrator's designate will supply a copy of the record. A written request for the information and a statement from a DYFS representative that the requested information was received (can be handwritten) must be obtained and forwarded to the Medical Records Department.

In-Service Training

All staff and departments potentially involved in the treatment and referral of child abuse/neglect cases will be involved in a minimum annual educational program. Staff Development will coordinate these education activities.

REFERENCES

"Child Abuse and Neglect: A Professional's Guide to Identification, Reporting, Investigation and Treatment," the Governor's Task Force on Child Abuse and Neglect, October 1988.
Joint Commission: PE. 1.8 (1996), R1.15 (1996)

Source: Adapted from Kennedy Health System, Voorhees, New Jersey.

4-30 Child Abuse and Neglect Indicators: Physical Abuse, Sexual Abuse, Physical Neglect, Emotional Maltreatment

Type	Physical Indicators	Behavioral Indicators	Emotional Indicators
Physical Abuse	Unexplained bruises and welts: • on head, face, lips, mouth • on torso, back, buttocks, thighs • in various stages of healing • clustered, forming regular patterns • reflecting shape of article used to inflict (electric cord, belt buckle) • on several different surface areas • regularly appear after absence, weekend or vacation	Wary of adult contacts Apprehensive when other children cry Behavior extremes: • aggressiveness • withdrawal Frightened of parents Afraid to go home Reports injury by parents	
Sexual Abuse	Difficulty in walking or sitting Torn, stained or bloody underclothing Pain or itching in genital area Foreign objects in vagina or rectum STD, especially in preteens Pregnancy	Unwilling to change for gym or participate in Physical Education Withdrawal, fantasy, or infantile behavior Bizarre, sophisticated, or unusual sexual behavior or knowledge Poor peer relationships Delinquent or runaway Reports sexual assault by caretaker	Infant & Toddler • Irritability • Feeding difficulty • Sleep disturbances • Altered levels of activity School Age Child • Behavioral problems • Anxieties • Sleep disturbances • Disturbing dreams • Withdrawn attitude Adolescent • Fright and confusion • Guilt feelings • Anger and acting out • Depressive affect
Physical Neglect	Consistent hunger, poor hygiene, inappropriate dress Consistent lack of supervision, especially in dangerous activities or long periods Constant fatigue or listlessness Unattended physical problems or medical needs Abandonment Malnutrition Decayed or painful teeth	Begging, stealing food Extended stays at school (early arrival or late departure) Constantly falling asleep in class Alcohol or drug abuse Delinquency (thefts) States there is no caretaker	
Emotional Maltreatment	Habit disorders (sucking, biting, rocking, etc.) Conduct disorders (anti-social, destructive, etc.) Neurotic traits (sleep disorders, speech disorders, inhibition of play) Psychoneurotic reactions (hysteria, obsession, compulsion, phobias, hypochondria)	Behavior extremes: Overly compliant, passive or aggressive, demanding Overly adaptive behavior • inappropriately adult • inappropriately infant Developmental lags (physical, mental, emotional) Attempted suicide	

Source: Adapted from Kennedy Health System, Voorhees, New Jersey.

4-31 Adult Violence Assessment

DEFINITIONS

For the purpose of this policy, adult violence includes any one of the following types inflicted upon any male or female over the age of 18:

- domestic violence
- sexual abuse
- physical assault
    1. Domestic violence is defined as any use of physical force, the threat of use of physical force, or psychological abuse between family members or significant others.
    2. Sexual abuse is forced, manipulated, or coerced sexual activity; it includes: rape, incest, same-sex assault, acquaintance rape, and marital rape.
    3. Physical assault may include aspects of defined domestic violence; in addition, it may include the use of weapons, and the alleged perpetrator may be known or unknown.

POLICY

In accordance with the following:

1. Prevention of Domestic Violence Act.
2. State Sexual Assault law.
3. State Assault Laws.

This Hospital will follow the outlined procedure.

IDENTIFICATION

Identification of adult violence can be supported by the attached guidelines.

PROCEDURE

Confidentiality

When abuse is suspected, provide the patient with a quiet, private environment to speak with associates and/or medical staff. Attempt to interview the patient privately. At the request of the patient, we will allow family/friend to accompany the patient during the interview process. If the family/friend accompanying the patient will not provide the patient privacy, security shall be called to intervene.

Guidelines for Security Department

The hospital needs to provide a safe environment for the victim of adult abuse throughout the hospital stay. Security may be called on to provide this protection to the patient. Security will:

1. respond when called by the emergency department, physician, social work department, or nursing unit

2. restrict or monitor visitation, if necessary
3. restrain or escort the perpetrator from the hospital premises
4. provide liaison with local law enforcement personnel if necessary to ensure the safety of victim, family, and/or staff

Security will need the following information:

- the name of the patient
- admitting number
- room number
- reason for assistance
- whether or not a police report has been filed
- familiarity with the Prevention of Domestic Violence Act

Interview/Assessment of Victim of Adult Violence

The following will serve as guidelines for all associates during the interview and assessment phase:

- in patient's own words with a brief summary of circumstances surrounding the incident
- maintain patient's attention to immediacy of situation
- clarify patient's support system availability

Patient Education

- Devise a Safety Plan.
- Provide information for the appropriate resources.

Referrals

- For admitted patients with children who may be at risk, coordinate children's care at relatives/friends or referral to Division and Family Services (DYFS).
- As warranted, facilitate police and/or legal counseling referral if patient chooses to pursue these avenues.
- Provide patient with knowledge for appropriate community resources:

  —shelter

  —counseling

  —medical follow-up

  —financial/insurance options

Documentation

Documentation on the medical record is essential. Document all findings and referral actions/plans. The medical record will include the following:

- chief complaint and description of the abusive event or violent situation; the patient's own words should be quoted whenever possible
- the physician's assessment

- complete medical history
- relevant social history
- for physical abuse, a detailed description of injuries, including type, number, size, location, stages of healing, color, resolution, possible causes, and explanations given
  —when applicable, the location and nature of the injuries should be recorded on a body chart or drawing
  —an opinion on whether the injuries were adequately explained during the assessment
  —results of all pertinent laboratory and other diagnostic procedures
  —imaging studies, if applicable
  —if the police or prosecutor are called, the name of the investigating officer and any actions taken

Documentation will also be performed on the Care Plan.

Staff Development

Adult violence, including domestic violence, sexual abuse, and physical assault, is a mandatory annual education program for the Emergency Department, Home Care, and Family Health Centers. All other departments potentially involved in the treatment and referral of adult violence are encouraged to participate.
Staff Development will coordinate education activities and provide a Self Learning Module upon request.

REFERENCE

Joint Commission: PE.1.8 (1996), RI.1.5 (1996)

Source: Adapted from Kennedy Health System, Voorhees, New Jersey.

4-32 Violent Injury or Domestic Violence Report

A. Reporting Party:	Name/Title		Signature of Reporting Party	
	Address		Facility	
	Phone ( )	Date of Report		
B. Report Sent To:	Agency @ Police Department @ Sheriff's Office	Official Contacted	Badge #	
	Phone ( )	Date/Time of Incident	Reason for Report: Domestic Violent ☐ Violent Injury ☐	
C. Involved Parties — Victim	Name (Last, First, Middle)	Lang.	Birthdate	Sex / Race
	Address	Phone Home / Phone Work		
	Whereabouts of patient after treatment	Phone	Can patient be safely contacted there? Yes ☐ No ☐	Special Instructions
	Safe Person to Contact	Relationship to Victim	Phone	
	Name and Ages of Children in Home		Were children present during incident? ☐ Yes ☐ No	
	Referral to Domestic Violence Services ☐ Yes ☐ No			
C. Involved Parties — Suspect	Name (Last, First, Middle)	Lang.	Birthdate	Sex / Race
	Address			
	Phone Home	Phone Work	Relationship to Victim	
D. Incident Information	1. Date/Time of Incident	Address of Incident		
	2. Type of injury: ☐ Bruises ☐ Fractures ☐ Choking ☐ Internal Injuries ☐ Lacerations ☐ Gunshot Wound ☐ Stab Wound ☐ Sexual Assault ☐ Other/Specify ☐ Self-inflicted ☐ Assault Against On-Duty Hospital Personnel			
	3. Location of injury: ☐ Face ☐ Neck ☐ Head ☐ Eyes ☐ Extremities ☐ Chest ☐ Upper Back ☐ Lower Back ☐ Ribs ☐ Abdomen ☐ Pelvis ☐ Other/Specify			
	4. Narrative Description. Summarize what the victim or person accompanying the victim said happened:			
	5. Explain known history of similar incident(s) for this victim:			

REPORTING

Reporting Decision Matrix:

	Patient has injury or condition caused by (or suspected to be caused by) DV, whether or not treatment is provided	No current injury or condition caused by DV
Patient admits abuse	Refer and Report	Refer only
Patient denies abuse; abuse suspected	Refer and Report	Refer only
Patient denies abuse, none suspected	Do not Report	Do not Report

Making a legal report:

- A health practitioner is required to make a report when providing medical services to a patient whom s/he knows or reasonably suspects is suffering from a wound or other physical injury that is the result of assaultive or abusive conduct.
- Reporting is mandated, even if the patient does not want a report to be filed.
- Inform patient that a report to law enforcement will be made.
- Make an immediate telephone report to the law enforcement agency in the jurisdiction where the injury occurred.
- Complete a Violent Injury/Domestic Violence Report and mail to law enforcement agency within 2 work days.
- File a copy of the report in the medical record.

Summary of Resources:

Battered Women's Services (24-hr Hotline) ______________________________

Domestic Violence InfoLine (Recording) ________________________________

United Way InfoLine (General Info) _____________________________________

QUICK GUIDE FOR SCREENING AND REPORTING DOMESTIC VIOLENCE

SCREENING
Routinely screen patients. At a minimum, screen as follows:

- Any emergency room visit
- Annual physical exam for women; initial obstetrical visit
- Any presentation of indicators which cause reasonable suspicion (i.e., repeat use of emergency or urgent care service, rape or assault; injuries inadequately explained).

Ask direct questions privately without family members present.

- "Because violence is so common in many women's lives, I've begun to ask about it routinely."
- "Are you in a relationship in which you have been physically hurt or threatened?" If no, "Have you ever been?"
- "Did someone cause these injuries? Who?"

If patient answers "no," but you suspect violence:

- Document clinical signs that may indicate abuse.
- Give patient information about resources and help.
- Decide whether you need to report.

If patient answers "yes," send important messages:

- "You are not alone"; "It is not your fault."
- "No one has to live with violence"; "Help is available."

Document findings in the medical record; use patient's words.

- "The patient states . . ."
- "She said her boyfriend, Joe Smith, struck her."
- Clearly document all injuries; use a body map.
- Take Polaroid photographs of injuries.

Complete a discharge safety assessment and plan:

- "Is it safe to leave with the person who brought you?"
- "Is it safe to go home?" "Do you need access to a shelter?"
- "Do you need to stay with family or friends?"

Refer to Community Domestic Violence Resources

- Written information
- Hotline phone numbers
- Remember, it may be dangerous for the patient to carry these items home. Do not insist that the patient take them.

Source: Aspen Publishers.

4-33 Elder Mistreatment ED Assessment

DEFINITIONS

For the purpose of this policy, elderly patients are those 60 years and above. Elder mistreatment is defined as any behavior that causes fear or intimidation, or harms an older person physically or mentally; misdirected aggression which endangers another person. It includes:

- physical mistreatment
- psychological mistreatment
- financial exploitation
- violation of one's rights
- neglect, both active and passive
- self neglect

POLICY

Every elderly person has the right to be protected from aggression/neglect at the hands of another person. Elderly patients are vulnerable to such mistreatment because of their increased dependency due to age and/or frailty. The goal of intervention is to protect the elderly patient from mistreatment. The rights of the elderly patient should be respected in all care planning, and alternative living arrangements should only be considered after all alternatives available to the patient have been explored, and with the patient's understanding of such consequences. Patients admitted from extended care facilities who are suspected of mistreatment while at a facility will be reported to the Office of the Ombudsman for the Institutionalized Elderly. Other suspected cases of elder mistreatment shall be reported, in accordance with State law, to the Board of Social Services, Adult Protective Service Unit.

PROCEDURE

1. The patient suspected to be a victim of elder mistreatment may present to the Health System's attention via the emergency room admission, at the time of the admission assessment by the physician and/or nurse, through a patient or family member/significant other's disclosure, or from a community agency.
2. Assessment of the patient should include cognitive status, health status, functional status, living arrangements, financial status, social supports, emotional/psychological status, and stresses in the patient's environment.
3. Any suspected case of elder mistreatment will be referred by any associate to the departmental social worker (i.e., home health, dialysis, acute care, family health services, behavioral health, long-term care facility) or designee for assessment.
4. When any associate has suspicion or substantial evidence exists regarding elder mistreatment, referrals will be made to the social worker, who will subsequently refer to the Adult Protective Services (APS) Unit at the appropriate County Board of Social Services or in the case of institutional mistreatment to the Office of the Ombudsman.
5. The social worker or designee will collaborate with the Adult Protective Services Unit and will refer to other community agencies/resources as appropriate to establish ongoing support, care and follow-up.
6. When the evidence is not substantiated, the social worker will assess and intervene if other interventions are needed.
7. Also it is important to recognize the needs of the perpetrator if that person is known. Should the perpetrator be the primary caregiver, intervention could include but not be limited to the following:
   - education on the patient's condition, prognosis, and needs
   - referral for counseling
   - referral for respite assistance
   - suggestions regarding changed living arrangements

Documentation Procedures for Suspected Abuse

Documentation on the medical record is essential. Document all findings and referral actions/plans. The medical record will include the following:

- chief complaint and description of the abusive event or neglectful situation; the patient's own words should be quoted whenever possible
- the physician's assessment
- complete medical history
- relevant social history
- for physical abuse, a detailed description of injuries, including type, number, size, location, stages of healing, color, resolution, possible causes, and explanations given
  - —when applicable, the location and nature of the injuries should be recorded on a body chart or drawing

—an opinion on whether the injuries were adequately explained during the assessment
—results of all pertinent laboratory and other diagnostic procedures
—imaging studies, if applicable
—if the police or prosecutor are called, the name of the investigating officer and any actions taken

Documentation will also be performed on the Care Plan.

STAFF DEVELOPMENT

Elder Mistreatment is a mandatory educational program for the Emergency Department, Home Care, and Family Health Centers. All other departments potentially involved in the treatment and referral of elder mistreatment are encouraged to participate. Staff Development will coordinate education activities and provide a Self Learning Module upon request.

REFERENCE

Joint Commission: PE.1.8 (1996), RI.1.5 (1996)

Source: Adapted from Kennedy Health System, Voorhees, New Jersey.

4-34 Detection: Indications of Elder Mistreatment Patient Signs and Symptoms

This list represents the most common indicators used to detect abuse and neglect. While the presence of any of these indicators may be caused by a variety of non-abusive factors, the combination of several should cause the professional to suspect mistreatment. *Italicized Behavioral and Emotional Indicators are not limited to any one type of mistreatment.*

Type of Mistreatment	Physical/Situational Indicators	Behavioral Indicators	Emotional Indicators
Physical	Unexplained injuries or explanation inconsistent with medical findings: • fractures • welts • lacerations • punctures • burns: unusual location, type or shape similar to object (i.e., iron, cigarette burn) • bruises: presence of old and new, shape similar to object (i.e., belt marks, fingers) bilateral on upper arms (from holding or shaking), clustered on trunk (from repeated striking)	*Denies problem despite evidence* *"Doctor shopping"* *Failure to seek health care* *Incomparability between history and injury* *Patient is accident prone* *Cries easily, frequently* *Is alcohol dependent and functioning is impaired by drinking* *Has nightmares and difficulty sleeping* *Shakes, trembles and cowers in presence of caregiver (abuser)* *Exhibits distrust of others* *Has suddenly become more dependent on the caregiver, adopting the role of the child*	*Talks about past, and avoids talking about future* *Is difficult to care for because of emotional outbursts* *Exhibits stress related illness (i.e., hypertension, asthmatic attacks, somatized pain)*

Type of Mistreatment	Physical/Situational Indicators	Behavioral Indicators	Emotional Indicators
Sexual	Torn, stained or bloody underclothing Difficulty in walking or sitting Pain, itching, bruising or bleeding in genital area Unexplained STD or genital infections		
Psychological/ Emotional	Unusual weight gain or loss	*Confusion* *Insomnia, sleep deprivation, or need for excessive sleep* *Change in appetite* *Loss of interest in self, activities or environment*	*Excessive fears* *Ambivalence* *Resignation* *Withdrawal* *Agitation* *Helplessness, hopelessness, depression* *Expresses a desire to die*
Financial/ Material	Disparity between income/assets and lifestyle Unprecedented transfer of assets from an older person to other(s) Extraordinary interest by family member in older person's assets Unexplained disappearance of valuables	Inaccurate, confused, or no knowledge of finances Hoarding money Unexplained or sudden inability to pay bills, purchase food or personal care items Lack of receptivity by older person or family member to any necessary assistance requiring expenditure, when finances are not a problem	Fear or anxiety when discussing finances
Neglect	Dehydration Malnutrition Hypo/Hyperthermia Excessive dirt or odor Inadequate or inappropriate clothing Absence of eye glasses, hearing aids, dentures or prostheses Unexpected or unexplained deterioration of health Decubitus ulcers (bedsores) Signs of excess drugging, lack of medication or other misuse	*Apathy, confusion and edema* *Is resistant to taking medication, being bathed, eating or allowing caregiver to provide care* *Decreased alertness, responsiveness and orientation*	*Obsesses, worries or is anxious about his or her own performance (i.e., losing dentures or being incontinent)*

DETECTION: INDICATIONS OF ELDER MISTREATMENT

History	Professional Observations	Risk Factors
Pattern of physician and/ or hospital hopping	Patient appears fearful of family member	Family member psychopathology; presence of mental illness, mental retardation, dementia or drug or alcohol abuse
Unexplained delay in seeking treatment	Patient appears reluctant to respond when questioned	Transgenerational violence: family history of violence
Series of missed medical appointments	Patient and family member provide conflicting accounts of incident	Dependency: patient or family member dependent on the other for housing, finances, emotional support, or caregiving
Previous unexplained injuries	Family member is indifferent or angry towards patient and refuses to provide necessary assistance	Isolation: patient does not have the opportunities to relate with people or pursue activities and interests in a manner he or she chooses
Explanation of past injuries inconsistent with medical findings	Family member appears overly concerned with costs of medical care and services	Stress: recent occurrence of stressful life events such as loss of a job, moving, or death of a significant other

History	Professional Observations	Risk Factors
Previous reports of similar injuries	Family member seeks to prevent the patient from interacting privately or speaking openly with health care provider Family member appears concerned about a particular patient problem but not the patient's overall health	Living arrangements: patient and family member live together

Source: Adapted from Kennedy Health System, Voorhees, New Jersey.

4-35 Clinical and Behavioral Decision Tree: To Restrain or Not to Restrain

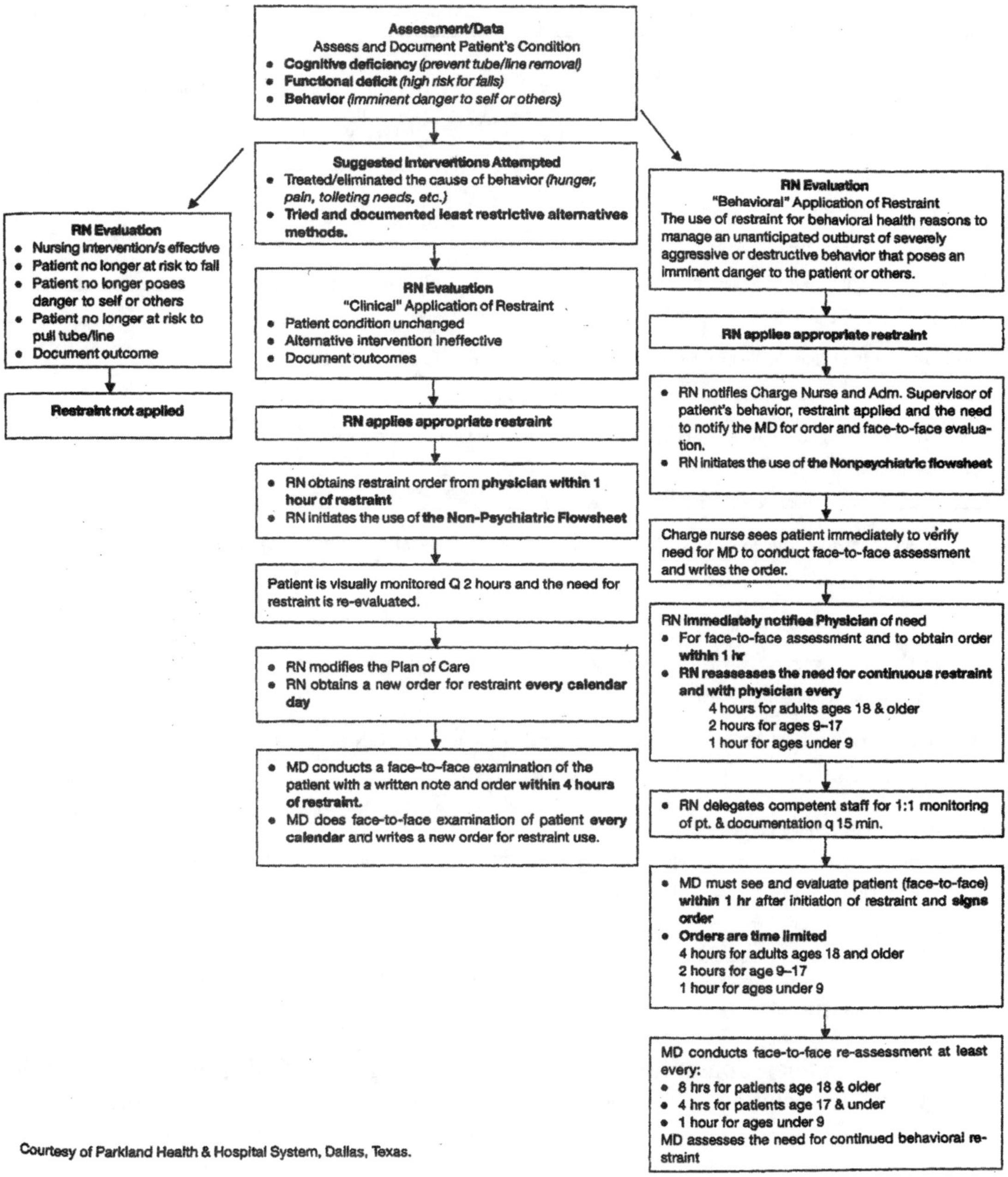

Courtesy of Parkland Health & Hospital System, Dallas, Texas.

4-36 ED Pain Screen

Date______/______/______

Resident Name____ Age______ Room_________

Diagnosis____

Physician______________________________ Nurse______________________________

Objective: This interview will help to identify the level of pain education and history of the resident to provide optimal resident comfort in the process of easing, controlling and/or diminishing pain. The following documentation may be mutually established with the help of the resident, family members and staff. If the resident is *non*verbal, ask a family member or significant other if they can answer any of the questions. If not, note "not able to obtain from resident or significant other."

Who Answered the following questions:

☐Resident Family Member (name)____________________________ Relationship to Resident:________________

RESIDENT INTERVIEW:

1. Do you have pain now? ☐Yes ☐No *Use Pain Rating Scale and indicate level of pain.*
2. Do you ever have pain? ☐Yes ☐No ☐If Yes, how often and where: ____________________
3. Are you able to report your pain to the nurse? ☐Yes ☐No ☐If No, why not: ____________________
4. Do you feel that it is normal to have pain? ☐Yes ☐No ☐If No, why not: ____________________
5. Do you feel that all pain should be treated? ☐Yes ☐No ☐If No, why not: ____________________
6. Do you have any cultural or religious beliefs that would influence the management of pain? ☐Yes ☐No
   ☐If Yes, please explain: ____________________
7. How intense does your pain need to be to be treated? ☐Rate on a Scale of 1—10_____ Or, explain: ________________
8. How have you treated your pain in the past? (Explain) (medications, other modalities): ____________________
9. Have you ever used alcohol to relieve your pain? ☐Yes ☐No
10. What drugs, legal or illegal, have you used in the past to relieve your pain? ☐None List drugs: ____________________

INTERVIEWER OBSERVATIONS:

1. If the resident is not able to describe pain, please check below if there are any current *non*verbal signs of pain:
   ☐Moaning/Yelling ☐Rocking ☐Restless Movements ☐Combative ☐Grimacing ☐Guarding ☐Rubbing Area
   ☐*No Signs of pain* ☐Other: ____________________
2. EDUCATION: ☐Resident educated to report pain to the nurse ☐Family/significant other educated to report signs of resident's pain to the nurse ☐Family/significant other not available at admission to discuss/educate re: pain management
3. OTHER OBSERVATIONS: ____

Source: Best Practices Committee, *HCANJ Pulse Management Guidelines*, 1/05 Revision. Health Care Association of New Jersey, Hamilton, New Jersey. Reprinted with permission.

4-37 ED Pain Rating Scale

Date_____/_____/_____

Resident Name____ Age______ Room__________

GENERAL INSTRUCTIONS: Choose only one appropriate scale based upon the resident's ability to respond. Identify the scale used and the score for that scale on the bottom of this form. *Any score above 0 requires a Pain Assessment.*

WONG-BAKER SCALE:

Initial Instructions: Explain to the resident that each face is for a person who feels happy because he or she has no pain (hurt) or sad because he or she has some or a lot of pain. **FACE 0** is happy because he or she doesn't hurt at all. **FACE 2** hurts just a little bit **FACE 4** hurts a little more. **FACE 6** hurts even more. **FACE 8** hurts a whole lot. **FACE 10** hurts as much as you can imagine, although you don't have to be crying to feel this bad. Ask the resident to choose the face that best describes how he or she is feeling.

NO HURT	HURTS LITTLE BIT	HURTS LITTLE MORE	HURTS EVEN MORE	HURTS WHOLE LOT	HURTS WORST
0	**2**	**4**	**6**	**8**	**10**

NUMERIC SCALE: Choose a number from 0 to 10 that best describes the level of pain.

0	1	2	3	4	5	6	7	8	9	10
NO PAIN		MILD PAIN, ANNOYING Pain is present but does not limit activity.		NAGGING PAIN, UNCOMFORTABLE, TROUBLESOME Can do most activities with rest periods.		MISERABLE, DISTRESSING Unable to do some activities because of pain.		INTENSE, DREADFUL, HORRIBLE Unable to do most activities because of pain.		WORST PAIN POSSIBLE, UNBEARABLE Unable to do any activities because of pain.

FLACC SCALE:

Initial Instructions: The FLACC is a behavior pain assessment scale for use with nonverbal residents who are unable to provide reports of pain. Rate the resident in each of the five measurement categories, add the scores together, and document the total pain score.

	0	1	2
FACE	No particular expression of smile.	Occasional grimace or frown, withdrawn, disinterested.	Frequent to constant frown, clenched jaw, quivering chin.
LEGS	Normal Position or relaxed.	Uneasy, restless, tense.	Kicking, or legs drawn up.
ACTIVITY	Lying quietly, normal position, moves easily.	Squirming, shifting back and forth, tense.	Arched, rigid, or jerking.
CRY	No crying (awake or asleep).	Moans or whimpers, occasional complaint	Crying steadily, screams or sobs, frequent complaints.
CONSOLABILITY	Content, relaxed.	Reassured by occasional touching, hugging, or "talking to." Distractible.	Difficult to console or comfort.

Scale Used: **□Wong-Baker Score:______**
□Numerical Score:______
□FLACC Score:______

Nurse Signature______________________________

Source: Best Practices Committee, *HCANJ Pulse Management Guidelines*, 1/05 Revision. Health Care Association of New Jersey, Hamilton, New Jersey. Reprinted with permission.

4-38 ED Pain Assessment

Date______/______/______

Resident Name____ Age______ Room__________

Diagnosis____

Initial Instructions: (1) Complete SECTION I. If the resident has pain now or has had pain recently, follow the instructions to assess each site of pain. Use another Pain Assessment Form if there are more than 2 sites of pain. (2) Complete SECTION II.

Who Answered the following questions?: (If the resident is nonverbal, ask a family member if they can answer any of the questions. If not, note "not able to obtain from resident or significant other.")

SECTION I—INDICATE THE BEST RESPONSE FOR RESIDENT ASSESSMENT:

1. COMMUNICATION: Is resident alert & oriented? ☐Yes ☐No Can resident verbalize pain? ☐Yes ☐No
2. PAIN SITE PHYSICAL LOCATION: *Instructions:* Circle the anatomical location on the anatomy charts in SECTION II. *Number the sites of pain from 1-2* and answer the questions for that site. More than 2 sites of pain, use an additional form.

Chest Pain____________________________ Headache Pain____________________________

Back Pain: *Upper* Back______ *Lower* Back______ *Middle* Back______ Hip Pain: *Right* Hip______ *Left* Hip______

Abdominal Pain: *Upper* Ab______ *Lower* Ab______ *Middle* Ab______ Arm Pain: *Right* Arm______ *Left* Arm______

Leg Pain: *Right* Leg_____ *Left* Leg_____ Knee Pain: *Right* Knee______ *Left* Knee______

Elbow Pain: *Right* Elbow______ *Left* Elbow______ Shoulder Pain: *Right* Shoulder______ *Left* Shoulder______

_____Incision Pain (specify):______________________________

_____Wound Pain (specify):______________________________

_____Joint Pain (specify):______________________________

_____Other (specify):______________________________

PAIN SITE #1 ASSESSMENT:

1. PAIN CHARACTERISTICS: ☐Dull Pain ☐Sharp/Stabbing Pain ☐Pressure ☐Throbbing and Radiating Pain ☐Burning ☐Itching ☐Other (specify)____________________
   ☐Pain *upon movement* (specify):____________________
   ☐Pain *upon touch* (specify):____________________
   ☐Other (specify):____________________
2. PAIN FREQUENCY AND TIME: ☐Pain is daily ☐Pain is less than daily ☐All Times ☐Intermittent / no pattern
   Time of day____________________ Pain Duration____________________
3. NON-VERBAL OBSERVATIONS: ☐Anger ☐Agitation, Fidgeting and Restless ☐Complaining ☐Sighing and/or breathing heavily ☐Crying, Moaning and/or Yelling ☐Depressed, Sad and Worried Look ☐Wincing and Wrinkled Brow ☐Frightened, Guarding and Withdrawn Look ☐Muscle Rigidity, Resistive, Tense Fingers/Fist
   ☐Other (specify) ____________________
4. PAIN INTENSITY: Score from Pain Rating Scale: ☐Wong-Baker ☐Numerical ☐FLACC Scale Score:_________
5. INSPECTION OF PAIN SITE: (specify findings of swelling, redness, heat, etc.) ____________________

PAIN SITE #1 ORIGIN AND DIAGNOSIS:

PAIN SITE #2 ASSESSMENT:

1. PAIN CHARACTERISTICS: ☐Dull Pain ☐Sharp/Stabbing Pain ☐Pressure ☐Throbbing and Radiating Pain ☐Burning ☐Itching ☐Other (specify)____________________
   ☐Pain *upon movement* (specify):____________________
   ☐Pain *upon touch* (specify):____________________
   ☐Other (specify):____________________
2. PAIN FREQUENCY AND TIME: ☐Pain is daily ☐Pain is less than daily ☐All Times ☐Intermittent / no pattern
   Time of day____________________ Pain Duration____________________
3. NON-VERBAL OBSERVATIONS: ☐Anger ☐Agitation, Fidgeting and Restless ☐Complaining ☐Sighing and/or breathing heavily ☐Crying, Moaning and/or Yelling ☐Depressed, Sad and Worried Look ☐Wincing and Wrinkled Brow ☐Frightened, Guarding and Withdrawn Look ☐Muscle Rigidity, Resistive, Tense Fingers/Fist
   ☐Other (specify) ____________________
4. PAIN INTENSITY: Score from Pain Rating Scale: ☐Wong-Baker ☐Numerical ☐FLACC Scale Score:_________
5. INSPECTION OF PAIN SITE: (specify findings of swelling, redness, heat, etc.) ____________________

PAIN SITE #2 ORIGIN AND DIAGNOSIS:

SECTION II—INDICATE LOCATION OF PAIN:

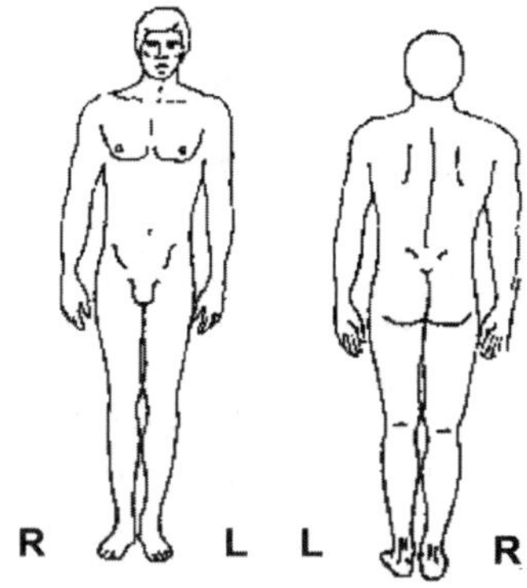

PAIN SITE #1 - PAIN MANAGEMENT HISTORY AND RESIDENT GOALS:

1. What causes or increases the pain?__________
2. What medications and other methods have been used to relieve the pain?__________
3. How well have these medications and methods worked?__________
4. What is the resident's goal for pain management? ☐Decrease pain ☐Improved mobility ☐Improved sleep
   ☐Other: (explain)__________

PAIN SITE #2 - PAIN MANAGEMENT HISTORY AND RESIDENT GOALS:

1. What causes or increases the pain?__________
2. What medications and other methods have been used to relieve the pain?__________
3. How well have these medications and methods worked?__________
4. What is the resident's goal for pain management? ☐Decrease pain ☐Improved mobility ☐Improved sleep
   ☐Other: (explain)__________

OBSERVATIONS AND/OR COMMENTS:

1. **Accompanying symptoms associated with pain:** (Example: Nausea, Headache) __________
2. **Appetite:** ☐No change ☐Loss of appetite ☐Difficult to sit and eat ☐Other: (explain)__________
3. **Sleeping:** ☐No change ☐Difficult to sleep at night ☐Other: (explain)__________
4. **Physical Activity:** ☐No change ☐Difficult to sit-up/get-up/walk ☐Non-participation in favorite activity
   ☐Other: (explain)__________
5. **Relationship to others:** ☐No change ☐Decrease in social action ☐Totally withdrawn from friends, family, etc.
   ☐Other: (explain)__________
6. **Concentration:** ☐No change ☐Loss of concentration ☐Other: __________
7. **Emotions** (complacent, agitated or aggressive behavior, etc.) ☐No change ☐Emotional change (Explain):__________
8. **Personal Hygiene:** ☐No change ☐Unable to wash, dress or perform personal care ☐Other:__________

Note: Information is to be used to formulate the Resident's Pain Treatment Plan. (Care Plan)

RN Signature____________________

Source: Best Practices Committee, *HCANJ Pulse Management Guidelines*, 1/05 Revision. Health Care Association of New Jersey, Hamilton, New Jersey. Reprinted with permission.

4-39 Guiding Principles for ED Cross-Cultural Clinical Practice Guidelines

The clinical guidelines are comprised of 10 statements that highlight the processes and skill sets necessary for physicians to effectively obtain an adequate medical history, ensure an accurate diagnosis, and develop a mutually agreeable treatment plan during the cross-cultural encounter.

The statements are intended to be used as a package to affect the entire spectrum of care including the individual, interpersonal, and institutional aspects of patient care.

The 10 Guiding Principles

1. Elicit the patient's views on illness and treatment practices to understand his or her health values, particular concerns, and expectations for care.
2. Assess the cultural norms, values, and customs that influence the patient's health-seeking behaviors, practices, and expectations for the physician-patient relationship.
3. Assess the patient's environmental context to determine what social experiences and resources may be affecting illness behaviors or health-seeking practices.
4. Identify a range of treatment goals for a given medical condition that can be mutually satisfactory and take into account the patient's cultural health beliefs, practices, norms, customs, and traditions.
5. Identify the social and environmental factors that may potentially interfere with adherence to treatment goals.
6. Work collaboratively with the patient to negotiate treatment plans that incorporate aspects of the biomedical model while integrating cultural concepts for treating illness familiar and important to the patient.
7. Develop communication skills that are respectful of the patient's cultural norms, values, and language to facilitate empathy in the clinical encounter.
8. Utilize patient education strategies during the clinical encounter that take into consideration literacy, cultural appropriateness, and language concordance.
9. Acknowledge that personal, professional, and institutional factors can affect aspects of clinical decision making which, in turn, may lead to disparities in care.
10. Take proactive steps to adapt institutional and system processes that support clinical practice aimed at delivering clinically appropriate and culturally responsive care.

The guidelines emphasize promoting skill sets for establishing a doctor-patient relationship based on respect and empathy for cultural and racial diversity as the basis for exchange and engendering trust. In addition, they offer a framework to avoid the pitfalls of stereotyping and generalizing about subgroup beliefs, practices, and behaviors.

Practitioners must recognize that developing knowledge and skills to deliver patient-centered care to culturally diverse populations is an ongoing developmental process that requires gaining a certain level of awareness, reflecting on current practice, and taking actions to continually modify care delivery processes.

The statements are intended to serve as standards to strive toward and are best adapted over time. Practitioners may choose to customize the guidelines depending on the predominant cultural characteristics of patients served by their practice settings.

An important component of these guidelines requires that practitioners have organizational and system supports consistent with national standards for Cultural and Linguistically Appropriate Services (CLAS) in health care settings. The successful adoption of Cross-Cultural Clinical Practice Guidelines not only depends on the knowledge, attitudes, behaviors, and resources of the physicians within the organization, but also on creating a practice environment that is committed to reducing barriers to guideline use.

It is recommended that each practice setting provide training and establish interdisciplinary teams to share responsibility in adopting the use of the guidelines. Training can be tailored to the type of patient practice, level of knowledge, and experience of physicians within a given setting.

Source: University of Massachusetts Medical School, Office of Community Programs (2004). *Physician Toolkit: To Implement Cross-Cultural Clinical Practice Guidelines for Medicaid Practitioners.* U.S. Department of Health and Human Services, Office of Minority Health, Washington, DC.

4-40 Transfer of Patients from the ED to Another Facility

PURPOSE

To ensure that all patients are evaluated, stabilized and, if necessary, transferred to another facility in a safe, efficient manner consistent with EMTALA guidelines.

POLICY

A medical screening will be provided to all patients who present to the ED for care. The ED will provide evaluation, treatment, and stabilization of emergency medical conditions prior to transfer when a more suitable facility is indicated. The following policy is adapted from EMTALA and applies to physicians, nursing staff, and the hospital.

A patient may be transferred to another facility if:

1. The patient has been examined by a qualified individual who has determined that the patient is not in "active labor" or is not suffering from an "emergency medical condition."
2. The patient is in "active labor" or suffers from an "emergency medical condition" that has <u>not</u> been stabilized, provided that all of the following conditions have been met:
   a. Patient or legally responsible person has signed the request for transfer or the physician has signed the certificate authorizing transfer.
   b. The receiving facility has available space and qualified personnel for the treatment of the patient and has agreed to accept transfer and to provide treatment.
   c. The transferring hospital provides copies of medical records of examination and treatment.
   d. Transfer is effected through qualified personnel and transportation equipment including appropriate life-support measures during transfer.
   e. The benefits of transfer outweigh the risks of transfer.

f. The "emergency medical condition" has been stabilized to the extent that deterioration is not reasonably anticipated during transfer.

3. The patient is no longer in "active labor" and the conditions of the mother and child have been stabilized.
   a. "Active Labor" means labor at a time which delivery is imminent and there is inadequate time to effect safe transfer to another hospital prior to delivery; or a transfer may pose a threat to the health and safety of the patient or unborn child.
4. The patient's "emergency medical condition" has been stabilized.
   a. "Emergency Medical condition" means a medical condition manifesting itself by acute symptoms of sufficient severity (including severe pain) such that the absence of immediate medical attention could be reasonably expected to result in serious jeopardy to the patient's health; serious impairment to bodily functions; or serious dysfunction of any bodily organ or part.

PROCEDURE

A. Any patient presenting to the ED and requesting examination or treatment will be seen by the ED physician or his or her private physician to determine whether or not an emergency medical condition exists. If a woman presents over 20 weeks gestation, she will be taken immediately to L&D, evaluated by qualified L&D personnel or her private physician as to whether she is a woman in active labor. (If facilities are not available on L&D for evaluation of labor, the attending obstetrical physician or the obstetrical physician on-call will evaluate the patient in the ED to determine if she is in active labor.) This evaluation may include all the resources routinely available to the ED, including ancillary services. The medical screening exam will not be delayed to inquire about method of payment.

B. If an emergency medical condition exists or the patient is in active labor, the patient will receive examination and treatment to ensure stabilization of the medical condition or the labor (unless the patient refuses to consent to further examination and treatment); or the patient will be transferred to another facility (unless the conditions under "Policy" are not met, or the patient refuses transfer).

C. If the decision is made to transfer the patient, the following steps will be taken:
   1. The patient's condition must be stabilized to the extent of the ability of the hospital; no patient will be transferred unless the patient is capable of withstanding the transfer.
   2. The reasons for the transfer, and the benefits and risks of the transfer, will be explained to the patient, or to the person legally responsible for the patient, by the physician. If the patient or legally responsible person requests or agrees to the transfer, the Consent to Transfer form will be signed. If the patient or legally responsible person refuses transport despite understanding of the risks of remaining in this hospital, the Refusal of Transfer form will be signed, and the patient will be cared for to the best extent of the hospital's ability. If a competent patient refuses both further treatment and transfer, the patient will be allowed to sign out AMA.
   3. The certification for transfer must be filled out and signed by the transferring physician for any patient with an emergency medical condition that has not been stabilized. It is recommended that it be filled out on all transfers.

4. If the patient consents to transfer, the receiving institution and physician are contacted, preferably by the transferring physician. They must accept transfer of the patient and confirm availability of space, equipment, and personnel to meet the needs of the patient.
5. Copies of all medical records, lab work, and X-rays pertinent to this admission, and the transfer consent will accompany the patient. (Notify Radiology before sending X-rays.)
6. Administration and/or Nursing supervisor will be notified prior to transfer.
7. Transfers to another facility will be via an appropriate vehicle and be accompanied by appropriately qualified personnel (e.g., MD, RN, Paramedic, etc.) as determined by the transferring physician. Transportation facilities will include sufficient personnel and equipment to maintain the stability of the transported patient en route.

D. Psych Staff and/or Security will escort psychiatric patients to the respective units (psychiatric units on campus). Contract security services will escort psychiatric patients to off-campus units.

Source: Parkview Medical Center, Pueblo, Colorado. Reprinted with permission.

4-41 Definitions for Level of Care Needed

PURPOSE

To clarify the terms used in the ED for the urgency of care needed. To rapidly assess and sort patients so as to expedite the sickest patients back into the ED as fast as possible while expeditiously placing other patients into the appropriate level and order of care.

POLICY

EMERGENT

Sudden onset of a medical condition manifesting itself by acute symptoms of sufficient severity (including severe pain) that the absence of immediate medical attention could reasonably be expected to result in a) the patient's health being placed in serious jeopardy, b) serious impairment to bodily functions, and/or c) serious dysfunction of any bodily organ or part.

PRIORITY 1—EMERGENT: NEED TO BE SEEN IMMEDIATELY, NOTIFY ER PHYSICIAN
Any condition requiring evaluation and/or treatment within a short period of time to prevent disability or physical impairment, not meeting the above requirements. Severe pain possibly indicative of a serious medical problem.

PRIORITY 2—MORE EMERGENT: (Keep in Triage Hold area after Triage OR MOVE TO MEDICAL HOLDING ROOM)
Need to be seen quickly by the ER physician and immediately by the nurse.

PRIORITY 3—SEEN BY ER PHYSICIAN AND NURSE IN A TIMELY MANNER. PATIENTS CAN BE SENT TO ER ADMISSION AFTER TRIAGE AND WAITING ROOM.

LESS URGENT: After Triage can return to Waiting Room to register. Conditions not appearing severe but likely to require IV therapy and/or significant workups.

PRIORITY 4—ERB NON-URGENT
Patients presenting themselves to the ED for primary care.

EXCLUSION CRITERIA: AT THE DISCRETION OF THE TRIAGE NURSE/ CHARGE NURSE

Less than 3 months of age
Greater than 60 years old with a medical complaint
Vaginal complaints
Complaints associated with pregnancy

Source: Parkview Medical Center, Pueblo, Colorado.

4-42 Emergency Contraception (EC)

OBJECTIVE: To develop a consistent method of protecting against pregnancy.

GENERAL GUIDELINES:
These are general guidelines and may not be applicable in all situations. Decisions must be made in the context of the situation and of judgmental parameters existent at the time of decision-making.
Emergency contraception will be offered to all nonpregnant patients whose breast or pubic hair development is Tanner Stage II or beyond, even if they have not begun to menstruate, unless they are reliable users of a hormonal contraceptive.

1. Obtain a gynecologic history.
   a. If the patient is a reliable user of hormonal contraception, EC is not indicated.
   b. If the patient was menstruating normally at the time of sexual intercourse, EC is not indicated.
   c. If the patient may be pregnant, be sure that her pregnancy test is negative before prescribing EC. Pregnancy is a contraindication to EC, not because it can injure the fetus, but because it is not indicated
2. Obtain verbal consent by informing the patient of the availability of EC and its complications and side effects:
   a. Women rarely experience nausea using Plan B as an EC.
   b. The failure rate for EC is not known, but it is thought to be low if used within 72 hours of sexual contact.
      1) The pregnancy rate will increase with increased time between sexual intercourse and the use of EC.
      2) Although EC is generally used up to 72 hours after intercourse, it may be used later after intercourse (up to 120 hours) but its effectiveness is not known.

3. There is no need to split the doses of Plan B by 12 hours. Prescribe both to be taken immediately.
4. Counsel the patient that a pregnancy test should be performed if she misses her period after using EC.

APPROVAL:
Approved by:
Director, Community Health Services
Signature ________________
Date ________________
Medical Director, CRC
Signature ________________
Date ________________
Reviewed by ________________
Date ___________________

Source: Pinnacle Health Hospitals.

4-43 Suicidal Patients in the Emergency Room

EVALUATION

1. Obtain medical clearance.
   - You do not want to be admitting a seriously medically ill patient to the psychiatry ward.
   - Watch for even what was thought to be a minor gesture—acetaminophen, aspirin.
2. Interview.
   - **ID**—Age, sex, psychiatric illness, medical illness, social environment, acute crisis/loss
   - **Intent**—Expression of intent, duration of desire, duration of plan, intensity of thoughts, specific plan, availability of plan, lethality of plan, preparation for death, past attempts
   - **State of mind**—Hopeless, intoxicated (impulsive), manipulative, angry, psychotic. Watch for a calm before the storm—decision to die is made and patient is at peace.
   - **Practicalities**—Do not leave the patient alone. If everything looks okay but your gut feeling is telling you something is wrong—trust that gut feeling and inquire further.
   - **Techniques**
     a. Be nonjudgmental—You are in a position of authority. Someone who is suicidal already has low self-esteem. If you are condescending or judgmental, their self-esteem will probably be made worse. Your approach could make their suicidal intentions stronger.
     b. Be calm and supportive. Display confidence in your abilities.
     c. Encourage self-disclosure.

SAMPLE QUESTIONS

- What has happened to make life so difficult?
- Are things hopeless?

- Have you recently had a serious loss or crisis (divorce, finances, job, legal)?
- Are you thinking of suicide?
- How long have you been thinking of suicide? frequency, intensity?
- Do you have a suicide plan?
- What preparations have you made to carry out this plan?
- Why do you want to take your life? Make it make sense to me.
- What would suicide solve?
- How much do you want to live?
- How much do you want to die?
- Have you attempted suicide in the past?
- What have you done to try and feel better?
- Have you been using alcohol or drugs?

Source: Gerard P. Clancy, MD, Dean, College of Medicine, University of Oklahoma, Tulsa, Oklahoma.

4-44 Care of ED Pregnant Trauma Policy and Procedure

SUBJECT: Pregnant Trauma, Care of
PRIMARY SERVICE: Emergency
EFFECTIVE DATE:
CONTRIBUTING SERVICES: Trauma

PURPOSE

To establish guidelines to be used in the treatment of a traumatized pregnant patient.

POLICY

Treatment priorities for a traumatized pregnant patient remain the same as for the non-pregnant patient. Initial management is directed at resuscitation and stabilization of the pregnant patient because the fetus' life is totally dependent on the integrity of the mother's life.

PROCEDURE

1. The traumatized pregnant patient will be triaged in the following manner:
   a. The following trauma patients may be transported to the Hospital for triage:
      1) *Unknown*—not knowing the patient is pregnant.
      2) *Unconscious*—unable to answer questions.
      3) *Unviable age of fetus*—less than 25 weeks gestation.
      4) *Unstable*—injuries require immediate attention regardless of the fetal gestation age.
      5) *Uncertain stability*—further transport may be a risk.
   b. The following pregnant trauma patients may be transported directly to an obstetrical/trauma center by appropriate transportation if **all** three conditions are met:

1) Conscious traumatized pregnant patient.
2) Traumatized pregnant patient is considered stable and additional transport time is considered safe.
3) Traumatized pregnant patient's fetus is most likely viable—more than 25 weeks gestation.

c. The trauma surgeon and obstetrician on call will be alerted and respond within 30 minutes of notification, as allowed by the Echelons of Care. If the patient is known to be in the first trimester of the pregnancy, the obstetrician does not need to respond within 30 minutes, but will be contacted at the time of admission and remain a consultant providing service as needed.

2. The following equipment will be gathered and placed in the Trauma Room:
   a. Fetal monitor
   b. Precipitous delivery tray
   c. Incubator
3. All female trauma patients (up to the age of 48) will have a STAT serum pregnancy test performed.
4. Nursing personnel will be required to attend an annual inservice on the use of fetal monitoring equipment.
5. Although needed X-rays of the traumatized pregnant patient must not be withheld, the fetus will be shielded for all radiological procedures unless the shielding interferes with a specific X-ray.
6. Caution will be used in administering medications with the direction of the attending physician and obstetrician.
7. Once the traumatized pregnant patient has been evaluated, a definitive plan of care will be developed by surgeon and obstetrician. The following options will be considered:
   a. Stabilize the pregnant patient and transfer to an obstetrical/trauma center as soon as possible for observation and monitoring.
   b. If the severity of injuries requires treatment and/or surgery at the Hospital, fetal monitoring and care will be continued as directed by the obstetrician.
   c. If the fetus needs to be delivered at the Hospital, there are two options available and are listed below definitive care for the neonate.
      1) If the neonate will require neonatal intensive care, notify the Neonatal Unit. They will provide telephone consultation and send a neonatal team to transport the neonate to their facility.
      2) If the neonate does not require neonatal intensive care, contact a local hospital with an Obstetrical Service to arrange transfer for the neonate. It will be this hospital's responsibility to transport the neonate to the receiving hospital.

Source: Suburban Hospital, Inc., Bethesda, Maryland.

4-45 Patient Restraint Policy in the ED

RATIONALE

A patient who appears to be dangerous to himself or others and is unable or unwilling to cooperate will be physically restrained in as safe and expeditious manner as possible. Prior to application of restraints, efforts will be made to help the patient regain control of his/her behavior through verbal means or medications. Security will be notified of all restraints and participate in any restraint where the patient is potentially dangerous to staff members.

PROCEDURE

1. Restraints will only be applied under a physician's order.
2. Verbal and written orders for restraint and seclusion are limited to the following:
   - 4 hours for patients ages 18 and older
   - 2 hours for children and youth ages 9 to 17
   - 1 hour for children under age 9

   The reason for the restraint will be documented in the order.
3. The patient will be placed on his/her back or stomach (as directed by the physician) on a locked gurney with one member of the restraint team controlling each limb.
4. Straps will be placed through the metal rings on the cuffs, then strapped to the frame of the gurney. Under no circumstances will the cuffs be directly attached to the gurney, nor will the straps be attached to the mattress or side rail. If needed, a leather chest strap will be placed to control the patient's torso.
5. A restraint flow sheet will be instituted at the time of the restraint. The patient will be checked at least every 15 minutes to note current behavior and to check circulation. Pressure point checks will be documented hourly and repositioning, hydration status, and elimination needs will be documented every 2 hours. The initial assessment and rationale for restraints, efforts to otherwise control behavior, periodic evaluation of the need for continued restraints, and explanation given to the patient/relative/guardian will be documented on the flow sheet or in the ED record.
6. Restraints will be removed by a physician's order, or when documented behavioral guidelines have been met. If restraint or seclusion needs to continue beyond the expiration of the time-limited order, a new order for restraint or seclusion is obtained from the ED MD responsible for the patient's ongoing care and treatment.
7. All leather restraint incidents must be logged and reviewed monthly by the Department director or designee and reported at the ED Committee Meeting.

Source: Parkview Medical Center, Pueblo, Colorado. Reprinted with permission.

4-46 Patient Restraint or Seclusion Policy

PURPOSE OF POLICY

To define restraints and seclusion, the appropriate use of restraints or seclusion based on patient behavior, the physician's ordering process, and the care and documentation required for patients for whom restraints or seclusion are used, regardless of where in the hospital the patient is receiving care.

DEFINITION OF RESTRAINTS

A device that restricts the movement of a patient, that is, to prevent the patient from hurting him- or herself or others, knowingly or not.

Category I Restraints

A device that limits the patient's mobility to the extent that the patient will not be able to independently reposition him- or herself or will otherwise be rendered helpless in an emergency. Such devices include four-point leather restraints.

Category II Restraints

Any device not considered by the facility to be a Category I Restraint. Such devices include soft restraints and Posey restraints.

DEFINITION OF SECLUSION

Under the direction of a physician or RN, the involuntary confinement of a patient alone in a room in which the patient is physically prevented from leaving.

EXCEPTIONS TO THE RESTRAINT/SECLUSION POLICY

This policy does not apply to

1. mechanisms usually and customarily employed during medical, diagnostic, or surgical procedures that are considered a regular part of such procedures (including but not limited to body restraints during surgery, limb restraints while intubated and ventilated, and arm restraints during intravenous administration)
2. devices used to protect the patient, such as side rails, tabletop chairs, helmets, orthopaedic devices, braces, or wheelchairs
3. devices used to secure patients for transfer, balance, and positioning or for postural support of the patient (e.g., temporarily placing a belt or sheet around the patient when he or she is seated in a chair)
4. situations in which a patient agrees to restraints and a written consent is obtained.

POLICY

When other, less-restrictive, measures have been ineffective, physician-ordered restraints/seclusion can be used only to prevent injury and to prevent disruption of the therapeutic environment.

Physician Orders

A. A physician order is required for any use of a restraint/seclusion.

B. All orders are to include
   1. *date and time* that the order was written
   2. *type* of restraint to be used
   3. the *maximum duration* of restraint/seclusion
   4. the *specific rationale* for the restraint/seclusion
   5. *special precautions*, if any, to safeguard the patient
   6. the physician's *signature*

C. A physician may write an order for restraints/seclusion for a maximum duration of up to, but not more than 24 hours.

D. No "standing," "as needed," or "prn" orders for restraints/seclusion can be given.

E. In emergency situations, an RN may place a patient in an appropriate restraint/seclusion and obtain a physician order within one hour.

F. If an oral order is obtained, the order must be signed, dated, and timed by the ordering or covering physician within 24 hours.

Nursing Management and Care

A. Explanation to patient/family:
   All patients requiring restraint/seclusion must receive an explanation of why restraint is needed and how long it will be used.

B. Care (to be documented):
   1. Keep patients who are in seclusion in view *at all times.*
   2. *Every 15 minutes* Patients in (Category I) four-point restraints or seclusion are observed for safety.
   3. Unless contraindicated by circumstances as assessed and documented by a physician or registered nurse *every hour* make and document personal contact.
      a. Determine if the patient has any special needs that require attention.
      b. Check circulation of extremities restrained.
      c. Adjust the restraint.
      d. Realign the body or massage the extremity restrained, or both.
   4. Unless contraindicated by circumstances as assessed and documented by a physician or registered nurse, *every two hours*:
      a. Range of motion of restrained limbs is checked.
      b. Toileting is offered.
      c. Fluids are offered.
      d. The appropriateness of continuing the restraint is assessed, and those factors are documented.
   5. *Meal* times/*daily hygiene*
      a. Nutrition is offered at meal times.
      b. Hygiene needs are met every 24 hours.
   6. *Children* younger than 12 years of age may not be placed in four-point restraints.
   7. When applying or repositioning a restraint, the application of force on long bone joints of children should be avoided.
   8. Unless circumstances suggest a medical problem may exist, staff may not disrupt a patient's sleep during the night to implement the clinical procedures described in the Nursing Management and Care section of this policy.

C. Documentation of implementation of restraint/seclusion:
   1. Document the implementation of restraint/seclusion in the patient's medical record.
   2. Include in the documentation the following information:
      a. a description of the specific behavior leading to restraint/seclusion
      b. whether and which less-restrictive techniques were used, such as medication, placing patient near nurses' station, etc.
      c. the readily observable physical condition of the patient
      d. the date and time of the restraint/seclusion
      e. whether the patient was permitted to wear his or her own clothes or other attire
      f. a description of any physical injury to the patient resulting from placement of the patient in restraint/seclusion

D. Release from restraint/seclusion
   1. When a physician clinically determines that a patient is to be released from restraint/seclusion, the physician shall
      a. order the release and write, sign, and date a note indicating the rationale for the release
      b. if orally ordering the release, write, sign, and date the note not later than 24 hours after an oral order to release
   2. When the registered nurse clinically determines that the release of the patient before the maximum period specified on the physician's order is appropriate, the registered nurse shall
      a. order termination of the restraints/seclusion with or without a physician's order, unless the physician's order specifically requires physician concurrence with the termination
      b. document, sign, and date the rationale for the termination of the restraint/seclusion in the patient's record

Source: Adapted from Holy Cross Hospital, Silver Spring, Maryland.

4-47 Restraint Record: Alternatives Attempted

Date: ______________

Check all that apply (must try alternatives prior to initiating restraints). Alternatives that failed must be documented.

☐ Assisted with toileting q 2 hrs while awake, after meals, and q 4 hrs during the night
☐ Bed exit alarm on
☐ Checked with physician that tube &/or line is still necessary
☐ Cover PEG tube with abdominal binder
☐ Cover peripheral IVs with kerlix or stockinet for protection
☐ Family/sitter staying with patient
☐ Instructed to dangle prior to ambulation, to sit if dizzy and call for help
☐ Moved closer to nursing station
☐ Pain relief/comfort measures
☐ Redirecting focus
☐ Reorientation of patient
☐ Repeated education as to purpose, function & necessity of tube &/or line
☐ Repeated instruction to ask for help when getting out of bed
☐ Routine safety measures *(bed in low position, top rails up as indicated, call light within reach, floor clear, bedside table within reach)*
☐ Verbal de-escalation *(attempt to calm)*
☐ Other:

Physician's order obtained within: ? 12 hours for non-emergency **OR** ? 1 hour for emergency (severely aggressive/destructive behavior)

☐Use of restraints, reason for application, behavior required to discontinue restraints discussed with ☐ patient

☐ family Name and relationship:

☐ Printed Patient/Family Information educational hand-out given to patient/family

Type of restraint utilized: ☐ Ankle ☐ Vest ☐ Wrist ☐ Other

Date restraint initiated: Time restraint initiated:

Initial Boxes	0000	0100	0200	0300	0400	0500	0600	0700	0800	0900	1000	1100	1200	1300	1400	1500	1600	1700	1800	1900	2000	2100	2200	2300
Visual Check Q 10																								
Circ ✓ Q 20																								
Reposition Q 20																								
Release/Exercise Q 20																								
Hygiene/Toilet Q 20																								
Fluids/Food Q 20																								
Reassess Q 40 *(RN only)*																								

Behavior Necessitating Restraints (if for severely aggressive or destructive behavior, Q 15 minute visual checks are required and are to be documented).

Behavior/Circumstances allowing DC			
Signature/Title/Initials	Signature/Title/Initials	Signature/Title/Initials	Signature/Title/Initials
Signature/Title/Initials	Signature/Title/Initials	Signature/Title/Initials	Signature/Title/Initials

Source: Rusty McNew, RN, MA, CPHQ, Dallas, Texas.

4-48 Care of the Psychiatric Patient

SUBJECT: Psychiatric Patient, Care of
PRIMARY SERVICE: Emergency
EFFECTIVE DATE:
CONTRIBUTING SERVICES: Mental Health Services

PURPOSE

To establish a standard of care for psychiatric and behavioral health patients.

POLICY STATEMENTS

Patients with mental and/or behavioral health problems will be treated with dignity and respect, while ensuring the safety of staff and patients alike.

PROCEDURE

A. Patients who present with psychiatric complaints will be interviewed by the triage nurse to determine patient's need for safety (i.e., harm to self, harm to others).
B. Mental health nursing, social and medical evaluations will be completed through a collaborative effort with physicians, nurses and crisis counselors.
C. Every effort will be made to place patients in a quiet room with family member, if appropriate.
D. Patient will be asked to undress and placed in a gown. Belongings will be searched and kept outside of the room at the discretion of the primary nurse. Primary nurse must have patient seen by the Emergency Physician and order received for seclusion or restraint as soon as possible.
E. The primary nurse will assess patient in terms of safety and determine the need for seclusion or restraints. Restraints or seclusion may be initiated by nurse, cosigned and changed or terminated by the Emergency Department Physician.
F. The Emergency Physician will evaluate patient and determine if crisis counselor is to be called.
G. Voluntary patients are required to sign voluntary admission form after full explanation by R.N. or crisis counselor.
H. Combative patients may need physical constraints to control their behavior. Leather restraints are applied by Security and Emergency Department staff and checked by

a nurse every 15 minutes for maintaining circulation within normval limits. Patients in leather restraints are in full view of the nursing staff at all times.

I. Restraints can be the locked seclusion room, chemical restraints (e.g., Haldol, Valium) or leather straps. The goal is to use the least restrictive means to keep patient and personnel safe. Documentation on observation sheet is initiated at the time of restraint application and circulation checks are done every 15 minutes along with patient assessment and offerings of bathroom privileges (may be bedpan), food, liquids.

J. A "Code 6" should be initiated if, in the Emergency Physician or Nurse's judgment, more help is required. (See Code 6 Protocol.)
   a. When requesting the Security staff for assistance, it is important that they be advised of the following:
      1. Who the primary nurse is (leadership role in Code 6).
      2. What behavior can be expected of the patient.
      3. What restraints, if any, will be utilized.
      4. What is the predicted time of involvement by the Security staff.
   b. The Security personnel may be requested to assist with observation or continued care of a patient for brief period of time.

K. Should a patient, in restraints, have to be transferred out of the department (i.e., Radiology), then it is necessary for a member of the nursing staff to accompany the patient.

L. A female needs to be in attendance when any care is rendered to a restrained female patient.

M. Should a situation develop where the other patients in the Emergency/Shock Trauma Center (E/STC), the staff, or hospital property may be in jeopardy because of the behavior of a violent patient, ________ the County Police Department may be requested to assist in the patient's management by the Security personnel or the E/STC charge nurse. If the E/STC charge nurse requests the assistance of the police, then the Security Department must be notified.

N. At times, a patient may be restrained at the order of a police officer. This patient is in police custody and the police officer must remain with the patient at all times. Documentation of police custody and restraint must be included in the patient's medical record.

O. Refer to the policy "Application and Removal of Physical Restraints."

P. Transfer of patients to a psych facility/hospital will follow the procedures in interfacility transfers.

Q. The patient who presents for alcohol and drug detoxification will have a mental health, nursing, social and medical evaluation completed through a collaborative effort of physicians, nurses and drug counselors, including but not limited to:
   a. A systematic mental status examination, emphasizing immediate recall and recent and remote memory, as well as any learning impairment that might influence diagnosis and treatment;
   b. A determination of current and past psychiatric disorders.
   c. A determination of the degree of danger the patient presents to self or others, and
   d. A neuropsychological assessment, if indicated by the psychiatric or psychological assessment.

e. Furthermore, the social assessment of such a patient includes:
   1. The family's history of alcohol and other drug dependence;
   2. The patient's educational level, vocational status, and job performance history;
   3. The patient's social support networks, including family and peer relationships;
   4. The patient's perception of his or her strengths and weaknesses;
   5. The patient's leisure, recreational, and vocational interests and hobbies;
   6. The patient's ability to participate with peers in programs and social activities;
   7. The patient's perception of his or her own dependence;
   8. The patient's daily activity patterns, including those that support, and those that are alternatives to, dependency.

Source: Suburban Hospital, Bethesda, Maryland.

4-49 Psychiatry Emergency Department: Seclusion Safety Guidelines

POLICY

Patients will be placed in locked seclusion rooms to protect themselves and other individuals.

PURPOSE

To provide safety for the patient and other individuals in the psychiatry emergency department.
To provide seclusion guidelines for staff assigned in the psychiatry emergency department.

PROCEDURE

1. Assess the patient's need for seclusion.
2. Assess the need for assistance from the Department of Public Safety (DPS).
3. Ensure seclusion room is a safe environment. It may contain a mattress/blanket if physician determines the items will not be used by the patient in a detrimental manner.
4. Explain to the patient the need for seclusion.
5. Remove the following from the patient:
   - eyeglasses
   - shoes
   - jewelry
   - belts
   - any items that may be potentially dangerous
6. Obtain written physician orders to initiate seclusion procedure, including the estimated length of time for seclusion. Order must be rewritten, if indicated.
7. DPS officers should be used to escort the patient to the toilet or if staff need to enter room for any reason.
8. Patients are **not** to be removed from seclusion without a physician order.

9. Nursing personnel will be responsible for initiating the Checklist for Seclusion Patient, indicating time seclusion initiated, monitored, reevaluated, and discontinued.
10. Nursing personnel will document in nursing notes "Seclusion protocols in place."
11. a. Nursing staff must observe the secluded patient every 15 minutes and document observation(s) per emergency department policy.
    b. Patients in seclusion rooms should be continuously monitored via video-monitoring/intercom systems.

Source: Rusty McNew, RN, MA, CPHQ, Dallas, Texas.

4-50 Psychiatry Emergency Department: Checklist for Seclusion Patients

Patient name: ______________________________ Date: __________

Reason for Seclusion: ☐ Danger to Self ☐ Danger to Others

Time secluded: ______________ Time restrained: ______________ Type of restraint: __________

Time seclusion discontinued: ______________ Time restraints discontinued: __________

Helmet: ________________________

Code explanation:	**0700-1500**	**INIT**	**1500-2300**	**INIT**	**2300-0700**	**INIT**
1. Hitting door	0700		1500		2300	
2. Yelling	0715		1515		2315	
3. Crying	0730		1530		2330	
4. Cursing	0745		1545		2345	
5. Laughing	0800		1600		2400	
6. Singing	0815		1615		0015	
7. Mumbling	0830		1630		0030	
8. Standing still	0845		1645		0045	
9. Pacing	0900		1700		0100	
10. Sitting	0915		1715		0115	
11. Quiet	0930		1730		0130	
12. Sleeping	0945		1745		0145	
13. Eating meal	1000		1800		0200	
14. Using toilet	1015		1815		0215	
15. Labs drawn	1030		1830		0230	
16. Medicated	1045		1845		0245	
17. Interview	1100		1900		0300	
18. Soiled room	1115		1915		0315	
19. Bathed	1130		1930		0330	
20. Moved to another room	1145		1945		0345	
21. Agitated	1200		2000		0400	
22. Drinking fluids	1215		2015		0415	
23. Fighting staff	1230		2030		0430	
24. Vomiting	1245		2045		0445	
25. Vital signs	1300		2100		0500	
26. Regular resp.	1315		2115		0515	
27. Verbal response	1330		2130		0530	
28. Hitting self	1345		2145		0545	
29. _______	1400		2200		0600	
30. _______	1415		2215		0615	
31. _______	1430		2230		0630	
32. _______	1445		2245		0645	
33. _______						

RN Signature:	__________	__________	__________
Psychiatric Assistant Signature:	__________	__________	__________
Physician Signature:	__________	__________	__________
Shift:	__________	__________	__________

Source: Rusty McNew, RN, MA, CPHQ, Dallas, Texas.

4-51 Emergency Treatment, Transfer, and Discharge to Home

POLICY

To ensure that all patients are evaluated, and/or stabilized for transfer to another facility or discharged to home, in a safe, efficient manner consistent with EMTALA guidelines. This policy is adapted from EMTALA and applies to Health Care providers, nursing staff, and hospital. (See Transport of Patient to Other Facility Policy.)

Emergency Medical Condition:
An individual has an emergency medical condition if his/her medical condition is marked by acute symptoms of sufficient severity, including severe pain, or the absence of immediate medical attention could reasonably be expected to result in:

- Placing the person's health in serious jeopardy;
- Serious impairment of body function; or
- Serious dysfunction of any body organ or part.

SPECIAL NOTE REGARDING PREGNANT WOMEN:
Women in active pre-term labor or other conditions that pose a threat to the health or safety to the mother and fetus will be presumed to have an emergency medical condition. All EMTALA guidelines apply to labor and delivery.
All pregnant women seeking unscheduled care must have a medical screening exam (MSE) to determine if they are in labor or have an emergency medical condition. The L&D nurse or ER physician or patient's primary physician will complete MSE.
All pregnant women who are in pre-term labor and/or with emergency medical condition must be stabilized or, if the benefits exceed the risks to the mother and/or the fetus, they will be transferred to an appropriate alternative facility through qualified personnel and transportation equipment, including the use of necessary and appropriate life-support measures. Ambulance and air services will be coordinated to provide continuity of patient care. Neither the initial screening nor any needed stabilizing treatment may be delayed by inquiries about payment or insurance status.

- If an unstable pregnant woman must be transferred, treatment must be provided to minimize the risk of transfer. The transferring care provider regarding the risks and benefits of transfer must counsel the patient. The care provider must certify the need for transfer.
- A reasonable effort must be made to obtain written informed patient refusal to consent to treatment or transfer.
- The facility maintains a list of care providers who are on-call after the initial examination to provide treatment necessary to stabilize an individual with an emergency medical condition or who are in pre-term labor.

- The facility may not penalize a care provider who refuses to transfer an unstable patient.
- The facility may not refuse to accept appropriate transfers if it has the capability to treat the patient.
- The facility must maintain records of patient transfer for 5 years or as required by the laws and regulations of the state in which the hospital is located.

GUIDELINES

1. The primary care provider will initiate the transfer by first contacting the receiving care provider and facility. Acceptance of the patient by the receiving facility must be confirmed. Name of the accepting care provider documented.
2. The receiving facility will provide the information about the method of transportation and the Estimated Time of Arrival (ETA) of the transport team. This information will be relayed to the appropriate staff.
   a. Charge nurse or the Nursing Supervisor, coordinates the transport process. Notify the emergency department of a maternal transport and ETA. If using helicopter of fixed wing, have the emergency department arrange for ambulance services. Notify security if helicopter pad is needed.
   b. Staff Nurse
      - Prepares the patient for transport.
      - Communicates information to the receiving facility.
      - Obtains transport, release of information, and treatment consents.

   c. Unit Secretary or OST obtains copies of chart and necessary forms for the receiving facility. Security clears the helicopter pad and opens front doors during off-shifts.
3. Medical Examination Screening: The hospital must provide an examination within the capability of the hospital's L&D Ante Partum emergency department and ancillary services that are routinely available to the ED to determine whether an individual who comes to the emergency room has an emergency medical condition.
4. Stabilization of Emergency Medical Condition: The hospital must provide for such treatment as may be required to stabilize the condition, within the staff and facilities available in the facility or, if the medical benefits outweigh the risks, take action to assure the appropriateness of transfer.
5. Responsibility of On-Call Care Providers: The hospital maintains a list of care providers who are on-call for duty after the initial examination to provide treatment necessary to stabilize an individual with an emergency medical condition. Any care provider, including an on-call care provider, responsible for the examination and treatment of such patients, is subject to a civil monetary penalty. The on-call physician who refuses or fails to appear within a reasonable period of time may be subject to these penalties.
6. Consent to Treatment: The patient is presumed to be stable if the hospital informs the patient of the risks and benefits of treatment and the patient refuses both examination and treatment. The hospital must take all "responsible steps" to obtain the patient's written "informed consent" (including patients who are drug abusers, psychotics, and crime victims) to refuse both examination and treatment; at this point the facility presumes to have stabilized the patient. In some cases, the only appropriate action may be to discharge the patient against medical advice.

7. Consent to Transfer: If the hospital desires to transfer a patient to another facility, the patient must be informed of the risks and benefits to the transfer. If the patient wants the transfer, the patient must sign a form that requests the transfer proceed unless the care provider executes a risk/benefit certification.
8. Certification: A woman in labor or in an unstable medical condition may not be transferred unless the care provider signs a certification at the time of transfer that the benefit of the treatment at the other facility outweighs the increased risk of the transfer. The care provider documents the risks and benefits as part of the certification. Specific penalties exist for signing a certification when the care provider knows or should know that the benefits do not outweigh the risks of transfer or for signing a false certification.
9. Appropriate Transfer: Unstable transfer must be "appropriate." An appropriate transfer to a medical facility is a transfer:
   - In which the transferring facility provides the medical treatment within its capacity that minimizes the risks of the individual's health and, in the case of a woman in labor, the health of the unborn child.
   - In which the receiving facility:
     —Has available space and qualified personnel for treating the patient, and
     —The facility and care provider has agreed to accept the transfer.
   - In which the transferring facility sends the patient to the accepting facility:
     —A copy of the medical records related to the individual's emergency medical condition.
     —A copy of the informed written consent or the physician's certification.
     —The name and address of the on-call care provider who refuses or fails to appear within a reasonable time to provide necessary stabilizing treatment.

The transfer must be affected through "qualified personnel and transportation equipment necessary and medically appropriate life-support measures. The transferring hospital must provide stabilizing treatment during the transfer."

Source: Parkview Medical Center, Pueblo, Colorado. Reprinted with permission.

4-52 Pediatric Trauma Transfer/Transport

POLICY

All patients are received and/or transferred according to the Pediatric Trauma Acceptance and Transfer Guidelines that follow. Any patient seen in the Emergency Department will be stabilized before transfer/transport.

Transfer of pediatric patients:

1. All transfers follow COBRA protocol.
   Physician-to-physician contact for patient acceptance and report.
   Nurse-to-nurse report.
   Bed availability confirmed through receiving facility nursing supervisor.
   COBRA forms completed and signed.

2. The ED nursing report will include:
   - History of trauma
   - Known allergies
   - Home medications
   - Health history
   - Patient weight
   - ED procedures and results
   - Medications given and response
   - Total I & O
   - Current condition and vital signs
   - Method of patient transport and ETA
   - Method of family/guardian transport and ETA
   - Family/guardian telephone number
3. Completed documents to be sent with transport crew:
   - Copy of ED chart (including nurse and MD notes)
   - Labs
   - Hard copies of diagnostics
   - COBRA documents
4. Prepare patient for transport:
   - Secure airway
   - Secure IV access (two lines)
   - Stabilize any bleeding wounds or fractures
   - Send medications and blood PRN
   - Send additional warm blankets
   - IV fluids will be per pump for any child under 12
5. All pediatric trauma patients will be transferred to ______ unless otherwise dictated by attending physician.

GUIDELINES FOR ACCEPTANCE AND TRANSFER OF PEDIATRIC PATIENTS

The following guidelines are for acceptance of pediatric patients and their subsequent transfer as necessary. These guidelines are specifically for trauma patients but may apply to patients within the community. Treatment is at the discretion of the individual physician.

______________ may accept and treat all pediatric patients over the age of two (2) years who meet the following criteria:

1. Any pediatric patient who is stable from a cardiovascular standpoint;
2. Any pediatric patient who is not ventilator dependent;
3. Any pediatric patient who does not have any major pulmonary injury.

We will not accept incoming transfers of pediatric patients who meet the following criteria:

1. Patients who are less than two (2) years of age;
2. Any pediatric patient who is unstable from a cardiovascular standpoint;
3. Any pediatric patients requiring a prolonged ventilator;
4. Any pediatric patient who has a major pulmonary injury;
5. All burns.

Pediatric patients who are initially treated in our ER will be stabilized prior to transfer. Such stabilization may include surgery.

The pediatrician on-call will assist in the stabilization of the patient and the subsequent transfer.

Source: Parkview Medical Center, Pueblo, Colorado. Reprinted with permission.

4-53 Request for Authorization for Autopsy

DATE: __________TIME: _____a.m./p.m.

In the hope that this authorization will further medical knowledge and help others suffering from similar ailments, I hereby consent to a post-mortem examination of the decedent, ________late as of:______________
(Address)

____________________.
(City and State)

I hereby verify that I am assuming custody of the body of the above decedent for purpose of burial, and that I bear the following relationship to the decedent

__________________.
(Relationship)

I hereby authorize the Pathology Department of this health care facility and its assistants and consultants to perform the post-mortem examination.

I hereby authorize the removal of any organs and tissues of the decedent for extended study, as the Pathology Department deems necessary. I further authorize the Department to obtain photographs as it deems necessary, and to use such photographs as well as information and data from the autopsy findings, for publication in scientific and professional journals in connection with medical research and teaching.

This authorization includes permission for a complete examination of all portions of the decedent with the following exceptions:

____

____

I direct that after the post-mortem examination, release of the decedent shall be made to the ___________________________________mortuary.

____

(Signature)

____

(Address)

Source: Parkview Medical Center, Pueblo, Colorado. Reprinted with permission.

4-54 Health Care for Homeless Patients: Summary of Recommendations

I. DIAGNOSIS & EVALUATION

A. **History**

- **Living conditions**—Ask where patient is staying. Explore access to food, water, restrooms, place to store medications; exposure to toxins, allergens, infection; threats to health/safety. Be alert to possible homelessness.
- **Prior homelessness**—What precipitated it; whether first time, episodic, chronic; history of foster care
- **Acute/chronic illness**—Ask about individual/familial history of asthma, chronic otitis media, anemia, diabetes, CVD, TB, HIV/STIs, hospitalizations, medications
- **Prior providers**—What worked well, does patient have regular source of primary care
- **Mental illness/cognitive deficit**—Problems with stress, anxiety, appetite, sleep, concentration, mood, speech, memory, thought process and content, suicidal/homicidal ideation, judgment, impulse control, social interactions
- **Developmental/behavioral problems**—Adaptive/maladaptive, underlying pathology
- **Alcohol/nicotine/other drug use**—Ask about use (amount, frequency, duration); look for signs of substance abuse/dependence
- **Health insurance/prescription drug coverage**—Entitlement assistance (Medicaid/SCHIP, SSI/SSDI)
- **Sexual**—Gender identity, sexual orientation, behaviors, partners, pregnancies, hepatitis/HIV/other STIs
- **History & current risk of abuse**—Emotional, physical, sexual abuse; knowledge of crisis resources, patient safety
- **Legal/violence history**—Legal problems, violence against persons or property, domestic/interpersonal violence, history of arrest/incarceration, treatment while incarcerated
- **Regular/strenuous activities**—Consistent routines (treatment feasibility); level of strenuous activity
- **Work history**—Longest time held a job, occupational injuries; vocational skills and interests
- **Literacy**—If "trouble reading," offer help with intake form; assess ability to read English
- **Nutrition/hydration**—Diet, food resources, preparation skills, liquid intake
- **Cultural heritage/affiliations/supports**—Involvement with family, friends, faith community, other sources of support
- **Strengths**—Coping skills, resourcefulness, abilities, interests

B. **Physical Examination**

- **Comprehensive exam**—At first encounter if possible, following standard clinical guidelines
- **Serial, focused exams**—For patients uncomfortable with full-body, unclothed exam at first visit
- **Dental assessment**—Age-appropriate teeth, obvious caries, dental/referred pain, diabetes patients

- **Special populations**—Victims of abuse, sexual minorities

C. **Diagnostic Tests**
- **Interpersonal violence**—Posttraumatic diagnostic scale for use with extremely low-income women
- **Mental health screenings**—Patient Health Questionnaire (PHQ-9, PHQ-2), MHS-III
- **Substance abuse screening**—SSI-AOD
- **Cognitive assessment**—Mini-Mental Status Examination (MMSE)
- **STI screening**—For chlamydia, gonorrhea, syphilis, HIV, HBV, trichomonas, bacterial vaginosis, monilia
- **Baseline labs**—Including liver function tests
- **PPD**—For patients living in shelters and others at risk for tuberculosis
- **Health care maintenance**—Cancer screening for adults, EPSDT for children
- **Developmental assessment**—Denver II or other standard screening tool
- **Forensic evaluation**—If strong evidence of child abuse

II. PLAN & MANAGEMENT

A. **Plan of Care**
- **Basic needs**—Food, clothing, housing may be higher priorities than health care
- **Patient goals & priorities**—Immediate/long-term health needs, what patient wants to address first
- **Action plan**—Simple language, portable pocket card
- **After hours**—Extended clinic hours, how to contact medical provider when clinic is closed
- **Safety plan**—If interpersonal violence/sexual abuse suspected; mandatory reporting requirements
- **Emergency plan**—Contacting PCP before going to ER, location of emergency facilities
- **Adherence plan**—Clarification of care plan/patient feedback; use of interpreter, lay educator if LEP

B. **Education, Self-Management**
- **Patient/parent instruction**—Simple language/illustrations, confirm comprehension; pocket card listing immunizations, chronic illnesses, medications
- **Prevention/risk reduction**—Protection from communicable diseases
- **Behavioral change**—Individual/small group/community interventions, motivational interviewing
- **Nutrition counseling**—Diet, dietary supplements, food choices, powdered formula for infants
- **Peer support**—Support groups, consumer advocates
- **Education of service providers (shelter/clinical staff)**—Re: special problems/needs of homeless people

C. **Medications**
- **Simple regimen**—Low pill count, once-daily dosing where possible; capsules/tablets for child > 5 yrs
- **Dispensing**—On-site; small amounts at a time to promote follow-up, decrease risk of loss/theft/misuse; avoid written prescriptions when possible

- **Storage/access**—In clinic/shelters; if no access to refrigeration, do not prescribe meds that require it
- **Patient assistance**—Entitlement assistance, free/low-cost drugs if readily available for continued use
- **Aids to adherence**—Harm reduction, outreach/case management, directly observed therapy
- **Potential for misuse**—Inhalants, bronchodilators/spacers, pain medications, clonidine, needles
- **Side effects**—Primary reason for non-adherence (diarrhea, frequent urination, nausea, disorientation)
- **Analgesia/symptomatic treatment**—Patient contract, single provider for refills of pain medications
- **Immunizations**—Per standard clinical guidelines; influenza, pneumococcus, HAV, HBV, Td for adults
- **Antibiotics**—Standard liquid measurements, importance of completing regimen, RSV prophylaxis
- **Dietary supplements**—Multivitamins with minerals, nutritional supplements with lower resale value
- **Managed care**—Prescribe medications that do not require pre-authorization, assistance getting Rx filled

D. **Associated Problems, Complications**
- **No place to heal**—Efficacy of medical respite/recuperative care, supportive housing
- **Masked symptoms/misdiagnosis**—e.g., weight loss, dementia, edema, lactic acidosis
- **Developmental discrepancies**—Focus on immediate concerns, not possible future consequences
- **Functional impairments**—Documentation of disabilities, assistance with SSI applications
- **Dual diagnoses**—Integrated treatment for concurrent mental illness/substance use disorders
- **Loss of child custody**—Support for parent of child abused by others, and for abused parent

E. **Follow-Up**
- **Contact information**—Phone numbers, e-mail addresses for patient/friend/family/case manager
- **Medical home**—To coordinate/promote continuity of health care
- **Frequency**—More frequent follow-up, incentives, nonjudgmental care regardless of adherence
- **Drop-in system**—Anticipate/accommodate unscheduled clinic visits
- **Transportation assistance**—Provide car fare/tokens, help with Medicaid transportation services
- **Outreach, case management**—Connect with community outreach programs, HCH providers
- **Monitor school attendance**—Address health/developmental problems with family/school
- **Peer support**—Client advocate to accompany patient to clinical appointments/ambulatory surgery

- **Referrals**—Linkage with specialists, pro bono care, providers sensitive to underserved populations

III. MODEL OF CARE

A. **Service Delivery Design**
   - **Multiple points of service**—Clinics, drop-in centers, outreach sites; electronic medical records, if feasible
   - **Integrated, interdisciplinary**—Coordinated medical and psychosocial services
   - **Flexible service system**—Walk-ins permitted, help with resolving systems barriers
   - **Access to mainstream health system**—Ready access to secondary/tertiary care

B. **Outreach and Engagement**
   - **Outreach sites**—Streets, soup kitchens, shelters, other homeless service sites
   - **Clinical team**—Use of outreach workers/case managers and medical providers to promote engagement
   - **Therapeutic relationship**—Based on trust, nonjudgmental care, frequent encounters
   - **Incentives**—To promote engagement: food, drink, vouchers, hygiene products, subway/bus fare (tokens)

C. **Standard of Care**
   Evidence-based medicine—Make elimination of health disparities a clinical goal

Source: Bonin E, Brehove T, Kline S, Misgen M, Post P, Strehlow AJ, Yungman J. *Adapting Your Practice: General Recommendations for the Care of Homeless Patients*, Nashville: Health Care for the Homeless Clinicians' Network, National Health Care for the Homeless Council, Inc., 2004.

4-55 Policy and Procedure: Discharge Instructions

I. PURPOSE

To provide procedures for effective patient discharge and follow-up.

II. POLICY

A. All patients will be assessed for medical stability, orientation, readiness to learn and barriers to learning.

B. All patients discharged from the Emergency Department will receive condition-appropriate instructions for home care and appropriate referrals.

III. RESPONSIBILITIES

A. The physician or nurse will verbally instruct patient on specific discharge instructions, including medications.

B. Patient will verbally state understanding or return demonstration of discharge instructions.

C. Patient will sign discharge instruction sheet:
    1. One copy is given to the patient.
    2. One copy is placed in patient's medical record.
D. Appropriate medical follow up referral will be given.
E. Assure that all medications and procedures ordered by the physician have been accomplished. Patient will be observed for at least twenty (20) minutes after receiving any antibiotic, narcotic or any other medications that the Emergency physician states appropriate to observe to insure there are no signs or symptoms of an untoward reaction. Take home medications must be dispensed by the physician.
F. Assure all patients have appropriate transportation arranged upon discharge. This may include arranging transportation through family, friends, ambulance services, taxi vouchers or bus token. The Emergency Services case manager or social worker may be involved in the process as appropriate.

IV. PERSONNEL

Registered Nurses, Licensed Vocational Nurses, Physicians

V. EQUIPMENT/SUPPLIES

Aftercare Instruction Forms

VI. BUSINESS UNIT ADDENDUM

A. Patient to be accompanied to Financial Counselor's Office or have the Financial Counselor come to the bedside if there are financial arrangements or payments to be made.
B. Employees treated for workers' compensation cases may be referred for one follow-up visit to the Urgent Care. Those employees who require follow-up for a wound recheck and a second follow-up visit for suture removal may also be referred to the Urgent Care. The employee should then be referred to Employee Occupational Health Services. Employees requiring more than one follow-up visit are to be referred directly to Employee Occupational Health Services. It is the responsibility of the Employee Occupational Health Nurse to make the appropriate physician referral.
C. Workers' compensation cases are to be referred to the Compensation coverage physician of that particular company, as listed in the Workers' Compensation Rolodex. If the patient has no physician and has undergone procedures, such as suturing for a laceration, care of a simple burn, and I&D of a wound, etc., the patient may be referred back to the Urgent Care for the initial follow-up wound check or suture removal. The Emergency Center physician will determine at the first follow-up visit what action will then be taken.

Source: Scripps Mercy Hospital, San Diego, California.

4-56 Physician Certification for Transfer of Patient from the Emergency Department

AUTHORIZATION FOR TRANSFER

Directions: This form must be completed by a physician who authorizes transfer to another medical facility of a patient determined by the Emergency Department to have an emergency medical condition or to be in active labor. An emergency medical condition and active labor are defined by the Consolidated Omnibus Budget Reconciliation Act (COBRA) of 1985 (42 U.S.C. § 1395dd) and amended by the Omnibus Budget Reconciliation Act of 1987 and 1989.

SECTION 1 COMPLETE AS INDICATED.

A. ☐ **The patient has been stabilized** such that, within reasonable medical probability, no material deterioration of the patient's condition is likely to result from or occur during the transfer. (A patient in active labor has been stabilized if she has delivered, including the placenta.)

B. ☐ **Patient's condition has NOT been stabilized.**

SECTION 2 COMPLETE AS INDICATED.

A. ☐ **Reason for transfer:** NOTE: if 1(B) was checked, RISKS AND BENEFITS MUST ALSO BE LISTED BELOW.
REMINDER: If the reason for transfer is because the on-call physician failed or refused to appear within a reasonable period of time, indicate the name and address of the on-call physician on the medical record.

____

____

____

SECTION 3 COMPLETE ONLY IF SECTION 1(B) ABOVE HAS BEEN CHECKED. IF NOT, PROCEED TO SECTION 4.

CHECK ONE OF THE FOLLOWING:

A. ☐ **Patient requests transfer** (or a legally responsible individual acting on the patient's behalf requests the transfer). TRANSFER BY UNSTABILIZED PATIENT on signature page of this form must be completed.

B. ☐ **Medical benefits outweigh risks:** Based on the reasonable risks and benefits to the patient, and based upon the information available at the time of the patient's transfer, the medical benefits reasonably expected from the provision of appropriate medical treatment at another medical facility outweigh the increased risks, if any, to the patient's medical condition [including, in the case of a pregnant woman, the risks to the unborn child(ren)] from effecting the transfer.

SECTION 4 OMIT THIS SECTION IF 3 (A) WAS CHECKED. OTHERWISE, COMPLETE A OR B AS APPROPRIATE.

A. ☐ **Patient consents to the transfer** (or a legally responsible individual acting on the patient's behalf consents to the transfer). TRANSFER CONSENT on signature page of this form must be completed.

B. ☐ **Transfer was offered but refused** by the patient or a legally responsible individual acting on the patient's behalf. TRANSFER REFUSAL on signature page of this form must be completed.

SECTION 5 COMPLETE AS INDICATED.

NOTE: The patient may not be transferred unless each of the following requirements is met:

A. ☐ The receiving facility has available space and qualified personnel for the treatment of the patient.
B. ☐ The receiving facility has agreed to accept transfer and to provide appropriate medical treatment.
1. Name of the receiving facility ______________________________
Please print
2. Name of individual accepting transfer ______________________________
Please print

C. ☐ The receiving facility will be provided with appropriate medical records of the examination and treatment of the patient.

D. ☐ The patient will be transferred by qualified personnel and transportation equipment as required, including the use of necessary and medically appropriate life support measures.
1. MEANS OF TRANSPORT
☐ Ground ambulance (☐ BLS ☐ ALS) ______________
Name
☐ Air ambulance (☐ BLS ☐ ALS) ______________________________
Name
☐ Transport Team______________________________
Name
☐ Private car
☐ Other ______________________
2. PERSONNEL ACCOMPANYING PATIENT (check all that apply)
☐ EMT—A
☐ EMT—P
☐ Physician
☐ Nurse
☐ Respiratory Therapist
☐ Other ______________________

I certify that I have answered the above questions based upon the information available to me at the time of the patient's transfer. I further certify that I have made the appropriate disclosures as indicated on this form.

______________________________ ______________________________
Name of Physician Authorizing Transfer (please print) Physician Signature

Date ________ Time ________

SIGNATURE PAGE FOR PATIENT'S REQUEST/REFUSAL/CONSENT TO TRANSFER

I. TRANSFER REQUEST BY UNSTABILIZED PATIENT

I acknowledge that my medical condition has been evaluated and explained to me by ______________________
Name of physician
who has recommended and offered to me further medical examination and treatment and has informed me of the hospital obligation to provide stabilizing treatment. The potential benefits of such further medical examination and treatment as well as the potential risks associated with transfer to another facility have been explained to me and I fully understand them. In spite of this understanding, I refuse to consent to the further medical examination and treatment that has been offered to me, and request transfer to ______________________.
Name of receiving facility

____
Signature of patient or legally responsible individual signing on patient's behalf

____
Date and time

____
Relationship to patient

II. TRANSFER CONSENT

I acknowledge that my medical condition has been evaluated and explained to me by ________________ who has recommended that I be transferred to the service of Dr. ____________________ at __________________________.
Name of receiving facility

The potential benefits of such transfer, the potential risks associated with such transfer, and the probable risks of not being transferred have been explained to me and I fully understand them. With this knowledge and understanding, I agree and consent to be transferred.

____
Date and time

____
Signature of patient or legally responsible individual signing on patient's behalf

____
Relationship to patient

III. TRANSFER REFUSAL

I acknowledge that my medical condition has been evaluated and explained to me by ________________
Name of physician

who has recommended that I be transferred to ____________________.
Name of receiving facility

The potential benefits of such transfer, the potential risks associated with such transfer, and the probable risks of not being transferred have been explained to me and I fully understand them. Even though the above named physician believes it is in my best interests to be transferred, I refuse to be transferred and I request instead to continue receiving treatment at ______________________ Hospital.

____
Date and time

____
Signature of patient or legally responsible individual signing on patient's behalf

____
Relationship to patient

Source: Aspen Publishers.

4-57 Protocol Approval Flowchart

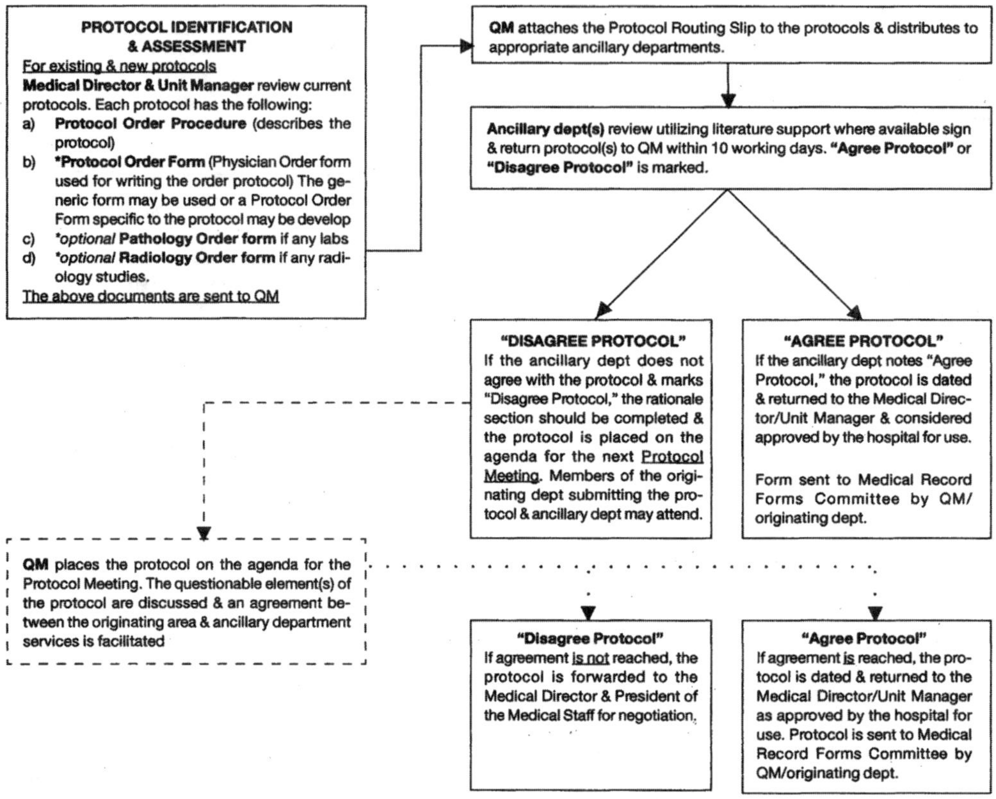

WHERE TO CATALOGUE DOCUMENTS

Individual units maintain the following:	Medical Records Committee minutes contain a copy of the following:	Quality Management maintains a copy of the following
☐ Approved Protocols ☐ *Approved Protocol Order form (Physician Order from used for writing the order protocol) ☐ *Approved Pathology Order form (PS5550-01) ☐ *Approved Radiology Order form (PS2482)	☐ *Approved Protocol Order form (order form MD/nurse uses for ordering protocol) ☐ *Approved Pathology Order form ☐ *Approved Radiology Order form	☐ Approved Protocols

**Order forms optional in ambulatory settings*

Clinical protocols are based on current medical literature as of the start date. Protocols are not intended to prevent the physician from using their clinical judgment in treating the individual patient. Each protocol should be based on current medical knowledge and practice as well as clinical circumstances of the patient.

Source: Rusty McNew, RN, MA, CPHQ, Dallas, Texas.

4-58 Physician-Patient Report Form

Date Report Called: ____________

Patient Name: ______________________________

AGE: ________

Physician Calling Report: ____

Presenting Complaint: ____

____

Order Requests: ____

____

____

Patient to be seen by ED physician?: YES OR NO (circle one)

Patient to by seen by PMD?: YES OR NO (circle one)

Patient to be admitted?: Yes OR NO (circle one)

Signature: ______________________
(PERSON TAKING REPORT)

Copy to be taken to the Triage Nurse.

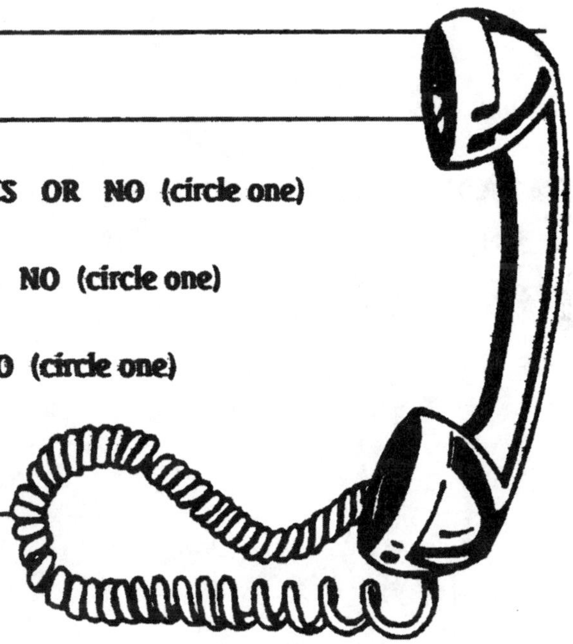

Source: Medical Center of Plano, Plano, Texas.

4-59 Emergency Department/Radiology Communication Form

INITIAL IMPRESSION BY ED PHYSICIAN

☐ Essentially Normal
Other Findings:

Date: ______________
X-ray Ordered: ______________

Chief Complaint: ______________

Time: ______________
Emergency Physician: ______________, MD

RADIOLOGIST'S REVIEW

☐ Agree, No Significant Discrepancy
☐ Disagree with ED physician's impression
Diagnosis:

☐ Final report dictated.

If radiologist disagrees with ED physician's impression:
Notified ______________ in ED at ________ on ________
(Time) (Date)

Radiologist: ______________, MD
Date: ________ Time: ________

EMERGENCY DEPARTMENT REVIEW AND FOLLOW-UP

☐ No Significant Discrepancy
☐ Discrepancy, No change in therapy required
☐ Discrepancy, Actions taken:

☐ *Patient notified at* ________ *on* ________ *and advised* ______________
(Time) *(Date)*

☐ Dr. ______________ was called at ________ on ________.
(Time) *(Date)*

☐ Patient's private physician, Dr. ______________ agreed to notify patient.

Completion, Review and Follow-up by: ______________, MD
(Emergency Department)

Anytown Medical Center
Emergency Department/Radiology
Communication Form

Source: ©2005 Medical Insurance Exchange of CA (MIEC), Oakland, California. Reprinted with permission.

4-60 X-Ray Release Form

I______________, hereby authorize and request the release of X-rays taken of me to:
(Please Print)

☐ Me (the patient) Address and Phone: ________________

☐ ________________________
Name of Relative/Other

☐ ________________________
Physician or Hospital

I understand that these X-rays are part of original medical records which belong to the _________. I accept responsibility for their care and prompt return.

Patient's Signature: ________________________
Signature of Borrower: ____________________ Date ________
Witnessed By: ________________________

Films Released (*type and date*) ____________________

Number of Films Released __________ By ________________
Doctor or Technologist

Number of Films Returned __________ Date ________________

Recorded By: ________________

4-61 Detoxification and Substance Abuse Treatment: Freestanding Urgent Care Center or Emergency Department

A freestanding urgent care center or emergency department reasonably can be expected to provide assessment and acute biomedical (including psychiatric) care. However, these settings often are unable to provide satisfactory psychosocial stabilization or complete biomedical stabilization (which includes both the initiation and taper of medications used in the treatment of substance withdrawal syndromes). Appropriate triage and successful linkage to ongoing detoxification services are essential. The ongoing detoxification services may be provided in an inpatient, residential, or outpatient setting. Patients with more than moderate biomedical or psychosocial complications are more likely to require treatment in an inpatient setting. Care in these settings can be quite costly and should be accessed only when there are serious concerns about a patient's safety.

A timely and accurate assessment in an emergency department is of the highest importance. This will permit the rapid transfer of the patient to a setting where complete care can be provided. Ideally, personnel in the emergency department will have at least a small amount of experience and expertise in identifying critically ill substance-using patients who may be about to experience or are already experiencing withdrawal symptoms. Three essential rules apply to emergency departments and their handling of intoxicated patients and patients who have begun to experience withdrawal:

- Emergency departments and their clinicians should never simply administer medications to intoxicated persons and then send them home.
- No intoxicated patient should ever be allowed to leave a hospital setting. All such persons should be referred to the appropriate detoxification setting if possible, although there are legal restrictions that forbid holding persons against their will under certain conditions.
- A clear distinction must be made between acute intoxication on the one hand and withdrawal on the other. Acute intoxication, it must be remembered, creates special issues and challenges that need to be addressed. The risk of suicidality in patients who present in a state of intoxication needs to be carefully assessed. Because of their volatility and often risky behavior, patients who are intoxicated, as well as those patients who have begun to experience withdrawal, merit special attention. For more on treating intoxicated patients, see "Detoxification and substance abuse treatment: an overview of psychosocial and biomedical issues during detoxification" (Chapter 3 in the original full-text guideline document).

LEVEL OF CARE

Care is provided to patients whose withdrawal signs and symptoms are sufficiently severe to require primary medical and nursing care services. The services are delivered under a defined set of physician-managed procedures or medical protocols. Both settings provide medically directed assessment and acute care that includes the initiation of detoxification for substance use withdrawal. Neither setting is likely to offer satisfactory biomedical stabilization or 24-hour observation. Generally speaking, triage to inpatient care can easily be facilitated from either setting.

Freestanding urgent care centers and emergency departments are outpatient settings that are uniquely designed to address the needs of patients in biomedical crisis. For patients with substance use disorders, care in these settings is not complete until successful linkage is made to treatment that is focused specifically on the substance use disorder. To accomplish this, a comprehensive assessment, taking into account psychosocial as well as biomedical issues, is recommended wherever possible.

Appreciation of the value of multidimensional patient assessment is central to the clinician's ability to decide which triage (linkage) options are least restrictive and most cost-effective for a given patient.

STAFFING

The same rules regarding who may provide care apply here as they did in the discussion of staffing of office-based detoxification. An RN or other licensed and credentialed nurse may provide primary nursing care and observation. Psychologists, social workers, addiction counselors, and acupuncturists usually are not available in these settings. The physician or attending nurse usually facilitates linkage to substance abuse treatment.

Source: Settings, levels of care, and patient placement. In: Center for Substance Abuse Treatment (CSAT). *Detoxification and substance abuse treatment.* Rockville (MD): Substance Abuse and Mental Health Services Administration (SAMHSA); 2006 Jan 18, p. 9-18. Treatment improvement protocol (TIP); no. 45.

4-62 ED EMTALA Transfer Tracker

South Fulton Medical Center
EMTALA/ Transfer Log

	Name	MR #	Account #	Date Transfer	Time Transfer	Reason Transfer	Transfer Location	Receiving Location	Financial Class	Chief Complaint/ Diagnosis	*MSE Complete ED & L&D	*MSE Complete OB Addendum	SFMC Transfer Form Complete	SFMC Transfer Form Scanned/ *MEDHOST*	PSYCH - PET/ Scanned *MEDHOST*	Pink Sheet Submitted Admin	Patient In *MEDHOST*	Patient In PBAR
1	**EXAMPLE 1**					Higher Level of Care - No SFMC ICU Bed	ED			Asthma	Y	NA	Y	Y	NA	Y	Y	Y
2	**EXAMPLE 2**					Higher Level of Care - No SFMC ICU Bed	L&D			Sanorg Syndrome	Y	Y	Y	Y	NA	Y	Y	Y
3	**EXAMPLE 3**					No Ortho MD On-Call	ED			Femur Fracture	Y	NA	Y	Y	NA	Y	Y	Y
4	**EXAMPLE 4**					No Capability - Psychiatry	ED			Suicide Ideation/ Plan	Y	NA	Y	Y	Y	Y	Y	Y
5																		
6																		
7																		
8																		
9																		
10																		
11																		
12																		
13																		
14																		
15																		
16																		
17																		
18																		
19																		
20																		
21																		
22																		
23																		
24																		
25																		

<u>Reason For Transfer:</u>

1.
2.
3.
4.
5.

Source: Rusty McNew, RN, MA, CPHQ, Dallas, Texas.

* Requires PI Tool Completion At The Time of Transfer.

4-63 EM Xpress Paramedic to ED Transfer System

Valley Hospital Emergency Department (Las Vegas, Nevada) Introduces New Initiatives to Decrease Waiting Times for Paramedics, Patients

"EM Xpress" to Alleviate Paramedic Waiting Time While Parallel Provider Triage Continues to Benefit Walk-In Patients

Introducing EM Express

The Emergency Department has created a new program to reduce the amount of time it takes for the "transfer of care" between paramedics and the hospital.

On February 26, 2006, EMS personnel, which includes paramedics and EMT-Is, began working in the Emergency department from 11 a.m. to 11 p.m.—traditionally the ER's busiest times—to offload ambulance patients and begin the necessary workup. "Even if we're waiting for an ER bed, our EM Xpress is available to care for the patients, allowing the paramedics to return to the streets more quickly," explained Jim Holtz, Director of Emergency Services for Valley Hospital.

Because the EMS personnel are Valley Hospital employees, they will also be able to assist in the Emergency department with other tasks and projects.

EM Xpress was developed to comply with Senate Bill 458, which was passed during the 2005 Nevada state legislative session. Essentially, this bill initiated an official study regarding the length of time it takes for the transfer of care to pass between paramedics and the hospital staff. Each Las Vegas hospital is equipped with Transfer of Care software that captures the time EMTs arrive onsite until the patient's transfer of care occurs. Because the software will track both first responders and hospitals, the study's intent is to examine problems that are leading to the delayed transfers while also reducing the EMS offload/ transfer time. The study began March 1, 2006.

Parallel Provider Triage Reduces Patients' Time to Be Seen by Physician

"The parallel provider triage has been very successful since we started it on October 31, 2005," said Holtz. "Before, patients were triaged by a registered nurse and then they returned to the lobby to wait for an available bed. Now, the ER physician works with the RN who is completing the assessment and orders necessary testing at the time of triage."

Background

Clark County hospitals use a color-coded "green-yellow-red-black system" to indicate the estimated waiting time to transfer patient care from the paramedics to the hospital team. A green status means no waiting for paramedics to offload their patients, while black status indicates a wait of 60 minutes or more.

Between February 1 and February 26, 2006, Valley Hospital was on green status 95.7 percent of the time. "Green status is a testament to a hospital-wide commitment to improving patient flow," said Kevin Stockton, Chief Operating Officer. "The sooner we can turn over patient beds in the ER, the sooner we can accommodate all ambulance and walk-in traffic. The efforts of the Emergency and Admitting departments, inpatient units and house supervisors have made a significant difference in reducing ER waiting times at Valley Hospital."

EM Xpress Position Description/Job Duties/Guide

ED Tech II / EM XPress Position

Description/Job Duties/Guide

1. Shift 1100 to 2330
2. Wear approved apparel for assignment.
3. After clocking in, proceed to the charge nurse desk, utilize Charge Nurse II radio/ cell phone. Receive update on unit status from Charge Nurse.
4. PRIMARY JOB DUTIES:
   a. Off-load EMS crews immediately into:
      i. EMXpress Locations 1-8
      ii. **Transfer the patient in the TOC (transfer of care) software, use immediate transfer as much as possible.** Advise crew to proceed to the charge nurse desk to give report.
   b. Assist Charge Nurse in triaging patients when necessary or directed by the Charge Nurse on duty. Usually this will occur when there is more than one crew waiting.
      i. If patient remains in an EMXpress location, place patient on monitor if required, obtain current set of vitals (including temperature) and document on the RN T-Sheet. Complete clothing list.
   c. Draw required labs and label as required by RN standing order sheet or Physicians order sheet, under the direction of the Charge Nurse.
   d. Monitor Patients in EMXpress location for the Charge Nurse on duty. Report any changes as required/needed.
   e. Assist Charge Nurse with patient flow.
5. Secondary Job Duties (NO EMS CREWS WAITING/AVAILABLE ER BEDS):
   a. Off-load EMS crews into available ER Bed
      i. Have patient change into patient gown, or assist patient with this requirement.
      ii. Place patient on bedside monitoring equipment.
      iii. Draw required labs and label as required by RN standing order sheet or Physician order sheet.
      iv. Advise primary nurse of patient's arrival and chief complaint.
   b. Assist ER staff as required or necessary.
6. THE DO NOT'S:
   a. Leave the unit without advising the Charge Nurse.
   b. Transport patients to the floor, unless under extreme conditions and with approval from the Charge Nurse.
   c. Assist RN's on the floor only with the approval of the Charge Nurse on duty.
7. REMINDERS:
   a. Your primary duty is to off-load EMS crews and monitor those patients for the Charge Nurse on duty.
   b. We have other ED Techs working in the ER, their duties remain the same.

This program is a work in progress. Its success depends on you, and your diligence in off-loading EMS crews to get them back on the street and out of the hospital within 30 mins. The TOC (transfer of care) software must be maintained and updated frequently. Your suggestions and ideas are always welcome.

Introductory Information for EMTs

Introducing EM Xpress

11 a.m. to 11 p.m. Daily

Goal: Reduce EMS waiting time so you can begin responding to other calls as soon as possible.

How It Works:

- Bring your patient to Valley Hospital
- Check-in with the Transfer of Care software
- Give report to the Charge Nurse or the EM Xpress personnel
- Offload your patient
- Done—the Charge Nurse will check you out—drive safely

Source: Reprinted with permission of Valley Hospital Medical Center, Las Vegas, Nevada.

4-64 Managing Surge Needs for Injuries

I. Emergency Medical Service Response

PURPOSE

To provide guidance for local emergency medical service (EMS) response and to operationalize additional EMS-related resources needed in a community within four hours of an explosion. These resources are intended to treat 300 injured patients for up to 72 hours.

BACKGROUND

The Madrid terrorist bombings were used as a model to help develop solutions for managing rapid surge problems during a mass casualty event.

On March 11, 2004, 10 terrorist explosions occurred almost simultaneously on commuter trains in Madrid killing 177 people instantly and injuring more than 2,000. That day, 966 patients were taken to 15 pubic community hospitals. More than 270 patients arrived at the closest facility between 0800 and 1030 hours. Federal resources should not be expected to arrive sooner than 72 hours from the time of the explosion. Resources can be delayed by the time taken to deploy them and by responding to multiple communities.

GOAL

To mobilize the appropriate number and type of EMS resources to adequately evaluate injuries, initiate triage, begin transporting 300 injured patients, and to establish ongoing EMS operations for up to 72 hours.

Note: This document is a resource guide. Local needs, preferences, and capabilities of affected communities may vary.

REQUIRED RESOURCES

1. Personnel must be:
   - Appropriately equipped and knowledgeable about chemical, biological, radiological, nuclear, and explosives (CBRNE) detection, personal protection, and decontamination.
   - Educated in the care of blast-related injuries for adult and pediatric patients.
   - Prepared to institute triage.
   - Prepared to institute and participate in unified incident command.
2. A communications system that is interoperable with public safety disciplines (fire, law enforcement, EMS, and emergency management) and with receiving hospitals and local public health officials.
3. Rapid access to sufficient ambulance resources to transport critically injured patients.
4. Rapid access to sufficient alternative resources (e.g., buses) to transport noncritical, injured persons.
5. Have the necessary material and the capability to detect CBRNE agents to assist with decontamination plans.
6. Decontamination equipment for ambulatory and non-ambulatory patients; equipment should be rapidly deployable to the explosion site, a secondary treatment site, or a hospital.
7. Determine/implement secondary triage and treatment sites within the community.

ASSUMPTIONS

1. EMS systems in the United States are highly variable, with a wide range of available resources, experience, and financing.
2. A functional EMS system is a critical component for planning the prehospital management of injured bombing victims.

ACTION STEPS

1. Education:
   - Train EMS officials in advanced ICS (ICS 700 or equivalent).
   - Train responding EMS personnel about how to treat primary, secondary, tertiary, and quaternary blast-related injuries. For guidance, go to *www.bt.cdc.gov/masstrauma/explosions.asp*.
   - Train EMS personnel about National Incident Management System (NIMS) compliance; Incident Command System (ICS Homeland Security Presidential Directive 5); and the importance of command, staging, triage, and treating initial casualties (regardless of rank of the provider) should be emphasized.

- Train EMS personnel about the use of personnel protective equipment (PPE) and the risks of transporting potentially contaminated patients. The relative importance of gross vs. technical decontamination should be reviewed.

2. Local policy and planning:

Fire, EMS, law enforcement, emergency management, hospitals, and public health should collaborate to develop and complete written plans within six months, as listed below. Within one year, other agencies listed in these plans (including mutual aid agencies, etc.) must be included in ongoing planning and evaluation.

- Plan for mobilizing 50 ambulances within 10 minutes after the blast. At least 75% of these resources should arrive at staging areas in the first hour with all arriving in the first 90 minutes. This should be accomplished using 9-1-1 EMS resources, mutual aid agreements with other EMS providers, or mutual aid agreements with nonemergency transport providers.
- Plan describing each agency's role in the command structure. This should include how critical functions of command, staging, triage, and treatment will be accomplished in the first 10 minutes of a response; how additional ICS elements will be filled over the first hour; and how the ICS structure will be formally filled by officials trained in advanced ICS (ICS-700 or equivalent) by the end of the first hour.
- Plan describing how alternative transport for 200 ambulatory patients will be initiated in the first 10 minutes after an explosion.
- Plan describing the details of interdisciplinary communications (primary and alternatives). Representatives from fire prevention, EMS, law enforcement, emergency management, hospitals, and public health must be included in this plan.
- Plan for decontaminating and protecting personnel that addresses the following:
  - Agency responsible for scene assessment and determining what (if any) decontamination measures are required.
  - Realistic assessment of the time required to deploy decontamination resources for ambulatory and non-ambulatory patients.
  - Deployment of decontamination resources to event site, secondary triage sites, or receiving hospitals.
  - Transport of patients after gross decontamination (technical decontamination of patients before transport; appropriate personal protective equipment, or PPE; and
  - appropriately equipped destination choices).
- Plan to establish secondary triage points for ambulatory patients (ideally, within the first hour after the explosion). This should address the following:
  - How sites can be activated and staffed with at least one transport ambulance, sufficient law enforcement personnel for security, and adequate support staff to record arrivals.
  - How gross and technical decontamination could be accomplished at affected site(s).
  - How medical care at secondary triage sites could be converted to treatment areas (e.g., provision of medical supplies, additional medical personnel, and other logistical concerns).
- Plan to establish criteria for determination of death at the scene, particularly in a mass casualty situation, and appropriately manage the deceased.

EVALUATION

1. Plan and conduct a community-wide drill. Afterwards, evaluate it by assessing overall operations and EMS resources such as personnel, ambulances, and PPE. Evaluate compliance with NIMS.
2. Assess and refine plan.

II. Emergency Department Response

PURPOSE

To activate additional emergency department resources needed within four hours of an explosion. These resources should treat 300 injured patients for up to 72 hours.

BACKGROUND

The experiences of the Madrid terrorist bombings were used as a model to help develop solutions for managing rapid surge problems during a mass casualty event.

GOAL

To establish policies, procedures, didactic training, and drills to improve institutional preparedness for treating 300 injured patients for up to 72 hours.

RESOURCES REQUIRED

There should be adequate medical, nursing, and support staff to provide initial triage, and to evaluate and stabilize 300 persons.

Note: This document is a resource guide. Local needs, preferences, and capabilities of affected communities may vary.

ASSUMPTIONS

1. Developed packets for each patient containing disaster bands (those from blood banks work best), manual charting forms, and manual lab and radiology order forms. These packets should be prepared in advance and stored in the ED.
2. Established procedures for obtaining additional personnel, equipment, supplies and beds; establish a mechanism for notifying and activating backup personnel.
3. Established procedures for triage, patient emergency identification of patients and discharge, and quick documentation.
4. Established temporary disaster log to document basic information.

ACTION STEPS

1. Implement and drill a hospital emergency incident command system (such as Hospital Incident Command System or "HICS"); include clinical care providers in the training and drill.

   If hospital personnel (e.g., practitioners, administrators, nurses) have not trained or drilled in a hospital incident command system, learned about the National Incident Management System (NIMS), or do not understand the function of a

Hospital Incident Command Center, this information should be included in training sessions.

2. Instruct clinical staff, especially surgeons and emergency physicians, about the unique aspects of blast-related injuries and care following an attack with a radiation dispersal device (RDD).
3. Establish an institutional lockdown process and drill on a regular basis; include radiation detection and decontamination of arriving patients.
4. Update the institutional call-down list and perform a functional call-down exercise.
5. Identify potential institutional surge staffing from employees with clinical training, but not currently tasked with clinical jobs.
6. Identify patient care supplies for a surge situation, such as additional IV equipment, bandages/dressings, gowns, gloves, masks, other operating room supplies, etc.
7. Develop a regional Unified Command Structure that includes local emergency management and area hospitals. This should be achieved under the guidance and leadership of the local emergency managers.
8. Identify non-patient care areas in the institution that could be converted to patient care to expand bed surge capacity.
9. Establish and drill a procedure for early patient discharge to increase bed capacity. This procedure should include evaluation of ICU patients for potential movement to a non-ICU bed and evaluation of all patients for potential early discharge or transfer to an alternative care site (internal or external to the institution).

EVALUATION

When appropriate, evaluation drills have been incorporated into the “Action Steps” listed above. The institutional disaster preparedness plan should be updated based on each drill experience.

Source: *In a Moment’s Notice: Surge Capacity for Terrorist Bombings—Challenges and Proposed Solutions*. April 2007. National Center for Injury Prevention and Control, Division of Injury Response, Centers for Disease Control and Prevention, Atlanta, Georgia.

MEDICATION MANAGEMENT

4-65 Dispensing of Medications from the Emergency Department

BACKGROUND

To best serve patient care needs, it is sometimes necessary to dispense medication from the emergency department to allow a patient enough medication until a prescription can be filled. This decision is based on the physician’s judgment that such medication is both expedient and necessary.

PURPOSE

To define the policy and procedure by which medications are dispensed to patients who are discharged from the emergency department.

POLICY

1. Medications will be dispensed solely at the physician's discretion.
2. Medication orders must be written on the ED chart.
3. Medications should be labeled appropriately, including date, patient name, physician name, type of medication, expiration date, lot number, and instruction for use.

PROCEDURE

1. RN verifies written medication order on ED chart.
2. RN obtains medication from pharmacy and places in *childproof container.* The patient will be given no more than four doses of non-controlled or two doses of controlled substances.
3. RN fills out self-adhering medication label (see the following example) that includes
   a. patient's name
   b. date
   c. medication name, dosage, and amount
   d. direction for administration
   e. physician's name
   f. expiration date
   g. lot number
4. Prior to peeling off label, *have physician initial* at bottom to indicate that physician
   a. confirms accuracy of order
   b. confirms accuracy of instructions
   c. will adhere signed label to medication container
5. Physician or RN gives medication to the patient, including instructions for use.
6. The back sheet behind the label will serve as the pharmacy log sheet to meet the state's standards of control.
7. Medications are charged to the patient on the ED chart.

THE HOSPITAL EMERGENCY DEPARTMENT

DATE ____________________________________

PATIENT NAME ____________________________

DRUG ____________________________________

INSTRUCTIONS ____________________________

____

DR/RN INITIALS __________________________

Source: Aspen Publishers.

4-66 Medication Discrepancy Tool

Medication Discrepancy Tool (MDT)

MDT is designed to facilitate reconciliation of medication regimen across settings and prescribers

Medication Discrepancy Event Description: *Complete one form for each discrepancy*

✓ **Causes and Contributing Factors: Check all that apply:**

Italicized text suggests patient's perspective and/or intended meaning

Patient Level

1. ☐ Adverse Drug Reaction or side effects
2. ☐ Intolerance
3. ☐ Didn't fill prescription
4. ☐ Didn't need prescription
5. ☐ Money/financial barriers
6. ☐ Intentional non-adherence
   "I was told to take this but I choose not to."
7. ☐ Non-intentional non-adherence (ie:Knowledge deficit)
   "I don't understand how to take this medication."
8. ☐ Performance deficit
   "Maybe someone showed me, but I can't demonstrate to you that I can."

System Level

9. ☐ Prescribed with known allergies/intolerances
10. ☐ Conflicting information from different informational sources.
    For example, discharge instructions indicate one thing and pill bottle says another.
11. ☐ Confusion between brand & generic names
12. ☐ Discharge instructions incomplete/inaccurate/illegible.
    Either the patient cannot make out the hand- writing or the information is not written in lay terms.
13. ☐ Duplication.
    Taking multiple drugs with the same action without any rationale.
14. ☐ Incorrect dosage
15. ☐ Incorrect quantity
16. ☐ Incorrect label
17. ☐ Cognitive impairment not recognized
18. ☐ No caregiver/need for assistance not recognized
19. ☐ Sight/dexterity limitations not recognized

✓ **Resolution: Check all that apply:**

- ☐ Advised to stop taking/start taking/change administration of medications
- ☐ Discussed potential benefits and harm that may result from non-adherence
- ☐ Encouraged patient to call PCP/specialist about problem
- ☐ Encouraged patient to schedule an appointment with PCP/specialist to discuss problem at next visit
- ☐ Encouraged patient to talk to pharmacist about problem
- ☐ Addressed performance/knowledge deficit
- ☐ Provided resource information to facilitate adherence
- ☐ Other ______________________________

4-67 Management of Asthma Exacerbations During Pregnancy and Lactation: ED and Hospital-Based Care*

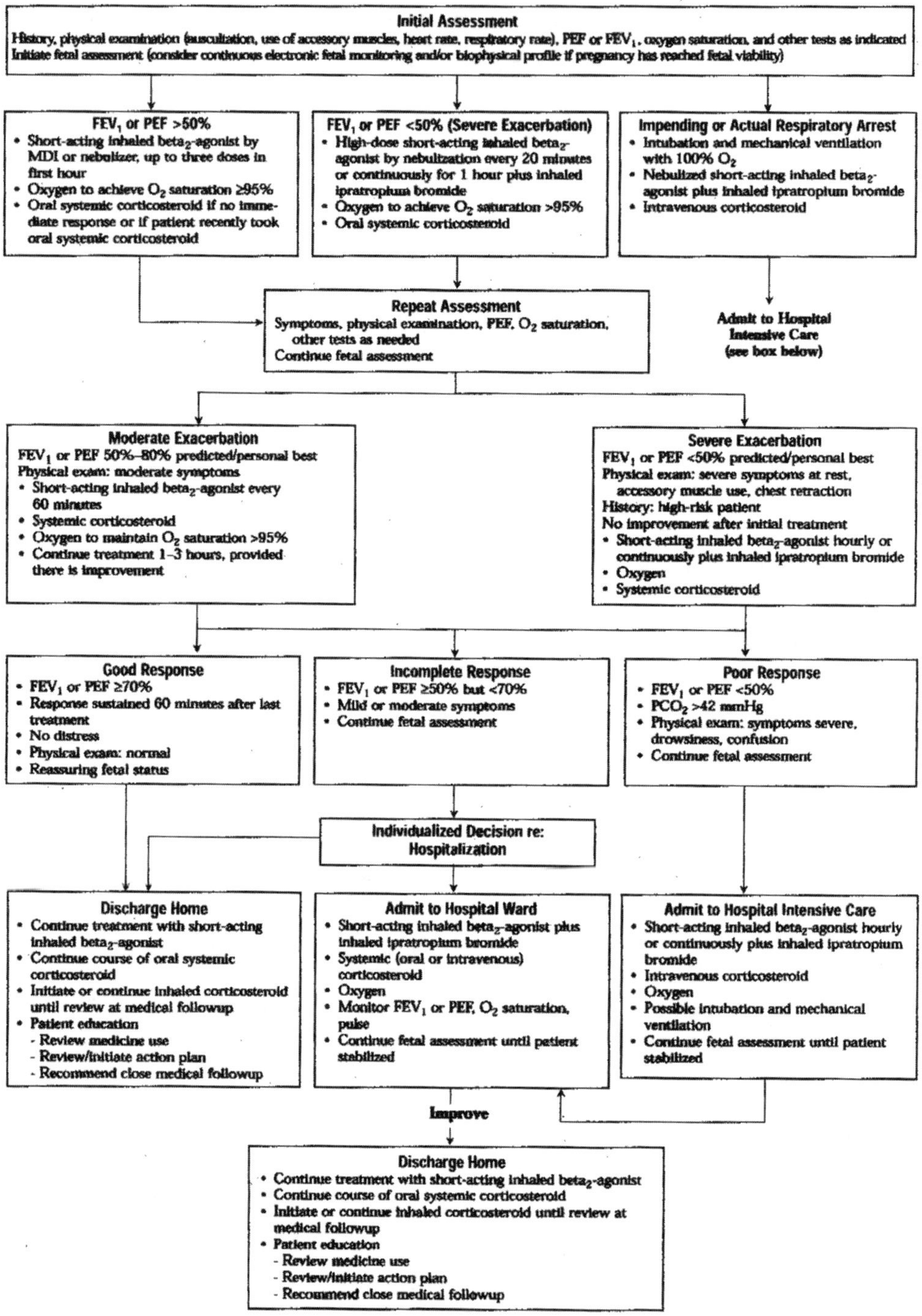

Medications and Dosages for Asthma Exacerbations During Pregnancy and Lactation*

Medications	Dosages		[illegible]
	Adult Dose	Child Dose	
Short-Acting Inhaled $Beta_2$-Agonists			
Albuterol Nebulizer solution (5.0 mg/mL, 2.5 mg/3mL, 1.25 mg/3mL, 0.63 mg/3 mL)	2.5–5 mg every 20 minutes for 3 doses, then 2.5–10 mg every 1–4 hours as needed, or 10–15 mg/hour continuously	0.15 mg/kg (minimum dose 2.5 mg) every 20 minutes for 3 doses, then 0.15–0.3 mg/kg up to 10 mg every 1–4 hours as needed, or 0.5 mg/kg/hour by continuous nebulization	Only selective $beta_2$-agonists are recommended. For optimal delivery, dilute aerosols to minimum of 3 mL at gas flow of 6–8 L/min.
MDI (90 mcg/puff)	4–8 puffs every 20 minutes up to 4 hours, then every 1–4 hours as needed	4–8 puffs every 20 minutes for 3 doses, then every 1–4 hours inhalation maneuver; use spacer/holding chamber	As effective as nebulized therapy if patient is able to coordinate.
Bitolterol Nebulizer solution (2 mg/mL)	See albuterol dose.	See albuterol dose; thought to be half as potent as albuterol on a mg basis.	Has not been studied in severe asthma exacerbations. Do not mix with other drugs.
MDI (370 mcg/puff)	See albuterol dose.	See albuterol dose.	Has not been studied in severe asthma exacerbations.
Levalbuterol (R-albuterol) Nebulizer solution (0.63 mg/3 mL, 1.25 mg/3 mL)	1.25–2.5 mg every 20 minutes for 3 doses, then 1.25–5 mg every 1–4 hours as needed, or 5–7.5 mg/hour continuously	0.075 mg/kg (minimum dose 1.25 mg) every 20 minutes for 3 doses, then 0.075–0.15 mg/kg up to 5 mg every 1–4 hours as needed, or 0.25 mg/kg/hour by continuous nebulization	0.63 mg of levalbuterol is equivalent to 1.25 mg of racemic albuterol for both efficacy and side effects.
Pirbuterol MDI (200 mcg/puff)	See albuterol dose.	See albuterol dose; thought to be half as potent as albuterol on a mg basis.	Has not been studied in severe asthma exacerbations.
Systemic (Injected) $Beta_2$-Agonists			
Epinephrine 1:1000 (1 mg/mL)	0.3–0.5 mg every 20 minutes for 3 doses sq	0.01 mg/kg up to 0.3–0.5 mg every 20 minutes for 3 doses sq	No proven advantage of systemic therapy over aerosol.
Terbutaline (1 mg/mL)	0.25 mg every 20 minutes for 3 doses sq	0.01 mg/kg every 20 minutes for 3 doses, then every 2–6 hours as needed sq	No proven advantage of systemic therapy over aerosol.
Anticholinergics			
Ipratropium bromide Nebulizer solution (0.25 mg/mL)	0.5 mg every 30 minutes for 3 doses, then every 2–4 hours as needed	0.25 mg every 20 minutes for 3 doses, then every 2 to 4 hours	May mix in same nebulizer with albuterol. Should not be used as first-line therapy; should be added to $beta_2$-agonist therapy.
MDI (18 mcg/puff)	4–8 puffs as needed	4–8 puffs as needed	Dose delivered from MDI is low and has not been studied in asthma exacerbations.
Ipratropium with albuterol Nebulizer solution (Each 3 mL vial contains 0.5 mg ipratropium bromide and 2.5 mg albuterol)	3 mL every 30 minutes for 3 doses, then every 2–4 hours as needed	1.5 mL every 20 minutes for 3 doses, then every 2–4 hours	Contains EDTA to prevent discoloration. This additive does not induce bronchospasm.
MDI (Each puff contains 18 mcg ipratropium bromide and 90 mcg albuterol)	4–8 puffs as needed	4–8 puffs as needed	
Systemic Corticosteroids	(Dosages and comments apply to all three corticosteroids)		
Prednisone **Methylprednisolone** **Prednisolone**	120–180 mg/day in 3 or 4 divided doses for 48 hours, then 60–80 mg/day until PEF reaches 70% of predicted or personal best	1 mg/kg every 6 hours for 48 hours, then 1–2 mg/kg/day (maximum = 60 mg/day) in 2 divided doses until PEF is 70% of predicted or personal best	For outpatient "burst" use 40–60 mg in single or 2 divided doses for adults (children: 1–2 mg/kg/day, maximum 60 mg/day) for 3–10 days.

* Adapted from EPR—Update 2002.

Notes:
- The most important determinant of appropriate dosing is the clinician's judgment of the patient's response to therapy.
- No advantage has been found for higher dose corticosteroids in severe asthma exacerbations, nor is there any advantage for intravenous administration over oral therapy provided gastrointestinal transit time or absorption is not impaired. The usual regimen is to continue the frequent multiple daily dose until the patient achieves an FEV_1 or PEF of 50 percent of predicted or personal best and then lower the dose to twice daily. This usually occurs within 48 hours. Therapy following a hospitalization or emergency department visit may last from 3 to 10 days. If patients are then started on inhaled corticosteroids, studies indicate there is no need to taper the systemic corticosteroid dose. If the followup systemic corticosteroid therapy is to be given once daily, one study indicates that it may be more clinically effective to give the dose in the afternoon at 3 p.m., with no increase in adrenal suppression.[54]

Source: National Asthma Education and Prevention Program Working Group Report on Managing Asthma During Pregnancy: Recommendations for Pharmacologic Treatment

Update 2004. U.S. Department of Health and Human Services, National Institutes of Health, National Heart, Lung, and Blood Institute. NIH Publication No. 05-5246. Originally Printed March 2004. Revised January 2005.

4-68 Policy and Procedure: Moderate Sedation by Non-Anesthesiologists

I. SUBJECT

Management of Patients Undergoing Procedures Receiving Moderate Sedation by Non-anesthesiologists.

II. PURPOSE

To provide a uniform hospital-wide standard of care for all patients undergoing Moderate Sedation by non-anesthesiologists.

III. DEFINITIONS

Sedation and Analgesia

Moderate Sedation is the administration of pharmacologic agents to provide a minimally depressed level of consciousness yet allow the patient to independently and continuously maintain an airway and respond to physical stimulation and verbal commands. The purpose of Moderate Sedation is to enhance the patient's comfort during therapeutic and diagnostic procedures.

Specifically excluded from governance by this policy are patients on life support, patients under the direct care of the formally organized Department of Anesthesia, patients receiving night-time sleep Sedation, other Sedation given on an inpatient nursing unit, pre-operative Sedation, or narcotics for pain.

IV. RESPONSIBILITY/CRITERIA

It is the responsibility of the physician performing the procedure to manage patients receiving Moderate Sedation.

The physician performing the procedure shall determine whether Moderate Sedation shall be used during any given procedure.

The physician performing the procedure must: 1) assess the needs of the patient and the demands of the procedure, 2) choose Moderate Sedation, and 3) appropriately monitor the patient.

For Moderate Sedation, the physician performing the procedure shall include pertinent history and physical on the record for the procedure. Consideration for NPO status and risk of aspiration shall be given prior to any Moderate Sedation procedure.

Nursing support shall be appropriate for the procedure.

Since Moderate Sedation may convert unexpectedly to Deep Sedation at any time, it is recommended that the Code Blue cart and defibrillator shall be available.

V. MODERATE SEDATION PROCEDURE

This policy shall be followed in conjunction with unit-specific protocols related to the specific procedure being performed.

1. Procedures requiring Moderate Sedation must meet the criteria in Section IV.
2. Moderate Sedation may be administered in all patient care areas satisfying the criteria stated in Section IV.
3. Administration of Moderate Sedation must be given in the presence of the physician performing the procedure he/she is credentialed to perform;
   a. individuals responsible for patients receiving Moderate Sedation shall understand the pharmacology of the agents that are administered, as well as the role of pharmacologic antagonists for opioids and benzodiazepines. Individuals monitoring patients receiving Moderate Sedation shall be able to recognize the associated complications. At least one individual capable of establishing a patent airway and positive pressure ventilation, as well as a means for summoning additional assistance, shall be present whenever Moderate Sedation is administered;
   b. Credentialing for a procedure assumes this competency;
   c. Anesthesia personnel and a code blue team are available 24 hours a day.
4. Moderate Sedation may be administered by appropriately licensed health care personnel who have documented competency in the administration and care of the patient undergoing Moderate Sedation;
5. The ongoing assessment process will be performed by a registered nurse or the physician performing the procedure. A designated individual other than the physician performing the procedure shall be present to monitor the patient throughout the procedure. This individual may assist with minor, interruptible tasks which do not interfere with such monitoring;
6. All medications given for Moderate Sedation during procedures will be written on the physician order sheet and will be signed by the physician according to current Hospital policy;
7. Only medications that are approved in the Hospital formulary will be given. Utilization of these drugs will be according to protocol acceptable to the Pharmacy and Therapeutics Committee;
8. The physician performing the procedure shall be physically available until patient's discharge from the procedure area;
9. The patient is discharged to the appropriate unit or home according to current Hospital policy post procedure;
10. Quality Assessment and Improvement: Monitoring of procedures performed with Moderate Sedation will be done according to the Hospital's Quality Assessment and Improvement Process. Summary results will be submitted to the Medical Staff's Anesthesia Department CQI Committee at regularly-defined intervals and the Quality Improvement Council as required.

VI. REQUIRED ELEMENTS

Pre-Assessment will include verification and documentation of:

1. Informed consent;
2. Relevant physician history and physical;

3. Nursing assessment:
   a. allergies to medications;
   b. level of consciousness;
   c. denture status;
   d. baseline vital signs;
   e. NPO status

Equipment needed includes:

1. Pulse oximeter;
2. Blood pressure cuff;
3. Sedation of choice;
4. Narcan-Mazicon;
5. IV access for IV Sedation;
6. Cardiac monitor available;
7. Oxygen setup with mask, nasal cannula and ambu bag available;
8. Suction setup with Yankauer available;
9. Code Blue cart and defibrillator available.

Intra-Procedure Assessment
Patients' ventilatory and oxygenation status and hemodynamic variables shall be recorded at a frequency to be determined by the type and amount of medication administered as well as the length of the procedure and the general condition of the patient. At a minimum, this should be 1) before the beginning of the procedure, 2) after administration of sedative and analgesic agents, 3) on completion of the procedure, 4) during initial recovery, and 5) at the time of discharge. If recording is performed automatically, device alarms should be set to alert the care team to critical changes in patient status.

1. Vital signs (BP, pulse and respirations) shall be measured at regular intervals, not less than Q15 minutes;
2. S_pO_2 will be monitored continuously and recorded Q15 minutes;
   a. equipment to administer supplemental oxygen shall be present when Moderate Sedation is administered. If hypoxemia is anticipated or develops during Moderate Sedation, supplemental oxygen shall be administered.
3. Monitoring of patient response to verbal and/or tactile stimulation shall be periodic (Q15 minutes);
4. Ventilatory function shall be monitored continually by observation and/or auscultation and recorded Q15 minutes;
5. Electrocardiographic monitoring shall be used in patients with significant cardiovascular disease as well as during procedures in which dysrhythmias are anticipated;

   Items 1-5 may be recorded in the doctor's progress notes, nursing notes, or procedure records.
6. Intravenous sedative and analgesic drugs should be given in small, incremental doses that are titrated to the desired endpoints of Moderate Sedation. Sufficient time must elapse between doses to allow the effect of each dose to be assessed before subsequent drug administration. When drugs are administered by non-intravenous routes (e.g., oral, rectal, intramuscular), allowance should be made for the time required for drug absorption before supplementation is considered.

7. In patients receiving intravenous medications for Moderate Sedation, vascular access shall be maintained throughout the procedure and until the patient is no longer at risk for cardiorespiratory depression. In patients who have received Moderate Sedation by non-intravenous routes or whose intravenous line has become dislodged or blocked, the physician performing the procedure shall determine the advisability of establishing or reestablishing intravenous access on a case-by-case basis. In all instances, an individual with the skills to establish intravenous access should be immediately available.
8. Specific antagonists shall be available whenever opioid analgesics or benzodiazepines are administered for Moderate Sedation. Naloxone and/or flumazenil may be administered to improve spontaneous ventilatory efforts in patients who have received opioids or benzodiazepines, respectively. This may be especially helpful in cases in which airway control and positive pressure ventilation are difficult. Before or concomitantly with pharmacologic reversal, patients who became hypoxemic or apneic during Moderate Sedation shall: 1) be encouraged or stimulated to breathe deeply, 2) receive positive pressure ventilation if spontaneous ventilation is inadequate, and 3) receive supplemental oxygen. After pharmacologic reversal, patients shall be observed long enough to ensure that cardiorespiratory depression does not recur.
9. Whenever possible, appropriate medical specialists should be consulted before administration of Moderate Sedation to patients with significant underlying conditions. The choice of specialists depends on the nature of the underlying condition and the urgency of the situation. For significantly compromised patients (e.g., severe obstructive pulmonary disease, coronary artery disease, congestive heart failure) or if it appears likely that Moderate Sedation to the point of unresponsiveness or general anesthesia will be necessary to obtain adequate conditions, physicians who are not specifically qualified to provide these modalities should consult an anesthesiologist.

Post-Procedure Assessment/Discharge Criteria

After Moderate Sedation, patients shall be observed until they are no longer at increased risk for cardiorespiratory depression. Vital signs and respiratory function shall be monitored at designated intervals until patients are suitable for discharge. Discharge criteria should be designed to minimize the risk of central nervous system or cardiorespiratory depression after discharge from observation by trained personnel.

The patient may be discharged from the procedure area to an in-house patient care area when the five-point Aldrete score is > 8 (8 to 10):

Modified Post-Anesthetic Recovery (PAR) score for patients having anesthesia on ambulatory basis:

I.	Able to move 4 extremities voluntarily or on command	2	
	Able to move 2 extremities voluntarily or on command	1	ACTIVITY
	Unable to move extremities voluntarily or on command	0	
II.	Able to breathe deeply and cough freely	2	
	Dyspnea, limited breathing or tachypnea	1	RESPIRATION
	Apneic or on mechanical ventilator	0	

III.	BP plus or minus 20% of pre-anesthetic level	2	
	BP plus or minus 20-49% of pre-anesthetic level	1	CIRCULATION
	BP plus or minus 50% of pre-anesthetic level	0	
IV.	Fully awake	2	
	Arousable on calling	1	CONSCIOUSNESS
	Not responding	0	
V.	Able to maintain O_2 saturation > 90% on room air	2	
	Needs O_2 inhalation to maintain O_2 saturation > 90%	1	O_2 SATURATION
	O_2 saturation < 90% even with O_2 supplement	0	

The patient may be discharged from the Hospital when the 10-point Aldrete score is > 18 (18 to 20).

VI.	Dry and clean	2	
	Wet but stationary or marked	1	DRESSING
	Growing area of wetness	0	
VII.	Pain free	2	
	Mild pain handled by oral medication	1	PAIN
	Severe pain requiring parenteral medication	0	
VIII.	Able to stand up and walk straight*	2	
	Vertigo when erect	1	AMBULATION
	Dizziness when supine	0	
IX.	Able to drink fluids	2	
	Nauseated	1	FASTING-FEEDING
	Nausea and vomiting	0	
X.	Has voided	2	
	Unable to void but comfortable	1	URINE OUTPUT
	Unable to void and uncomfortable	0	

*May be substituted by Romberg's test, or picking up 12 clips in one hand.

These standards are acceptable minimum criteria. Unit-specific protocols mandating measures in excess of these are appropriate.

VII. PERFORMANCE IMPROVEMENT (PI)

The PI monitoring tool attached shall be used for monitoring Moderate Sedation procedures. The results shall be summarized and submitted to the Medical Staff Anesthesia Department CQI Committee at regularly-defined intervals. Appropriate peer review shall be directed to department chairs for review. PI shall be reported to Quality Improvement Council per reporting schedule as required.

APPENDIX
GUIDE TO DOSAGES FOR MODERATE SEDATION

Intravenous sedative and analgesic drugs should be given in small, incremental doses that are titrated to the desired endpoints of Moderate Sedation. Sufficient time must elapse between doses to allow the effect of each dose to be assessed before subsequent drug administration. When drugs are administered by non-intravenous routes (e.g., oral, rectal,

intramuscular), allowance should be made for the time required for drug absorption before supplementation is considered.

ADULT PATIENTS

1.	Diazepam (Valium)	2.5 to 5 mg
2.	Midazolam (Versed)	1 to 2 mg
3.	Morphine Sulfate	1 to 5 mg
4.	Meperidine HCL (Demerol)	25 mg
5.	Sublimaze (Fentanyl)	2 micrograms/kilogram
6.	Naloxone (Narcan)	0.1 to 0.4 mg
7.	Flumazenil (Romazicon)	0.2 mg

PEDIATRIC PATIENTS

1.	Chloral Hydrate	75 mg/kg p.o.
2.	Diazepam (Valium)	0.04 to 0.3 mg/kg
3.	Midazelam (Versed)	0.02 to 0.05 mg/kg
4.	Morphine Sulfate	0.05 to 0.1 mg/kg
5.	Sublimaze (Fentanyl)	1-2 micrograms/kilogram
6.	Naloxone (Narcan)	5 to 10 micrograms/kg Q 3-5 min
7.	Flumazenil (Romazicon)	0.2 mg IV over 15 seconds, repeat Q 1 min., up to 1 mg total dose

Adjustment of the above dosages on a time-weighted basis is the responsibility of the physician performing the procedure.

This guide is not meant to be exhaustive. As new drugs become available and are appropriate for use during Moderate Sedation, it will be the responsibility of the physician performing the procedure to incorporate such drugs into practice.

Source: Adapted from Holy Cross Hospital, Silver Spring, Maryland.

4-69 Ketamine: Emergency Applications

PURPOSE

The purpose of an emergency department protocol for ketamine is to define the guidelines for the administration, monitoring, and recovery of patients undergoing sedation with ketamine.

Introduction

Ketamine produces a unique sedative state that is characterized by the following:

- Dissociation: Following administration of ketamine, the patient rapidly passes into a trance. This trance is first characterized by nystagmus and a glassy-eyed stare. The patient's eyes usually remain open, but the patient does not respond.
  This state is unique to ketamine and is termed dissociation because, while brainstem function is maintained normally, higher cognitive awareness is disconnected from somatic sensory input. Because brainstem function is preserved, normal or slightly enhanced muscle tone is maintained. On occasion, the patient may move or be moved into a position that is self-maintaining.

- Analgesia: Ketamine produces profound somatic analgesia that is adequate for most surgical procedures.
- Amnesia: Ketamine produces a complete lack of recall of events and procedures performed under sedation.
- Maintenance of airway and breathing reflexes: Upper airway reflexes remain intact and active. Airway reflexes are preserved in a manner superior to most other sedative agents. Sonorous respirations are observed frequently and may be managed by repositioning the patient's head and airway. Stimulation of the vocal cords by instrumentation or secretions rarely produces mild laryngospasm. Brief apnea may occur (albeit rarely) when ketamine is administered via rapid IV push.
- Cardiorespiratory stability: Unlike other sedatives, ketamine usually causes cardiac stimulation, not depression. Therefore, it is a preferred agent in patients who are hypotensive but still require sedation.

POLICY

Ketamine may be administered only by a physician specifically credentialed to administer Ketamine. Ketamine may be used for the sedation and analgesia of children and adult patients in the ED. *It is important to understand that Ketamine is an anesthetic agent.* Ketamine is appropriate for painful procedures, such as dressing changes, central line or chest tube placement, cardioversion, rapid sequence intubation, orthopedic manipulation, and emergency surgical procedures. Ketamine is suitable for most age groups provided that the physician supervising its use is versed in its age-related effects and contraindications. (Emergence phenomena are less frequently dramatic in children and elderly patients, and apnea is observed more frequently in children <3 mo.) Ketamine is relatively contraindicated in the following cases:

- Airway instability or tracheal pathology (unless used with endotracheal intubation to provide a higher margin of safety)
- High predisposition to laryngospasm or apnea (active pulmonary infection or children <3 mo)
- A full meal within last 3 hours (because of higher aspiration risk)
- Severe cardiovascular disease, such as angina, heart failure, or malignant hypertension (because of cardiostimulant effects of ketamine; however, this is controversial)
- CSF obstructive states (e.g., severe head injury, central congenital, or mass lesions; however, this is controversial)
- Intraocular pressure pathology (e.g., glaucoma or acute globe injury; however, this is controversial)
- Previous psychotic illness (because of potential activation of psychoses)
- Hyperthyroidism or thyroid medication use (because of potential for severe tachycardia or hypertension)
- Porphyria (because of possibility of triggering a porphyric reaction)

These are relative contraindications, and most are unconfirmed by rigorous methods. In cases necessitating emergency sedation, the benefits of ketamine may outweigh the risks listed above, particularly if substituting other sedative agents brings greater risks. The literature demonstrates that ketamine has a safety profile that outperforms many other sedative agents. This makes it the agent of choice for many potentially difficult emergency situations.

Potential adverse effects

Potential adverse effects of ketamine administration include hypersalivation, muscle hypertonicity, transient clonus, transient stridor, emesis, transient rash, and agitation.

PROCEDURE

Prior to administration of ketamine, chart an initial patient assessment with weight, vital signs, initial oxygen saturation, and baseline level of consciousness. As with all sedative techniques, make resuscitative equipment for advanced airway management readily available and initiate and continue pulse oximetry with audible alarms until the patient meets recovery criteria. (In regions without pulse oximetry, ketamine is not contraindicated and is preferred over sedation with other agents.) If possible, place the patient in a private treatment room to minimize stimulation during the recovery period. During the procedure, ensure that medical staff continuously attends the patient. Once the procedure is complete and the recovery period is well underway, ensure that staff or family members attend the patient until recovery criteria are met.

Some clinicians routinely premedicate all patients with promethazine or a benzodiazepine to reduce postprocedure agitation, though this may greatly prolong the recovery period. Promethazine is used widely in Africa for adult premedication and may have some advantage over the benzodiazepines because of its additional antiemetic effects; however, controlled studies are lacking. Ketamine may be combined with an antisialagogue to reduce its stimulant effect on oral and respiratory secretions. Either glycopyrrolate, in a dose of 0.01 mg/kg (not to exceed 0.2 mg), or atropine, in a dose of 0.01 mg/kg (0.1 mg minimum, not to exceed 0.5 mg), is acceptable. Pretreatment 30 minutes prior to ketamine administration is best; however, both glycopyrrolate and atropine may be mixed in the same syringe as ketamine if time is short.

Some physicians forego the use of an antisialagogue (more often in adults), preferring ketamine-induced hypersalivation to the additional tachycardia caused by atropine or glycopyrrolate.

Ketamine may be dosed via IM injection, IV injection or infusion, intranasal drops, rectal injection, or oral elixir. For children, IM injection is usually the least traumatic method of obtaining effective sedation, and it may be safely performed without routine need for IV access. For adults, continuous IV infusion is usually the safest and most easily titratable to effect.

IM ketamine is usually dosed initially at 4 mg/kg (with a typical range of 2-10 mg/kg, depending on procedural requirements). Analgesia alone is usually obtained with a dose of 1 mg/kg IM. Complete dissociation is usually obtained with a dose of 4-10 mg/kg IM. Onset of action (glazed eyes and nystagmus) usually occurs within 5 minutes and lasts for up to 30 minutes, depending on the dose used. Prior to beginning any painful procedure, test analgesic effect by pricking the patient with a needle. Booster doses of 2-5 mg/kg IM every 10 minutes (without additional antisialagogue) may be administered if initial sedation is inadequate. A 100 mg/mL ketamine solution is preferred for IM administration to reduce the volume of injected solution.

Perform IV infusion of ketamine by mixing ketamine with saline or D5W to make a 1 mg/mL solution (500 mg ketamine in 500 mL fluid). To prevent inadvertent overdosage, the total amount of ketamine mixed can be limited to the maximum safe dosage (3 mg/kg IV).

Using a regular nonmicrodrip IV chamber (15 drops/mL), open the IV to flow at a rapid drop rate (about 2 drops/kg/min). Onset of action (glazed eyes and nystagmus) usually occurs within 2 minutes and lasts until 10 minutes after the infusion is terminated. Prior to beginning any painful procedure, test analgesic effect by pricking the patient with a needle. Once sedation is deep enough, turn down the drip to approximately one half of the induction rate (1 drop/kg/min). Stop the drip 10 minutes prior to the end of the procedure.

IV slow bolus injection is the most commonly used alternative to the 2 methods described above. Initially dose ketamine IV bolus at 1 mg/kg (with a typical range of 0.5-2 mg/kg, depending on procedural requirements). Onset of action (glazed eyes and nystagmus) usually occurs within 1 minute. Surgical anesthesia lasts about 15 minutes, with full recovery in about 60 minutes. As above, prior to beginning any painful procedure, test analgesic effect by pricking the patient with a needle. Booster doses of 0.5-1 mg/kg IV every 10 minutes (without additional antisialagogue) may be administered if initial sedation is inadequate. The maximum dose for routine use is 3 mg/kg, except in patients with alcoholism, who may require much more. The more dilute 10-50 mg/mL ketamine solutions are preferred for IV administration. Perform the injection slowly to avoid ketamine-induced apnea (rare).

It is important to note that in some states nurse practice acts do not allow nurses to administer ketamine because it is considered an anesthetic agent. Check your state law for clarification.

Recovery guidelines

In many studies, the incidence of unpleasant emergence experiences is less than 1% in adults and children. Unless safer methods of sedation are available, the fear of the ketamine recovery experience should not preclude its use. Indeed, management of this period requires a certain finesse that may separate the physician experienced in ketamine sedation from the novice. Because of the unique effects of dissociation, patients undergoing ketamine sedation experience a sense of semiconscious bodily detachment as they awaken. During this period, imagination can be confused with actual environmental stimuli. Partially conducted stimuli may be interpreted as pleasant or not. Because of this, the physician potentially has much control of the patient's recovery experience and may direct this experience positively by simple and repeated suggestion and by controlling the recovery environment.

By the same mechanism, misinterpreted or noxious stimuli may cause patients to have a frightening recovery. During this period, minimize physical contact, noise, and stimulation and instruct caretakers not to awaken the patient prematurely. Blood pressure monitoring during this period is discouraged by some anesthesiologists who note undue disruption of recovery from cuff stimulation. Recovery reactions are less frequently dramatic in children and patients who are elderly.

For patients who are recovering poorly, administration of any number of sleep-inducing agents during recovery is helpful. Patients at high risk for agitated recovery can be medicated prior to initiation of the procedure. Such agents sedate the active but partially dissociated mind, blunting the confusion between imagination and reality. If such medication is used, promethazine is effective and provides antiemetic effects. Many practitioners in developing countries consider it to be the drug of choice. Lorazepam, droperidol, haloperidol, and midazolam demonstrate efficacy as well. Diazepam has a variable effect in different studies. Note that sedative agents are not essential for smooth recovery. By using reassurance alone, adult patients in one series experienced no unpleasant reactions during recovery from ketamine sedation.

Recovery criteria

Anticipated recovery time is 0.5-2 hours following administration of ketamine. The patient may be discharged from the hospital when all of the following criteria are met:

- At least 30 minutes has passed since the administration of ketamine.
- The patient's level of consciousness has returned to baseline. (Note that the level of consciousness may be depressed normally following the procedure because of fatigue, and a guardian may be able to validate normal behavior for the patient under these circumstances.)
- The patient is able to stand unassisted without falling.

The physician should record the patient's level of consciousness, as well as the patient's ability to stand, at the time of discharge. Discharge a patient in the company of a guardian or other caregiver. The physician should advise the caregiver that the patient may vomit and have mild disequilibrium, and that the patient should not be administered anything by mouth and not be allowed independent ambulation for 2 hours after discharge. Restrict driving for a full day following ketamine administration.

Source: Excerpted from James Li, MD, "Ketamine: Emergency Application," eMedicine Journal.

4-70 Pain Management: Rating/Medication Administration Record

Month:__________________ Year:______

Instructions: Complete this form as you would complete a Medication Administration Record (MAR) document specifying the pain site, pain rating, & post treatment pain rating. (see other side for Pain Scale)

Pain Rating Scale used: **W** ONG-BAKER SCALE **N**UMERICAL SCALE **F**LACC SCALE

Medication	Date:	Date:	Date:	Date:	Date:	Date:	Date:
	Scale___ Level___ Pain Site________ ________ Time_____ am pm Initial________ **RESULTS:** Scale___ Level___ Time_____ am pm Initial________	Scale___ Level___ Pain Site________ ________ Time_____ am pm Initial________ **RESULTS:** Scale___ Level___ Time_____ am pm Initial________	Scale___ Level___ Pain Site________ ________ Time_____ am pm Initial________ **RESULTS:** Scale___ Level___ Time_____ am pm Initial________	Scale___ Level___ Pain Site________ ________ Time_____ am pm Initial________ **RESULTS:** Scale___ Level___ Time_____ am pm Initial________	Scale___ Level___ Pain Site________ ________ Time_____ am pm Initial________ **RESULTS:** Scale___ Level___ Time_____ am pm Initial________	Scale___ Level___ Pain Site________ ________ Time_____ am pm Initial________ **RESULTS:** Scale___ Level___ Time_____ am pm Initial________	Scale___ Level___ Pain Site________ ________ Time_____ am pm Initial________ **RESULTS:** Scale___ Level___ Time_____ am pm Initial________
Medication	Date:	Date:	Date:	Date:	Date:	Date:	Date:
	Scale___ Level___ Pain Site________ ________ Time_____ am pm Initial________ **RESULTS:** Scale___ Level___ Time_____ am pm Initial________	Scale___ Level___ Pain Site________ ________ Time_____ am pm Initial________ **RESULTS:** Scale___ Level___ Time_____ am pm Initial________	Scale___ Level___ Pain Site________ ________ Time_____ am pm Initial________ **RESULTS:** Scale___ Level___ Time_____ am pm Initial________	Scale___ Level___ Pain Site________ ________ Time_____ am pm Initial________ **RESULTS:** Scale___ Level___ Time_____ am pm Initial________	Scale___ Level___ Pain Site________ ________ Time_____ am pm Initial________ **RESULTS:** Scale___ Level___ Time_____ am pm Initial________	Scale___ Level___ Pain Site________ ________ Time_____ am pm Initial________ **RESULTS:** Scale___ Level___ Time_____ am pm Initial________	Scale___ Level___ Pain Site________ ________ Time_____ am pm Initial________ **RESULTS:** Scale___ Level___ Time_____ am pm Initial________
Medication	Date:	Date:	Date:	Date:	Date:	Date:	Date:
	Scale___ Level___ Pain Site________ ________ Time_____ am pm Initial________ **RESULTS:** Scale___ Level___ Time_____ am pm Initial________	Scale___ Level___ Pain Site________ ________ Time_____ am pm Initial________ **RESULTS:** Scale___ Level___ Time_____ am pm Initial________	Scale___ Level___ Pain Site________ ________ Time_____ am pm Initial________ **RESULTS:** Scale___ Level___ Time_____ am pm Initial________	Scale___ Level___ Pain Site________ ________ Time_____ am pm Initial________ **RESULTS:** Scale___ Level___ Time_____ am pm Initial________	Scale___ Level___ Pain Site________ ________ Time_____ am pm Initial________ **RESULTS:** Scale___ Level___ Time_____ am pm Initial________	Scale___ Level___ Pain Site________ ________ Time_____ am pm Initial________ **RESULTS:** Scale___ Level___ Time_____ am pm Initial________	Scale___ Level___ Pain Site________ ________ Time_____ am pm Initial________ **RESULTS:** Scale___ Level___ Time_____ am pm Initial________

Resident Name:______________________________ Room #__________ Doctor:______________________________ Side 1 of 2

Diagnosis:____

General Instructions:

1. Choose only one appropriate scale based upon the resident's ability to respond.
2. Identify the scale used and the score for that scale on the other side of this form by using the following key:

W ONG-BAKER SCALE

N UMERICAL SCALE

F LACC SCALE

Side 2 of 2
of Pain Management: Rating / **MEDICATION** Administration Record

WONG-BAKER SCALE:

Initial Instructions: Explain to the resident that each face is for a person who feels happy because he or she has no pain (hurt) or sad because he or she has some or a lot of pain. **FACE 0** is happy because he or she doesn't hurt at all. **FACE 2** hurts just a little bit **FACE 4** hurts a little more. **FACE 6** hurts even more. **FACE 8** hurts a whole lot. **FACE 10** hurts as much as you can imagine, although you don't have to be crying to feel this bad. Ask the resident to choose the face that best describes how he or she is feeling.

NO HURT	HURTS LITTLE BIT	HURTS LITTLE MORE	HURTS EVEN MORE	HURTS WHOLE LOT	HURTS WORST
0	2	4	6	8	10

NUMERIC SCALE: Choose a number from 0 to 10 that best describes the level of pain.

0	2	4	6	8	10
NO PAIN	MILD PAIN, ANNOYING Pain is present but does not limit activity.	NAGGING PAIN, UNCOMFORTABLE, TROUBLESOME Can do most activities with rest periods.	MISERABLE, DISTRESSING Unable to do some activities because of pain.	INTENSE, DREADFUL, HORRIBLE Unable to do most activities because of pain.	WORST PAIN POSSIBLE, UNBEARABLE Unable to do any activities because

0 1 2 3 4 5 6 7 8 9 10

FLACC SCALE:

Initial Instructions: The FLACC is a behavior pain assessment scale for use with nonverbal residents who are unable to provide reports of pain. Rate the resident in each of the five measurement categories, add the scores together, and document the total pain score.

	0	1	2
FACE	No particular expression of smile.	Occasional grimace or frown, withdrawn, disinterested.	Frequent to constant frown, clenched jaw, quivering chin.
LEGS	Normal Position or relaxed.	Uneasy, restless, tense.	Kicking, or legs drawn up.
ACTIVITY	Lying quietly, normal position, moves easily.	Squirming, shifting back and forth, tense.	Arched, rigid, or jerking.
CRY	No crying (awake or asleep).	Moans or whimpers, occasional complaint	Crying steadily, screams or sobs, frequent complaints.
CONSOLABILITY	Content, relaxed.	Reassured by occasional touching, hugging, or "talking to." Distractible.	Difficult to console or comfort.

Source: Best Practices Committee, *HCANJ Pain Management Guidelines*, 1/05 Revision. Health Care Association of New Jersey, Hamilton, New Jersey. Reprinted with permission.

4-71 Pain Management: Rating/Treatment Administration Record

Instructions: Complete this form as you would complete a Medication Administration Record (MAR) document specifying the pain site, pain rating, & post treatment pain rating. (see other side for Pain Scale)

Pain Rating Scale used: **W** ONG-BAKER SCALE **N**UMERICAL SCALE **F**LACC SCALE

Treatment	Date:	Date:	Date:	Date:	Date:	Date:	Date:
	Scale___ Level___ Pain Site________ ____________ Time_____ am pm Initial__________ **RESULTS:** Scale___ Level___ Time_____ am pm Initial__________	Scale___ Level___ Pain Site________ ____________ Time_____ am pm Initial__________ **RESULTS:** Scale___ Level___ Time_____ am pm Initial__________	Scale___ Level___ Pain Site________ ____________ Time_____ am pm Initial__________ **RESULTS:** Scale___ Level___ Time_____ am pm Initial__________	Scale___ Level___ Pain Site________ ____________ Time_____ am pm Initial__________ **RESULTS:** Scale___ Level___ Time_____ am pm Initial__________	Scale___ Level___ Pain Site________ ____________ Time_____ am pm Initial__________ **RESULTS:** Scale___ Level___ Time_____ am pm Initial__________	Scale___ Level___ Pain Site________ ____________ Time_____ am pm Initial__________ **RESULTS:** Scale___ Level___ Time_____ am pm Initial__________	Scale___ Level___ Pain Site________ ____________ Time_____ am pm Initial__________ **RESULTS:** Scale___ Level___ Time_____ am pm Initial__________
Treatment	Date:	Date:	Date:	Date:	Date:	Date:	Date:
	Scale___ Level___ Pain Site________ ____________ Time_____ am pm Initial__________ **RESULTS:** Scale___ Level___ Time_____ am pm Initial__________	Scale___ Level___ Pain Site________ ____________ Time_____ am pm Initial__________ **RESULTS:** Scale___ Level___ Time_____ am pm Initial__________	Scale___ Level___ Pain Site________ ____________ Time_____ am pm Initial__________ **RESULTS:** Scale___ Level___ Time_____ am pm Initial__________	Scale___ Level___ Pain Site________ ____________ Time_____ am pm Initial__________ **RESULTS:** Scale___ Level___ Time_____ am pm Initial__________	Scale___ Level___ Pain Site________ ____________ Time_____ am pm Initial__________ **RESULTS:** Scale___ Level___ Time_____ am pm Initial__________	Scale___ Level___ Pain Site________ ____________ Time_____ am pm Initial__________ **RESULTS:** Scale___ Level___ Time_____ am pm Initial__________	Scale___ Level___ Pain Site________ ____________ Time_____ am pm Initial__________ **RESULTS:** Scale___ Level___ Time_____ am pm Initial__________
Treatment	Date:	Date:	Date:	Date:	Date:	Date:	Date:
	Scale___ Level___ Pain Site________ ____________ Time_____ am pm Initial__________ **RESULTS:** Scale___ Level___ Time_____ am pm Initial__________	Scale___ Level___ Pain Site________ ____________ Time_____ am pm Initial__________ **RESULTS:** Scale___ Level___ Time_____ am pm Initial__________	Scale___ Level___ Pain Site________ ____________ Time_____ am pm Initial__________ **RESULTS:** Scale___ Level___ Time_____ am pm Initial__________	Scale___ Level___ Pain Site________ ____________ Time_____ am pm Initial__________ **RESULTS:** Scale___ Level___ Time_____ am pm Initial__________	Scale___ Level___ Pain Site________ ____________ Time_____ am pm Initial__________ **RESULTS:** Scale___ Level___ Time_____ am pm Initial__________	Scale___ Level___ Pain Site________ ____________ Time_____ am pm Initial__________ **RESULTS:** Scale___ Level___ Time_____ am pm Initial__________	Scale___ Level___ Pain Site________ ____________ Time_____ am pm Initial__________ **RESULTS:** Scale___ Level___ Time_____ am pm Initial__________

Resident Name:______________________ Room #__________ Doctor:______________________ Side 1 of 2

Diagnosis:____

General Instructions:

1. Choose <u>only one</u> appropriate scale based upon the resident's ability to respond.
2. Identify the scale used and the score for that scale on the other side of this form by using the following key:

W ONG-BAKER SCALE

N UMERICAL SCALE

F LACC SCALE

Side 2 of 2
of Pain Management: Rating /
TREATMENT Administration Record

WONG-BAKER SCALE:

Initial Instructions: Explain to the resident that each face is for a person who feels happy because he or she has no pain (hurt) or sad because he or she has some or a lot of pain. **FACE 0** is happy because he or she doesn't hurt at all. **FACE 2** hurts just a little bit **FACE 4** hurts a little more. **FACE 6** hurts even more. **FACE 8** hurts a whole lot. **FACE 10** hurts as much as you can imagine, although you don't have to be crying to feel this bad. Ask the resident to choose the face that best describes how he or she is feeling.

NO HURT	HURTS LITTLE BIT	HURTS LITTLE MORE	HURTS EVEN MORE	HURTS WHOLE LOT	HURTS WORST
0	2	4	6	8	10

NUMERIC SCALE: Choose a number from 0 to 10 that best describes the level of pain.

0	1	2	3	4	5	6	7	8	9	10
NO PAIN		MILD PAIN, ANNOYING Pain is present but does not limit activity.		NAGGING PAIN, UNCOMFORTABLE, TROUBLESOME Can do most activities with rest periods.		MISERABLE, DISTRESSING Unable to do some activities because of pain.		INTENSE, DREADFUL, HORRIBLE Unable to do most activities because of pain.		WORST PAIN POSSIBLE, UNBEARABLE Unable to do any activities because

FLACC SCALE:

Initial Instructions: The FLACC is a behavior pain assessment scale for use with nonverbal residents who are unable to provide reports of pain. Rate the resident in each of the five measurement categories, add the scores together, and document the total pain score.

	0	1	2
FACE	No particular expression of smile.	Occasional grimace or frown, withdrawn, disinterested.	Frequent to constant frown, clenched jaw, quivering chin.
LEGS	Normal Position or relaxed.	Uneasy, restless, tense.	Kicking, or legs drawn up.
ACTIVITY	Lying quietly, normal position, moves easily.	Squirming, shifting back and forth, tense.	Arched, rigid, or jerking.
CRY	No crying (awake or asleep).	Moans or whimpers, occasional complaint	Crying steadily, screams or sobs, frequent complaints.
CONSOLABILITY	Content, relaxed.	Reassured by occasional touching, hugging, or "talking to." Distractible.	Difficult to console or comfort.

Source: Best Practices Committee, *HCANJ Pain Management Guidelines*, 1/05 Revision. Health Care Association of New Jersey, Hamilton, New Jersey. Reprinted with permission.

4-72 Medication Management Team Joint Commission Tracking Tool

General Hospital

JOINT COMMISSION TEAM TRACKING LIST
Medication Management Team

Responsibility	Issue	Start Date	Due Date	Notes
1.				
2.				
3.				
4.				
5.				
6.				
7.				
8.				
9.				
10.				
11.				
12.				
13.				
14.				
15.				
16.				
17.				
18.				
19.				
20.				
21.				
22.				
23.				
24.				
25.				
26.				
27.				
28.				

Source: Rusty McNew, RN, MA, CPHQ, Dallas, Texas.

IMPROVING ORGANIZATION PERFORMANCE

4-73 Physician Peer/Chart Review

Date of Review: **Patient Medical Record:** **Treatment Area:**

Yes = Documentation supports compliance **No** = No documentation to support compliance ***NA*** = Not Applicable	**Yes**	**No**	***NA***	**Comments** **Document % in completion** *(i.e., 5/10 lab reports initialed)*
A. SYSTEMS REVIEW/NON-CLINICAL				
1. Time Seen by Resident				
1.1 1-60 minutes				
1.2 61-120 minutes				
1.3 >120 minutes				
2. Time Placed in ESD Bed or Stretcher				
2.1 1-60 minutes				
2.2 61-120 minutes				
2.3 >120 minutes				
3. Resident Signature				
4. Faculty Signature				
B. CLINICAL REVIEW				
Neuro				
5. Neuro CC: Neuro Exam Completed				
6. Seizure: Dstix Post Ictal Documented				
7. Head Trauma: GCS Documented				
Respiratory				
8. Asthma: Peak Flow Documented				
9. Pneumonia: Pulse Oximeter Documented				
10. SOB: Pulse Oximeter Documented				
Cardiovascular				
11. Chest Pain Requiring EKG: Read				
GI/GU				
12. Female Lower Abd Pain: Pelvic Exam Completed				
13. Female Dysuria: Pelvic Exam Completed				
14. Abdominal Pain: Rectal Exam				

Endocrine
15. Diabetes: Dstix Documented
16. Diabetes: Ketones Measured; Serum or Urine if indicated
Other
17. Wounds: Tetanus Assessed
18. ETOH: Thiamin Administered
19. Procedure Note Completed

Source: Rusty McNew, RN, MA, CPHQ, Dallas, Texas.

4-74 Survey Primer: Emergency Services Visit

During the emergency services visit, the physician surveyor assesses the setting where emergency services are performed. This activity lasts approximately 45 minutes. It is important to note areas maybe surveyed prior to the scheduled visit. Surveyors may jump ahead of the schedule or even return to your area if they have free time.

WHO WILL PARTICIPATE?

- Clinical director or manager emergency services
- Other staff you may designate

WHAT WILL OCCUR?

The visit consists of the following:

- a brief discussion with the director about the volume and scope of services provided and the purpose of the visit
- a tour of the area
- a meeting with staff members
- a review of medical records

Conversations with patients and families generally do not occur, but observations about privacy, dignity, and confidentiality are made during the tour of the area.

WHAT DOCUMENTS NEED TO BE AVAILABLE?

Open medical records of patients who are in the area at the time of the visit or who have received services.

SAMPLE QUESTIONS THE SURVEYOR MAY ASK DURING THE VISIT.

1. How does your hospital demonstrate respect for the following patient needs?
   - confidentiality
   - privacy
   - security
   - resolution of complaints
   - use of pastoral services
   - communication
2. Does the environment provide for patients' privacy?
3. Does the initial patient assessment address physical, psychological, and social status?
4. In the initial assessment, how is the patient's pain identified?
5. When warranted by the patient's condition, is there a more comprehensive pain assessment?
6. Are there reports of required diagnostic testing?
7. Is the assessment process for adolescent patients highly individualized?
8. Have you addressed the special needs of patients who are possible victims of alleged or suspected abuse or neglect?

9. How is physician coverage provided?
10. Do storage, distribution, and control of medications reflect policies and procedures?
11. How do policies and procedures support safe medication prescription and ordering?
12. How does medication preparation and dispensing adhere to law, regulation, licensure, and professional standards of practice?
13. Are medication preparation and dispensing appropriately controlled?
14. Is important patient medication information considered when medications are prepared and dispensed?
15. How does the hospital ensure that emergency medications are consistently available, controlled, and secure?
16. Describe how you monitor the effects of medications on patients.
17. Do you use restraint or seclusion with adequate and appropriate clinical justification?
18. Are staff educated and assessed for competence in minimizing the use of restraint and seclusion?
19. Does staff apply techniques such as redirecting the patient's focus or verbal de-escalation before employing restraint and seclusion?
20. Is restraint and seclusion used pursuant to an order of the licensed independent practitioner primarily responsible for the patient's ongoing care?
21. If authorized and approved by the patient, is the patient's family promptly notified of the initiation of restraint and seclusion?
22. Is the patient released as soon as he or she meets the behavior criteria?
23. Are all episodes of restraint and seclusion documented in the patient's medical record?
24. Is there appropriate equipment available and accessible should patients require resuscitation services?
25. During the entry process, how do you provide patients and families with information about proposed care?
26. How do you provide for coordination among the health professional(s) and service(s) or setting(s) involved in patient care?
27. Describe the process(es) for referral, transfer, or discharge of a patient to another level of care, health professional, or setting.
28. How do you provide for the exchange of appropriate patient care and clinical information when patients are admitted, referred, transferred, or discharged?
29. What aspects of the care provided in this setting do you measure, assess, and improve?
30. How does performance in this service relate to your hospital's mission and strategic planning processes?
31. Are the services appropriate to the scope and level of care?
32. What information is available relative to patient satisfaction with the services provided?
33. Are services available in a timely manner to meet patient needs?
34. Do the leaders collaborate with departmental staff for the development of department budgets?
35. Are there any issues relating to uniform performance of patient care processes?
36. Are the goals and scope of the setting's services defined?
37. What programs do you have to promote recruitment, retention, development, and recognition of staff members, especially job-related educational programs?

38. Has the hospital considered clinical practice guidelines in the design or improvement of clinical processes?
39. If clinical practice guidelines are used, how do hospital leaders identify or set criteria to guide the selection and implementation of the guidelines?
40. Who is involved in the review and approval of clinical practice guidelines selected prior to implementation?
41. Describe the process for how clinical practice guidelines are monitored for their effectiveness.
42. Is there evidence of communication across the hospital? If so, what?
43. Within this patient care setting, is there evidence of plans and performance standards for the following programs:
    - safety
    - security
    - hazardous materials and waste
    - emergency preparedness
    - life safety
    - medical equipment
    - utilities
44. Have staff members been oriented to the environment of care and educated about environment of care issues? Do they perform their responsibilities under the environment of care management plans?
45. Do you have regular emergency drills?
46. Do you have fire drills on a quarterly basis?
47. Have you performed hazard surveillance surveys in this setting at least every six months?
48. Has your setting maintained, tested, and inspected life safety elements of the environment of care? Has your hospital documented the required testing of fire alarm, detection, and extinguishing systems?
49. Have you maintained, tested, and inspected medical equipment in this setting?
50. Has your department maintained, tested, and inspected utility systems, including the emergency power system?
51. Is there adequate privacy to reflect sensitivity to and respect for the patient?
52. How do your leaders define the following:
    - other qualifications and responsibilities of staff working in this setting
    - a system to evaluate how well staff responsibilities are met
    - the number of staff needed to fulfill the setting's mission
53. How do you monitor and adjust staffing levels based on patient needs?
54. How do you encourage and support staff self-development and learning?
55. Do staff members receive an orientation to the department and initial job training and information?
56. Does each staff member participate in ongoing in-service education sessions and other related training to increase his or her knowledge of specific work-related issues?
57. How does the department manager determine whether staff are competent to perform assigned duties and, when appropriate, provide care for the special needs and behaviors of specific age groups?
58. Are the information and data you require for patient care provided in an accurate and timely fashion?

59. What types of aggregate data do you have available to emergency services staff of the setting to support patient care and operations decisions?
60. Do you have adequate resources and services available to meet the knowledge-based information needs of the medical staff?
61. Do those who need poison-control information have appropriate access?
62. Describe the following:
    - the process for reporting information about infections
    - actions you have taken to reduce the risk of or prevent nosocomial infections
    - actions you have taken to control outbreaks of identified nosocomial infections

Source: Rusty McNew, RN, MA, CPHQ, Dallas, Texas.

4-75 Nursing Outcome Report Action Plan

	Knowledge	Policy	Communication	Documentation	System Process	Performance Practice
1.	D/C Planning Initiated on Admit					
2.	Pre- D/C orders written: Date & Time					
3.	D/C teaching completed: Ed. Plan					
4.	D/C teaching completed: Teaching Method					
5.	D/C teaching completed: Evaluation of learning					
6.	D/C teaching completed: F/U Plan					
7.	D/C assessment completed					
8.	Appointments: In hand or telephone #/referrals					
9.	LOS was increased due to lack of D/C Planning					
10.	Pain assessment/screen/ reassessment performed q 4 hrs					
11.	MD notified for > level 4 pain post intervention					
12.	Nonpharmacological interventions documented: Positioning					
13.	Nonpharmacological interventions documented: Ice pack/Sitz bath					
14.	Nonpharmacological interventions documented: Other					
15.	Pharmacological interventions documented: Break through pain med.					
16.	Pharmacological interventions documented: Preprocedure med.					
17.	Pharmacological interventions documented: Timely Renewal					

	Knowledge	Policy	Communication	Documentation	System Process	Performance Practice
18.	Reassessment performed q 60 minutes post pain event					
19.	LOS was increased due to lack of Pain Mgmt					
20.	Pts. Learning needs assessed/screened on admit/encounter					
21.	Barriers to learning documented					
22.	Teaching/needs plan: Developed					
23.	Teaching plan: Implemented					
24.	Teaching plan: Evaluated					
25.	Evaluation of learning, understand assessed					
26.	LOS was increased due to lack of Patient & Family Ed.					

Source: Rusty McNew, RN, MA, CPHQ, Dallas, Texas.

4-76 Emergency Department Performance Improvement Plan for Physician Assistants

Performance improvement in the emergency department is performed by the medical director, assistant medical director, physician assistant director, or the departmental designee. A summary of the plan is as follows:

A. The scope of care and aspects of care are reviewed annually and are revised as needed.
B. Chart review: 5 percent of the physician assistant monthly charts will be reviewed using the following sentinels:
   - legibility of charts
   - timeliness of patient evaluation
   - adequate history and physical exam for the severity of the patient complaint
   - interpretation of test results
   - consideration of differential diagnosis and appropriateness of discharge diagnosis
   - discharge instructions
   - consultation with attending physicians
   - discrepancy between nurse and MD/PA notes are adequately addressed
C. X-ray, EKG, and culture variances are reviewed daily.
D. Focused audits are performed monthly.
E. Departmental referrals and patient complaints are reviewed on an as needed basis.

Aspect of Care: MEDICAL RECORD REVIEW

These indicators are suggested guidelines for review rather than mandatory requirements.

REVIEW FREQUENCY: ______________ REVIEW MONTH/YEAR: ______________

CASE SELECTION GUIDELINES

Select a random sample of 5 percent of charts and include all emergency physicians in review.

DATE													
REVIEWER'S INITIALS													
CODE NO.													

TOTALS

SENTINEL EVENT

PHYSICIAN CODE														TOTAL #	TOTAL # MET	TOTAL % MET	THRES-HOLDS
DOCUMENTATION 1. Chart is legible.																	90%
2. Time patient seen by MD is noted.																	90%
3. Adequate information is documented to identify why high-risk, high-cost or problem-prone tests are ordered, and to provide adequate information for interpretation.																	95%
4. Results and interpretation of all ordered tests are documented.																	95%
5. Consideration of appropriate differential diagnoses is documented and all considered diagnoses are listed (for seriously ill patients).																	98%
6. Time of consultation request and response noted.																	96%
7. Discrepancy between nurse and MD notes adequately addressed.																	100%
8. Appropriate patient instructions ordered and given.																	98%
9. Diagnosis is substantiated by documented results of diagnostic studies and treatment.																	100%

Blank Box = Criterion Met X = Criterion Not Met G = Non-Applicable Criterion

Remarks: ______________________________

Note: Thresholds do not demonstrate or imply that a problem exists, but merely indicate that a more detailed review should be undertaken.

Source: Suburban Hospital, Inc., Bethesda, Maryland.

4-77 Emergency Department Quality Indicators

PROCEDURE

- ED quality indicators will be addressed for findings, conclusions, actions, and evaluation at the quarterly management of care team meeting.
- The ED monthly report will be used as a guide for discussion by the co-chairs of the team. (The monthly report will be produced by the executive secretary.)
- The minutes from the team meeting will serve as documentation of the above.
- Quarterly, the indicators will be trended.
- The minutes from the team meeting will serve as documentation of the above.

INDICATORS

1. Mortality and morbidity
2. 72-hr. unplanned readmission
3. 72-hr. unplanned readmission admit
4. Specimen errors
5. Medication errors
6. Patient falls
7. Patient satisfaction
8. Patients residing in the emergency department > 24 hr.

Evaluating Quality Indicators

- Mortality and Morbidity
  Number of Deaths ÷ Total Number of Patients Seen
  Number of Preventable Deaths ÷ Total Number of Deaths
  - 72-hr. Bounceback
    Number of Bouncebacks ÷ Number of Patients Seen
  - 72-hr. Bounceback Death
    Number of Bounceback Deaths ÷ Number of Patients Seen
  - Bounceback Admit
    Number of Bounceback Admits ÷ Number of Patients Seen
  - 72-hr. Bounceback Admit Death
    Number of Bounceback Deaths ÷ Number of Patients Seen
  - Specimen Errors
    Number of Specimen Errors ÷ Number of Patients Seen
  - Medication Errors
    Number of Medication Errors ÷ Number of Patients Seen
  - Patient Falls
    Number of Falls ÷ Number of Patients Seen
- Patient Satisfaction
- Nursing Documentation
- Medical Staff Documentation
  - Invasive Procedures
    Number of Procedures Performed per Criteria ÷ Total Number of Procedures Performed

- Patients Residing in the ED > 24 hr.
Number of Stays > 24 hr. ÷ Total Number of Patients Seen

Source: Rusty McNew, RN, MA, CPHQ, Dallas, Texas.

4-78 Conducting an FMEA

Failure Mode Effect and Analysis (FMEA) is similar to a root cause analysis. Both are excellent quality improvement tools. A root cause analysis is used reactively to analyze problems after an occurrence, while the FMEA is a proactive tool used to analyze systems/processes/behaviors in an attempt to prevent adverse occurrences. FMEA has been used in engineering, aviation and the general business sector for many years however, only recently has it been introduced in health care.

FMEA begins by outlining the current high risk processes/activities in an organization (or within a department). A vulnerability scale is applied by using a weighting system to determine which processes, based on the current practice, have the highest potential for failure/error. Once the priorities are identified, a project management or CQI team is formed to act upon the identified weakness in the safe practice or process. FMEA can also be used when designing new systems.

Joint Commission standards require that health care organizations conduct at least one FMEA annually and incorporate the findings into their Pl program.

CONDUCTING A FAILURE MODE AND EFFECTS ANALYSIS

- Assemble a team. The team may be structured as an organization-wide Patient Safety Committee or developed within each department. Start with high-risk departments.
- Outline the high-risk activities in the organization or department. Identify what the outcome should be.
- Identify potential occurrences, which are at risk for poor patient outcomes or medical errors, i.e. the possible failures that could occur (i.e. the failure mode).
- For each "failure mode," estimate its criticality by
  —severity of the potential effect*
  —probability the failure will occur (based on current procedures, policies, personnel, equipment, etc.)*
- Calculate the score of each "failure mode" to determine the priority of addressing them with improvement projects. Scores of 8 or above should be addressed first.
- Conduct an analysis of each potential failure issue using a cause & effect diagram, flow chart, root cause analysis or other appropriate tools.
- Utilizing Pl principles, redesign the process or activity to minimize the risk of that failure mode and protect patients from the failure effects.
- Analyze and test the redesigned process.
- Implement the redesigned process
- Monitor the redesigned process.
- Implement a strategy for maintaining the effectiveness of the redesigned process over time.

---

* See FMEA tool.

4-79 Failure Mode Analysis Tool

Procedure/Treatment/ Process at risk	Failure Potential	Severity Rating	Probability Rating	*Outcome Score	Action Date	Responsi-bility	Plan

Probability Score	Severity Score
Frequent = 4	Catastrophic = 4
Occasional = 3	Major Permanent = 3
Uncommon = 2	Major Temporary = 2
Remote (Unlikely) = 1	Minor = 1

Source: Quality Resource Groups, LLC, Arlington, Texas.

4-80 Quality Management Patient Complaint/Grievance Committee Flowchart

Division VP forwards completed Patient Complaint/Grievance form to QM for placement on the next scheduled Complaint/Grievance Committee agenda.

[If the Complaint/Grievance is considered an emergency, the committee may meet within 24-hrs notice. Fifty-percent attendance plus one is required to conduct an emergency meeting.]

STEPS

Step #1
☐ Refer to Manager
If Patient is still NOT satisfied after speaking with Manager, go to Step #2

***Step #2**
☐ Refer to Director
If Patient is still NOT satisfied after speaking with Director, go to Step #3

Step #3
☐ Refer to VP
If Patient is still NOT satisfied after speaking with VP, go to Step #4

Step #4
Patient Complaint Grievance Committee
*Complaints sent directly to Administration will be accelerated to Step #3 of the process.

→ QM distributes the agenda prior to scheduled meetings with copies of Patient Complaint/Grievances to committee members.

QM telephones the patient(s) & sends a letter inviting them to the Patient Complaint/Grievance meeting.

↓ The committee convenes with an overview of the patient's perception of the Complaint/Grievance. The patient is thanked & excused from the meeting. The VP from the respective division states their perception of the Patient Complaint/Grievance.

↓ The committee assesses, concludes & makes a decision regarding how or if they can resolve the grievance.

↓ QM initiates a letter to the patient with the committee's decision within 10 working days.

↓ QM enters the above into the Patient Complaint/Grievance Committee report for trending/analysis.

↓ QM presents Patient Complaint/Grievance trended data to District Performance Improvement Committee (DPIC) & to the Board of Mangers no less than quarterly.

↓ Each Division VP presents Patient Complaint/Grievance data to their respective Division Performance Improvement Committee for division's specific actions to improve patient satisfaction.

Where to Catalogue Documents

All Grievance Committee documents are maintained in the Quality Management Department

Source: Rusty McNew, RN, MA, CPHQ, Dallas, Texas.

4-81 Patient Complaints/Grievance Log

#	Status	Division	Unit	Patient Name	MR #	Incident Date	Referred to	Date Referred	Description	Step #1 Refer to Unit	Step #2 Refer to Director	Step #3 Refer to VP	Step #4 Refer to Grievance Committee/ QM	Comments

Source: Rusty McNew, RN, MA, CPHQ, Dallas, Texas.

4-82 Emergency Department Callback Questionnaire

Date called: ____________
Time of call: ____________
Nurse calling: ____________

1. Service Date:

   ☐☐ / ☐☐ / ☐☐
   month day year

2. Medical Record Number

   __ __ __ __ __ __

3. Patient age

   __ __

4. Time of visit (registration time):
   ___ Day 7 AM–3 PM
   ___ Evening 3 PM–11 PM
   ___ Night 11 PM–7 AM

5. Category:
   ___ emergency ___ urgent ___ nonurgent

6. Express Care:
   ___ yes ___ no

---

7. The information below was given by: ___ Patient ___ Family Member ___ Other

8. Did you (the patient) schedule follow-up care? ___ YES ___ NO ___ N/A

9. Did you (the patient) fill the prescription? ___ YES ___ NO ___ N/A

10. Did the nurse introduce him/herself to you (the patient) and/or your family? ___ YES ___ NO ___ N/A

11. Did the physician introduce him/herself to you (the patient) and/or your family? ___ YES ___ NO ___ N/A

12. Did you (the patient) receive an ID band? ___ YES ___ NO ___ N/A

13. Were treatments and procedures explained to you before they were started? ___ YES ___ NO ___ N/A

14. Were delays in care and treatment explained to you (the patient) and/or your family? ___ YES ___ NO ___ N/A

15. Did you (the patient) understand the discharge instructions? ___ YES ___ NO ___ N/A

16. Were you (the patient) satisfied with the care and attention you received? ___ YES ___ NO ___ N/A

17. How would you (the patient) describe your present condition? ___ Improved ___ Same ___ Worse

18. Comments: ____________

Source: Kennedy Health System, Voorhees, New Jersey.

4-83 Occurrence Report Form

B.

Date of Occurrence

Time

Location of happening ______

Location assigned or visiting ______

Inpatient ____Outpatient____Visitor_____

Addressograph
Inpatient
Outpatient

C. Complete if visitor or no addressograph:

Name: ______
Last First I.

______
City State Zip

______
Street Address

( )______
Telephone

D. Diagnosis or Chief complaint ______

Service ______ Admission or Visit Date ______

Attending Physician ______

Complete one form per occurrence.

E. Type of Occurance—Complete appropriate occurrence type and then go to Section F.

E1. Treatment/Test/Procedure (*Circle one*)
Invasive/Non-Invasive (*Circle one*)
(*Select one only*)

______ Delay in Performing
______ Not Done
______ Unordered
______ Incorrect Counts
___S___N___I

______ Delay in Obtaining Results
______ Incomplete/Inaccurate documentation
______ Complication during or after
______ Other ______

MDR

Was there a faulty medical device or piece of equipment found during this occurrence?
______ Yes ______ No (select one)

If yes, complete the following:

Equipment Name ______ Serial # ______

Lot # ______ Model #______ Biomed # ______

Follow malfunctioning Equipment Policy. Send device to Biomed.
Call Risk Management. Go to F.

E2. Medication/Blood (*Circle One*) Name of: ______
(*Select One only*)

______ Incorrect Dose/Route
______ Incorrect Time/date omitted
______ Infiltration

______ Incorrect med/unordered
______ Reaction
______ Other ______

If faculty medical device or piece of equipment, complete MDR box above.
Follow Adverse Drug Reaction policy and call pharmacy.
Follow Blood Transfusion policy. Go to F.

Complete one form per occurence.

E. Type of Occurence — Complete appropriate occurence type and then go to Section F.

E3. Trauma (*Select One*)

_______ Slip
_______ Burn
_______ Slip and Fall
_______ Needlestick
_______ Fall
_______ Other Injury _______

Observed staff ____ Y ____ N   Observed by other ____ Y ____ N

Witnesses: *(Names/Relation to Patient/Visitor)* _______

(Select One)

_______ From bed/Chair/Stretcher
_______ While standing/Walking
_______ In BR
_______ Other _______

(Select One)

Object/Substance contributed to trauma?

____ Y ____ N ____ Briefly describe _______

(Select One)

Did age or condition contribute to trauma?

____ Y ____ N ____ Unknown

Outpatients and visitors should be escorted to the Emergency Department for evaluation and treatment.

Did patient accept offer? ____ Y ____ N.

Call Risk Management Department.   Go to F.

E4. Miscellaneous (*Select one*)

_______ High Risk AWOL
_______ Confidentiality Issues
_______ Verbal Abuse
_______ Property Damage/Loss
_______ Physical Abuse
Briefly describe _______
_______ Other _______

Follow policy regarding AWOL, Abuse or Property Situations.

Was Security contacted? ____ Y ____ N

Go to F.

F. Expected Outcome (*Select One*)

_______ Near miss situation. Staff identified before patient involvement.
_______ Requires significant medical intervention but likely to recover fully.
_______ Requires no nursing/medical intervention.
_______ Requires significant medical intervention, not likely to recover or death.
_______ Requires some medical intervention but not likely to be admitted or increase L.O.S
_______ Reportable for administrative evaluation

Go to F.

G. Print Name and ID number or Person Completing Report

Name: _______   ID #: _______

Source: Rusty McNew, RN, MA, CPHQ, Dallas, Texas.

4-84 Risk Management Process

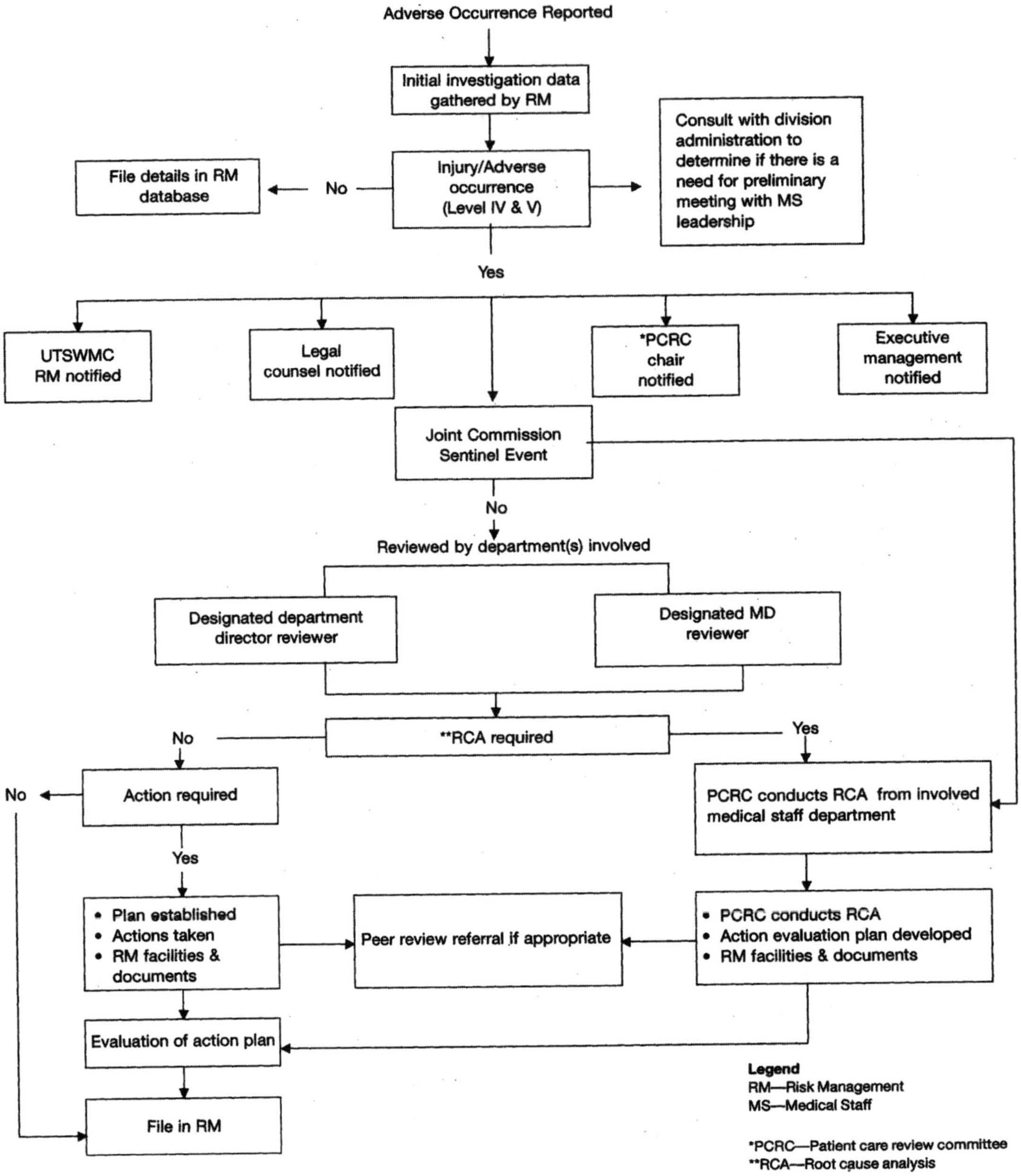

Source: Rusty McNew, RN, MA, CPHQ, Dallas, Texas.

4-85 Adverse Occurrence/Sentinel Event Procedure

GOAL

Identify and investigate adverse occurrences and sentinel events in order to reduce likelihood of reoccurrence. Following an adverse occurrence or sentinel event, ________ will promptly act to investigate, assess processes and systems involved in order to take corrective actions as appropriate. The focus on the investigation is to evaluate possible factors that led to the occurrence/event in order to make improvements.

PURPOSE

The purpose of this procedure is to

1. clarify risk management, (RM), medical staff department and management responsibilities related to adverse occurrences
2. identify process for reporting, investigating and conducting **a thorough and credible** root cause analysis that maintains quality assurance protection and/or client attorney discovery privilege
3. ensure compliance with OIG, CMS, and Joint Commission regulations/standards related to quality improvement.

DEFINITIONS

- **Adverse occurrence**—Any untoward event that either causes actual injury or has the direct potential to cause injury or loss of function. Adverse occurrences include events that are due to commission or omission.
- **Near miss**—Event that "almost occurred" but was averted that had the potential for having caused injury or loss of function
- **Sentinel event**—An adverse occurrence that causes injury or significant loss of function or death to a patient including, but not limited to
  - unanticipated death or major permanent loss of function, not related to the natural course of the patient's illness or underlying condition
  - suicide of an inpatient
  - infant/child abduction
  - discharge of an infant to the wrong family
  - rape of an inpatient
  - hemolytic transfusion reaction with major blood group incompatibilities
  - surgery on the wrong patient or wrong body part
- **Root cause analysis (RCA)**—Root cause analysis is a process for identifying the basic or causal factors that underlie variation in performance, including the occurrence or possible occurrence of a sentinel event. A root cause analysis focuses primarily on systems and processes, not individual performance. A root cause analysis should develop an action plan that will likely decrease the likelihood of such events in the future, or determines, after analysis, that no such improvement opportunities exist. To be thorough, the root cause analysis must consider
  - all pertinent factors associated with the event
  - analysis of the specific systems and processes related to the event

- a determination of potential improvement processes or systems that will reduce the likelihood of such events in the future

To be credible, the root cause analysis must

- include participation by leadership and individuals closely involved in the processes and systems under review
- provide an explanation if the findings in the analysis are deemed "not applicable" or "a known complication"
- include consideration of any relevant literature

- **Department physician reviewer**—A faculty physician appointed by the department chair to review risk management level IV and V and sentinel cases that occur in the specific department. Physician review assists risk management determine whether or not further investigation or referrals are needed or if a root cause analysis group should be convened.
- **Patient care review committee (PCRC)**—A permanent subcommittee of the medical advisory council charged with ensuring that adverse occurrence/sentinel event investigations are thorough and credible and that appropriate actions are taken to reduce the likelihood of reoccurrence. Ad hoc members are appointed as appropriate.
- **Risk management**—Risk management consults with legal services, administration and PCRC to direct investigations, reports occurrences to medical staff and executive management, coordinates and facilitates root cause analysis process, documents and reports as action plans are implemented and follow-up occurs.

RISK IDENTIFICATION REPORTING OF ADVERSE OCCURRENCES/SENTINEL EVENTS

Adverse Occurrences and Sentinel Events shall be reported to the risk management department as soon as the event is known. Reporting may be by the physician, nurse, or any other person with knowledge of the occurrence. The hospital risk identification form shall be completed and submitted within 24 hours of the event. If there is patient injury of a catastrophic nature or a sentinel event identified, risk management should be notified by phone (__________) or pager (__________).

RISK MANAGEMENT PROCESS

1. Screen all risk identification reports regardless of source of information.
2. Categorize according to the severity of the occurrence.
   - Level I—No actual occurrence. No patient or person involved (near miss). Information is entered into a database for aggregate reporting.
   - Level II—Limited or no harm to the patient or persons involved. Limited or no intervention required. Information entered into a database for aggregate reporting.
   - Level III—Moderate adverse occurrence. Intervention required, but not likely to have lasting effect. Not likely to increase a patient's acuity or length of stay. Investigated as necessary to establish above information and entered into RM database for aggregate reporting.
   - Level IV—Moderate adverse occurrence. Increased intervention, transfer to higher level of care (admission to hospital, or transfer to an ICU), or increased

length of stay. Investigation actions as appropriate and follow-up to resolution required.
- Level V—Severe adverse occurrence or death. Permanent harm or loss of function. Cause may be unknown. Investigation, actions as appropriate and follow-up to resolution required.

3. Inform hospital legal affairs, executive management, vice president of the involved division and risk management about a sentinel event or a Level IV or V adverse occurrences immediately.
4. Investigate—Level III, IV, and V adverse occurrences Investigation may include any of the following:
   - review of medical record
     - A. initial meeting with division administration to determine if there is need for a preliminary meeting with medical staff leadership
     - B. initial evaluation meeting with chair of PCRC to direct further investigation
     - C. refer to physician reviewer of specific department for clinical evaluation
     - D. refer to nurse or other clinical staff of involved department(s) for review and evaluation
   - review of relevant policies, procedures and standards of care
   - patient care review committee chair call for a root cause analysis (RCA) to be conducted
   - if RCA is to be conducted, PCRC chair will appoint co-chair from involved department
   - when necessary, coordinate and facilitate the completion of a root cause analysis with the patient care review committee and appropriate physicians, nurses and other health care professionals involved in the case. Legal counsel will be invited to attend as appropriate.
   - document findings, conclusions, actions, and evaluation plan
   - prepare a thorough and credible root cause analysis summation within 45 calendar days after a sentinel event has been reported.
   - refer action plan to division performance improvement committee through quality management

REPORTING SENTINEL EVENTS AND LEVEL IV & V ADVERSE OCCURRENCES

- Root cause analysis (RCA) action plans will be reported to respective performance improvement committee within 45 days for follow-up monitoring, as appropriate.
- RCA and action plans will be reported to executive management when designed
- Board of managers shall receive aggregate data on risk occurrences quarterly and information regarding sentinel events and Level IV & V at the next board meeting
- The Joint Commission or other regulatory agencies, upon request, may receive information regarding root cause analysis procedure and documentation regarding action plans for improving care and processes. Due to legal implications, sentinel events are **not** voluntarily reported to Joint Commission.

Approved hospital president, medical staff ______________________

Source: Rusty McNew, RN, MA, CPHQ, Dallas, Texas.

4-86 Response after a Significant Adverse Occurrence

To swiftly and effectively manage the personal and organizational impacts of a significant adverse occurrence (patient, visitor or employee injury or death related to health care delivery), an interdepartmental, multidisciplinary meeting will be held within a day or two of the occurrence. The purpose of this meeting is to

- provide support to those involved in the occurrence
- obtain information about what happened (chronology of events)
- determine what processes and/or procedures may have impacted the course of events
- direct communication
- determine what additional information, discussion and/or investigation is needed and summarize next steps

When an adverse occurrence is reported to risk management, the risk management staff will validate the type and severity of the occurrence. The risk manager will contact hospital and medical staff leadership to discuss the occurrence and determine what type of response should occur. The following outlines the role and responsibilities of leadership and risk management (before, during, and after the initial response).

Hospital and medical staff leadership shall

- identify persons directly involved with the occurrence and determine who should attend the initial response meeting
- provide support for the purpose of system and process review for improvement purposes and eliminate finger pointing or blame identification/shifting
- designate person(s) to manage communications with the patient and family
- encourage limiting/reducing unit/department discussions regarding the occurrence (rumor control)
- arrange for staff and leadership to meet within a day or two of the occurrence
- participate actively in the initial review, follow-up discussions and, when applicable, a root cause analysis for the development and implementation of action plans
- educate and/or update staff on process improvements

Risk manager will

- Facilitate initial response meeting and promote the completion of follow-up activities
- Document process and system changes and educational efforts
- Report to hospital senior management and legal department as needed
- Ensure that root cause analysis is conducted according to Joint Commission standards

Source: Rusty McNew, RN, MA, CPHQ, Dallas, Texas.

4-87 Creation of a Hospital-Wide Patient Flow Team
Sample Patient Flow Team Structure

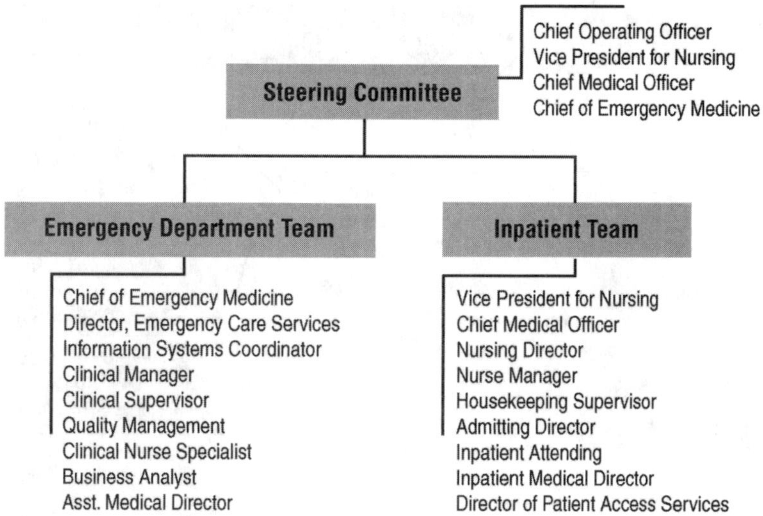

Creation of a Hospital-Wide Patient Flow Team

Creating hospital-wide teams to participate in decisions and guide changes is a critical factor for improving patient flow. Figure shows one model for constructing such teams. In this model, a steering committee of senior hospital leadership is responsible for overseeing all change efforts and provides high visibility for those efforts. Separate teams are created to focus on problems in the Ed and on the inpatient side. Each of these teams has broad representation from departments throughout the hospital including ancillary services, housekeeping, and patient transport. Equally important is ensuring that the ED and inpatient teams include members from each side to the foster an understanding of the problems and issues that each team faces. Teams include both managers' front-line staff to encourage the generation of new strategies or initiatives and to engage all levels of employees in the change process.

Source: *Perfecting Patient Flow: America's Safety Net Hospitals and Emergency Department Crowding.*

4-88 Emergency Department Input/Throughput/Output Model of Patient Flow Diagram

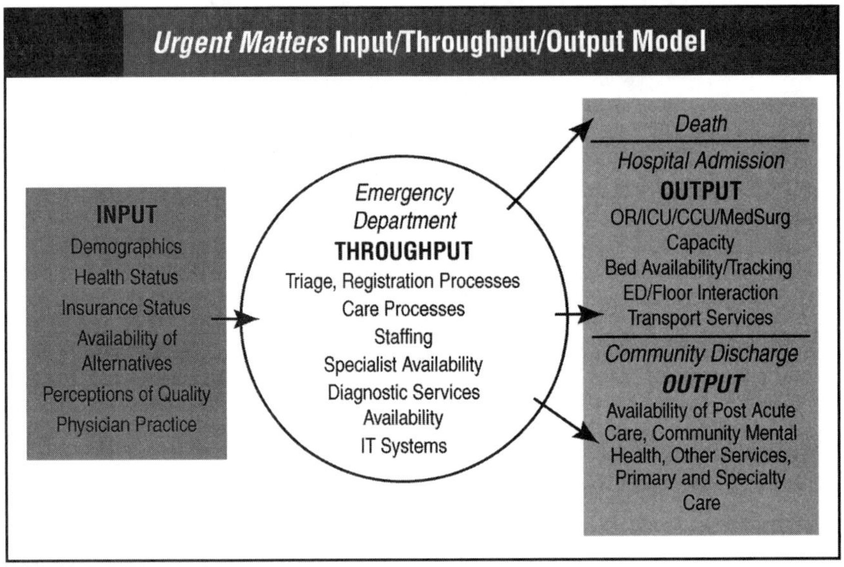

Source: *Perfecting Patient Flow: America's Safety Net Hospitals and Emergency Department Crowding.*

4-89 Patient Flow Key Performance Indicators

<table>
<tr><th>Factor</th><th colspan="2">Indicator</th><th>Reporting Interval</th></tr>
<tr><td rowspan="4">ED Throughput</td><td colspan="2">1. Total ED throughput time — time from patient's arrival in the ED → time of patient disposition*</td><td rowspan="4">Weekly</td></tr>
<tr><td rowspan="3">2. By treatment path:
Admitted/Fast Track /Other ED Discharged</td><td>a. Time from arrival to bed placement — patient arrival in the ED → time the patient is first placed in a bed for exam and treatment</td></tr>
<tr><td>b. Time from bed placement to examination — time patient is first placed in a bed → time the patient is first seen by a physician</td></tr>
<tr><td>c. Time from disposition decision to departure — time physician issues a discharge or admit order → time patient has left the ED</td></tr>
<tr><td rowspan="3">Inpatient Flow</td><td colspan="2">3. Time from inpatient bed assignment to bed placement — inpatient bed available and assigned → patient arrives in unit and placed in bed</td><td rowspan="3">Weekly</td></tr>
<tr><td colspan="2">4. Time of day of discharge — average time of day that inpatients are discharged**</td></tr>
<tr><td colspan="2">5. Bed turnaround time — time that a bed becomes empty → time that the bed is reported as cleaned and available for use by a new patient</td></tr>
<tr><td rowspan="2">Clinical Processes (Choose one)</td><td colspan="2">6. Time to heart treatment — patient arrival at the ED → time thrombolytic medication is administered or a vessel is opened</td><td rowspan="2">Monthly</td></tr>
<tr><td colspan="2">7. Time to pain management (fractures/dislocations) — time of arrival → 1st administration of pain management, e.g., medication or ice packs</td></tr>
<tr><td rowspan="3">Other ED</td><td colspan="2">8. Hours on diversion — if hospitals are allowed to go on diversion, total number of hours on diversion</td><td rowspan="3">Monthly</td></tr>
<tr><td colspan="2">9. Percent incomplete treatment — percent of patients that leave prior to completion of treatment (left without being seen, against medical advice, or for any other reason before medical treatment is completed)</td></tr>
<tr><td colspan="2">10. Patient Satisfaction — use existing measures of patient satisfaction</td></tr>
</table>

* Disposition is when the physician's orders have been written to admit or discharge the patient and the patient has left the ED.

** Time of discharge is when the physician's discharge orders have been written and the patient has left the hospital.

Source: *Perfecting Patient Flow: America's Safety Net Hospitals and Emergency Department Crowding.*

4-90 Emergency Department Priority Improvement List

1. *Service*
2. *Disadvantaged Business Enterprise*
3. *Environment*
4. *Employee Centered Workplace*
5. *Access for Patients*
6. *Financial Performance*

DCHD Goals	Improvement Topics	Improvement Goals	Status Report	Working Teams Membership ***Psych. PIC Responsible person(s)***	Target Dates
1 5 6	**Trauma routine ED lab panels**	• To reduce patient charges by 50% • To reduce hospital costs by 10% • To improve utilization to meet standards of care.	Lab panels have been developed in conjunction with Pathology. Awaiting Information Systems to make screens available on the LIS.		
1 5 6	**Psychiatric ED Patient Involuntary Patient's Rights**	• To reduce potential and/or actual risk for litigation • To communicate the Patient Rights to the patient or family when appropriate. • To reduce potential risk for elopement. • To comply with all local, state and federal statues • To comply with TDH, HCFA & JCAHO	After discussion with the hospital's Legal Department, it was discovered that the Psychiatry Patient Rights did not have to be read to patients who are put under a county Order of Protective Custody. Issues resolved—no further actions necessary.		
1 5 6	**Utilization Review Process** *Phase I: design & implement* *Phase II: monitor ESD unplanned returns*	• To monitor unplanned returns to the ED within 72 hours from the initial visit.			

Rating Scale: 1=immediate implementation, 2=to be implemented in 2007–2008, 3=Long term planning required. p-prio

4-91 Emergency Department Patient Complaint Report

EMERGENCY DEPARTMENT PATIENT COMPLAINT
QUARTERLY PERFORMANCE IMPROVEMENT REPORT

	Oct	*Nov*	*Dec*	**1st Qtr**	*Jan*	*Feb*	*Mar*	**2nd Qtr**	*Apr*	*May*	*Jun*	**3rd Qtr**	*Jul*	*Aug*	*Sep*	**4th Qtr**	Year to Date
Professional Care																	
RN Response/Care/Delay	0	0	0	**0**	0	0	0	**0**	0	0	0	**0**	0	0	0	**0**	**0**
MD Response/Care/Delay	0	0	0	**0**	0	0	0	**0**	0	0	0	**0**	0	0	0	**0**	**0**
Staff Response/Care/Delay	0	0	0	**0**	0	0	0	**0**	0	0	0	**0**	0	0	0	**0**	**0**
Lack of Privacy/Confidentiality	0	0	0	**0**	0	0	0	**0**	0	0	0	**0**	0	0	0	**0**	**0**
Pain Management	0	0	0	**0**	0	0	0	**0**	0	0	0	**0**	0	0	0	**0**	**0**
Attitude/Rudeness	0	0	0	**0**	0	0	0	**0**	0	0	0	**0**	0	0	0	**0**	**0**
Other	0	0	0	**0**	0	0	0	**0**	0	0	0	**0**	0	0	0	**0**	**0**
total Professional Care	**0**	**0**	**0**	**0**	**0**	**0**	**0**	**0**	**0**	**0**	**0**	**0**	**0**	**0**	**0**	**0**	**0**
Financial																	
Bill/Adjustment/Questions	0	0	0	**0**	0	0	0	**0**	0	0	0	**0**	0	0	0	**0**	**0**
Financial Communication	0	0	0	**0**	0	0	0	**0**	0	0	0	**0**	0	0	0	**0**	**0**
Classification/Reclassification	0	0	0	**0**	0	0	0	**0**	0	0	0	**0**	0	0	0	**0**	**0**
Refunds	0	0	0	**0**	0	0	0	**0**	0	0	0	**0**	0	0	0	**0**	**0**
Financial Aid	0	0	0	**0**	0	0	0	**0**	0	0	0	**0**	0	0	0	**0**	**0**
other	0	0	0	**0**	0	0	0	**0**	0	0	0	**0**	0	0	0	**0**	**0**
total Financial Care	**0**	**0**	**0**	**0**	**0**	**0**	**0**	**0**	**0**	**0**	**0**	**0**	**0**	**0**	**0**	**0**	**0**
Records/Forms																	
Insurance Forms	0	0	0	**0**	0	0	0	**0**	0	0	0	**0**	0	0	0	**0**	**0**
Name Change	0	0	0	**0**	0	0	0	**0**	0	0	0	**0**	0	0	0	**0**	**0**
Medical Records	0	0	0	**0**	0	0	0	**0**	0	0	0	**0**	0	0	0	**0**	**0**
Birth Certificates	0	0	0	**0**	0	0	0	**0**	0	0	0	**0**	0	0	0	**0**	**0**
Work release Form	0	0	0	**0**	0	0	0	**0**	0	0	0	**0**	0	0	0	**0**	**0**
School Release Form	0	0	0	**0**	0	0	0	**0**	0	0	0	**0**	0	0	0	**0**	**0**
Prescriptions	0	0	0	**0**	0	0	0	**0**	0	0	0	**0**	0	0	0	**0**	**0**
Clinic cards	0	0	0	**0**	0	0	0	**0**	0	0	0	**0**	0	0	0	**0**	**0**
Other	0	0	0	**0**	0	0	0	**0**	0	0	0	**0**	0	0	0	**0**	**0**
total Records/Forms	**0**	**0**	**0**	**0**	**0**	**0**	**0**	**0**	**0**	**0**	**0**	**0**	**0**	**0**	**0**	**0**	**0**

	Oct	*Nov*	*Dec*	**1st Qtr**	*Jan*	*Feb*	*Mar*	**2nd Qtr**	*Apr*	*May*	*Jun*	**3rd Qtr**	*Jul*	*Aug*	*Sep*	**4th Qtr**	Year to Date
Operations/Systems																	
Waiting Time/Delay	0	0	0	**0**	0	0	0	**0**	0	0	0	**0**	0	0	0	**0**	**0**
Registration/Admission	0	0	0	**0**	0	0	0	**0**	0	0	0	**0**	0	0	0	**0**	**0**
Smoking	0	0	0	**0**	0	0	0	**0**	0	0	0	**0**	0	0	0	**0**	**0**
Overhead Speaker	0	0	0	**0**	0	0	0	**0**	0	0	0	**0**	0	0	0	**0**	**0**
Temperature Control	0	0	0	**0**	0	0	0	**0**	0	0	0	**0**	0	0	0	**0**	**0**
Appointment/Scheduling	0	0	0	**0**	0	0	0	**0**	0	0	0	**0**	0	0	0	**0**	**0**
Cleanliness	0	0	0	**0**	0	0	0	**0**	0	0	0	**0**	0	0	0	**0**	**0**
Visitors/Noise	0	0	0	**0**	0	0	0	**0**	0	0	0	**0**	0	0	0	**0**	**0**
Parking Facilities	0	0	0	**0**	0	0	0	**0**	0	0	0	**0**	0	0	0	**0**	**0**
Menu/Food	0	0	0	**0**	0	0	0	**0**	0	0	0	**0**	0	0	0	**0**	**0**
Transportation	0	0	0	**0**	0	0	0	**0**	0	0	0	**0**	0	0	0	**0**	**0**
Patient Property/Misplaced	0	0	0	**0**	0	0	0	**0**	0	0	0	**0**	0	0	0	**0**	**0**
Other	0	0	0	**0**	0	0	0	**0**	0	0	0	**0**	0	0	0	**0**	**0**
total Records/Forms	**0**	**0**	**0**	**0**	**0**	**0**	**0**	**0**	**0**	**0**	**0**	**0**	**0**	**0**	**0**	**0**	**0**
Total # of Complaints	**0**	**0**	**0**	**0**	**0**	**0**	**0**	**0**	**0**	**0**	**0**	**0**	**0**	**0**	**0**	**0**	**0**
Total # of Patients/Visitors making Complaints	**0**	**0**	**0**	**0**	**0**	**0**	**0**	**0**	**0**	**0**	**0**	**0**	**0**	**0**	**0**	**0**	**0**
Total # Patients > 3 complaints per form	**0**	**0**	**0**	**0**	**0**	**0**	**0**	**0**	**0**	**0**	**0**	**0**	**0**	**0**	**0**	**0**	**0**

Source: Rusty McNew, RN, MA, CPHQ, Dallas, Texas.

4-92 ED Quality Management Study Description

Study Title: ____________________

Study Category

Studies should measure either outcome and/or process. Please indicate which applies to this study.

Evaluation Grid

1–4 Meaningful
5–6 Least Meaningful
7–8 Start Over

Outcome	Process		Known Problem	High Risk	Low Risk High Volume	Low Risk Low Volume
Customer Satisfaction	Documentation					
Effectiveness	Efficiency					
Complication Prone	Cost Analysis	OUTCOME	1	3	5	7
Status Improvement	Compliance to Standard	PROCESS	2	4	6	8

INDICATOR STATEMENT: *Your outcome indicator or a statement of of what should happen.*
RATIONALE FOR STUDY: *Why you are doing the study.*
STUDY PARTICIPANTS: *Who is collecting the data?*
PATIENT POPULATION: *Who are you studying and the volume to be studied.*

Criteria	Goal (Threshold)	Results
Measurable objectives, or what is necessary for the outcome indicator to occur.	*The "action point," or the established minimum level of acceptable performance*	*% of compliance to the "action point" or threshold*

Source: Rusty McNew, RN, MA, CPHQ, Dallas, Texas.

4-93 Daily Unit Rounding Checklist

Unit: ______________ **Surveyor:** ______________ **Date:** ______________

Directions 1. Complete this tool for each unit each day by 12:00 noon. 2. Mark compliant areas with a check. Mark non-compliant areas with an X. 3. Document your actions to correct each item marked with an X on the bottom of this tool. 4. Turn in one tool per unit each Monday morning by 10:00 a.m. to Administration.	Monday	Tuesday	Wednesday	Thursday	Friday	Saturday	Sunday
All Patient Care Areas							
QC for ACT, glucometer, nitrazine, guiac, dipstick, urine preg.							
Curtains closed—ED, ICU/CCU, PACU, OR, Imaging, MRI							
Audio—ED, ICU/CCU, PACU, OR holding, Admitting							
Clean syringes & needles locked							
Medical records, electronic, charts & exp. paper protected							
No food, drinks in ED workstation							
No names/dx/procedures linked on boards in view of public							
No patient names visible for sign-in rosters							
Radiology films not visible to the public							
Visual privacy of patients not protected							
II. Medications							
Automated dispensing machine reconciliation completed per shift							
All food is labeled & dated (patient food refrigerators)							
Emergency medications locked at all times							
Extra crash cart locks not kept on unit							
Different types of insulin not stored together in same bin							
IV bags locked							
Keys to medications not in drawers							
Look alike sound alike drugs segregated							
Medication cabinet doors locked							
Medication carts clean, preparation areas							
Medication refrigerator temps documented daily, within range							
Medication refrigerators have no food in them							
Medication resource/ reference books current							
Medication rooms locked							

Directions 1. Complete this tool for each unit each day by 12:00 noon. 2. Mark compliant areas with a check. Mark non-compliant areas with an X. 3. Document your actions to correct each item marked with an X on the bottom of this tool. 4. Turn in one tool per unit each Monday morning by 10:00 a.m. to Administration.	Monday	Tuesday	Wednesday	Thursday	Friday	Saturday	Sunday
Medications in refrigerators locked							
Medications labeled (Pt name, account #, Rm #, medication, strength, quantity, expiration date							
Medications not expired							
Medications not left on top of med carts							
Medications not taken out of packages & left in soufflé cup							
Multi-dose vials dated = 30 days > opened or manufacturer's date which ever comes first							
Narcotics locked at all times							
Narcotics wasted & documented–2 licensed signatures							
Neuroparalytics secure							
No disinfectants or cleaners stored with medications							
No injectibles w/ topicals on the same shelf							
No leftover food stored without label, date in pt. refrigerators							
No single use medications/ vials used for multi-dose admin							
Only appropriate personnel have access to narcotics							
Only approved medications stocked in approved locations on unit							
Patient food refrigerators have no medications in them							
Refrigerators clean, defrosted							
Syringes & needles locked							
Syringes labeled							
Thermometers in ALL patient refrigerators							
III. Safety/Security							
No > than 12 "E" (small green) cylinder O_2 tanks stored in an area							
IV. Hazardous Materials							
EVS carts locked with no cleaning products accessible to public							
Formalin stored upright with spill kit							
MSDS sheet on unit for each hazardous material							
MSDS sheets/book clearly labeled, visible & accessible to staff							
V. Life Safety (fire safety)							
18" ceiling rule EVERYWHERE							

Directions 1. Complete this tool for each unit each day by 12:00 noon. 2. Mark compliant areas with a check. Mark non-compliant areas with an X. 3. Document your actions to correct each item marked with an X on the bottom of this tool. 4. Turn in one tool per unit each Monday morning by 10:00 a.m. to Administration.	Monday	Tuesday	Wednesday	Thursday	Friday	Saturday	Sunday
8' hallway rule EVERYWHERE (1 side of hall, on wheels & only temporary storage)							
All electrical & mechanical rooms locked							
Exit signs illuminated & point the correct direction							
Fire extinguishers current (dated monthly)							
No (flammable) papers on walls, doors							
No door props							
No holes in the walls or ceilings							
No missing, broken, or stained ceiling tiles							
No penetrations present in closets, hallways, rooms, etc.							
O_2 tanks, etc. in proper holders or chained							
Paper boxes, etc. stored on floor							
VI. Electrical Safety							
Biomedical equipment has current sticker							
VII. Infection Control							
All supplies & linen carts have solid bottoms							
Biohazard boxes labeled, covered, not available to the public							
Clean/dirty linen not stored in the same area							
Fans clean							
HVAC vents clean							
Ice machines clean with no calcium, rust, lime, dirt, stains							
Isolation rooms well marked							
Linen chutes latched/protected from public							
Linen covered, not ripped, solid bottom on cart							
Negative ventilation for isolation, dirty utility, decontam rooms							
No chipped or peeling paint							
No dust on the floor, waist high, equipment, shoulder, above							
No dust, dirt on vents or in vent space							
No mold in tubs, showers, sinks, ceiling tiles, etc.							
No rust anywhere							

Directions 1. Complete this tool for each unit each day by 12:00 noon. 2. Mark compliant areas with a check. Mark non-compliant areas with an X. 3. Document your actions to correct each item marked with an X on the bottom of this tool. 4. Turn in one tool per unit each Monday morning by 10:00 a.m. to Administration.	Monday	Tuesday	Wednesday	Thursday	Friday	Saturday	Sunday
No tears or cracks on bed or stretcher mattresses							
No torn stretchers							
PPE equipment stocked where hazardous work occurs							
Sharps containers not more than 2/3 full							

A. ACTIONS

Source: Rusty McNew, RN, MA, CPHQ, Dallas, Texas.

4-94 Emergency Department Open Medical Record Review Tool

			Medical Records					YES	NO	%
			1	2	3	4	5			
		Diagnosis, Procedure								
	Standard	Unit, ED, Diagnostic								
RI	IM.6.20	Advanced Directives								
H&P	PC.2.120	H&P								
	PC.2.120	Update								
	IM.6.30	H&P Prior to Procedure								
Assess	PC.2.120	RN Admit Assessment								
	PC.2.130	Initial Assessment Conducted W/ Timeframe								
	PC.2.120	Nutrition Screen								
	PC.2.120	Functional Screen								
	PC.3.10	Abuse Screen								
	PC.15.20	Discharge Screen								
	PC.8.10	Initial Pain Assessment								
	PC.8.10	Pain Reassessment								
	PC.8.10	Pain Non-Cognitive Scale								
NPSG / Patient Safety	1A	2 Identifiers								
	2A	Read Back T/O V/O								
	2A	Read Back Critical Test Results								
	2B	Abbreviations								
	2B	No Abbreviations on Preprinted Forms								
	2E	Hand Off								
	8A	Medication Reconciliation: Initial Inventory								
	8A	Medication Reconciliation: Compared w/ MD Order								
	7A	Handwashing								
	8B	Medication Reconciliation Communicated Next Provider								
	8B	Medication Reconciliation; Next Provider Compare List/ Orders								
	8B	Medication Reconciliation: Provided Pt On D/C								
	9B	Fall Reduction Screen								
	9B	Fall Reduction Interventions								
	9B	Fall Reduction: Patient/ Family Education								
	15A	Risk for Suicide: Screen								
	15A	Risk for Suicide: Interventions								
	15A	Risk for Suicide: Hotline Information								
	UP Protocol 1B	Performer Marks Site								
	UP Protocol 1C	Time Out								
	MM.3.20 §482.25	Resume/ Blanket Orders								
Anesthesia	RI.2.40 §482.51(b)(2)	Informed Consent: Procedure Present								
	RI.2.40 §482.52(b)	Informed Consent: Anesthesia Present								
	RI.2.40	Informed Consent Blood Present								
	RI.2.40	Informed Consent Verbiage: Procedure, Anesthesia, Blood								
	PC.13.20	ASA								
	PC.13.20, §482.52(b)(1)	Pre-Moderate Sedation Assessment								
	PC.13.20	Plan for Anesthesia: Moderate Sedation Documented								
	PC.13.20	Immediate Pre-Induction Assessment Prior to Moderate Sedation								
	PC.13.40	Discharge Aldrete/ LIP Order After Moderate Sedation								
Procedure Note	§482.51(b)(5)	Pre-op Diagnosis								
	IM.6.30	Post-op Diagnosis								
	IM.6.30	Name of Surgeon/ LIP/ Assistants								
	IM.6.30	Procedure								
	IM.6.30	Description of Procedure								
	IM.6.30	Findings								
	§482.51(b)(5)	Complications								
	IM.6.30	EBL								
	IM.6.30	Specimen Removed								
Date	MS.3.20	Legible								
	IM.6.10	Dated								
	§482.23(c)(2)	Timed								
	IM.6.10	Author ID								
	IM.6.50 §482.23(c)(2)(ii)	Verbal Orders Authenticated Per State Law								

Source: Rusty McNew, RN, MA, CPHQ, Dallas, Texas.

4-95 Joint Commission Team Tracking Tool

JCAHO/ CMS Chapter	Accountable A Team Member	Chapter Leader	Standard/ Chapter Team	Jan	Feb	Apr	May	Jun	Jul	Aug	Sep	Oct	Nov	Dec
National Patient Safety (NPSG)														
			Patient Safety Annual Report (LD.4.40 EP8)											
			Patient Safety Annual Evaluation (LD.4.40 EP8)											
			Goal 1 Improve Accuracy Patient Identification											
			1A Two patient identifiers											
			Goal 2 Improve of Communication Among Caregivers											
			2A Telephone order/ critical test results read-back											
			2B Standardize list abbreviations											
			2C Measure/ improve critical test result reporting											
			2E Hand-off											
			Goal 3 Improve Safety Using Medications											
			3B Standardize/ limit number of drug concentrations											
			3C Look-alike/sound-alike drugs: (Annual Review MM.2.20 EP)											
			3D Label all medications											
			Goal 7 Reduce Health Care-Associated Infections											
			7A Hand hygiene											
			7B Health care-associated infection/ SE											
			Goal 8 Medication Reconciliation											
			8A Implement reconciliation on admission											
			8B List is communicated to next provider											
			Goal 9 Fall Risk											
			9B Implement fall reduction program											
			Goal 15 Suicide Assessment											

JCAHO/ CMS Chapter	Accountable A Team Member	Chapter Leader	Standard/ Chapter Team	Jan	Feb	Apr	May	Jun	Jul	Aug	Sep	Oct	Nov	Dec
			15A Risk Assessment											
Ethics, Rights and Responsibilities (RI)			**Staff Safety Perception Survey** (PI.1.10 EP2)											
			Staff - Opinions & needs *(Consider)*											
			Staff - Risks & Suggest To Improve *(Consider)*											
			Staff - Willingness To Report *(Consider)*											
			Patient Safety Perception Survey (PI.1.10 EP3)											
			Patient - Care *(Consider)*											
			Patient - Specific Needs & Expectations											
			Patient - Needs & Expectations Meet *(Consider)*											
			Patient - How Hospital Improve Pt Safety *(Consider)*											
			Patient - Effectiveness Pain Mgt. *(Consider)*											
			Patient Complaints/ Grievances (RI.2.120 EP2)											
			Grievance Resolved 7 Day *(Recommend)*											
			Unresolved > 7 Day *(Recommend)*											
			Complaints By Type *(Recommend)*											
			Number per Month *(Recommend)*											
			Complaint Location *(Recommend)*											
			Organ & Tissue Donation (PI.1.10 EP19)											
			Notify OPO 100%											
			Conversion >95%											
Provision of Care, Treatment, and Services (PC)														
			Restraint (PI.1.10 EP6. PC.11.20 EP1)											
			Appropriateness Of Use, P&P Compliance											
			Anesthesia/ Moderate Sedation (PI.2.20 EP8)											
			Pain											
			Plan for Patient Care											
			Operative/ Invasive High Risk Process (PI.1.10 EP10)											

JCAHO/ CMS Chapter	Accountable A Team Member	Chapter Leader	Standard/ Chapter Team	Jan	Feb	Apr	May	Jun	Jul	Aug	Sep	Oct	Nov	Dec
Medication Management (MI)														
			Medication High Risk Process/ FMEA (PI.1.10 EP4)											
			Medication Error (PI.2.20 EP6)											
			Formulary Approval (MM.2.10 EP5)											
			Verbal Orders (MM.3.20 EP7)											
			Serious adverse Drug Events (PI.2.20 EP5)											
Surveillance, Prevention, and Control of Infection (IC)														
			Vent, CVL, UTI Nosocomial (PI.1.10 EP16\)											
			IC Plan (IC.5.10 EP1)											
			IC Evaluation (IC.5.10 EP1)											
			IC Risk Analysis (IC.2.10 EP2)											
			Vaccine Program Evaluation (Annual) (IC.4.15 EP4)											
Improving Organizational Performance (PI)														
			PI Plan (For Approval)											
			PI Evaluation											
			Leadership Priorities (LD.4.50 EP1)											
			FMEA (PI.3.20 EP1)											
			Sentinel Event Alert Assessment/ Activity (PI.2.30 EP4)											
			RCA (PI.3.10 EP1)											
			UM (PI.1.10 EP14)											
			Research (PI.1.10 EP17)											
			QC (PI.1.10 EP15)											
			Pathology Discrepancies (PI.2.20 EP7)											
			Core Measures (PI.2.20 EP13)											
			Autopsies (PI.1.10 EP18)											
			Resuscitation & Outcomes (PI.1.10 EP12)											
			Risk Management (PI.1.10 EP13)											
			Blood (PI.2.20 EP4)											
			Hazardous Conditions (PI.2.20 EP9)											
			Sentinel Event Improvements (PI.2.30 EP4)											

JCAHO/ CMS Chapter	Accountable A Team Member	Chapter Leader	Standard/ Chapter Team	Jan	Feb	Apr	May	Jun	Jul	Aug	Sep	Oct	Nov	Dec
Management of Information (IM)														
			Medical Record Pertinence (IM.6.10 EP12)											
			Medical Record Delinquency (CON05, IM.6.10 EP10)											
			Information Assessment (IM.1.10 EP1)											
			Information Flow (IM.1.10 EP2)											
Leadership (LD)														
			Board Self Evaluation (LD.1.20 EP7)											
			Budget Review: Operating & Capital (LD.2.50 EP1)											
			Annual Financial Audit (LD.2.50 EP5)											
			Outside Services Contracts Review/Approval (LD.3.50 EP6)											
			Accreditation & Regulatory Reports (LD.1.30 EP2)											
			Patient Flow (LD.3.15 EP1)											
			Safety Management Plan (EC.1.10, EP1)											
			Safety Management Evaluation (EC.1.10, EP1)											
			Safety Risk Assessment (EC.1.10 EP4)											
			Product Safety Recalls (EP.1.10 EP8)											
			EOC Tours: Clinical (EC.1.20 EP2)											
			EOC Tours: Non-Clinical (EC.1.20 EP3)											
			Smoking P&P Compliance (EC.1.30 EP6)											
			Security Management Plan (EC.2.10, EP1)											
			Security Management Evaluation (EC.2.10, EP1)											
			Security Risk Assessment (EC.2.10 EP3)											
			Emergency Management Plan (EC.4.10, EP3)											
			Emergency Management Evaluation (EC.4.10, EP3)											
			HVA (EC.4.10 EP5)											

JCAHO/ CMS Chapter	Accountable A Team Member	Chapter Leader	Standard/ Chapter Team	Jan	Feb	Apr	May	Jun	Jul	Aug	Sep	Oct	Nov	Dec
Management of Environment of Care (EC)			Emergency Management Drills (EC.4.30 EP1)											
			Life Safety Management Plan (EC.5.10, EP1)											
			Life Safety Management Evaluation (EC.5.10, EP1)											
			Qtr. fire Drills (EC.5.30, EP1)											
			OR, L&D Fire Drill (Annual) (EC.5.30, EP1)											
			SOC (EC.5.20 EP5)											
			Supervisory Signal Devices (Except Valve Tamper Switches) (Qtr.) (EC.5.40 EP1)											
			Valve Temper Switches & H20 Flow Devices (Semi-Annual) (EC.5.40 EP1)											
			Duct Detectors, E-mechanical Release Devices, Heat Detectors, Manual Fire Alarm Boxes, Smoke Detectors (Annual) (EC.5.40 EP10)											
			E-mechanically Release Devices (Annual) (EC.5.40 EP1)											
			Heat Detectors (Annual) (EC.5.40 EP1)											
			Manual Fire Alarm Boxes (Annual) (EC.5.40 EP1)											
			Occupant Alarm Notification Devices (All Audible Devices, Speakers, Visual Devices) (Annual) (EC.5.40 EP20)											
			Transmission Equipment Fire Notification (Qtr.) (EC.5.40 EP3)											
			Fire Pimps - Churn: No Flow (Weekly) (EC.5.40 EP4)											
			Fire Pumps - Churn: Full Flow (Annual) (EC.5.40 EP9)											
			Water Tank high & Low Level Alarm (Semi-Annual) (EC.5.40 EP5)											
			Water Tank Low Temp Alarm (Monthly in cold Weather) (EC.5.40 EC 6)											
			Main Drains (Annual) (EC.5.40 EP7)											
			Fire Dept Connections (Qtr.) (EC.5.40 EP8)											
			Kitchen Ansel (Annual) (EC.5.40 EP10)											
			Portable Fire Extinguish (Monthly) Inspection (Annual) (EC.5.40 EP12)											

JCAHO/ CMS Chapter	Accountable A Team Member	Chapter Leader	Standard/ Chapter Team	Jan	Feb	Apr	May	Jun	Jul	Aug	Sep	Oct	Nov	Dec
			Occupant Hose (1 ½ IN.) 5 Years After Install: Then 3 Years (EC.5.40 EP13)											
			Fire Dampers Test & Maintain 4 Years (Operate Damper) (EC.5.40 EP14)											
			Smoke Dampers Test & Maintain Every 4 years (Operate Damper) (EC.5.40 EP14)											
			HVAC Smoke Detection Shutdown Devices (Annual) (EC5.40 EP14)											
			Sliding Rolling Fire Doors (Annual) (EC.5.40 EP16)											
			Battery Powered Lights/ Egress: Functional 30 Day/ 30 Seconds (EC.7.40 EP3)											
			EOC - Utility Management Plan (EC.7.10, EP7)											
			EOC - Utility Management Evaluation (EC.7.10, EP7)											
			EOC - Medical Equipment Plan (EC. 6.10, EP1)											
			EOC - Medical Equipment Evaluation (EC. 6.10, EP1)											
			Safe Medical Device (EC.6.10 EP7)											
			EOC - Hazardous Materials Plan (EC.3.10, EP1)											
			EOC - Hazardous Materials Evaluation (EC.3.10, EP1)											
Management of Human Resources (HR)														
			Staffing Effectiveness (PI.2.20 EP10, HR.1.30 EP11)											
			Staffing Effectiveness Plan											
			Staffing Effectiveness Evaluation											
Medical Staff (MS)														
			Graduate Medical Education (MS.2.30 EP6)											
			Peer Review											
			Credentialing/ Privileging (MS.4.10 EP2) MS Recommends											
			Credentialing/ Privileging (MS.4.10 EP3) GB Approves											

Steps	Jan	Feb	Mar	Apr	May	Jun	Jul	Aug	Sep	Oct	Nov	Dec
Step 1 - Meet With Team												
Determine Who May Already Be Working On This												
Determine Scope of Work												
Name Members												
Copy JCAHO Standards												
Set Meeting Date & Time												
Review Roles & Responsibilities												
Set Timeframes For Deliverables												
Step 2 - Review Current Process, Tools & Forms And Make Recommendations												
Determine Who May Already Be Working On This												
Flowchart Current Process												
Identify Compliance "Hot-Spots"												
Review Relevant Policy & Procedures												
Review Relevant Documentation Tools & Forms												
Review Relevant Data already Collected												
Step 3 - Pilot Process, P&P, Tools & Forms												
Determine Who May Already Be Working On This												
Develop Indicators & Monitoring Process												
Pilot New/ Revised Process, Tools & Forms												
Monitor To Determine Compliance												
Use Data To Refine Process, P&P, Tools & Forms												
Step 4 - Measure & Report Data												
Determine Who May Already Be Working On This												
Monitor												
Develop Indicators												
Develop Reporting Process												
Report Data												
Step 5 - Educate												
Determine Who May Already Be Working On This												
Develop Education Process												
Directors/ Managers												
Staff												
Medical staff												
Step 6 - Full Implementation												
Determine Who May Already Be Working On This												

Steps	Jan	Feb	Mar	Apr	May	Jun	Jul	Aug	Sep	Oct	Nov	Dec
Step 5 - Process To Report Compliance To Administration & Appropriate MD/ Staff												
Determine Who May Already Be Working On This												
Monitoring												
Develop Indicators												
Develop Process												
Report												
Communication Department Directors												
Monthly Unit Flyer												
Communication Staff												
Monthly Unit Flyer												
Communication Department MD												
MEC												
Medical Staff Lounge												

Source: Rusty McNew, RN, MA, CPHQ, Dallas, Texas.

4-96 General Hospital Joint Commission Roles and Responsibilities

	JCAHO Steering Committee	JCAHO Standards & Chapter Teams	Managers	Medical Staff	Administrative Team
1. Role	Steering committee for JCAHO Compliance	JCAHO Standards & Chapter Teams To Meet Compliance w/ Specific JCAHO Standards	Department Compliance	Participation & Recommendations For JCAHO Standards & Chapter Teams MEC Receives Timely Reports From JCAHO Steering Committee	Oversee the entire JCAHO process
2. Core Responsibilities	Interpret JCAHO Standards Assign JCAHO Steering Committee Member To Each JCAHO Subgroup Attends JCAHO Steering Committee Meetings Serve As A Resource To JCAHO Standards & Chapter Teams	Attends Meetings Identify Specific Standards To Review Review Standards vs.: Hospital P&P, Forms, Tools Recommend, Develop & Implement Solutions Measure & Report Data Develop Education For Managers, Staff, MD	Implements Changes in P&P, Forms, etc Within Department Monthly Staff Meeting Attends Monthly Leadership Meeting Collects Data As Needed Serves On JCAHO Standards & Chapter Teams	Approve P&P's That Impact Credentialing/ Privileging Processes & Quality Of Care Attends, Review and Make Recommendations To JCAHO Standards & Chapter Teams	
3. Communicates With	Managers Monthly Medical Staff Hospital Committees Administrative Team	JCAHO Steering Committee & Managers Monthly	Receive Communication From JCAHO Steering Committee and/or JCAHO Standards & Chapter Teams, Then Communicates w/ Staff		
4. Education	Receives Education Content From JCAHO Standards & Chapter Teams Streamlines Process w/ Coordinated Approach	Develops Educational Content	Educates Staff In Collaboration w/ JCAHO Steering Committee & JCAHO Standards & Chapter Teams		

Source: Rusty McNew, RN, MA, CPHQ, Dallas, Texas.

4-97 CMS Guidance on Hospital Emergency Services Requirements

Guidance Applies to Specialty and All Other Hospitals Except Rural Critical Access Hospitals

On April 26, 2007, the Centers for Medicare & Medicaid Services (CMS) issued a guidance clarifying the responsibility of hospitals providing emergency services if they participate in the Medicare program. The guidance makes it clear that nearly all hospitals—including specialty hospitals and others without emergency departments—must be able to evaluate persons with emergencies, provide initial treatment, and refer or transfer these individuals when appropriate. The guidance does not apply to critical access hospitals (CAHs), which are small, rural hospitals that are subject to separate regulation.

The guidance was issued in a Survey and Certification letter. The announcement was made at the annual meeting between CMS and the Directors of the State Agencies that contract with CMS to survey hospitals and other Medicare providers and suppliers to ensure compliance with quality of care standards.

Survey and Certification letters guide State Agency surveyors in determining whether hospitals meet all conditions of participation required to participate in the Medicare program. Today's letter reiterates Medicare's long-standing requirement that hospitals have appropriate policies and procedures in place to address individuals' emergency care needs 24 hours per day, 7 days per week.

"Any hospital participating in Medicare, regardless of the type of hospital and apart from whether the hospital has an emergency department, must have the capability to provide basic emergency care interventions," said Leslie V. Norwalk, Esq., Acting Administrator of the Centers for Medicare & Medicaid Services. "The guidance we are issuing today is part of an overall strategy to ensure quality care by assuring the rapid response to emergencies for all people with Medicare."

Three key requirements are (a) the capability to appraise the emergency situation, (b) providing initial treatment, and (c) referral when appropriate. The letter clarifies that the Medicare Conditions of Participation (CoPs) do not permit a hospital to rely upon 9-1-1 services as a substitute for the hospital's own ability to provide these services.

In a separate development, CMS issued a proposed rule on April 13, 2007 that would increase transparency and public disclosure concerning emergency services. The FY 2008 acute care hospital inpatient prospective payment system (IPPS) proposed rule would require a hospital to notify all patients in writing if a doctor of medicine or doctor of osteopathy is not present in the hospital 24 hours a day, 7 days per week. The hospital would be required to disclose how it would meet the medical needs of a patient who develops an emergency condition while no doctor is on site. CMS also invited comments on whether current requirements for emergency service capabilities in hospitals with and without emergency departments should be strengthened in certain areas, such as the types of clinical personnel that should be present at all times and their competencies; the type of emergency response equipment that should be available; and whether hospital emergency departments should be required to operate 24 hours per day, 7 days per week.

Although the survey guidance issued today applies to all hospitals, it also implements one element of the *Strategic and Implementing Plan for Specialty Hospitals* that CMS reported to Congress in August of 2006, in accordance with the provisions of section 5006 of the Deficit Reduction Act of 2005. Other actions CMS has taken to implement the *Plan's* elements include the following:

1. Continue making improvements in the inpatient hospital and ambulatory surgical center (ASC) payment systems to address the perception that specialty hospitals select more profitable DRGs and more profitable patients within those DRGs.

Inpatient Prospective Payment System (IPPS). In the FY 2006 and 2007 final IPPS rules, CMS refined selected diagnosis related groups (DRGs), including the cardiac DRGs, to reflect the severity of a patient's illness. In the FY 2008 proposed IPPS rule, CMS is proposing a more comprehensive revision to the DRGs that would further improve the accuracy of inpatient acute care payments, while providing additional incentives for hospitals to engage in quality improvement efforts. The proposed rule would replace the existing 538 DRGs with 745 new DRGs to account more fully for the severity of the patient's condition.

CMS is also transitioning from basing DRG weights on hospital charges to estimated hospital costs. Studies by the Medicare Payment Advisory Commission have indicated that hospitals charge significantly more than their costs for some types of services, such as medical supplies and radiology. As a result, certain services are relatively more profitable, potentially contributing to the development of specialty hospitals which focus on high margin conditions. By basing DRG weights on estimated costs, rather than hospital charges, hospital payments will be more closely aligned with the actual costs of patient care, and the incentive for hospitals to take higher margin cases will be reduced. In October 2006, CMS began to phase in the new cost-based weights. The phase-in will take three years.

ASC Payment System. Consistent with its payment reform goals, CMS published its proposal for reforming the payment system for ambulatory surgical centers on August 23, 2006. The proposal was intended to improve payment accuracy under the revised ASC payment system by more logically aligning payment rates across payment systems to eliminate financial incentives favoring one care setting over another. The proposal would significantly expand the list of covered ASC services and provide ASC payment generally based on the Ambulatory Payment Classification relative payment weights used in the Outpatient Prospective Payment System to improve access to surgical services and payment accuracy. At the same time, the proposed rule recommended capping ASC payments at the physician non-facility practice expense payment rate for services that are frequently performed in the physician office setting and that would be new to the ASC list of covered procedures in CY 2008. CMS is reviewing the public comments on that proposed rule and expects to publish a final rule in the summer of 2007, with the revised ASC payment system to be implemented January 1, 2008.

2. *Transparency and Required Disclosure of Hospital Investment and Ownership Information.*

Disclosure to Patients of Physician Ownership in Hospital. In the FY 2008 IPPS proposed rule issued on April 13, 2007, CMS proposed to require hospitals to disclose to patients whether they are owned in part or in whole by physicians, and if so, to make available the names of the physician owners. In addition, as a condition of continued medical staff membership, physicians would be required to inform patients of their ownership interests in a hospital at the time they refer patients to that hospital.

Disclosure to CMS. Using its existing authority, CMS will be requiring hospitals to disclose information concerning physician investment and compensation arrangements. By July 2007, approximately 500 hospitals will be required to complete a Financial Relationship Disclosure Report and submit information to CMS for review. CMS is studying ways to implement a regular mandatory disclosure process that will apply to all Medicare participating hospitals.

3. Transparency in Emergency Services Capability.

Disclosure to Patients. The FY 2008 IPPS proposed rule would require a hospital to notify all patients in writing if a doctor of medicine or doctor of osteopathy is not present in the hospital 24 hours a day, 7 days per week. The hospital would also be required to disclose how it would meet the medical needs of a patient who develops an emergency condition while no doctor is on site.

4. Obligations of Hospitals with Specialized Capabilities to Accept Appropriate Transfer of Individuals with Emergency Medical Conditions, as Required by the Emergency Medical Treatment and Labor Act (EMTALA).

Accepting Emergency Transfers. The FY 2007 IPPS rule added language to the EMTALA rules clarifying that every participating hospital with specialized capabilities, *regardless of whether or not it operates an emergency department (ED)*, must accept an appropriate transfer for which it has capacity and the necessary specialized capabilities to treat the patient.

5. Changes to Enrollment Form to Capture Type of Hospital.

Identifying the Type of Hospital. CMS is developing changes to the Medicare provider enrollment application form and accompanying instructions that would clearly identify specialty hospitals as a separate category of hospitals. Implementation of the revised form is expected by September 2007.

For more information on the emergency services guidance issued, see: www.cms.hhs.gov/SurveyCertificationGenInfo/PMSR/list.asp#TopOfPage

For more information about Specialty Hospitals, including the DRA Report to Congress, see:

www.cms.hhs.gov/PhysicianSelfReferral/

Source: Press Release. CMS Office of Public Affairs, April 26, 2007.

LEADERSHIP

4-98 Emergency Department Committee Meeting Template

Emergency Department Committee
Area: ______________

Date: __________
Time: __________

Place: __________
Co-Chairs: ______________ ______________

1. Minutes/Attendance list

______ Approved as read.
______ Approved with additions/deletions.

2. Old Business

2.1 Management of Care Study
Name of Study____________________________________
** See Clinical Indicator Sheet for findings, conclusions, actions, and evaluation.*

3. Reports

3.1 Quality Indicator Report
______ ** See Quality Indicator Report for findings, conclusions, actions, and evaluation.*

3.2 Patient Satisfaction
______ ** See Patient Satisfaction Report for findings, conclusions, actions, and evaluation.*

3.3 Referrals

4. New Business

Agenda Number: __________

Quality Issue:

Findings:

Conclusions:

Actions/Responsibility:

Evaluation Date: __/__/___

Results of Evaluation:

Agenda Number: __________

Quality Issue:

Findings:

Conclusions:

Actions/Responsibility:

Evaluation Date: __/__/___

Results of Evaluation:

Emergency Services Department Management of Care Team Meeting Minutes

Agenda Number/Issue: Action/Responsibility:	Findings/Conclusions: Evaluation:

Source: Rusty McNew, RN, MA, CPHQ, Dallas, Texas.

4-99 Emergency Department Provider Satisfaction Survey

Below are some things people say about their doctors. Please give us your opinion about your doctor.	Strongly Disagree	Disagree	Not Sure	Agree	Strongly Agree
1. The Emergency Department doctor listened to me.					
2. The Emergency Department doctor took enough time with me and/or my child.					
3. The Emergency Department doctor or nurse explained the effects my medications may have on me and/or my child.					
4. The Emergency Department doctor or nurse told me what I need to know about my or my child's treatment and follow-up plans.					

Comments:

____

____

____

____

____

____

Provider Name: ______________________________

Comments are confidential.

Source: Rusty McNew, RN, MA, CPHQ, Dallas, Texas.

4-100 Emergency Department Staff Survey of Management

YES	NO	1. Does ED Management set goals that are reasonable and measurable?
YES	NO	2. Are the deadlines ED Management set usually fair and realistic?
YES	NO	3. Is ED Management sympathetic/empathetic when it comes to personal problems—sick children, family crises, day care, elderly relatives? What measures would be of help to you? Flextime? Job sharing? More personal days off? Company day care? Company-sponsored emergency day care?
YES	NO	4. Do you dare to disagree with ED Management? If not, why not?
YES	NO	5. In general, does ED Management stress results and allow you to handle the details of projects? Or does ED Management often oversupervise?
YES	NO	6. Are your complaints given the attention they deserve? Do you feel ED Management is in your corner even when it can't offer concrete assistance?
YES	NO	7. Do you feel you can admit your mistakes without fear of being judged too harshly?
YES	NO	8. Do you feel like a valuable member of the team? If not, why not?
YES	NO	9. Is ED Management usually available when you need it?
YES	NO	10. Do you feel ED Management meddles in your work or makes changes that don't improve it?
YES	NO	11. Does ED Management approach projects with an open mind, make its goals and expectations clear, then allow you to figure out how you'll accomplish them?
YES	NO	12. When ED Management offers criticism, is it usually constructive?
YES	NO	13. Does the ED Management treat department members with courtesy and respect?
YES	NO	14. Is ED Management consistent and fair? If not, can you give examples?
YES	NO	15. Do you have faith ED Management helps you grow in your job, develop your skills, and move on when you're ready? If not, why not?
YES	NO	16. Do you get enough feedback from ED Management—especially positive feedback?
YES	NO	17. Do you believe ED Management takes your ideas—and your answers to this questionnaire—seriously? If not, why not?

Source: Rusty McNew, RN, MA, CPHQ, Dallas, Texas.

4-101 Emergency Department Committee/Team Effectiveness Evaluation

Ineffective Effective		
1. Confused; vague; disagreement	**Priorities/Goals** 1 2 3 4 5 **Least Greatest**	Clear; shared by committee members priorities/ goals obtained
2. Indifference; lack of commitment	**Involvement/Commitment of Team** 1 2 3 4 5 **Least Greatest**	Everyone is actively involved in getting the work done
3. Members distrust one another, are careful, closed, afraid to criticize or be criticized	**Trust** 1 2 3 4 5 **Least Greatest**	Members trust one another; are not afraid to say what they feel, freely express negative ideas
4. Disagreements are ignored or covered up	**Conflict/Resolution** 1 2 3 4 5 **Least Greatest**	Conflicts are acknowledged and discussed openly
5. Members try to win; dissenters are overruled or ignored; decisions are supported only by those who made them	**Decision Making** 1 2 3 4 5 **Least Greatest**	People try to understand other members' views; differences are appreciated and used to improve decisions; decisions are supported by the entire group
6. Group depends too much on a single person or a few persons	**Leadership** 1 2 3 4 5 **Least Greatest**	As needs for leadership arise, various members meet them; shared leadership
7. Members and group in a rut; operate routinely; persons stereotyped and rigid in their roles	**Creativity** 1 2 3 4 5 **Least Greatest**	Group flexible, spontaneous; imaginative; tries new ways of doing things
8. All remarks are directed to the leader; members interrupt each other and try to dominate the conversation	**Communication** 1 2 3 4 5 **Least Greatest**	Members speak freely to each other; do not interrupt; encourage others to speak
9. Met few or no goals	**Set Goals/Timeline Measurements** 1 2 3 4 5 **Least Greatest**	Team has met all goals, proceeding by trial and error

Source: Rusty McNew, RN, MA, CPHQ, Dallas, Texas.

4-102 Joint Commission Leadership Communication Tool

General Hospital

JCAHO Leadership Communication

________ Department
________ # Staff
________ # Staff Attend/ Reviewed Information
________ % Staff Attend/ Review Information

JCAHO Chapter/ Standard	Policy & Procedure (REVISION)	Summary	Comments	Unit Education (DUE DATE)	General Hospital Education (DUE DATE)
Abbreviations *JCAHO Medication Mgt. Team*	(YES) Admin – 2.006 Revised 3/2007 Effective Immediately	If unacceptable abbreviations or designations are used the appropriate discipline (pharmacy, nursing, therapy, dietitians, etc) will clarify by calling the LIP and an order will then be written as "Order Clarification….."	Physician will be called to clarify.	(YES) Manager - March Department Meetings (3/31/07)	No
Restraints *JCAHO Provision of Care Team*	(NO) Admin – 3.209	Initially and every 24 hours: LIP must sign, date and TIME orders LIP must note reason for restraints LIP must note Acute Med/Surgical or Behavioral LIP must note type of restraint LIP must note assessment of patient	Separate consent sheet, document in progress notes. Do Not order PRN	(YES) Manager - Restraint team will provide unit education tools. (Manager) Education due to 100% staff by (5/1/07)	(YES) Educator - Will include in annual carnival day education (8/15/07)
Read Back - Verbal Order - Phone Orders - Critical Test *JCAHO Read Back Team*	(NO) Admin – WKRP.90	Verbal orders are discouraged, use only in emergencies and during sterile procedures Telephone and verbal orders are written on an order form with the initials VO or TO The nurse will read back verbatim to the physician Documentation is done by using the stamp "Order re-read and verified" or by writing RBV VO or TO followed by the physician's name/accepting person's name and title.	Decrease use of verbal orders when at all possible.	(YES) Manager - Poster will be provided to manager by JCAHO Read Back Team. Post on unit. (5/1/07)	(YES) Educator - Will include in annual carnival day education (8/15/07)

Instructions: 1. Communicate the following information during or before your monthly department/ area staff meeting.	2. Attach a sign in sheet to this document indicating 100% attendance or review of information and file in your office.	3. Place a copy this document on your staff communication board. Leave each copy posted for 12 months.

Source: Rusty McNew, RN, MA, CPHQ, Dallas, Texas.

MANAGEMENT OF THE ENVIRONMENT OF CARE

4-103 ESD Fire Drill Quality Control

PURPOSE

To protect patients, staff, and visitors from the hazards of fire
To ensure that the hospital is in compliance with Fire Dept. and JCAHO standards

RESPONSIBILITY:

As delegated by a manager.

FREQUENCY:

Once per shift per quarter.

REPORTED TO:

Area manager/director

TARGETED GOAL:

100%

INITIATIVE TRIGGER:

90%

METHODOLOGY:

1. Audit for documentation of one completed 1. *Department Fire Drill Report* per shift per quarter. Report should be scored as number of yes answers divided by 16.
2. Report % compliance with 2. *Departmental Fire Drill Report* criteria as an average of at least 3 completed drills.
3. Include your interpretation of data as Findings and Conclusions, action 3. plan, and evaluation date.

MEASUREMENT:

$$\frac{\text{Scores on 3 or more completed } \textit{Departmental Fire Drill Reports}}{\text{3 or more completed Reports}}$$

REPORTING TIMELINE:

Report completed by the 5th of the last month of the quarter.

Results:

Shift	Score on *Departmental Fire Drill Report*
7 to 3	
3 to 11	
11 to 7	
Other	
% Compliance	

Findings & Conclusions:

Plan of Action:

Note: Code Green Drills are conducted monthly and monitored in a few designated areas by Safety Management. Each area remains accountable for documentation of departmental fire drills.

Source: Rusty McNew, RN, MA, CPHQ, Dallas, Texas.

4-104 Cardiopulmonary Resuscitation Emergency Equipment Policy

POLICY

All patient care units and many specialty areas in the hospital, such as clinics, diagnostic procedure areas, physical therapy, recreation therapy, and the cafeteria, have their own resuscitation equipment.

Emergency equipment is specified by the CPR committee and should include

1. locked resuscitative cart with
    - airway equipment (intubation kit(s) and ventilation kit(s) with CO_2 detectors) in appropriate sizes for patients served (e.g., neonate, infant, pediatric, adult)
    - drug tray
    - miscellaneous supplies and equipment
    - accessory emergency equipment (tracheostomy tray, extension cord)
    - compression board
    - contents book listing emergency equipment and supplies with chart indicating their placement on the cart
    - CPR records for documenting resuscitative efforts
    - emergency equipment checklist with current date and signature indicating completion of the daily review
2. defibrillator
3. ECG monitor
4. oxygen (wall or cylinder)
5. suction (wall or portable)

RESPONSIBILITY FOR MAINTAINING EQUIPMENT

Equipment Checks

At the beginning of each 12-hour shift, the charge nurse or his/her designee checks the resuscitation equipment defibrillator, ECG monitor, and laryngoscope handles and blades for proper functioning; the ventilation kit for expiration date of the CO_2 detector; and the CPR cart for expiration date and integrity of the breakaway lock. Special care units must check all of the above every shift. Resuscitation equipment for recreation therapy and the cafeteria is secured in locked closets and must be checked weekly. Equipment in recreation therapy is checked by the department's staff; equipment in the cafeteria is checked by the peritoneal dialysis nursing staff.

Equipment checks must be documented.

Resuscitative Cart

Resuscitative carts in the ED are equipped in accordance with recommendations of the CPR committee. The integrity of all carts is maintained with a standardized security device, such as a breakaway lock. A CPR cart should be entered only for resuscitative measures. Each cart is labeled with an expiration date and equipped with a locator chart so that it will not need to be opened for purposes of checking expiration dates or educating staff.

The resuscitative cart is exchanged by central sterile services (CSS) Monday through Friday (8 AM to 12 midnight) and by the patient equipment department at all other times and on holidays. Carts are exchanged after each use and whenever the lock is broken. Expired carts will only be exchanged by CSS Monday through Friday, 8 AM to 12 midnight.

Airway Equipment

Intubation kits are supplied/exchanged by central distribution during times specified above. For areas included in the cart exchange, intubation kits will be exchanged with the cart. Areas excluded from the exchange must notify central distribution for an exchange. Laryngoscopes that do not light should be exchanged in central distribution. Ventilation kits are exchanged by respiratory care.

RESUSCITATIVE CART EXCHANGE PROCEDURE

Responsibilities

CSS or the patient equipment department will initiate an ED cart exchange within 30 minutes of a paged code for all areas in the main hospital included in the exchange. The user department must notify CSS of the need for a cart exchange when an item in the cart expires (as shown by the date on top of the cart) or when a cart's lock is broken. When a replacement cart is delivered and not needed (after a paged code), it is the responsibility of the user department to see that the delivered cart is returned to CSS following the code.

If an occasion should arise when CSS or patient equipment fails to exchange the cart, the user department should initiate the exchange.

CSS maintains a log of all cart exchanges by date, user department, and reason.
For a replacement cart following a paged code, no request is usually needed. CSS or patient equipment will initiate delivery of a replacement cart within 30 minutes. (The user department should initiate a request if the cart is not delivered within 30 minutes or if code is not paged.) The user department must return the used cart to CSS if the cart is not ready for return when the replacement cart is delivered.
For replacement cart due to an outdated item or broken lock, exchanges cannot be accommodated within the 30-minute time frame. The user department should notify CSS/ patient equipment of the reason for the requested exchange. Exchanges for expired contents should be scheduled with CSS one week prior to the cart's expiration date. Note: The cart should not be opened prior to calling CSS for exchange.

PROCEDURE

1. Prior to the exchange, the ED shall do the following:
   a. Remove from exterior of cart the ventilation kit, clipboards, CPR records, emergency equipment checklists, and cart contents book. Note: Areas with portable oxygen and suction should remove the portable suction and the oxygen regulator (leave the oxygen tank on cart).
   b. Clean CPR compression board with approved antimicrobial solution and return to cart. (If the board accompanies the patient during transfer to ICU, it is the responsibility of the user department to retrieve and clean the compression board and to return it to CSS.)
   c. Stamp a miscellaneous charge requisition and a pharmacy charge requisition (located with the drug tray) with the patient's name and the department number, and place them on top of the cart. Note: If the cart is exchanged for reasons other than patient use, stamp a miscellaneous requisition with the user's department number and the reason for the exchange.
2. After receipt of the cart, the user department shall do the following:
   a. Check cart for expiration date and integrity of the lock.
   b. Return to the cart the ventilation kit, clipboards, CPR records, emergency equipment checklists, and cart contents book. Note: Areas requiring portable oxygen and suction should connect the oxygen regulator to the new tank and return the portable suction to the top of the cart.

Cart Locks

Designated representatives for areas excluded from the cart exchange may obtain locks and prongs from CSS (Monday through Friday, day shift). CSS maintains a log of all locks and prongs issued. Locks may be reused by replacing prongs only.

This card copy is slipped into a plastic sleeve located on top of the code cart. The expiration date is checked when the code cart is checked.

Drugs and Supplies with Expiration Date

Indicate below the item name, drawer number, and expiration date of the next item to expire. Cross out last entry.

Name	Drawer Number	Date

Source: Adapted from the University of North Carolina Hospitals, Chapel Hill, North Carolina.

4-105 Emergency Department Safety Assessment Checklist

PHYSICAL ENVIRONMENT

1. Are separate entrances available for ambulatory ED patients and ambulances?
2. Does the ambulance entrance (if provided) open directly to a nursing station?
3. Does the ambulance entrance stay locked when not in use and how does staff know when to open it? _____ Is there a means for communication from this area to the inside?
4. Is there a means to observe what is going on outside of the ambulance entrance either by direct observation or by closed circuit television?
5. Is the ambulatory entrance from the outside capable of being locked if a lock-down is ordered?
6. Are areas around the ambulance and ambulatory entrance, including adjacent parking areas well lit?
7. Are there shrubs or other areas where persons considering assaultive behavior could hide? ______ In general, are parking areas for staff, patients and visitors using the ED, especially at night, safe and secure?
8. Is the waiting area staffed by a receptionist and/or triage nurse at all times? ________ Is there a protected area that will make it difficult for a person to grab them or jump over the counter? ________ Is the counter protected by some means (acrylic glazing above counter)? ________ Does the reception area open up to the waiting area?
9. Is a comfortable waiting area provided? ________ Is it clean, are washrooms provided, vending equipment, functional television, informational materials and telephone? __ Is a separate grieving room provided?
10. Is the triage area separated from the walk-in area? Does the door from the waiting area lock? __________ Does the triage area have an entry into the treatment area?
11. Has an area or room been designated as a safe room for staff or patients if violence erupts? ________ Is this room lockable? ________ Is it centrally located? ________ Is it equipped with a means of communication?
12. Has a room been designated as a seclusion room? ________ Is it specially equipped? ________ How?

OTHER COMMENTS AND OBSERVATIONS

EQUIPMENT

1. Do security personnel carry weapons and if so, what do they carry? _______ Has staff been trained (formal and documented) on their use?
2. Is security staff equipped with portable two-way radios? _______ Do they also carry either a cell phone or does the portable two-way radio have a cell phone?
3. Is Closed Circuit TV available for the ED? _______ Is the quality of the picture good? _______ Does it have storage capacity and for how long? _______ What areas of the ED are covered by the CCTV?
4. Are there any panic alarms in the ED? _______ How do staff request assistance if they need immediate assistance, and is this system effective?
5. Does the facility have a handheld and/or pass through metal detector(s) and have staff been trained in their use?
6. Are outside entryways adequately marked indicating weapons are prohibited?
7. Are weapons collected from visitors and if so, how do they store them?

OTHER COMMENTS AND OBSERVATIONS

STAFF TRAINING

1. Have staff been trained in
   a. access control to the ED?
   b. ED vulnerabilities?
   c. Dealing with emergencies involving violence?
   d. Nonviolent crisis intervention?
   e. Other departmental policies? (list)
2. Is there a system in place that informs forensic staff (law enforcement) of their responsibilities and are these responsibilities provided in writing?
3. Is the ED adequately staffed? __ Are waiting times documented?
4. Is someone available to periodically check on patients and their family during these waits to communicate and help reduce stress while waiting?
5. Have security personnel received outside formal training or in the process of taking a certification program in security?

OTHER COMMENTS AND OBSERVATIONS

POLICIES AND PROCESSES

1. Assessment policies for victim of domestic and other forms of violence?
2. Workplace violence?
3. Access policy?
4. Visitor (ED) policy?
5. Restraint policy?
6. Hostage plan?
7. Weapons policy? (staff, visitors)
8. Policy on staff debriefing/counseling following violence incident?
9. System for flagging charts and records?
10. Incident reporting (appropriate definition) and analysis system?
11. Emergency procedures? (list)
12. System for conducting periodic security assessments?
13. Forensic policies?
14. Policies for dealing with patient stress?
15. Policies for weapons searches of visitor and patients?

OTHER COMMENTS AND OBSERVATIONS

Source: Phoenix Area Indian Health Service, Phoenix, Arizona.

4-106 Security Risk Assessment*

Department: Emergency

			TOTAL
COMMUNITY RISK (*for Security Risk Occurrence*)			
Violent crime in area	15	[ ]	
Nonviolent crime	10	[ ]	
Nontypical behavior	5	[X]	
			5
ACCESS FROM OUTSIDE TO INSIDE OF HOSPITAL			
Open to all—no time restrictions	30	[X]	
Open to all—normal hours	25	[ ]	
Restricted to staff—no time restrictions	20		
Open to staff only—normal hours	15	[ ]	
Security key restricted	10	[ ]	
Entrance security monitored	5	[ ]	
			30
SECURITY RISK OCCURRENCE PER YEAR: *(Consider patients, staff, and facility)*			
5 or more	20	[ ]	
3 or more	15	[X]	
1 or more	5	[ ]	
None	0	[ ]	
			15
STAFF AVAILABILITY:			
Roaming	25	[ ]	
Central location	20	[X]	
1:3	15	[ ]	
1:2	10	[ ]	
1:1	5	[ ]	
			20
RESOURCE AVAILABILITY:			
No communication or monitoring	20	[ ]	
Telephone communication (Internal or 911)	15	[ ]	
Overhead paging	10	[ ]	
Alarm system/Lifeline/nurse call	5	[X]	
			5
	WORK SHEET TOTAL		75

ACTION:	
	105
Administrative review and/or change in policy/Procedure/ practice	↓
	80
	↓
Policy/procedure/security education	
	50
	↓
No change	
	20

*Security Risk assessment to be communicated to Environment of Care Committee.

Source: Tillamook County General Hospital, Tillamook, Oregon.

4-107 Security Presence in the ED

A Security Officer is assigned to the ED during the hours of darkness. Security will be called at the request of the triage nurse, and Security will respond promptly for the following kinds of patients:

- Patients brought in by law enforcement officers.
- Patients requiring restraints.
- Suicidal patients not accompanied by competent relatives or caretakers.
- Intoxicated patients.
- Patients who have exhibited out-of-control behavior in the past.
- Agitated patients at risk for escalation.
- Any patient who has a potential for violence.

Security will check each patient for any weapons or contraband when notified by nursing staff.

- Security will apply sticker to the chart indicating the time they checked the patient for any weapons or contraband.

In addition, Security will be called and will promptly respond when relatives or visitors exhibit behavior, which may escalate into or presents a threat to the staff, patients or other visitors.
Security will accompany patients outside for smoking if, in the opinion of the ED staff or Psych Liaison, not smoking may lead to an escalation of potentially violent behavior.

Source: Parkview Medical Center, Pueblo, Colorado.

4-108 Emergency Department Disaster Plan

Usual Hours of Business: 24 hours a day, 7 days a week

POLICY

The Emergency Department shall have a plan, based on the department's internal capabilities, to adequately prepare for any disaster. The plan will be in accordance with the Medical Centers Disaster Manual. Any member of the emergency department staff who becomes aware of a potential disaster will immediately notify the ED physician, charge nurse, ED administrator and ED Hazmat Coordinator.

PROCEDURE

In following the plan, the Hospitals Disaster Manual should be referenced and followed at all times. In the event of a Code Orange, the Emergency Department Disaster Manual will be followed as well. The Emergency Department disaster Manual includes specific instruction for each role to be assumed.

NOTIFICATION OF PERSONNEL

During normal business hours, notification will be made via the overhead speaker system, personal pagers or telephone extensions. After hours, home telephone numbers cellular phones or pagers will be used as appropriate to notify employees, the ED Operator will initiate the department recall (the recall list is kept in the department). The Disaster Call List will be followed sequentially in alphabetical order starting with the director.

PUBLIC ADDRESS CODES

A. ABDUCTIONS **(CODE GREEN)**
   Follow the hospital-wide Abduction Procedure in the Disaster Manual.
B. BOMB THREATS **(CODE BLACK)**
   Follow the hospital-wide Bomb Threat procedure in the Disaster Manual.
C. FIRE/EXPLOSION/VISIBLE SMOKE **(CODE RED)**
   Follow the hospital-wide Fire/smoke procedure in the Disaster Manual.
D. **CODE RESPOND**
   Follow the hospital-wide Code Respond procedure in the Disaster Manual.
E. DISASTERS **(CODE ORANGE)**
   Follow the hospital-wide Disaster Response procedure in the Disaster Manual.
F. TORNADO/SEVERE WEATHER **(TORNADO WARNING IS NOW IN EFFECT)**
   Follow the hospital-wide Tornado Threat procedure in the Disaster Manual.
G. WEAPONS AND VIOLENCE
   Follow the Weapons and Violence procedure in the Disaster Manual.
H. HAZARDOUS MATERIAL SPILL
   Follow the hospital-wide procedure for Hazardous Materials/Chemical Spill or Release procedure in the Disaster Manual.
I. BIOTERRORISM
   Follow the hospital-wide procedure of Bioterrorism in the Disaster Manual.

CONTINUATION OF SERVICES

If, by the nature of the event, the Emergency Department must be continued throughout the disaster, the department director or designee shall coordinate these activities. The department director or designee will initiate whatever actions he/she deems necessary for the continuation of services.

A. STAFF SCHEDULES: Staffing schedules will be made available to account for all Emergency Department staff.
B. PARKING: Follow the directions for staff parking in the Disaster Manual.
C. ENTRANCE INTO THE BUILDING: Follow the directions for staff entrance in the Disaster Manual.
D. ON-DUTY: All personnel will be considered on-duty until such time that the disaster is terminated or with prior approval from the director/designee of Emergency Department.
E. ELEVATOR USAGE: Follow the hospital-wide Disaster Manual for Elevator Location and Security Procedures and Evacuation Procedures and Continuation

of Care **ELEVATORS ARE NOT TO BE USED IN THE EVENT OF FIRE OR STRUCTURAL DAMAGE TO THE FACILITY UNLESS CLEARED BY SECURITY OR ADMINISTRATOR-ON-CALL.**

F. EVACUATION—Follow the directions for Evacuation Procedure in the Disaster Manual.

Source: Parkview Medical Center, Pueblo, Colorado.

4-109 Use of Cellular Telephones and All Two-Way Communication Devices

POLICY SUMMARY/INTENT: To ensure that Electromagnetic Interference (EMI) from cellular telephones and all two-way communication devices does not interrupt proper operation of any medical device within the hospital or patient care buildings.

DEFINITIONS:

EMI: Electromagnetic Interference.

EMI-producing devices include the following:
<u>Category 1 (High Risk)</u>

1. Cell phones and cell phone like devices (including cell phones with camera capability)
2. 2-way pagers
3. Personal Digital Assistant (PDA); for example, hand-held device that combines computing, telephone/fax, Internet, and networking features; also called palmtops, hand-held computers, and pocket computers with cell phone capabilities that cannot be turned off
4. Analog, digital and personal communication services

<u>Category 2 (Medium Risk)</u>

5. All walkie-talkies or wireless transceiver

<u>Category 3 (Low Risk)</u>

6. Cordless telephones
7. Wireless headsets
8. 1-way pagers
9. Personal Digital Assistant (PDA); for example, handheld device that combines computing, telephone/fax, Internet, and networking features; also called palmtops, hand-held computers, and pocket computers without cell phone capabilities or with cell phone capabilities that can be turned off.
10. All forms of Wireless Network Systems (WANS) including wireless phones

* Note: 1-way pagers do not transmit and therefore, do not produce EMI
AFFECTED DEPARTMENTS/SERVICES: All patient care departments.

POLICY: COMPLIANCE—KEY ELEMENTS

A. Category 1 and 2 devices are prohibited within six feet of all patients and in the following "cell phone prohibited" areas:
   Any patient care area with operational electrical clinical equipment
   Family Birth Place
   ICU
   Post Anesthesia Care Unit
   Emergency Department
   Operating Room
   Med/Surg Rooms

Category 1 devices must be turned off within six feet of all patients and in the above cell phone prohibited areas.
Category 2 devices may be used in a "listen only" mode in the "cell phone prohibited" areas and/or within six feet of all patients. If there is a need to respond the user must step six feet away from the patient and/or leave the "cell phone prohibited" area.

B. Category 3 devices can be used throughout the hospital.
C. Signage prohibiting the use of cellular phones and two-way communication devices will be posted in all "cell phone prohibited" areas. Signage designating "cell phone safe" areas will be posted in designated areas.
D. Individuals using Category 1 or 2 devices in "cell phone prohibited" areas will be directed to a "cell phone safe" area.

PROCEDURE:

1. All staff members are to be informed of this policy and made aware of the possible EMI (electromagnetic interference) danger to medical equipment such as telemetry monitors, incubators/infant warmers, infusion pumps, and defibrillators.
2. Appropriate signage as described above will be posted throughout the facility.
3. The use of staff-owned cellular telephones and two-way communication devices is only allowed in the event of:
   a. An emergency/disaster.
   b. An employee working in a celling with another employee assisting on the ground; in such cases, if the work is being done in a patient care area, the staff must be informed that a cellular telephone or two-way communication device is in use and may cause EMI. If any trouble with medical equipment is reported, the cellular telephone or two-way communication device must be turned off immediately. In the event an equipment problem is noted, the user should step away from the patient or turn the device off immediately.
4. Areas where it is safe to use cell phones within the hospitals are: Lobby areas, Waiting Rooms, Cafeteria, as well as Business office areas, such as Admitting, Administration, PBO and Nursing Offices outside of Patient care areas.
5. Any patient care injuries resulting from the EMI should be reported immediately to the Risk Manager and/or Nursing Supervisor as per Administrative Policy.
6. The use of cell phones for the purpose of transmitting digital pictures is prohibited in all areas of the hospital.

7. Avoid discussing or transmitting patient identifiable information that could give rise to allegations of breech of confidentiality.
8. Be aware of the potential for community transmissions that utilize these types of equipment to be overheard, listened in on, or even recorded.

Source: Tillamook County General Hospital, Tillamook, Oregon.

4-110 Abduction, Infant and Child

POLICY SUMMARY/INTENT: To protect infants and children from removal from hospital by unauthorized persons.

Responsible Persons:

1. All Medical—Surgical Nursing Personnel
2. All Medical—Surgical Ancillary Personnel

KEY WORDS/PHRASES		DIRECTIONS
PREPARATION	1.	On admission to the ED, infant or child will be placed in a room close to the nurses' station.
IMPLEMENTATION		
	1.	Identification band with patient name, age, physician, date of birth will be placed on ankle or wrist.
	2.	Parents are encouraged to stay with infants as much as possible.
	3.	Nursing staff will introduce self at beginning of shift.
	4.	Anyone carrying a baby (the patient) in the hallway will be questioned by ED staff.
EDUCATION		
	1.	Upon hire, and yearly, staff will be Instructed on the above procedures.
	2.	Instruction will Include creating an awareness of the real risk of Infant/child abduction and what to look for when observing activity on the unit; i.e., individuals loitering, persons In piecemeal hospital garb without proper I.D. badges. a. Please note the "The typical Infant Abductor" on page two of this procedure. b. Supervise infant and children at all times. Be aware that a disturbance in another part of the hospital could be a diversion to draw attention away from the child. c. Report unidentified persons carrying infant or child from hospital.
	3.	Nursing Supervisor will be notified of questionable individuals or if suspicious behavior is observed.
	4.	ED Manager shall be notified If discrepancies In this procedure are observed In hospital staff.

COMMON CHARACTERISTICS OF THE TYPICAL INFANT ABDUCTOR

- Female, aged 15–44, often overweight
- Emotionally immature and compulsive
- Frequently has lost a baby or is incapable of having one
- Often married or cohabitating; companion's desire for a child may motivate the abduction
- Considers the baby her own once the abduction occurs
- Usually lives in community where abduction occurs
- Often visits nursery and asks detailed questions about hospital procedures and layout
- Usually plans abduction but does not necessarily target a particular infant
- Frequently impersonates nurse or other hospital personnel
- Often acquainted with hospital personnel or victim's parents

Source: Tillamook County General Hospital, Tillamook, Oregon.

4-111 Emergency Department Overcrowding

POLICY

It is the policy of Parkview Emergency Department that all patients be seen by the ER physician as soon as possible. Under no circumstances will a medical screening exam be delayed on the basis of insurance or ability to pay to facilitate ER flow during over crowding situations.

PURPOSE

To facilitate patient flow during patient over crowding. To ensure patient safety and crowd control in the Emergency Room.

Criteria

Meets more than 2 to 3 of the following criteria. The ER charge nurse will notify Director or Lead Clinical Nurse:

1. No beds available in the emergency room.
2. The charge nurse is using hall beds for patient.
3. Priority 2 patients waiting greater than 30 minutes.
4. Triage Holding and E-3 have been used as treatment and holding area.
5. Consider using Emergency Room Holding Area Criteria policy.

PROCEDURE

1. The charge nurse and ER physician determine ER Over Crowding policy needs to be implemented.
2. The charge notifies Director or LCN about staffing.
3. Rooms X1, X2, X3 used for priority 3 patients.
4. The charge nurse or designee assist with triage.
5. ER tech is placed in triage to assist with point of care and procedures.
6. Notify Radiology and Lab about patients and ordering.

Source: Parkview Medical Center, Pueblo, Colorado.

4-112 Fall Risk Assessment and Prevention

PURPOSE

To maintain a safe environment for all patients
To identify those at an increased risk of fall by a Fall Risk Assessment

EQUIPMENT

Computer or manual assessment initially
Clinical Notes documentation

SIDE RAIL USAGE AND CRITERIA

1. Side rails are specifically raised if the patient meets one or more of the following criteria:
    a. Patient is sedated
    b. Patient is somnolent
    c. Patient is on life support equipment
    d. Patient requests the lower side rails to be up
    e. Physician Order to have the lower side rails up

FALL PRECAUTIONS

Consider the following if you judge the patient to be at risk for a fall:

1. Educate patient to call, and how to call for help.
2. Provide a room near the ED Nurses Station.
3. Ensure call device is available: call light, bell, etc. Answer promptly.
4. Offer assistance for ambulation.
5. Ensure bed and wheelchair brakes are locked.
6. Provide antiskid footwear.
7. Keep environment free of clutter or spills.
8. Place walker and assistive devices near patient.
9. Utilize bedside commode if appropriate to gait.
10. Keep urinal within reach as appropriate.
11. Anticipate patient needs and make frequent rounds and offer to assist patient to bathroom.
12. Monitor medication effects and side effects.
13. Observe for dehydration, perform orthostatic BP checks as indicated.

AGE SPECIFIC

Children age 2 and under shall have a crib available. The child shall be in the crib when unattended by parent or care provider. The crib sides shall be up at all times when patient is not directly attended. The crib top shall be on if the child is able to climb up the side rail and has the potential to fall.

* A fall mat will be placed on the floor by the bed if the patient's parent or care giver takes the child out of the crib and uses the full size bed.

* NOTE: Recommendation by Quality Council 4/01 and Safety Committee 6/01.

Source: Tillamook County General Hospital, Tillamook, Oregon.

4-113 Prohibited Abbreviations in Physician's Orders

POLICY

This nursing administrative policy and procedure outlines the steps for the Health Unit Coordinator (HUC) and the nurse to take when prohibited abbreviations appear in physician's orders. The procedure differs slightly for handwritten orders and Computerized Provider Order Entry (CPOE) medication orders. Other CPOE orders (non-medication orders) do not require clarification since they are not transcribed to other portions of the permanent medical record (this is a JCAHO time limited exception for computer systems).

The HCS Abbreviations Policy outlines prohibited abbreviations and the approved reference for other abbreviations. See for the list of prohibited abbreviations.

Handwritten Orders

HUCs and Nurses cannot accept or process any written orders containing prohibited abbreviations. Medication orders with prohibited abbreviations may not be transcribed to the Medication Administration Record (MAR). Orders containing prohibited abbreviations cannot be implemented until the orders are clarified and rewritten. Pharmacy is responsible for contacting physicians/providers for clarification of medication orders. Nurses are responsible for clarification of all other orders (non-medications). If a medication needs to be given immediately as with STAT orders or for patient care needs such as pain, then the RN must contact the physician/provider for medication order clarification.

CPOE Medication Orders

HUCs and nurses cannot accept CPOE medication orders with prohibited abbreviations. Medications orders with prohibited abbreviations cannot be transcribed to the MAR. Medications cannot be administered until the order is clarified by revision in CPOE. Most prohibited abbreviations will be found in comment lines or in free text orders. This only applies to medication orders. The nurse is responsible for contacting the physician about medication order revision in CPOE. Non-medication orders do not require clarification.

Areas with Unit Stock Medications and Pyxis Non-Profile Machines

In some clinical care areas, pharmacy does not review all medications orders prior to administration. The nurse directly accesses medication supplies in stock locations or Pyxis non-profile machines. In this situation the nurse is responsible for contacting the provider for medication order clarification. These nursing units and clinical care areas include: Emergency Department, Pediatric Urgent Care, Urgent Care Center, Labor & Delivery, Newborn Nursery, General Clinical Research Center, Main Operating Room (OR), Post Anesthesia Care Unit (PACU), Procedural Care Suites (PCS), Women's & Children's OR, Women's and Children's PACU, Women's and Children's PCS, ACC Day-Op, and most procedural areas and outpatient clinics.

PROCEDURE

I. <u>For Handwritten Physician's Orders:</u>

A. HUC or RN

1. Review orders for prohibited abbreviations. See example below.

DATE: **6/9/04**	TIME: **0800**	PM	ROOM NO. **9999**	University of North Carolina Hospitals Chapel Hill, NC 27514
Digoxin 0.25 mg po QD				
Flush feeding tube with 25 cc free H2O q4h				
P. Abbreviation, MD 999999 6/9/04			TRANSCRIBED BY:	CHECKED BY:

2. Highlight any orders containing prohibited abbreviations in yellow. In the example the digoxin contains the prohibited abbreviation "QD" and the flush order contains "cc."

DATE: **6/9/04**	TIME: **0800**	PM	ROOM NO. **9999**	University of North Carolina Hospitals Chapel Hill, NC 27514
Digoxin 0.25 mg po QD				
Flush feeding tube with 25 cc free H2O q4h				
P. Abbreviation, MD 999999 6/9/04			TRANSCRIBED BY:	CHECKED BY:

3. Notify the RN caring for the patient.
4. Make a note to the right of the order: "RN Notified."

DATE: **6/9/04**	TIME: **0800**	PM	ROOM NO. **9999**	University of North Carolina Hospitals Chapel Hill, NC 27514
Digoxin 0.25 mg po QD *RN Notified*				
Flush feeding tube with 25 cc free H2O q4h *RN Notified*				
P. Abbreviation, MD 999999 6/9/04			TRANSCRIBED BY:	CHECKED BY:

5. Transcribe other orders as usual. Highlighted orders are not transcribed.
6. Sign the "Transcribed By" box on the order sheet when complete.

B. RN

1. Notify the physician/provider for any non-medication orders containing a prohibited abbreviation. The physician/provider needs to rewrite the order for clarification. Orders cannot be implemented until rewritten. Make a note on the order sheet: "MD Notified."
2. For STAT or urgently needed medication orders, contact the physician/provider for order clarification prior to administering the medications. For other medication orders, pharmacy will contact the physician.
   Note: For nursing units or areas where pharmacy does not review all medication orders prior to administration, the nurse is responsible for contacting the physician/provider for medication order clarification.
3. The RN may need to take a verbal order to support patient care needs.
4. Verify all other orders.
5. Sign "Checked By" box on the order sheet when complete.
6. During Chart Checks (24 hour or 12 hour in ICUs) review the orders to see if all yellow highlighted orders have been revised. If needed, notify the physician/provider again.

II. <u>For CPOE Medication Orders</u>:

A. HUC or RN

1. Review orders for medication orders with prohibited abbreviations. See example below.

```
^&13G                                                        Page:    1

UNC HOSPITALS                               00001202001-2
CHAPEL HILL, NORTH CAROLINA 27514           BAGGINS ,FRODO T          M - 6
                                            02/14/1981    23
PHYSICIANS ORDERS                            1202001143            P   P
                                            8BT    8306P1
                                                        06/09/04

Medicare will only pay for services that it determines to be reasonable and
necessary under section 1862(a)(1) of the Medicare Law.  When ordering tests
for which Medicare reimbursement will be sought, physicians should order only
those individual tests that are necessary for the diagnosis and treatment of a
patient, rather than for screening purposes.
-------------------------------------------------------------------------------
ALLERGIES:
AMOXICILLIN
-------------------------------------------------------------------------------

ORDER#  DESCRIPTION                                          START / STOP

   4 ALUM/MAGN HYDROX + SIMETHICONE 30. CC PO ONCE DAILY    06/09/04 08:28
                                                              /  /      :

   5 DIGOXIN 250. MCG PO ONCE DAILY                          06/09/04 08:28
                                                              /  /      :
     HOLD IF PULSE LT 60          CHECK APICAL PULSE QD PRE DOSE
```

2. Highlight any medication orders containing prohibited abbreviations in yellow.
3. Notify the RN caring for the patient.
4. Make a note to the right of the order: "RN Notified."
5. Transcribe other orders as usual. Highlighted orders are not transcribed to the MAR.
6. Sign the "Transcribed By" line on the order sheet when complete.

B. RN

1. Notify the physician/provider that a medication order contains a prohibited abbreviation. The physician/provider needs to clarify the order by revising the order in CPOE. Make a note on the order sheet: "MD Notified."
2. Medications cannot be administered until the orders are clarified by revision in CPOE.
3. The RN may need to take a verbal order to support patient care needs.
4. Verify any remaining orders.
5. Sign "Checked By" line on the order sheet when complete.
6. During Chart Checks (24 hour or 12 hour in ICUs) review the orders to see if all yellow highlighted orders have been revised. If needed, notify the physician/provider again.

Source: UNC Health Care, Chapel Hill, North Carolina.

4-114 Elements of a Hospital Emergency Response Plan

This Emergency Response Plan is intended for hospitals involved in a community response to a hazardous substance incident. The plan should address the following elements:

- pre-emergency drills implementing the hospital's emergency response plan;
- practice sessions using the Incident Command System (ICS) with other local emergency response organizations;
- lines of authority and communication between the incident site and hospital personnel regarding hazards and potential contamination;
- designation of a decontamination team, including emergency department physicians, nurses, aides and support personnel;
- description of the hospital's system for immediately accessing information on toxic materials;
- designation of alternative facilities that could provide treatment in case of contamination of the hospital's Emergency Department;
- plan for managing emergency treatment of non-contaminated patients;
- decontamination procedures and designation of decontamination areas (either indoors or outdoors);
- hospital staff use of Personal Protective Equipment (PPE) based on routes of exposure, degree of contact, and each individual's specific tasks;
- prevention of cross-contamination of airborne substances via the hospital's ventilation system;
- air monitoring to ensure that the facility is safe for occupancy following treatment of contaminated patients; and
- post-emergency critique of the hospital's emergency response.

When a hospital has been designated by the Local Emergency Planning Committee (LEPC), it must prepare to fulfill its role in community emergency response. This is accomplished by engaging in emergency response planning activities that involve all segments of the community (i.e., employers, other emergency response organizations, local government, and the emergency medical community). With this in mind, the hospital should consider the following:

- The hospital must define its role in community emergency response by pre-planning and coordinating with other local emergency response organizations, such as the fire department. In particular, the hospital must be familiar with the ICS used by other local organizations during emergencies and should participate in training and practice sessions using the ICS.
- All hospital personnel who are expected to respond in emergencies where hazardous substances are released must be trained in handling contaminated patients and objects including body fluids.
- Training must be based on the duties and responsibilities of each employee.
- Hospitals should have a contingence plan for managing other patients in the emergency response system when contaminated patients are being treated.
- There should be communication between other members of the ICS, the incident site, and the hospital personnel regarding the hazards associated with potential contaminants.
- Hospitals should have access to a database that is compiled by the LEPC to provide immediate information to hospital staff on the hazards associated with exposure to toxic materials that may be used by local employers.

Source: *Hospitals and Community Emergency Response—What You Need to Know.* Emergency Response Safety Series. U.S. Department of Labor, Occupational Safety and Health Administration, Washington, DC. OSHA Publication No. 3152.

4-115 CMS Guidance on Use of Alcohol-Based Skin Preparations

Center for Medicaid and State Operations/Survey and Certification Group

Ref: S&C-07-11

DATE: **January 12, 2007**

TO: State Survey Agency Directors

FROM: Director
Survey and Certification Group

SUBJECT: Use of Alcohol-Based Skin Preparations in Anesthetizing Locations

Memorandum Summary

- This letter addresses risk reduction techniques to permit safe use of alcohol-based skin preparations in inpatient or outpatient anesthetizing locations in hospitals, Critical Access Hospitals (CAH) or Ambulatory Surgical Centers (ASC).
- Alcohol-based skin preparations are considered the most effective and rapid-acting skin antiseptic, but they are also flammable and contribute to risk of fire.
- When alcohol-based skin antiseptics are used in anesthetizing locations that have *not* implemented effective fire risk reduction measures, then the use of such antiseptics should be cited as evidence of noncompliance with §482.41(b), §485.623(d), or §416.44(b).

It is estimated that approximately 100 surgical fires occur each year in the United States, resulting in roughly 20 serious patient injuries, including one to two deaths annually.[1] Fires occur when an ignition source, a fuel source, and an oxidizer come together. Heat-producing devices are potential ignition sources, while alcohol-based skin preparations provide fuel. Procedures involving electro-surgery or the use of cautery or lasers involve heat-producing devices. There is concern that an alcohol-based skin preparation, combined with the oxygen-rich environment of an anesthetizing location, could ignite when exposed to a heat-producing device in an operating room. Specifically, if the alcohol-based skin preparation is improperly applied, the solution may wick into the patient's hair and linens or pool on the patient's skin, resulting in prolonged drying time. Then, if the patient is draped before the solution is completely dry, the alcohol vapors can become trapped under the surgical drapes and channeled to the surgical site.[2]

On the other hand, surgical site infections (SSI) also pose significant risk to patients; according to the Centers for Disease Control and Prevention (CDC), such infections are the third most commonly reported nosocomial, or hospital-acquired infections.[3] Although the CDC has stated that there are no definitive studies comparing the effectiveness of the different types of skin antiseptics in preventing SSI, it also states that "Alcohol is readily available, inexpensive, and remains the most effective and rapid-acting skin antiseptic."[4] Hence, in light of alcohol's effectiveness as a skin antiseptic, there is a need to balance the risks of fire related to use of alcohol-based skin preparations with the risk of surgical site infection.

The use of an alcohol-based skin preparation in inpatient or outpatient anesthetizing locations is not considered safe, *unless* appropriate fire risk reduction measures are taken, preferably as part of a systematic approach by the hospital, CAH or ASC to preventing surgery-related fires. A review of recommendations produced by various expert organizations concerning use of alcohol-based skin preparations in anesthetizing locations indicates there is general consensus that the following fire risk reduction measures are appropriate:[5]

- Using skin prep solutions that are: 1) packaged to ensure controlled delivery to the patient in unit dose applicators, swabs, or other similar applicators; and 2) provide clear and explicit manufacturer/supplier instructions and warnings. These instructions for use should be carefully followed.

- Ensuring that the alcohol-based skin prep solution does not soak into the patient's hair or linens. Sterile towels should be placed to absorb drips and runs during application and should then be removed from the anesthetizing location prior to draping the patient.

- Ensuring that the alcohol-based skin prep solution is completely dry prior to draping. This may take a few minutes or more, depending on the amount and location of the solution. The prepped area should be inspected to confirm it is dry prior to draping.

- Verifying that all of the above has occurred prior to initiating the surgical procedure. This can be done, for example, as part of a standardized pre-operative "time out" used to verify other essential information to minimize the risk of medical errors during the procedure.

Hospitals, CAHs, and ASCs that employ alcohol-based skin preparations in anesthetizing locations should establish appropriate policies and procedures to reduce the associated risk of fire. They should also document the implementation of these policies and procedures in the patient's medical record.

Failure by a hospital, CAH or ASC to develop and implement appropriate measures to reduce the risk of fires associated with the use of alcohol-based skin preparations in anesthetizing locations should be cited as condition-level noncompliance at §482.41, §485.623, or §416.44, as applicable.

In situations where a fire has occurred in an anesthetizing location and an alcohol-based skin preparation was in use, surveyors should evaluate whether an immediate jeopardy situation is present.

If you have any questions concerning this memorandum, please call David Eddinger at (410) 786-3429 or via e-mail at David.Eddinger@cms.hhs.gov; or Mayer Zimmerman at (410) 786-6839 or via e-mail at Mayer.Zimmerman@cms.hhs.gov.

Effective Date: Please ensure that all appropriate staff are fully apprised of this information within 30 days.

Training: This information should be shared with all appropriate survey and certification staff, surveyors, their managers, and state fire authorities and their staff.

/s/
Thomas E. Hamilton

cc: Survey and Certification Regional Office Management

---

[1] Association of Operating Room Nurses AORN Guidance Statement: Fire Prevention in the Operating Room (AORN website: http://www.aorn.org/), citing ECRI, "Surgical fire safety," *Health Devices* 35 no 2 (February 2006) 45-66.
[2] Prepared by ECRI for the Pennsylvania Patient Safety Reporting System, *Patient Safety Advisory* June 2005 (Vol. 2 No. 2) 13.
[3] CDC Hospital Infection Control Practices Advisory Committee, "Guideline for Prevention of Surgical Site Infection, 1999," *Infection Control and Hospital Epidemiology* April 1999 (Vol. 20 No. 4) 251.
[4] *Ibid.*, 257.
[5] Tentative Interim Amendment (TIA 05-02) to NFPA 99, 2005 edition, 13.4.1.2.2. Germicides and Antiseptics, issued July 29, 2005 and effective August 18, 2005. See also AORN Guidance Statement: Fire Prevention in the Operating Room; and *Patient Safety Advisory* June 2005 (Vol. 2 No. 2) 14, Prepared by ECRI for the Pennsylvania Patient Safety Reporting System.

Source: Memo from Director of Survey & Certification Group to State Survey Agency Directors, January 12, 2007. Ref. S&C-07-11. Centers for Medicaid and State Operations. Available online at: http://www.cms.hhs.gov/SurveyCertificationGenInfo/downloads/SCLetter07-11.pdf

4-116 Patients in Police Custody

Policy: Patients in Police Custody (Nonclinical Forensics Personnel)	**Manual:** Human Resources
Function: Management of the Environment of Care	**Policy Number:**
Effective:	**Page:** 1 of 2
Revised:	
Author: Security Work Group	**Distriction:** Systemwide

POLICY

It is the policy of this health system to ensure that patients under law enforcement custody receive proper medical treatment, while also providing a safe environment for its patients, visitors, and staff. The law enforcement officer requires an appropriate orientation to the organization, the procedures, and responses to emergency and disaster codes.

PROCEDURE

A. The Admissions Department or other department of entry into the system will notify Security or designee that a law enforcement officer or individual with a patient in custody is in the hospital. Security Officer or designee will then meet the law enforcement officer and review with them a Nonclinical Forensic Orientation Pamphlet and a Pocket Guide. Unit/department staff will also be available to the officers to answer questions and provide clarification on policy.
   1. Orientation Pamphlets and Pocket Guides will be available on individual units and in the Security or Administrative office at each facility.
   2. Officers will receive any necessary additional unit-specific orientation from the department manager or designated associate in charge.

B. The orientation will include, but not be limited to the following:
   1. fire safety
   2. safety/security
   3. right to know
   4. infection control
   5. hospital channels of communication
   6. patient rights.

C. The health system representative will confirm the identity of the officer and the patient and verify:
   1. name, badge, and agency of the officer,
   2. patient identity by name, date of birth, and patient number,
   3. patient is in legal custody by contacting the law enforcement agency if questions arise.

D. Upon admission, the health system representative will work with the Healthcare Access Department and unit staff to:
   1. Have patient placed in a private room as needed.
   2. Coordinate other law enforcement needs that arise.

E. Patient care units:
   1. The law enforcement officer will be solely responsible for guarding the patient while in a health system facility.
   2. All personal clothing and property will be removed by health system staff on the patient care unit and will be released to the officer.
   3. For law enforcement purposes, the officer will communicate with the medical team on the use of administrative restraints that do not interfere with medical care to ensure a safe environment.
   4. Medical restraints are applied according to the organization's administrative policy (Restraints and Seclusion).

F. Visitors:
   1. All visitors to patients in officer custody will require approval of the physician and the responsible officers. The officer assigned to the patient will screen visitors.
   2. The Healthcare Access Department will ensure that the Information desk card and other records are marked "Law Enforcement Custody." All inquiries should then be directed to the Security Department or the designated unit representative.
   3. Phone service will not be extended to the patient's room without the approval of the officer responsible for the patient.

G. Outpatient transfer:
   1. If a patient under custody is brought to the hospital for outpatient treatment, the department manager or associate in charge will immediately contact the Security Department.
   2. Security will obtain proper identifying information as outlined in C above.
   3. If a patient under custody is brought to a nonhospital health system facility for outpatient treatment, the department manager or the designated unit representative will obtain proper identifying information.
   4. Security or the designated unit representative will coordinate with the responsible officer to provide a secluded area while awaiting treatment, if necessary, so as not to present a threat to other patients or Kennedy staff.

RESPONSIBILITIES

A. Healthcare Access or other department of entry.
   1. Will notify Security of presence of a patient under custody in the hospital.
   2. Healthcare Access will mark records as indicated in F above.
   3. Nonhospital departments will designate a "unit representative" to identify the officer and the patient.

B. The Information desk will refer all inquiries for patients in custody to Security.

C. Department manager or designated unit representative will coordinate room placement, visitor contacts, etc. with Security.

D. Security will coordinate activities and responsibilities for hospital and nonhospital departments as outlined in this policy.

Source: Kennedy Health System, Voorhees, New Jersey.

4-117 Required ED EMTALA Signage

A hospital or other Dedicated Emergency Department (DED) that is subject to EMTALA is required to post signs explaining a patient's right to receive emergency service under EMTALA [42 C.F.R. 489.20(q)]. The Center for Medicare and Medicaid Services has described the signage requirement as follows:

- The sign(s) must specify the rights of individuals with emergency conditions and women in labor who come to the emergency department for health care services;
- It must indicate whether the facility participates in the Medicaid program;
- The wording of the sign(s) must be clear and in simple terms and language that are understandable by the population served by the hospital;
- The signs must be readable at a distance of 20 feet or the expected vantage point of the emergency department patron; and
- The sign(s) must be posted in a place or places likely to be noticed by all individuals entering the emergency department, as well as those individuals waiting for examination and treatment (e.g., entrance, admitting area, waiting room, treatment area).

The specific sign language as provided by CMS is illustrated on the sample EMTALA sign that follows. Any other signs posted in the same areas may not in any way conflict with the information in the EMTALA signage; be especially careful about how signs about patient insurance information are phrased.

IT'S THE LAW!

IF YOU HAVE A MEDICAL EMERGENCY OR ARE IN LABOR, YOU HAVE THE RIGHT TO RECEIVE, within the capabilities of this hospital's staff and facilities:

An appropriate Medical SCREENING EXAMINATION

Necessary STABILIZING TEATMENT (including treatment for an unborn child) and, if necessary, An appropriate TRANSFER to another facility Even if YOU CANNOT PAY or DO NOT HAVE MEDICAL INSURANCE or YOU ARE NOT ENTITLED TO MEDICARE OR MEDICAID

This hospital (DOES/DOES NOT) participate in the Medicaid Program

Source: Rozovsky, FA & Conley, JL. *Health Care Organizations Risk Management*, 2d Ed. Aspen Publishers, Inc. (2007).

4-118 Search of Emergency Department Patients and/or Visitors

POLICY

Patients and/or visitors may be searched by Hospital Security over concern that the patient or visitor may be a danger to self or others, if probable cause exits. Emergency staff may request a search, or Security may initiate the search; such searches shall be performed by security personnel.

PROCEDURE

The suspected patient or visitor may be asked to empty his/her pockets, purses, bags, cases, etc., for inspection, and a pat-down search may be conducted if deemed necessary.

- Weapons will be confiscated by Hospital Security and the Police Department will be notified for disposition.
- Street drugs or suspected street drugs, i.e., pot, cocaine, crack, etc., will be confiscated by Hospital Security and the Police Department will be notified for disposition.
- The medical staff will deal with abuse and/or suspected abuse of prescribed drugs on a case-by-case basis.

Probable cause for conducting a patient search may include, but may not be limited to:

- Person known to carry weapons (guns, knives, etc.)
- Weapons are seen on person
- Threats being made to self or others
- Weapon accessories (sheath for knife, holster, bullets, etc.)
- Suspicious behavior (hanging onto bag, etc.)
- Overdose
- Suicide attempt
- Psychiatric evaluation while in ED

Source: Parkview Medical Center, Pueblo, Colorado. Reprinted with permission.

MANAGEMENT OF HUMAN RESOURCES

4-119 Rationale for Patient Care Staffing

1. The ED is staffed based on patient acuity levels, unit census, scheduled appointments and established national guidelines.
2. Data related to census and acuity shall be collected and monitored at different intervals specific to the care area.
3. Managers respond to this data by adjusting staffing mixes at the appropriate interval.
4. Options to respond to staffing needs varies by service area. Each service area may respond to varying staffing needs for short term and long term solutions.
5. The ED utilizes appropriate solutions to varying staffing needs which include area-specific float pools, staff who have been trained to provide care in different areas, managers who may provide direct patient care, as well as the use of contract nursing when appropriate.
6. The Risk Management Root Cause Analysis Tool is used to assess for staffing related issues when as warranted.
7. Monitoring activities such as the ED Nursing Quality Report, Risk Management Reports and Patient Satisfaction data are used to monitor trends related to staffing.

A staffing variance is handled by a variety of methods:

- use of qualified ED float pool staff

- managers work with each other, floating of qualified staff
- incentive pay for staff, voluntary overtime is offered to staff
- management staff accept patient assignments
- use of case management staff
- pharmacy staff has assumed additional duties
- increased support by transportation
- delivery of supplies by disciplines other than nursing
- elective surgeries may be rescheduled
- patient beds may be closed

Source: Rusty McNew, RN, MA, CPHQ, Dallas, Texas.

4-120 Delineation of Privileges: Department of Emergency Medicine

Name:

Please specify below all categories requested, and initial:

_______ Evaluation of patient health care needs and provision of such services as are indicated

_______ Performance of definitive treatment, as falls within my areas of competence, and when appropriate, referral to other physicians for definitive care

_______ Care of life-threatening situations, with the facilities and staff available until such time as another physician or facility assumes responsibility for the patient's care.

Requested	Privilege	Approved	Denied
	Emergency Care of all systemic diseases within my capabilities as an Emergency Physician, or under the direction of an attending physician		
	Burns: Emergency or Initial Care only		
	Initial patient stabilization and care in cases of major trauma		
	Other:		
	Anesthesia:		
	Local		
	Regional		
	Nerve Blocks		
	Sedation & Analgesia		
	Other:		
	Cardiac Management:		
	Defibrillation		
	External pacemaker		
	Intra-cardiac injection		
	Pericardiocentesis		
	Open/Closed chest massage		
	Advanced Cardiac Life Support (ACLS)		
	Pediatric Advanced Life Support (PALS)		
	Preparation/Administration of Thrombolytics in Acute MI		
	Control of Hemorrhage by:		
	Packing		
	Cautery		
	Suture		
	Silver nitrate		
	Delivery of Baby/Fetus		
	Delivery of placenta (does not include retained placenta)		

Requested	Privilege	Approved	Denied
	Sexual Assault Evaluation & Treatment		
	Advanced Trauma Life Support (ATLS)		
	Initial assessment & stabilization of psychiatric patients		
	SPECIAL STUDIES AND PROCEDURES:		
	Arterial puncture		
	Arterial catheterization		
	Arthrocentesis		
	Aspiration		
	Joint		
	Lymph node		
	Biopsy		
	Skin		
	Other:		
	Catheterization		
	CVP or Subclavian		
	Foley		
	Splint Application		
	Noncircular casting		
	Continuous Positive Airway Pressure		
	Cricothyroidotomy		
	EKG (with interpretation)		
	Excision of minor lesion/cyst		
	Excision of nail		
	Endotracheal intubation		
	Gastric Lavage		
	Incision (w/without drainage or FB removal)		
	Abscess/Cyst		
	Hematoma		
	Skin/subcutaneous tissue		
	Injection of dye for radiologic studies (IVP, CT scan)		
	Insertion of:		
	Arteriovenous dialysis fistula		
	Chest tube		

Requested	Privilege	Approved	Denied
	Intubation (Endotracheal/nasotracheal)		
	Lumbar puncture		
	Pacemaker insertion—temporary		
	Paracentesis		
	Pericardiocentesis		
	Peritoneal dialysis		
	Rapid sequence intubation		
	Reduction		
	Dislocation		
	Fracture (closed only)		
	Removal of foreign body (w/without incision)		
	Repair of simple laceration		
	Facial		
	Other sites:		
	Sedation: IV/Conscious		
	Splinting		
	Suprapublic cystostomy		
	Tracheostomy—temporary		
	Thoracotomy/thoracostomy		
	Thrombolytic agent administration		
	Venous cutdown		

I understand that the completion of these forms at the present time does not preclude me from requesting additional privileges in accordance with the medical staff bylaws.

I also understand that, in conjunction with such privileges, occasional consultations are suggested, particularly when unexpected complications develop, failure to respond as expected occurs, or unfamiliar features arise.

I understand that I shall be authorized to treat any medical disease or perform any medical or surgical procedures at the hospital in an emergency situation. For these purposes, an emergency is defined as any situation in which any delay in administering treatment would result in serious harm or an immediate threat to the life of the patient.

I have no mental or physical condition that would impair my ability to perform the above procedures, and I am proficient and qualified to perform all such procedures.

________ ____________________________________

Date Signature of Applicant

ACTION OF THE CHIEF OF EMERGENCY MEDICINE:

_______ Clinical Privileges Approved as requested

_______ Clinical Privileges Approved WITH THE FOLLOWING CHANGES:

____

____

______ ______________________________________

Date Signature of Chief

ACTION OF THE MEDICAL BOARD

________ Approved

________ Approved WITH THE FOLLOWING CHANGES:

____

____

Copy sent to physician Date: ____________________

Date ______________ Signature of Chief of Staff: ____________________

Source: Huntington Hospital, Huntington, New York.

4-121 Delineation of Emergency Physician Privileges

PURPOSE

To delineate the privileges of emergency physicians.

POLICY

Category I

Those physicians who have shown by proficiency that they are capable of initially managing the areas of Emergency Medicine listed below, but are not yet board certified in Emergency Medicine.

Category II

Those physicians who are certified by the American Board of Emergency Medicine. The categories of Emergency Medicine are as follows:

1. Establishment and maintenance of airways
2. Initial recognition and treatment of cardiac arrhythmias and threat to life
3. Control of bleeding and replacement of blood
4. Recognition, control, and correction of shock
5. Initial diagnosis and treatment of the comatose patient
6. Diagnosis and treatment of acute infections
7. Diagnosis and treatment of allergy and asthma
8. Diagnosis and treatment of abdominal emergencies
9. Initial assessment and treatment of fractures and dislocations
10. Recognition and treatment of endocrine disorders and emergencies
11. Initial handling of obstetrical, gynecological, and urinary tract problems
12. Repairing lacerations of the skin
13. Recognition and treatment of drug problems
14. Recognition and treatment of emergencies involving the neurological system
15. Competence in various emergency procedures
16. Management of emergency systems
17. Management of pain, including IV sedation techniques

Source: Parkview Medical Center, Pueblo, Colorado. Reprinted with permission.

4-122 LPN/LVN Competency Record

Name: ....
Date of Employment: ....
Dates of Orientation: ....
Date Record Initiated: ....
Assigned Preceptors: ....
....

Certifications

Title	Exp. Date

I. Purpose
The LPN/LVN Competency Record has been developed to
   A. facilitate orientee self-assessment prior to orientation and promote his or her involvement in the learning process;
   B. facilitate the Staff Development process in providing an individualized orientation;
   C. provide a current and objective assessment of the nurse's performance in the delivery of patient care services;
   D. provide documentation of individual nurse competence, as necessary, for assigning clinical responsibilities.

II. Policy
   A. The LPN/LVN Competency Record will be initiated by staff development at the beginning of orientation.
   B. The LPN/LVN orientee will complete the self-assessment section and collaborate with staff development in planning for specific orientation needs.
   C. Asterisked competency statements require completion of the appropriate competency checklist.

Orientation Self Assessment											
Competent	Needs Review	No Experience	Skills & Competencies	END ORIENTATION		END PROBATION		YEAR ____		YEAR ____	
				Date	Init	Date	Init	Date	Init	Date	Init
			I. Maintenance of Safe, Effective Care Environment								
			A. Knowledge of Legal/Ethical Framework for Care								
			1. Verbalizes protocol for reporting child and elder abuse								
			2. Verbalizes knowledge of rape policy and kit location								
			B. Environment Safety								
			1. Describes the physical plan of the ED								
			2. Demonstrates awareness of ED Policy and procedure book								
			3. Verbalizes calling a code in the ED								
			4. Demonstrates location and correct use of adult and pediatric crashcart checklist and pediatric work cart								
			5. Demonstrates correct use of the Lifepak 6-S defibrillator Nihon Kohen monitors								
			6. Demonstrates correct use of IV fluid warmer								
			7. Demonstrates ability to set up and assist with specific procedures in the ED including, but not limited to, phlebotomy, paracentesis, peritoneal tap, thoracentesis, sigmoidoscopy, lumbar, puncture, and minor procedures as scheduled in ED								
			II. Maintenance of Physiologic Integrity								
			A. Medications/IV therapy								

continues

Orientation Self Assessment			Skills & Competencies	END ORIENTATION		END PROBATION		YEAR ___		YEAR ___	
Competent	Needs Review	No Experience		Date	Init	Date	Init	Date	Init	Date	Init
			1. Demonstrates ability to perform venipuncture for IV administration								
			2. Demonstrates ability to initiate IVPB medications as directed by RN								
			B. Application of Nursing Process for Emergent Patients								
			1. Applies general elements of nursing process for emergent patients								
			a. Verbalizes ED policy/procedure for triage								
			b. Discusses ED policy re initial and ongoing assessment of patient								
			c. States ED policy re: fast track methodology								
			d. Explains standing orders implementation								
			e. Verbalizes transfer policy and procedure								
			f. Verbalizes discharge policy and procedure								
			2. Uses nursing process to render care appropriate and specific to emergent patients with impairment of the INTEGEMENTARY SYSTEM								
			a. Assesses status of patient's skin								
			b. Demonstrates the ability to implement the emergency nursing protocol for patients presenting with surface trauma, as directed by RN, inclusive of, but not limited to								
			1. abrasions								
			2. avulsions								
			3. contusions								

continues

Orientation Self Assessment			Skills & Competencies	END ORIENTATION		END PROBATION		YEAR		YEAR	
Competent	Needs	No Experience		Date	Init	Date	Init	Date	Init	Date	Init
			4. lacerations								
			5. puncture wounds								
			6. foreign body injury								
			7. traumatic amputation								
			8. human bites								
			9. animal bites								
			c. Demonstrates the ability to implement the emergency nursing protocol for patients presenting with thermal injuries								
			1. Verbalizes thermal injury protocol for patients presenting with thermal injuries								
			2. Implements nursing interventions appropriate to thermal injury classification as directed by RN								
			3. Implements protocol for transfer of major burns to burn treatment center as directed by RN								
			3. Uses nursing process to render care appropriate and specific to emergent patients with impairment of HEAD AND NECK/NEUROLOGICAL SYSTEM								
			a. Assesses status of emergent patients presenting with neurologic impairment including head, neck, and face								

continues

Orientation Self Assessment											
Competent	Needs Review	No Experience	Skills & Competencies	END ORIENTATION		END PROBATION		YEAR ___		YEAR ___	
				Date	Init	Date	Init	Date	Init	Date	Init
			b. Demonstrates the ability to assist in the implementation of the emergency nursing protocol for patients presenting with head, neck, and facial trauma inclusive of, but not limited to								
			1. CVA								
			2. Seizures/status epilepticus								
			3. Unconsciousness								
			4. Spinal cord and neck								
			4. Uses nursing process to render care appropriate and specific to emergent patients with impairment of the CARDIOVASCULAR SYSTEM.								
			a. Achieves a score of 70 or better in basic cardiology exam								
			b. Achieves and maintains ACLS certification								
			c. Assesses patient's cardiovascular status								
			d. Implements standing orders for patients presenting with chest pain as directed by RN								
			e. Demonstrates ability to implement the emergency nursing protocol for patients presenting with chest pain								
			1. Demonstrates ability to use Dinemapp								
			2. Demonstrates ability to analyze basic rhythm strips								
			3. Recognizes lethal dysrhythmias								

continues

Orientation Self Assessment			Skills & Competencies	END ORIENTATION		END PROBATION		YEAR ____		YEAR ____	
Competent	Needs Review	No Experience		Date	Init	Date	Init	Date	Init	Date	Init
			4. Demonstrates ability to apply monitor leads and set parameters for individual patients								
			5. Verbalizes protocol for transfer of patient to CCU or telemetry								
			6. Demonstrates ability to do an EKG								
			7. Assists in transport with orderly to 3E, CCU, ICU, as directed by RN								
			5. Uses nursing process to render care appropriate and specific to emergent patients with impairment of the PULMONARY SYSTEM								
			a. Assesses patient's pulmonary status								
			b. Demonstrates the ability to recognize and implement the emergency nursing protocol for patients presenting with a pulmonary emergency inclusive of, but not limited to								
			1. pulmonary edema								
			2. asthma/status asthmatics								
			3. emphysema								
			4. smoke inhalation								
			5. croup								
			6. Uses nursing process to render care appropriate and specific to emergent patients with impairment of the MUSCULOSKELETAL SYSTEM								
			a. Assesses status of patients presenting with musculoskeletal emergencies								

continues

Orientation Self Assessment											
Competent	Needs Review	No Experience	Skills & Competencies	END ORIENTATION		END PROBATION		YEAR ___		YEAR ___	
				Date	Init	Date	Init	Date	Init	Date	Init
			b. Demonstrates the ability to recognize and implement the emergency nursing protocol for patients presenting with musculoskeletal emergencies as directed by RN, inclusive of but not limited to								
			1. soft tissue injuries								
			a. strains								
			b. sprains								
			2. fractures: closed, open								
			a. extremities—arm, leg, shoulder								
			b. pelvis								
			c. hip								
			3. dislocations								
			4. assists with cast application								
			c. Provides nursing interventions, including patient education, related to								
			1. crutch walking								
			2. cervical collar								
			3. knee immobilizer								
			4. buddy-taping								
			5. ace bandage								
			6. cast care								
			7. arm sling								
			7. Demonstrates the ability to implement the emergency nursing protocol for patients presenting for conscious sedation								

continues

Orientation Self Assessment											
Competent	Needs Review	No Experience	Skills & Competencies	END ORIENTATION		END PROBATION		YEAR		YEAR	
				Date	Init	Date	Init	Date	Init	Date	Init
			a. Verbalizes the protocol for caring for a patient undergoing conscious sedation								
			8. Uses nursing process to render care appropriate and specific to emergent patients with impairment of the METABOLIC SYSTEM								
			a. Demonstrates the ability to recognize and implement the emergency nursing protocol for patients presenting with a potential or actual metabolic emergency as directed by RN, inclusive but not limited to								
			1. hypoglycemia								
			2. DKA								
			3. HHNKS								
			b. Demonstrate ability to perform BGM testing								
			9. Uses nursing process to render care appropriate and specific to emergent patients with impairment of the GENITOURINARY SYSTEM								
			a. Assesses status of patients with genitourinary emergencies								
			b. Demonstrates the ability to implement the emergency nursing protocol for patients presenting with genitourinary emergencies as directed by an RN, inclusive of, but not limited to								
			1. urethral trauma								
			2. urinary retention								
			3. hematuria								

continues

Orientation Self Assessment: Competent	Needs Review	No Experience	Skills & Competencies	END ORIENTATION Date	Init	END PROBATION Date	Init	YEAR ___ Date	Init	YEAR ___ Date	Init
			4. cystitis								
			5. acute epididymitis								
			6. testicular Torsion								
			7. clotted graft in dialysis patients								
			10. Uses nursing process to render care appropriate and specific to emergent patients with impairment of the GYNECOLOGICAL/OBSTETRICAL SYSTEM								
			a. Assesses status of patients with gynecologic/ obstetrical emergencies.								
			b. Demonstrates ability to recognize and implement the emergency nursing protocol for patients presenting with obstetrical or gynecological emergencies as directed by RN, inclusive of, but not limited to								
			1. ectopic pregnancy								
			2. abruptio placenta								
			3. placenta previa								
			4. emergency delivery								
			5. post-partum hemorrhage								
			6. abortion								
			7. sexual assault								
			a. Implements nursing interventions appropriate for patient who has been sexually assaulted								

continues

Orientation Self Assessment											
Competent	Needs Review	No Experience	Skills & Competencies	END ORIENTATION		END PROBATION		YEAR ___		YEAR ___	
				Date	Init	Date	Init	Date	Init	Date	Init
			11. Uses nursing process to render care appropriate and specific to emergent patients with impairment of the EARS/NOSE/THROAT								
			a. Demonstrates the ability to implement the emergency nursing protocol for patients presenting with ear emergencies as directed by RN, inclusive of, but not limited to								
			1. FB ear								
			2. bleeding, discharge or wax in external canal								
			3. frostbite								
			b. Demonstrates ability to implement nursing interventions appropriate for ear emergencies as directed by RN, inclusive of, but not limited to								
			1. location and set up ENT tray and instruments								
			2. otoscope								
			3. ear syringe								
			4. tuning fork								
			5. controlling bleeding								
			c. Demonstrates the ability to implement the emergency nursing protocol for patients presenting with nose emergencies as directed by RN, inclusive of but not limited to								
			1. epistaxis								
			2. FB								

continues

Orientation Self Assessment											
Competent	Needs Review	No Experience	Skills & Competencies	END ORIENTATION		END PROBATION		YEAR ___		YEAR ___	
				Date	Init	Date	Init	Date	Init	Date	Init
			d. Assesses status of patient's throat								
			e. Demonstrates the ability to implement the emergency nursing protocol for patients presenting with throat emergencies								
			12. Uses nursing process to render care appropriate and specific to emergent patients with impairment of EYES								
			a. Assesses status of a patient's eyes								
			b. Tests for visual acuity								
			c. Demonstrates the ability to implement the emergency nursing protocol for patients presenting with eye emergencies as directed by RN								
			13. Uses nursing process to render care appropriate and specific to emergent patients with MULTIPLE SYSTEM TRAUMA								
			a. Assesses status of patients presenting with multiple system trauma as directed by RN								
			1. Verbalizes knowledge of primary trauma survey using ABC4. (airway, breathing, circulation, cervical spine, chest, consciousness)								
			2. Verbalizes knowledge of secondary survey								
			3. Verbalizes knowledge of general management following completion of systemic assessment								

continues

Orientation Self Assessment			Skills & Competencies	END ORIENTATION		END PROBATION		YEAR ____		YEAR ____	
Competent	Needs Review	No Experience		Date	Init	Date	Init	Date	Init	Date	Init
			4. Verbalizes knowledge of hospital medical policy for patients presenting with multiple trauma—surgeon on call is								
			14. Uses nursing process to render care appropriate and specific to emergent patients with INFECTIOUS DISEASE								
			a. Demonstrated ability to recognize and implement the emergency nursing protocol for patients presenting with a potential infectious disease as directed by RN								
			1. isolates for possible infectious disease, including rash.								
			2. labels room appropriately								
			3. demonstrates ability to implement and use								
			15. Uses nursing process to render care appropriate and specific to patients with TOXICOLOGIC emergencies								
			a. Assesses status of patients who present with a potential or actual toxicologic emergency								
			b. Demonstrates the ability to recognize and implement the emergency nursing protocol as directed by RN, with a toxicologic emergency inclusive of, but not limited to								
			1. acetaminophen								
			2. food poisoning								

continues

Orientation Self Assessment: Competent	Orientation Self Assessment: Needs Review	Orientation Self Assessment: No Experience	Skills & Competencies	END ORIENTATION Date	END ORIENTATION Init	END PROBATION Date	END PROBATION Init	YEAR ___ Date	YEAR ___ Init	YEAR ___ Date	YEAR ___ Init
			3. Salicylates, NSAIDS								
			4. Narcotics								
			16. Uses nursing process to render care appropriate and specific to patients with PEDIATRIC emergencies								
			a. Assesses status of pediatric patients who present with a chronic or acute emergency, using the following criteria								
			1. visual assessment								
			2. level of activity								
			3. skin color								
			4. breathing pattern								
			5. rectal temperature								
			6. heart rate								
			7. respiratory rate								
			8. blood pressure (if over 4 years)								
			9. weight								
			b. Demonstrates the ability to implement the emergency nursing protocol for Pediatric patients as directed by RN, inclusive of but not limited to								
			1. hypoxia								
			2. nasopharyngeal obstruction								
			3. oropharyngeal obstruction								
			4. upper airway obstruction—(croup, FB)								

continues

Orientation Self Assessment											
Competent	Needs Review	No Experience	Skills & Competencies	END ORIENTATION		END PROBATION		YEAR ____		YEAR ____	
				Date	Init	Date	Init	Date	Init	Date	Init
			5. lower airway obstruction (asthma, bronchiolitis)								
			6. fevers								
			7. set up infant radiant warmer								
			III. Maintenance of Psychosocial Integrity								
			A. Assesses the general level of patients psychosocial adaptation								
			B. Demonstrates the ability to recognize and implement the emergency nursing protocol for patients presenting with a psychiatric emergency inclusive of, but not limited to								
			1. acute anxiety attack								
			2. acute depression								
			3. suicidal ideation								
			4. assaultive behavior								
			5. acute psychotic reactions								
			6. drug-related psychiatric emergencies								
			IV. Health Promotion/Maintenance								
			A. Provides special need referrals								
			1. emergency housing								
			2. Pederson-Krag Clinic								
			3. Family Service League								
			4. drug abuse hot line								

continues

Orientation Self Assessment			Skills & Competencies	END ORIENTATION		END PROBATION		YEAR ____		YEAR ____	
Competent	Needs Review	No Experience		Date	Init	Date	Init	Date	Init	Date	Init
			5. Alcohol abuse hot line								
			6. Department of Health								
			7. Haven House for Battered Women								
			8. Well Baby Clinic								
			B. Makes support group referrals								
			1. Victims Information Bureau								
			2. Alcoholics Anonymous								
			3. Drugs and Alcohol Withdrawal								
			4. Women's Coalition								
			C. Special Procedures								
			1. Maintains well stocked environment								
			2. Demonstrates ability to provide a sterile field								
			3. Assists with collection, accurate labeling, and delivery of specimens obtained during procedure to the lab								
			4. Obtains consent, site verification for procedure as indicated								
			5. Requests H & P from physicians as necessary								
			6. Documents pertinent information to charge nurse								
			7. Reports pertinent information to charge nurse								

continues

Orientation Self Assessment											
Competent	Needs Review	No Experience	**Skills & Competencies**	END ORIENTATION		END PROBATION		YEAR ____		YEAR ____	
				Date	Init	Date	Init	Date	Init	Date	Init
			8. Cleans instruments and sends back to central supply								

Source: Huntington Hospital, Huntington, New York.

4-123 Emergency Department Physician Assistant (PA) Orientation Checklist

INTRODUCTION

Purpose of Orientation

- ☐ Provide knowledge necessary to perform ED responsibilities.
- ☐ Meet Joint Commission requirements.
- ☐ Avoid potential pitfalls.
- ☐ Decrease medicolegal risk.

PA ADMINISTRATIVE RESPONSIBILITIES

Scheduling and Staffing

- ☐ Procedures for shift requests, including due dates and necessary materials
- ☐ Procedures for vacation requests, due dates and necessary materials
- ☐ Shift swapping, illness and other emergencies which impact a scheduled shift
- ☐ Sign-in sheet, double coverage provisions
- ☐ Punctuality

Credentialing

- ☐ Current medical license
- ☐ Recredentialling AAPA & EMSA requirements
- ☐ Other certifications (e.g., ACLS, ATLS, PALS)

General Performance Expectations

- ☐ Clinical expectations
- ☐ Appearance
- ☐ Meeting attendance

Medical Staff Relationships

- ☐ Referral of private patients to specialists
- ☐ Call list
- ☐ HMO: Department-specific policies including use of call list
- ☐ Disagreements about disposition: how to handle
- ☐ Importance of providing service to medical staff
- ☐ Social interaction with medical staff
- ☐ General conflict resolution guidelines

Nursing Relationships

- ☐ Nursing capabilities (RN, LPN/LVN, Aides, Techs)
- ☐ Standing orders
- ☐ Triage protocols on test ordering and order patient seen
- ☐ Triage out of ED and management of HMO patients
- ☐ Prompt response to nursing requests
- ☐ Conflict resolution
- ☐ Notifying nurses whenever PA leaves department
- ☐ Praise and constructive criticism: appropriate way
- ☐ Nurses are the greatest asset to success of the ED: efforts to ensure their operation

Patient Satisfaction

- □ We are in a service role
- □ Empathetic attending behavior: appearance, name tag, identification, eye contact, touch
- □ Explanation of waiting times
- □ Pain relief
- □ Managing chronic pain patients
- □ Physician-Patient communication
- □ Communicating discharge instructions
- □ Dealing with problem patients

General Administrative Issues

- □ ED administration: Chain of command; names and telephone numbers
- □ Mail
- □ Reference books
- □ Long-distance and private telephone use
- □ CME
- □ Employee health program
- □ Meal breaks

EMSA Employee Issues

- □ Interface with corporate office
- □ Bloodborne pathogen manual

CLINICAL PRACTICE

Introductions to Department Staff and Hospital Administration

- □ Highlights regarding key hospital administrative and medical staff leaders
- □ Tour of Facility

Patient Flow Overview

- □ Patient demographics
- □ Patient flow through department
- □ Problem solving (i.e., lab, X-ray)
- □ Direct admissions
- □ Visitors
- □ Triage

Charting Documentation

- □ ED Medical Record
- □ Flow of medical record
- □ Legibility
- □ Dictation capabilities
- □ Discharge instructions
- □ Patient consents
- □ Patient transfers
- □ Voice BillStat (intro to key parameters)

Nursing Orders

- □ Method of conveying orders to nursing and clerical staff

Radiology Services

- □ Availability of CT/MRI, ultrasound, IVP, nuclear medicine
- □ Daily coverage in-house, specific tests
- □ After-hour coverage, specific tests
- □ Obtaining radiologists' readings
- □ Completing temporary reports
- □ Receipt of review of radiology readings
- □ Follow-up of discordant X-ray readings

Laboratory Services

- □ Availability of various lab results
- □ Mechanism for ordering lab tests
- □ Procedure for managing lab tests or type specific blood on an emergent basis
- □ Follow-up on culture results and abnormal lab studies received after patient discharge
- □ Blood bank (indications for blood products)

Cardiopulmonary Services

- □ EKG, blood gases
- □ How to order
- □ Stat. vs. I Stat.

Specialty Services

- □ Poison control
- □ Social services
- □ Inpatient care units: types/availability
- □ Psychiatric

EMS

- □ System overview
- □ Emergency physician's medical control and/or interaction
- □ Standing orders
- □ Bypass procedures

Equipment and Supplies

- □ Mechanism for requesting new or different type of equipment
- □ Documenting deficiencies in equipment or supplies
- □ Formulary: medications available in ED and process for obtaining different medications

Technical Procedures and Protocols

- □ Equipment availability and location

Chest tubes
CVP lines
Splinting
Epistaxis
Doppler
Airway mgmt.
Surgical trays
Spinal taps

Arterial lines
Temporary pacing
Suturing
Laryngoscopy
Slit lamp
Peritoneal lavage
Deliveries

- ☐ Medical staff considerations
- ☐ Procedures not to be done in ED
- ☐ ED clinical protocols (i.e., thrombolytics)

Patient Disposition

- ☐ Philosophy on admission vs. discharge
- ☐ Admission orders process
- ☐ Transfers: procedures, consent, COBRA, state regulations, documentation, destination
- ☐ Patient holding and observation
- ☐ Discharges: procedures, discharge instructions, follow-up referrals
- ☐ Rechecks

Reimbursement

- ☐ Changing guidelines
- ☐ Documentation
- ☐ Site-specific considerations

Participation in Performance Improvement Program (PI)

- ☐ Discussion of indicators and thresholds
- ☐ Responsibilities in PI data collection and evaluation
- ☐ Attendance at PI peer-review meetings
- ☐ Hospital Integration with PI
- ☐ Recredentialing use of PI data

Participation in Risk Management Program

- ☐ Incident reporting to EMSA Risk Management
- ☐ Risk management alerts and audiotapes

Policy and Procedure Issues

- ☐ Hospital policy and procedure manual
- ☐ ED policy and procedure manual
- ☐ Disaster manual
- ☐ Infection control manual
- ☐ Bloodborne pathogens

Physician Assistant Name: ______________________________ **Date:** __________

Orientation Conducted by: ______________________________ **Date:** __________

Source: Suburban Hospital, Inc., Bethesda, Maryland.

4-124 Physician Assistant (PA) Orientation: Minimum Standards of Care

PEDIATRICS

Subjective

- Interaction with parents/guardians, pre/post-natal course/PARA/PMD/last visit/allergies
- Appropriate interaction with environment based on age; onset of complaint (improved/status quo/worsening) fever/TMAX/how temperature was determined, i.e., PO/rectal/ear
- Response to treatment/home remedies
- Associates S/S/diarrhea/vomiting/number of wet diapers/able to cry
- Behavior changes
- Exposures
- Meningeal signs, responsiveness to parents/ambulatory
- Medications
- Allergies
- Growth/development

Objective

- Examine from least invasive (chest, arm) to most invasive (ENT)
- General—listen to parents, hydration, nasal flare, capillary refill, color vital signs
- Neuro—appropriateness, consolable, alert, smile, plays, good suck, ambulation
- Chest—retractions/abnormal sounds
- Lung—diminished, wheezes, cough, races, referred
- Heart sounds—rate, rub murmur
- Abdominal—bowel sounds, tone guarding, rebound, localized tenderness, organomegaly, masses
- Head fontanelles/deformities/asymmetry
- Ears—adjust auricle, do not force ophthalmoscope, tmS, Fb, cerument obstruction, cannals
- Eyes—perl, follows objects, discharge, injection
- Nose—foreign body, odor discharge
- Mouth—dentation, lesions, odor especially if ingestion is suspected
- Throat—lesions, nodes
- Neck—supple
- Skin—rashes, genitalia (sexual abuse/physical abuse)

Intervention

- Fever without a source, consider the following based on appearance of child: chest X-ray, urine, CBC, culture, SMA6
- In general—oxygenation, O_2 sat, hydration, teaching, parenting, pain relief

Common Drugs

- Tylenol—15 mg/kg for pain and fever (toxic is 150 mg/kg)
- Pediaprofen—10 mg/kg/tid
- Amoxicillin—40 mg/kg/tid
- Septra—10 kg = 5 mg bid
- Ceclor—40 mg/kg/bid/tid

- Augmentin—40 mg/kg (animal bites)
- Suprax—qd
- EES—3-50 mg/kg qid
- Pediazole—50 mg/kg 8 kg = 2.5 ml, 16 kg = 5 ml qid
- Rocephin—50 mg/kg IM (100 mg/kg if meningitis)
- Phenogran—.5 mg/lb q4-6
- Proventil Syrup—.1 mg/kg (2 mg = 5 ml) tid
- Nystatin Suspension—100,000 units/ml qid
- Duricef—30 mg/kg bid

MEDICAL ILLNESSES

Diabetes

Subjective
- Oral or Sub-Q insulin/last taken/duration of DM
- Pain/fever
- DKA (breath)—ABG/.9NSS
- Complications/risks/silent MI
- Neuropathy/foot problems
- Cellulitis/abscesses
- Abdominal pain
- New onset, polyuria, polydipsia, frequent abscesses, frequent yeast infections, family history

Objective
- Neurological (LOC and peripheral neuropathy)
- Breath
- HR, RR, adventitious sounds
- ABD-BS, point tenderness, rebound, guarding

Interventions
- IV .9NSS, SMA7, CBC, urine (CXR, EKG, amylase dependent upon history)
- Ketones dependent on urine dip
- Hypoglycemic reactions: oral vs. insulin

Seizure Disorder

Subjective
- Duration, time, type
- Injuries, preceding, after
- Etiology
- Complaint with medications
- Additional medical history
- Allergies

Objective
- Postical/injuries
- Head to toe assessment
- Hypoglycemia, hypothermia

- ETOH, drug abuse
- Medications

Sickle Cell

Subjective

- Onset, duration of pain, similar to previous crisis
- Pain medication used
- Caution if pregnancy or abdominal pain
- Is there a H/O drug seeking?

Objective

- Head to toe/often icteric
- Pain relief, CBC, Hgb, retic

ENT

Subjective

- Onset, duration of symptoms, associated malaise, fever, rash, H/O swimming or URI
- H/O trauma, nasal bleed
- Check risk factors/hypertension
- Anticoagulants
- Trauma
- If no risk factors, often infectious

Objective

- Ears—TMS, cannals, FB, auricle, lymphadenopathy
- Nose—septal hematoma, subcutaneous emphysema, discharge, bleeding
- Fractures
- Mouth—jaw, TMJ, dentition (number, pointing, abscess)
- Lesions, palate uvula, salivation, stridor, loose teeth (aspiration)
- Risk
- Throat—lesions, lymphadenopathy

Intervention

- Nosebleed—direct pressure, packing, if packing is done place on antistaph coverage
- Teaching—vaseline in nares
- Follow-up—in 24 hours for packing removal
- Pharyngitis vs. mono vs. lymphadenitis vs. AIDS
- History and appropriate F/U
- Able to handle secretions
- Medications
- Amox—250/500 tid
- Pen-VK—250/500 qid
- Cavities vs. abscess: pain relief vs. drug seek follow-up, antibiotics (teeth numbered when record)
- Foreign body ear—4 percent lidocaine and irrigate with WARM water or use alligators, cerumen spoon, operating head of ophthalmoscope

Dermatology

Subjective

- Onset duration, distribution and appearance when initiated, painful or pruritic, exacerbating, and relieving symptoms, associated symptoms, i.e., SOB. Self-treated?
- Prior history, medications, topics, and exposures

Objective

- Allergic reactions: check respiratory status, urticaria, angioedema, H1 or H2 inhibit (Atarax, Benadryl, or Cimetidine, if severe, steroids, epi) (check cardiovascular first)
- Cellulitis—warm, red, tender, check DM and fever, treat antibiotics (Duricef, Keflex)
- Chicken pox—respiratory S&S, 7- to 21-day incubation, dew drop on rose petal, vesicles, crusting, often initiate on trunk, crops of lesions
- Chronic discoid lupus erythematous
- Contact dermatitis—pruritic, exposed areas, linear, prevent with soap and water after exposure. Rx steroids (poison ivy)
- Corns—shoes, podiatry follow-up
- Cutaneous candidiasis—(check oral and anal area) keep dry, Lotrimin, if oral
- Nystatin or Mycelex (immunocompromised)
- Dandruff (seborrhea)—Sebulex or other shampoo
- Decubitis ulcers—positioning, dressings, debridement, infection
- Dyshidroses—sweat blisters
- Drug eruptions—onset, Atarax, Benadryl
- Eczema—history of steroids, cool compresses (atopic dermatitis)
- Erythema multiform
- Erysipelas
- Folliculitis—warm wash cloths, antibiotics, check nodes
- Fungal—tinea capitis, corporis, circinata, cruris, pedis . . . Lotrimin
- Furuncles (boils) and carbuncles
- Herpes simplex—cold sores
- Herpes zoster—shingles, painful, nerve distribution, ophthalmologist if near eyes, Acyclovir
- Impetigo—gold exudate . . . antibiotics p.o. or Bactroban
- Intertrigo—fat folds
- Insect bites—Td status and antihistamines, if infected—antibiotics
- Miliaria—"baby acne" hormonal change 4 to 12 weeks
- Pediculosis—K well, contacts
- Pityriasis rosea—viral, Christmas tree distribution, herald patch
- Psoriasis—steroids
- Skin tumors
- Tinea versicolor—Tegrin shampoo

Assessment

In general, wet needs, drying and vice versa. Although most rashes represent benign or self limiting problems, DO NOT think of them as minor. Some rashes represent diseases, meningitis, AIDS, renal failure, liver failure, syphillis, Rocky Mountain spotted fever, Lymes. Be aware of petechia (pinpoint flat, purplish red, caused by intradermal and submucous hernorrhage. ALWAYS check for bleeding disorders, liver, etc.)

Intervention

- Teaching, infection, spread, scratching (short nails, bandaids)
- Itching: cool compresses H1 or H2 inhibitor, steroid creams, consider oral steroids or Decadron, epinephrine .2 mg SC in adult, .01 mg/kg in child
- Referral to derm clinic; Refer to private derm

Wounds

Subjective

Mechanism, onset, tetanus status, foreign body

Objective

Shock, bleeding, size, depth, FB, function, N/V status, degree and body percentage if burns

Intervention

- Subungual hematomas use cautery
- Burns—major, treat shock first; if minor, pain relief—iced saline, narcotic, silvadene and dressing
- Puncture wounds—depth, foreign body; Teaching potential for infection or osteo, dimple cleaning. Consider X-ray or antibiotics.
- Suturing—Refer to text book anesthesia after N/V check. Palpate FB, fracture, plan closure. If unsure get help. Controversy about closing old wounds . . . 8 hours or more on body, 24 hours or more on face. Ortho involvement if tendon or joint space involved. Be aware of all hand wounds. Consult hand surgery when indicated.
- Suture materials: Need to add gloves, suture, and anesthetic to tray.
- Knots—In general, simple interrupted sutures are best. Vertical mattress has fallen into disfavor (good subQ closure eliminates need). Tunning sutures for long straight wounds distribute tension. Horizontal mattress for "loose skin" dorsum of hand, eyelid. Bury the knot for subcutaneous, subcuticular.
- Suture/staple removal guidelines—
  Face 5-7 days
  Scalp 10-14 days
  Trunk 10 days
  Extremity 10-14 days (extensor surfaces—14 days)
- Topical anesthetic—Tetracaine (4% lidocaine)—4 cc
  Adrenaline (1:1000 epinephrine)—2 cc
  Cocaine 10 percent—4 cc
- Buffer: Lidocaine with bicarbonate (1:10)
- Close skin with a monofilament suture material

Intervention

Demonstrate simple closure, refer for suture removal to private or HMO unless you desire to see follow-up

Psych

Potential violent . . . decrease stimulation, restraints, position near door, call for security if needed, never jeopardize self.

Subjective
Suicidal, homicidal, auditory or visual hallucinations, medications, of no prior history, and > 35 look for metabolic cause.

Objective
Heart, lungs, abdomen, screening CBC, or SMA

Assessment
Commitment voluntary vs. involuntary, CIS consult.

Detox

Subjective
Type and amount of drug, last used, usual use, prior rehab, psych exam.

Objective
Heart, lungs, abdomen, chest pain, DT's.

Intervention
Consult, CIS.

Ophthalmology

Onset, mechanism, photophobia, visual acuity, Alcaine, Slit lamp, fluorescein, PERL without "A," irrigation of Morgan lens, patching, X-ray, tetanus, follow-up, to ophthalmologists

OB/Gyn

Subjective
Onset, duration, LMP, GPA, BC, GI, GU

Objective
Open vs. closed OS, cervical motion tenderness, cultural media viral vs. bacterial, results to PMD/HMO.

1. PID/vaginitis; all cultures need results to private doc, OPC, or health dept. Partners to be referred to health dept, "Safe Sex"
2. Suspect ectopic: check pallor, conjunctiva, VS, consider T&screen with CBC; 6 weeks from LMP is classic.
3. Dysfunctional uterine bleed: consider Provera or BCP depending on age, and last PAP.
4. Bartholin's
5. Miscarriage
6. Ultrasound

Intervention
Perform pelvic exam, do not contaminate, size of uterus

Ortho

Before calling Ortho consult, know your anatomy.

Subjective
Mechanism and PMH

Objective
Back pain, point tenderness, joint stability, ROM strength, sensation, joints above and below. Back pain—check straight leg raising, extremities, ask about bowel and bladder.

Intervention
Pain relief: consider Toradol, morphine esp if dislocation. Only good X-rays, comparison views, growth plates, casting . . . no circular, crutches, R.I.C.E., knees should follow-up in 24 hours, referrals know your anatomy, demonstrate splinting.
If snuff box tenderness is detected on exam with X-ray, the patient should be discharged with a thumb slicer splint or a wrist splint with additional thumb immobilization which should be worn until the patient is evaluated by an orthopedic physician in follow-up.
If an acute spinal cord injury presents, implement the high dose methylprednisolone protocol.
Immobilize and make non-weight bearing in most acute orthopedic injuries until the follow-up visit.

Surgery

Subjective
N/V, onset, last meal, fever

Objective
Abscess, cyst, may I/D, consider ethylene chlorid as well as xylocaine to numb. Abdomen appendicitis, gallbladder, cellulitis often staph, mark streaks, DVT-Doppler studies, DAA.
If the patient presents with a complaint related to previous surgery within 30 days of the surgical procedure, the patient's surgeon should be consulted.

Asthma

COPD, pneumonia, bronchiolitis, asthma, protocols, O2 saturation, peak flow, teaching. Use multiple respiratory treatments, steroids, check abdominal pain, N/V and tachypnea in children.

Headaches

Subjective
Onset, duration, trauma, similar to past, worst of life

Objective
Neurocranial II-XII, drift, reflexes, discs, muscle strength, gait, change from baseline mental status

Intervention
Consider relaxation, IV compazine 10 mg, Toradol IM 60 or 30 mg, Thorazine IV. Check with MD and consider CT if worst of life or focal findings or new onset seizure.

Urology

Obtain an IVP on every patient presenting with known or suspected urolithiasis. If there is an allergy to IVP dye, a sonogram should be performed.

Facial Trauma

Pay specific attention to air fluid levels in the facial sinuses which may indicate a blow-out facial fracture.
In general, HMO patients treated here should be given follow-up with their HMO, unless prearranged with the HMO authorizing agent.
For orthopedic/foot/surgery consultation: If HMO, contact the HMO.

Source: Suburban Hospital, Inc., Bethesda, Maryland.

4-125 Nursing Direction in the Emergency Department

PURPOSE

To define the duties and organizational guidelines for the Director of Emergency Nursing and to provide an alternative plan for Nursing direction in the absence of the Director of Emergency Nursing.

POLICY

A designate registered nurse who is qualified by relevant training, experience, and current competence in emergency care will act as the Director of Emergency Nursing to supervise the care provided by all nursing services personnel within the Emergency Department. The Director of Emergency Nursing will participate in committee activities concerned with the emergency department.

In the absence of the Director of Emergency Nursing, the Charge Nurse will be the nurse in charge and will make decisions regarding policy. An attempt to reach the Nursing Director or her designee by telephone should be made. In the event of an extended absence of the Nursing director, a designee will be appointed to carry on administrative duties. This nurse will be responsible for over-seeing nursing functions in the Department, until the Nursing Director returns to her regular duties.

Source: Parkview Medical Center, Pueblo, Colorado.

4-126 Physician Compliance with EMTALA Responsibilities for Back-up Emergency Room Call

OBJECTIVE

To provide access and care of trauma and other emergency patients who present to ________ and provide for care through the continuum.

POLICY

As a condition of appointment to the Medical Staff, each medical staff appointee, by agreeing to abide by the medical staff bylaws and rules and regulations, accepts assignment on a rotational basis for back-up Emergency Department call in his/her specialty based on his/her medical staff category when requested to do so. When assigned s/he agrees to comply with EMTALA regulations to accept responsibility for patients who present to the Emergency Department without an existing physician relationship for primary care or care appropriate to the patient's injury, regardless of ability to pay.

The medical staff member is expected to respond promptly when called by the Emergency Department and to treat those patients, when requested to do so, without regard to the patient's ability to pay. On-call medical staff members who are requested by the emergency physician to provide care and who direct the emergency physician in providing stabilizing care for the patient without being present in the Emergency Department are expected to provide follow-up care for the patient if needed.

The medical staff member may make arrangements with another provider to provide follow-up care for the patient prior to or after the first visit.

Patients seen and treated in the emergency room by the emergency department physician without consultation with the on-call medical staff member and who require follow-up, will be provided with a list of providers in the appropriate specialty. It is the patient's responsibility to arrange for appropriate care after the stabilizing emergency care.

PURPOSE

To have appropriate specialty assistance in a timely manner for patients needing specialty care in the Emergency Department.

PROCESS

1. ED physicians will refer to the "On-Call List" generated by the medical staff office to determine who to call for specialty care.
2. The ED unit clerk will call the listed number at the request of the ED physician.
3. If no response is obtained in 10 minutes, a second call will be made.
4. If still no response, then a call will be made directly to the physician's home.
5. If the physician is unavailable, then the Chairman of the on-call physician's department will be contacted for assistance, followed by the on-call administrator and chairman of the medical staff, if necessary.

6. If appropriate care cannot be made available in a safe and effective time frame as determined by the patient's condition, a transfer process will be initiated.
7. If a physician did not respond to his or her on-call responsibilities and other care or transfer occurred, an incident report shall be filed with Medical Staff Services and Risk Management for investigation and follow-up.

Source: Parkview Medical Center, Pueblo, Colorado. Reprinted with permission.

MANAGEMENT OF INFORMATION

4-127 Emergency Department Management System

POLICY

The EDM system is used for the initial reception of patients, nursing and physician documentation, treatment and diagnostic ordering, and discharging of ER patients.

PURPOSE

To establish guidelines for the use of emergency department management EDM.

PROCEDURE

1. System Access
   a. Access to the EDM stations will be via a user ID combined with a password. A bar-coded badge will also be used to 'swipe' access into the system.
   b. The user ID will be the Meditech vendor system mnemonic.
   c. The user chooses confidential passwords. The bar-coded badge will be re-set every 90 days.
   d. Purposeful disclosure of system password is grounds for immediate termination of employment.
   e. Passwords are 6 alpha-numeric characters.
   f. Access privileges will be based on specific location and specific job titles.
   g. Passwords will have an expiration of 90 days. A user at anytime may change passwords. A user must change their password/swipe badge if there is a chance the confidentiality of the password has been compromised.
2. Reception
   a. The triage nurse or the nurse who receives the patient into the ER will fill out the reception screen, which puts the patient onto the active patient tracker.
3. Nursing/Physician Documentation
   a. The triage nurse will fill out the triage assessment screen as indicated.
   b. The primary nurse will fill out the following screens:
      - Arrival History (required)
      - Assessment (required)
      - Outgoing disposition assessment (required)
      - IV fluid flow sheet (as indicated)
      - Medication/Vital signs flow sheet (as indicated)
      - Ortho/Procedure flow sheet (as indicated)

   c. The physician will complete the Physician Chart (required).
3. Orders
   a. The ER physician, nurse, or unit clerk may enter orders into EDM.
   b. ER physicians will e-sign all orders entered by the unit clerk or nurse
   c. All orders entered by the nurse will be 'verbal' orders.
   d. The unit clerk will enter orders, which are written, on a physician order form. A hard copy of this physician order will be maintained with the patient record.
   e. Any orders entered by the ER unit clerk will be checked and noted by the ER RN.
   f. Outside physicians will give written orders and therefore e-signature will not be used.
5. Printing Reports
   a. Admitted patients will have their EDM record printed via the "Reports" function and will be sent to the admitting unit at the time of transport to that unit.
   b. When private physicians, specialists, etc arrive to the ER to care for their patients, the ER unit clerk will print a copy of the EDM record as well as any diagnostic test results and the order summary for them to review.
6. Problem Solving
   a. A number of resource people are available to assist with problem solving on each shift.
   b. The EDM quick start manual is available.
   c. For problems unable to be resolved, contact the ER administrator on call or designee.
7. EDM Down Time
   a. Paper charts/forms will be kept on hand in the event that Meditech is unavailable for a period of time. These charts/forms will be stocked and kept in the ER triage area cabinets.

Source: Parkview Medical Center, Pueblo, Colorado.

4-128 Emergency Department Psychiatry Documentation Standard

POLICY

It is the policy of the psychiatry emergency department to document in the patient's medical record according to the following standards.

PURPOSE

To provide documentation standards to physicians and nurses assigned in the psychiatry emergency department.

PROCEDURE

Physician Documentation Responsibilities

1. Patient allergies
2. Time patient is examined

3. Patient history indicating chief complaint
4. Current patient medications
5. Physician assessment
6. Time seclusion or restraint orders activated
7. Diagnosis, discharge or admission
8. Patient disposition
9. Patient condition or discharge
10. Time and date of disposition
11. Signature

Registered Nurse Documentation Responsibilities

1. The following data will be documented:
   a. initial nursing assessment time/date
   b. mode of arrival to department
   c. patient allergies
   d. patient's chief complaint
   e. physical nursing assessment addressing chief complaint findings
   f. initial vital signs
   g. medical history
   h. current medications
   i. community resources/support groups
   j. initial treatment implemented
   k. signature/title
2. The RN will document the medications administered in the emergency department, including
   a. name of medications
   b. dosage
   c. route/site
   d. time
   e. initials
   f. signature
3. Documentation will be based on level of care, as follows:

Level of Care	Initial Assessment	Assessment and Documentation	Vital Signs
I	Immediately upon arrival	Every hour	Every hour
II	Immediately upon arrival	Every four hours	Every four hours
III	Within 30 minutes of arrival	Every four hours	Every four hours
IV	Within two hours of arrival	Upon discharge	Upon admission
V	Within two hours of arrival	Upon discharge	Upon admission

4. Any changes in the patient's condition will be documented and the physician will be notified.
5. Patient response to treatments, procedure, or medications administered will be documented.

6. Level of care IV and V—The patient's chief complaint will be reassessed at time of discharge and documented in the nursing notes.
7. Level of care I, II, and III—The plan of care will be reviewed and documented every four hours.

Source: Rusty McNew, RN, MA, CPHQ, Dallas, Texas.

4-129 Emergency Department Nurses' Notes

Bed # __________

Time	Temp.	Pulse	Resp.	BP	Output	IVs and Meds.	Pain (1–10)	No change in status	Nursing Observations, Treatments and Signature

BELONGINGS LIST:
__ Shirt/Blouse
__ Trousers/Pants/ Shorts
__ Dress/Skirt
__ Shoes/Slippers
__ Underwear
__ Robe/Pajamas
__ Coat/Sweater/ Gloves

VALUABLES:
__ Wallet/Purse
__ Watch
__ Ring
__ Necklace/ Bracelet
__ Earrings
__ Money
__ Dentures
__ Upper/Lower/ Partial
__ Glasses/ Contacts
__ Prosthesis
__ Ambulatory Aid
__ Other

DISPOSITION OF BELONGINGS AND VALUABLES
__ With Patient
__ With Family
__ To Safe
__ Other

Nurses' Signature Initial
____
____
____
____
____

Source: Johnston Memorial Hospital, Abingdon, Virginia.

4-130 Managers' HIPAA Guide

Here's a quick guide to help you remember some of the most compelling things that should be going on to comply with HIPAA.

1. Notice of Privacy Practices is displayed in clinics, admissions, ER, and posted on the hospital's web site.
2. Give patients a copy of the Notice of Privacy Practices . . . and make good-faith efforts to obtain written acknowledgment of receipt.
3. Avoid verbal discussions of protected health information (PHI) on the phone, public areas, or in reception/waiting areas that are within earshot of people who don't have a need to know.
4. Don't leave sensitive information on telephone answering machines.
5. Limit or use minimum necessary PHI in announcements made in clinic waiting rooms.
6. You may share PHI with family, friends, personal representative identified by the patient as someone involved in their care.
7. Limit patient information on whiteboards, X-ray boxes, computer screens and other areas that may be visible to the public and others who don't need access to PHI.
8. Follow safeguards for PHI that is transmitted by fax or e-mail.
9. File away promptly and secure folders that contain patient medical records.
10. Make sure that computer/network security measures are in place (e.g., that screen-savers kick in quickly, passwords are not taped to the monitor, machines are turned off at night, and access from off site is carefully restricted).
11. Do not share passwords.
12. Make sure the physical plant is locked down at night, with windows closed and doors locked.
13. Remind people that only the "minimum necessary" PHI should be disclosed except for treatment purposes.
14. Make sure separated employees turn in their keys and building cards and terminate their network access.
15. Enter required disclosures of PHI in the Disclosure Tracking Database.
16. Make sure written authorizations to use and disclose PHI are received except for treatment, payment, operations, and exceptions permitted in the policy.
17. Make sure new and existing employees participate in HIPAA privacy training.
18. Make sure everyone is aware of the rights patients have to review (and get copies of) their records and what procedures will be followed.
19. Make sure everyone knows who patients should speak with if they have questions about their HIPAA privacy rights.
20. Be sure everyone in your work force knows who the privacy officer is and who they should contact with patient privacy questions or problems. The Privacy Officer is __________, extension __________.

Source: University of California-Davis Compliance Department, Sacramento, California.

4-131 Sample Protected Health Information Policy and Procedure

POLICY

Protected health information (PHI) is individually identifiable health information that is transmitted or maintained by electronic media or any other form or medium, excluding information in educational records and inmate records. PHI will be used and disclosed in accordance with the Health Insurance Portability and Accountability Act (HIPAA) Privacy Standards and other applicable law; deidentified information is not subject to these regulations.

PROCEDURE

1. PHI includes oral, written, or otherwise recorded information that is created or received by [COVERED ENTITY].
2. PHI may relate to an individual's physical or mental health, payment, or health care services provided to an individual.
3. PHI may pertain to a health condition or payment in the past, present, or future, and the person who is the subject of the information may be alive or deceased.
4. PHI will be protected in any form, including, but not limited to, telephone conversations and voice mail, paper records, computers, transmissions over the Internet, dial-up lines, private networks, fax machines, electronic memory chips, magnetic tape, magnetic disk, CD-ROM.
5. Deidentified information is not subject to [COVERED ENTITY'S] privacy policies and procedures.
6. PHI may be deidentified by removing, coding, encrypting, or otherwise eliminating or concealing the information that makes the PHI individually identifiable, including the following identifiers of the individual or of relatives, employers, or household members of the individual: names, all geographic subdivisions smaller than a state (except for the initial three digits of a ZIP code if the total population in the ZIP code areas covered by such three digits of a ZIP code exceeds 20,000), all elements of date (except year), telephone numbers, fax numbers, electronic mail addresses, Social Security numbers, medical record numbers, health plan beneficiary numbers, account numbers, certificate/license numbers, vehicle identifiers and serial numbers, Web universal resource locators (URLs), Internet protocol (IP) address numbers, finger or voice prints, photographic images, and any other unique identifying numbers, characteristics, or codes regardless of whether the covered entity has actual knowledge that the information could identify an individual.

Source: Knag, Paul. *HIPAA: A Guide to Health Care Privacy and Security Law.* Aspen Publishers (2004).

4-132 ED Disclosure Consent and Authorization Checklist

Review with your organization to determine whether these types of disclosures are made—also use as a guide as requests for disclosure occur.

Purpose of Disclosure	Consent or Authorization Requirement
Mandatory Disclosures	
__ Individual requests own information	
__ DHHS requests for compliance enforcement purposes	
Treatment, Payment, or Health Care Operations:	**Consent Required**
__ Treatment	
__ Payment	
__Operations (quality assessment, professional evaluations, insurance rating, medical audits, business planning, business management)	
Certain Types of Public Purposes:	**Authorization Not Required**
__Public health activities (public health authorities, child abuse reporting, FDA-regulated companies, persons at risk of communicable disease, employers for work-related injury, or medical surveillance of workplace)	
__ Victims of abuse, neglect, or domestic violence (can disclose to authorized governmental authority if required by law or individual approves)	
__ Health oversight purposes (audits, investigations, inspections, licensure, discipline)	
__ Judicial and administrative proceedings (court order, subpoena—see law enforcement checklist if requesting party is law enforcement official)	
__ Law enforcement purposes (see law enforcement checklist)	
__ Decedents (coroners, medical examiners, funeral directors)	
__ Cadaveric organ, eye, or tissue donation purposes	
__ Research purposes (need waiver of authorization form approved by IRB or privacy board)	
__ Avert a serious threat to health or safety (if imminent threat to individual or public health or safety)	
__ Specialized government functions (military, veterans, national security, intelligence, medical suitability determinations, correctional institutions, government programs providing public benefits)	
__ Workers' compensation	
Special Cases	
__ Facility directory	**Opportunity to Orally Agree/Object Required**
__ Person involved in care	**Opportunity to Orally Agree/Object Required**
__ Psychotherapy notes	
__ Research involving treatment	

Source: Knag, Paul. *HIPAA: A Guide to Health Care Privacy and Security Law.* Aspen Publishers (2004).

4-133 Access to Medical Records by or on Behalf of an ED Patient

INFORMATION

While the medical record is the property of the hospital, the hospital recognizes an individual's right to examine and/or obtain a copy of their medical record.
The hospital also recognizes the right of an individual, or the individual's designee, to be provided with one free copy of their medical record.

INSTRUCTIONS

1. When a patient requests to examine or obtain copies of the medical records, designated medical records personnel will review the medical record.
2. In all cases in which the patient's request for access to the medical records is granted, the patient must complete an authorization for release of information form, or its equivalent, before he or she will be provided with copies of the record. The form and a record of the transaction will be filed in the medical record.
3. Medical records personnel will provide requested copies of medical records, prepared for mailing to or for pick-up by the requester, within 7 business days of the written request.

Charges for Copies of Medical Records

A patient or patient's designee is entitled to one free copy of the medical records; all additional copies cost $1.00 per page.

Note: Third-party payers are not considered first requesters and are charged in accordance with contractual agreements with the hospital.

Medical records will release the free copy of the medical record on a first-come, first-served basis. Patients, as well as third parties who hold a release signed by the patient and dated within sixty (60) days of the date of the request, may receive a free copy of the medical records by being the first requester.

Medical records are copied by service dates. Any part of a specific service date record that has been copied and released as the first free copy will be copied at a charge of $1.00 per page for additional copies. Those parts of a specific service date record that have not yet been provided as a first free copy will remain available to be requested as the first free copy.

Health care providers are not charged for copies of a medical record and will not be considered a first requester.

The department of disability determination pays $10.00 per request for copies of medical record and will not be considered a first requester.

Source: University of Kentucky Hospital, Lexington, Kentucky.

4-134 HIPAA Privacy and Disclosures in Emergency Situations

Persons who are displaced and in need of health care as a result of a severe disaster need ready access to health care and the means of contacting family and caregivers. We provide this bulletin to emphasize how the HIPAA Privacy Rule allows patient information to be shared to assist in disaster relief efforts, and to assist patients in receiving the care they need.

Providers and health plans covered by the HIPAA Privacy Rule can share patient information in all the following ways:

TREATMENT. ***Health care providers can share patient information as necessary to provide treatment.***

- *Treatment* includes:
  - —sharing information with other providers (including hospitals and clinics),
  - —referring patients for treatment (including linking patients with available providers in areas where the patients have relocated), and
  - —coordinating patient care with others (such as emergency relief workers or others that can help in finding patients appropriate health services).
- Providers can also share patient information to the extent necessary to seek payment for these health care services.

NOTIFICATION. ***Health care providers can share patient information as necessary to identify, locate and notify family members, guardians, or anyone else responsible for the individual's care of the individual's location, general condition, or death.***

- The health care provider should get verbal permission from individuals, when possible; but, if the individual is incapacitated or not available, providers may share information for these purposes if, in their professional judgment, doing so is in the patient's best interest.
  - —Thus, when necessary, the hospital may notify the police, the press, or the public at large to the extent necessary to help locate, identify or otherwise notify family members and others as to the location and general condition of their loved ones.
- In addition, when a health care provider is sharing information with disaster relief organizations that, like the American Red Cross, are authorized by law or by their charters to assist in disaster relief efforts, it is unnecessary to obtain a patient's permission to share the information if doing so would interfere with the organization's ability to respond to the emergency.

IMMINENT DANGER. Providers can share patient information with anyone as necessary to prevent or lessen a serious and imminent threat to the health and safety of a person or the public—consistent with applicable law and the provider's standards of ethical conduct.

FACILITY DIRECTORY. Health care facilities maintaining a directory of patients can tell people who call or ask about individuals whether the individual is at the facility, their location in the facility, and general condition.

Of course, the HIPAA Privacy Rule does not apply to disclosures if they are not made by entities covered by the Privacy Rule. Thus, for instance, the HIPAA Privacy Rule does not restrict the American Red Cross from sharing patient information.

Source: Hurricane Katrina Bulletin: HIPAA Privacy and Disclosure Bulletin. September 2, 2005. Director, U.S. Department of Health and Human Services Office for Civil Rights, Washington, DC.

4-135 HIPAA Privacy—Disclosure of PHI and Interpreters

Must a covered health care provider obtain an individual's authorization to use or disclose protected health information to an interpreter?

No, when a covered health care provider uses an interpreter to communicate with an individual, the individual's authorization is not required when the provider meets the conditions below. Covered entities may use and disclose protected health information for treatment, payment and health care operations without an individual's authorization. [45 C.F.R. 164.506(c)] A covered health care provider might use interpreter services to communicate with patients who speak a language other than English or who are deaf or hard of hearing, and provision of interpreter services usually will be a health care operations function of the covered entity as defined at 45 C.F.R. 164.501.

When using interpreter services, a covered entity may use and disclose protected health information regarding an individual without an individual's authorization as a health care operation, in accordance with the Privacy Rule, in the following ways:

- When the interpreter is a member of the covered entity's workforce (i.e., a bilingual employee, a contract interpreter on staff, or a volunteer) as defined at 45 C.F.R. 160.103;
- When a covered entity engages the services of a person or entity, who is not a workforce member, to perform interpreter services on its behalf, as a business associate, as defined at 45 C.F.R. 160.103. A covered entity may disclose protected health information as necessary for the business associate to provide interpreter services on the covered entity's behalf, subject to certain written satisfactory assurances set forth in 45 C.F.R. 164.504(e). For instance, many providers—including those that are recipients of federal financial assistance and are required under Title VI of the Civil Rights Act of 1964 to take reasonable steps to provide meaningful access to persons with limited English proficiency—will have contractual arrangements with private commercial companies, community-based organizations, or telephone interpreter service lines to provide such language services. If a covered entity has an ongoing contractual relationship with an interpreter service, that service arrangement should comply with the Privacy Rule business associate agreement requirements.

In addition, a covered health care provider may, without the individual's authorization, use or disclose protected health information to the patient's family member, close friend, or any other person identified by the individual as his or her interpreter for a particular health care encounter. In these situations, that interpreter is not a business associate of the health care provider. As with other disclosures to family members, friends, or other persons identified by an individual as involved in his or her care, when the individual is present, the covered entity may obtain the individual's agreement or reasonably infer, based on the exercise of professional judgment, that the individual does not object to the disclosure of protected health information to the interpreter. [45 C.F.R. 164.510(b)(2)] For example, if a covered health care provider encounters a patient who speaks a language for which the provider has no employee, volunteer member of the workforce, or contractor who can competently interpret, but then is able to identify a telephone interpreter service to communicate with the patient, the provider may contact the telephone interpreter service and identify the language used by the patient, so that the interpreter may explain to the patient that the interpreter is available to assist the patient in communicating with the provider. If the provider reasonably concludes that the patient has chosen to be assisted by the interpreter, and, by the patient's willingness to continue the health care encounter using the interpreter, reasonably infers that the individual does not object to the disclosure, protected health information may be disclosed in accordance with 45 C.F.R. 164.510(b) without a business associate contract.

Organizations that are subject to both HIPAA and Title VI must comply with the requirements of both laws, though not all HIPAA-covered entities are recipients of federal financial assistance and thus, required to comply with Title VI; and not all recipients of federal financial assistance are also HIPAA-covered entities, subject to the Privacy Rule. For information about the obligation of recipients of federal financial assistance to take reasonable steps to provide meaningful access to persons who are limited English proficient, see Guidance to Federal Financial Assistance Recipients Regarding Title VI Prohibition Against National Origin Discrimination Affecting Limited English Proficient Persons available at *http://www.hhs.gov/ocr/lep/*. This guidance includes information for recipients of federal financial assistance about important considerations for determining the competency of interpreters, such as their understanding of applicable confidentiality requirements, that should be taken into account when using interpreters arranged by the provider or when individuals elect to use friends, family, or others as interpreters.

HIPAA-covered entities may also be required to comply with the Americans with Disabilities Act and/or Section 504 of the Rehabilitation Act of 1973, both of which have requirements for the provision of sign language and oral interpreters for people who are deaf or hard of hearing. The use of communications assistants as part of a Telecommunications Relay Service (TRS) was the subject of a previous FAQ available at *http://www.hhs.gov/ocr/hipaa* (click on Your Frequently Asked Questions About Privacy).

Source: Answer ID: 760, Health Information Privacy and Civil Rights, Questions & Answers, 2/28/05. U.S. Department of Health & Human Services. Accessed August 18, 2006, at *http://www.hhs.gov/ocr/hipaa*.

4-136 PHI Disclosures for Emergency Preparedness: A Decision Tool

Background

Emergency preparedness and recovery planners are interested in the availability of information they need to serve people in the event of an emergency. For example, planners seek to meet the special needs of the elderly or persons with disabilities in the event of an evacuation. The federal Health Insurance Portability and Accountability Act of 1996 (HIPAA) Privacy Rule protects individually identifiable health information held by "covered entities." The information protected is referred to as protected health information, or PHI. The HIPAA Privacy Rule permits covered entities to disclose PHI for a variety of purposes. This tool presents avenues of information flow that could apply to emergency preparedness activities. The rules regarding the use and disclosure of PHI apply to all individuals; no special rules apply to particular populations, such as persons with disabilities. We anticipate that emergency planners may organize their activities in a variety of ways; we hope this guidance will provide useful information to a range of potential programs.

This tool does not address other federal, state, or local confidentiality laws that may apply in specific circumstances. For example, disclosures permitted by the Privacy Rule for public health would generally be prohibited under federal substance abuse confidentiality law. Because this tool focuses on issues relevant to emergency preparedness, this tool does not present all the uses and disclosures permitted by the Privacy Rule, nor does it discuss all of the Rule's requirements. For comprehensive guidance on the Privacy Rule, see the educational materials on the OCR web site.

How to Use this Tool

To guide you in determining how the Privacy Rule applies to the disclosure in question, this tool focuses on the source of the information being disclosed, to whom the information is being disclosed, and the purpose of the information being disclosed. To make your determination, go to the question that is most relevant to your emergency preparedness planning need and follow the information flow to find the appropriate answer.

Decision Tool

Who is the source of the information to be disclosed?

1. **A covered entity**
2. **The individual consumer**
3. **Other agency or organization that is not a covered entity**

A Covered Entity is:

- **A health plan.** An individual or group plan that provides, or pays the cost of, medical care. Health plans include private entities (e.g., health insurers and managed care organizations) and government organizations (e.g., Medicaid, Medicare, and the Veterans Health Administration).

- **A health care provider.** A provider of health care services and any other person or organization that furnishes, bills, or is paid for health care in the normal course of business. Health care providers (e.g., physicians, hospitals, and clinics) are covered entities if they transmit health information in electronic form in connection with a transaction for which a HIPAA standard has been adopted by HHS (e.g., billing).
- **A health care clearinghouse.** A public or private entity, including a billing service, repricing company, or community health information system, that processes non-standard data or transactions received from another entity into standard transactions or data elements, or vice versa.

For more specific decision tool options to determine if you are a covered entity, go to *http://www.cms.hhs.gov/apps/hipaa2decisionsupport/default.asp.*

To whom is the information being disclosed?

1. **Public Health Authority**
2. **A health care provider for treatment**
3. **Other agency for public health purposes**
4. **Other person(s)/agency**

Has the individual consumer signed an authorization permitting the disclosure?
Yes
No

PROCESS CHART

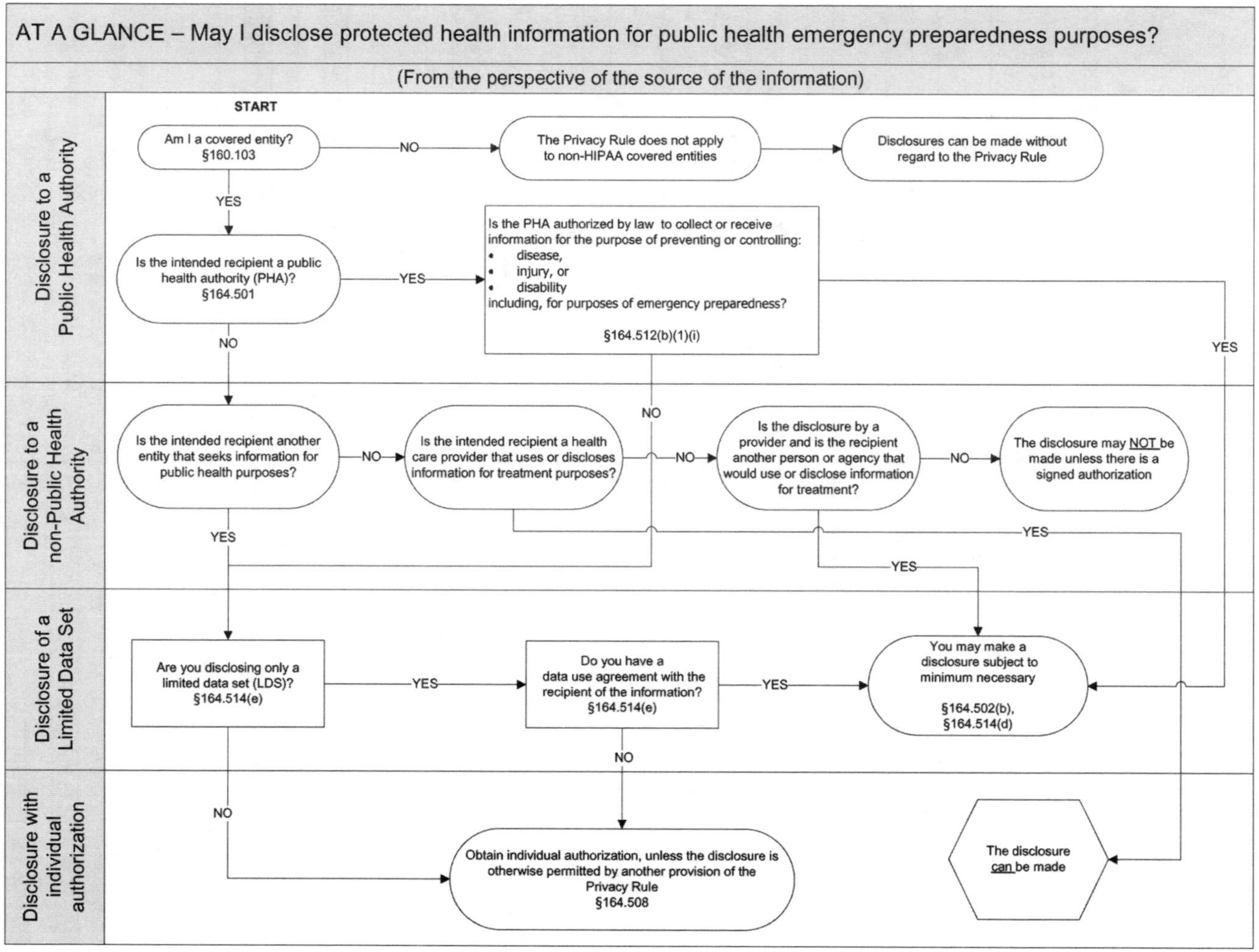

Source: HHS Office for Civil Rights. *HIPAA Privacy Rule: Disclosures for Emergency Preparedness—A Decision Tool. Last revised: June 27, 2006, http://www.hhs.gov/ocr/hipaa/decisiontool/*

4-137 Emergency Department Encounter Record

PATIENT NAME

TIME | LOGICARE C/O

TRIAGE NOTES

PAIN RATING: ____ 0-10 Numeric ____ 0-10 Faces ____ 0-10 FLACC (or)

Observed Behavior: ____

INTERVENTIONS @ TRIAGE | SOURCE OF INFO | DATE/TIME OF ACCIDENT/ILLNESS

PRIORITY OF ADMISSION ❑ 1 ❑ 2 ❑ 3 ❑ 4

VITAL SIGNS (Triage) Temp ____ P ____ R ____ BP ____

LMP | WEIGHT | HEIGHT | OFC | TET

IMMUNIZATIONS REVIEWED ❑ UTD ❑ Not UTD, Information Given

❑ Developmental age is appropriate OR

❑ Developmental screening is required

PMD NAME

Police: ____ Animal Control: ____ ME: ____

Mode of Arrival: ❑ Wheelchair ❑ Ambulatory ❑ Carried ❑ FD

PTA | MEDS GIVEN:

❑ Backboard ❑ C-Collar ❑ CID ❑ IV ❑ Oxygen ❑ Splints ❑ Monitor

MEDICAL - SURGICAL HISTORY

CURRENT MEDICATIONS

ALLERGIES

NURSE'S SIGNATURE

MD TIME		MD TIME		MD TIME	
	CBC		UA		PORTABLE STRETCHER W/C
	BMP		CCMS I/O		Skull
	CMP		Wet Prep		Soft Tissue Neck
	CP Profile		Gram Stain		C-Spine 1 2 3
	Trauma Profile		CG Culture		T-Spine 1 2 3
	CKMB		Chlamydia		LS-Spine 1 2 3
	Troponin				CXR IV 2V
	PT/PTT				
	Lipase				ABD KUB 2 V
	Amylase		Monitor		Pelvis
	ETOH		EKG		Extremity
	Tylenol		O2 Liters		R L ____
	ASA		PEFR		R L ____
	Pregnancy Test		UABD		R L ____
	Quant. HCG		2		R L ____
	Urine HCG		3		
	Urine Drug Scr		Continuous		
			Pulse OX		IVP
			Room Air Y or N		Sono ____
					Sono ____
			Blood Culture		CT
			X1 X2		VQ Scan
			Throat CS		Head
			RSV Culture		Head Angio
			Rapid Strep		Chest IV Contrast
			Urine CS		Chest Angio
					Abd IV Rectal PO
					Pelvis IV Rectal PO

TIME ORDERED	TREATMENTS / MEDICATIONS / PROCEDURES	TIME DONE	INITIALS

INITIALS	SIGNATURE - RN/TECH	INITIALS	SIGNATURE - RN/TECH

M.D. TIME | PHYSICIAN DOCUMENTATION

TIME ORDERED	ORDERS AT TIME OF DISCHARGE	TIME DONE	INITIALS

CLINICAL IMPRESSION

PHYSICIAN SIGNATURE

CONDITION OF DISCHARGE: ❑ Stable ____ Time ❑ Home ❑ Nursing Home

❑ Admit - Rm. # ____ ❑ Other: ____ ❑ Transfer: ____

PAIN RATING: ____ 0-10 Numeric ____ 0-10 Faces ____ 0-10 FLACC (or)

Observed Behavior: ____

DISCHARGE INSTRUCTIONS: (Time Ordered: ____)

____ F/U Physician ❑ PRN ____ day(s)

❑ Appointment in ____ day(s) ❑ And if not better, call in ____

❑ Return to ED in ____ day(s) or ____ hour(s) for ____

❑ Return to Work in ____ day(s) with ____ limitations.

Pain Management Plan: ____

MEDS/OTHER/DISCHARGE TOPIC: ____

FORM #31800 (Rev. 5/02) **1st COPY** - MEDICAL RECORDS **2nd COPY** - DEPARTMENT **3rd COPY** - QUEST CARE

Source: Medical Center of Plano, Plano, Texas.

4-138 Emergency Unit Nursing Record

BED #: | TIME

MD/TIME

AIRWAY: ❑ Patent ❑ Denies Sx ❑ Secretions/blood ❑ Stridor
❑ Obstruction: ____
Treatment: ❑ Airway: Oral / Nasal ❑ ETT# ________ Oral / Nasal
❑ Cricothyroidotomy ❑ Tracheostomy
Time: __________, by ____

RESPIRATORY: ❑ Denies Sx ❑ Spontaneous ❑ Unlabored
❑ Labored ❑ Assisted ❑ Mechanical / BVM
Chest: ❑ Symmetrical Expansion ❑ Accessory Muscle Use
❑ Injury / Tenderness (See Diagram)
Breath Sounds: Right: ❑ Present ❑ Absent ❑ Clear ❑ Diminished
❑ Wheezes ❑ Crackles ❑ Rhonchi
Left: ❑ Present ❑ Absent ❑ Clear ❑ Diminished
❑ Wheezes ❑ Crackles ❑ Rhonchi
Treatment: ❑ O2 ______ L/min ❑ Nasal Cannula ❑ Non-rebreather
❑ Venti-mask ______ % ❑ Face mask ❑ Other: ______
TB Risk Assessment:
Possibly has Pneumonia with Bloody Sputum ❑ Yes ❑ No
❑ Notify M.D., Request Resp. Isolation and Notify Infection Control.

CARDIOVASCULAR: ❑ Denies Sx ❑ Palpitations
❑ Chest Pain Level: ______ (0-10)
Pulse: ❑ Regular ❑ Irregular ❑ Thready ❑ Diminished
❑ Absent (See CPR Record)
Rhythm: ____
Skin: ❑ Warm ❑ Hot ❑ Cool ❑ Dry ❑ Moist ❑ Diaphoretic
Color: ❑ WNL ❑ Pale ❑ Flushed ❑ Cyanotic

NEURO: ❑ AA&O X ________ ❑ Responds to verbal
❑ Responds to pain ❑ Unresponsive ❑ +LOC
❑ Pedi: ❑ Alert / Active / Playful ❑ Age appropriate
Pupils: Right: ❑ Reactive ❑ Sluggish ❑ Unreactive ❑ Size ____ mm
Left: ❑ Reactive ❑ Sluggish ❑ Unreactive ❑ Size ____ mm

GLASGOW COMA SCALE INFANT / TODDLER			GLASGOW COMA SCALE CHILDREN / ADULT			INITIAL	ONE HOUR
EYE OPENING	SPONTANEOUS	4	EYE OPENING	SPONTANEOUS	4		
	TO VOICE	3		TO VOICE	3		
	TO PAIN	2		TO PAIN	2		
	NONE	1		NONE	1		
BEST VERBAL RESPONSE	SMILES, INTERACTS	5	BEST VERBAL RESPONSE	ORIENTED	5		
	CONSOLABLE	4		CONFUSED	4		
	CRIES TO PAIN	3		INAPPROPRIATE WORDS	3		
	MOANS TO PAIN	2		INCOMPREHENSIBLE WORDS	2		
	NONE	1		NONE	1		
BEST MOTOR RESPONSE	NORMAL SPONT. MOVEMENT	6	BEST MOTOR RESPONSE	OBEYS COMMAND	6		
	LOCALIZES PAIN	5		LOCALIZES PAIN	5		
	WITHDRAWS TO PAIN	4		WITHDRAWS (PAIN)	4		
	ABNORMAL FLEXION	3		FLEXION (PAIN)	3		
	ABNORMAL EXTENSION	2		EXTENSION (PAIN)	2		
	NONE	1		NONE	1		

ABDOMEN: ❑ Denies Sx ❑ C/O Pain: ❑ RUQ ❑ RLQ ❑ LUQ ❑ LLQ
Palpitation: ❑ Soft ❑ Distended ❑ Rigid ❑ Pregnant ❑ Non-Tender
❑ Tender: ❑ RUQ ❑ RLQ ❑ LUQ ❑ LLQ
Bowel Sounds: ❑ Active X 4 quads ❑ Hypoactive ❑ Hyperactive ❑ Absent
Symptoms: ❑ Nausea ❑ Vomit ❑ Diarrhea ❑ Hematemesis ❑ Melena

GYN: ❑ N/A
LMP: ____ Gravida ____ Para ____
Pregnant: ❑ N/A: Hyst / Tubal
❑ Neg ❑ Pos: ______ weeks
❑ Abd Cramping
Genitalia: ❑ Pain ❑ Discharge
❑ Itching
Vag Bleeding: ❑ None ❑ Spotting
❑ #/pads/hr: ______ ❑ Gross

GU: ❑ Denies Sx ❑ Pain
❑ Burning ❑ Discharge
❑ Odor ❑ Frequency/Urgency
❑ Retention ❑ Hematuria
❑ Dip UA: + / –
Genitalia (Male): ❑ Denies Sx
❑ Testicular Pain
❑ Sudden Onset

MUSCULOSKELETAL: ❑ Denies Sx
❑ Pain/Swelling/Deformity/Injury (See Diagram)
Extremities: ❑ Sensory Intact X 4 ❑ Deficit: ❑ RUE ❑ LUE ❑ RLE ❑ LLE
❑ Motor Intact X 4 ❑ Deficit: ❑ RUE ❑ LUE ❑ RLE ❑ LLE
❑ Equal Strength: ❑ Upper Ext ❑ Lower Ext
Pulses: Right: ❑ Carotid ❑ Radial ❑ Femoral ❑ Dorsalis Pedis
Left: ❑ Carotid ❑ Radial ❑ Femoral ❑ Dorsalis Pedis
Pelvis: ❑ Stable ❑ Unstable **Spine Precautions:** ❑ C-Collar ❑ Backboard

INITIALS	NURSE'S SIGNATURE

❑ N/A

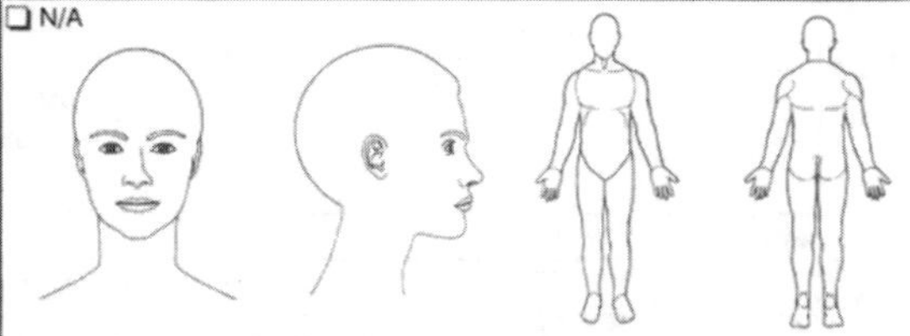

1. Abrasion
2. Amputation
3. Avulsion
4. Bite
5. Burn
6. Contusion
7. Crush
8. Deformity
9. Open Fracture
10. GSW
11. Hematoma
12. Laceration
13. Puncture
15. Stab Wound / Impalement
16. Swelling
17. Wound Unknown
18. Pain
20. Rash/Hives

EYES: ❑ Denies Sx ❑ Redness ❑ Vision Changes ❑ Drainage
❑ Foreign Body ❑ Trauma ____
Visual Acuity: Corrected: ______ OD ______ OS ______ OU ❑ N/A
Uncorrected: ______ OD ______ OS ______ OU

PSYCHOSOCIAL:
❑ Cooperative ❑ Calm ❑ Combative
❑ Anxious ❑ Tearful ❑ Uncooperative

REASSURANCE:
❑ Patient ❑ Family

PAIN ASSESSMENT: PAIN RATING: ___ 0-10 Numeric ___ 0-10 Faces ___ 0-10 FLACC
(or) Observed Behavior: ____
Location: ____ Severity 0 1 2 3 4 5 6 7 8 9 10
Quality: ❑ Sharp ❑ Dull ❑ Stabbing ❑ Pressure ❑ Twisting ❑ Tearing
❑ Other ____ Onset: ____
Duration: ❑ Constant ❑ Intermittent
Worsened by: ❑ Cough ❑ Movement ❑ Deep Breath ❑ Pressure ❑ Other ____
Eased by: ❑ Nothing ❑ Rest ❑ Splinting ❑ Heat ❑ Cold ❑ Meds ❑ Other ____

INTERVENTIONS: ❑ Notify Phys. ❑ Monitor ❑ O2 ❑ Ice/Elevate
❑ Comfort Measures ❑ Safety ❑ Reassure
Siderails: ❑ Up x 2 ❑ Up x 1 **ID Band:** ❑ Yes ❑ No

DIAGNOSTIC	TIME	RADIOLOGY	TIME	RETURN
Blood Drawn		X-Rays		
UA		IVP		
EKG		CT		
ABG		Ultrasound		
RT Treatment		Nuclear Medicine		

IV FLUIDS

TIME	IV #	SITE	GA.	SOLN.	LTC/TOTAL	INT
					/	
					/	
					/	

TOTAL INTAKE: ____ cc | **TOTAL OUTPUT:** ____ cc

COMMENTS: ____

DISPOSITION: ❑ Home ❑ Admit ❑ Transfer ❑ Death ❑ AMA ❑ LWBS
MODE: ❑ Ambulatory ❑ Carried ❑ Stretcher ❑ Ambulance
D/C: ❑ Instructions given to: ❑ Patient ❑ Parent ❑ Other: ____
❑ Verbalizes Understanding
VITAL SIGNS: BP: ____ **PULSE:** ____
RESP: ____ **TEMP:** ____
PAIN RATING: _____ 0-10 Numeric _____ 0-10 Faces _____ 0-10 FLACC
(or) Observed Behavior: ____
TIME: ______ **SIGNATURE:** ____

Source: Medical Center of Plano, Plano, Texas.

4-139 Operative/Invasive Checklist Report

	LEFT SIDE PROCEDURES (Complete Form on Left side)	ALL OTHER PROCEDURES (Complete In Center)	RIGHT-SIDED PROCEDURES (Complete on the Right Side)
PRE-TESTING		Patient Identity Verified by NAME and DOB:	
		Scheduled Surgery/Procedure:	
		Consent for: Same as above: Y N If no:	
		* Orally verified procedure/site/side with whom: ______________if not verified, reason:	
		* * The side/site was initialed by: If not initialed, reason:	
Signature:		Date:	Time:
FLOOR / OSU / ICC / ENDO / ED (circle one)		Patient Identity Verified by NAME and DOB:	
		Scheduled Surgery/Procedure:	
		Consent for: Same as above: Y N If no:	
		* Orally verified procedure/site/side with whom: ______________if not verified, reason:	
		* * The side/site was initialed by: If not initialed, reason:	
Signature:		Date:	Time:
PRE-PROCEDURAL AREA		Unit or Area:	
		Patient Identity Verified by NAME and DOB:	
		Scheduled Surgery/Procedure:	
		Consent for: Same as above: Y N If no:	
		* Orally verified procedure/site/side with whom: ______________if not verified, reason:	
		* * The side/site was initialed by: If not initialed, reason:	
Signature:		Date:	Time:
PROCEDURALAREA		**Final Verification ("TIME-OUT")**	
		Unit or Area:	
		TeamVerified Patient Identity by Name and DOB:	
		Procedure to be performed verified by team:	
		Procedure:	
		Side/Site Verified by Team:	
		Correct equipment/supplies/implants available:	
		Physician:	
		Anesthesia;	
		Nursing Staff Member(s):	
		Radiology Staff Member(s):	
Signature:		Date:	Time:

* Verify procedure/side/site, upon entry to facility and when care is transferred to another caregiver with patient awake and aware, if possible.
* *With patient awake and aware if possible, the person performing the procedure is to initial the procedural site in all cases involving lateralitv. multiple structures (fingers, toes, lesions), or multiple levels (spine). Initialing is to be done by the person doing the procedure. Initialing the procedural site on pediatric patients 2 years or younger is done at the discretion of the physician.

PATIENT IDENTIFICATION

GF-335A (Rev 7/04) MAC 844

☐ This side of form is waived for bedside procedures not involving the surgical team.____________________RN

ID Band: Y / N
Allergy Band: Y / N
Blood Band: Y / N / NA
NPO after: ____________________
H&P present: Y / N H&P current: Y / N
Procedural consent complete: Y / N Blood Consent complete: Y / N
Height: ______________ Weight: ______________

Time: __________ Blood Pressure: __________ Pulse: ________
Respirations: Temperature: 02 Sat:
Lab Tests Done: Y / N / NA Current Labs Printed and on Chart: Y / N / NA
X-Rays Done: Y / N / NA
EKG Done: Y / N / NA

Dentures Removed: Y / N / NA
Disposition: ________________________________
Jewelry/Piercings Removed: Y / N / NA
Disposition: ________________________________
Contact Lenses Removed: Y / N / NA
Disposition: ________________________________
Hearing Aid(s) Removed: Y / N / NA
Disposition: ________________________________
Glasses Removed: Y / N / NA
Disposition: ________________________________
List patient cosmetic implants (e.g. breast, chin): ☐ None

List patient implants that contain metal (e.g. metal plates, screws, total joints, etc): ☐ None

Current MAR printed for in-house patients: Y / N / NA
Special Needs/Comments (if none, write none): ____________________

Significant others waiting: Y / N Location:____________________

EMERGENCY DEPARTMENT CONSIDERATIONS:
X-Rays sent with patient: Y / N / NA
If no, Radiology Notified: Y / N

Signature of sender: Date: Time:

Exceptions noted by receiving unit:

PATIENT IDENTIFICATION

GF-335B (Rev 7/04) MAC 188

Source: Medical Center of Plano, Plano, Texas.

4-140 Post-Mortem Record

ROUTINE INQUIRY

On every death, contact Southwest Transplant Alliance (STA) at 1-800-201-0527 to determine what organs and/or tissues can be donated and discuss the family approach.

Name of STA contact person: ______________________ Confirmation # ________________ Date/Time of Call: __________________

☐ Patient/decedent was determined medically unsuitable for donation due to: (Please write reason for unsuitability): ____________________

____

☐ Patient/decedent was determined to be medically suitable candidate for donation.

Name of designated requestor who offered the option of donation to the family: ______________________________

Name of relationship of family member who was approached for consent:

Name: ______________________________ Relationship: ______________________

Did the family agree to donate? ☐ Yes ☐ No If yes, then a consent form must be completed and placed in the patient's chart.

Name and Title of person completing routine inquiry: ______________________________ Date/Time: ________

MEDICAL EXAMINER

Meets hospital criteria ☐ Yes ☐ No If no autopsy being done, explain why: ______________________________

Meets Medical Examiner's Criteria* ☐ Yes ☐ No Medical Examiner notified by: ______________________ at ______ ☐ AM ☐ PM

Body release by: ____

Medical Examiner postmortem ordered by: ______________________________________ Date: ______________

* Listed on back of top Copy

CONSENT FOR GENETIC TESTING

Medical Center of Plano is authorized to remove tissue specimens and perform genetic testing on ______________________________
who expired on ____________________ at ________ ☐ AM ☐ PM

Signature: X ______________________________________ Relationship: ______________________

Witness Signature: X ______________________________________ Date: ________________

CONSENT FOR POSTMORTEM EXAMINATION

Postmortem Examination ______________________________________ Postmortem Examination Date: ________________

I (we) being the next of kin of the decreased, hereby grant permission for the performance of a complete postmortem examination upon the body of the above patient by the staff pathologists. Authority is also granted for the preservation and study of any and all tissues that may be removed. This authority shall be limited only by the conditions expressly stated below:

____

____

Signature: X ______________________________________ Relationship to deceased: ______________________

Witness Signature: X ______________________________________ Date: ________________

RELEASE OF BODY

Medical Center of Plano is authorized to release the body of ______________________________________
who expired on ________________ at ________ ☐ AM ☐ PM ______________________________ Funeral Home.

Articles of clothing or valuables to accompany the body are (if none, write the word NONE): ______________________________

____ Date: __________ Time: ________ ☐ AM ☐ PM

Signature: X ______________________________________ Relationship to deceased: ______________________

(Signature and relationship of nearest relative of person authorized to release).

REMOVAL OF BODY

The body of the above named deceased person has been received by the undersigned person. Articles of clothing and/or valuables are to be disposed of as instructed by the person or persons authorizing the release of the body from Medical Center of Plano.

X ____________________	________	________	X ____________________	________
SIGNATURE	DATE	TIME	NAME OF FUNERAL HOME	LICENSE NUMBER

PATIENT IDENTIFICATION

Medical Examiner Criteria

All duties of death investigation are the responsibility of the Collin County Medical Examiner. The following criteria are used to report hospital deaths:

1. **All Emergency Department deaths.**
2. **All trauma deaths, obvious and suspected.**
3. **All deaths under anesthesia and the immediate post-anesthesia period.**
4. **All deaths within 24 hours of entry into the hospital.**
5. **All deaths occurring as a result of, during, or following a diagnostic procedure.**
6. **When the suspected cause of death is work-related, whether traumatic or natural.**
7. **All dead on arrival cases.**
8. **When the attending physician has no reasonable cause of death.**
9. **Stillbirths and instantiates if the delivery took place outside the hospital or if the delivery and/or death is related to, or suspected to be related to trauma.**
10. **Maternal deaths during or after delivery or where abortion is suspected.**

If there is any doubt as to whether the death needs to be reported, call the Medical Examiner's Office. Don't guess or make a decision if you are not absolutely sure. Medical Examiner's Office 1-972-548-3775.

Hospital Autopsy Criteria

It is the responsibility of the attending physician to request and encourage the family of the deceased to permit an autopsy. The permit will be maintained in the permanent medical record. Indications for autopsy are as follows:

- **Autopsy may help explain unknown or unanticipated complications;**
- **Cause of death is not known with certainty based on the clinical findings;**
- **Unexplained or unexpected death occurred during or following any medical or surgical diagnostic procedure or therapy;**
- **Unexplained or unexpected death that is apparently natural and not subject to a forensic medical jurisdiction;**
- **Death occurred during participation in a clinical trial of an investigational drug or device;**
- **Death occurred following an injury sustained while hospitalized;**
- **Death resulting from high-risk infectious and contagious diseases;**
- **Obstetrical death;**
- **Pediatric or neonatal death;**
- **Suspected illness may have bearing on survivors or recipients of transplant organs;**
- **Death known or suspected to have resulted from environmental or occupational hazards.**

The attending physician's request and the family's permission or refusal for autopsy should be documented in the medical record. The attending physician will notify the Pathology Department of cases referred for autopsy.

	PATIENT IDENTIFICATION
GF-070B (Rev 11/02) MAC 303	

Source: Medical Center of Plano, Plano, Texas.

4-141 HIPAA Security Guidance for Remote Use of Electronic Devices Containing Electronic Protected Health Information (EPHI)

Introduction

There have been a number of security incidents related to the use of laptops, other portable and/or mobile devices and external hardware that store, contain or are used to access Electronic Protected Health Information (EPHI) under the responsibility of a HIPAA covered entity. All covered entities are required to be in compliance with the HIPAA Security Rule[1], which includes, among its requirements, reviewing and modifying, where necessary, security policies and procedures on a regular basis. This is particularly relevant for organizations that allow remote access to EPHI through portable devices or on external systems or hardware not owned or managed by the covered entity.

This guidance document has been prepared with the main objective of reinforcing some of the ways a covered entity may protect EPHI when it is accessed or used outside of the organization's physical purview. In so doing, this document sets forth strategies that may be reasonable and appropriate for organizations that conduct some of their business activities through (1) the use of portable media/devices (such as USB flash drives) that store EPHI and (2) offsite access or transport of EPHI via laptops, personal digital assistants (PDAs), home computers or other non corporate equipment.

The Centers for Medicare & Medicaid Services (CMS) has delegated authority to enforce the HIPAA Security Standards, and may rely upon this guidance document in determining whether or not the actions of a covered entity are reasonable and appropriate for safeguarding the confidentiality, integrity and availability of EPHI, and it may be given deference in any administrative hearing pursuant to 45 C.F.R. § 160.508(c)(1), the HIPAA Enforcement Rule[2].

The kinds of devices and tools about which there is growing concern because of their vulnerability, include the following examples: laptops; home-based personal computers; PDAs and Smart Phones; hotel, library or other public workstations and Wireless Access Points (WAPs); USB Flash Drives and Memory Cards; floppy disks; CDs; DVDs; backup media; Email; Smart cards; and Remote Access Devices (including security hardware).

In general, covered entities should be extremely cautious about allowing the offsite use of, or access to, EPHI. There may be situations that warrant such offsite use or access, e.g., when it is clearly determined necessary through the entity's business case(s), and then only where great rigor has been taken to ensure that policies, procedures and workforce training have been effectively deployed, and access is provided consistent with the applicable requirements of the HIPAA Privacy Rule[3]. Some examples of appropriate business cases might include:

[1] The HIPAA Security Rule: Health Insurance Reform: Security Standards, February 20, 2003, 68 FR 8334.

[2] The HIPAA Enforcement Rule: Administrative Simplification: Enforcement, February 16, 2006, 45 FR 8390.

[3] The HIPAA Privacy Rule: Standards for Privacy of Individually Identifiable Health Information, December 28, 2000, 65 FR 82462, as amended August 14, 2002, 67 FR 53182

- ❑ A home health nurse collecting and accessing patient data using a PDA or laptop during a home health visit;
- ❑ A physician accessing an e-prescribing application on a PDA, while out of the office, to respond to patient requests for refills;
- ❑ A health plan employee transporting backup enrollee data on a media storage device, to an offsite facility.

We recognize that there may be additional business cases that will require the offsite use of, or access to, EPHI. This guidance is not intended to provide a comprehensive list of applicable business cases nor does it attempt to identify all covered entity compliance scenarios. A covered entity must evaluate its own need for offsite use of, or access to, EPHI, and when deciding which security strategies to use, must consider those factors identified in § 164.306(b)(2):

"*(i)* *The size, complexity, and capabilities of the covered entity.*
(ii) *The covered entity's technical infrastructure, hardware, and software security capabilities.*
(iii) *The costs of security measures.*
(iv) *The probability and criticality of potential risks to [EPHI].*"

Specifically, with respect to remote access to or use of EPHI, covered entities should place significant emphasis and attention on their:

- ❑ Risk analysis and risk management strategies;
- ❑ Policies and procedures for safeguarding EPHI;
- ❑ Security awareness and training on the policies & procedures for safeguarding EPHI.

Risk analysis and risk management drive policies

Once the covered entity has completed the analysis of the potential risks and vulnerabilities associated with remote access to, and offsite use of, EPHI, it must develop risk management measures to reduce such risks and vulnerabilities to a reasonable and appropriate level in compliance with § 164.306(a).

We group some of the risks associated with remote access and offsite use of EPHI into three areas: *access, storage and transmission*. Risk management planning takes all three areas into account, based on the unique vulnerabilities they introduce to covered entities that rely on remote operations involving EPHI.

A covered entity's analysis of the risks associated with accessing, storing and transmitting EPHI will form the basis for the policies and procedures designed to protect this sensitive information. Each area presents a unique set of challenges and should be individually addressed. Below is a brief summary of considerations to help guide the development or enhancement of these policies:

Data access policies and procedures focus on ensuring that users only access data for which they are appropriately authorized. Remote access to EPHI should only be granted to authorized users based on their role within the organization and their need for access to EPHI.

Storage policies and procedures address the security requirements for media and devices which contain EPHI and are moved beyond the covered entity's physical control. Such media and devices include laptops, hard drives, backup media, USB flash drives and any other data storage item which could potentially be removed from the organization's facilities.

Transmission policies focus on ensuring the integrity and safety of EPHI sent over networks, and include both the direct exchange of data (for example, in trading partner relationships) and the provisioning of remote access to applications hosted by the organization (such as a provider's home access to ePrescribing systems or "web mail" in organizations where EPHI might be included in internal communications).

Policies require training

No amount of risk analysis and policy development will be effective if the workforce does not have an appropriate security workforce awareness and training program; it is important that a covered entity's workforce awareness and training program specifically address any vulnerabilities associated with remote access to EPHI. Training should provide, at minimum, clear and concise instructions for accessing, storing and transmitting EPHI. If applicable, covered entities should include in their workforce awareness and training programs, password management procedures (for changing and safeguarding passwords); remote device/media protection to reinforce policies that prohibit leaving devices/media in unattended cars or public thoroughfares; as well as training on policies prohibiting the transmission of EPHI over open networks (including email) or downloading EPHI to public or remote computers.

It is imperative to again stress that in situations involving remote use of, and access to, EPHI, covered entities must make reasonable efforts to ensure that any such use or access is authorized and limited as required by the HIPAA Security Rule at §164.308(a)(4) and the HIPAA Privacy Rule.

Addressing security incidents and non-compliance

Should a covered entity experience loss of EPHI via portable media, the entity's security incident procedures must specify the actions workforce members must take to manage harmful effects of the loss. Procedures may include securing and preserving evidence; managing the harmful effects of improper use or disclosure; and notification to affected parties. Needless to say, such incidents should be evaluated as part of the entity's ongoing risk management initiatives.

A sanction policy must be in place and effectively communicated so that workforce members understand the consequences of failing to comply with the security policies and procedures of the covered entity related to offsite use of, or access to EPHI. When addressing the development and implementation of sanction policies, a covered entity should consider at least requiring employees to sign a statement of adherence to security policies and procedures as a prerequisite to employment.

Possible Risk Management Strategies

The tables in this section list risks applicable to each category identified earlier (access, storage, transmission), paired with risk management strategies. The "Risk" column includes general problems that could occur with the use of remote devices, or work done off-site, and lists risks in order of those that may be likely to occur followed by those that may be less likely to occur but are still pertinent to the overall risk analysis. Where applicable, the "Possible Risk Management Strategies" column suggests basic solutions first, followed by solutions that may be more complex and therefore, possibly more appropriate for organizations with advanced technical capabilities.

Covered entities that allow or require offsite use of, or access to EPHI, and are capable of implementing all of the strategies described below, are strongly urged to do so. Furthermore, since the lists are not comprehensive, entities should strive to incorporate any other appropriate strategies to ensure the protection of EPHI. In the Strategies column, we do not repeat the same strategy multiple times even though a strategy may be appropriate to address more than one of the listed risks. For example, in the category of storing EPHI, there are risks related to the loss of a laptop or risks associated with inadvertently saving a file containing sensitive information as a temporary file or cache on a foreign computer. Assuming the files on the laptop, and those launched from an email onto an offsite system are protected by passwords, the use of a strong password to protect access to the device or file would be an appropriate and expected risk management strategy. However, "use of strong passwords" may only appear once in the entire table for that section. The tables should be read so that a number of different strategies can be considered appropriate for any or all of the risks listed, and for others that may be identified by the covered entity.

Accessing EPHI

Covered entities must develop and implement policies and procedures for authorizing EPHI access in accordance with the HIPAA Security Rule at §164.308(a)(4) and the HIPAA Privacy Rule at §164.508. It is important that only those workforce members who have been trained and have proper authorization are granted access to EPHI.

Risks	Possible Risk Management Strategies
➢ Log-on/password information is lost or stolen resulting in potential unauthorized or improper access to or inappropriate viewing or modification of EPHI.	➢ Implement two-factor authentication for granting remote access to systems that contain EPHI. This process requires factors beyond general usernames and passwords to gain access to systems (e.g., requiring users to answer a security question such as "Favorite Pet's Name"); ➢ Implement a technical process for creating unique user names and performing authentication when granting remote access to a workforce member. This may be done using Remote Authentication Dial-In User Service (RADIUS) or other similar tools.
➢ Employees access EPHI when not authorized to do so while working offsite.	➢ Develop and employ proper clearance procedures and verify training of workforce members prior to granting remote access; ➢ Establish remote access roles specific to applications and business requirements. Different remote users may require different levels of access based on job function. ➢ Ensure that the issue of unauthorized access of EPHI is appropriately addressed in the required sanction policy.
➢ Home or other offsite workstations left unattended risking improper access to EPHI.	➢ Establish appropriate procedures for session termination (time-out) on inactive portable or remote devices. Covered entities can work with vendors to deliver systems or applications with appropriate defaults.
➢ Contamination of systems by a virus introduced from an	➢ Install personal firewall software on all laptops that store or access EPHI or connect to networks on which EPHI is

Risks	Possible Risk Management Strategies
infected external device used to gain remote access to systems that contain EPHI.	accessible; ➢ Install, use and regularly update virus-protection software on all portable or remote devices that access EPHI.

Storing EPHI

Covered entities must develop and implement policies and procedures to protect EPHI that is stored on remote or portable devices, or on potentially transportable media (particularly backups).

Risks	Possible Risk Management Strategies
➢ Laptop or other portable device is lost or stolen resulting in potential unauthorized/improper access to or modification of EPHI housed or accessible through the device.	➢ Identify the types of hardware and electronic media that must be tracked, such as hard drives, magnetic tapes or disks, optical disks or digital memory cards, and security equipment and develop inventory control systems; ➢ Implement process for maintaining a record of the movements of, and person(s) responsible for, or permitted to use hardware and electronic media containing EPHI; ➢ Require use of lock-down or other locking mechanisms for unattended laptops; ➢ Password protect files; ➢ Password protect all portable or remote devices that store EPHI; ➢ Require that all portable or remote devices that store EPHI employ encryption technologies of the appropriate strength; ➢ Develop processes to ensure appropriate security updates are deployed to portable devices such as Smart Phones and PDAs; ➢ Consider the use of biometrics, such as fingerprint readers, on portable devices.
➢ Use of external device to access corporate data resulting in the loss of operationally critical EPHI on the remote device.	➢ Develop processes to ensure backup of all EPHI entered into remote systems; ➢ Deploy policy to encrypt backup and archival media; ensure that policies direct the use of encryption technologies of the appropriate strength.
➢ Loss or theft of EPHI left on devices after inappropriate disposal by the organization.	➢ Establish EPHI deletion policies and media disposal procedures. At a minimum this involves complete deletion, via specialized deletion tools, of all disks and backup media prior to disposal. For systems at the end of their operational lifecycle, physical destruction may be appropriate.
➢ Data is left on an external device (accidentally or intentionally), such as in a library or hotel business center.	➢ Prohibit or prevent download of EPHI onto remote systems or devices without an operational justification; ➢ Ensure workforce is appropriately trained on policies that require users to search for and delete any files intentionally or unintentionally saved to an external device; ➢ Minimize use of browser-cached data in web based applications which manage EPHI, particularly those accessed remotely.
➢ Contamination of systems by a	➢ Install virus-protection software on all portable or remote

Risks	Possible Risk Management Strategies
virus introduced from a portable storage device.	devices that store EPHI.

Transmitting EPHI

Covered entities must establish and implement appropriate policies and procedures to secure EPHI that is being transmitted over an electronic communications network.

Risks	Possible Risk Management Strategies
➢ Data intercepted or modified during transmission.	➢ Prohibit transmission of EPHI via open networks, such as the Internet, where appropriate; ➢ Prohibit the use of offsite devices or wireless access points (e.g. hotel workstations) for non-secure access to email. ➢ Use more secure connections for email via SSL and the use of message-level standards such as S/MIME, SET, PEM, PGP etc.; ➢ Implement and mandate appropriately strong encryption solutions for transmission of EPHI (e.g. SSL, HTTPS etc.). SSL should be a minimum requirement for all Internet-facing systems which manage EPHI in any form, including corporate web-mail systems.
➢ Contamination of systems by a virus introduced from an external device used to transmit EPHI.	➢ Install virus-protection software on portable devices that can be used to transmit EPHI.

Summary

The HIPAA Security and Privacy Rules require all covered entities to protect the EPHI that they use or disclose to business associates, trading partners or other entities. New standards and technologies have significantly simplified the way in which data is transmitted throughout the healthcare industry and created tremendous opportunities for improvements in the healthcare system. However, these technologies have also created complications and increased the risk of loss and unauthorized use and disclosure of this sensitive information.

This document provides a review of some strategies that may be reasonable and appropriate under the HIPAA Security Rule, for certain covered entities to follow (based upon their individual technological capabilities and operational needs), for offsite use of, or access to, EPHI. For a more detailed review of the HIPAA Security Rule, please visit www.cms.hhs.gov and follow the link under "Regulations and Guidance" for HIPAA Educational Materials. There you will find the "Security Series of Papers" which provide an overview of the regulatory requirements of the HIPAA Security Rule (www.cms.hhs.gov/EducationMaterials/). Please note that the HIPAA Privacy Rule also requires covered entities to implement appropriate administrative, technical, and physical safeguards for protected health information (PHI) in any form, including non-electronic. These provisions are enforced by the Office for Civil Rights (OCR). For more information on the Privacy requirements please visit www.hhs.gov/ocr/hipaa or call the HIPAA Privacy Hotline at 1-866-627-7748 (TDD: 1-800-537-7697).

To provide feedback regarding this guidance document, you may write to Michael Phillips in the Office of eHealth Standards and Services at RemoteAccessGuidance@cms.hhs.gov.

Source: HIPAA Security Guidance for Remote Use of and Access to Electronic Protected Health Information, 12/28/06. CMS HIPAA Security Education Materials. Available online at http://www.cms.hhs.gov/SecurityStandard.

SURVEILLANCE, PREVENTION, AND CONTROL OF INFECTION

4-142 Infectious Diseases in ED Settings

The following are infectious diseases that may be transmitted and/or acquired in health care settings and therefore are possible Healthcare Associated Infections (HAIs).

Acinetobacter
Bloodborne Pathogens
Burkholderia cepacia
Chickenpox (Varicella)
Clostridium Difficile
Clostridium Sordellii
Creutzfeldt-Jakob Disease (CJD)
Ebola (Viral Hemorrhagic Fever)
Gastrointestinal (GI) Infections
Hepatitis A
Hepatitis B
Hepatitis C
HIV/AIDS
Influenza
MRSA—Methicillin-resistant *Staphylococcus Aureus*
Mumps
Norovirus
Parvovirus
Poliovirus
Pneumonia
Rubella
SARS
S. pneumoniae (Drug resistant)
Tuberculosis
Varicella (Chickenpox)
Viral Hemorrhagic Fever (Ebola)
VISA—Vancomycin Intermediate *Staphylococcus aureus*
VRE—Vancomycin-resistant *enterococci*

Source: CDC Division of Healthcare Quality Promotion (DHQP), Date last modified: January 3, 2006. Available at *http://www.cdc.gov/ncidod/dhqp/id.html.*

4-143 Infection Control Policies

I. Employees

A. All employees receive an education to house-wide infection control policies and procedures as well as ED-specific practices during their orientation. Formal and informal inservice programs are provided thereafter specific to the employee's work-related responsibilities in the ED.

B. Employees are required to report illnesses due to infection or contagious diseases to the Occupational Health Nurse. If an illness is due to infection or contagious disease, a physician's statement is required stating that the employee is non-infectious and is able to return to work.

C. Universal precautions are used for the care of all patients using appropriate protective equipment (gloves, gowns, masks, goggles, etc.) for contact with blood and body fluids. This equipment is readily accessible in the department.

D. Employees are to wash their hands before and after contact with patients and after contact with contaminated objects.

E. Attire:

1. Emergency & Shock Trauma Center nursing personnel wear scrub uniforms in accordance with the departmental dress code.
2. While acting as a member of the Trauma Team, the established Trauma Protocols are followed.

F. Communicable Disease Exposure
   1. The Occupational Health Section of the Infection Control Manual contains the appropriate procedures to be followed. An Employee Accident Report must be completed.
   2. The Infection Control Nurse/Nursing Supervisor are notified as per the protocol outlined in the Infection Control Manual.

G. All employees are offered and encouraged to receive the Hepatitis B vaccination. The Emergency Department is considered to be a high-risk area for exposure.

II. Care of ED Patients With Infectious Diseases/Conditions

A. Patients admitted to the Emergency Department who have a known or suspected infectious or communicable disease should be treated and released/admitted as soon as possible. Isolation policies and procedures as outlined in the Infection Control Manual shall be followed while the patient remains in the Emergency Department. Every attempt is made to separate the patient from other patients and visitors. Room 14 is used for isolation whenever possible.

B. Documentation on the patient's Emergency Department record should include specific isolation procedures followed while the patient is in the Emergency Department.

C. The Infection Control Nurse is notified on weekdays; the Nursing Supervisor, on weekends, nights, and evenings. The Nursing Supervisor will contact the Infection Control Nurse after hours as appropriate.

D. For patients being admitted, the Admitting Office will be notified of the type of isolation required so that an appropriate bed assignment can be made.

E. The department/nursing unit to which the patient is being admitted is notified of the type of isolation or precautions required.

F. When transporting patients on Strict of Respiratory Isolation, the patient will wear a surgical mask.

III. ED Physical Layout

A. Clean and sterile supplies are stored in the clean utility room. Contaminated equipment is stored in the appropriate utility room.

B. Only authorized personnel are admitted to the supply areas in order to minimize traffic.

C. The performance of incision and drainage of abscesses, wound irrigation's, etc., that could possible cause cross-contamination is done such that all materials used are contained at the bedside, and disposed of (or prepared for CSS reprocessing) as appropriate. The surrounding area is cleaned after use.

IV. Specimen Collection

A. All specimens are considered contaminated.

B. Appropriate precautions will be used as needed (gloves, mask, goggles, etc.) when collecting specimens. All specimens are placed in ziploc plastic bags prior to transport to the laboratory.

V. Instruments/Equipment

A. All reusable instruments or equipment will be returned to Central Sterile Supply (CSS) for sterilization. Reusable instruments will be rinsed to remove any gross soilage and placed in red biohazard containers kept in dirty utility room to soak. CSS is responsible for picking up dirty instruments. Used laryngoscope blades are sent to CSS for exchange.

B. Electronic thermometers with disposable probe covers are used routinely. For patients on Strict Isolation or VRE Precautions, glass thermometers are used.
C. EKG machines, monitors, and cables are wiped off daily with the approved hospital disinfectant. See the Infection Control Policy Manual.
D. All stretchers/wheelchairs are wiped with the hospital approved disinfectant solution after use where soiling or contamination has occurred, and weekly per schedule.
E. IV Pumps/Controllers are wiped with disinfectant weekly.

VI. Linen

A. All dirty linen is placed in a fluid-resistant bag and sent to the Laundry via the laundry chute. Laundry chutes are to remain locked when not in use.

VII. Housekeeping

A. Daily cleaning of the department is provided according to a schedule provided by the Housekeeping Department.
B. Nursing staff will direct Housekeeping staff in required terminal cleaning procedures. AORN standards will be used for terminal cleaning.

VIII. Communicable Disease Reporting

The Emergency Department physician who examines a patient with one of the communicable diseases listed, shall complete the "Maryland Confidential Morbidity Report" (DHMH-1140, 12-74). This form shall be mailed to the Montgomery County Health Department. Attached list of REPORTABLE DISEASES.

IX. A. Attached follow-up of Communicable Disease Exposure incidents occurring in the ER/Hospital Personnel.

1. The physician involved in the case shall consult with the Infection Control Nurse to discuss whether follow-up measures are indicated. Consultation will be sought from the Infection Control Committee Chairman when necessary.
2. Infection Control will coordinate employee follow-up with the Employee Health Service, and provide counseling to those concerned.
3. Any prophylactic medications recommended will be ordered by the ER physician or the Employee Health Nurse.

B. Follow-up of the Exposed persons not employed by the Hospital (medics, Police) or concerned community members.
ANY PUBLIC/PARAMEDICAL INQUIRIES FOR INFORMATION ON EXPOSURES SHALL BE DIRECTED TO INFECTION CONTROL, OR CONTACT THROUGH NURSING SUPERVISOR ON WEEKENDS OR OFF-SHIFTS.

1. The Infection Control notifies the appropriate facility where the exposed person is employed to explain the circumstances. Follow-up is conducted by that facility.

2. The Infection Control Nurse reports the case to the Health Department (if it is a reportable disease/condition).

Source: Suburban Hospital, Inc., Bethesda, Maryland.

4-144 Employee Health/Infection Control Policy

POLICY

________________________ provides Employee Health Services to its employees to protect them from communicable diseases and to identify and control diseases and infections that may pose a risk to patients that are employee transmissible.

1. The Infection Control Committee will have input into the employee health program requirements.
2. All communicable or infectious diseases experienced by employees that are reported to the Employee Health Nurse will be reported to the Infection Control Committee. Employee name and unique identifiers will be redacted from any reports to the committee.
   A. All reportable employee communicable diseases will be reported to the Health Department by the Employee Health Nurse.
   B. An Accident Report will be filled out if infection is job related.
   C. The Employee Health Nurse may require a work release from the employee's physician.
3. Work restrictions for employees with an infectious disease will be according to the *CDC Guideline for Infection Control in Hospital Personnel.*
4. In addition to the guidelines set forth by the CDC, employees known to have HIV Virus, Hepatitis B Virus and/or Hepatitis C Virus:
   A. Will be evaluated by the Employee Health Medical Director to determine if they can safely be allowed to perform the duties of their position.
   B. Employees with impaired immune systems resulting from HIV infection or other causes are at increased risk of acquiring or experiencing serious complications of infectious disease. Of particular concern is the risk of severe infection following exposure to patients with infectious diseases that are easily transmitted if appropriate precautions are not taken (e.g., measles, varicella). Any employee known to have an impaired immune system should be counseled about the potential risk associated with any transmissible diseases and the importance of observing standard precautions. A physician's release stating fitness for duty may be requested.
   C. Employees with impaired immune systems that work in areas where risk of exposure to tuberculosis exists will be counseled about the risks and not assigned to care for patients suspected of having or diagnosed with tuberculosis.
5. The following guidelines have been developed to protect employees from patients with certain conditions.
   A. Employees known to be pregnant
      1. Must not be assigned to care for patients with rubella, rubeola, or infants with congenital rubella syndrome or cytomegalovirus infections.
      2. Must not care for patients receiving riboviran therapy.

B. Employees with known immunity, active or passive, to infectious diseases such as measles, mumps, chicken pox, small pox, or influenza, should be assigned to care for patients with those diseases.
C. Employees with known immune deficiencies will be evaluated on a case- by-case basis.

6. Immunization and screening records will be kept in the employee's health file.

Requirements are as follows:

A. Screening for Tuberculosis
1. A Mantoux (PPD) two-step skin test is done on all potential new hires who do not have a documented negative test within the last 12 months at the time of the pre-placement screen.
2. If the potential new hire has documentation of a negative test within the last 12 months, a one-step test is done.
3. A chest x-ray is done on those potential new hires with a history of a positive PPD (unless the new hire has documentation of a recent CXR) and on those who test positive at the time of the pre-placement screen.
4. For all applicants whose skin test and/or chest x-ray is positive, a TB Referral Form is filled out by the EHN and sent to the ______ County Health Department. A copy is placed in the potential new hire's chart.
5. Employees with positive skin tests and negative follow-up chest x-rays will be allowed to work after the Employee Health Nurse consults with the ______ County Health Department.
6. Applicants with positive chest x-rays must provide the Employee Health Nurse with a medical release prior to reporting to work.
7. Skin testing will be done post exposure as recommended by CDC guidelines and for contact investigation.
8. Employees will be given a PPD test annually, or as determined by the Annual Community TB Risk Assessment. Employees who work in the Business Office or who are Home Transcriptionists will be given a TB test on hire only.
9. Employees with a positive PPD and negative chest x-ray will not be tested yearly, but will complete an annual surveillance questionnaire. This form will be kept in their employee health file and not in their human resource file. If any answers are positive, the EHN reviews them with the EH Medical Director and a CXR is done if indicated. Positive results are reported to the Health Department.
10. Contract workers will be able to show documentation of testing upon request.

B. Hepatitis B Vaccine
1. Hepatitis B Vaccine is offered (not required) at no cost to all employees.
2. Employees must:
   a. Read and sign an informational consent form or sign a declination form. These will be kept in the employee's health file.
   b. The employee is responsible for completing the series of three vaccinations.
   c. After completion of the series, a titer will be drawn and follow up done according to CDC Guidelines.
3. Bloodborne pathogen initial training is done in EH at hire.
4. All employees are given the opportunity to receive the vaccinations as of their first day of work or at any time during the course of their employment.

5. Hepatitis B Vaccine will be given to pregnant women or nursing mothers according to manufacturer's guidelines and only with employee's physician's written approval.
6. If an employee separates from the hospital and has started his/her immunization series, he/she may obtain copies of his/her records from the Employee Health Office and complete the series elsewhere.

C. Measles Immunity
1. All applicants born after January 1, 1957, must provide proof of their Rubeola (hard measles) and Rubella (German measles) immunity status. Active immunity will be confirmed by at least one of the following:
   a. Written proof; a copy of immunization record indicating the two dose measles/Rubella vaccine was given after 1967 and after the age of 15 months.
   b. A physician-signed medical record showing the applicant has had the active disease.
   c. Documentation of a titer showing active immunity to the disease.
2. If the applicant does not provide proof of immunity during their first calendar month of employment, or receive the vaccine from their physician or in the Employee Health office, they will be so noted in the computer. This will provide identification of at-risk employees in the event of a measles outbreak. In the event of exposure, the at-risk employee would be excluded from work during the incubation period of the disease without pay. The employee will be notified of this possibility and strongly urged to receive the vaccine.

D. Meningococcal Disease
1. The meningococcal vaccine is offered at no charge to employees who are hired to work in microbiology.
2. Employees exposed to meningococcal disease should be treated prophylactically according to CDC guidelines: if an employee has had "intensive, unprotected contact (i.e., without wearing a mask) with infected patients (e.g., intubating, resuscitating, or closely examining the oropharynx of patients".
   a. Current recommendation in adults is Rifampin 600 mg BID x 2 days. However, Rifampin is NOT recommended for pregnant women. Ceftriaxone may be recommended for pregnant women.
   b. Ciprofloxacin and Cettriaxone in single-dose regimens are reasonable alternatives to the multidose rifampin.

E. Records of respirator fit testing for those employees affected will be maintained in the Employee Health office.

Source: Courtesy of Judy Sikes, PhD, CPHQ, Parkview Medical Center, Pueblo, Colorado.

4-145 Guidelines for Significant Blood/Body Fluid Exposures

A tetanus-diphtheria booster should be offered if the employee has not had one in 5 years. Immune Globulin, 0.06 ml/kg, gluteal muscle should be offered as soon as possible.

KNOWN SOURCE:

TEST	IF SOURCE NEGATIVE:	IF SOURCE POSITIVE:
HBSAG	• Employee's Employee Health Antibody Hepatitis B Surface Antigen (EHAHBS) will be tested as part of EH/PANEL. • No Rx. Offer vaccine to those who have not initiated series. Offer booster dose to those whose Hepatitis B Surface Antibody (AHBS) is negative and have previously been immunized (for up to a total of two complete series of three).	• Employee's EHAHBS will be tested as part of EH/PANEL. • Offer HBIG, 0.06 ml/kg, gluteal muscle, as soon as possible. • If employee has completed Hepatitis B vaccination series, and AHBS is positive, no further RX. • If employee has completed Hepatitis B vaccination series, and EHAHBS is negative, offer vaccination booster. • If employees has initiated Hepatitis B vaccination series, continue on series schedule. • If employee's EHAHBS is negative, employee's Hepatitis B Surface Antigen (HBSAG) will be tested at 3 months, 6 months, and 12 months.
HCVAB	• Employee's Employee Health Hepatitis C Virus Antibody (EHHCVAB) will be tested as part of EH/PANEL. • No Rx.	• Employee's EHHCVAB will be tested as part of EH/PANEL. • No Rx—according to the CDC there is no licensed tx or prophylaxis for Hepatitis C exposure. Employee EHHCVAB will be retested at 3 months, 6 months, 12 months.
HIV	• Employee's Employee Health HIV Antibody (EHHIVAB) will be tested as part of Employee Health series of tests (EH/PANEL). • In accordance with Maryland state law, Source EHHIVAB may not be baseline tested unless employee also agrees to be tested. • Retest employee EHHIVAB at 3 months and 6 months.	• (Know positive or confirmed by Western Blot) • Employee's baseline EHHIVAB will be tested as part of EH/PANEL. • Employee's EHHIVAB will be retested at 6 weeks, 3 months, 6 months and 12 months. See Protocol for Occupational HIV Post-Exposure Chemoprophylaxis.

UNKNOWN SOURCE:

- Employee will be baseline tested (EHHIVAB, EHAHBS, and EHHCVAB).
- If employee has not completed or initiated Hepatitis B vaccination series, it should be offered at this time.
- Retest employee's EHHIVAB at 3 months, 6 months, and 12 months.

Source: Suburban Hospital, Inc., Bethesda, Maryland.

4-146 Management of Occupational Blood Exposures

Provide immediate care to the exposure site.

- Wash wounds and skin with soap and water.
- Flush mucous membranes with water.

Determine risk associated with exposure by

- type of fluid (e.g., blood, visibly bloody fluid, other potentially infectious fluid or tissue, and concentrated virus) and

- type of exposure (i.e., percutaneous injury, mucous membrane or nonintact skin exposure, and bites resulting in blood exposure).

Evaluate exposure source.

- Assess the risk of infection using available information.
- Test known sources of HbsAg, anti-HCV, and HIV antibody (consider using rapid testing).
- For unknown sources, assess risk of exposure to HBV, HCV, or HIV infection.
- Do not test discarded needles or syringes for virus contamination.

Evaluate the exposed person.

- Assess immune status for HBV infection (i.e., by history of hepatitis B vaccination and vaccine response).

Give PEP for exposures posing risk of infection transmission.

- HBV
- HCV: PEP not recommended.
- HIV

  —Initiate PEP as soon as possible, preferably within hours of exposure.

  —Offer pregnancy testing to all women of childbearing age not known to be pregnant.

  —Seek expert consultation if viral resistance is suspected.

  —Administer PEP for 4 weeks if tolerated.

Perform follow-up testing and provide counseling.

- Advise exposed persons to seek medical evaluation for any acute illness occurring during follow-up.

HBV exposures

- Perform follow-up anti-HBs testing in persons who receive hepatitis B vaccine.

  —Test for anti-HBs 1-2 months after last dose of vaccine.

  —Anti-HBs response to vaccine cannot be ascertained if HBIG was received in the previous 3 4 months.

HCV exposures

- Perform baseline and follow-up testing for anti-HCV and alanine amino-transferase (ALT) 4-6 months after exposures.
- Perform HCV RNA at 4-6 weeks if earlier diagnosis of HCV infection desired.
- Confirm repeatedly reactive anti-HCV enzyme immunoassays (EIAs) with supplemental tests.

HIV exposures

- Perform HIV-antibody testing for at least 6 months post-exposure (e.g., at baseline, 6 weeks, 3 months, and 6 months).
- Perform HIV antibody testing if illness compatible with an acute retroviral syndrome occurs.
- Advise exposed persons to use precautions to prevent secondary transmission during the follow-up period.

- Evaluate exposed persons taking PEP within 72 hours after exposure and monitor for drug toxicity for at least 2 weeks.

Source: Centers for Disease Control *MMWR Reports & Recommendations*, June 29, 2001/ 50(RR11);43-4. *http://www.cdc.gov/mmwr/previous/mmwrhtml/rr5011a2.htm.* Accessed 8/14/01.

4-147 Procedure for Employee Exposures (During Office Hours)

Contact Nursing Supervisor for evening/weekend/holiday exposures.

EMPLOYEE:

1. IMMEDIATELY AFTER CONTACT WITH BLOOD OR BODY FLUIDS:
   - Wash hands and any other affected skin area(s) with soap and water. Or
   - Flush mucous membranes with water.
2. Notify immediate supervisor.
3. Notify Employee/Occupational Health & Safety immediately and report to Employee/ Occupational Health & Safety before the end of shift.
4. Complete Potential Exposure Report.
5. Have blood drawn for baseline lab tests after reporting to Employee/Occupational Health & Safety.

MANAGER/SUPERVISOR:

1. Notify Employee/Occupational Health & Safety of exposure.
2. Obtain source HIV consent for medically determined exposures (applies to Nursing Managers/Charge Nurses).
3. Forward ALL exposure related forms to Employee Health.

HIV orders related to employee exposures are not documented on patient chart.

Source: Suburban Hospital, Inc., Bethesda, Maryland.

4-148 Procedure for Employee Exposures (Evening/Weekends/Holidays)

1. IMMEDIATELY AFTER CONTACT WITH BLOOD OR BODY FLUIDS:
   - Wash hands and any other affected skin area with soup and water.
     or
   - Flush mucous membranes with water.
2. Notify immediate supervisor.
3. The employee contacts the Nursing Supervisor who will evaluate the incident to assess whether this is an actual exposure to source blood/body fluids. If the incident is an actual exposure, the employee completes the Potential Exposure Report.
4. The Nursing Supervisor will determine via policy and procedure if the employee needs to be seen in the ER for a tetanus booster, Hepatitis B vaccine, H-BIG, immune globulin, human immunodeficiency virus (HIV) Post-Exposure Chemoprophylaxis, or other treatment.

5. The Nursing Supervisor will obtain source HIV consent.
6. Nursing Supervisor:
   - Due to the fact that Employee/Occupational Health & Safety lab work is now irretrievable, the employee may now be admitted using their own name, SS#, date of birth, and address.
   - Admit source patient using the patient's own name, SS#, date of birth, and address.
7. Order the following labs:
   Employee: EH/DIAGNOSTIC PANEL
   Source: EHP/DIAGNOSTIC PANEL
8. Employee reports to Ambulatory Testing/Outpatient Lab (or the ER if they are closed) for blood work and calls Employee/Occupational Health & Safety the following day/Monday.
9. If the source is HIV+, the employee should read and be counseled on the Protocol for Occupational HIV Post-Exposure Chemoprophylaxis. If the employee elects to begin HIV Post-Exposure Chemoprophylaxis, the employee should be seen in the ER immediately for counseling, treatment, Rx, and baseline lab work. The following lab work should also be ordered: EELR, ECBC, EHHEPPA. Post-HIV exposure counseling documentation includes the signature of the employee exposed and the counselor.
10. Forward ALL exposure forms to Employee/Occupational Health & Safety. These forms are filed in the employee heath office and not in the human resource file.

If the employee is seen in the ER, the ER physician completes/signs The Statement of Medical Findings. The employee should follow up with Employee/Occupational Health & Safety the following day if not seen in the ER. If it is a Friday evening or Saturday, ER evaluation is recommended.

Source: Suburban Hospital, Inc., Bethesda, Maryland.

4-149 Potential Exposure Report

EXPOSURE DATE: ____/____/____

NAME: ______________________ SS#: ________________________ DEPT: ______________________
BIRTHDATE: ___/___/___ TIME OF EXP: ________________________ LOCATION OF EXP: ________________
DATE REPORTED: ___/___/___ TO WHOM: ________________________ WITNESS: ________________
SOURCE (PATIENT) NAME: ______________________________ SS#: ______________________________
SOURCE BIRTHDATE: ___/___/___ ADDRESS: ____

Please check exposure type:

__________ Needle puncture
__________ Eye splash
__________ Mucous membrane contact
__________ Open wound contact (includes chapped skin)
__________ Contaminated Sharp
__________ Other (specify) ____

Describe incident in detail: (What employee was doing, how exposure occurred, exposure site)

____
____
____

I request that efforts be made by _______ to seek the informed consent of the source to test his/her blood for the presence of HIV if there is a medically determined exposure. I agree to submit a sample of my blood to be tested for HIV.

______________________________ ______________________________
Employee Signature Date Supervisor Signature Date

STATEMENT OF MEDICAL FINDINGS

VACCINATION STATUS: Last tetanus date ____________________ (if applicable, i.e., puncture wound)
Hepatitis B Vaccinations? _____ yes _____ no Date completed: ____________________
NATURE OF EXPOSURE/TREATMENT/FOLLOW-UP:

____

MEDICAL DETERMINATION OF EXPOSURE: (see exposure criteria)

______ Massive Exposure
______ Definite Exposure
______ Probable Exposure
______ Doubtful Exposure

____
Examiner's signature

Source: Suburban Hospital, Inc., Bethesda, Maryland.

4-150 Exposure Criteria

MASSIVE EXPOSURE

- Transfusion of blood
- Injection of more than 1ml of blood/body fluids
- Parenteral exposure to lab specimens containing a high titer of virus

DEFINITE EXPOSURE

- Injection of blood/body fluids (less than 1ml)
- Deep intramuscular injury with a blood/body fluid contaminated needle
- Laceration or wound produced by a visibly blood/body fluid contaminated instrument which causes bleeding in the health care worker
- Laceration or fresh wound inoculated with blood/body fluids

PROBABLE EXPOSURE

- Subcutaneous (superficial) injury with blood/body fluid contaminated needle
- Wound produced by blood/body fluid contaminated instrument which does not cause spontaneous bleeding
- Prior wound/skin lesion contaminated with blood/body fluid
- Mucous membrane inoculation with blood/body fluid

DOUBTFUL EXPOSURE

- Subcutaneous (superficial) injury with a needle or device contaminated with non-infectious, non-bloody fluid (e.g., urine, feces, sweat, tears)
- Laceration produced by non-infectious body fluid contaminated instrument
- Prior wound/skin lesion contaminated with non-infectious body fluid
- Mucous membrane inoculation with non-infectious body fluid

Source: Suburban Hospital, Inc., Bethesda, Maryland.

4-151 Employee Consent for Treatment

- The recommendations for employees who experience a potential contaminated exposure have been explained to me. I have had the opportunity to ask questions about the risks associated with this exposure, and to request additional information.
- I understand the necessity for base-line lab tests for me and the source individual, and follow-up tests for myself. I understand that these tests will be done, and records will be maintained, using confidential practices.
- I understand that test results will not be given to me or to others over the phone. If the results so indicate, I will be informed of possible follow-up treatment.
- If the source patient is **known to be positive for human immunodeficiency virus (HIV),** I will read and be counseled on The Protocol for Occupational HIV Post-Exposure Chemoprophylaxis.
- Compliance with recommended follow-up is my responsibility.

I hereby agree:

_________ • to be tested for HIV, AHBS (Hepatitis B surface antibody), & Hepatitis C
(initial)

_________ • choose/decline/N/A (circle) HIV Post-Exposure Chemoprophylaxis, if the source patient is known to be positive for HIV.
(initial)

_______________________________ ____
Employee Name (print) Date Employee Signature

____
Witness Signature

Report the following symptoms to Employee Health:

a. Infection—redness, swelling, pain, drainage from the site.
b. Hepatitis—fever, malaise, anorexia, dark urine or jaundice.
c. Acute viral symptoms within 6 weeks of exposure—fever, rash, lymph node inflammation.

Source: Suburban Hospital, Inc., Bethesda, Maryland.

4-152 Informed Consent and Agreement to HIV Testing

With my signature below I acknowledge that I have read (or have had read to me) and understand the following information:

Facts About HIV Testing

I HAVE BEEN TOLD THAT: (1) My blood or other body fluid or tissue sample will be tested for signs of an infection by the human immunodeficiency virus (HIV), the virus that causes acquired immunodeficiency syndrome (AIDS); (2) My consent to have my blood tested for HIV should be FREELY given; and (3) Every attempt will be made to keep the results of this test confidential, but that confidentiality cannot be guaranteed.

What a NEGATIVE Result Means:

A negative test means that the laboratory has not found evidence of HIV infection in my blood sample.

What a POSITIVE Test Result Means:

A. A positive HIV test means that I have HIV infection and can spread the virus to others by having sex or by sharing needles;
B. A positive HIV test DOES NOT mean that I have AIDS—other tests are needed;
C. If my test result is positive, I may experience emotional discomfort and, if my test result becomes known to the community, I may experience discrimination in work, personal relationships, and insurance.

What Will Be Done for Me if My Test is Positive:

A. I will be given a copy of the Department of Health and Mental Hygiene's publication, "Information for HIV Infected Persons," which contains information about counseling services which may help me;
B. I will be told how to keep from spreading my HIV infection by; (1) Avoiding sexual intercourse, or practicing SAFER sex; (2) Not sharing drug needles—better still, getting off drugs; (3) Not donating or selling my blood, plasma, organs, or sperm; (4) Avoiding pregnancy; and (5) Not breastfeeding, or donating breast milk;
C. Unless my test is performed at a designated anonymous test site approved by the Department of Health and Mental Hygiene, my unique patient identifying number will be given to the local health department and, if I have signs or symptoms of HIV infection, my name will be reported to the local health department to assist me in obtaining services and help the health department understand and control the AIDS problem;
D. I know that my local health department or doctor may assist me in notifying and referring my partners for medical services—without giving my name to my partners;
E. If I refuse to notify my partners, my doctor may either notify them or have the local health department do so. In this case, my name will not be used. Where required by law, when a local health department knows of my partners, it must refer them for care, support, and treatment and
F. I have had a chance to have my questions about this test answered. My counselor has explained to me about the use of a portion of my Social Security number in the unique patient identifying number and I have indicated below whether or not a portion of my Social Security number can be used for this purpose.

   —YES, I allow the use of a portion of my Social Security number.

   —NO, I DO NOT allow the use of a portion of my Social Security number.

I hereby agree to have my blood drawn for an HIV test.

Name of Person Tested	Date
Signature of Patient or Authorized Substitute	Signature of Counselor

Source: Suburban Hospital, Inc., Bethesda, Maryland.

4-153 Potential Exposure to Hepatitis B

Vaccination and antibody response status of exposed workers*	**Treatment**		
	Source HBsAg[†] positive	**Source HBsAg[†] negative**	**Source Unknown or not available for testing**
Unvaccinated	HBIG[§] × 1 and initiate HB vaccine series	Initiate HB vaccine series[¶]	Initiate HB vaccine series
Previously vaccinated			
Known responder**	No treatment		No treatment
Known nonresponder[††]	HBIG × 1 and initiate revaccination or HBIG × 2[§§]	No treatment	If known high risk source, treat as if source were HBSAg positive
Antibody response unknown	Test exposed person for anti-HBS[¶¶] 1. If adequate,** no treatment is necessary 2. If inadequate,[††] administer HBIG × and vaccine booster	No treatment	Test exposed person for anti-HBs 1. If adequate,[¶] no treatment is necessary 2. If inadequate,[¶] administer vaccine booster and recheck titer in 1-2 months

*Persons who have previously been infected with HBV are immune to reinfection and do not require postexposure prophylaxis.

[†]Hepatitis B surface antigen.

[§] Hepatitis B immune globulin; dose is 0.06 mL/kg intramuscularly.

[¶]Hepatitis B vaccine.

**A responder is a person with adequate levels of serum antibody to HBsAg (i.e., anti-HBs $\geq$ 10 mIU/mL).

[††]A nonresponder is a person with inadequate response to vaccination (i.e., serum anti-HBs < 10 mIU/mL).

[§§] The option of giving one dose of HBIG and reinitiating the vaccine series is preferred for nonresponders who have not completed a second 3-dose vaccine series. For persons who previously completed a second vaccine series but failed to respond, two doses of HBIG are preferred.

[¶¶]Antibody to HBsAg.

Source: Centers for Disease Control and Prevention. Updated U.S. Public Health Service Guidelines for the Management of Occupational Exposures to HBV, HCV, and HIV and Recommendations for Postexposure Prophylaxis. *MMWR* 2001; 50(No RR-11):22.

4-154 Written Opinion Regarding Occupational Exposure

You have sustained an exposure to blood or body fluids which may require preventive immunizations or further evaluation or treatment. Indications for hepatitis B vaccination have been reviewed by your health care provider and are listed below:

_____ Your AHBS (hepatitis B antibody) is positive. Vaccination is not indicated.

_____ Hepatitis B vaccination is indicated. Please call our office at _____ to schedule this immediately.

_____ You have received one or two hepatitis vaccinations. Future immunization(s) are due on the following date(s): __________

Please call _____ to schedule appointment(s).

I acknowledge that I have been informed of the results of the evaluation regarding my exposure incident. I have been told about any medical conditions resulting from exposure to blood or other potentially infectious materials which may require further evaluation or treatment.

I realize that Employee/Occupational Health & Safety will contact me for follow-up.
Remarks:

____

____

____

____

______________________________	______________________________
Employee Signature	Date
______________________________	______________________________
Print Name CLEARLY	Department

Source: Suburban Hospital, Inc., Bethesda, Maryland.

4-155 ED Decontamination Room Preparation and Use Policy and Procedure

SUBJECT:

ED Decontamination Room Preparation and Use

PRIMARY SERVICE:

Emergency

EFFECTIVE DATE:

CONTRIBUTING SERVICES:

PURPOSE

To outline the basic setup and use of the Decontamination Area for those patients who have been exposed to radiation and/or hazardous materials. The type of exposure will determine the type of care required. Further guidance and direction will be given by the Emergency Physician on duty and the Safety Officer.

POLICY

To ensure safe decontamination of hazardous materials the following procedure must be carefully followed.

PROCEDURE

1. For those patients with minor exposures to chemicals, the following are general steps to be followed:
   - A. Admit to the Emergency Department. Designated area depends upon the type of chemical involved. Most patients will be treated in the main Emergency Department areas without the need for special decontamination procedures.
   - B. Treat symptomatically for specific chemical, if known, including oxygen and observation.
   - C. Admission depends on specific chemical, if known, and symptoms.
   - D. Reassure all patients
   - E. Body Surface Decontamination
     1. Attendant will gown and glove
     2. Clothing and dressing removal—place in appropriate labeled container (red bags)
     3. Wound irrigation and debridement
     4. Save all F.B. and tissue; place in appropriate labeled container (sterile cups)
     5. Washing techniques
        - a. Type of solution, H_2O and/or soap and detergent
        - b. Ambulatory; shower at 45 degree angle top to bottom
        - c. Stretcher borne; washcloth top to bottom
2. Approach to the Radiation Exposed Patient
   - A. If you have prior warning of radiation exposure event:
     1. Communication of event from accident site—possible prior decontamination;
     2. Check patient in ambulance;
     3. Treat life-threatening injuries;
     4. Prevent contamination of facility by covering floor, emergency radiation area (ERA), equipment and supplies (see B below);
     5. Rope off the Emergency Department Area (Decontamination Room);

6. Monitor patient and personnel;
7. Double gown personnel appropriately (caps, masks, gowns, foot covers, gloves);
8. Decontaminate body while protecting wounds from contamination, then decontaminate wounds;
9. Use shield, if necessary;
10. Consider short exposure periods for personnel and maintain distance if possible;
11. All patient's clothing and effects should be collected and placed in containers for surveillance and disposal;
12. Effluent should be collected in containers for surveillance and disposal whenever possible;
13. Patient should be treated for any injuries and when stabilized transferred to hospital setting with care being taken to protect the facility from contamination;
14. All attendant personnel should be monitored and decontaminated and their garments appropriately disposed of.

B. Site Preparation
1. Designate arrival triage area—separate entrance through Decontamination Room.
2. Establish radiation control zone
   a. Triage area
   b. Decontamination + Rx area
3. Establish buffer zone; backup clean Rx area
4. Prepare radiation control zone
   a. D/C air circulation
   b. Utilize radiation kit
   c. Rope off
   d. Plastic floor covering
   e. Close vents

3. Decontamination Procedures
A. Patient management—decontaminate
1. Triage assessment
   a. ABCs
   b. Hazard assessment
2. Patient transport to radiation control zone;
3. Repeat hazard assessment;
4. Historical assessment—It is important to differentiate the individual types of radiation accidents. There are three (3) main radiation accidents of significance:
   a. External contamination—external contamination complicated by wound/s;
      1. Wound/s necessitate that cross-contamination between the wound/s and surrounding tissue be avoided;
      2. Cleanse wounds and surrounding tissue separately;
      3. Irrigate all dirty tissue;
      4. Debride early.

THIS IS A POTENTIAL HAZARD TO ALL ATTENDANTS, OTHER PATIENTS AND THE ENVIRONMENT. STRICT ISOLATION TECHNIQUE IS MANDATORY.

b. Internal contamination—This involves inhalation or ingestion. Treatment is basically cleansing of the contaminated material deposited on the body surface during airborne exposure. Collection and retainment of body waste for measurement of nuclear isotopes is also done to determine the appropriate therapy.

THERE IS NO HAZARD TO ATTENDANTS OR OTHER PATIENTS OR THE ENVIRONMENT. HOWEVER, MAINTAIN ISOLATION TECHNIQUE.

c. External radiation—Whole or partial body involvement. There is no basic hazard to attendants or other patients or the environment.

HOWEVER, ALL THREE ARE TREATED WITH THE FOLLOWING DECONTAMINATION PROCEDURE:

B. Decontamination
   1. Clothing and dressing removal; place in appropriate labeled container;
   2. Wound irrigation and debridement;
   3. Save all F.B. and tissue; place in appropriate labeled container;
   4. Washing technique
      a. Type of solution, H_2O and/or soap and detergent;
      b. Ambulatory; shower at 45 degree angle top to bottom;
      c. Stretcher borne; washcloth top to bottom; REMEMBER; H_2O with detergent removes 90% of contamination

SAVE ALL MATERIALS USED AND PLACE IN APPROPRIATE CONTAINERS "RADIOACTIVE DO NOT DISCARD."

5. Additional information can be obtained in the Safety Policies and Procedures #29 "Hazardous Materials and Waste Management."
6. The Hazardous Materials (Hazmat) Team may be contacted through the Emergency Operations Center (EOC) for guidance and/or assistance in caring for a contaminated patient or potential Hazmat situations.

Source: Suburban Hospital, Inc., Bethesda, Maryland.

4-156 Practice Recommendations for Health Care Facilities Implementing the U.S. Public Health Service Guidelines for Management of Occupational Exposures to Bloodborne Pathogens

Practice Recommendation	Implementation Checklist
Establish a bloodborne pathogen policy.	All institutions where health care personnel (HCP) might experience exposures should have a written policy for management of exposures. The policy should be based on the U.S. Public Health Service (PHS) guidelines. The policy should be reviewed periodically to ensure that it is consistent with PHS recommendations.
Implement management policies.	Health care facilities (HCF) should provide appropriate training to all personnel on the prevention of and response to occupational exposures. HCF should establish hepatitis B vaccination programs. HCF should establish exposure-reporting systems. HCF should have personnel who can manage an exposure readily available at all hours of the day. HCF should have ready access to postexposure prophylaxis (PEP) for use by exposed personnel as necessary.
Establish laboratory capacity for bloodborne pathogen testing.	HCF should provide prompt processing of exposed person and source person specimens to guide management of occupational exposures. Testing should be performed with appropriate counseling and consent.
Select and use appropriate PEP regimens.	HCF should develop a policy for the selection and use of PEP antiretroviral regimens for HIV exposures within their institution. Hepatitis B vaccine and HBIG should be available for timely administration. HCF should have access to resources with expertise in the selection and use of PEP.
Provide access to counseling for exposed HCP.	HCF should provide counseling for HCP who might need help dealing with the emotional effect of an exposure. HCF should provide medication adherence counseling to assist HCP in completing HIV PEP as necessary.
Monitor for adverse effects of PEP.	HCP taking antiretroviral PEP should be monitored periodically for adverse effects of PEP through baseline and testing (every 2 weeks) and clinical evaluation.
Monitor for seroconversion.	HCF should develop a system to encourage exposed HCP to return for follow-up testing. Exposed HCP should be tested for HCV and HIV.
Monitor exposure management programs.	HCF should develop a system to monitor reporting and management of occupational exposures to ensure timely and appropriate response. **Evaluate** • exposure reports for completeness and accuracy, • access to care (i.e., the time of exposure to the time of evaluation), and • laboratory result reporting time.

Review

- exposures to ensure that HCP exposed to sources not infected with bloodborne pathogens do not receive PEP or that PEP is stopped.

Monitor

- completion rates of HBV vaccination and HIV PEP and
- completion of exposure follow-up.

Source: Centers for Disease Control *MMWR Reports & Recommendations*, June 29, 2001/ 50(RR11);43-4. *www.cdc.gov/mmwr/preview/mmwrhtml/rr5011a2.htm.* Accessed 8/14/01.

4-157 Guidelines for Hand Hygiene in Health Care Settings Recommendations of the Health Care Infection Control Practices Advisory Committee and the HICPAC/ SHEA/APIC/IDSA Hand Hygiene Task Force

Prepared by John M. Boyce, M.D.1 Didier Pittet, M.D.2 1 *Hospital of Saint Raphael New Haven, Connecticut*
2 University of Geneva Geneva, Switzerland

Summary

The Guideline for Hand Hygiene in Health-Care Settings provides health-care workers (HCWs) with a review of data regarding handwashing and hand antisepsis in health-care settings. In addition, it provides specific recommendations to promote improved hand-hygiene practices and reduce transmission of pathogenic microorganisms to patients and personnel in health-care settings. This report reviews studies published since the 1985 CDC guideline (Garner JS, Favero MS. CDC guideline for handwashing and hospital environmental control, 1985. Infect Control 1986;7:231-43) and the 1995 APIC guideline (Larson EL, APIC Guidelines Committee. APIC guideline for handwashing and hand antisepsis in health care settings. Am J Infect Control 1995;23:251-69) were issued and provides an in-depth review of hand-hygiene practices of HCWs, levels of adherence of personnel to recommended handwashing practices, and factors adversely affecting adherence. New studies of the in vivo efficacy of alcohol-based hand rubs and the low incidence of dermatitis associated with their use are reviewed. Recent studies demonstrating the value of multidisciplinary hand-hygiene promotion programs and the potential role of alcohol-based hand rub in improving hand-hygiene practices are summarized. Recommendations concerning related issues (e.g., the use of surgical hand antiseptics, hand lotions or creams, and wearing of artificial fingernails) are also included.

Recommendations

Categories

These recommendations are designed to improve hand-hygiene practices of HCWs and to reduce transmission of pathogenic microorganisms to patients and personnel in health-care settings. This guideline and its recommendations are not intended for use in food processing or food-service establishments, and are not meant to replace guidance provided by FDA's Model Food Code.

As in previous CDC/HICPAC guidelines, each recommendation is categorized on the basis of existing scientific data, theoretical rationale, applicability, and economic impact. The CDC/HICPAC system for categorizing recommendations is as follows:
Category IA. Strongly recommended for implementation and strongly supported by well-designed experimental, clinical, or epidemiologic studies.
Category IB. Strongly recommended for implementation and supported by certain experimental, clinical, or epidemiologic studies and a strong theoretical rationale.
Category IC. Required for implementation, as mandated by federal or state regulation or standard.
Category II. Suggested for implementation and supported by suggestive clinical or epidemiologic studies or a theoretical rationale.
No recommendation. Unresolved issue. Practices for which insufficient evidence or no consensus regarding efficacy exist.

Recommendations:

1. Indications for handwashing and hand antisepsis
A. When hands are visibly dirty or contaminated with proteinaceous material or are visibly soiled with blood or other body fluids, wash hands with either a non-antimicrobial soap and water or an antimicrobial soap and water (IA).
B. If hands are not visibly soiled, use an alcohol-based hand rub for routinely decontaminating hands in all other clinical situations described in items 1C-J (IA). Alternatively, wash hands with an antimicrobial soap and water in all clinical situations described in items 1C-J (IB).
C. Decontaminate hands before having direct contact with patients (IB).
D. Decontaminate hands before donning sterile gloves when inserting a central intravascular catheter (IB).
E. Decontaminate hands before inserting indwelling urinary catheters, peripheral vascular catheters, or other invasive devices that do not require a surgical procedure (IB).
F. Decontaminate hands after contact with a patient's intact skin (e.g., when taking a pulse or blood pressure, and lifting a patient) (IB).
G. Decontaminate hands after contact with body fluids or excretions, mucous membranes, non-intact skin, and wound dressings if hands are not visibly soiled (IA).
H. Decontaminate hands if moving from a contaminated-body site to a clean-body site during patient care (II).
I. Decontaminate hands after contact with inanimate objects (including medical equipment) in the immediate vicinity of the patient (II).
J. Decontaminate hands after removing gloves (IB).
K. Before eating and after using a restroom, wash hands with a non-antimicrobial soap and water or with an antimicrobial soap and water (IB).
L. Antimicrobial-impregnated wipes (i.e., towelettes) may be considered as an alternative to washing hands with non-antimicrobial soap and water. Because they are not as effective as alcohol-based hand rubs or washing hands with an antimicrobial soap and water for reducing bacterial counts on the hands of HCWs, they are not a substitute for using an alcohol-based hand rub or antimicrobial soap (IB).

M. Wash hands with non-antimicrobial soap and water or with antimicrobial soap and water if exposure to *Bacillus anthracis* is suspected or proven. The physical action of washing and rinsing hands under such circumstances is recommended because alcohols, chlorhexidine, iodophors, and other antiseptic agents have poor activity against spores (II).
N. No recommendation can be made regarding the routine use of non-alcohol-based hand rubs for hand hygiene in health-care settings. Unresolved issue.

2. Hand-hygiene technique
A. When decontaminating hands with an alcohol-based hand rub, apply product to palm of one hand and rub hands together, covering all surfaces of hands and fingers, until hands are dry (IB). Follow the manufacturer's recommendations regarding the volume of product to use.
B. When washing hands with soap and water, wet hands first with water, apply an amount of product recommended by the manufacturer to hands, and rub hands together vigorously for at least 15 seconds, covering all surfaces of the hands and fingers. Rinse hands with water and dry thoroughly with a disposable towel. Use towel to turn off the faucet (IB). Avoid using hot water, because repeated exposure to hot water may increase the risk of dermatitis (IB).
C. Liquid, bar, leaflet or powdered forms of plain soap are acceptable when washing hands with a non-antimicrobial soap and water. When bar soap is used, soap racks that facilitate drainage and small bars of soap should be used (II).
D. Multiple-use cloth towels of the hanging or roll type are not recommended for use in health-care settings (II).

3. Surgical hand antisepsis
A. Remove rings, watches, and bracelets before beginning the surgical hand scrub (II).
B. Remove debris from underneath fingernails using a nail cleaner under running water (II).
C. Surgical hand antisepsis using either an antimicrobial soap or an alcohol-based hand rub with persistent activity is recommended before donning sterile gloves when performing surgical procedures (IB).
D. When performing surgical hand antisepsis using an antimicrobial soap, scrub hands and forearms for the length of time recommended by the manufacturer, usually 2-6 minutes. Long scrub times (e.g., 10 minutes) are not necessary (IB).
E. When using an alcohol-based surgical hand-scrub product with persistent activity, follow the manufacturer's instructions. Before applying the alcohol solution, prewash hands and forearms with a non-antimicrobial soap and dry hands and forearms completely. After application of the alcohol-based product as recommended, allow hands and forearms to dry thoroughly before donning sterile gloves (IB).

4. Selection of hand-hygiene agents
A. Provide personnel with efficacious hand-hygiene products that have low irritancy potential, particularly when these products are used multiple times per shift (IB). This recommendation applies to products used for hand antisepsis before and after patient care in clinical areas and to products used for surgical hand antisepsis by surgical personnel.
B. To maximize acceptance of hand-hygiene products by HCWs, solicit input from these employees regarding the feel, fragrance, and skin tolerance of any products under

consideration. The cost of hand-hygiene products should not be the primary factor influencing product selection (IB).

C. When selecting non-antimicrobial soaps, antimicrobial soaps, or alcohol-based hand rubs, solicit information from manufacturers regarding any known interactions between products used to clean hands, skin care products, and the types of gloves used in the institution (II).

D. Before making purchasing decisions, evaluate the dispenser systems of various product manufacturers or distributors to ensure that dispensers function adequately and deliver an appropriate volume of product (II).

E. Do not add soap to a partially empty soap dispenser. This practice of "topping off" dispensers can lead to bacterial contamination of soap (IA).

5. Skin care

A. Provide HCWs with hand lotions or creams to minimize the occurrence of irritant contact dermatitis associated with hand antisepsis or handwashing (IA).

B. Solicit information from manufacturers regarding any effects that hand lotions, creams, or alcohol-based hand antiseptics may have on the persistent effects of antimicrobial soaps being used in the institution (IB).

6. Other Aspects of Hand Hygiene

A. Do not wear artificial fingernails or extenders when having direct contact with patients at high risk (e.g., those in intensive-care units or operating rooms) (IA).

B. Keep natural nails tips less than 1/4-inch long (II).

C. Wear gloves when contact with blood or other potentially infectious materials, mucous membranes, and nonintact skin could occur (IC).

D. Remove gloves after caring for a patient. Do not wear the same pair of gloves for the care of more than one patient, and do not wash gloves between uses with different patients (IB).

E. Change gloves during patient care if moving from a contaminated body site to a clean body site (II).

F. No recommendation can be made regarding wearing rings in health-care settings. Unresolved issue.

7. Health-care worker educational and motivational programs

A. As part of an overall program to improve hand-hygiene practices of HCWs, educate personnel regarding the types of patient-care activities that can result in hand contamination and the advantages and disadvantages of various methods used to clean their hands (II).

B. Monitor HCWs' adherence with recommended hand-hygiene practices and provide personnel with information regarding their performance (IA).

C. Encourage patients and their families to remind HCWs to decontaminate their hands (II).

8. Administrative measures

A. Make improved hand-hygiene adherence an institutional priority and provide appropriate administrative support and financial resources (IB).

B. Implement a multidisciplinary program designed to improve adherence of health personnel to recommended hand-hygiene practices (IB).

C. As part of a multidisciplinary program to improve hand-hygiene adherence, provide HCWs with a readily accessible alcohol-based hand-rub product (IA).
D. To improve hand-hygiene adherence among personnel who work in areas in which high workloads and high intensity of patient care are anticipated, make an alcohol-based hand rub available at the entrance to the patient's room or at the bedside, in other convenient locations, and in individual pocket-sized containers to be carried by HCWs (IA).
E. Store supplies of alcohol-based hand rubs in cabinets or areas approved for flammable materials (IC).

Performance Indicators

1. The following performance indicators are recommended for measuring improvements in HCWs' hand-hygiene adherence:
A. Periodically monitor and record adherence as the number of hand-hygiene episodes performed by personnel/number of hand-hygiene opportunities, by ward or by service. Provide feedback to personnel regarding their performance.
B. Monitor the volume of alcohol-based hand rub (or detergent used for handwashing or hand antisepsis) used per 1,000 patient-days.
C. Monitor adherence to policies dealing with wearing of artificial nails.
D. When outbreaks of infection occur, assess the adequacy of health-care worker hand hygiene.

Source: Centers for Disease Control and Prevention. Guideline for Hand Hygiene in Health-Care Settings: Recommendations of the Healthcare Infection Practices Advisory Committee and the HICPAC/SHEA/APIC/IDSA Hand Hygiene Task Force. *MMWR* 2002; 51 (No. RR-16):31-34, 45.

4-158 Sharps-Safety and Needlestick-Prevention Device Assessment Form

Device: ______________________________

Supplier/trade name: ______________________________

Applications: ______________________________

Reviewer: ______________________________

Date: ______________________________

For each question, circle the appropriate response for the protective device being evaluated.

Health care worker safety

1.	A.	Does the protective device prevent needlesticks or other sharps injuries during use (i.e., before disposal)?	Yes	No
	B.	Does it do so after use (i.e., does the safety mechanism remain activated through disposal of the protective device)?	Yes	No
2.	A.	Does protective device provide protection in one of the following ways: either intrinsically or automatically? (Answer "No" if a specific action by the user is required to activate the safety mechanism.)	Yes	No
	B.	If "No," is the mechanism activated in one of the following ways: either by a one-handed technique or by a two-handed technique accomplished as part of the usual procedure?	Yes	No

3. During the use of protective device, do the user's hands remain behind the needle or sharp until activation of the safety mechanism is complete?		Yes	No
4. Is the safety mechanism reliable when activated properly?		Yes	No
5. Does the protective device minimize the risk of user exposure to the patient's blood?		Yes	No

Patient safety and comfort

6. Does the protective device minimize the risk of infection to the patient (e.g., through cross-contamination)?		Yes	No
7. Can the protective device be used without causing more patient discomfort than a conventional device?		Yes	No
8. *For* intravenous (IV) protective devices: Does the protective device attach comfortably (i.e., without causing patient discomfort) at the catheter port or IV tubing)?		Yes	No

Ease of Use and Training

9. Is device operation obvious? That is, can the device be used properly without extensive training?			Yes	No
10. Can the protective device be used by a left-handed person as easily as by a right-handed person?			Yes	No
11. Is the technique required for using the protective device the same as that for using a conventional device?			Yes	No
12. Is it easy to identify the type and size of the product from the packaging?			Yes	No
13. For IV catheters and blood collection needle sets: Does the protective device provide a visible blood flashback during initial insertion?			Yes	No
14. Please rate the ease of using this protective device				
A. Under normal conditions	Excellent	Good	Fair	Poor
B. When using the device with wet gloves	Excellent	Good	Fair	Poor
15. Please rate the quality of the in-service training	Excellent	Good	Fair	Poor

Compatibility

16. Is the protective device compatible with devices (e.g., blood collection tubes) from a variety of suppliers?	Yes	No
17. For IV protective devices:		
A. Is the protective device compatible with intralipid solutions?	Yes	No
B. Does the protective device attach securely at the catheter port?	Yes	No
C. Does the protective device attach securely or lock at a Y-site (e.g. for piggybacking)?	Yes	No
18. Is the protective device easy to dispose of in sharps containers of all sizes (if required)?	Yes	No
19. Does using the protective device instead of a conventional device result in only a modest (if any) increase in sharps container waste volume? (Answer "No" if the protective device will increase waste volume significantly.)	Yes	No

Overall

20. Would you recommend using this device?	Yes	No

Comments (e.g., describe problems, list incompatibilities)

____

____

____

4-159 Sample Sharps Injury Log

Please complete a Log for each employee exposure incident involving a sharp.
Fill in the one circle corresponding to the most appropriate answer. Use block print and avoid touching lines.

Institution: ______ Department: ______
Address: ______ Page # ______ of ______
City: ______ State: ______ ZIP code: ______
Date filled out: ______ by: ______ Phone number: ( ) ______
Facility Injury ID#: ______ Date of injury: ______ (month day year) Time of injury: ______

Sex: __ Male __ Female   Age ______

Description of the exposure incident
______
______
______
______
______

Job classification
__ MD __ Nurse
__ Medical assistant
__ Phlebotomist/lab tech
__ Housekeeper/Laundry
__ CNA/HHA
__ Student, type ______
__ Other ______

Department/Location
__ Patient room __ Emergency dept
__ Operating room __ Procedure room
__ OCU/ICU __ Home
__ Clinical laboratory
__ Medical/outpatient clinic
__ Service/utility area (disp rm./laundry)
__ Other ______

Procedure
__ Draw venous blood __ Heparin/saline flush
__ Draw arterial blood __ Cutting
__ Injection, through skin __ Suturing
__ Start IV/set up heparin lock
__ Unknown/not applicable
__ Other ______

Did the exposure incident occur
__ During use of sharp __ Disassembling
__ Between steps of a multistep procedure
__ After use and before disposal of sharp
__ While putting sharp into disposal container
__ Sharp left, inappropriate place (table, bed, etc)
__ Other ______

Body part
(check all that apply)
__ Finger __ Face/head
__ Hand __ Torso
__ Arm __ Leg
__ Other ______

Identify sharp involved
(if known)
Type: ______
Brand: ______
Model: ______
e.g., 18g needle/ABC Medical/"no stick" syringe

Did the device being used have engineered sharps injury protection?
__ yes __ no __ don't know
Was the protective mechanism activated?
__ yes, fully __ yes, partially __ no
Did the exposure incident occur?
__ before? __ during? __ after activation?

Exposed employee: If sharp had no engineered sharps injury protection, do you have an opinion that such a mechanism could have prevented the injury? __ yes __ no
Explain: ______
______

Exposed employee: Do you have an opinion that any other engineering, administrative or work practice control could have prevented the injury? __ yes __ no
Explain: ______
______

Source: Sharps Injury Control Program (Sharps), Department of Health Services, Occupational Health Branch/University of California.

4-160 Model Exposure Control Plan

The following model for an Exposure Control Plan includes all elements required by the OSHA bloodborne pathogens standard (29 CFR 1910.1030). The intent of this model is to provide employers with an easy-to-use format that may be used as a template to develop a written exposure control plan tailored to the individual requirements of their establishments.

POLICY

The (Your facility name) is committed to providing a safe and healthful work environment for our entire staff. In pursuit of this goal, the following Exposure Control Plan (ECP) is provided to eliminate or minimize occupational exposure to bloodborne pathogens in accordance with OSHA standard 29 *C.F.R.* 1910.1030, "Occupational Exposure to Bloodborne Pathogens."

The ECP is a key document to assist our organization in implementing and ensuring compliance with the standard, thereby protecting our employees. This ECP includes:

- Determination of employee exposure
- Implementation of various methods of exposure control, including:
  —Universal precautions
  —Engineering and work practice controls
  —Personal protective equipment
  —Housekeeping
- Hepatitis B vaccination
- Post-exposure evaluation and follow-up
- Communication of hazards to employees and training
- Recordkeeping
- Procedures for evaluating circumstances surrounding exposure incidents Implementation methods for these elements of the standard are discussed in the subsequent pages of this ECP.

PROGRAM ADMINISTRATION

- (Name of responsible person or department) is (are) responsible for implementation of the ECP. (Name of responsible person or department) will maintain, review, and update the ECP at least annually, and whenever necessary to include new or modified tasks and procedures. Contact location/phone number: ___.
- Those employees who are determined to have occupational exposure to blood or other potentially infectious materials (OPIM) must comply with the procedures and work practices outlined in this ECP.
- (Name of responsible person or department) will provide and maintain all necessary personal protective equipment (PPE), engineering controls (e.g., sharps containers), labels, and red bags as required by the standard.

- (Name of responsible person or department will ensure that adequate supplies of the aforementioned equipment are available in the appropriate sizes. Contact location/ phone number: ________________.
- (Name of responsible person or department) will be responsible for ensuring that all medical actions required by the standard are performed and that appropriate employee health and OSHA records are maintained. Contact location/phone number: ________________.
- (Name of responsible person or department) will be responsible for training, documentation of training, and making the written ECP available to employees, OSHA, and NIOSH representatives. Contact location/phone number: ________________.

EMPLOYEE EXPOSURE DETERMINATION

The following is a list of all job classifications at our establishment in which all employees have occupational exposure:

Example:

Job Title	*Department/Location*
Phlebotomists	Clinical Lab

(use as many lines as necessary) ____

____

The following is a list of job classifications in which some employees at our establishment have occupational exposure. Included is a list of tasks and procedures, or groups of closely related tasks and procedures, in which occupational exposure may occur for these individuals:

Example:

Job Title	*Department/Location*	*Task/Procedure*
Housekeeper	Environmental Services	Handling Regulated Waste

(use as many lines as necessary) ____

____

NOTE: Part-time, temporary, contract, and per diem employees are covered by the bloodborne pathogens standard. The ECP should describe how the standard will be met for these employees.

METHODS OF IMPLEMENTATION AND CONTROL

Universal Precautions

All employees will utilize universal precautions.

Exposure Control Plan

Employees covered by the bloodborne pathogens standard receive an explanation of this ECP during their initial training session. It will also be reviewed in their annual refresher training. All employees can review this plan at any time during their work shifts by contacting (Name of responsible person or department). If requested, we will provide an employee with a copy of the ECP free of charge and within 15 days of the request.

(Name of responsible person or department) is responsible for reviewing and updating the ECP annually or more frequently if necessary to reflect any new or modified tasks and procedures that affect occupational exposure and to reflect new or revised employee positions with occupational exposure.

Engineering Controls and Work Practices

Engineering controls and work practice controls will be used to prevent or minimize exposure to bloodborne pathogens. The specific engineering controls and work practice controls used are listed below:

- (For example: non-glass capillary tubes, SESIPs, needleless systems)
- ______________________________
- ______________________________

Sharps disposal containers are inspected and maintained or replaced by (Name of responsible person or department) every (list frequency) or whenever necessary to prevent overfilling.

This facility identifies the need for changes in engineering controls and work practices through (Provide examples: Review of OSHA records, employee interviews, committee activities, etc.).

We evaluate new procedures and new products regularly by discussing them in the ED Committee and staff meetings as needed.

ED staff and management officials are involved in this process in the following manner.

Personal Protective Equipment (PPE)

PPE is provided to our employees at no cost to them. Training in the use of the appropriate PPE for specific tasks or procedures is provided by (Name of responsible person or department).

The types of PPE available to employees are as follows: (gloves, eye protection, etc.) ______________________________

____

____

PPE is located in the main hallways in the ED. Additional PPE is maintained in the clean supply room.

All employees using PPE must observe the following precautions:

- Wash hands immediately or as soon as feasible after removing gloves or other PPE.
- Remove PPE after it becomes contaminated and before leaving the work area.
- Used PPE may be disposed of in (List appropriate containers for storage, laundering, decontamination, or disposal.)
- Wear appropriate gloves when it is reasonably anticipated that there may be hand contact with blood or OPIM, and when handling or touching contaminated items or surfaces; replace gloves if torn, punctured or contaminated, or if their ability to function as a barrier is compromised.
- Utility gloves may be decontaminated for reuse if their integrity is not compromised; discard utility gloves if they show signs of cracking, peeling, tearing, puncturing, or deterioration.
- Never wash or decontaminate disposable gloves for reuse.
- Wear appropriate face and eye protection when splashes, sprays, spatters, or droplets of blood or OPIM pose a hazard to the eye, nose, or mouth.
- Remove immediately or as soon as feasible any garment contaminated by blood or OPIM, in such a way as to avoid contact with the outer surface.

The procedure for handling used PPE is as follows:
(may refer to specific procedure by title or number and last date of review; include how and where to decontaminate face shields, eye protection, resuscitation equipment)

____

____

____

Housekeeping

Regulated waste is placed in containers which are closable, constructed to contain all contents and prevent leakage, appropriately labeled or color-coded (see the following section "Labels"), and closed prior to removal to prevent spillage or protrusion of contents during handling.

The procedure for handling sharps disposal containers is:
(may refer to specific procedure by title or number and last date of review)

____

The procedure for handling other regulated waste is: *(may refer to specific procedure by title or number and last date of review)*

____

____

Contaminated sharps are discarded immediately or as soon as possible in containers that are closable, puncture-resistant, leak proof on sides and bottoms, and appropriately labeled or color-coded.

Sharps disposal containers are available at (must be easily accessible and as close as feasible to the immediate area where sharps are used).

Bins and pails (e.g., wash or emesis basins) are cleaned and decontaminated as soon as feasible after visible contamination.

Broken glassware that may be contaminated is only picked up using mechanical means, such as a brush and dustpan.

Laundry

The following contaminated articles will be Laundry:

____

____

Laundering will be performed by _______________________

The following laundering requirements must be met:

- handle contaminated laundry as little as possible, with minimal agitation
- place wet contaminated laundry in leak-proof, labeled or color-coded containers before transport. Use (specify either red bags or bags marked with the biohazard symbol) for this purpose.
- wear the following PPE when handling and/or sorting contaminated laundry: (List appropriate PPE).

Labels

The following labeling methods are used in the ED:

Equipment to be Labeled (specimens, contaminated laundry, etc.)	*Label Type (size, color) (red bag, biohazard label)*

(Name of responsible person or department) is responsible for ensuring that warning labels are affixed or red bags are used as required if regulated waste or contaminated equipment is brought into the facility. Employees are to notify (Name of responsible person or department) if they discover regulated waste containers, refrigerators containing blood or OPIM, contaminated equipment, etc., without proper labels.

HEPATITIS B VACCINATION

(Name of responsible person or department) will provide training to employees on hepatitis B vaccinations, addressing safety, benefits, efficacy, methods of administration, and availability.

The hepatitis B vaccination series is available at no cost after initial employee training and within 10 days of initial assignment to all employees identified in the exposure determination section of this plan. Vaccination is encouraged unless: 1) documentation exists that the employee has previously received the series; 2) antibody testing reveals that the employee is immune; or 3) medical evaluation shows that vaccination is contraindicated.

However, if an employee declines the vaccination, the employee must sign a declination form. Employees who decline may request and obtain the vaccination at a later date at no cost. Documentation of refusal of the vaccination is kept at (List location). Vaccination will be provided by (List health care professional responsible for this part of the plan) at (location).

Following the medical evaluation, a copy of the health care professional's written opinion will be obtained and provided to the employee within 15 days of the completion of the evaluation. It will be limited to whether the employee requires the hepatitis vaccine and whether the vaccine was administered.

POST-EXPOSURE EVALUATION AND FOLLOW-UP

Should an exposure incident occur, contact the ED Charge Nurse. An immediately available confidential medical evaluation and follow-up will be conducted by (name of licensed health care professional). Following initial first aid (clean the wound, flush eyes or other mucous membrane, etc.), the following activities will be performed:

- Document the routes of exposure and how the exposure occurred.
- Identify and document the source individual (unless the employer can establish that identification is infeasible or prohibited by state or local law).
- Obtain consent and make arrangements to have the source individual tested as soon as possible to determine HIV, HCV, and HBV infectivity; document that the source individual's test results were conveyed to the employee's health care provider.
- If the source individual is already known to be HIV, HCV and/or HBV positive, new testing need not be performed.
- Assure that the exposed employee is provided with the source individual's test results and with information about applicable disclosure laws and regulations concerning the identity and infectious status of the source individual (e.g., laws protecting confidentiality).
- After obtaining consent, collect exposed employee's blood as soon as feasible after exposure incident, and test blood for HBV and HIV serological status.
- If the employee does not give consent for HIV serological testing during collection of blood for baseline testing, preserve the baseline blood sample for at least 90 days; if the exposed employee elects to have the baseline sample tested during this waiting period, perform testing as soon as feasible.

ADMINISTRATION OF POST-EXPOSURE EVALUATION AND FOLLOW-UP

House Supervisor ensures that health care professional(s) responsible for employee's hepatitis B vaccination and post-exposure evaluation and follow-up are given a copy of OSHA's bloodborne pathogens standard.

Employee Health Nurse ensures that the health care professional evaluating an employee after an exposure incident receives the following:

- a description of the employee's job duties relevant to the exposure incident
- route(s) of exposure
- circumstances of exposure
- if possible, results of the source individual's blood test
- relevant employee medical records, including vaccination status

(Name of responsible person) or department provides the employee with a copy of the evaluating health care professional's written opinion within 15 days after completion of the evaluation.

PROCEDURES FOR EVALUATING THE CIRCUMSTANCES SURROUNDING AN EXPOSURE INCIDENT

Employee Health Nurse will review the circumstances of all exposure incidents to determine:

- engineering controls in use at the time
- work practices followed
- a description of the device being used (including type and brand)
- protective equipment or clothing that was used at the time of the exposure incident (gloves, eye shields, etc.)
- location of the incident (O.R., E.R., patient room, etc.)
- procedure being performed when the incident occurred
- employee's training

(Name of Responsible Person) will record all percutaneous injuries from contaminated sharps in a Sharps Injury Log.

NOTE: If revisions to this ECP are necessary (Responsible person or department) will ensure that appropriate changes are made. (Changes may include an evaluation of safer devices, adding employees to the exposure determination list, etc.)

EMPLOYEE TRAINING

All employees who have occupational exposure to bloodborne pathogens receive initial and annual education.

All employees who have occupational exposure to bloodborne pathogens receive training on the epidemiology, symptoms, and transmission of bloodborne pathogen diseases. In addition, the training program covers, at a minimum, the following elements:

- a copy and explanation of the OSHA bloodborne pathogen standard
- an explanation of our ECP and how to obtain a copy
- an explanation of methods to recognize tasks and other activities that may involve exposure to blood and OPIM, including what constitutes an exposure incident
- an explanation of the use and limitations of engineering controls, work practices, and PPE
- an explanation of the types, uses, location, removal, handling, decontamination, and disposal of PPE
- an explanation of the basis for PPE selection
- information on the hepatitis B vaccine, including information on its efficacy, safety, method of administration, the benefits of being vaccinated, and that the vaccine will be offered free of charge
- information on the appropriate actions to take and persons to contact in an emergency involving blood or OPIM
- an explanation of the procedure to follow if an exposure incident occurs, including the method of reporting the incident and the medical follow-up that will be made available
- information on the post-exposure evaluation and follow-up that the employer is required to provide for the employee following an exposure incident

- an explanation of the signs and labels and/or color coding required by the standard and used at this facility
- an opportunity for interactive questions and answers with the person conducting the training session.

Training materials for this facility are available at (name location).

RECORDKEEPING

Training Records

Training records are completed for each employee upon completion of training. These documents will be kept for at least three years in the ED.
The training records include:

- the dates of the training sessions
- the contents or a summary of the training sessions
- the names and qualifications of persons conducting the training
- the names and job titles of all persons attending the training sessions

Employee training records are provided upon request to the employee or the employee's authorized representative within 15 working days. Such requests should be addressed to (Name of responsible person or department).

Medical Records

Medical records are maintained for each employee with occupational exposure in accordance with 29 *C.F.R.* 1910.1020, "Access to Employee Exposure and Medical Records."

(Name of Responsible person or department) is responsible for maintenance of the required medical records. These confidential records are kept in (List location) for at least the duration of employment plus 30 years. Employee medical records are provided upon request of the employee or to anyone having written consent of the employee within 15 working days. Such requests should be sent to (Name of responsible person or department and address).

OSHA Recordkeeping

An exposure incident is evaluated to determine if the case meets OSHA's Recordkeeping Requirements (29 C.F.R. 1904). This determination and the recording activities are done by (Name of responsible person or department).

Sharps Injury Log

In addition to the 1904 Recordkeeping Requirements, all percutaneous injuries from contaminated sharps are also recorded in a Sharps Injury Log. All incidences must include at least:

- date of the injury
- type and brand of the device involved (syringe, suture needle)
- department or work area where the incident occurred
- explanation of how the incident occurred.

This log is reviewed as part of the annual program evaluation and maintained for at least five years following the end of the calendar year covered. If a copy is requested by anyone, it must have any personal identifiers removed from the report.

HEPATITIS B VACCINE DECLINATION (MANDATORY)

I understand that due to my occupational exposure to blood or other potentially infectious materials I may be at risk of acquiring hepatitis B virus (HBV) infection. I have been given the opportunity to be vaccinated with hepatitis B vaccine, at no charge to myself.

However, I decline hepatitis B vaccination at this time. I understand that by declining this vaccine, I continue to be at risk of acquiring hepatitis B, a serious disease. If in the future I continue to have occupational exposure to blood or other potentially infectious materials and I want to be vaccinated with hepatitis B vaccine, I can receive the vaccination series at no charge to me.

Signed: (Employee Name) ____________________ Date:____________________

Source: *Model Plans and Programs for the OSHA Bloodborne Pathogens and Hazard Communications Standards.* OSHA 3186-06N. 2003. Available online at: ***http://www.osha.gov.***

4-161 Influenza Vaccination of Health Care Personnel Recommendations of the Health Care Infection Control Practices Advisory Committee (HICPAC) and the Advisory Committee on Immunization Practices (ACIP)

The recommendations were drafted after review of peer-reviewed scientific articles, and whenever possible are based on well-designed studies; certain recommendations are based on strong theoretic rationale and expert opinion. All recommendations have been approved by HICPAC and ACIP. The committees involved in drafting and reviewing these recommendations included persons with expertise in infectious diseases, infection control, pediatrics, vaccinology, internal medicine, and public health.

The committees' recommendations are as follows:

- Educate HCP regarding the benefits of influenza vaccination and the potential health consequences of influenza illness for themselves and their patients, the epidemiology and modes of transmission, diagnosis, treatment, and non-vaccine infection control strategies, in accordance with their level of responsibility in preventing health care-associated influenza.
- Offer influenza vaccine annually to all eligible HCP to protect staff, patients, and family members and to decrease HCP absenteeism. Use of either available vaccine (inactivated and live, attenuated influenza vaccine [LAIV]) is recommended for eligible persons. During periods when inactivated vaccine is in short supply, use of LAIV is especially encouraged when feasible for eligible HCP.
- Provide influenza vaccination to HCP at the work site and at no cost as one component of employee health programs. Use strategies that have been demonstrated to increase influenza vaccine acceptance, including vaccination clinics, mobile carts, vaccination access during all work shifts, and modeling and support by institutional leaders.

- Obtain a signed declination from HCP who decline influenza vaccination for reasons other than medical contraindications.
- Monitor HCP influenza vaccination coverage and declination at regular intervals during influenza season and provide feedback of ward-, unit-, and specialty-specific rates to staff and administration.
- Use the level of HCP influenza vaccination coverage as one measure of a patient safety quality program.

Source: *Morbidity and Mortality Weekly Report*, Recommendations and Reports, February 24, 2006/Vol. 55/No. RR-2.

4-162 Respiratory Hygiene/Cough Etiquette in Health Care Settings

To prevent the transmission of all respiratory infections in health care settings, including influenza, the following infection control measures should be implemented at the first point of contact with a potentially infected person. They should be incorporated into infection control practices as one component of Standard Precautions.

1. Visual Alerts

Post visual alerts (in appropriate languages) at the entrance to the ED instructing patients and persons who accompany them (e.g., family, friends) to inform health care personnel of symptoms of a respiratory infection when they first register for care and to practice Respiratory Hygiene/Cough Etiquette.

- *Notice to Patients to Report Flu Symptoms*
  (Available at: *www.cdc.gov/ncidod/dhqp/pdf/Infdis/RespiratoryPoster.pdf*). Emphasizes covering coughs and sneezes and the cleaning of hands
- *Cover Your Cough*
  (Available at: *www.cdc.gov/flu/protect/covercough.htm*) Tips to prevent the spread of germs from coughing
- *Information about Personal Protective Equipment*
  (Available at *www.cdc.gov/ncidod/dhqp/ppe.html*) Demonstrates the sequences for donning and removing personal protective equipment

2. Respiratory Hygiene/Cough Etiquette

The following measures to contain respiratory secretions are recommended for all individuals with signs and symptoms of a respiratory infection.

- Cover the nose/mouth when coughing or sneezing;
- Use tissues to contain respiratory secretions and dispose of them in the nearest waste receptacle after use;
- Perform hand hygiene (e.g., handwashing with non-antimicrobial soap and water, alcohol-based hand rub, or antiseptic handwash) after having contact with respiratory secretions and contaminated objects/materials.

Health care facilities should ensure the availability of materials for adhering to Respiratory Hygiene/Cough Etiquette in waiting areas for patients and visitors.

- Provide tissues and no-touch receptacles for used tissue disposal.
- Provide conveniently located dispensers of alcohol-based hand rub; where sinks are available, ensure that supplies for handwashing (i.e., soap, disposable towels) are consistently available.

3. Masking and Separation of Persons with Respiratory Symptoms

During periods of increased respiratory infection activity in the community (e.g., when there is increased absenteeism in schools and work settings and increased medical office visits by persons complaining of respiratory illness), offer masks to persons who are coughing. Either procedure masks (i.e., with ear loops) or surgical masks (i.e., with ties) may be used to contain respiratory secretions (respirators such as N-95 or above are not necessary for this purpose). When space and chair availability permit, encourage coughing persons to sit at least three (3) feet away from others in common waiting areas. Some facilities may find it logistically easier to institute this recommendation year-round.

4. Droplet Precautions

Advise health care personnel to observe Droplet Precautions (i.e., wearing a surgical or procedure mask for close contact), in addition to Standard Precautions, when examining a patient with symptoms of a respiratory infection, particularly if fever is present. These precautions should be maintained until it is determined that the cause of symptoms is not an infectious agent that requires Droplet Precautions (*www.cdc.gov/ncidod/dhqp/gl_isolation.html*).

Stop the spread of germs that make you and others sick!
Cover your Cough
Cover your mouth and nose with a tissue when you cough or sneeze
or
cough or sneeze into your upper sleeve, not your hands.
Put your used tissue in the waste basket.
You may be asked to put on a surgical mask to protect others.
Clean your Hands after coughing or sneezing.
Wash hands with soap and warm water for 20 seconds or
clean with alcohol-based hand cleaner.
Soap
CDC
SAFER·HEALTHIER·PEOPLE
MINNESOTA
MDH
DEPARTMENT OF HEALTH
Minnesota Department of Health
717 SE Delaware Street
Minneapolis, MN 55414
612-676-5414 or 1-877-676-5414
www.health.state.mn.us
Minnesota Antibiotic Resistance Collaborative
APIC

¡Pare la propagación de gérmenes que lo enferman a usted y a otras personas!

Cubra su tos

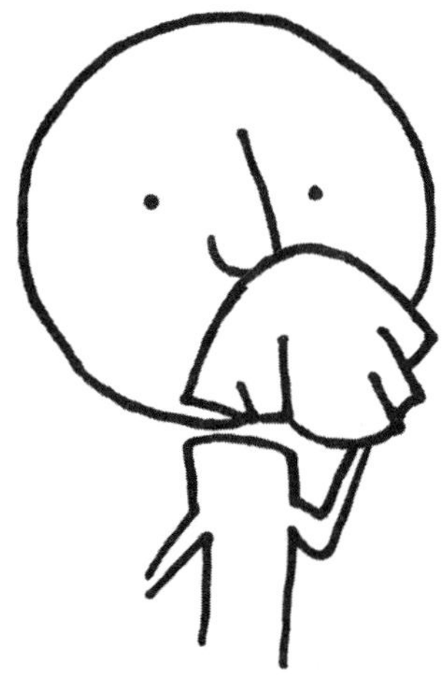

Cubra su boca y nariz con un kleenex cuando tosa o estornude

o

tosa o estornude en la manga de su camisa, no en sus manos.

Deseche el kleenex sucio en un basurero.

Quizás le pidan ponerse una mascarilla quirúrgica para proteger a otras personas.

Lávese las manos

después de toser o estornudar.

Lávese las manos con jabón y agua tibia por 20 segundos

o

límpielas con un limpiador de manos a base de alcohol.

Source: These recommendations are based on the *Draft Guideline for Isolation Precautions: Preventing Transmission of Infectious Agents in Healthcare Settings.* Recommendations of the Healthcare Infection Control Practices Advisory Committee (HICPAC), Centers for Disease Control and Prevention, Atlanta, Georgia.

4-163 Emergency Wound Management for Health Care Professionals

The risk for injury during and after a natural disaster is high. Tetanus (*see http://www.cdc.gov/ncidod/diseases/submenus/sub__tetanus.htm*) is a potential health threat for persons who sustain wound injuries. Tetanus is a serious, often fatal, toxic condition, but is virtually 100% preventable with vaccination. Any wound or rash has the potential for becoming infected and should be assessed by a health-care provider as soon as possible.

These principles can assist with wound management and aid in the prevention of amputations. In the wake of a flood disaster resources are limited. Following these basic wound management steps can help prevent further medical problems.

Evaluation

- Ensure that the scene is safe for you to approach the patient, and that if necessary; it is secured by the proper authorities (police, fire, civil defense) prior to patient evaluation.
- Observe universal precautions, when possible, while participating in all aspects of wound care.
- Obtain a focused history from the patient, and perform an appropriate examination to exclude additional injuries.

Treatment

- Apply direct pressure to any bleeding wound, to control hemorrhage. Tourniquets are rarely indicated since they may reduce tissue viability.
- Examine wounds for gross contamination, devitalized tissue, and foreign bodies.
- Remove constricting rings or other jewelry from injured body part.
- Cleanse the wound periphery with soap and sterile water or available solutions, and provide anesthetics and analgesia whenever possible.
- Irrigate wounds with saline solution using a large bore needle and syringe. If unavailable, bottled water is acceptable.
- Leave contaminated wounds, bites, and punctures open. Wounds that are sutured in an unsterile environment, or are not cleansed, irrigated, and debrided appropriately, are at high risk for infection due to contamination. Wounds that are not closed primarily because of high risk of infection should be considered for delayed primary closure by experienced medical staff using sterile technique.
- Remove devitalized tissue and foreign bodies prior to repair as they may increase the incidence of infection.
- Clip hair close to the wound, if necessary. Shaving of hair is not necessary, and may increase the chance of wound infection.
- Cover wounds with dry dressing; deeper wounds may require packing with saline soaked gauze and subsequent coverage with a dry bulky dressing.

- If wound infections develop see "**Guidance for Management of Wound Infections**" (below).
- Follow tetanus prophylaxis guidelines (see: *http://www.cdc.gov/ncidod/diseases/submenus/sub__tetanus.htm*) for all wounded patients.

Other Considerations

- Be vigilant for the presence of other injuries in patients with any wounds.
- Ensure adequate referral, follow-ups, and reevaluations whenever possible.
- Dirty water and soil and sand can cause infection. Wounds can become contaminated by even very tiny amounts of dirt.
- Puncture wounds can carry bits of clothing and debris into wound resulting in infection.
- Crush injuries are more susceptible to infection than wounds from shearing forces.

Guidance for Management of Wound Infections

Most wound infections are due to staphylococci and streptococci. This would likely hold true even in the post-hurricane setting.

- For initial antimicrobial treatment of infected wounds, beta-lactam antibiotics with antistaphylococcal activity (cephalexin, dicloxacillin, ampicillin/sulbactam, etc.) and clindamycin are recommended options.
- Of note, recently an increasing number of community associated skin and soft tissue infections appear to be caused by methicillin-resistant *Staphylococcus aureus* (MRSA). Infections caused by this organism will not respond to treatment with beta-lactam antibiotics and should be considered in patients who fail to respond to this therapy. Treatment options for these community MRSA infections include trimethoprim-sulfamethoxazole (oral) or vancomycin (intravenous). Clindamycin is also a potential option, but not all isolates are susceptible.
- Incision and drainage of any subcutaneous collections of pus (abscesses) is also an important component of treating wound infections.

Special Considerations Related to Flood Conditions

Contamination of wounds with water (fresh or sea water) can lead to infections caused by waterborne organisms. Though infections with these organisms are uncommon, even after floods, this possibility should be considered in patients who fail to respond to initial therapies described above. Water-borne organisms often implicated in these infections include: *Aeromonas* spp., non-cholera *Vibrio* spp. And sometimes Pseudomonas or other Gram-negative rods.

Trimethoprim/sulfamethoxazole, amoxicillin/clavulanate and newer fluoroquinolones (levofloxacin, moxifloxacin, gatifloxacin) will treat *Aeromonas* and the fluoroquinolones will also treat *Pseudomonas* and many other Gram-negative pathogens.

Clinicians should consider *Vibrio* as a possible causative organism of wound infections incurred in coastal waters or from contact with shellfish or marine wildlife. *Vibrio vulnificus* wound infections may require extensive debridement and mortality can be high. These infections often manifest with bullous lesions that may be hemorrhagic. Persons with underlying hepatic disease or other immunocompromising illness are at highest risk of *Vibrio vulnificus* infection. When this infection is suspected, the recommendation is that patients be treated with a combination of ceftazidime and doxycycline.

Source: 6th Edition *Emergency Medicine: A Comprehensive Study Guide*, 2004; and 34th Edition. *The Sanford Guide to Antimicrobial Therapy*, 2004. In *CDC Disaster Safety Information for Healthcare Providers*, September 6, 2005. Available at: *www.bt.cdc.gov/disasters.*

4-164 MRSA—Infection Control Policies and Procedures Checklist

"What to do about MRSA in Outpatient Clinics/Offices"

Infection Control Polices and Procedures Checklist

Review recommended policies and procedures below. **Use tool to document current policies and procedures; those you would like to implement; and target dates for implementation.**	**Policy in Place (X)**	**Need to implement (X)**	**Target date**
Waiting Room Infection Control Policy, including:			
Using plastic seating or vinyl covered seating (should be easy to clean & disinfect)			
Covering open lesions in waiting area (client is given dressings)			
Hand Hygiene for Staff Policy, including:			
Minimizing hand and wrist jewelry (watch only)			
Changing gloves between clean/dirty procedure			
Keeping natural nails less than ¼" long. No acrylic nails/extenders			
Washing hands using soap and warm water			
➢ Prior to starting work day			
➢ If hands are soiled			
➢ After using the restroom			
Using 60% or greater **alcohol based hand sanitizer** (Prefer stationary dispensing units) **OR** Using soap and water to wash hands			
➢ Upon staff entering/leaving exam room			
➢ Between all patient contacts			
➢ Between clean and dirty steps of a procedure			
➢ Prior to accessing and setting up supplies			
Hand Hygiene for Patients Policy, including:			
Using 60% or greater alcohol based sanitizer before entering exam room (Prefer stationary dispensing units)			
Prevention of Cross Contamination Policies/Procedures, including:			
Having comprehensive infection control policies/procedures readily available			
Soaking stainless steel instruments in high level disinfectant (HLD) or sterilize			
Collecting/handling/transporing specimens appropriately			
Covering contaminated instruments/equipment during transport			
Initialing and dating all opened containers (bottles,ointments, creams, etc.)			
Discarding open bottles of irrigation fluid at end of day			
Checking supply expiration dates before use			
Using sterile <u>disposable</u> scissors to cut off dressings, discarding scissors after use. ***Do not use pocket scissors.***			
Using sterile, <u>non-disposible</u> scissors to cut off dressings. Then washing scissors in enzymatic detergent, rinsing & drying. Follow by immersing in HLD (per label directions), rinsing thoroughly and drying before using again. ***Do not use pocket scissors .***			

	Policy in Place	Need to implement	Target date
Use of Personal Protective Equipment (PPE) Policy/Procedure, including:			
Wearing gloves when touching non-intact skin, wound and mucous membranes			
Wearing masks with face shield during wound irrigation or when expect splashing			
Wearing gowns during wound care as appropriate			
Environmental Cleaning & Disinfecting Procedure, including:			
Using plastic wrapping to protect non-disposable equipment *(BP cuff, Doppler)* from wound or other non-intact skin			
Wiping down equipment that comes in contact with wound or non-intact skin			
Cleaning and disinfecting environmental areas contaminated by body substances or wound drainage			
Cleaning visibly soiled surfaces with friction first. Then wiping with EPA-approved low level disinfectant (LLD)-saturated *disposable* cloth allowing 30-60 seconds of wet time and air drying			
Wearing gloves when handling contaminated linen			
Washing uniforms at home in warm water and bleach, if tolerated. Use hot dryer.			
Cleaning and disinfecting stethoscopes after each use with EPA-approved LLD or 70% isopropyl alcohol (IPA)			
Cleaning pulse ox probe with 70% IPA or other LLD after each use			
Knowing what, when and where housekeeping cleans and names of products used.			
Wound Care Procedures, including:			
Wound Irrigation			
Covering all items within 3-5 feet area of wound irrigation			
Using barrier on surfaces to prevent contamination from wound site			
Bagging soiled items close to point of use			
Using biohazard bags for saturated items (blood or bodily fluids)			
Wound Culturing			
Obtaining culture prior to antibiotic use			
Listing all antibiotics patient is taking on lab slip			
Removing excess debris prior to culturing, using normal saline			
Staff Training Policy, including:			
All new staff receive training on infection control policies and procedures			
Infection control training for staff is provided on an ongoing / regular basis			

Signature ________________________________ **Date** _______________

Title ____

Source: Reprinted with permission of Tacoma-Pierce County Health Department, Tacoma, Washington. *www.tpchd.org.*

4-165 MRSA—Assessing Infection Control Policy Compliance

What to do about MRSA in Outpatient Clinics/Offices
Assessing Clinical Practice

Instructions for Use of Assessment Tool		
Instructions for Use of Assessment Tool Selecting Date/Time: Choose one or two hours during a "typical" clinic day & observe clinical practice to see how much of the time behaviors follow policies and procedures. Give feedback to staff on how well they are doing, and what needs to be improved. Use this assessment tool periodically to monitor progress. Scoring: Use the adjacent scale to score each item listed. Record how often available opportunities are taken...0%, 25%, 50%, 75% or nearly 100% of the time.	0=	0%
	1=	1- 25%
	2=	26 - 50%
	3=	51 - 75%
	4=	76 - 100%
	NA=	Not applicable

Name of Facility:	
Name of person performing assessment:	
Assessment Date:	

Section 1 *(Include in every assessment)*	Number of Opportunities	Opportunities taken	Score (1, 2,3, or 4)
Waiting Room Infection Control			
Use plastic seating or vinyl covered seating (should be easy to clean & disinfect)			
Cover open lesions in waiting area (Client is given dressings)			
Hand Hygeine - Worker Behaviors			
Minimize hand and wrist jewelry (watch only)			
Change gloves between clean/dirty procedure			
Keep natural nails less than ¼" long. No acrylic nails/extenders			
Wash hands using soap and warm water			
➢ Prior to starting work day			
➢ If hands are soiled			
➢ After using the restroom			
Use 60% or greater **alcohol based hand sanitizer** (Prefer stationary dispensing units) OR use soap and water to wash hands			
➢ Upon staff entering/leaving exam room			
➢ Between all patient contacts			
➢ Between clean and dirty steps of a procedure			
➢ Prior to accessing and setting up supplies			
Hand Hygiene - Patient Behaviors			
Use 60% or greater alcohol based sanitizer before entering exam room (Prefer stationary dispensing units)			
Prevention of Cross Contamination			
Have comprehensive infection control policies/procedures readily available			
Soak stainless steel instruments in high level disinfectant (HLD) or sterilize			
Collect/handle/transport specimens appropriately			
Cover contaminated instruments/equipment during transport			
Initial and date all opened containers (bottles, ointments, creams, etc.)			
Discard open bottles of irrigation fluid at end of day			
Check supply expiration dates before use			
Use sterile disposable scissors to cut off dressings, discard scissors after use. ***Do not use pocket scissors.***			
Use sterile non-disposable scissors to cut off dressings. Then wash scissors in enzymatic detergent, rinse & dry. Follow by immersing in HLD (per label directions), rinse thoroughly and dry before using again. ***Do not use pocket scissors*.**			

Scoring: Use the adjacent scale to score each item listed. Record how often available opportunities are taken…0%, 25%, 50%, 75% or nearly 100% of the time.	0=	0%	
	1=	1 - 25%	
	2=	26 - 50%	
	3=	51 - 75%	
	4=	76 - 100%	
	NA=	Not applicable	
Section 1 (continued)	**Number of Opportunities**	**Opportunities Taken**	**Score (1,2,3 or 4)**
Use of Personal Protective Equipment (PPE)			
Wear gloves when contacting non-intact skin, wounds, and mucous membranes			
Wear masks with face shield during wound irrigation or when expect splashing			
Wear gowns during wound care as appropriate			
Environmental Cleaning & Disinfecting			
Use plastic wrapping to protect non-disposable equipment (*BP cuff, Doppler*) from wound or other non-intact skin			
Wipe down equipment that comes in contact with wound or non-intact skin			
Clean and disinfect environmental areas contaminated by body substances or wound drainage			
Clean visibly soiled surfaces with friction first. Then wipe with EPA-approved low level disinfectant (LLD)-saturated *disposable* cloth, allow 30-60 seconds of wet time and air dry			
Wear gloves when handling contaminated linen			
Clean and disinfect stethoscopes after each use with EPA-approved LLD or 70% isopropyl alcohol (IPA)			
Clean pulse ox probe with 70% IPA or other LLD after each use			
Know what, when and where housekeeping cleans and names of products used.			
Add scores for Section I total - (maximum score: 136) (Optimal score for each behavior is between 3 and 4)			
Section 2 *(Include in assessment only if procedures can be observed)*			
Wound Care Procedures			
Wound Irrigation (if observed)			
Cover all items within 3-5 feet area of wound irrigation			
Use barrier on surfaces to prevent contamination			
Bag soiled items close to point of use			
Use biohazard bags for saturated items (blood or bodily fluids)			
Wound Culturing (if observed)			
Obtain culture prior to antibiotic use			
List all antibiotics patient is taking on lab slip			
Remove excess debris prior to culturing, using normal saline			
Add scores for total of Section 2 (maximum score: 28)			
Add scores for total of Sections 1 and 2 - maximum score: 164 (Optimal score for each behavior is between 3 and 4)			

Source: Reprinted with permission of Tacoma-Pierce County Health Department, Tacoma, Washington. *www.tpchd.org*.

4-166 MRSA—Chain of Infection Poster

How to Break the Chain of Infection in your Outpatient Clinic/Medical Office

INFECTIOUS AGENT
(Germ that causes the disease) =

MRSA
(Methicillin resistant *Staphylococcus aureus*)

How to break the chain:
Kill or remove agent

- Identify individuals who are infected or colonized & treat appropriately
- Clean surfaces, then disinfect them with an EPA-registered disinfectant following manufacturer's instructions
- **Wash hands!**

SUSCEPTIBLE PERSON
(How likely a person is to get sick after being exposed to the germ) =

Anyone can get MRSA,
but it is more likely if there are:

- Crowded living conditions
- Lack of cleanliness
- Frequent skin-to-skin contact
- Abraded skin
- Shared sports equipment
- Shared personal hygiene items
- Lack of healthcare access
- Overuse of antibiotics

How to break the chain:
Stop germs from entering

- Practice good personal hygiene
- **Wash hands!**
- Maintain a strong immune system through healthy living practices
- Take antibiotics appropriately – only when needed; take all prescribed

RESERVOIR
(Where the germ normally lives) =

Skin and Nose of individuals infected or colonized with MRSA

How to break the chain:
Eliminate or reduce reservoir

- Incise and drain (I & D) abscesses
- Do culture and sensitivity (C & S) of skin/soft tissue infection
- **Wash hands!**
- Prescribe antibiotics, if indicated, based on results of C & S report
- Consider decolonization

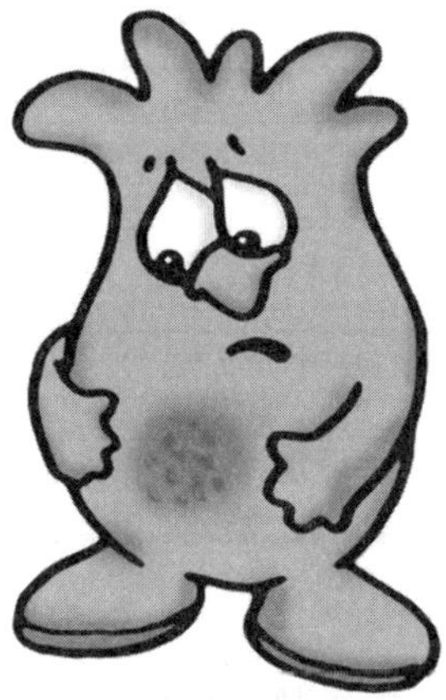

MEANS OF TRANSMISSION
(How the germ travels from the reservoir to a person) =

Hands, Infection Site and Fomites
(Fomites-items or environmental surfaces contaminated with body fluids containing MRSA)

How to break the chain:
Do not allow germs to escape and travel

- **Wash hands** / Use alcohol-based hand sanitizers
- Keep nails short. Acrylic nails should not be worn
- Avoid touching own nose, face while providing care
- Keep skin infections covered with clean, dry bandages
- Use contact precautions
- Clean and disinfect exam room and equipment
- Do not share sports equipment, towels, soap, clothing, razors, linens....

Source: Reprinted with permission of Tacoma-Pierce County Health Department, Tacoma, Washington. *www.tpchd.org.*

4-167 MRSA—Environmental Cleaning Quick Reference

How to clean equipment and surfaces, when to clean, what to use			
Visibly soiled surfaces must be cleaned with friction first then re-wiped. Non-visibly soiled surfaces may be wiped thoroughly with friction once. When using spray disinfectant, spray/saturate towel and wipe surface with friction. Spraying the surface and letting it dry is not adequate to clean and disinfect. Wear gloves.			
Item to clean	**Wipe down what?**	**When?**	**With what?**
Blood pressure cuff (Disposable preferred)	Cuff, tubing, bulb (if manual)	After each use	Wipe with low-level (LL) disinfectant; if visibly soiled, wash in soap and water, rinse and hang to dry.
Pulse ox probe (Disposable preferred)	Inside and outside of reusable probe, discard if disposable	After each use	Wipe with 70% isopropyl alcohol (IPA) or low-level (LL) disinfectant.
Stethoscope	Bell and tubing	After each use	Wipe with IPA or low-level disinfectant.
Reflex hammer	Handle and head	After each use	Wipe with IPA or low-level disinfectant.
Otoscope speculae (Disposable preferred)	If reusable, wash and disinfect	All surfaces after each use	IPA may be used for non-disposable oto speculae, soak for 20 minutes.
Otoscope handle	Handle	All surfaces after each use	Wipe with LL disinfectant and air dry.
Nasal, vaginal and rectal specula (Disposable preferred)	If reusable, clean after each use	After each use	If reusable, clean in enzymatic detergent. Then autoclave or soak in high-level disinfectant (HLD).
Metal basin (Disposable preferred)	Basin	After each use	Wash in enzymatic detergent and rinse well, then autoclave.
Flexible endoscopes	Scope	After each use	Wash in enzymatic detergent per manufacturer's instructions. Soak in HLD according to manufacturers instructions.
Vascular/Fetal Doppler	Head of doppler	After each use	Wipe with 70% isopropyl alcohol (IPA).
Hyfrecator (Change the tip after each use)	Wand and controls on the unit	After each use	Wipe with low-level (EPA) disinfectant.
Cloth appliances-neck and arm traction, etc.	All cloth	After each use	Wash with laundry detergent in hot/warm water, rinse well and hang to dry.
Canes, walkers, crutches, wheelchairs, rehab equipment	Special attention to surfaces that are in contact with people	Between patients	If visibly soiled, clean first with friction. Then wipe down with low-level disinfectant.

Visibly soiled surfaces must be cleaned with friction first then re-wiped. Non-visibly soiled surfaces may be wiped thoroughly with friction once. When using spray disinfectant, spray/saturate towel and wipe surface with friction. Spraying the surface and letting it dry is not adequate to clean and disinfect. Wear gloves.			
Item to clean	**Wipe down what?**	**When?**	**With what?**
Exam tables, gurneys, papoose boards, etc.	Top of table, other areas that came in contact with patient and/or bodily fluids	After each use	If visibly soiled, clean first with friction. Then wipe down with low-level disinfectant.
Baby scale/changing table	Surfaces that come in contact with patient or staff	After each use	If visibly soiled, clean first with friction. Then wipe down with low-level disinfectant.
Toys (Eliminating toys from office/clinic is preferred; use videos)	If office/clinic has toys - Use only washable toys; OR Give child 3-4 crayons in a baggie with individual sheets of pictures to color and let child keep	After each use - between children	Wash "used" toys with dish soap and hot water, air dry. May use dishwasher.
Door knobs, phones, keyboards, light switches, other "hand touch" items	Front door, inside and out, and "community" pen at the desk; Shared keyboards, counters, telephones, doorknobs, drawer pulls, and other "hand touch" areas (Avoid sharing pens, pencils)	At least twice daily	If visibly soiled, clean first with friction. Then wipe down with low-level disinfectant. Disinfect keyboards for 5 seconds daily and when visibly dirty by wiping with LL disinfectant or IPA.
Waiting room: chairs, tables, etc. (Vinyl furniture preferred)	All surfaces that can come in contact with patient	First thing in the morning (or at the end of the day) and at lunchtime	If visibly soiled, clean first with friction. Then wipe down with low-level disinfectant.
Patient restrooms	Doorknobs, faucets, toilet seat, handles, etc.	At least twice daily	Wipe with low-level disinfectant.

Note: Surfaces must be moisture-resistant to be able to disinfect them. *Upholstered furniture that is not vinyl covered, soft toys, etc. cannot be disinfected and their use is discouraged.* 08/2006

Guide to Sterilization and Disinfection of Equipment & Surfaces		
You MUST thoroughly clean items to remove all visible soil before disinfecting or sterilizing		
Intended Use	**Level of Process Required**	**Products*** ***Brand names are used as examples only, no endorsement is implied.**
Critical Intended use: Objects that enter normally sterile tissue, the vascular system or through which blood flows should be sterile (*instruments*).	**Sterilization** (Steam, gas, hydrogen peroxide plasma, or chemical sterilization)	**For Chemical Sterilization** Glutaraldehyde (≥ 2.0%) (Cidex, Metricide) Hydrogen peroxide – HP (7.5%) (Sporox) Peracetic acid – PA (0.2%) HP (1.0%) & PA (0.08%) HP (7.5%) & PA (0.23%) Glut (1.12%) & Phenol/phenate (1.93%) (*Exposure time on all per manufacturers' recommendations*) HP is NOT your clinic wound cleaning product!
Semi-critical Objects that touch mucous membranes or skin that is not intact require an HLD process (*scissors, flexible scopes*)	**High Level Disinfection (HLD)** (FDA regulates products)	**Germicide** — **Concentration** Glutaraldehyde — ≥ 2.0% Ortho-phthalaldehyde (OPA) *(12 min)* — 0.55% Hydrogen peroxide (HP) — 7.5% HP and paracetic acid (PA) — 1.0%/0.08% HP and PA — 7.5%/0.23% Hypochlorite (free chlorine)* — 650-675ppm *May cause cosmetic and functional damage *(Exposure time ≥ 12 min to 30 min @ 20° C, see manufacturers' recommendations)*
Non-critical Objects that will not come in contact with mucous membranes or non-intact skin (e.g., environmental surfaces) require a low level process that kills vegetative bacteria, fungus and some viruses (Hepatitis B, C, MRSA and HIV).	**Low Level Disinfectant (LLD)** (EPA regulates hospital-level products)	**Germicide** — **Concentration** Ethyl or isopropyl alcohol — 70-90% Chlorine — 100ppm (1:500 dilution)** Phenolic — * Iodophor — * Quaternary ammonium (quat) — * **Use manufacturers' recommendations for concentrations* ***5.25-6.15% household bleach diluted 1/500provides > 100ppm available chlorine* *(Exposure time ≥ 1 min)* EPA registered, pop-up towelettes are usually quat and are effective low-level disinfectants.

Note: Intermediate level disinfectants - usually used for therapy or whirlpool tubs.

Source: Reprinted with permission of Tacoma-Pierce County Health Department, Tacoma, Washington. *www.tpchd.org.*

4-168 MRSA—Wound Culture Protocols

<table>
<tr><th colspan="2">Wound Culture Protocols</th></tr>
<tr><td colspan="2">Applies to patients presenting with:
• Soft skin and tissue infections with open or draining lesions
• (Appearance of) insect/spider bite with necrotizing center, drainage & erythema
• Abscess - ulcer
• Infected laceration
⇒ Culture wound prior to initiation of antibiotics if signs or symptoms of infection are present. If Culture & Sensitivity is obtained after antibiotics have been started, list the drug on the laboratory C& S request.</td></tr>
<tr><td colspan="2">Supplies</td></tr>
<tr><td>For swab culture</td><td>Additional supplies for aspiration culture</td></tr>
<tr><td>Supplies for cleaning/irrigating wound
Gloves
Biohazard plastic lab transport bag
Culture collection/transport kit with gel for aerobic C&S
Culture collection/transport kit without gel (for gram stain)</td><td>10ml sterile syringe
22 gauge needle
Syringe end cap
Sterile gloves
Skin antiseptic (betadine, etc.)</td></tr>
<tr><td colspan="2">Wound Cleansing: Wound must be thoroughly cleaned prior to culturing. Do not culture purulent or necrotic debris or drainage over hard eschar. See also Wound Irrigation Procedure.</td></tr>
<tr><td>Procedure</td><td>Comments</td></tr>
<tr><td>1. Cleanse wound by removing excess debris from wound base with normal saline (pink saline fish or saline bullet).
2. Thoroughly flush wound with sterile saline.
3. Gently blot excess saline from wound bed with sterile gauze.
4. Remove soiled gloves; apply hand sanitizer.
5. Apply clean gloves.</td><td>Maintain aseptic environment.
When flushing/irrigating wound wear gown and face protection – see PPE section above.</td></tr>
<tr><td colspan="2">Culture Method – Swab Technique</td></tr>
<tr><td>Procedure</td><td>Comments</td></tr>
<tr><td>1. Open sterile culture collection/transport kit containing Amies or Stuarts transport medium and remove swab.
2. If wound is dry, moisten tip of swab with transport fluid at the bottom of the transport sleeve or sterile preservative-free saline (pink saline fish or saline bullet). If wound is moist (weepy) after cleaning, this might not be necessary.
3. Without touching swab to surrounding wound edges or skin, rotate tip of swab</td><td>Culture collection/transport kit contains a synthetic swab (rayon or Dacron). Cotton tip swabs are not recommended. Note: for a Gram Stain use a non gel culture collection kit
Apply sufficient pressure to cause tissue fluid to be expressed. It is the bacteria in the tissue fluid that is desired for culture.
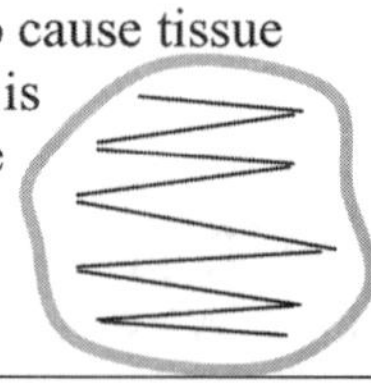
10-point culture of wound</td></tr>
</table>

over a 1cm area of open wound for 5 seconds (preferred method), or rotate the swab while making a zigzag pattern across the wound at 10 points. 4. Place swab in culture transport sleeve. Make sure swab tip is in contact with the liquid transport medium at the base of the sleeve. Break ampule containing transport fluid if present in the collection kits being used. 5. Label culture collection/transport kit with name, birth date, specimen source, date and time of culture. 6. Place in lab biohazard transport bag.	Avoid contaminating outside of culture collection/transport kit.

Culture Method – Tissue Aspiration Technique (MD, PA, ARNP Responsibility)	
Procedure	**Comments**
1. Perform hand hygiene and apply sterile gloves. 2. Face shield and gown may be necessary to avoid potential exposure to inadvertent wound spray. 3. Cleanse *intact skin* with antiseptic and allow to dry. 4. Expel all air from a 10mL syringe with a 22 gauge needle prior to aspiration. Insert needle into intact skin and apply suction (aspirate). 5. Aspirate approximately 0.5mL of wound fluid. 6. Discard needle, then cap syringe with sterile cap used for blood gases. 7. Label syringe (see Swab Culture, above). 8. After labeling syringe, place in lab biohazard transport bag and send aspirate immediately to lab.	Involves insertion of a needle into the tissue adjacent to the wound to aspirate tissue fluid. This is a sterile procedure. *Intact skin* next to the wound is disinfected and allowed to air dry. Do not fan area to speed drying as it allows the organisms in environment to settle on the skin surface. The needle is moved backward and forward at different angles for 2-4 explorations. Remove needle with hemostat and place immediately in sharps container. Place end cap on syringe to prevent leakage.
Culture Method – Incision and Drainage (I&D) (MD, PA, ARNP Responsibility)	
Procedure	**Comments**
1. Follow the clinic/office procedure for incision & drainage. 2. Follow the procedure for swab culture technique (above).	Culture the drainage from the incision regardless of appearance.

Note: Reviewed by microbiologists from all Pierce County acute care hospitals (07/2006).

Source: Reprinted with permission of Tacoma-Pierce County Health Department, Tacoma, Washington. *www.tpchd.org*.

4-169 Interim Guidelines for Management of Suspected *Staphylococcus aureus* Skin and Soft Tissue Infections*

Clinical presentation

- Looks like insect or spider bite
- Folliculitis, pustular lesions
- Furuncle, carbuncle (boils)
- Abscess (esp. w/ tissue necrosis)
- Cellulitis
- Impetigo
- Infected wound

Risk factors associated with MRSA

- History of MRSA infection, colonization
- History (within past 12 months) of: hospitalization, surgery, long term care residence, indwelling catheter or medical device; dialysis, renal failure, diabetes, or other co-morbidities
- Injection drug use, incarceration
- Close contact with someone known to be infected or colonized with MRSA
- High prevalence of MRSA in community or population
- Local risk factors: consult local public health department

Incision & drainage (I & D) of abscesses – If I & D not performed, consider culture of draining wounds, or aspirate or biopsy of central area of inflammation

Culture & antimicrobial susceptibility testing
Include "D-test" for clindamycin resistance if MRSA

Patient education
To decrease spread of infection, provide education on infection control measures and wound care to all patients and/or caregivers of patients with *S. aureus* infections, esp. those with MRSA per WAC 246.101.105(7)

Mild
Afebrile, healthy other than SSTI

Moderate
Febrile, appears ill, but no unstable co-morbidities

Severe/Critically Ill
Appears toxic, unstable co-morbidity, sepsis syndrome, or limb-or life threatening infection, e.g., necrotizing fasciitis

Outpatient management (Mild)

- <u>Local care, I & D, +/- topical antibiotics may be sufficient</u>
- ***If oral antibiotics used*** – β-lactam preferred for MSSA
- **If increased suspicion for MRSA based on presence of ≥ 1 risk factor**: Consider empiric therapy active against MRSA
- Adjust antibiotics based on results of culture & susceptibility testing
- Monitor response to therapy

Outpatient management (Moderate)

- **Low suspicion for MRSA**: β-lactam antibiotics effective against S. aureus preferred for MSSA
- **If increased suspicion for MRSA based on presence of ≥ 1 risk factor:** Empiric therapy active against MRSA
- Adjust antibiotics based on results of culture & susceptibility testing
- Monitor response to therapy

Hospital management (Severe/Critically Ill; also Moderate as indicated)

- Empiric broad-spectrum IV antibiotics including vancomycin for activity against S. *aureus*, including MRSA
- Adjust antibiotics based on results of culture & susceptibility testing
- Monitor response to therapy
- Consult ID specialist if no improvement or considering alternative agents (e.g., linezolid, daptomycin)
- Switch to oral therapy based on susceptibility testing if:
  - Afebrile for 24 hours
  - Clinically improved
  - Able to take oral therapy
  - Close follow-up possible

MSSA: *Methicillin susceptible S. aureus*
MRSA: *S. aureus resistant to all penicillins & cephalosporins*
β-lactam antibiotics*: Includes all penicillins & cephalosporins*

*For details, see full text of Interim Guidelines for Evaluation & Management of Community-Associated Methicillin Resistant *Staphylococcus aureus* Skin and Soft Tissue Infections in Outpatient Settings

Table 1. Interim Guidelines for Empiric Oral Antimicrobial Treatment of Outpatients with Suspected MRSA Skin and Soft Tissue Infections (SSTI)

Selection of empiric therapy should be guided by local *S. aureus* susceptibility and modified based on results of culture and susceptibility testing. The duration of therapy for most SSTI is 7-10 days, but may vary depending on severity of infection and clinical response. ***NOTE: Before treating, clinicians should consult complete drug prescribing information in the manufacturer's package insert or the PDR.***

Antimicrobial	Adult Dose	Pediatric Dose
Trimethoprim-sulfamethoxazole (TMP-SMX) DS	1 tablet (160 mg TMP/800 mg SMX) PO bid	Base dose on TMP: 8-12 mg TMP (& 40-60 mg SMX) per kg/day in 2 doses; not to exceed adult dose
Minocycline or doxycycline	100 mg PO bid	***Not recommended for pediatric use – suggest consultation with infectious disease specialist before use***
Clindamycin	300-450 mg PO qid	10-20 mg/kg/day in 3-4 doses; not to exceed adult dose

[a] **If considering clindamycin, isolates resistant to erythromycin and sensitive to clindamycin should be evaluated for inducible clindamycin resistance (MLS_B phenotype) using the "D test."** Consult with your reference laboratory to determine if "D testing" is routine or must be specifically requested. If inducible resistance is present, an alternative agent to clindamycin should be considered.

- If Group A streptococcal infection is suspected, oral therapy should include an agent active against this organism (β-lactam, macrolide, clindamycin). Tetracyclines and Trimethoprim-sulfamethoxazole, although active against many MRSA, are not recommended treatments for suspected GAS infections.
- Outpatient use of quinolones or macrolides: Fluoroquinolones (e.g., ciprofloxin, levofloxacin, moxifloxacin, gatifloxacin) and macrolides (e.g., erythromycin, clarithromycin, azithromycin) are NOT recommended for treatment of MRSA because of high resistance rates. If fluoroquinolones are being considered, consult with infectious disease specialist before use.
- Outpatient use of linezolid in SSTI: Linezolid is costly and has great potential for inappropriate use, inducing antimicrobial resistance, and toxicity. Although it is 100% bioavailable and effective in SSTI, it is not recommended for empiric treatment or routine use because of these concerns. It is strongly recommended that linezolid only be used after consultation with an infectious disease specialist to determine if alternative antimicrobials would be more appropriate.

Table 2. Eradication of MRSA Colonization

Efficacy of decolonization in preventing re-infection or transmission in the outpatient setting is not documented, and is NOT routinely recommended. Consultation with an infectious disease specialist is recommended before eradication of colonization is initiated.

Possible eradication regimens include:
Rifampin (Adult dose: 300mg PO bid x 5 days; pediatric dose: 10-12 mg/kg/day in 2 doses not to exceed 600 mg/d x 5 days) may be used in combination with TMP-SMX, **OR** rifampin with doxycycline, **OR** rifampin with minocycline, for recurrent MRSA infection despite appropriate therapy. ***Never use rifampin monotherapy, due to the rapid emergence of resistance. Rifampin interacts with methadone, oral hypoglycemics, hormonal contraceptives, anticoagulants, protease inhibitors, phenytoin, theophylline, cardiac glycosides and other drugs.***
Topical intranasal mupirocin may be used bid for 5 days with or without systemic antimicrobial therapy.
Skin antisepsis with chlorhexidine or other agents may be used in addition to one or both of the above regimens.

Source: Reprinted with permission of Tacoma-Pierce County Health Department, Tacoma, Washington. *www.tpchd.org*.

4-170 CDC Recommendations on Multi-Drug Resistant Organisms

General Recommendations for Routine Prevention and Control of MDROs in Healthcare Settings - Tier 1.

Administrative Measures/Adherence Monitoring	MDRO Education	Judicious Antimicrobial Use	Surveillance	Infection Control Precautions to Prevent Transmission	Environmental Measures	Decolonization
Make MDRO prevention/control an organizational priority. Provide administrative support and both fiscal and human resources to prevent and control MDRO transmission. *(IB)* Identify experts who can provide consultation and expertise for analyzing epidemiologic data, recognizing MDRO problems, or devising effective control strategies, as needed. *(II)* **Implement systems to communicate information about reportable MDROs to administrative personnel and state/local health departments. *(II)*** Implement a multi-disciplinary process to monitor and improve HCP adherence to recommended practices for Standard and Contact Precautions.*(IB)* Implement systems to designate patients known to be colonized or infected with a targeted MDRO and to notify receiving healthcare facilities or personnel prior to transfer of such patients within or between facilities. *(IB)* Support participation in local, regional and/or national coalitions to combat emerging or growing MDRO problems.*(IB)* Provide updated feedback at least annually to healthcare providers and administrators on facility and patient-care unit MDRO infections. Include information on changes in prevalence and incidence, problem assessment and performance improvement plans. *(IB)*	Provide education and training on risks and prevention of MDRO transmission during orientation and periodic educational updates for HCP; include information on organizational experience with MDROs and prevention strategies. *(IB)*	In hospitals and LTCFs, ensure that a multi-disciplinary process is in place to review local susceptibility patterns (antibiograms), and antimicrobial agents included in the formulary, to foster appropriate antimicrobial use. *(IB)* Implement systems (e.g., CPOE, susceptibility report comment, pharmacy or unit director notification) to prompt clinicians to use the appropriate agent and regimen for the given clinical situation. *(IB)* Provide clinicians with antimicrobial susceptibility reports and analysis of current trends, updated at least annually, to guide antimicrobial prescribing practices. *(IB)* In settings with limited electronic communication system infrastructures to implement physician prompts, etc., at a minimum implement a process to review antibiotic use. Prepare and distribute reports to providers. *(II)*	Use standardized laboratory methods and follow published guidelines for determining antimicrobial susceptibilities of targeted and emerging MDROs. Establish systems to ensure that clinical micro labs (in-house and outsourced) promptly notify infection control or a medical director/designee when a novel resistance pattern for that facility is detected. *(IB)* In hospitals and LTCFs: …develop and implement laboratory protocols for storing isolates of selected MDROs for molecular typing when needed to confirm transmission or delineate epidemiology of MDRO in facility. *(IB)* …establish laboratory-based systems to detect and communicate evidence of MDROs in clinical isolates *(IB)* …prepare facility-specific antimicrobial susceptibility reports as recommended by CLSI; monitor reports for evidence of changing resistance that may indicate emergence or transmission of MDROs *(IA/IC)* …develop and monitor special-care unit-specific antimicrobial susceptibility reports (e.g., ventilator-dependent units, ICUs, oncology units). *(IB)* …monitor trends in incidence of target MDROs in the facility over time to determine if MDRO rates are decreasing or if additional interventions are needed. *(IA)*	Follow Standard Precautions in all healthcare settings. *(IB)* Use of Contact Precautions (CP): --- In <u>*acute care settings*</u> : Implement CP for all patients known to be colonized/infected with target MDROs.*(IB)* --- In <u>*LTCFs:*</u> *Consider the individual patient's clinical situation and facility resources in deciding whether to implement CP (II)* --- *In ambulatory and home care settings, follow Standard Precautions (II)* ---In <u>*hemodialysis units*</u>: Follow dialysis specific guidelines *(IC)* No recommendation can be made regarding when to discontinue CP. *(Unresolved issue)* Masks are not recommended for routine use to prevent transmission of MDROs from patients to HCWs. Use masks according to Standard Precautions when performing splash-generating procedures, caring for patients with open tracheostomies with potential for projectile secretions, and when there is evidence for transmission from heavily colonized sources (e.g., burn wounds). Patient placement in hospitals and LTCFs: When single-patient rooms are available, assign priority for these rooms to patients with known or suspected MDRO colonization or infection. Give highest priority to those patients who have conditions that may facilitate transmission, e.g., uncontained secretions or excretions. When single-patient rooms are not available, cohort patients with the same MDRO in the same room or patient-care area. *(IB)* When cohorting patients with the same MDRO is not possible, place MDRO patients in rooms with patients who are at low risk for acquisition of MDROs and associated adverse outcomes from infection and are likely to have short lengths of stay. *(II)*	Follow recommended cleaning, disinfection and sterilization guidelines for maintaining patient care areas and equipment. Dedicate non-critical medical items to use on individual patients known to be infected or colonized with an MDRO. Prioritize room cleaning of patients on Contact Precautions. Focus on cleaning and disinfecting frequently touched surfaces (e.g., bed rails, bedside commodes, bathroom fixtures in patient room, doorknobs) and equipment in immediate vicinity of patient.	Not recommended routinely

Recommendations for Intensified MDRO control efforts - Tier 2.

Institute one or more of the interventions described below when 1) incidence or prevalence of MDROs are not decreasing despite the use of routine control measures; or 2) the *first* case or outbreak of an epidemiologically important MDRO (e.g., VRE, MRSA, VISA, VRSA, MDR-GNB) is identified within a healthcare facility or unit (*IB*) Continue to monitor the incidence of target MDRO infection and colonization; if rates do not decrease, implement additional interventions as needed to reduce MDRO transmission.

Administrative Measures/Adherence Monitoring	MDRO Education	Judicious Antimicrobial Use	Surveillance	Infection Control Precautions to Prevent Transmission	Environmental Measures	Decolonization
Obtain expert consultation from persons with experience in infection control and the epidemiology of MDROS, either in-house or through outside consultation, for assessment of the local MDRO problem and guidance in the design, implementation and evaluation of appropriat4e control measures. *(IB)* Provide necessary leadership, funding and day-to-day oversight to implement interventions selected. *(IB)* Evaluate healthcare system factors for role in creating or perpetuating MDRO transmission, including staffing levels, education and training, availability of consumable and durable resources; communication processes, and adherence to infection control measures.*(IB)* Update healthcare providers and administrators on the progress and effectiveness of the intensified interventions. *(IB)*	Intensify the frequency of educational programs for healthcare personnel, especially for those who work in areas where MDRO rates are not decreasing. Provide individual or unit-specific feedback when available. *(IB)*	Review the role of antimicrobial use in perpetuating the MDRO problem targeted for intensified intervention. Control and improve antimicrobial use as indicated. Antimicrobial agents that may be targeted include vancomycin, third-[d] generation cephalosporins, anti-anaerobic agents for VRE; third generation cephalosporins for ESBLs; and quinolones and carbapenems. *(IB)*	Calculate and analyze incidence rates of target MDROs (single isolates/patient; location-, service-specific) *(IB)* Increase frequency of compiling, monitoring antimicrobial susceptibility summary reports *(II)* Implement laboratory protocols for storing isolates of selected MDROs for molecular typing; perform typing if needed *(IB)* Develop and implement protocols to obtain active surveillance cultures from patients in populations at risk. *(IB)* (See recommendations for appropriate body sites and culturing methods.) Conduct culture surveys to assess efficacy of intensified MDRO control interventions. Conduct serial (e.g., weekly) unit-specific point prevalence culture surveys of the target MDRO to determine if transmission has decreased or ceased.*(IB)* Repeat point-prevalence culture-surveys at routine intervals and at time of patient discharge or transfer until transmission has ceased. *(IB)* If indicated by assessment of the MDRO problem, collect cultures to assess the colonization status of roommates and other patients with substantial exposure to patients with known MDRO infection or colonization. *(IB)* Obtain cultures from HCP for target MDROs when there is epidemiologic evidence implicating the staff member as a source of ongoing transmission. *(IB)*	**Use of Contact Precautions:** **Implement Contact Precautions (CP) routinely for all patients colonized or infected with a target MDRO. *(IA)*** **Don gowns and gloves *before or upon entry* to the patient's room or cubicle. *(IB)*** **In LTCFs, modify CP to allow MDRO-colonized/infected patients whose site of colonization or infection can be appropriately contained and who can observe good hand hygiene practices to enter common areas and participate in group activities** **When active surveillance cultures are obtained as part of an intensified MDRO control program, implement CP until the surveillance culture is reported negative for the target MDRO *(IB)*** No recommendation is made for universal use of gloves and/or gowns. (*Unresolved issue*) **Implement policies for patient admission and placement as needed to prevent transmission of the problem MDRO. *(IB)*** When single-patient rooms are available, assign priority for these rooms to patients with known or suspected MDRO colonization or infection. Give highest priority to those patients who have conditions that may facilitate transmission, e.g., uncontained secretions or excretions. When single-patient rooms are not available, cohort patients with the same MDRO in the same room or patient-care area. *(IB)* When cohorting patients with the same MDRO is not possible, place MDRO patients in rooms with patients who are at low risk for acquisition of MDROs and associated adverse outcomes from infection and are likely to have short lengths of stay. *(II)* **Stop new admissions to the unit or facility if transmission continues despite the implementation of the intensified control measures. *(IB)***	Implement patient.-dedicated use of non-critical equipment *(IB)* Intensify and reinforce training of environmental staff who work in areas targeted for intensified MDRO control. Some facilities may choose to assign dedicated staff to targeted patient care areas to enhance consistency of proper environmental cleaning and disinfection services *(IB)* **Monitor cleaning performance to ensure consistent cleaning and disinfection of surfaces in close proximity to the patient and those likely to be touched by the patient and HCWs (e.g., bedrails, carts, bedside commodes, doorknobs, faucet handles) *(IB)*.** Obtain environmental cultures (e.g., surfaces, shared equipment) only when epidemiologically implicated in transmission *(IB)* **Vacate units for environmental assessment and intensive cleaning when previous efforts to control environmental transmission have failed *(II)***	Consult with experts on a case-by-case basis regarding the appropriate use of decolonization therapy for patients or staff during limited period of time as a component of an intensified MRSA control program *(II)* When decolonization for MRSA is used, perform susceptibility testing for the decolonizing agent against the target organism or the MDRO strain epidemiologically implicated in transmission. Monitor susceptibility to detect emergence of resistance to the decolonizing agent. Consult with microbiologists for appropriate testing for mupirocin resistance, since standards have not been established. Do not use topical mupirocin routinely for MRSA decolonization of patients as a component of MRSA control programs in any healthcare setting. *(IB)* Limit decolonization to HCP found to be colonized with MRSA who have been epidemiologically implicated in ongoing transmission of MRSA to patients. *(IB)* No recommendation can be made for decolonization of patients who carry VRE or MDR-GNB.

Source: Healthcare Infection Control Practices Advisory Committee (HICPAC), Management of Multidrug-Resistant Organisms In Healthcare Settings, 2006. Centers for Disease Control and Prevention, Atlanta, GA. Available online at: www.cdc.gov/ncidod/dhqp/pdf/ar/mdroGuideline2006.pdf.

4-171 Components of a Protective Environment

CDC Isolation Guidelines, 2007

I. **Patients: Allogeneic Hematopoeitic Stem Cell Transplant (HSCT) Only**
   - Maintain in PE room except for required diagnostic or therapeutic procedures that cannot be performed in the room, e.g. radiology, operating room
   - Respiratory protection, e.g., N95 respirator, for the patient when leaving PE during periods of construction

II. **Standard and Expanded Precautions**
   - Hand hygiene observed before and after patient contact
   - Gown, gloves, mask NOT required for health care workers (HCWs) or visitors for routine entry into the room
   - Use of gown, gloves, mask by HCWs and visitors according to Standard Precautions and as indicated for suspected or proven infections for which Transmission-Based Precautions are recommended

III. **Engineering**
   - Central or point-of-use high efficiency particulate air [filtration] (HEPA) (99.97% efficiency) filters capable of removing particles 0.3 μm in diameter for supply (incoming) air
   - Well-sealed rooms
     - ➢ Proper construction of windows, doors, and intake and exhaust ports
     - ➢ Ceilings: smooth, free of fissures, open joints, crevices
     - ➢ Walls sealed above and below the ceiling
     - ➢ If leakage detected, locate source and make necessary repairs
   - Ventilation to maintain >12 ACH
   - Directed air flow: air supply and exhaust grills located so that clean, filtered air enters from one side of the room, flows across the patient's bed, exits on opposite side of the room
   - Positive room air pressure in relation to the corridor
     - ➢ Pressure differential of >2.5 Pa [0.01" water gauge]
   - Monitor and document results of air flow patterns daily using visual methods (e.g., flutter strips, smoke tubes) or a hand held pressure gauge
   - Self-closing door on all room exits
   - Maintain back-up ventilation equipment (e.g., portable units for fans or filters) for emergency provision of ventilation requirements for PE areas and take immediate steps to restore the fixed ventilation system
   - For patients who require both a PE and Airborne Infection Isolation, use an anteroom to ensure proper air balance relationships and provide independent exhaust of contaminated air to the outside or place a HEPA filter in the exhaust duct. If an anteroom is not available, place patient in an airborne infection isolation room (AIIR) and use portable ventilation units, industrial-grade HEPA filters to enhance filtration of spores.

IV. Surfaces

- Daily wet-dusting of horizontal surfaces using cloths moistened with EPA-registered hospital disinfectant/detergent
- Avoid dusting methods that disperse dust
- No carpeting in patient rooms or hallways
- No upholstered furniture and furnishings

V. Other

- No flowers (fresh or dried) or potted plants in PE rooms or areas
- Use vacuum cleaner equipped with HEPA filters when vacuum cleaning is necessary

Source: Siegel JD, Rhinehart E, Jackson M, Chiarello L, and the Healthcare Infection Control Practices Advisory Committee, *2007 Guideline for Isolation Precautions: Preventing Transmission of Infectious Agents in Healthcare Settings,* June 2007. Table 5, p. 131-132. *http://www.cdc.gov/ncidod/dhqp/pdf/isolation2007.pdf*

4-172 Hospital Pandemic Flu Checklist

HOSPITAL PANDEMIC INFLUENZA PLANNING CHECKLIST

Planning for pandemic influenza is critical for ensuring a sustainable healthcare response. The Centers for Disease Control and Prevention (CDC), with input from other Federal partners, have developed this checklist to help hospitals assess and improve their preparedness for responding to pandemic influenza. Because of differences among hospitals (e.g., characteristics of the patient population, size of the hospital/community, scope of services), each hospital will need to adapt this checklist to meet its unique needs and circumstances.[1] This checklist should be used as one of several tools for evaluating current plans or in developing a comprehensive pandemic influenza plan. Additional information can be found at www.pandemicflu.gov.

An effective plan will incorporate information from state, regional, tribal and local health departments, emergency management agencies/authorities, hospital associations and suppliers of resources. In addition, hospitals should ensure that their pandemic influenza plans comply with applicable state and federal regulations and with standards set by accreditation organizations, such as the Joint Commission on Accreditation of Healthcare Organizations (JCAHO). Comprehensive pandemic influenza planning can also help facilities plan for other emergency situations.

1. Structure for planning and decision making.

Completed	In Progress	Not Started	
☐	☐	☐	Pandemic influenza has been incorporated into disaster planning and exercises for the hospital.[2]
☐	☐	☐	A multidisciplinary planning committee has been identified to specifically address pandemic influenza preparedness planning and preparedness testing.[3]
☐	☐	☐	Primary and backup responsibility has been assigned for coordinating preparedness planning. (Insert names, titles and contact information) Primary: ______________________ (Name) (Title) (Contact info) Backup: ______________________ (Name) (Title) (Contact info)
☐	☐	☐	Members of the planning committee include (as applicable to each setting) the following: (Check categories below that apply and develop a list of committee members with the name, title, and contact information for each personnel category checked below, and attach to this checklist.) ☐ Hospital administration ☐ Legal counsel/risk management ☐ Infection control/hospital epidemiology ☐ Disaster coordinator ☐ Public relations coordinator/public information officer ☐ Medical staff (e.g., internal medicine, pediatrics, hospitalist, infectious disease) ☐ Nursing administration ☐ Human resources (personnel, including Equal Employment Opportunities) ☐ Facility personnel representative (e.g., union representative) ☐ Occupational health ☐ Physical therapy ☐ Intensive care ☐ Emergency department ☐ Respiratory therapy

1 Checklists applicable to other healthcare settings (e.g., residential and long-term care facilities, emergency medical services, physician offices and clinics, and home health care) are available. See www.pandemicflu.gov/plan/healthcare/index.html.

2 Hospitals using the Hospital Incident Command System (HICS) may wish to modify the terminology and planning structure in this checklist to be consistent with that model.

3 An existing emergency or disaster preparedness committee may be assigned this responsibility.

June, 2007
Version 1

CDC SAFER·HEALTHIER·PEOPLE

1. Structure for planning and decision making. *(continued)*

Completed	In Progress	Not Started	
			☐ Diagnostic imaging (radiology) ☐ Discharge planning ☐ Staff development/education ☐ Engineering and maintenance ☐ Environmental (housekeeping) services ☐ Central (sterile) services ☐ Security ☐ Dietary (food) services ☐ Pharmacy services ☐ Information technology ☐ Purchasing agent /materials management ☐ Laboratory services ☐ Expert consultants (e.g., ethicist, mental/behavioral health professionals) ☐ Other member(s) as appropriate (e.g., volunteer services, community representative, clergy, local coroner, medical examiner, morticians)
☐	☐	☐	Points of contact for information on pandemic influenza planning resources have been identified within local, state and tribal health departments and the state hospital association (insert names, titles, and contact information.) Local health department: ______________________________ (Name) (Title) (Contact info) State health department: ______________________________ (Name) (Title) (Contact info) State hospital association: ______________________________ (Name) (Title) (Contact info) Tribal health association: ______________________________ (Name) (Title) (Contact info)
☐	☐	☐	Local, regional or state emergency preparedness groups[4], including bioterrorism/communicable disease coordinators points of contact, have been identified. (Insert name, title and contact information for each) City: ______________________________ (Name) (Title) (Contact info) County: ______________________________ (Name) (Title) (Contact info) Other regional (and/or tribal): ______________________________ (Name) (Title) (Contact info)
☐	☐	☐	Local or regional pandemic influenza planning groups have been contacted for information on coordinating the facility's plan with other pandemic influenza plans.

[4] State health deparments should be contacted for information on pandemic influenza preparedness planning.

2. Development of a written pandemic influenza plan.

Completed	In Progress	Not Started	
☐	☐	☐	Copies of relevant sections of the HHS Pandemic Influenza Plan (available at www.hhs.gov/pandemicflu/plan/) and policy documents that may be forthcoming (available at www.pandemicflu.gov) have been obtained and reviewed for incorporation into the facility's plan.
☐	☐	☐	Copies of relevant sections of other available plans (i.e., state, tribal, regional, or local) have been obtained and reviewed for incorporation into the facility's plan. ☐ State ☐ Regional ☐ Local ☐ Tribal
☐	☐	☐	A copy of the facility plan and other relevant materials are available in Administration and Infection Control. (List other locations where information is available, including facility intranet sites.) ____________________ (Location) ____________________ (Other locations)
☐	☐	☐	The plan includes strategies for collaborating with local and regional planning and response groups and hospitals and other healthcare facilities in order to coordinate response efforts at the community level (e.g., staffing, material and other resources, triage algorithms, etc.).
☐	☐	☐	The facility plan includes the elements listed in #3 below.
☐	☐	☐	The plan identifies the person(s) authorized to implement the plan and the organizational structure that will be used, including the delegation of authority to carry out the plan 24/7.
☐	☐	☐	The plan stratifies implementation of specific actions on the basis of the WHO Pandemic Phases, US Government Pandemic Stages, and the pandemic severity index level worldwide, in the United States and at the local level. (See section IV and Appendix 3 of the "Community Strategy for Pandemic Influenza Mitigation" at www.pandemicflu.gov/plan/community/commitigation.html)
☐	☐	☐	Responsibilities of key personnel and departments within the facility related to executing the plan have been described.
☐	☐	☐	Personnel who will serve as back-up (e.g., B team) for key personnel roles have been identified.
☐	☐	☐	A tabletop simulation exercise or other exercises have been developed to test the plan. ☐ Date performed (__________) ☐ Date performed (__________)
☐	☐	☐	A full scale drill/exercise has been developed to test the plan. ☐ Date performed (__________)
☐	☐	☐	The plan is updated regularly and includes current contact information and lessons learned from exercises and drills.

3. Elements of an influenza pandemic plan.

Completed	In Progress	Not Started	
☐	☐	☐	**A plan is in place for surveillance and detection of pandemic influenza in hospital patients and staff.** ☐ A method for performing and reporting syndromic surveillance for persons with influenza-like illness has been tested and evaluated during the regular influenza season in preparation for using the system for pandemic influenza surveillance. Hospital sites for syndromic surveillance should include the emergency department, hospital clinics, and occupational health. Surveillance reports are sent to hospital epidemiology/infection control personnel and to the local health authority. (The frequency of reporting should be determined by the local health authority and reflect the pandemic severity level, as well as any applicable federal or state recommendations.)

3. Elements of an influenza pandemic plan. *(continued)*

Completed	In Progress	Not Started	
			☐ Responsibility has been assigned for monitoring public health advisories (federal and state) and for updating the pandemic response coordinator and members of the pandemic influenza planning committee when pandemic influenza has been reported in the United States and is nearing the geographic area. (For more information see www.cdc.gov/flu/weekly/fluactivity.htm.) Primary: ____________ (Name) (Title) (Contact info) Backup: ____________ (Name) (Title) (Contact info)
			☐ A written protocol has been developed for monitoring and reporting seasonal influenza-like illness among hospitalized patients, volunteers, and staff (e.g., weekly or daily number of patients and staff with influenza-like illness). (Having a system for tracking illness trends during seasonal influenza will ensure that the hospital can detect stressors that may affect operating capacity, including staffing and supply needs, during a pandemic.) Information on the clinical signs and diagnosis of influenza is available at www.cdc.gov/flu/professionals/diagnosis/.)
			☐ A protocol has been developed for the evaluation and diagnosis of hospitalized patients and/or staff with symptoms of pandemic influenza. Information on the clinical signs and diagnosis of influenza is available at www.cdc.gov/flu/professionals/diagnosis/.
			☐ A protocol has been developed for the management of persons with possible pandemic influenza who are seen in the emergency department, hospital clinics, or are transferred from another facility or referred for hospitalization by an admitting physician. The protocol includes criteria for detecting a possible case, the diagnostic work-up to be performed, infection control measures to be implemented, medical treatment, and directions for notifying infection control.
			☐ Protocols include triggers for different levels of action that are based on the Pandemic Severity Index (See www.pandemicflu.gov or www.cdc.gov/flu.)
			☐ A system is in place to monitor for and internally review healthcare-associated transmission of seasonal influenza among patients and staff in the facility. Information used from this monitoring system is used to implement prevention interventions (e.g., isolation, cohorting). (This system will be necessary for assessing pandemic influenza transmission.)
☐	☐	☐	**A facility communication plan has been developed and is coordinated with the local health authority. For more information, see www.hhs.gov/pandemicflu/plan/sup10.html.**
			☐ Key public health points of contact for communication[5] during an influenza pandemic have been identified. (Insert name, title and contact information for each.) Local health department communication contact: ____________ (Name) (Title) (Contact info) State health department communication contact: ____________ (Name) (Title) (Contact info) Tribal health department communication contact: ____________ (Name) (Title) (Contact info)
			☐ Responsibility has been assigned for communications with public health authorities (i.e., case reporting, status updates) during a pandemic. (Insert names, titles and contact information of primary and backup persons.) Primary: ____________ (Name) (Title) (Contact info) Backup: ____________ (Name) (Title) (Contact info)

[5] Public health points of contact for communicating or reporting during a pandemic may be different from those who are involved in pre-pandemic planning.

3. Elements of an influenza pandemic plan. ***(continued)***

Completed	In Progress	Not Started	
			☐ Responsibility has been assigned for communicating with the public. (Insert name, title and contact information of primary and backup persons for each) Clinical spokesperson: Primary: ____________________ (Name) (Title) (Contact info) Backup: ____________________ (Name) (Title) (Contact info) Public relations spokesperson: Primary: ____________________ (Name) (Title) (Contact info) Backup: ____________________ (Name) (Title) (Contact info)
			☐ Methods of communicating with the public (e.g., public service announcements (PSAs), message mapping) and the subjects that will be addressed have been discussed.
			☐ Plans and responsibilities for communicating with hospital staff, volunteers, and private medical staff have been developed. Anticipate employee fear/anxiety and plan communications accordingly.
			☐ Plans and responsibilities for communication with patients and their family members have been developed.
			☐ Responsibility has been assigned for internal communications with staff regarding the status and impact of pandemic influenza in the hospital. (Insert names, titles and contact information of primary and backup persons.) Primary: ____________________ (Name) (Title) (Contact info) Backup: ____________________ (Name) (Title) (Contact info)
			☐ The types of communication needs (e.g., staff and community updates) and methods of communication (e.g., intranet, PSAs, and newspaper reports) have been identified and are appropriate for individuals with visual, hearing, or other disabilities, or limited English proficiency.
			☐ A list has been created of other healthcare entities, including their points of contact, within the region (e.g., other hospitals, long-term care and residential facilities, local hospital's emergency medical services, clinics, relevant community organizations [including those involved with disaster preparedness]) with which it will be necessary to maintain communication in real-time and be able to report information in a timely and accurate manner during a pandemic (Insert location of the list of contacts and attach a copy to the pandemic plan:) ____________________ (location of list)
			☐ The facility has been represented in discussions with other hospitals regarding local plans for inter-facility communication during a pandemic.
☐	☐	☐	**A plan is in place to provide education and training for personnel and information for patients and visitors to ensure that the implications of and basic prevention and control measures for pandemic influenza are understood. (For more information and resources see www.cdc.gov/flu/professionals/index.htm.)**
			☐ A person has been designated with responsibility for coordinating education and training on pandemic influenza (e.g., identifies and facilitates access to available programs, maintains a record of personnel attendance). (Insert name, title and contact information.) ____________________ (Name) (Title) (Contact info)

3. Elements of an influenza pandemic plan. *(continued)*

Completed	In Progress	Not Started	
			☐ Current and potential opportunities for long-distance (e.g., Web-based) and local (e.g., health department- or hospital-sponsored) influenza training programs have been identified. (See www.cdc.gov/flu/professionals/training/.)
			☐ Language, format (i.e., prepared for individuals with visual, hearing or other disabilities) and reading-level appropriate materials for clinical and non-clinical personnel have been identified to supplement and support education and training programs (e.g., materials available through state and federal public health agencies and through professional organizations), and a plan is in place for obtaining these materials.
			☐ Education and training for hospital personnel includes information on differences in pandemic influenza infection prevention and control measures if necessary and are provided in languages and format (i.e., prepared for individuals with visual, hearing or other disabilities) appropriate for hospital personnel. Regular education and training should include, but not be limited to: training in Standard and Droplet Precautions; use of respiratory protection; social distancing and respiratory hygiene/cough etiquette.
			☐ Education and training includes information on the hospital's pandemic influenza plan, including relevant personnel policies, and operational changes that will occur once the plan is implemented.
			☐ A plan has been established for expediting the identification of, credentialing and training of non-facility staff brought in from other locations within the region to provide patient care when the hospital reaches a staffing crisis.
			☐ Informational materials (e.g., brochures, posters) on pandemic influenza and relevant hospital policies (e.g., visitation) have been developed or identified for patients and their families. These materials are language format (i.e., prepared for individuals with visual, hearing or other disabilities) and reading-level appropriate and a plan is in place to disseminate these materials to hospital patients and visitors.
☐	☐	☐	**A plan has been developed for triage (e.g., initial patient evaluation) and admission of patients during a pandemic that includes the following:**
			☐ A designated location, separate from other clinical triage and evaluation areas, (utilizing the principles of social distancing) for the triage of patients with possible pandemic influenza.
			☐ Assigned responsibility to specifically-trained healthcare personnel overseeing the triage process.
			☐ Use of signage to direct and instruct patients with possible pandemic influenza on the triage process that is language, format (i.e., prepared for individuals with visual, hearing or other disabilities) and reading-level appropriate.
			☐ A telephone triage system for prioritizing patients who require a medical evaluation (i.e., those patients whose severity of symptoms or risk for complications necessitate being seen by a physician).
			☐ Criteria for prioritizing admission of patients to those in most critical need.
			☐ Coordination with local emergency medical services and 9-1-1 services for transport of suspected flu patients.
			☐ A method to specifically track admissions and discharges of patients with pandemic influenza
☐	☐	☐	**A plan has been developed to address the needs of specific patient populations that may be disproportionately affected during a pandemic or that may need services normally not provided by the hospital (e.g., pediatric and adult hospitals may need to extend services to other populations).**
			Populations to consider
			☐ Children and their families
			☐ Frail elderly and their caretakers
			☐ Young adults
			☐ Patients with chronic diseases (e.g., diabetes, hemodialysis)
			☐ Physically or mentally challenged/individuals with disabilities
			☐ Pregnant women
			☐ Immunocompromised children and adults
			☐ Others (specify)____________________

3. Elements of an influenza pandemic plan. *(continued)*

Completed	In Progress	Not Started	
			Issues to consider
			☐ Clinical expertise available
			☐ Need for specialized equipment, medical devices, and medications
			☐ Transportation
			☐ Mental health concerns
			☐ Need for social services
			☐ Translation services/medical interpreters
			☐ Cultural issues affecting behavioral response
☐	☐	☐	**A plan has been developed for facility access during a pandemic that includes the following:**
			☐ Criteria and protocols for modifying admission criteria on the basis of current bed capacity.
			☐ Criteria and protocols for closing the facility to new admissions and referrals to other facilities.
			☐ Criteria and protocols for limiting or restricting visitors to the hospital, including specific plans for communicating with patients' families about hospital rules for visiting hospitalized family members.
			☐ A contingency plan has been developed in the event of hospital quarantine in conjunction with local jurisdictions to ensure quarantine is enforced and necessary supplies, equipment, and basic necessities can be delivered and maintained.
☐	☐	☐	**A plan has been developed for facility security during a pandemic that includes the following:**
			☐ Hospital security personnel input into procedures for enforcing facility access controls.
			☐ Plans for facilitating identification (e.g., special badges) of non-facility healthcare personnel and volunteers by security staff and facilitating their access to the facility when deployed.
			☐ The identity of key and essential personnel who would have access to the facility during a pandemic.
			☐ Recruitment and training of additional security personnel (e.g., local police, national guard) that is coordinated by the local health authority.
			☐ Plans for establishing a controlled, orderly, flow of patients within the facility.
☐	☐	☐	**An infection control plan that includes the following is in place for managing hospital patients with pandemic influenza: (For the most recent information on pandemic influenza infection control recommendations for staff in a healthcare setting, see** www.pandemicflu.gov/plan/healthcare/maskguidancehc.html.)
			☐ An infection control policy[6] that requires healthcare personnel to use at a minimum Standard Precautions (www.cdc.gov/ncidod/dhqp/gl_isolation_standard.html and Droplet Precautions (i.e., mask for close contact) (www.cdc.gov/ncidod/dhqp/gl_isolation_droplet.html) with symptomatic patients.
			☐ A communication plan is developed to inform all hospital staff and employees about appropriate need for and use of infection control measures, social distancing practices, and personal protective equipment.
			☐ Use of respiratory protection (i.e., N-95 or higher-rated respirator as feasible) by personnel who are performing aerosol-generating procedures (e.g., bronchosocopy, endotrachael intubation, open suctioning of the respiratory tract). Use of N-95 respirators for other direct care activities involving patients with confirmed or suspected pandemic influenza is also prudent. If supplies of N-95 or higher-rated respirators are not available, surgical masks can provide benefits against large droplet exposures. (Additional guidance available at www.pandemicflu.gov/plan/healthcare/maskguidancehc.html.)
			☐ A strategy for implementing Respiratory Hygiene/Cough Etiquette throughout the hospital. (For information, see www.cdc.gov/flu/professionals/infectioncontrol/resphygiene.htm.)
			☐ A plan for cohorting patients with known or suspected pandemic influenza in designated units or areas of the facility.

[6] Refer to HHS recommendations for infection control for pandemic influenza for recent updates or changes in recommendations. (www.hhs.gov/pandemicflu/plan/sup4.html)

3. Elements of an influenza pandemic plan. *(continued)*

Completed	In Progress	Not Started	
			☐ Responsibility has been assigned for regularly monitoring www.pandemicflu.gov for updates/revisions of infection control recommendations and implementing recommended changes. Once a pandemic influenza virus is detected and its transmission characteristics are known, HHS/CDC will provide updated guidance on any need to modify infection control recommendations. Any changes to current recommendations will be published on www.pandemicflu.gov. Primary: ______________________________ (Name) (Title) (Contact info) Backup: ______________________________ (Name) (Title) (Contact info)
			☐ A plan for monitoring adherence to infection control procedures and for monitoring the effectiveness of the infection control plan.
☐	☐	☐	**The facility's human resource and payment policies should be reviewed to identify and eliminate language that may encourage staff to work when ill or even when they are symptomatic with influenza-like illness and especially when they are within the period of communicability. An occupational health plan for addressing staff absences and other related occupational issues has been developed that includes the following:**
			☐ A liberal/non-punitive sick leave policy that addresses the needs of ill and symptomatic personnel and facility staffing needs during various levels of a pandemic health crisis. The policy considers the following: ☐ The handling of personnel who develop symptoms while at work. ☐ Allowing and encouraging ill people to stay home until no longer infectious. ☐ When personnel may return to work after having pandemic influenza. ☐ Personnel who need to care for family members who become ill or affected by closed care centers. ☐ Personnel who must stay home to care for children if schools and childcare centers close ☐ A plan to educate staff and volunteers to self-assess and report symptoms of pandemic influenza before reporting for duty; consider a phone triage system similar to that used for patients. ☐ A list of mental/behavioral health, community and faith-based resources that will be available to provide counseling to personnel during a pandemic. ☐ A system to track annual influenza vaccination of personnel. (Having a system in place to track annual vaccination will facilitate documentation and tracking of pandemic influenza vaccine in personnel.) ☐ A plan for managing personnel who at the time of a pandemic are at increased risk for influenza complications[7] (e.g., pregnant women, immunocompromised workers, employees 65 yrs of age and over). A plan might include, for example, placing them on administrative leave, altering their work location, or other appropriate alternative.
☐	☐	☐	**A vaccine and antiviral use plan has been developed. (For useful information on this subject see www.hhs.gov/pandemicflu/plan/sup6.html and www.hhs.gov/pandemicflu/plan/sup7.html.)**
			☐ CDC and state health department websites have been identified for obtaining the most current recommendations and guidance for the use, availability, access, and distribution of vaccines and antiviral medications during a pandemic.
			☐ Local and/or state health departments and the hospital have agreed upon the hospital's role, if any, in a large scale program to distribute vaccine and antivirals to the general population.
			☐ A list has been developed of key healthcare and other personnel who are essential for maintaining hospital operations during an influenza pandemic who would be the first priority for influenza vaccination.
			☐ A plan is in place for expediting administration of influenza vaccine to patients as recommended by the state health department.
			☐ A plan is in place for expediting provision of antiviral prophylaxis/treatment to patients as recommended by the state health department

[7] Persons at increased risk for influenza complications may not be known prior to a pandemic. The subject, however, should be considered as part of the planning process.

3. Elements of an influenza pandemic plan. *(continued)*

Completed	In Progress	Not Started	
			☐ A plan is in place for expediting administration of influenza vaccine to staff as recommended by the state health department.
			☐ A plan is in place for expediting provision of antiviral prophylaxis/treatment to staff as recommended by the state health department.
			☐ The vaccine/antiviral plan considers the following:
			☐ How decisions on allocation of limited vaccine or antivirals will be made.
			☐ How persons who receive antiviral prophylaxis/treatment will be followed for adverse events.
			☐ Security issues have been identified and addressed in the influenza vaccine and antivirals use plans.
☐	☐	☐	**Issues related to surge capacity during a pandemic have been addressed and discussed with the local and/or State health department and other pandemic influenza planning partners.**
			Healthcare services
			☐ Plans include strategies for maintaining the hospital's core missions and continuing to care for patients with chronic diseases (e.g., hemodialysis and infusion services), women giving birth, emergency services, and other types of required care unrelated to influenza.
			☐ Criteria have been developed for determining when to cancel elective admissions and surgeries.
			☐ Plans for shifting healthcare services away from the hospital, e.g., to home care or pre-designated alternative care facilities, have been discussed with local, state, tribal, or regional planning contacts.
			☐ Ethical issues concerning how decisions will be made in the event healthcare services must be prioritized and allocated (e.g., decisions based on probability of survival) have been discussed.
			☐ A procedure has been developed for communicating changes in hospital status to health authorities and the public.
			Staffing
			☐ A contingency staffing plan has been developed that identifies the minimum staffing needs and prioritizes critical and non-essential services on the basis of essential facility operations.
			☐ The contingency staffing plan considers how health professions students assigned to the facility will be utilized.
			☐ A plan has been developed for utilizing non-facility volunteer staff, such as those who may be made available through a State Emergency System for Advanced Registration of Volunteer Health Professionals (ESAR-VHP) to provide patient care when the hospital reaches a staffing crisis.
			☐ The contingency staffing plan includes a strategy for training of non-facility volunteers (e.g., retired clinicians, trainees) and includes a procedure for rapid credentialing/privileging (consistent with the JCAHO disaster privileging standard MS.4.110) and badging for easy identification by security and access to the facility when deployed.
			☐ The contingency staffing plan includes a strategy for cross-training and reassignment of personnel to support critical services.
			☐ The contingency staffing plan considers alternative strategies for scheduling work shifts in order to enable personnel to work longer hours without becoming overtired.
			☐ Responsibility has been assigned for conducting a daily assessment of staffing status and needs during an influenza pandemic. (Insert name, title and contact information of primary and backup persons.)
			Primary: ______________________________ (Name) (Title) (Contact info)
			Backup: ______________________________ (Name) (Title) (Contact info)
			☐ Define criteria for declaring a "staffing crisis" that would enable the use of emergency staffing alternatives.

3. Elements of an influenza pandemic plan. ***(continued)***

Completed	In Progress	Not Started	
			☐ Strategies have been developed for supporting personnel whose family and/or personal responsibilities or other barriers prevent them from coming to work (e.g., strategies that take into account the principles of social distancing when schools are closed, care of elders, transportation, reasonable accommodation or state governmental mandate).
			☐ The staffing plan includes strategies for collaborating with local and regional planning and response groups to address widespread healthcare staffing shortages during a crisis, including the development of memorandums of advanced agreement (MAAs) and memorandums of understanding (MOUs) with regional and tribal healthcare partners.
			Consumable and durable medical equipment and supplies
			☐ Estimates have been made of the quantities of essential patient care materials and equipment (e.g., intravenous pumps and ventilators, pharmaceuticals, diagnostic testing materials) and personal protective equipment (e.g., masks, respirators, gowns, gloves, and hand hygiene products), that would be needed during an eight-week pandemic with subsequent eight-week pandemic waves.
			☐ Estimates have been shared with local, regional, and tribal planning groups to better plan stockpiling agreements.
			☐ A strategy has been developed for how priorities would be made in the event there is a need to allocate limited patient equipment (e.g., ventilators), pharmaceuticals (e.g., antiviral and antibacterial therapy), and other resources.
			☐ A plan has been developed to address related shortages of supplies (e.g., intravenous fluids, personal protective equipment), including strategies for using normal and alternative channels for procuring needed resources.
			☐ A list of alternative vendors for medical devices, pharmaceuticals, and contracted services (e.g., laundry, housekeeping, food services) has been developed.
			☐ A plan has been developed for maintaining critical laboratory testing capability in-house and priorities for tests that require shipping; back-up plans are in place for testing services that will remain in-house.
			☐ A process is in place to track and report to public health and other response partners, in real-time, information regarding the status of the hospital and resources available that would identify burden on the system.
			Bed capacity
			☐ Surge capacity plans include strategies to help increase hospital bed capacity.
			☐ Signed agreements have been established with area hospitals and long-term-care facilities to accept or receive appropriate non-influenza patients who need continued inpatient care to optimize utilization of acute care resources for seriously ill patients.
			☐ Facility space has been identified that could be adapted for use as expanded inpatient beds and this information has been provided to local, regional, and tribal planning contacts.
			☐ Plans are in place to increase physical bed capacity (staffed beds), including the equipment, personnel and pharmaceuticals needed to treat a patient with influenza (e.g., ventilators, oxygen, antivirals).
			☐ Logistical support has been discussed with local, state, tribal and regional planning contacts to determine the hospital's role in the set-up, staffing, and provision of supplies and in the operation of pre-designated alternate care facilities.
			Postmortem care
			☐ A contingency plan has been developed for managing an increased need for post mortem care and disposition of deceased patients.
			☐ An area in the facility that could be used as a temporary morgue has been identified.
			☐ Logistical support for the management of the deceased has been discussed with local, state, tribal, or regional planning contacts and local coroners/medical examiners.
			☐ Local morticians have been involved in planning discussions.
			☐ Mortality estimates have been used to anticipate and supply needed body bags and shroud packs.
			☐ Plans for expanding morgue capacity have been discussed with local, State, tribal and regional planning contacts.

CS111288

Source: *HHS Pandemic Influenza Plan*, Supplement 3: Healthcare Planning. Appendix 2: Hospital Preparedness Checklist. U.S. Department of Health and Human Services. Washington, DC. Available online at: http://www.hhs.gov/pandemicflu/plan/sup3.html

4-173 Avoiding Hazards with Use of Cleaners and Disinfectants on Electronic Medical Equipment

This notification describes the hazards of using excess cleaning and disinfecting liquids on certain electronic medical equipment and recommends ways to avoid these hazards. The Food and Drug Administration (FDA), Centers for Disease Control and Prevention (CDC), Environmental Protection Agency (EPA), and Occupational Safety and Health Administration (OSHA) collaborated to develop this notification.*

BACKGROUND

A broad perspective on contamination drives current infection control strategies that focus on cleaning and disinfecting frequently touched surfaces that contribute to cross-transmission of infections. Contaminated surfaces can include:

- Surfaces and equipment with blood or other potentially infectious material
- Surfaces touched by gloved hands after glove contact with patients
- Surfaces touched by patients, and surfaces contacted by or in the vicinity of aerosols and spatter
- Surfaces about whose state of cleanliness the healthcare professional is uncertain

Contaminating substances can include:

- blood
- semen
- vaginal secretions
- respiratory secretions
- fecal material
- cerebrospinal fluid
- synovial fluid
- pleural fluid
- pericardial fluid
- peritoneal fluid
- amniotic fluid
- saliva in dental procedures
- body fluids that might harbor potential pathogens
- any body fluid that is visibly contaminated with blood
- all body fluids in situations where it is difficult or impossible to differentiate between body fluids

---

** The content of this notification reflects the products that are currently available, current versions of any relevant regulations and regulatory directives, and current infection control statements from Federal agency guidance. With respect to electronic medical equipment, this notification is limited to that which is regulated by the Food and Drug Administration (FDA) as medical devices. Barrier products that might be marketed to protect this equipment from contamination also are regulated by FDA as medical devices. Hospital disinfectants that might be used on electronic medical equipment are regulated primarily by the U.S. Environmental Protection Agency (EPA) as pesticides, and secondarily by FDA as medical devices. The Occupational Safety and Health Administration (OSHA) regulates occupational exposure of employees to blood or other potentially infectious materials (OPIM) which may occur during the handling of contaminated medical equipment. Other OSHA regulations (e.g., Hazard Communication; Use of [Electrical] Equipment) may also be applicable. Recommendations for general infection control strategies, including cleaning and disinfecting electronic medical equipment are published in guidelines from the Centers for Disease Control and Prevention (CDC), a non-regulatory agency.*

Over the past two years the relevant Federal agencies have learned about and collaborated to address problems associated with inappropriate use of liquids on electronic medical equipment. The problems included equipment fires and other damage, equipment malfunctions, and healthcare worker burns. These problems involved infusion pumps, ventilators, patient-controlled analgesia pumps, sequential compression device pumps, telemetry physiological signal receivers and transmitters, infusion fluid warmers, and infant anti-abduction sensors. This notification, however, is not limited to these equipment types and may be relevant to any equipment that has unsealed electronic circuitry or components, such as computer workstations, handheld devices and other monitoring equipment. The equipment malfunctions could result in life-threatening events to patients such as over-infusion of medications, loss of life-supporting drug therapy, and loss of patient ventilation.

The root cause of the problems mentioned above was likely corrosion of electronic circuitry by disinfecting or cleaning solutions that penetrated the equipment housings. Healthcare workers routinely sprayed the housings with disinfectants or wrapped the housings with disinfectant-soaked towels. These practices are generally not consistent with the equipment manufacturers' directions for use, which typically recommend wiping the housing with a soft cloth dampened with a mild detergent and water.

RECOMMENDATIONS

To avoid the hazards described above, review your facility policies on equipment management and assignment of responsibility for key tasks associated with said management. The relevant Federal agencies recommend the following in conjunction with your facility's equipment management policies:

- **Identify the equipment for which this notification applies**
  - Obtain the manufacturer's labeling which may include information attached to the equipment, instructions accompanying the equipment (such as the user manual), and information on the manufacturer's website.
  - Review the labeling for any cautions, precautions, or warnings about wetting, immersing, or soaking the equipment. If you find any of these, then this notification applies to that equipment.
- **Review the manufacturer's cleaning and maintenance instructions and ensure all staff are trained and will follow these instructions.**
- **Protect equipment from contamination whenever possible.**
  - Use engineering controls and careful work practices to avoid contaminating the equipment. Such work practices generally include:
    - ➢ Avoid unnecessary touching of the equipment during care delivery, especially with contaminated hands or gloves.
    - ➢ Position equipment to avoid contact with anticipated spatter.
    - ➢ Avoid laying contaminated items on unprotected equipment surfaces.
  - Use barriers on equipment surfaces that you expect to touch with contaminated hands or when contact with spatter cannot be avoided.
- **If there is suspicion of equipment contamination with microorganisms that might pose a transmission risk in healthcare settings (e.g., those requiring contact precautions), do the following:**
  - Clean equipment surfaces in accordance with instructions from both the equipment manufacturer and the chemical manufacturer.

    - If disinfection is necessary, alternative strategies to avoid wetting should be explored in consultation with the equipment manufacturer.
- **Always adhere strictly to all the chemical manufacturer's warnings, precautions and cautions, and carefully follow all directions for use.**
    - The manufacturer's directions for use are the primary source for information on disinfectants. All relevant Federal regulations, recommendations, and guidelines support and promulgate this position. This includes information on how to apply disinfectants to the equipment and the time required to achieve disinfection.
    - All manufacturers of regulated medical equipment and disinfectants are required to include adequate directions for use of their products. If directions for use are not included with the equipment or disinfectant, obtain the directions from the manufacturer(s).
    - It is a violation of Federal law [Federal Insecticide, Fungicide, and Rodenticide Act (FIFRA 7 USC § 136 et seq.)] to use a disinfectant in a manner inconsistent with its labeling. Furthermore, if a disinfectant labeled for immersion is applied by wiping or spraying, then disinfection may not result, especially if the recommended conditions for use (such as remaining wet for the required contact time) are not met.
- **If equipment is contaminated with blood or other potentially infectious material (OPIM), the equipment must be decontaminated per OSHA regulations**
    - Follow the equipment manufacturer's directions for cleaning to remove as much soil as possible.
    - It may be necessary to remove the equipment from service for thorough cleaning and disinfection (see Additional Information).

ADDITIONAL INFORMATION

In addition to the cleaning instructions, some equipment manufacturers' labels list disinfectants that the equipment housing can tolerate and refer the user to the disinfectant's label for use on the equipment. FDA allows this type of labeling for equipment that it regulates because it would be overly burdensome for every regulated device to provide specific, current instructions for the use of all compatible disinfectants. Interpreting such labeling as well as interpreting the Federal regulations and guidances relevant to disinfection of equipment, requires the user to understand infection control principles and to use sound judgment. The language of relevant labeling and regulations is purposefully non-specific to accommodate the users' individual circumstances. The relevant Federal agencies do not intend this notification to modify current regulatory authority. Instead, this notification is intended to clarify current Federal regulations and guidances previously issued by these agencies.

The best strategy to avoid damaging equipment is to avoid equipment contamination to minimize the need for disinfectants. Using work practice controls and barriers on equipment can prevent equipment contamination. The use of barriers in healthcare facilities is recognized by OSHA regulation as a contamination control measure and is supported by the CDC in its environmental infection control guidance. Use of work practice controls and barriers on equipment in the patient care environment minimizes contamination with all microorganisms, including drug-resistant microorganisms such as vancomycin-resistant *Enterococcus* (VRE).

OSHA's *Bloodborne Pathogens Standard* (29 CFR 1910.1030) requires use of an appropriate chemical disinfectant on contaminated equipment. OSHA considers an item or surface contaminated if it:

- has blood or OPIM on it, or
- is reasonably anticipated to be contaminated with blood or OPIM during a procedure that involves blood or OPIM contact.

All disinfectants that meet OSHA's definition of "appropriate" include directions to keep the item or surface wet for a specified contact time. Equipment that cannot tolerate this exposure to liquids may require special handling if the equipment becomes contaminated and the equipment may need to be removed from use. To avoid wetting the circuitry, the contaminated equipment housing may need to be disassembled, washed, and soaked in the liquid disinfectant. Disassembly of electronic medical equipment may require the services of trained technical staff and/or servicing by the equipment manufacturer before the equipment can be returned to use. This may necessitate shipping the affected piece of equipment to another location. Healthcare facilities must comply with OSHA requirements for handling, servicing or shipping contaminated equipment, which include removal of as much soil as possible and labeling the equipment as contaminated. Once cleaning is accomplished, package the equipment for safe movement within the facility for repairs or in preparation for off-site shipping. If the equipment is sent off-site for decontamination and service, label the equipment package to alert those handling the package that it may contain potentially infectious material per all relevant Federal and local regulations. Send the package per the manufacturer's recommendations for service. These recommendations will indicate whether the equipment should be sent directly to the manufacturer or can be sent to an authorized repair service. Please note that some service facilities may require users to provide instructions for decontamination and processing after the equipment is disassembled.

Be advised that not all equipment handling or patient contact results in the need for disinfection. None of the documents from the relevant Federal agencies is intended to require disinfection of equipment that has not become contaminated.

Source: Public Health Notification from FDA, CDC, EPA and OSHA. Issued October 31, 2007. Center for Devices and Radiological Health / CDRH, U.S. Food & Drug Administration. Available online at: ***http://www.fda.gov/cdrh/safety/103107-cleaners.html.***

PART 5

CMS and Joint Commission Standards Checklist

The following materials serve as examples. Hospitals should consult with counsel or other appropriate advisors before adapting the materials in this part to suit particular purposes.

INTRODUCTION

"Hospital Checklist: CMS and Joint Commission Standards" is a tool designed to reference similarities and differences between CMS regulations and Joint Commission accreditation standards for hospital compliance. It is an invaluable tool for quality assurance nurses, directors of nursing, infection control nurses, medical records personnel, risk managers, and hospital administrators.

CMS regulations are cited in the Code of Federal Regulations (C.F.R.). The Hospital Conditions of Participation (COPs) at 42 C.F.R. Subpart E is cited as 42 C.F.R. 482. CMS expects the hospital, as part of its participation agreement, to implement a demonstrable process and system to produce the desired outcome for compliance with the regulations. Citations or Statements of Deficiency (SODs) are written when the hospital fails to maintain a system to produce the desired outcome or when the hospital fails to monitor and correct undesirable outcomes. CMS can take termination actions if the intent of the regulation is not objectively met by the hospital.

"Hospital Checklist: CMS and Joint Commission Standards" compares CMS regulations to Joint Commission accreditation standards in a table format. The table contains a section for the user to enter applicable state laws for a complete reference guide. Remember, the hospital's policies, procedures, and protocols (PPPs) must reflect the requirements of CMS, the Joint Commission, and the state to be in compliance, so it makes sense to include all of the requirements in one easy-to-use checklist.

This checklist is intended for use as a reference guide to aid the user in determining the most stringent requirements for compliance, so the user can formulate PPPs that meet or exceed the most restrictive requirement. It is not intended to be utilized as a complete set of regulations, conditions, standards, or laws governing hospitals or compliance.

Source: Denise Atwood, Paralegal, RN, BSS, a teeny tiny corporation, dba C.A. Enterprises.

AREAS OF ASSESSMENT

Requirement	CMS		Joint Commission	State
Compliance Federal, State, Local Laws	**482.11(a)** **482.11(c)**		**LD.1.10**—The hospital identifies how it is governed **LD.1.30**—Hospital complies with applicable law and regulation	
Governing Body (GB)/ Administration	**482.12**	Legally responsible for the conduct of the hospital **(a)** Appoint medical staff (MS) **(a)(4)** Approve MS bylaws and rules/regulations **(a)(5)** Ensure MS is accountable to the GB for quality of care provided **(c)** Patients under the care of a physician and delegation of care recognized under State law **(c)(2)** Patient admitted by licensed independent practitioner (LIP) **(d)** Institutional plan and budget **(d)(6)** Plan revised/updated annually **(d)(7)** Plan prepared under the direction of the GB **(e)** GB responsible for contracted services furnished	**LD.1.20**—Governance responsibilities defined in writing, as applicable **LD.2.10**—Individual(s) responsible for operating hospital according to authority conferred by governance **HR.1.20**—Hospital has process to ensure person's qualifications are consistent with job responsibilities **LD.3.10**—Leaders engage in short- and long-term planning **LD.2.50**—Develop and monitor annual operating budget **LD.3.50**—Services provided by contractual arrangements are provided safely and effectively	

Requirement	CMS		Joint Commission	State
Patients' Rights (PR)	**482.13**	Hospital must promote and protect each PR **(a)(1)** Inform patient or representative (as allowed under State law) of PR before furnishing or discontinuing care **(a)(2)** Establish a patient grievance process that is approved by the GB **(b)(1)** Patients have the right to participate in plan of care **(b)(2)** Patient or representative (as allowed under State law) has the right to make informed decisions for care **(b)(3)** Patient has the right to formulate advanced directives **(c)(1)** Right to personal privacy **(c)(2)** Right to receive care in a safe setting **(c)(3)** Right to be free from abuse or harassment **(d)(1)** Right to confidentiality of medical records (MR) **(e)(1)** Right to be free from restraints (physical or chemical) unless medically necessary **(e)(2)** Restraint used only to improve the patient's well-being **(e)(3)** Use of a restraint must be **(e)(3)(i)** used when less restrictive measures ineffective **(e)(3)(ii)** in accordance with a physician's/LIP's order (permitted by the State). The order must— **(e)(3)(ii)(A)** never be written as a standing or as needed order **(e)(3)(iii)** according to written changes to patient's plan of care **(e)(3)(iv)** implemented in the least restrictive manner possible **(e)(3)(v)** in accordance with safe restraining techniques **(e)(3)(vi)** ended at earliest possible time **(e)(4)** Patient must be continually assessed, monitored, reevaluated **(e)(5)** Direct patient care staff must have ongoing education and training in safe use of restraints **(f)(1)** Patient has the right to be free from seclusion and restraint imposed as coercion or discipline **(f)(2)** Only used in emergency situations **(f)(3)(ii)(C)** Physician/LIP must see and evaluate restraint/seclusion within 1 hour of intervention **(f)(3)(ii)(D)** Restraint or seclusion orders max: 4 hours adults, 2 hours age 9-17, 1 hour if under 9—for a total of 24 hours **(f)(4)(i)** Restraint ***and*** seclusion require continual face-to-face monitoring *OR* **(f)(4)(ii)** continuous video and audio monitoring **(f)(7)** Hospital must report to CMS any death that occurs while a patient is restrained or secluded	**RI.2.10**—Hospital respects PR **RI.2.20**—Patients receive information about PR **RI.2.120**—Hospital addresses the resolution of complaints **RI.2.30**—Patients involved in decisions about care **RI.2.40**—Informed consent obtained **RI.2.80**—Hospital addresses wishes of patient for end-of-life issues **RI.2.130**—Hospital respects confidentiality, privacy, and security **RI.2.150**—Right to be free from abuse, neglect, and exploitation **PC.12.60**—Restraint or seclusion limited to emergencies where risk of patient harming self or others and nonphysical interventions ineffective **PC.12.50**—Nonphysical techniques are preferred **PC.12.70**—LIP orders restraint/seclusion **PC.12.90**—LIP sees and evaluates patients in person **PC.12.100**—Written or verbal orders for initial or continuing use are time limited **PC.13.70**—Behavior management conforms to treatment plan **PC.12.140**—Patients are monitored **PC.12.110**—Regularly evaluated **PC.12.30**—Staff is trained and competent **PC.12.150**—Discontinued when patient meets behavior criteria **PC.11.50**—Orders for initiation and renewing are consistent with PPP and patient condition **PC.11.70**—Patients in restraint are monitored **PC.12.180**—Hospital collects data on use of restraint and seclusion	

Requirement	CMS		Joint Commission	State
Quality Assessment (QA)/ Performance Improvement (PI)	**482.21**	GB ensures there is an effective hospital-wide, data-driven program **(a)** Program scope **(a)(1)** Ongoing program that shows measurable improvement **(a)(2)** Hospital must measure, analyze, and track quality indicators **(b)** Program data **(b)(1)** Must incorporate quality indicator data **(b)(2)** Hospital must use the data collected **(b)(3)** Data collection must be specified by the GB **(c)** Program activities **(c)(1)** Hospital must set priorities for performance improvement activities **(c)(2)** Activities must track medical errors and adverse patient events **(c)(3)** Hospital must measure its success, and track performance to ensure improvements are sustained **(d)** Performance improvement projects **(e)** Executive responsibilities. The GB, MS, and administrative officials are responsible and accountable **(e)(1)** Ongoing program **(e)(2)** Assessment addresses priorities for improved quality of care and patient safety **(e)(3)** Clear expectations for safety are established **(e)(4)** Resources allocated for sustaining hospital performance and reducing risk to patients **(e)(5)** Annual determination of the number of projects	**LD.5.40**—Leaders evaluate outcomes and improve processes **LD.3.50**—Services provided by contractual arrangements are provided safely and effectively **PI.1.10**—Hospital collects data to monitor performance **PI.2.10**—Data are systematically aggregated and analyzed **PI.3.10**—Information from data analysis used to make changes to improve performance and patient safety **PI.2.30**—Process to identify and manage sentinel events **PI.3.20**—Ongoing program for identifying and reducing adverse events **PC.11.20**—PI process identifies way to reduce risks associated with restraint use **LD.4.10**—Leaders use process to assess and improve the hospital's activities **LD.4.50**—PI organization priorities in response to unusual or urgent events **LD.4.60**—Resources for measuring, assessing and improving performance and safety **MS.3.10**—MS has leadership role in PI activities **MS.3.20**—MS participates in PI processes **ORYX specific requirements are not included in the scope of this manual.**	
Medical Staff (MS)	**482.22**	Organized MS responsible for the care of patients **(a)** Composition of MS **(a)(1)** Periodic appraisals of members **(a)(2)** Credentialing **(b)** MS organization and accountability to the GB **(b)(2)** If MS has executive committee, majority of members are MDs or DOs **(b)(3)** Responsibility for the organization and conduct of MS assigned to an MD or DO **(c)** MS bylaws adopted and enforced **(c)(1)** Approved by the GB **(c)(2)** Statement of privileges of each category of MS **(c)(3)** Describe MS organization **(c)(4)** Describe qualifications for MS appointment **(c)(5)** History and physical (H&P) are completed 7 days before or 48 hours after admission by an MD, DO, or oromaxillofacial surgeon **(c)(6)** Criteria for determining privileges	**MS.2.10**—MS oversees quality of patient care, treatment, and services **MS.1.10**—Organized, self-governing MS **MS.4.10**—MS has credentialing process **MS.1.40**—There is an MS executive committee **MS.4.40**—MS evaluates individuals for ability to provide quality care **MS.1.20**—MS bylaws **MS.2.20**—Patient's care responsibility of practitioner with privileges **MS.2.30**—Process to monitor LIP **PC.2.130**—Initial assessments performed as defined by hospital **MS.4.20**—Process for clinical privileges	

Requirement	CMS		Joint Commission	State
Nursing Services (NS)	**482.23**	Organized, 24-hour NS under the supervision of an RN **(a)** Plan of administrative authority and delineation of responsibilities for patient care Director of Nursing (DON) must be an RN **(b)** Staffing and delivery of care ensures immediate availability of an RN for patient care **(b)(2)** Procedure to ensure nurses have valid, current licenses **(b)(3)** RN supervises/evaluates care for each patient **(b)(4)** Current nursing care plans for each patient **(b)(5)** RN makes patient care assignments **(b)(6)** Responsibility for non-employee nurses (registry) **(c)** Preparation and administration of drugs and biologicals **(c)(2)** Orders for drugs and biologicals must be in writing and signed by the practitioner responsible for the patient's care **(c)(2)(i)** Telephone orders per PPP **(c)(3)** Blood transfusions and IV medications are administered per approved MS PPP **(c)(4)** Reporting transfusion and adverse drug reactions and errors in administration of drugs	**NR.2.10**—Nurse Executive is an RN **NR.1.10**—Nurse Executive directs nursing services **NR.3.10**—Nurse Executive establishes PPP **NR.1.10**—Nurse Leader coordinates the quality of nursing care, treatment, and services for patients **HR.1.20**—Hospital has a process to ensure a person is qualified **PC.4.10**—Development of plan of care **PC.2.130**—Initial assessments performed as defined by hospital **PC.2.150**—Patients are reassessed as needed **MM.5.10**—Medications are safely and accurately administered **IM.6.50**—Qualified personnel accept and transcribe verbal orders **MM.6.10**—Effects of medications are monitored **MM.6.20**—Actual or adverse drug events and medication errors	
Medical Records Services (MR)/ Information Management (IM)	**482.24**	MR must be maintained for every person evaluated or treated **(a)** Must employ personnel to ensure prompt completion, filing, and retrieval of records **(b)** Form and retention of MR: accurate, promptly filed, retained, and accessible and system of author identification that protects security of entries **(b)(1)** Retained at least 5 years **(b)(2)** Coding and indexing system **(b)(3)** Procedures for ensuring confidentiality and release **(c)** Content of MR: reason for admission, patient's progress, and response to treatment **(c)(1)** Legible, complete, and authenticated (name and discipline) and dated promptly **(c)(1)(ii)** Authentication: signatures, written initials, or computer entry **(c)(2)** MR must document the following: **(c)(2)(i)** H&P 7 days before or 48 hours after admission **(c)(2)(ii)** Admitting diagnosis **(c)(2)(v)** Properly executed informed consent forms **(c)(2)(vi)** Information necessary to monitor the patient's condition **(c)(2)(vii)** Discharge summary, outcome, and follow-up care **(c)(2)(viii)** MR completed in 30 days after discharge	**IM.6.10**—Complete and accurate MR for every patient assessed or treated **IM.6.60**—Access to all relevant information from MR **IM.2.10, 2.20 and 2.30**—Confidentiality, security, and integrity of data/information are maintained **IM.5.10**—Information resources readily available and current **IM.6.20**—Records contain patient-specific information to care, treatment and services **IM.4.10**—IM system provides information for use in decision making **IM.6.40**—MR contains summary list diagnoses, procedures, drug allergies, medications **PC.2.130**—Initial assessments performed as defined by hospital **RI.2.40**—Informed consent obtained	

Requirement	CMS		Joint Commission	State
Pharmaceutical Services (PS)	**482.25**	PS to meet the needs of patients. MS is responsible for developing PPP that minimize drug errors **(a)** Pharmacy or drug storage is administered in accordance with professional principles **(a)(1)** Full-time, part-time, or consulting pharmacist is responsible for developing, supervising, and coordinating activities of PS **(a)(2)** Adequate number of personnel to ensure quality of PS **(a)(3)** Current, accurate records on receipt and disposition of all scheduled drugs **(b)(1)** Compounding, packaging, and dispensing under the supervision of a pharmacist **(b)(2)** Drugs and biologicals must be kept in a locked storage area **(b)(3)** Outdated, mislabeled, or unusable drugs and biologicals must not be available for patient use **(b)(4)** PPP for removing drugs when pharmacist is not available **(b)(5)** Protocol for automatic stop orders determined by the MS **(b)(6)** Drug administration errors, drug reactions, and incompatibilities reported immediately to physician **(b)(7)** Reporting of abuse and loss of controlled substances **(b)(9)** Established formulary	**MM.4.10**—Review of prescriptions or orders **MM.4.20**—Medications prepared safely **MM.4.30**—Medications labeled appropriately **MM.4.40**—Medications dispensed safely **LD.2.20**—Each program, service, department has effective leadership **HR.1.20**—Hospital has a process to ensure a person is qualified **MM.2.30**—Emergency medications available, controlled and secured **MM.4.50**—System for safely providing medications to meet patient needs **MM.4.70**—Medications are retrieved when recalled or discontinued **MM.5.10**—Medications safely and accurately administered **MM.6.20**—Responds appropriately to actual or potential adverse drug events or medication errors	
Radiologic Services (RS)	**482.26**	**(a)** Hospitals must maintain, or have available, diagnostic RS **(b)** Must be free from hazards for patients and personnel **(b)(2)** Periodic equipment inspections including prompt correction of hazards **(b)(3)** Use of exposure meters or badge tests **(b)(4)** Provided only on the order of practitioners with privileges **(c)(1)** Personnel: full-time, part-time, or consulting radiologist **(d)** Record of RS must be maintained **(d)(1)** Signed reports of interpretations **(d)(2)** Retained at least 5 years	**LD.2.20**—Each program, service, department has effective leadership **HR.1.20**—Hospital has a process to ensure a person is qualified	

Requirement	CMS		Joint Commission	State
Laboratory Services (LS)	**482.27**	**(a)** Hospitals must maintain, or have available, adequate LS **(b)(1)** Emergency LS must be available 24 hours a day **(b)(2)** Written description of LS must be available to the MS **(b)(4)** MS and a pathologist must determine tissue specimens that require macroscopic or macroscopic and microscopic examinations **(c)(1)** Potentially HIV infectious blood and blood products **(c)(2)** Services furnished by an outside blood bank **(c)(4)** Patient notification of administration of potentially HIV infectious blood or blood products **(c)(5)** Time frame for notification **(c)(6)** Content of notification **(c)(7)** Policies and procedures for notification **CLIA- (waived testing) specific requirements are not included in the scope of this manual. They can be found at 42 C.F.R. 493, Subparts A, B, C, D, E, F, H, I, J, K, M, Q, R, and T.**	**LD.3.30**—Hospital demonstrates a commitment to community by providing essential services in a timely manner **PC.16.30**—Staff performing tests have training and demonstrate competence **PC.16.40**—Approved PPP governing testing processes are current and available **PC.16.50**—Quality control checks, as defined by hospital, are conducted on each procedure **PC.16.60**—Quality control and test records are maintained	
Food and Dietetic Services (FDS) and Nutrition Care	**482.28**	Must have an organized FDS that is directed and staffed by adequate personnel **(a)(1)** Must have a full-time employee who— **(a)(1)(i)** serves as the director **(a)(1)(ii)** is responsible for the daily management of FDS **(a)(2)** There must be qualified dietitian (full-time, part-time, or consulting) **(b)(1)** Therapeutic diets must be prescribed by the practitioner(s) responsible for the care of the patient **(b)(2)** Nutritional needs must be met in accordance with recognized dietary practices **(b)(3)** Therapeutic diet manual approved by the MS and dietitian and available to staff	**LD.2.20**—Each program, service, department has effective leadership **HR.1.20**—Hospital has a process to ensure a person is qualified **PC.7.10**—Process for preparing and/ or distributing food and nutrition products **PC.2.120**—Time frame(s) for initial assessment(s) are in writing	
Utilization Review (UR) or Continuum of Care	**482.30**	**(a)** This section applies except in the following circumstances: **(a)(1)** A Utilization and Quality Control Quality Improvement Organization (QIO) has assumed binding review for the hospital **(a)(2)** CMS has determined the UR procedures by the state under Title XIX of the Act are superior to the procedures required in this section **(b)** UR committee composition **(c)** Scope/frequency of review **(d)** Determination regarding admissions or continued stays **(e)** Extended stay review **(f)** Review of professional services **These sections are compared for total content only. DO NOT compare line by line.**	**PC.1.10**—Hospital accepts for care those patients whose needs it can meet **PC.5.60**—Hospital coordinates the care, treatment and services provided **PC.15.10**—Process addresses need for continuing care and services after discharge or transfer **PC.15.20**—Patient's transfer or discharge to another level of care is based on patient's assessed needs and hospital's capabilities **RI.1.40**—When care and services are subject to review resulting in denial of care or services, the hospital makes the decision regarding ongoing care and services **These sections are compared for total content only. DO NOT compare line by line.**	

Requirement	CMS		Joint Commission	State
Physical Environment (PE)	**"Life Safety Code"** **482.41**	**(a)** PE must be constructed and maintained to ensure safety of patients **(a)(1)** There must be emergency power and lighting **(a)(2)** There must be facilities for emergency gas and water **(b)** Life safety from fire **(b)(2)** Must have procedures for the storage and disposal of trash **(b)(3)** LSC does not apply in a State where CMS finds State law adequate **(b)(4)** Emergency lighting **(c)(2)** Facilities, supplies, and equipment must be maintained to ensure safety and quality **(c)(4)** Must be proper ventilation, light, and temperature controls in PS and FDS	**EC.5.50**—Hospital develops and implements activities to protect occupants when building does not meet Life Safety Code ® **EC.4.10**—Addresses emergency management **EC.7.20**—Provides emergency electrical power source **EC.1.10**—Manages safety risks **EC.1.20**—Maintains a safe environment **EC.3.10**—Manages hazardous materials and waste risks **EC.5.10**—Manages fire safety risks **EC.6.10**—Manages medical equipment risks **EC.7.10**—Manages utility risks **EC.5.40**—Maintains fire-safety equipment and building features	
Infection Control (IC)	**482.42**	The hospital must have an active program for the prevention, control, and investigation of infections and communicable diseases **(a)** Have designated infection control officer(s) develop and implement policies **(a)(1)** Infection control officer(s) must develop a system for identifying, reporting, investigating, and controlling infections and communicable diseases **(a)(2)** Must maintain a log of incidents related to infections and communicable diseases **(b)** The CEO, MS, and DON must— **(b)(1)** ensure hospital-wide QA and training programs address problems identified by infection control officer(s) **(b)(2)** be responsible for implementation of successful corrective action plans	**IC.1.10**—Hospital-wide infection control program **IC.2.10**—IC program identifies risks on an ongoing basis **IC.3.10**—Goals for preventing development of health care-associated infections **IC.5.10**—Evaluation of effectiveness of IC interventions **IC.7.10**—IC program is managed effectively **IC.9.10**—Hospital leaders allocate resources for IC program **IC.4.10**—Strategies implemented to achieve IC goals	

Requirement	CMS		Joint Commission	State
Discharge Planning (DP)	**482.43**	Must have DP policies and procedures that apply to all patients **(a)** Must identify all patients who are likely to suffer adverse health consequences on discharge if there is no DP **(b)(2)** An RN, social worker, or other qualified personnel must develop or supervise the DP evaluation **(b)(3)** Evaluation must include patient's need for post-hospital services and availability of services **(b)(4)** Evaluation must include patient's capacity for self-care or care in the environment from which they entered the hospital **(b)(5)** Evaluation must be completed in a timely manner, to avoid delays in discharge **(b)(6)** Evaluation must include discussion of the plan with the patient or the individual acting on the patient's behalf and must be in the MR **(c)(3)** Hospital must arrange for the initial implementation of the DP **(c)(4)** Hospital must reassess DP if needs change **(d)** Transfer or referral of patients as needed for follow-up care **(e)** Reassessment must be done on an ongoing basis	**PC.15.20**—Patient's transfer or discharge to another level of care is based on patient's assessed needs and hospital's capabilities **PC.6.10**—Patient receives education and training specific to needs **PC.2.120**—Time frame(s) for initial assessment(s) are in writing **PC.2.20**—Hospital defines in writing data and information gathered during assessment and reassessment **PC.15.10**—Process addresses needs for continuing care and services after discharge or transfer **PC.15.30**—When patients transferred or discharged, information related to care and services is provided	
Organ, Tissue, and Eye Procurement (OTEP)	**482.45**	**(a)** Must have and implement written protocols **(a)(1)** Agreement with a designated organ procurement organization (OPO), which the hospital must notify in a timely manner of all deaths **(a)(2)** Agreement with at least one tissue bank and one eye bank **(a)(3)** Ensures families of potential donors are informed of donation options **(a)(4)** Use discretion and sensitivity with respect to potential donors **(a)(5)** Ensure that staff is educated on donation issues, death records are reviewed to improve identification of potential donors, and potential donors are maintained while testing and placement of organs is done **(b)(1)** A hospital where transplants are performed must be a member of the Organ Procurement and Transplantation Network (OPTN) and abide by its rules. **(b)(2)** "Organ" means human kidney, liver, heart, lung or pancreas **(b)(3)** A transplanting hospital must provide data to OPTN, the Scientific Registry, and the OPOs	**LD.3.110**—Implement policies and procedures, developed with MS participation, for procuring and donation of organs and tissues **RI.2.80**—Hospital addresses wishes of patient relating to end-of life decisions	
	These sections are compared for total content only. DO NOT compare line by line.		**These sections are compared for total content only. DO NOT compare line by line.**	

Requirement	CMS		Joint Commission	State
Surgical Services (SS)	**482.51**	SS must be well organized and provided in accordance with acceptable standards of practice **(a)(1)** OR must be supervised by RN, MD, or DO **(a)(2)** LPNs and scrub techs work under the supervision of an RN **(a)(3)** RNs perform circulating duties **(a)(4)** SS must maintain a roster specifying surgical privileges **(b)** Must develop policies governing surgical care **(b)(1)** Must be an H&P in every patient's chart before surgery (except in emergencies) **(b)(2)** Properly executed informed consent form for the operation must be in every patient's chart before surgery (except in emergencies) **(b)(3)** Must have the following equipment: call system, cardiac monitor, resuscitator, defibrillator, aspirator and tracheotomy set **(b)(4)** Must have provisions for postoperative care **(b)(5)** OR register complete and must be up-to-date **(b)(6)** Operative report written or dictated immediately following surgery and signed by surgeon	**LD.2.20**—Each program, service, department has effective leadership **HR.1.20**—Hospital has a process to ensure a person is qualified **PC.13.20**—Procedures that require administration of moderate or deep sedation or anesthesia are planned **PC.13.30**—Patients are monitored during administration of moderate or deep sedation or anesthesia **PC.13.40**—Patients are monitored immediately after the administration of moderate or deep sedation or aesthesia **RI.2.40**—Informed consent is obtained **EC.4.10**—Hospital addresses emergency management **IM.6.30**—MR documents procedures use moderate or deep sedation or anesthesia	
Anesthesia Services (AS)	**482.52**	Must be provided in a well-organized manner under the supervision of a physician **(a)** Organization of AS must be appropriate to scope of services anesthesia administered by— **(a)(1)** A qualified anesthesiologist **(a)(2)** Doctor of medicine or osteopathy **(a)(4)** Certified RN anesthetist (CRNA) is under the supervision of the operating practitioner or anesthesiologist who is immediately available **(a)(5)** Anesthesiology assistant is under the supervision of an anesthesiologist who is immediately available **(b)** Policies on anesthesia procedures must include delineation of pre-anesthesia responsibilities. The policies must ensure the following are provided: **(b)(1)** Pre-anesthesia evaluation performed within 48 hours prior to surgery by an individual qualified to administer anesthesia **(b)(2)** Intraoperative anesthesia record **(b)(3)** Post-anesthesia follow-up report written within 48 hours after surgery for inpatients **(b)(4)** Post-anesthesia follow-up evaluation for anesthesia recovery in accordance with PPP approved by MS for outpatients **(c)(1)** State exemption. A hospital may be exempted from the physician supervision of CRNA's requirement if the State in which the hospital is located submits a letter to CMS signed by the Governor.	**LD.2.20**—Each program, service, department has effective leadership **HR.1.20**—Hospital has a process to ensure a person is qualified **MS.4.20**—Process for clinical privileges **PC.13.20**—Procedures that require administration of moderate or deep sedation or anesthesia are planned **PC.13.30**—Patients are monitored during administration of moderate or deep sedation or anesthesia **PC.13.40**—Patients are monitored immediately after the administration of moderate or deep sedation or aesthesia **IM.6.30**—MR documents procedures use moderate or deep sedation or anesthesia	

Requirement	CMS		Joint Commission	State
Nuclear Medicine Services (NMS)	**482.53**	**(a)** Organization of NMS must be appropriate to scope of services **(a)(1)** Director must be a doctor of medicine or osteopathy qualified in nuclear medicine **(a)(2)** Qualifications, training, and responsibilities of NMS personnel must be approved by NMS director and MS **(b)** Radioactive materials are handled in accordance with acceptable standards of practice **(b)(1)** In-house preparation **(b)(2)** Storage and disposal **(c)** The equipment must be— **(c)(1)** maintained in safe operating condition **(c)(2)** inspected, tested, and calibrated at least annually by qualified personnel **(d)(1)** NMS reports must be maintained for at least 5 years **(d)(2)** The practitioner approved by the MS to interpret diagnostic procedures must sign and date test interpretations **(d)(3)** Must maintain records of receipt and disposition of radiopharmaceuticals **(d)(4)** NMS is ordered only by a practitioner whose scope of licensure and defined privileges allow such referrals	**LD.3.30**—Hospital demonstrates a commitment to community by providing essential services in a timely manner **LD.2.20**—Each program, service, department has effective leadership **HR.1.20**—Hospital has a process to ensure a person is qualified **EC.3.10**—Hospital manages hazardous materials and waste	
Outpatient Services (OS)	**482.54**	**(a)** Must be organized and integrated with inpatient services **(b)(1)** Assign an individual to be responsible for the OS **(b)(2)** Have appropriate professional and nonprofessional personnel available	**IM.6.40**—Continuing ambulatory care services MR must contain summary list all significant information **LD.2.20**—Each program, service, department has effective leadership **HR.1.20**—Hospital has a process to ensure a person is qualified **MS.4.20**—Process for clinical privileges	
Emergency Services (ES)	**482.55**	**(a)(1)** Must be organized and under the direction of a qualified member of the MS and **(a)(2)** Services must be integrated with other hospital departments **(a)(3)** PPP governing medical care are established by and a continuing responsibility of the MS **(b)(2)** Must be adequate medical and nursing personnel qualified in emergency care to meet the needs of the facility	**LD.2.20**—Each program, service, department has effective leadership **HR.1.20**—Hospital has a process to ensure a person is qualified **MS.2.20**—Patient's care responsibility practitioner with privileges **LD.3.30**—Hospital demonstrates a commitment to community by providing essential services in a timely manner **LD.3.70**—Leaders define number of staff to provide care, treatment, and services	
	NOTE: THESE ARE NOT THE REQUIREMENTS FOR EMTALA. EMTALA is found at 42 C.F.R. 489.20 and 489.24.			

Requirement	CMS		Joint Commission	State
Rehabilitation Services (RS)	**482.56**	**(a)** Organization of the RS must be appropriate to the scope of services offered **(a)(1)** The director of RS must have knowledge, experience, and capabilities to properly supervise and administer RS **(a)(2)** RS must be provided by staff who meet the qualifications specified by the MS consistent with state law **(b)** Services must be furnished in accordance with a written plan of treatment. RS must be given in accordance with MS orders, and the orders must be incorporated in the patient's record	**LD.2.20**—Each program, service, department has effective leadership **HR.1.20**—Hospital has a process to ensure a person is qualified	
Respiratory Care Services (RCS)	**482.57**	**(a)** Organization of RCS must be appropriate to the scope and complexity of services offered **(a)(1)** Director of RCS must be a doctor of medicine or osteopathy. The director may be full- or part-time **(b)** Services are delivered in accordance with MS directives **(b)(1)** Written procedures for personnel and supervision **(b)(2)** Blood gases or other clinical laboratory tests **(b)(3)** Services must be provided in accordance with doctor's orders	**LD.2.20**—Each program, service, department has effective leadership **HR.1.20**—Hospital has a process to ensure a person is qualified **MS.2.20**—Patient's care responsibility of practitioner with privileges **IM.6.50**—Qualified personnel accept and transcribe verbal orders	
Human Resources (HR)	No COP titled "Human Resources"		**LD.3.70**—Leaders define qualification and sufficient number qualified/ competent persons to provide care *Planning* **HR.1.10** through **HR.1.30** *Orientation, Training, and Education* **HR.2.10** through **HR.2.30** *Competence Assessment* **HR.3.10** through **HR.3.20**	
Environment of Care (EC)	No COP titled "Environment of Care"		*Planning and Implementation Activities* **EC.1.10** through **EC.8.30** *Measuring and Improving Activities* **EC.9.10** through **EC.9.30**	

DEEMED STATUS

Background

The Social Security Act §§ 1861(e) and 1865(a) permit for deemed status of hospitals. Deemed status means that institutions accredited as hospitals by the Joint Commission or the American Osteopathic Association (AOA) are deemed to meet all of the Medicare Conditions of Participation, except

- The requirement for utilization review as specified in § 1861(e)(6) of the Act in 42 C.F.R. 482.30
- The additional special requirements necessary for the provision of active treatment in psychiatric hospitals §§ 1861(f) of the Act and 42 C.F.R. 482.60

- Any requirements under § 1861(e) of the Act and implementing regulations that CMS, after consulting with the Joint Commission or AOA, identifies as being higher or more precise than the requirements for accreditation in § 1865(a)(4) of the Act.

Procedure

A hospital deemed to meet program requirements must authorize the accreditation organization to release to CMS, or the state agency responsible for licensing, a copy of the most current accreditation survey. The hospital must furnish the accreditation survey report to the government agency that processes the deemed status requests (CMS or the state agency).

Determination

CMS or the state agency will review the survey, and related survey information, and make a determination to grant or deny deemed status to the hospital.

If deemed status is granted, the hospital is considered in compliance with the Medicare Conditions of Participation for the period of time the accreditation is valid (usually a period of three years).

CMS may use a validation survey (42 C.F.R. 488.7) or an accreditation survey or any other survey information (such as Life Safety Code requirements) to determine that a hospital does not meet the Medicare Conditions of Participation. In this case, the hospital is not granted deemed status, and may be required to submit a Plan of Correction to CMS to maintain Medicare certification.

ADDITIONAL RESOURCES

www.jcaho.org
www.cms.hhs.gov
www.cdc.gov
www.cms.hhs.gov/quality/hospital
www.organdonor.gov
www.fda.gov
www.osha.gov
www.jcrinc.com
wwwn.cdc.gov/clia/regs/toc.aspx
www.gpoaccess.gov/cfr/retrieve.html